Canadian Unit, Formation, and Command Histories

Units – regiments, corps, squadrons, and ships – form the foundation of the Canadian military. This new series from Wilfrid Laurier University Press critically explores the organizational, personal, societal, and cultural themes of those units by blending traditional operational history with innovative approaches in military scholarship.

A Canadian Gun-pit, 1918, by Wyndham Lewis. (National Gallery of Canada no. 8356)

Loyal Gunners

3rd Field Artillery Regiment (The Loyal Company)
and the History of New Brunswick's Artillery, 1893 to 2012

Lee Windsor • Roger Sarty • Marc Milner

with J. Brent Wilson • Shawn McPherson • Kendall French
Joe Foote and the Loyal Company Association

WILFRID LAURIER
UNIVERSITY PRESS
www.wlupress.wlu.ca

Wilfrid Laurier University Press acknowledges the support of the Canada Council for the Arts for our publishing program. We acknowledge the financial support of the Government of Canada through the Canada Book Fund for our publishing activities. This work was supported by the Research Support Fund.

Library and Archives Canada Cataloguing in Publication

Windsor, Lee A., 1971–, author
    Loyal gunners : 3rd Field Artillery Regiment (The Loyal Company) and the history of New Brunswick's Artillery, 1893 to 2012 / Lee Windsor, Roger Sarty, Marc Milner ; with J. Brent Wilson, Shawn McPherson, Kendall French, Joe Foote and the Loyal Company Association.

(Canadian unit, formation, and command histories)
Includes bibliographical references and index.
Issued in print and electronic formats.
ISBN 978-1-77112-237-5 (hardback).—ISBN 978-1-77112-255-9 (pdf).—ISBN 978-1-77112-256-6 (epub)

    1. Canada. Canadian Army. Field Artillery Regiment, 3rd—History. 2. Canada. Canadian Armed Forces. Field Artillery Regiment, 3rd—History. 3. Canada. Canadian Army. New Brunswick Regiment of Artillery—History. I. Milner, Marc, author II. Sarty, Roger, 1952–, author III. Title. IV. Series: Canadian unit, formation, and command histories

UA602.F338W55 2016   355.3'1097151   C2016-903720-7
                                                   C2016-903721-5

Front cover: The 3rd Canadian Garrison Brigade parades victoriously past General Sir Arthur Currie after the armistice of November 1918 (LAC PA-003502). Back cover: Soldiers from D Battery, 2nd Regiment, Royal Canadian Horse Artillery (2 RCHA) at the Canadian Forward Operating Base (FOB) at Sperwan Ghar, Afghanistan, fire their M777 155 mm howitzer, 25 June 2007 (Canadian Forces Combat Camera IS2007-7309). Inside front flap: Partridge Island looking south in 1943 (LAC PA-108409). Inside back flap: The Colours of the 3rd Field Artillery Regiment (The Loyal Company) (Loyal Company Association Collection). Spine: Cap badge of the 9th Overseas Siege Battery (Loyal Company Association Collection). Cover, text, and map design by Mike Bechthold.

© 2016 The 3rd Field (The Loyal Company) Regimental Association

Wilfrid Laurier University Press
Waterloo, Ontario, Canada
www.wlupress.wlu.ca

This book is printed on FSC® certified paper and is certified Ecologo. It contains post-consumer fibre, is processed chlorine free, and is manufactured using biogas energy.

Printed in Canada

Every reasonable effort has been made to acquire permission for copyright material used in this text, and to acknowledge all such indebtedness accurately. Any errors and omissions called to the publisher's attention will be corrected in future printings.

No part of this publication may be reproduced, stored in a retrieval system, or transmitted, in any form or by any means, without the prior written consent of the publisher or a licence from the Canadian Copyright Licensing Agency (Access Copyright). For an Access Copyright licence, visit http://www.accesscopyright.ca or call toll free to 1-800-893-5777.

To those Loyal Gunners who served New Brunswick and Canada so well over the last two centuries, and to those men and women who continue to serve. They truly give meaning to *Quo fas et gloria ducunt.*

Contents

List of Maps — ix
Foreword by Brigadier-General James J. Selbie, O.M.M., C.D. (ret'd) — xi
Foreword by Lieutenant-Colonel Stephen Strachan — xiii
Preface by Honorary Colonel John K.F. Irving — xv

Chapter 1	The Second Century of Service Begins, 1893–1914	1
Chapter 2	Seeking and Finding a Role at Home and Abroad, 1914–16	23
Chapter 3	Building the Corps Artillery, 1915–16	53
Chapter 4	War on Two Fronts, 1917	97
Chapter 5	The Guns of Victory, 1918	135
Chapter 6	The Long Armistice, 1919–39	167
Chapter 7	War on the Home Front, 1939–45	203
Chapter 8	The Long Road to Combat in Europe, 1939–44	239
Chapter 9	Sicily and Italy: New Brunswick's Batteries in I Canadian Corps, 1943–45	281
Chapter 10	Northwest Europe, 1944–45	337
Chapter 11	Cold War and Turbulent Peace, 1946–2001	381
Conclusion	Afghanistan: The Regiment's Latest Test, 2001–12	429

Appendix 1	**Commanding Officers of The Loyal Company, 1793–2016**	445
Appendix 2	**Regimental Sergeants Major, 1866–2016**	447
	Note on Sources	449
	Acknowledgements	453
	Index	457

List of Maps

New Brunswick	xx
The Canadian Corps on the Western Front, 1915–18	22
The Second Battle of Ypres, April–May 1915	42
The Somme, July–November 1916	78
Vimy Ridge Artillery Positions, March–April 1917	103
The Battle of Vimy Ridge, 9–12 April 1917	112
The Arras–Vimy–Lens–Hill 70 sector	116
Amiens, August 1918	145
Arras, 26 August–5 September 1918	150
Canal du Nord and Cambrai, 27 September–11 October 1918	157
Cambrai to Mons, 12 October–11 November 1918	162
Fortress Saint John, 1880–1956	198
Sicily, July–August 1943	282
Italy, July 1943–February 1945	300
Crossing the Moro and Ortona, December 1943–January 1944	304
The Gustav and Hitler Lines, May 1944	316
Operation Olive, August–October 1944	326
Normandy: Juno to Caen, 6 June–10 July 1944	342
Normandy: Caen to Argentan, 18 July–21 August 1944	355
Normandy to the Scheldt, September–November 1944	364
The Scheldt, October–November 1944	369
The Final Months, February–May 1945	374
Afghanistan	435

Foreword by the Colonel Commandant of the Royal Canadian Artillery

From the first recorded use of artillery in Canada by Jacques Cartier in 1534, gunners have played a key role at many important junctures in the history of our nation. During war, the deterrence of conflict, and in peace, they have faithfully and skilfully applied the science and art of their calling to the defence and security of their country and the well-being of its people. Today, regiments and batteries of the Royal Regiment of Canadian Artillery make their homes from Victoria to Halifax. All modern-day members of the Regiment may find inspiration in the exploits of their predecessors, and in no unit is this more the case than in 3rd Field Artillery Regiment (The Loyal Company), RCA – proud steward of a New Brunswick artillery heritage more than 220 years in the making.

In taking up the story of the "Loyal Gunners" where Captain John Baxter left it in 1893, and bringing it all the way to 2012, the Loyal Company Association and the Gregg Centre for the Study of War and Society at the University of New Brunswick have made an exceptionally valuable contribution to the preservation and interpretation of the noble record of service of not only New Brunswick Gunners, but of the Royal Regiment as a whole. The authors' descriptions of the vicissitudes of war and peace experienced through the years by The Loyal Company and its many perpetuated and associated regiments and batteries raised in the province will ring true in the ears of gunners across the country. So too, will be familiar and equally stirring their portrayal of the great constant of this account, which is the dedication, courage, and sacrifice of the citizen-soldiers of Saint John and New Brunswick who have filled the ranks of these fine gunner units to serve their country at home and abroad. On behalf of all members of the Royal Regiment of Canadian Artillery, I congratulate and thank all of those who have taken a hand in the completion of this most worthy undertaking.

> Brigadier-General James J. Selbie, O.M.M., C.D. (ret'd)
> Colonel Commandant
> The Royal Regiment of Canadian Artillery

Foreword by the Commanding Officer of The Loyal Company

The writing of this book has been a long and challenging process, punctuated by false starts, changes in direction, and awe-inspiring discoveries of our rich history and the relatively unknown contributions made by New Brunswick gunners in the defence of Canada.

The Loyal Company was initially formed in 1793 in response to threats to the City of Saint John and New Brunswick. The story of the first 100 years of the unit was told by Captain John B.M. Baxter in *Historical Records of the New Brunswick Regiment of Canadian Artillery*, published in 1896. As the unit's Bicentennial took place in 1993, discussions ensued regarding the requirement to officially record its history during a century that included two World Wars, the Korean conflict, and the Cold War. The project was launched by Honorary Colonel William Turnbull and Honorary Lieutenant-Colonel Neil McKelvey, and it was proposed that the book cover the regimental history for the second hundred years, from 1893 to 1993.

Despite the best efforts of the regimental leadership, the project suffered through a period of limited progress. In 2011, in an effort to re-energize the project, a partnership was formed between the Loyal Company Association and the Gregg Centre for the Study of War and Society at the University of New Brunswick. Lee Windsor, the Deputy Director of the Gregg Centre, was designated the lead for the project, and as a direct result of his dedication and enthusiasm, he was able to recruit a small army of researchers, who quickly became inspired by their discovery of the exploits of the New Brunswick Gunners and what their story revealed about Canada's military history.

While writing this book, we have endeavoured to add personal accounts from a variety of former members of the regiment to help us tell the story of the unit from the perspective of the soldiers behind the guns. This was accomplished through the use of journals, letters home to family and friends, and direct testimony. It had originally been planned to focus the research solely on 3rd Field Regiment, but as the work progressed it became clear that our history was in fact linked to the many batteries raised and trained by 3rd Field Regiment for service overseas and all those that no longer exist but whose honours and heritage are perpetuated by 3rd Field Regiment. It was also decided that this book would cover the period from 1893 until 2012, when the unit addendum "The Loyal Company" was officially returned to the unit title.

Many individuals have played major roles in producing this book. On behalf of the regiment, I would like to thank Honorary Colonel John Irving for taking over from Colonel Turnbull and Lieutenant-Colonel McKelvey and for being the driving force in the effort to complete the book. I would also like to thank Lee Windsor, Marc Milner, and the Gregg Centre for their outstanding support of this project, and Roger Sarty of Wilfrid Laurier University for giving freely of his time and effort. I am certain that they appreciate the significance of the history of the unit, for it is its history that gives a unit its strength to endure during difficult and trying times. Prior to the publication of this book, our recent history was an untold story.

This book tells the story of 3rd Field Regiment (The Loyal Company) and the soldiers who served in it over the past 120 years. It will inspire future generations of the regiment and will highlight the extraordinary accomplishments of New Brunswick Gunners. I urge all Canadians to take pride in what has been achieved by the members of this unit on behalf of Canada.

Stephen Strachan
Lieutenant-Colonel
Commanding Officer, 2011–2015
3rd Field Artillery Regiment (The Loyal Company),
Royal Canadian Artillery

Quo fas et gloria ducunt.
(Whither right and glory lead)

Preface by the Honorary Colonel of the Regiment: Why The Loyal Company of Artillery Matters

For almost as long as there has been a place called New Brunswick there has existed an organized body of very special volunteer soldiers: New Brunswick's gunners. For well over two centuries this group of citizen-soldiers has guarded Canada's shores against threat and served Canada – and the wider international community – abroad.

They have gone by many names. The Loyal Company of Artillery was formed in Saint John on 4 May 1793 to defend the port from French raiders. Two decades later, The Loyal Company earned its first battle honour during the War of 1812. In the early nineteenth century a regiment of New Brunswick Artillery coalesced around The Loyal Company. It included volunteer field batteries, among them one in Woodstock, where gunners of this regiment still muster today as 89th Battery. In 1861, The Loyal Company earned the rare distinction of being given its own regimental colours, which it carried until they were laid up in the Stone Church in Saint John in 1925. These colours were on hand when The Loyal Company, and the entire Regiment of New Brunswick Artillery, were called out in 1866 to defend the province from an army of Fenians forming just across the border in Maine.

The story of the New Brunswick gunners in the nineteenth century was one of defence, both from the sea and overland from the Great Republic to the south. Captain John Baxter told that story, in the style of the era, in his 1896 work *Historical Records of the New Brunswick Regiment of Artillery 1793–1896*. The regiment's first century was, in many ways, a tale of vigilance and quiet service in defence of hearth and home. No shots were fired in anger, no units deployed to operational theatres outside the province. But New Brunswick and Canada had been protected from those who would have done her and her citizens harm.

The regiment's story since 1896 is one of sharp contrast with Baxter's account. It involved gunners from all around the province as well as the rest of the Maritimes. There was no way that members of the regiment in 1896 could have foreseen the incredible conflict, destruction, and towering obstacles that those who followed them in service of the guns would endure and overcome. Indeed, since 1899 New Brunswick's gunners have been at the forefront of the action in Canada's overseas military activities, and at the cutting edge of modern artillery developments.

Less than three years after Baxter's book was published, New Brunswick's gunners were serving overseas, in the South African War (also known as the Boer War), and they have continued to do so ever since. During the Great War of 1914–18, New Brunswick's gunners fought a two-front war. For The Loyal Company the centre of that war the home front, in the newly constructed Barrack Green Armories in Saint John, and in the Composite Battery on Partridge Island and the training batteries it supported. The gunners' perennial task of guarding Canada's major year-round commercial port remained. Soon enough, however, that task changed: the New Brunswickers began providing heavy artillery for the Canadian Corps on the Western Front, where they adapted their coastal gunnery skills to the modern siege warfare needed to smash the German defences. As this new history of The Loyal Company and the gunners of New Brunswick reveals, because of the unique battery on Partridge Island, gunners from this province came to dominate the Canadian Corps Heavy Artillery. These New Brunswickers, and the heavy batteries raised in this province, were key to Canada's victory at Vimy Ridge, Hill 70, and Passchendaele in 1917, and were at the heart of the fire plans that blasted the final holes in the German defences during the 100 Days campaign of 1918. New Brunswick's 6th Siege Battery pursued the defeated German army retreating from Cambrai, and on 9 November 1918, near Mons, 1st Heavy Battery commanded by Major Inches of Saint John fired the war's final shots by the Canadian Garrison Artillery.

In the aftermath of the Great War, most of these accomplished soldiers returned to New Brunswick and to Canada, resolved to build a better life and a better country. Fortunately, many of them also stayed active in their local units, keeping alive critical gunnery skills in the expectation – indeed, fear – that Canada would need these again. Their worst fears became reality as Hitler rose to power in the 1930s and Germany renewed her aggression.

By 1939, tanks and aircraft, and the shift to oil-fired warships – especially the further development of diesel-electric submarines – presented new challenges on all fronts. Steady, dedicated training in basic gunnery skills would serve these units well during the transition to a new, more complicated battleground. What was now 3rd Coast Brigade mobilized again to defend Saint John, but this time as the heart of a massive project to protect Canada's most important winter port. The resulting Saint John Fortress complex drew some 3,000 to 4,000 men and women from across Canada into an integrated web of coastal defence, counter-bombardment, and anti-aircraft batteries, supported by an infantry brigade, machine-gun companies, anti-tank units, and engineer, service corps, and RCAF units.

Meanwhile, batteries from across the province went overseas to meet the new challenges of the modern war. Two of these batteries, the 8th from Moncton and the 28th from Newcastle, served throughout the war as field artillery batteries. Most of the others converted to the new anti-tank role, which involved wrestling high-velocity guns into direct fire positions on the forward edge of the battle zones. The 90th Battery from Fredericton landed in Sicily in July 1943 and evolved into perhaps the most innovative anti-tank unit in the Canadian army. The 104th joined them for the Italian campaign. Another, the 105th from St George, stormed the beaches of Normandy in June 1944, while the 103rd from Campbellton formed the backbone of the famous Canadian stand at St-Lambert-sur-Dives against a tide of Germans escaping the Falaise Gap in August 1944. Meanwhile the 89th Battery from Woodstock served in three roles: as field artillery, anti-aircraft artillery, and – briefly – front-line infantry in northern Italy in late 1944.

The vital importance of gunners for Canadian defence and mobilization planning was evident in the growth of New Brunswick's artillery after 1945. As the Cold War deepened, the province's artillery establishment reached its peak in size and complexity. By the early 1950s there were four and a half regiments of artillery in the province: two field regiments, two heavy anti-aircraft regiments – tasked primarily with defending Saint John from long-range Soviet bombers – and two batteries of a regional anti-tank regiment.

The advent of nuclear weapons confronted the province's gunners with their greatest existential crisis. Rapid changes in defence policy stripped units from the order of battle through the late 1950s and 1960s until only 3rd Field Regiment remained. And even the 3rd was under constant threat, with the result that senior New Brunswick gunners were forced to find creative ways to task-train as artillerymen. However, the establishment of Canadian Forces Base Gagetown outside Oromocto in 1950s was of incalculable help in preserving a strong artillery community in New Brunswick. CFB Gagetown became the home of the Canadian army, and its role as a key training centre and its proximity to the United States, the port of Saint John, and Europe established it as a national centre of excellence for preparing new soldiers and army leaders to defend Canada. Gagetown's size and the similarity of its terrain to that of northwest Europe allowed it to play a key role in the Canadian army. Because all of this activity took place halfway between Saint John (home of 115th Battery) and Woodstock (home of 89th Battery), it was always possible to get men – and, increasingly, women – of the regiment into the field and onto the gun line. It goes without saying that it was equally valuable for the Royal Canadian Artillery School to be able to draw on the talented gunners of 3rd Field Regiment.

The perseverance and foresight of a dedicated band of New Brunswick gunners has served Canada well. As the twentieth century drew to a close, well-trained gunners were once again needed on Canadian missions overseas. When the Royal Canadian Artillery were sent back into action in Afghanistan, gunners of 3rd Field Artillery Regiment were ready to deploy using the latest technologies. The specialist skills sustained and nurtured by 3rd Field Regiment every day since the regiment was formed in 1793 proved yet again the importance and adaptability of Canada's reserve (militia) soldiers in time of need.

The 3rd Field Regiment (The Loyal Company) remains Canada's oldest serving artillery unit. For more than 220 years, it has answered New Brunswick's call, and Canada's, in times of peace and war. The regiment has evolved, adapted, endured, and succeeded as an artillery unit since its founding. The Loyal Company and the gunners of New Brunswick have met the challenge. They have served their community and their country with dedication and distinction from the dusty veldt of South Africa to the dusty hills of South Asia and in myriad places in between. The motto of the Royal Regiment of Artillery and the Royal Regiment of Canadian Artillery is Ubique – "everywhere." That motto has been well lived up to by the men and women of New Brunswick who have in the past and will in the future serve Canada's guns. We look forward to our third century of service.

> John K.F. Irving
> Honorary Colonel, 2010–2018
> 3rd Field Artillery Regiment (The Loyal Company)
> Royal Canadian Artillery

New Brunswick

Chapter 1

The Second Century of Service Begins, 1893–1914

On 4 May 1893 the New Brunswick Battalion of Garrison Artillery, the oldest in Canada, celebrated its centenary. A 100-gun salute was fired from positions around Saint John, and the day was capped by a concert at the Mechanics' Institute. While there was much to celebrate – a century of service in defence of one of the great ports of British North America and the winter gateway to the Canadas – it had been a quiet century.

That said, The Loyal Company had served its sovereign, its province, and its city well during its first hundred years. Wars with France and the United States in the late eighteenth and early nineteenth centuries had presented real and immediate dangers to the port city and the commerce of the area, besides threatening winter communications with British colonies along the St. Lawrence and the Great Lakes that were isolated half the year. A complex network of batteries had grown to guard the city and the seaward end of the road to Canada. The fact that the defences were never tested was, in no small way, mute testimony to their success. By midcentury, when war was a distant memory and threats seemed remote, The Loyal Company had dwindled to a handful of diehards, and for a year the administration of the unit lapsed. That brief and apparently harmless pause was forgotten in the new wave of volunteerism and the rising threats of the 1860s, when Saint John once again guarded the road to Canada during the tense years of the American Civil War. But that low point was enough for the Militia Department of the new

Dominion of Canada to claim a break in the chain of continuity. When the Militia Act of 1868 formally established the Dominion's new Militia, The Loyal Company joined the ranks of "Canadian" regiments, but the distinction of senior artillery was awarded to another unit of the new Canadian Militia.

The only major mobilizations following the War of 1812 were against the Fenian threat, most notably in 1866. That year, thousands of Fenians, many of them battle-hardened veterans of the American Civil War, gathered around Eastport, Maine, to invade New Brunswick. This threat led to the only full mobilization of the province's colonial militia and its artillery component, during which the Saint John defences were brought to complete readiness. This was the last time New Brunswickers stood ready to defend their province from invasion. Subsequent war scares with the Russians in the 1870s highlighted the enduring importance of The Loyal Company, its skills, and the fortifications it manned. Some volunteers were accepted for service in the North-West Rebellion of 1885, but no actual units – and no artillery – joined in from New Brunswick. By the time of The Loyal Company's centennial in 1893, the New Brunswick Battalion of Garrison Artillery and the province's two field batteries (in Newcastle and Woodstock) had an honourable legacy of home defence. They had demonstrated a commitment to service and an adaptability to change that would characterize the service of New Brunswick gunners for the next hundred years or more. But the province's artillery units had not yet fired a gun in anger. The twentieth century would change all that.

In the late nineteenth and early twentieth centuries, the gunners of New Brunswick were swept up in major changes to the world around them, including organizational and technological changes. The late nineteenth century was characterized by the rise of imperial powers to challenge British supremacy and by the growing threat of major wars. The British home government responded by urging closer imperial cooperation, especially from the self-governing Dominions like Canada; meanwhile, military reforms throughout the Empire sought to build effective and more cohesive imperial armed forces. Those pressures, coupled with active service in the South African War of 1899–1902, transformed New Brunswick gunners on the eve of the outbreak of the Great War in August 1914.

In the early 1890s the New Brunswick Militia's artillery establishment consisted of two field batteries and one battalion of garrison artillery. The 10th (Woodstock) Field Battery had been established on 30 May 1866 as part of the NB colonial militia, and the 12th (Newcastle) Battery had been formed on 18 December 1868 as part of the new Canadian Militia. These field batteries were to provide light, mobile fire support to infantry and cavalry units on the battlefield. In 1893, each field battery consisted of seventy-nine all ranks. They included six officers (major, captain, lieutenant, second lieutenant, surgeon, and veterinary surgeon); seven sergeants (battery sergeant major, battery quartermaster sergeant, sergeant of farriers, and four sergeants); and sixty-six rank and file, including four corporals, four

Colonel Beaufort Henry Vidal, Commander of Militia District No. 8 (NB) between 1898 and 1900, reviews the guns of 4th (NB) Brigade, Canadian Field Artillery, Camp Sussex, ca. 1898. (PANB P13/160)

bombardiers, one trumpeter, thirty-four gunners, and twenty-three drivers. Each battery was equipped with four iron-rifled muzzle-loading 9-pounder field guns. Each gun was six feet long, weighed 800 pounds, and had a 3-inch calibre. When first purchased in 1872, the 9-pounder was a state-of-the-art direct-fire field gun; it would be used on active service during the 1885 North-West Rebellion. But by the early 1890s, it was obsolescent and about to be replaced. Each battery also had two ammunition wagons. Twenty-nine horses were used by the officers and riders, and to pull the guns and wagons.

By 1893, field batteries were receiving twelve days of training each year at local headquarters in Newcastle and Woodstock and at Camp Sussex, which they reached by rail. Unit strength at summer camps varied enormously. In 1892 the Newcastle Battery, commanded by Lt.-Col. R. Call, had only five officers and fifty-nine other ranks present, leaving them fifteen men short. But in 1894 they were fully up to strength. The field batteries also underwent annual firing tests on the Île d'Orléans in Quebec. In 1894, New Brunswick field gunners distinguished themselves nationally at this annual gun practice. The final test involved firing thirty-two common shells and sixteen shrapnel shells at two targets at different ranges. The Woodstock Battery scored 321 points, 114 ahead of its closest competitor, and won first prize from the Dominion Artillery Association, the organization formed in 1876 to develop artillery skills and to disseminate knowledge of gunnery practices. The Newcastle Battery came fourth with 187 points.

New Brunswick's field artillery deployed for action, Sussex, ca. 1898. (PANB P13/145)

In contrast to the field gunners, garrison artillery – as the term implies – was considered largely immobile. In the British terminology, garrison artillery was responsible for coast defence and employed heavy guns, typically in fixed fortifications. The Saint John unit, designated the "New Brunswick Battalion of Garrison Artillery" on 1 January 1893, was responsible for defence of the port. This was an old task, but the coming of the railways had changed Saint John's role in the life of the new Dominion. The main overland route, the Intercolonial Railway, now ran through eastern New Brunswick (having been built partly with imperial money diverted from defence schemes for Saint John) and connected directly with the imperial naval base in Halifax. That Nova Scotia port also handled Canada's winter passenger traffic and had an important liner terminal. Saint John, by contrast, was now Canada's major east coast commercial port, with more cargo-handling capacity than Halifax. It was linked to the Intercolonial Railway by a branch line to Moncton, and in 1889 when the link through Maine to Montreal was completed it became the eastern terminus of the Canadian Pacific Railway.

In 1893, the establishment strength of the New Brunswick Battalion of Garrison Artillery was 232 all ranks. That included twenty-two officers: a lieutenant-colonel and a major; five captains, lieutenants, and second lieutenants; and an adjutant, quartermaster, surgeon, assistant surgeon, and paymaster. Among the NCOs were fifteen sergeants for the regimental staff and batteries: a regimental sergeant major, regimental quartermaster sergeant, orderly room sergeant, paymaster sergeant, bandmaster, and ten sergeants. The battalion was completed by 195 rank and file: fifteen corporals, five trumpeters, twenty bandsmen, and 155 gunners. The battalion was divided into headquarters and five companies (the equivalent of batteries), each of which consisted of three officers and forty-two other ranks. In early 1893, the battalion was commanded by Lt.-Col. John Russell Armstrong, and the batteries by Captains Stanley Crawford, John Baxter, Charles Harrison, George Jones, and James Steeves.

As the nineteenth century drew to a close, the Dominion government moved on militia reforms that would, in the end, modernize Canada's artillery. In the new age of steamships and a British-controlled global system of submarine telegraph cables, threats to distant ports in the Empire grew remote. Naval dockyards like Halifax and Esquimalt still needed defending, but attacks on Saint John and other commercial ports were increasingly unlikely. The Royal Navy ruled the seas, especially the North Atlantic, and there was no place for coal-fired raiders to refuel without being found. So by 1896, when the number "3" was added to the title of the Saint John battalion, making it the "3rd New Brunswick Battalion of Canadian Garrison Artillery," the rationale for garrison artillery in the port city seemed to be fading. The unit's new number cemented its place on the seniority list of the Dominion's artillery and for that reason was not received warmly by its members. In their view, the Saint John garrison artillery pre-dated the 1st in Halifax and the 2nd in Montreal by many years.

Like the field artillery batteries, the garrison battalion underwent twelve days of training each year. The annual gun practice, held in either Saint John or Halifax, usually took place on the day of the annual inspection. In 1892, the strength of the batteries undergoing training varied from twenty-eight to forty-one men. The inspecting officer was highly complementary of their performance at camp that year: "Very smart and well turned out. The average efficiency of the Batteries was excellent." It was also noted that the 3rd NB Battalion had a very good band.

By the end of the nineteenth century the New Brunswick Battalion of Garrison Artillery oversaw an arsenal that was all obsolescent, cast-iron, muzzle-loading guns, dating to the war scares of the mid-century. In 1896, gun practice consisted of detachments firing antiquated 64-pounder rifled muzzle-loaders, which had been allocated to Saint John in the 1870s. These and other ancient pieces were still spread around the city in a system that had been developed to meet an American threat in the 1860s: Fort Dufferin, Carleton Martello Tower, Fairville, Fort Howe, Red Head, Partridge Island, and Dorchester Battery. The guns included 12, 18, 24, 32, and 68-pounder cast, smooth-bore cannon, 12- and 24-pounder howitzers, and one 8-inch mortar. The gunners' only chance to fire relatively modern guns like the 64-pounder rifled muzzle-loaders (formerly the smooth-bore 32-pounder, rebored to take a conoidal-shaped modern shell) and 20-pounder rifled breech-loaders came during the annual competitions.

As with most militia units of the era, much of the time of NB gunners was taken up with ceremonial activities. Each year, 3rd Battalion celebrated Dominion Day and Loyalist Day in Saint John with a gun salute from Fort Dufferin. The 3rd was in fact the only Canadian artillery unit entitled to fire a full salute on Loyalist Day, and the only unit designated to fire the salute on the opening of the NB Legislature – distinctions it retains to this day. In August 1893 the 3rd celebrated the visit of the Governor General, the Earl of Aberdeen, by firing a Royal Salute. One of the army's highlights in 1897 was the commemoration of Queen Victoria's Diamond Jubilee; a large contingent travelled to London that summer to participate in various events, including a grand parade. Among the troops representing the Canadian army were two soldiers from 3rd NB Battalion of the Canadian Garrison Artillery and one from 10th (Woodstock) Field Battery. In October 1901, gunners also participated in the Royal Review in Halifax, during which His Royal Highness the Duke of Cornwall presented South African war medals to Maritime recipients.

By 1899 the garrison unit had been renamed yet again, this time 3rd (New Brunswick) Regiment, Canadian Garrison Artillery. It would retain that name for the next decade or so. The name change brought no substantive organizational changes: the regiment, like the battalion, still consisted of the regimental headquarters at Saint John and five companies, two of which were located in the city proper, with the others in Carleton, Portland, and Fairville.

The Dominion government woke from its lethargy concerning military matters in the mid-1890s when the possibility of war between Britain and the United States arose during a boundary dispute between Venezuela and British Guiana. In 1896 the Canadian Militia Department, under the guidance of minister Frederick Borden, began increasing military expenditures and taking steps to modernize the Canadian army, including the artillery. That year the Militia Department ordered new 12-pounder breech-loading field guns from England to replace the obsolete 9-pounder muzzle-loaders. The 12-pounders had several advantages over the 9-pounders: they had a longer range of 5,000 yards; the guns' light-weight steel carriages made them more mobile; they used steel shells with more advanced fuses that allowed for either instantaneous detonation on contact or air bursts against troops in the open; and the new shells' smokeless cordite propellant would help conceal the batteries' positions from observation.

The new guns began arriving for distribution in 1897, but it was not until 1900 that the two New Brunswick field batteries received theirs. When they arrived, the batteries expanded from four guns to six, organized into "Left" and "Right" sections of three guns each. Militia units also began to receive replacement small arms and equipment. On 1 March 1897, 3rd NB Regiment was issued with Martini-Henry rifles to replace its aging Snider-Enfields, and by 1900 its men were outfitted with the Oliver pattern belts and cartridge pouches.

As the artillery units modernized, training at annual camps became more advanced. This improved training was largely based on the work of Major Charles William Drury, who in time became known as the "Father of Modern Artillery" in Canada. Drury had been born and raised in Saint John and learned about gunnery while serving as an officer with the New Brunswick Brigade of Garrison Artillery. After a transfer to the Permanent Force, he served in the North-West Rebellion. Later, he developed realistic training by combining moving targets with gun practice at the new central camp at Deseronto near Kingston, Ontario. By 1900, field artillery batteries were attending nine-day camps at Deseronto using their own equipment, horses, and personnel. Here they carried out gun practice along more modern lines that approximated conditions encountered on active service.

By the time Drury's realistic training was in place, many New Brunswick gunners had experienced the real thing in South Africa. In 1899, after years of tension and manipulation, the British government finally went to war with two quasi-independent Boer republics: the Transvaal and the Orange Free State. Both had been founded by Dutch settlers who had moved north in the mid-nineteenth century to escape the Cape Colony, a former Dutch possession that had been taken over by Britain after the Napoleonic Wars. The Boers' fierce independence was undermined by the discovery of gold on their new territories, an influx of British miners who threatened the political stability and independence of the two republics, and the machinations of British imperialists who wanted Transvaal and the Orange Free State under British suzerainty. Formal talks between the Boers and the British broke down in September 1899; the following month, the Boers were goaded into declaring war on Britain. When that happened, Britons and settlers in the Dominions flocked to the colours to defend "British rights."

Canada was not obliged to send troops to South Africa, but the government allowed volunteers to go. Between October 1899 and 1902, when the war ended, about 7,300 Canadian soldiers served in South Africa. Among them were at least seventy-three soldiers from New Brunswick's artillery units. They served overseas with eight different Canadian units, mostly with the infantry. New Brunswick gunners served in 2nd (Special Service) Battalion of the Royal Canadian Regiment, E Battery of the Royal Canadian Field Artillery, the Royal Canadian Dragoons, 2nd, 4th, and 6th Battalions of the Canadian Mounted Rifles, the Canadian Scouts, and the South African Constabulary. This was a modest contribution to be sure, but the South African War marked the beginnings of the overseas service that has characterized the experience of New Brunswick gunners ever since.

The first New Brunswick gunners to serve overseas went as infantry. Recruiting for the First Contingent's Special Service Battalion began in mid-October 1899. The battalion consisted of eight independent companies (A through H) of 125 men each. Members of 3rd New Brunswick Regiment were quick to enlist. In October, fifteen regimental officers agreed unanimously to notify Ottawa that they were ready to participate in whatever form that troops were to be raised. The next day, Captain Beverley R. Armstrong, son of the commanding officer of 3rd NB Regiment and a member of its No. 1 Company, notified Lt.-Col. Armstrong that he wished to join the "Transvaal contingent." Like many men, he was "willing to accept any rank which may be allotted to me." The younger Armstrong would get his chance, but not until the Second Contingent was organized. At least twenty-one gunners from 3rd NB Regiment enlisted in the First Contingent. They served as infantrymen with G Company of 1st Special Service Battalion, which was loosely affiliated with Canada's only permanent infantry unit, the Royal Canadian Regiment of Infantry (later renamed the Royal Canadian Regiment), and thus comprised almost one-fifth of that company. Among the company's officers was Captain F.C. Jones, adjutant of 3rd NB Regiment, who became a lieutenant in G Company. They departed Saint John on 25 October to join the rest of the battalion in Quebec and sailed for South Africa five days later.

The 1st Special Service Battalion arrived in South Africa on 29 November 1899. By then the British had suffered a number of serious setbacks. British garrisons were under siege at Ladysmith and Mafeking, and a relief column under General Revers Buller had been defeated by a much smaller Boer force at Colenso. On 1 December the battalion left Cape Town for the front, reaching Belmont on 11 December, where it engaged in outpost duty and training for the next two months. In early February of 1900 the battalion joined the British 19th Brigade in time for its advance on Boer positions on the Modder River as part of the campaign to relieve the embattled garrisons at Ladysmith and Mafeking. It was there, along the Modder, that a ten-day battle began that culminated in the surrender of Boer General Cronje's force at Paardeberg on 27 February.

The Battle of Paardeberg is generally viewed as the baptism of fire for the Royal Canadian Regiment, and New Brunswickers from G Company played a prominent part in the outcome. General Cronje had been forced by the sudden arrival of the British to dig in, which led to a ten-day siege of his position. Outnumbered three to one, the Boers repelled repeated attempts to overwhelm them by direct assaults, including one involving the RCR, and were subjected to continuous shelling. When the RCR's turn came around again to lead the assault, the regiment – led by G Company – moved by night instead, and by dawn had occupied positions overlooking the Boer lines. The next morning, faced with withering fire from the Canadians, Cronje surrendered. A separate column relieved Ladysmith the next day, but it took until May to lift the siege around Mafeking.

During the battle of Paardeberg, seven members of 3rd NB Regiment became casualties. William Donahue, Fred Kirkpatrick, Henry Marley, John Rawlings, Alfred Simpson, and Frank Sprague were all wounded. Corporal Fred W. Withers, formerly of No. 1 Company of the 3rd, was killed on 27 February. He was buried near General Cronje's laager on the north bank of the Modder River. On 4 March,

Carleton County Detachment of E Battery, South African campaign, photographed prior to their departure. Back row, L–R: Frank Brewer, Norman Cameron, Robert Smith, William Kenney, Harry Hall, Harry McLean, George Parker, and Fred Everett. Middle row, L–R: Robert Hughes, Wheeler Leighton, Harold Grey, Major Good, Harry Dysart, and A.S. Tibbits. Front row, L–R: J. Allie Hazen, Frank Buck, Robert Welch, George Searle, and W.P. Lynn. George Glew absent. (PANB P37/357)

3rd NB Regiment held a memorial service for Withers at Saint John's Stone Church. Withers was the first member of the regiment to be killed in action overseas; many more were soon to follow. His name appears on the provincial South African War Memorial on Douglas Avenue in Saint John. Paardeberg Day remains an important date on the regiment's calendar, and until the 1950s it was honoured with special significance by the NB militia.

By mid-1900 the Boers were on the defensive, adopting guerrilla hit-and-run tactics. During the final stages of its tour in South Africa, G Company did much marching but saw little action. Bloemfontein, Johannesburg, and then Pretoria were captured, and on 4 June the Canadians took part in the British army's grand victory parade at Pretoria. G Company returned home on 1 October 1900. On 28 October a reception that included 3rd NB Regiment was held at the Saint John train station to greet the returning gunners.

In the dark days of December 1899, while British garrisons lay under siege and General Buller's field army was retreating ignominiously from Colenso, Ottawa announced that a Second Contingent would be sent to South Africa. This would be a much bigger force, consisting of two battalions of the Canadian Mounted Rifles and a brigade of artillery consisting of three batteries of field artillery. Lt.-Col. C.W. Drury, RCA, the Saint John native and former member of the New Brunswick Battalion of Garrison Artillery, commanded the artillery brigade. When it was decided not to call out the Permanent Force batteries, three Special Service batteries (C, D, and E) were raised from drafts of the Regular Force (A and B batteries), and volunteers from militia field batteries. E Battery was raised in Quebec and the Maritimes at several enrolment and concentration locations, including Woodstock and Newcastle.

Recruitment for a one-year tour of duty overseas began during the week before Christmas 1899. Among the members of E Battery were at least forty New Brunswickers, including fourteen from Newcastle's 12th Field Battery and twenty from Woodstock's 10th Field Battery. At least six others came from 3rd NB Regiment, which in early January had received a request for gunners from headquarters. E Battery was commanded by Major G. Hunter Ogilvie, RCA; among its other officers were Major R. Costigan of 3rd NB Regiment, who became battery captain, and Captain W.C. Good of 10th Field Battery, who was the lieutenant in charge of 3rd Section.

On January 21, D and E Batteries sailed from Halifax aboard the transport *Laurentian*, with a strength of five officers, eight staff sergeants and sergeants, two trumpeters, 136 other ranks, and 137 horses. The Militia and Regular Force gunners were mixed, with one section of each battery composed of RCA personnel and the remainder from the Militia. Each battery was armed with six of the recently acquired 12-pounder breech-loading guns. The guns were taken from A and B Batteries, RCA, and 2nd Field Battery (Montreal), leaving those batteries "crippled" until their guns could be replaced. The Special Service batteries also brought ammunition limbers, store and forge wagons, and other transport equipment required for active service, as well as ammunition, fuses, and cartridges. A column to supply the batteries with reserve ammunition was not organized in Canada. This was to be organized locally, but the transport wagons, oxen, and drivers secured in South Africa were soon found to be inadequate. Once they took to the field, these local ammunition wagons often lagged miles behind the guns, and the batteries lost some of their mobility. Canada would not make this mistake the next time it deployed guns overseas.

By the time E Battery arrived at Cape Town on 16 February 1900, many of its horses had died of influenza, and they could not be easily replaced. Riding horses had to be used on the gun teams; mules pulled the battery transport wagons. After being re-equipped, the battery underwent collective training on the new guns for more than three weeks. On 27 February, news arrived of Cronje's surrender at Paardeberg. During the subsequent British advance on Bloemfontein and Pretoria, infantry was in short supply, so the Second Contingent's two mounted rifle battalions headed for the front. Artillery, however, was plentiful, so the Canadian gunners remained behind.

The gunners' chance came a month later. When a rebellion broke out in the Karoo District of the Cape Colony, the Canadian batteries were called on to join a punitive force to quell the uprising. On 13 March the brigade (less C Battery, which arrived later) moved north by train to join the Canarvon Field Force. Once the revolt ended the batteries were sent to different districts within the theatre of war. E Battery was sent to guard a 180-mile stretch of railway from Victoria to Belmont. The battery began a pattern of operations where it was often broken up and scattered over a wide area; when concentrated in a larger column, it often served alongside British and Australian gunners.

The Canadian artillery brigade finally got into action in mid-May, when it marched with a column northwest into the Griqualand country near Kimberley. On 30 May the column was surprised by an early morning Boer attack at Faber's Putt. Here the battery "experienced the hottest fire of the campaign." During the attack on its bivouac, E Battery suffered the division's highest casualties of the campaign: one gun detachment (seven men) lost one man killed and five wounded. Another four from other gun crews were wounded. Among the casualties was Gunner Norman P. McLeod from Fredericton. According to the battery commander, Major Ogilvie, "no seasoned troops could have been steadier or behaved better, obeying every order as quietly as on parade, than these young Canadian gunners."

For the gunners of the Second Contingent, the rest of the campaign was a dreary routine of marching across the veldt or standing guard. The action at Faber's Putt was followed by another month of mobile operations; then E Battery returned to guarding another stretch of railway north of Kimberley. In mid-November they began preparing for their return to Canada, arriving at Cape Town on 1 December. By then, the battery had been trekking constantly across the arid landscape, marching about 2,000 miles over nine months in the field. They sailed for home on 13 December and arrived in Halifax on 8 January 1901.

The experiences of the members of 3rd NB Regiment who had joined the Second Contingent's mounted rifle battalions were similar. They marched, guarded lines of communication, and suffered the occasion ambush. Among these gunners turned mounted infantry was Captain Beverley Armstrong, who had resigned his commission and enlisted in 1st Battalion of the Canadian Mounted Rifles as a trooper, rising eventually to lance corporal. Armstrong fought at Johannesburg on 29 May, Pretoria on 4 June, and Diamond Hill on 11–12 June. While campaigning in the Transvaal on 9 July 1900, he was shot in the right foot. The wound refused to heal, and surgeons later removed his leg from the mid-calf. He arrived in England in November and visited Queen Victoria at Windsor Castle on the last occasion in which she saw outsiders before her death. Armstong was presented with the Queen's Medal and four clasps, and was fêted upon his return to Saint John. Although his amputation was rated as a "total disability," Armstrong returned to duty with 3rd NB Regiment. As would later be revealed during the Great War, Armstrong was anything but disabled.

Some New Brunswick gunners served with more than one contingent. At least fifteen members served on two different tours, and one – Gunner George Frederick McLeod of 3rd Regiment – served overseas with three units: E Battery, the Canadian Scouts, and the South African Constabulary. William Good, a Militia major, returned to South Africa in the summer of 1902 as a captain in 4th Regiment of the Canadian Mounted Rifles. He was accompanied by Captain T.W. Lawlor of 12th Field Battery, who served as a lieutenant in 4th Canadian Mounted Rifles.

Canadian gunners learned many valuable lessons during the war in South Africa. First, they saw that they needed to exert greater centralized control over their batteries. Although they were brigaded together on occasion, at no time did they actively campaign alongside one another. For much of the time, the batteries were subdivided, with their sections serving in composite formations, sometimes made up of various national contingents. Second, they saw the need for heavier ordnance. The Boers were well equipped with modern Krupp artillery, and they knew how to handle it. The Canadian gunners soon realized that their 12-pounders were inferior to the Boer artillery, especially in range. British batteries fared better with their 15-pounders, which were reconstructed breech-loaders to which recoil buffers had been fitted. Some thought it had been a mistake to order the 12-pounder in the 1890s when the 15-pounder was already available – a belief that experiences in South Africa confirmed. Third, they learned the value of concealment. The practice of deploying guns in the open and engaging the enemy over open sights had exposed Canadian gunners to long-range Boer rifle fire. In the future, new techniques of indirect fire from cover would be taught in artillery schools and training camps. However, some practices would not change; for example, field batteries would continue to be used to fire on enemy personnel rather than on the enemy's guns. Counter-battery work belonged to the big guns, and Canada deployed none of these in South Africa. More generally, the war awakened the interest of the Canadian people and government in the army, especially the artillery, which would receive greater appropriations in the future.

While the Canadian troops were on active service in South Africa, the Militia carried on at home. The 3rd NB Regiment found various ways to support the overseas war effort. In December 1899, officers presented Captain Jones with a watch before he departed for the front with G Company, and the regimental band gave a concert at the Saint John opera house to support the Transvaal Fund, a benevolent organization supporting widows and orphans of soldiers killed on active service. In January 1900 the regiment held a concert at the Mechanics' Institute to raise funds for the Soldiers' Wives League.

The 3rd NB Regiment band leads a parade down King Street, June 1908. (PANB P210/3008)

The 3rd NB Regiment also carried on with its various Militia duties. On 30 August 1900, seventy-five Fenian Raid medals for the members of the Saint John Volunteer Battalion then living in New Brunswick were presented at the Drill Shed. One of those receiving the medal, Sergeant Major Samuel Hughes, was still serving in 3rd NB Regiment. In fact, Hughes had served in the Royal Artillery during the Crimean War and had later immigrated to New Brunswick. He had joined the regiment in August 1866 during the Fenian Raids and was appointed sergeant major. According to regimental orders dated 17 September 1901:

> During this long period, though at times suffering from a wound received at the siege of Sebastopol, he has never been absent from drill through sickness or otherwise nor has he been late on parade. He has not only been the Sergeant-Major of the Regiment but he has also acted as a most competent Drill Instructor to Officers as well as men. Ever cheerful and efficient in the discharge of his duties he has won and maintained the admiration of every past and present Officer, Non-Commissioned Officer and Gunner in the Regiment and now retiring at his own request he still holds the esteem, good will and best wishes of all his comrade[s].

Hughes retired on that day in September 1901, after thirty-five years of continuous service with the unit. At the close of the day the regiment formed a hollow square around him, presented him with gifts, and sang "Auld Lang Sine" as he marched off for the last time.

The 3rd NB Regiment contingent at the summer gun camp training in their new role as field gunners at Petawawa, August 1906. The Boer War influence shows clearly in the adoption of slouch hats. (NBM X8713)

In 1901, the field and garrison artillery batteries from New Brunswick conducted their annual gun practice at central camps. Members of 10th and 12th Field Batteries attended Camp Deseronto, where they fired percussion and timed shrapnel shells and case shot from 12-pounder breech-loading guns. Similarly, gun detachments from 3rd NB Regiment's four batteries carried out their gun practice on 40-pounder rifled breech-loading guns and 5-inch breech-loading howitzers at the garrison artillery camp on the Île d'Orléans.

Meanwhile, 3rd Regiment continued with its many ceremonial duties. On 22 February 1901 the regiment marked the passing of Queen Victoria with a memorial service and an eighty-one-minute and eighty-one-gun salute from Dorchester Battery, timed to end at sundown. In October 1901, Saint John was visited by the Duke and Duchess of Cornwall and York (the future King George V and Queen Mary), along with the Governor General, Lord Minto, and the prime minister, Sir Wilfrid Laurier. As the train arrived, the guns of 3rd Regiment fired a twenty-one-gun salute. The Royal Procession then travelled to the Exhibition Grounds, where a military review was staged and campaign medals were presented to Boer War veterans, along with a "sword of honour" to Captain F.C. Jones, the adjutant of 3rd Regiment.

Borden's reforms of the Canadian Militia and army begun in the 1890s were spurred on by the experience in South Africa and continued until 1911. As a result, the Militia saw major changes in the period leading up to the Great War aimed at creating a self-contained, modern, and effective citizen army. By 1914, the Canadian army was not big, but it was comparatively modern and well equipped. These reforms had largely been driven by Major-General E.T.H. Hutton, the Militia's General Officer Commanding between 1898 and 1900, who made several recommendations aimed at transforming the army into a modern all-arms force capable of taking to the field on active operations.

For the artillery, Hutton's reforms meant the creation of new batteries and the formation of permanent field brigades. On 9 May 1905 two new units were added to New Brunswick's artillery establishment. The 19th Battery of field artillery was organized, with its headquarters in Moncton. In September 1907, command of the battery fell to Major S. Boyd Anderson, an officer who would leave an indelible mark on Canadian artillery over the next decade. An Ammunition Column unit was also created, with its headquarters in Newcastle. The requirement for proper support of guns had been amply demonstrated in South Africa, and the Canadian militia reforms reflected that lesson. Although it took some time to form, by mid-1914 the Ammunition Column was operational and under the command of Captain A.E. Barton. Then, in June 1905, the 10th, 12th, and 19th Field Batteries and the Ammunition Column were organized as the 4th Brigade of the Canadian Field Artillery with brigade headquarters at Woodstock. The formation of 4th Brigade marked a milestone in the history of artillery in the province. At first, the brigade was commanded by Lt.-Col. F.H.J. Dibblee, the former commanding officer of 10th Field Battery. On 22 September 1910, Lt.-Col. William Good, a veteran of two tours in the South African War and Dibblee's successor at 10th Field, took command.

The 19th (Moncton) Battery on parade, Sussex, July 1909. The mounted officer in the front is Major Boyd Anderson. (PANB P210/163)

Further reorganization in 1911 intended to put the army on a more efficient wartime footing took place when military districts across the country were reconstituted to form divisional commands. The 6th Infantry Division was created in the Maritimes, headquartered in Halifax. In addition to its infantry brigades, it would include three field artillery brigades, each with three four-gun batteries armed with new, more powerful 18-pounders (the new standard field gun of the British army), plus a howitzer brigade of three batteries, each armed with four 4.5-inch or 5-inch howitzers; and a heavy battery of four 60-pounder or 4.7-inch guns suitable for counter-battery work. The division would also include a divisional ammunition column as well as ammunition columns allotted to each field and howitzer brigade and the heavy battery. The creation of 6th Division and its artillery component would have a profound impact on New Brunswick's contribution to Canadian artillery.

In the meantime, Canadian field artillery was modernized. In 1909 the 18-pounder quick-firing gun began arriving. The "quick-firing" revolution had started in the 1890s with the development of guns with a new recoil system capable of firing fixed ammunition at an impressive rate. The recoil system absorbed the gun's kick when fired, eliminating the need to re-lay the gun; the fixed nature of the new combined cartridge case and projectile also speeded up the loading process. The net result of all this was an enormously capable gun. The 18-pounder could fire twenty rounds per minute, delivering nearly 8,000 shrapnel pellets from its bursting shells over roughly an acre. A three- or four-gun battery could totally dominate the area to its front.

Training opportunities also improved. A new training camp for field artillery was opened at Petawawa near Pembroke, Ontario, with a more spacious training area and longer artillery ranges than at Deseronto, and it became the site of the annual gun camps. In 1912, New Brunswick's entire 4th Brigade attended for the full sixteen-day schedule. However, sending the whole brigade was too expensive to repeat in 1913. So while the brigade trained as a formation locally at Sussex, thirty-man detachments travelled to Petawawa for the annual firing competition. When they arrived at Petawawa, the competition crews received some preliminary training that involved firing 130 live 18-pounder shells at ranges varying from one to two and a half miles. On the last day of camp, gunners from across Canada fired against a variety of targets that simulated action against advancing enemy infantry as well as against hostile artillery – a major change for field artillery following the Boer War experience. The advancing enemy infantry were represented by movable screens representing troops. The men of Major Anderson's 19th Field Battery from Moncton came first in the competition and received a prize of $50.

Training was also becoming more comprehensive, extending beyond the simple – but critical – skills of loading, laying, and firing. Visual signalling had become the chief means of carrying out tactical communication in the field and was now recognized as one of the most important military skills. So many gunners underwent training in flag, lamp, and field signalling, which was provided by Signal Corps instructors from Halifax and from local units.

New Brunswick's field artillery was expanded and modernized after the Boer War. The increased emphasis on modern, deployable field pieces – and the concurrent decline in threat from coal-fired warships – would also have a profound impact as 3rd NB Regiment of Garrison Artillery endured repeated changes in armament and faced an uncertain future. In August 1901 the garrison artillery's firing practice was held again on the Île d'Orléans after a lapse of almost two years. Gunners from 3rd Regiment used 40-pounder rifled breech-loaders and 5-inch breech-loading howitzers, neither of which they were familiar with. In 1902 the regiment received two pedestal-mounted 12-pounder quick-firing guns. This light modern weapon could fire as many as 20 rounds per minute; it had been recently procured by Canada for coastal defence and also to arm government steamers as auxiliary warships in wartime. In the summers of 1902, 1903, and 1904 these guns, together with pedestal-mounted Hotchkiss 6-pounder quick-firing guns, were mounted in temporary positions at Fort Dufferin for firing practice by the regiment and by Permanent Force gunners from Quebec City. They fired at canvas targets towed by a boat on the open water at ranges between 1,300 and 1,800 yards. Planning was under way in Ottawa at that time to rebuild the Saint John defences with modern batteries of 12-pounder quick-firing guns and heavier calibres of pedestal-mounted modern breech-loaders, and the regiment was being prepared to operate the new weaponry. The planning abruptly ended in 1904, however, with the decision to follow British policy and concentrate coastal defences at major military and naval ports, meaning Quebec City, one of the main stations of Canada's regular army, and Halifax, where the British had always maintained up-to-date defences.

Despite the fact that the future of 3rd NB Regiment was unclear in the years following the Boer War, new recruits continued to join. Edward "Ned" Slader of Saint John enlisted in 1904. Years later he cited the influence of Crimean War veteran Sergeant Hughes and other veterans of Victorian era wars. These men, who turned out wearing their medals and told stirring stories of their exploits, inspired him to enlist. So too did his father's stories of the Franco-Prussian war, as well as G.A. Henty's adventure books, and stories about Brock's defence of Queenston Heights, the Charge of the Light Brigade, and the defence of Rorke's Drift. All of these sources implanted in Slader's "mind the germ of what is known as the military spirit and influenced me to the extent of joining the Militia with the idea in the back of my mind if war came, I wanted to be in it." After the Great War, he reflected that in 1904 he did not appreciate "that 'War is Hell' and not romance, and far different from flashy uniforms, bands, colorful reviews and spectacular Church parades."

The year Slader joined, 3rd NB Regiment began nearly a decade of renaming, re-equipping, and re-roling, as the Canadian government wrestled with the

The British BL (breech-loading) 4.7-inch gun, seen here in Canadian service in 1915. This is the gun that equipped 3rd NB Regiment in 1904–11, and then was deployed to Partridge Island in August 1914. (LAC MIKAN 3405480)

challenges of modernizing the organization and equipment of both coastal defences and mobile field forces. Canada had to be more self-reliant, and indeed that was the policy of the government of Sir Wilfrid Laurier. In 1904 the Royal Navy withdrew from its bases at Halifax and, on the west coast, at Esquimalt, BC. Then in 1905–6 the British army garrisons that had protected those stations also departed, and were replaced by troops from the newly expanded Canadian Permanent Force. Much more needed to be done, however, so that Canada could independently raise effective field forces for home defence, or for service overseas, on a scale possibly much larger than the battalion-sized contingents sent to South Africa. In 1904 the 3rd Regiment was re-equipped with 4.7-inch guns, a naval gun on a field carriage with specially designed recoil buffers. The gun had been used without the recoil system in South Africa for long-range counter-battery work. The importance of silencing the enemy's guns was not lost on the British or Canadian armies, and the rebuilt 4.7-inch was adopted as a stopgap until a proper gun, designed for just this work – what emerged as the 60-pounder – was available.

Given that counter-battery work was very similar to long-range coast gunnery (indirect fire at very small targets), this new task suggested a role for Saint John gunners in any future force mobilized for overseas service. The 4.7-inch gun was modern equipment, but much heavier than the 6-pounder and 12-pounder quick-firing guns the regiment had practised with in 1902–4. The 4.7-inch could fire its 45-pound (20 kg) shells accurately to a range of 9,000 yards, well over the horizon.

For the next seven years, what became, on 2 April 1907, 3rd "New Brunswick" Regiment (Heavy Brigade) (and on 2 May 1910, the 3rd "New Brunswick" Heavy Brigade, Canadian Garrison Artillery) trained as a heavy field brigade. In addition to annual training at local headquarters, in 1906 to 1911 the unit sent over one hundred personnel for a week's further training and firing practice at the large new camp at Petawawa, Ontario. The camp had been developed specifically to allow modern artillery safely to fire at long range. The regiment learned how to find firing positions concealed by forest and ground, as well as how to get their targets and adjustments from Forward Observation Officers (FOOs). The regiment even developed its own signals section, which connected the FOOs to the guns by means of flags, lamps, and heliographs. By the time the Great War came, hundreds of New Brunswickers – officers, NCOs, and gunners – were adept in the art and science of counter-battery work. No one yet suspected how useful those skills were about to become.

By 1911 there were more heavy batteries than needed for the field forces and a reorganization of the Canadian Garrison Artillery brought the continued existence of the 3rd "New Brunswick" Brigade into question. The 3rd Brigade, moreover, had recently been unable to send its most experienced and senior personnel on the long journey to Petawawa for annual firing practice because these people could not be spared from their civilian employment; the brigade had sent too many boys.

Captain Abner Belyea and the men of B Company (the Carleton Battery), 3rd NB Regiment at Sussex, July 1909. (PANB P210/215)

It was a common problem for urban units and especially so for a unit in a city so far from central Ontario. The Inspector General recommended that the brigade be disbanded. Further consideration at Headquarters, however, recognized the long-standing importance of Saint John as a centre for recruiting and training artillery units. Thus the unit was reorganized and re-equipped for a new role: operating the "movable" artillery that protected the landward approaches to the Halifax fortress. On 15 April 1912 the brigade was renamed – 3rd "New Brunswick" Regiment, Canadian Garrison Artillery – and received 15-pounder field guns, the armament left by the departing British garrison in 1906 for the mobile defences at Halifax. The 15-pounder was an interim design, superseded in field artillery units by the new 18-pounders. In the summers of 1912 and 1913 one hundred strong detachments from the 3rd Regiment fired the 15-pounders during week-long training camps at Petawawa, and the advance body of thirteen NCOs and forty-three gunners arrived there in August 1914 just when the war broke out. Senior personnel were still unable to attend because of their civilian employment, but the hope was that a land artillery range could be developed in the Maritime Provinces in the not too distant future, an intention that did not survive the upheavals of the war.

The Barracks Green Armories, Saint John, shortly after they were completed in January 1912. It has served since then as the focal point for Saint John Militia units, the heart of the port city's fortress system in two world wars, and the home of 3rd Field Regiment (The Loyal Company) in all its twentieth-century permutations. (PANB P210/2495)

Canadian field artillery was modern in 1914, equipped with the standard British 18-pounder gun, like this one seen at Valcartier in the fall of 1914. (LAC PA-004975)

By 1914, 3rd Regiment consisted of a regimental staff and three companies under the command of Lt.-Col. Beverley R. Armstrong, whose lack of a right lower leg had not prevented him from serving his country, rising through the ranks, and assuming command of the regiment in September 1912. No. 1 Company, located in Saint John, was commanded by Major W.H.E. Harrison; Major J.T. McGowan commanded No. 2 Company from Carleton; and No. 3 Company from Portland was led by Major F.C. Magee.

By 1914, the province's artillery units had received more of the latest weapons and equipment and were being provided with longer and more realistic opportunities for training. The three field batteries – 10th, 12th, and 19th of 4th Brigade – were each equipped with six modern 18-pounder field guns, and each was organized into two three-gun sections. They had all undergone reorganization and re-equipping that better prepared them for participation in the war, especially for an expeditionary force. The 3rd NB Regiment of the Canadian Garrison Artillery was ready to take its 15-pounders down the road and defend Halifax from assault. In light of what transpired over the next four years, it is clear that more could have been done. But New Brunswick's gunners already possessed unique and valuable skills, and like militiamen across the country their dedication to service was unquestionable. They would soon have ample opportunity to demonstrate all of that.

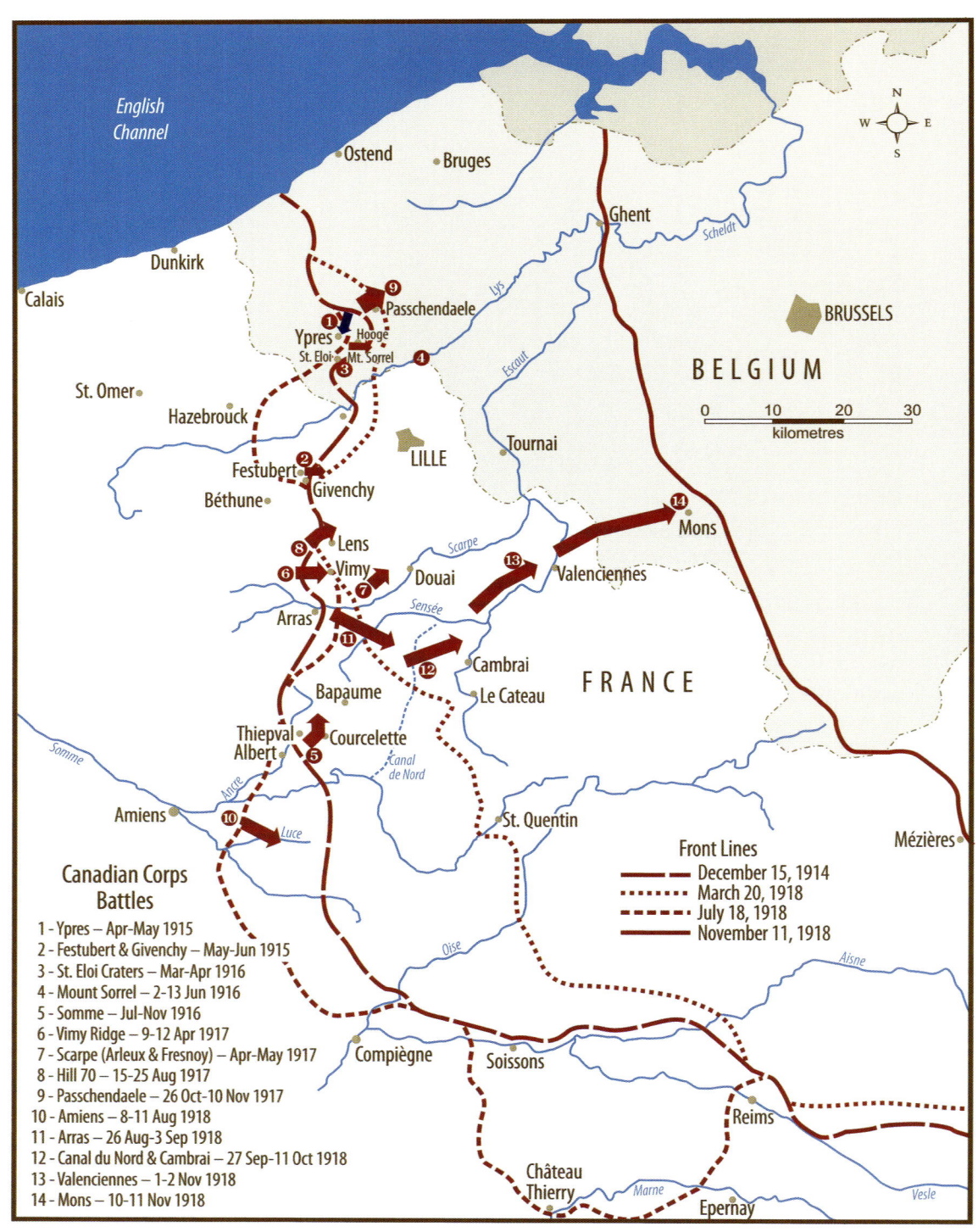

The Canadian Corps on the Western Front, 1915–18

Chapter 2

Seeking and Finding a Role at Home and Abroad, 1914–16

New Brunswick's gunners played a significant role in the Great War. The province's artillery units made an early contribution, notably at the Second Battle of Ypres – Canada's first major battle – in circumstances that could have been only faintly glimpsed before the outbreak of war. Their contribution reveals that, contrary the view that Canada's mobilization was chaotic, Canada's gunners were ready for war in 1914. More importantly, New Brunswick's artillery organization was uniquely adapted to the changing nature of modern war. This was especially true in terms of the increasing importance of long-range siege and heavy artillery fire delivered against precise targets – just the stuff of garrison artillery, especially coastal gunners. By 1916, New Brunswick's artillery establishment was poised to make a disproportionate contribution to Canada's burgeoning force of heavy guns on the Western Front. Finding that role, and finding a way to achieve some kind of recognition for New Brunswick's contribution – which was being lost as its officers and men filled out the ranks of units that represented other cities and regions – were the greatest challenges of the first two years of the Great War.

By 1914 the Canadian Artillery had been organized into two branches, on the model of Britain's Royal Artillery. The Canadian Garrison Artillery was responsible for heavy mobile guns (generally 4.7-inch and larger) and for fortress armament,

Men of the 12th Newcastle Field Battery who volunteered for the 1st Contingent, outside the armoury on Pleasant Street just prior to their departure for Quebec, August 1914. Their commanding officer, Major Randolph Crooker, is in the suit centre-right. (PANB P6-503)

principally at the defended ports of Halifax, Quebec City, and Esquimalt. These defended ports also had mobile batteries assigned; thus, on mobilization, 3rd NB Regiment, Canadian Garrison Artillery, was to head to Halifax with its three batteries of 15-pounders, ready to move rapidly with infantry and cavalry to resist enemy landing forces. Lt.-Col. Beverley R. Armstrong's drive, professionalism, and organizational acumen had prepared them well for this task.

New Brunswick's other artillery units belonged to the Canadian Field Artillery, a form of artillery deployed for close support of combat units on the battlefield, and the type generally expected to serve with expeditionary forces. NB's 4th Brigade, Canadian Field Artillery, included 10th Battery in Woodstock, 12th in Newcastle, and 19th in Moncton, as well as an ammunition column based in the Miramichi. Well-trained and equipped with modern guns, it was as ready to serve as any unit in Canada.

On 29 July 1914, Britain dispatched a "precautionary" war telegram to all parts of the Empire, and its dominions and colonies began partial mobilization of forces to secure strategic centres, especially on the seacoasts. On Canada's east coast, militia detachments arrived to supplement the permanent fortress garrisons at Halifax and Quebec City. Mobilization stepped into higher gear on 3 August based on a report from Heart's Content, Newfoundland, that two German cruisers had been sighted. The Maritime provinces' command, known as 6th Division, headquartered at Halifax under Maj.-Gen. R.W. Rutherford, took the threat seriously, and within hours full mobilization was under way.

Rutherford and his staff, however, had to change the mobilization plan on the fly. The fortress and the dockyard had been turned over to Canada eight years earlier, but Halifax remained the most important British naval and military base in the northwest Atlantic. The mobilization plan had been based on the worst-case scenario of war with the United States. To isolate Canada from British military assistance, the Americans would have to seize Halifax, and the expectation was that they would try to do so by landing some distance away and approaching the city from the landward side – hence the need for mobile field batteries as part of the fortress system. By contrast, the greatest danger from Germany was hit-and-run long-range bombardments of coastal towns by fast and elusive cruisers. The goal would be to terrorize the commercial shippers and thus interfere with the ocean trade on which Britain's economy and war-making potential depended. In an age of coal-fired ships, such a threat would be fleeting at best.

Saint John, the most important commercial port on the east coast, was a logical target for such a terror campaign. So 6th Division cancelled 3rd NB Regiment's deployment to Halifax and instead ordered the unit to defend its own city. To do this, 3rd NB was to raise a single "Composite Battery" of six officers and 113 other ranks to crew four 4.7-inch mobile guns, which were being rushed to Saint John for a coast defence role. The local press covered the mobilization on 4 August, with the *Saint John Globe* reporting: "Colonel B.R. Armstrong, of the 3rd N.B. Regiment, Canadian Artillery, has been ordered by the Military authorities at Halifax to call out a portion of his Regiment … One battery will be mobilized and Major F.C. Magee will be in command … There are some big 4.7-inch guns expected to arrive today from Petawawa for the local corps." It seems likely that the regiment's summer training cadre at Petawawa had been tasked with bringing the big guns home. The next morning, 5 August, 3rd NB Regiment's newly organized "composite" battery, commanded by Major Frank Magee, assembled for drill. "The local Regiment possessed in full measure the battle spirit of the Empire," reported the *Globe*. In the ranks were "found all classes of the city's young manhood. All other duties – many of them pressing ones – were sacrificed to the duty lying nearest them, i.e., the defence of their native city from possible invaders … Arrangements are to be made later for volunteers for foreign service. The battery on duty must remain indefinitely." That same day, the *Globe* printed a report from Portland, Maine, that gunfire

The 4.7-inch gun, seen here in Canadian service in 1915, had always been an interim design for counter-battery work: a naval gun on land carriage. The decision to deploy four of these obsolete guns on Partridge Island in August was entirely political, but the long-range impact on the NB artillery establishment proved profound. (LAC PA-022703)

had been heard off the coast. A further report, this one from New York, added: "Eight cruisers – three German, three British and two French are hovering somewhere off this coast … The firing may have marked the first engagement."

The 4.7-inch guns from Petawawa arrived on 5 August and on the next day were moved out to Partridge Island. The *Globe* was reassuring about the effectiveness of the new defences: the range of the guns was six miles, meaning that fire from Partridge Island, three miles from the city, would hold sea raiders nine miles out to sea. "The company of artillery men … are the older men in the service who have seen much drill at Petawawa. Using the same guns that were used on drill, the gunners will be able to give a splendid account of themselves if called upon by the events of the great war." In an interview with the press, Armstrong stated that the guns were in position on the island by 1500 hours on 6 August. "The men are quartered in the detention hospital on the Island and the best of spirits prevail." As the *Globe* commented: "Persons who think that this sort of soldier is child's play should have been present at the Island on Thursday afternoon [6 August] and watched the troops tailing up the steep slope with a four and one half ton gun as a tow."

The detailed coverage of the defence preparations in the press, the result of the government not yet imposing effective censorship, had the good effect of reassuring the local population. So did the frantic naval preparations to meet the looming threat. Royal Navy cruisers rushed from the West Indies to Halifax, and others then came from Great Britain. Although it soon became clear that German warships were not in northern waters – the alarmist reports had all been false – a half-dozen cruisers remained on station at Halifax. Forty percent or more of Britain's overseas trade passed close by Nova Scotia and Newfoundland, and by the fall virtually all of Canada's winter trade on the east coast would start funnelling through Saint John. It was also known that a large number of fast German merchant ships had taken refuge in US ports and that some were capable of carrying guns. While the navy established a watch off US ports, the gunners on Partridge Island stood poised to defend Saint John.

In fact, the 4.7-inch battery defending Saint John was a sham, and the gunners knew it. The wheeled carriages of the guns could not be levered about readily enough to track and engage a moving ship. A proper coastal gun sat on a carriage perfectly balanced on a heavy steel pivot set in concrete so that it could swing rapidly and precisely on a wide arc. As the battery commander complained early in 1915: "I find myself … with orders to fire on a hostile vessel and with such material on hand that the result would be to aggravate the situation rather than better it."

None of this came as a surprise to General W.G. Gwatkin, the highly competent British officer who served as Chief of the General Staff in Ottawa. Gwatkin had agreed to send the 4.7-inch guns to Partridge Island during the panic in early August 1914 to "soothe the citizens of St. John [sic]." But he resisted all new calls from coastal and border towns for defences. It was an uphill struggle. Colonel Sam Hughes, the Minister of Militia and Defence, although no less keen than Gwatkin to make the largest possible effort overseas, was extremely sensitive to political pressure. In the case of Partridge Island, Gwatkin wrote privately that "if it rested with me I would withdraw the 4.7-inch guns, as I believe their presence at St. John [sic] to be unnecessary from a military point of view. But they were mounted for other than military purposes, and I am powerless."

Many of the members of the regiment who came out for active service on Partridge Island also had little interest in German sea raiders. They had joined the Composite Battery hoping for a chance to serve overseas, and soon there was good news. On 14 August, 3rd NB's regimental orders announced it had the authority to raise a "Foreign Service Battery" that would form part of the Canadian Expeditionary Force. Major Frank Magee took charge of the new unit, and was replaced in command of the Composite Battery by Major W.H. "Harry" Harrison. Four of the six other officers who had come out with Composite Battery also transferred to the overseas unit, and were replaced on Partridge Island by four officers from the regiment. Lt.-Col. Armstrong's regimental staff attended to recruiting, both for the overseas unit and for replacements for the men who had transferred from the Composite Battery. No one could have imagined in those heady days of August 1914 where all this would eventually lead.

The recruiting efforts were vigorous and wide-ranging, with an officer coming from the Directorate of Artillery in Ottawa to help the regiment. Sergeant Major E.M. "Ned" Slader travelled on a recruiting mission with Captain Ralph Hayes to the NB coal-mining town of Minto, some 160 kilometres from Saint John. "We brought back a mixed bag, mostly Belgians and Russians," Slader recalled. "All proved good soldiers. I recall particularly Christopher Rudic, a Cossack. He had been a Cavalry Sergeant in the Russo-Japanese War, a superb horseman and later in the war Colonel Penhale's groom."

By the end of August, the overseas battery, consisting of five officers and 254 other ranks, was ready to leave. It included Lieutenants William Vassie, Lawrence Kelly, and Ralph Hayes, and a number of long-serving non-commissioned members of the regiment like Ned Slader, Charlie Cunard, Ed Puddy, A.E. Locket, Jim Stackhouse, Jack Edwards, and Alfred Dodge, along with a few new volunteers. The battery marched to Union Station on 28 August, led by Major Magee through a crowd of well-wishers. Grey skies threatened but could not dampen the enthusiasm. Slader remembered "crowds cheering, flags flying, the Artillery Band directed by Bandmaster Charlie Williams playing *Our Director* march. I admit I was somewhat exhilarated." Pouring rain greeted the train as it slid to a halt in Moncton to load 19th Field Battery led by Major S. Boyd Anderson and Sergeant Major Ernie Whitebone. The Moncton gunners had brought along a Westmoreland County black bear cub named Lee. Apparently they were not the only unit travelling with such a mascot.

Rain fell hard all the way to Valcartier, Quebec, where the First Contingent was mustering under canvas while the new camp rose around them. In the earliest days at Valcartier, shelter was scarce and food even more so. Stories of confusion, shortages, and deprivation were legion as the Minister of Militia, Sam Hughes, drove the Canadian army towards a hasty dispatch of the First Contingent. Less well known and perhaps more remarkable is how quickly militia-trained officers and NCOs along with the Permanent Force personnel pulled things together. Saint John's Regimental Quartermaster Sergeant Charlie Cunard, a South African War veteran, scrounged bedding and ground sheets. The 3rd NB Regiment's Lieutenant Cyrus Inches was waiting in Valcartier for the New Brunswickers to arrive. He had arrived early to link up with his new commanding officer, Lt.-Col. John Penhale from Sherbrooke, Quebec. A Permanent Force regimental sergeant-major was appointed as well – Jim Slade. "A veteran of the Northwest Rebellion and the South African War, a warrant officer of long standing in the Royal Canadian Horse Artillery, he was an expert in what is known in the army as 'Man Management.'" Shelter and rations were sorted quickly so that organization of the divisional artillery and training might commence.

If the misery of Valcartier was not enough, the men of 3rd NB Regiment's Overseas Battery soon learned that their skills at long-range gunnery, perfected

A Canadian BL 60-pounder at Valcartier, Quebec, in 1914. The British designed the gun in light of Boer War experience to conduct counter-battery work and to replace the interim 4.7-inch gun.
(LAC CNRP16208-41)

between 1905 and 1910 on 4.7-inch guns and honed on 15-pounders, were not yet required. Much to their dismay, Major Magee and most of his men were remustered as No. 4 Section, 1st Canadian Division Ammunition Column, alongside other sections from Charlottetown and Montreal. Their "armament" was now the General Service Wagon, and their mission was to haul shells to feed the division's hungry guns. Major Anderson's 19th Moncton Battery had disappeared as well. It had been combined with a section from Sydney, Nova Scotia's, 17th Battery to form 6th Field Battery, equipped with six modern 18-pounder field guns. The new 6th Field Battery joined batteries from Montreal and Sherbrooke to form 2nd Canadian Field Brigade. The Montreal field gunners were led by a young major named Andrew McNaughton. Second Field Brigade's structure was not to last, but its eastern Canadian flavour would.

Even at this early stage, Saint John gunners were assuming an increasingly prominent role in Canada's heavy artillery. That started in late September, when Major Magee was transferred to command 1st Canadian Heavy Battery. The "1st Heavies" served four modern breech-loading 60-pounder heavy field guns, which had been designed and built to replace the 4.7-inch, which 3rd NB Regiment had mastered years before and now operated again on Partridge Island. The battery was initially assembled from the Montreal Heavy Brigade but was liberally mixed with 3rd NB Regiment officers and men assigned to follow Magee, who brought their expertise in long-range indirect fire with them. This was the start of a close partnership between New Brunswick and Montreal gunners and of a process that would see NB gunners find a distinct role in heavy and siege artillery.

Barely thirty days after arriving at Valcartier, the First Contingent was equipped, organized into 1st Canadian Division, and ready to sail for Britain. Men, horses, wagons, guns, ammunition, and other equipment marched to the Quebec City docks late in September to load aboard SS *Megantic* and SS *Montezuma*. "The men, who expected to sleep in hammocks, are in the L and third-class staterooms, much better accommodation than most of them had ever enjoyed before," Ned Slader recorded. In fact, he and RSM Slade had a stateroom all to themselves, "provided with luxurious beds complete with silken covers and electric heaters to be turned on and off at our pleasure." Few could see the irony, given the conditions they were soon to encounter. They steamed down the St. Lawrence River on 1 October. Two days later they joined the convoy carrying the entire Canadian force in the Gaspé Basin and set out into the open Atlantic. With them went virtually all of Canada's modern equipment. Problems with faulty boots, leather webbing, and the Ross rifle notwithstanding, 1st Canadian Division was fully kitted out for modern war.

The convoy arrived at Plymouth after eleven days at sea, and within days, 1st Canadian Division was encamped on West Down North, in the British army's field training area on the Salisbury Plain. Here the benefits of employing coastal gunners trained in long-range indirect fire began to assert themselves. Major Magee soon had Lieutenant Cyrus Inches transferred to 1st Heavy Battery. Inches wrote home that he was glad for the assignment. "I think I can work in better with Frank than any other – he appreciates my capacities and incapacities better." Both officers were destined to accomplish great things before the war was over. That autumn, 1st Heavy Battery's New Brunswick flavour increased as more experienced Saint John gunners transferred in. Among them was Gunner Frank Hall, assigned as Inches's batman. Those officers and men, already trained and experienced as a Heavy Brigade, formed the nucleus that later grew to lead the Canadian Corps Heavy Artillery.

But those developments lay far off in the future. First, the gunners faced an unusually wet fall and winter on the Salisbury Plain. The rain began days after their arrival and proved unrelenting. By 2 November it had rained for ten days straight. Lieutenant Inches wrote home that the locals were warning that all "indications were not for better weather." The wet days carried through to December, when Gunner John Bovard wrote home to Moncton to report that "there hasn't been 12 hours of fine weather day or night since we have been here. I was on guard duty last night and it rained as hard as I've ever seen it rain … the water was about 3 inches deep in the guard tent. Imagine sleeping in that with nothing but blankets over you." Sergeant Noah Steeves wrote to his sister that packages from home were helping fend off the unending dampness. "The Daughters of the Empire at Moncton sent socks, sleeping caps, housewives (darning kits), handkerchiefs, and I got my share of them."

During that miserable winter the Moncton gunners received orders to re-form their battery. The whole 2nd Field Brigade reorganized from three six-gun batteries to four four-gun batteries to conform to the new British standard designed to spread the limited number of field guns evenly across the rapidly expanding army. The 1st Canadian Divisional Artillery conformed to the change but retained all its guns and trained gunners. As a result, while new British divisions operated thirty-six field guns in nine batteries, the Canadians kept fifty-two guns now spread across thirteen batteries. One of the "new" batteries was the 8th, composed of men from 19th Moncton Battery under their old battery commander, Major Boyd Anderson. Under this new number, Moncton's gunners would make history. The recognition of their unique NB bonds made "Anderson's Battery" a happy lot. Gunner George McMullen wrote home that their mascot black bear, Lee, was "as fat as a pig. We have him in a tent in a box and he wanders around all day." Conditions on the Salisbury Plain, however, made it difficult to train. Thankfully, by January 1915, Magee's 1st Heavy Battery, Ned Slader's No. 4 Section of the Divisional Ammunition Column, and Anderson's 8th Battery moved into billets in nearby villages. Leave passes became available to London and other nearby destinations, which improved morale.

By early 1915 more New Brunswick gunners were on their way to the Salisbury Plain. Even before 1st Canadian Divisional Artillery completed its training in England, it was clear that the war was going to last for some time. Canada responded by assembling a second division for service overseas, and New Brunswickers were now asked to form three more units. The 3rd NB Garrison Regiment recruited the Headquarters and No. 1 Section of 2nd Canadian Divisional Ammunition Column under the command of Lt.-Col. W.H. "Harry" Harrison. The total strength of 2nd Divisional Ammunition Column, as the unit was now known, was 852 all ranks. Of these, some 158 had been recruited at Saint John and Fredericton, and around seventy had previously served with 3rd NB Regiment, including eleven of the nineteen officers. Twenty of the 217 officers and men of 2nd Canadian Heavy Battery, primarily a Charlottetown unit, were NB gunners who had transferred to the Halifax fortress when the war started. Meanwhile, Militia field battery depots in Fredericton, Moncton, Woodstock, and Chatham recruited for 23rd and 24th Field Batteries, which drew officers and men from all over the Maritimes. The 3rd New Brunswick Garrison Regiment contributed the experienced Battery Sergeant Major Holly Patchell, among others, to stiffen the force.

The mobilization of men for the Second Contingent left the Composite Battery on Partridge Island, now under the command of Captain J.E. Sayre, seriously under strength. Of the seventy-nine gunners on the island at the end of January 1915, thirty-one had joined just that month. In fact, the demands on 3rd NB Regiment

Officers of HQ and No. 1 Section, 2nd Division Ammunition Column, prior to their departure overseas in June 1915. Back row, L-R: William Vassie, Norman MacLeod, S.K.L. MacDonald, and T.E. Ryder. Middle row: L-R, V.C. Johnson, Walter A. Harrison, William "Harry" Harrison, George Gamblin, and D.F. Pidgeon. Front row: L-R, W.G. Church and W.H. Edgar. (Loyal Company Association Collection)

had just begun. Early in March, 6th Division in Halifax directed 3rd NB Regiment and the PEI Heavy Brigade each to provide a detachment of seventy-five personnel for duty in the Halifax forts. The Halifax garrison was too small to keep the coastal batteries adequately crewed for what was now going to be a long war. Rear Admiral R.S. Phipps Hornby, commander of the Royal Navy cruisers operating from Halifax, would not consider a reduction in the defences; the existing level was essential to the security of his warships. Regimental orders that announced the organization of the detachment required all other ranks not already on duty on Partridge Island or enlisted in the new CEF contingent to report to the island or the armouries within forty-eight hours. The orders applied the whip, which certainly reflected the urgent need for reinforcements at Halifax, and might also have shown awareness that personnel did not relish the prospect of prolonged, unglamorous home service. "All N.C.O.'s and men who receive notices and do not report as above will be considered as having no objection to going on active service in home defence and will be called out," the order read. "Of those that report, those making no objection will be called out first and the balance of the required number will be made up first from the single men and those from the married men who will suffer least financially." A detachment comprised of Captain Lawrence T. Allen, Lieutenant H.A. Bruce, Lieutenant Herb A. West, and seventy-two other ranks left Saint John by train to Halifax on 16 March 1915, and immediately on their arrival took up duties in the coastal defence batteries. A second detachment, Lieutenant Colin MacKay and fifteen gunners, entrained for Halifax on 20 March. They joined a new unit, No. 6 Company RCGA, to establish and garrison batteries at Port Castries in the West Indies. By early 1915 it seemed clear that the role of Regimental Headquarters and the Composite Battery stuck on Partridge Island was recruiting and training gunners for others to employ.

Meanwhile, the men already in England prepared for the front. During that bleak winter on the Salisbury Plain, batteries and ammunition columns practised gun drill in the field for attack and defence, as well as methods for staging ammunition supplies for a sustained action. They exercised replenishing casualties in the field brigades and with men and horses from the ammunition columns, hence the need to train all ammunition column members to serve the guns. Battery commanders and staffs practised telephone and other forms of communication with Brigade Headquarters and with FOOs. Royal Artillery instructors emphasized the selection and preparation of covered and concealed firing positions and ammunition dumps – things many NB gunners were already well versed in – as well as the skill of hitching up guns and wagons in darkness for crash moves in and out of positions. The lessons learned from the South African War were reinforced by

Friends and family gather in Saint John to say goodbye to 26th NB Battalion and 2nd Canadian Division Ammunition Column commanded by Lt.-Col. Harry Harrison, whose headquarters and No. 1 Section were composed of NB gunners. (LAC C-026121)

34 | Chapter 2

Horses had to be trained, too. Here an unknown group of Canadian gunners put their horses through their paces at Whitley Camp, England. (LAC PA-005494)

the experience thus far in France, which had already made it clear that guns must be dug in and dispersed in depth behind the front-line infantry and connected to observers at the front with clear lines of vision and good communications to the guns behind them. Training in England culminated in January 1915 with live practice firing from covered positions and correcting fire based on reports from FOOs. According to the *Moncton Times*, Anderson's 8th Battery "made the highest record of any Canadian battery or any of the batteries of Kitchener's army."

New Brunswick's first three artillery units depended entirely on horses to move guns and wagons. Officers and men alike invested considerable time caring for horses, saddlery, wagons, and limbers after a long day in the mud. When the units moved into billets in January 1915, the animals could finally be stabled and sheltered from the cold, steady barrage of rain. Most horses had been brought all the way from Canada, but those of 1st Heavy Battery proved too light to haul Frank Magee's 60-pounder guns, each of which weighed some 5.5 tons. British draught animals were acquired, while the Canadian horses stayed within the battery to haul ammunition wagons and carry on other tasks.

On 4 February 1915, days before they were to sail to France, Germany declared a naval blockade of Britain, and the convoy carrying 1st Canadian Division to France was diverted from Le Havre all the way around the Brittany Peninsula to St-Nazaire. It was a long, rough voyage. Two of 1st Heavy Battery's horses were thrown to the deck, breaking bones and forcing broken-hearted drivers to shoot them and throw them over the side. After a rousing welcome at St-Nazaire, they boarded trains emblazoned with the now infamous stencil "40 Hommes, 8 Chevaux" and set off on a two-day journey across Normandy and the Somme and finally to Hazebrouck in the Nord-Pas-de-Calais region of France, close to the Belgian border and the front line. Ned Slader remembered the approach: "To the east we could see very lights and flashes and hear the steady rumble of the guns."

On arrival, the entire Canadian Divisional Artillery, under the command of then-Colonel Henry Burstall, ran through exercise rides to recondition the horses after long days of cramped travelling. Most battery personnel went to a British unit to get a taste of the front. Anderson's 8th Battery shadowed a British 18-pounder brigade at Le Bizet on the north edge of Armentières. While officers went forward to observation posts, NCOs and men worked with the guns "doing the same duties and learning all possible from the experienced soldiers." They were especially impressed by efforts to conceal gun pits from German aircraft. Frank Magee went forward with a Royal Garrison Artillery 60-pounder battery dug in behind Armentières. The 1st Divisional Ammunition Column officers moved to Meteren on the main highway and railway link connecting Dunkirk to Armentières to see how British 4th Division ran its ammunition supply.

While these first tastes of active service alongside British units proved rewarding, it took something else to get used to the local farms that served as ammunition dumps, gun positions, and homes for men and horses. Lieutenant Inches wrote: "French Farmers put Godliness first and cleanliness last with a vengeance. The filth about the barnyards is nauseating." Sgt.-Maj. Slader felt no better about the farm assigned as home to the New Brunswick section of the ammunition column. It was "filthy and stunk to high heaven … One night in the barn was sufficient time to louse up the whole outfit." So began the gunners' battle with the skin-irritating insects – a battle that lasted longer than the war with Germany.

Canadian gunners' introduction to the Western Front coincided with preparations for a minor British offensive that would demonstrate just how hard it was to master this new kind of warfare. At the end of February, 1st Canadian Division and all its guns moved a few miles south to relieve British 7th Division around Sailly-sur-la-Lys. Their new positions, facing Aubers Ridge, were just north of British and Indian divisions preparing to attack Neuve Chapelle. On 1 March, 1st Canadian Heavy Battery rolled its 60-pounders into positions vacated by two British 4.7-inch gun batteries in an orchard at Pont Vanuxeem, north of Sailly. Major Magee concealed his guns among the orchard's hedges and branch canopy. In early 1915 the war was still too new for shells to have laid waste to everything above ground. Among the hedges and fruit trees, 1st Heavy Battery signallers ran telephone lines from gun positions back to Magee's headquarters and forward to an observation post. The low, flat, wet country around Sailly and the River Lys made observation of shot difficult, but stone churches and larger buildings in Aubers, Fromelles, and Le Maisnil were visible atop Aubers Ridge, offering points of reference. Fromelles's church tower still stood proudly on the German-held ridge.

The next morning, 2 March 1915, Magee's battery fired the first Canadian rounds of the Great War. It began with registration shoots confirming the siting of the guns and the positions of targets, followed by counter-battery fire with 60-pounder shrapnel shells bursting over two German batteries. They also burst shrapnel around the Fromelles church tower to force German artillery observers to take cover. Lyddite and high-explosive shells with contact fuses would have been more effective, but these were in short supply in the early days of the war. Much of what was available was being dumped at British gun pits closer to the centre of the coming storm at Neuve Chapelle.

The same day, 2 March, Moncton's 8th Battery arrived at the Divisional Headquarters area at Sailly with the rest of 2nd Field Brigade. There they waited for darkness to conceal their move over the River Lys and into positions at Barlette Farm, just west of Fleurbaix, 2,500 yards behind the British front-line trench system facing Fromelles and Le Maisnil. When daylight had gone, drivers and teams pulled 18-pounder guns and ammunition limbers quickly into positions taken over from a Royal Horse Artillery brigade. The 8th Battery formed the reserve. Major Anderson left one two-gun section on the north side of the Lys and moved the other section in depth, behind 5th, 6th, and 7th Canadian Field Batteries at Barlette Farm. On 3 March the sun was hidden by threatening grey clouds, but once it was light enough to observe the fall of shot, the forward batteries registered on known aiming points on the enemy front, while horses and wagons moved to the rear at Sailly. For the next week their routine consisted of firing small numbers of shrapnel rounds to burst over enemy trenches, with occasional firing at houses and farm buildings that the infantry reported as concealing German snipers. Much to the field gunners' frustration, if not surprise, shrapnel shells – designed for a war of movement and composing some 80 percent of their ammunition supply – had little effect in this new war of trenches, dugouts, and barbed wire. Overall, 2nd Field Brigade and 1st Heavy Battery did not fire much that week. Still, the dozen or so shells each battery fired per day tested gun crews, telephone connections to the FOOs, and skills at fuse setting. On 7 March, 1st Heavy Battery's 60-pounders finally blew down the Fromelles Church Tower. Lieutenant Inches wrote later that the tower was a known "enemy observation post which dominated the whole divisional front … The battery was brought into prominence almost immediately by its destruction."

The Battle for Neuve Chapelle, the first British offensive on the Western Front, was set to open on the morning of 10 March 1915. Six British and Indian divisions were to attack the two German divisions holding Aubers Ridge. The Canadian mission was to convince German commanders that the attack frontage extended north to Fleurbaix and thus encourage them to disperse their artillery fire and reserve troops. At 0730 hours all of 2nd Field Brigade's batteries (except the 8th, still in reserve) opened fire, along with riflemen and machine-gunners from Canadian infantry battalions facing Aubers Ridge. Anderson's men had to watch as their

A 60-pounder of 2nd Canadian Heavy Battery in action in July 1917. About twenty NB gunners served with this PEI battery in 1915–16, but by this stage the bulk of NB's heavy gunners were with Frank Magee's 1st Canadian Heavy Battery. (LAC PA-001401)

brigade fired their biggest shoot of the war so far – 437 shells. Meanwhile, 1st Heavy Battery shelled Aubers village itself as well as suspected enemy gun positions in the woods east of Fromelles, all as part of the general Canadian deception effort. The main attack at Neuve Chapelle was supported by the largest British artillery barrage of the war so far, employing sixty-six heavy guns and hundreds of 18-pounder field guns. The principle was sound, but in reality, there were too few guns with too little ammunition to accomplish the goal.

The small Canadian diversionary barrage at Aubers nonetheless incited German artillery to retaliate. Thus commenced a three-day low-level gunnery duel. Each morning, Canadian batteries fired small dummy barrages of ten to fifteen rounds per gun. The German guns fired similar numbers back and more, including high-explosive shells from their very effective medium 5.9-inch howitzers. The German army had been well equipped with heavy artillery so that it could pound its way through frontier fortresses. These powerful guns gave the Germans a decided advantage in the new static warfare on the Western Front. The 1st Heavy Battery answered the German guns as best it could, but four 60-pounders and pitifully low stocks of ammunition could not begin to silence them. Each of three mornings, 2nd Field Brigade's FOOs counted fewer German kitchen wagon fires to their front as enemy infantry thinned and shifted south to seal off the initial British gains at Neuve Chapelle. Magee's 60-pounders tried to prevent their movement. On 15 March they ranged in on a train that was loading and unloading German men and equipment at Fromelles station, hitting three cars and the locomotive pulling them.

In the end, the Germans kept their grip on Aubers Ridge with superior artillery fire, which could concentrate on the narrow British attack front.

The Battle of Neuve Chapelle had ended by 15 March 1915. Only then did the Moncton gunners of 8th Field Battery come forward for their turn to range in, but by then daily ammunition quantities were used up. The Germans continued their retaliation. They aggressively pushed a 77 mm field battery into their trench line, close to a new front-line redoubt or strongpoint. In the spirit of medieval siege warfare, 2nd Field Brigade burst shrapnel rounds over the new German redoubt to slow the work. On 16 March, 2nd Field's 18-pounders joined their efforts with 1st Heavies to destroy the new strongpoint. They massed as much 60-pounder and 18-pounder shrapnel fire as possible on the Germans, who appeared to be rushing their work to completion. Frank Magee felt that the shoot "destroyed enemy gun emplacement in trench." The 2nd Field Brigade reported that "a great deal of damage was done." The Germans responded to the Canadian barrage the next day with a concentration of 5.9-inch howitzer high-explosive shells fired deep into the Canadian divisional rear, smashing apart houses used as billets for Canadian infantry units. A mixture of good shooting and good luck by the Canadians was not enough to counter superior German firepower. This first real taste of war cost the Canadian Divisional Artillery no losses in men or guns, but offered a glimpse of what lay ahead. Until the Allies deployed enough heavy artillery to match German firepower, and until Allied factories could turn out more heavy shells, German artillery would dominate the battlefield.

On 1 April 1915 all of 1st Canadian Divisional Artillery came out of the line and into reserve behind the Aubers Ridge front. Easter Sunday fell on 4 April that year and provided the occasion to parade all batteries in the division, including the Divisional Ammunition Column and 1st Heavy Battery. It proved to be the last time they would serve directly together for nearly two years. Senior British commanders recognized the need to concentrate heavy guns, which were properly a corps or army level asset. The 1st Canadian Heavy Battery was thus detached from 1st Canadian Division and pooled with the very limited numbers of other imperial heavy and siege guns massing in the Aubers Ridge sector. When the Canadian divisional artillery received orders to head north to the Ypres Salient, 1st Heavy Battery remained facing Aubers. The British Expeditionary Force planned to attack there again in support of the French spring offensive in the Artois and Champagne regions. The decision to assist the French attack was controversial under the circumstances, but the British and their dominions could not, in the words of Dominick Graham, "stand on the defensive while her allies bled to death."

The 1st Canadian Division and its field artillery contributed to the French effort by freeing a French division manning the Ypres Salient for service in the main spring offensive. That set the stage for the first Canadian battles of the Great War. The story of the Second Battle of Ypres is well known, and the tale is dominated by the exploits of infantry units, all from central and western Canada at this stage. But New Brunswickers were there, too. They manned guns that on several occasions turned the tide of the battle.

The 1st Canadian Divisional Ammunition Column were the first Canadian gunners in the Ypres Salient, arriving on 13 April to set up an ammunition depot and replenishment network based at Vlamertinge, two miles west of Ypres. From there they initially fed small-arms ammunition and grenades to Canada's three infantry brigades. The 2nd Field Brigade's advance party arrived on 16 April to meet the French artillery counterparts they were to relieve near Wieltje, 2,500 yards northeast of Ypres. The guns of 5th and 8th (Moncton) Batteries followed the next day. The Moncton Battery's four subsections prepared gun pits on the front right of the brigade area on a farm a few hundred yards south of Fortuin, shielded behind the crest of Zonnebeke Ridge – a spur off the sandy Messines–Passchendaele Ridge, which dominated the Ypres Salient. The area was badly scarred from the First Battle of Ypres in late 1914 but had not yet turned into the moonscape associated with later battles. When the sun came up on 18 April, Major Anderson's battery found two houses still standing behind the German front-line trenches on which they could register their fire. The next day, when German 77 mm "whiz-bang" field guns shelled 2nd Canadian Infantry Brigade's front-line trenches in front of Gravenstaffel Ridge, 8th Battery fired in retaliation. Thus, New Brunswickers were the first Canadian gunners to fire in the Ypres Salient.

Overall, those first days at Ypes were quiet enough that on 21 April, Brigadier Burstall ordered practice reliefs-in-place between 2nd and 3rd Field Brigades in the front line and 1st Brigade in reserve at Ypres. Reliefs began by half-batteries that night. The 8th Battery's Right Section relieved an 11th Battery (Hamilton, Ontario) section in the northern (or left) section of Canada's front near St-Julien. Meanwhile, Anderson's 8th Battery Headquarters and his Left Section were joined behind Zonnebeke Ridge by a section from 3rd "Gananoque" Battery, leaving his battery temporarily separated. The Germans attacked before the second half of the relief was completed. For the next week, through the height of Canada's role at Second Ypres, the Moncton Battery remained divided: one two-gun section and Battery Headquarters remained with their parent 2nd Field Brigade, while the other section served with 3rd Field Brigade. The 8th Battery gunners therefore served nearly everywhere on the Second Ypres battlefield. So too did Battery Sergeant Major Slader's 4th (New Brunswick) Section of 1st Divisional Ammunition Column. As the artillery motto "Ubique" claims, New Brunswick gunners were "everywhere" in what became known as the Second Battle of Ypres.

On the afternoon of 22 April 1915, Lt.-Gen. E.A.H. Alderson, 1st Canadian Division's commanding officer, and Brigadier Burstall were in the gun line behind Gravenstaffel ridge when French rifle fire drew their attention north, to "the two clouds of yellowish-green smoke each of which expanded until they blended into a

No photos exist of Canadian gunners at the Second Battle of Ypres, but all the Canadian batteries that fought there were equipped with the reliable and accurate 18-pounder field gun. This Canadian 18-pounder is seen in training early in the war. (LAC PA-022712)

single body." This cloud of chlorine gas choked and then panicked the French Colonial soldiers and virtually collapsed the northern rim of the Ypres Salient. Then the guns started. The Germans had massed field and heavy artillery pieces of six divisions, reinforced with 147 heavy guns and howitzers in calibres up to 170 mm, and struck the French with crushing fire. Trenches caved in and strongpoints blew apart, burying or obliterating men and silencing French artillery batteries.

The German effort to capture Ypres was a local attack designed to disrupt French attacks on the Western Front that might interfere with a massive German offensive in Poland designed to defeat Russia. Ypres was already viewed as symbol of Allied resistance to the full occupation of Belgium. It therefore also underscored, for both Britain and Canada, the very reasons they had gone to war. The Allies were compelled to hold Ypres at all costs.

The assault on 22 April opened three days of intense fighting, during which Canadians won lasting fame at a hideous cost – the highest of the entire war. Between 22 and 25 April, the 18,000 men of 1st Canadian Division suffered more than 6,000 casualties, including 2,000 dead. The Canadians were vastly outnumbered in men, weapons, and artillery, and beset by chlorine gas, but in the end, through willpower and skill-at-arms, they were able to check German attempts to capture Ypres and wipe out the salient. Afterwards, the British War Office proclaimed: "The

Canadians had many casualties but their gallantry and determination undoubtedly saved the situation."

Canadian gunners are less well known for their exploits at Second Ypres. The most famous of them are Major William King's 10th Field Battery from St. Catharines, Ontario. The 10th found itself north of St-Julien in a sharp corner in the new front line formed after 45th Algerian Division collapsed on the left. The St. Catharines battery fired over open sights, helping to break the German attack on the Canadian flank. But their four guns were not the only 18-pounders in action during those desperate days. New Brunswick's 8th Battery, its two sections separated by the disrupted relief begun on 21 April, fought alongside 2nd and 3rd Field Brigades. These brigades were connected by field telephones to FOOs on Gravenstaffel Ridge, who could see well to the northeast and east (and poorly due north, into the old French sector). At 1800 hours on 22 April, while the St. Catharines gunners were firing directly into the advancing Germans, Lt.-Col. Creelman's 2nd Field Brigade telephone exchange received calls for fire on enemy troops in the open. All batteries opened up almost immediately. So, too, did heavy German counter-battery fire, and a strong whiff of gas lingered in the air. Moncton Gunner Clyde Mollins, who was in the telephone exchange, wrote in a letter home:

> In the afternoon the enemy attacked. The shells were flying all around us, shrapnel hitting the building. This kept up all afternoon and they were using those gas shells. They were awful; we were all going around with sore eyes and half-asleep. About 6pm they broke through our lines and our infantry (Canadians) had to fight. The enemy was so close to us that enemy rifle bullets were hitting the barn we were in, and one of them got George McDougall.

McDougall was the first New Brunswick gunner to die in the Great War.

In two hours, 2nd Field Brigade fired 645 shrapnel shells in response to observers' calls. Their shells burst in the air, hurling lead balls down onto the closely packed ranks of German infantry. German accounts blame Canadian shellfire for stopping their attack. "A medical officer with 234th Reserve Regiment," historian Andrew Iarocci writes, "later reported that many of the casualties in his first-aid station were caused by shrapnel fire." Sergeant Neil McKinnon wrote home to his father in Scotch Settlement, New Brunswick, about what he called the Battle of Langemarck, "that it takes the 8th Battery of Moncton to 'do' the Germans."

For a time only the gunners of 3rd Field Brigade, including 8th Battery's Right Section, held the new northern "front." Brigadier Burstall worried that the forward Canadian batteries might be encircled and overrun: 2nd London Heavy Battery's four old 4.7-inch guns – the kind New Brunswick gunners were training with on Partridge Island – had already fallen into German hands. So he ordered both Canadian field artillery brigades to hitch up and withdraw to the prepared second line of defence, known as the GHQ Line. With 3rd Field Brigade's lines at the apex of the Canadian position around St-Julien already burdened by Canadian and French

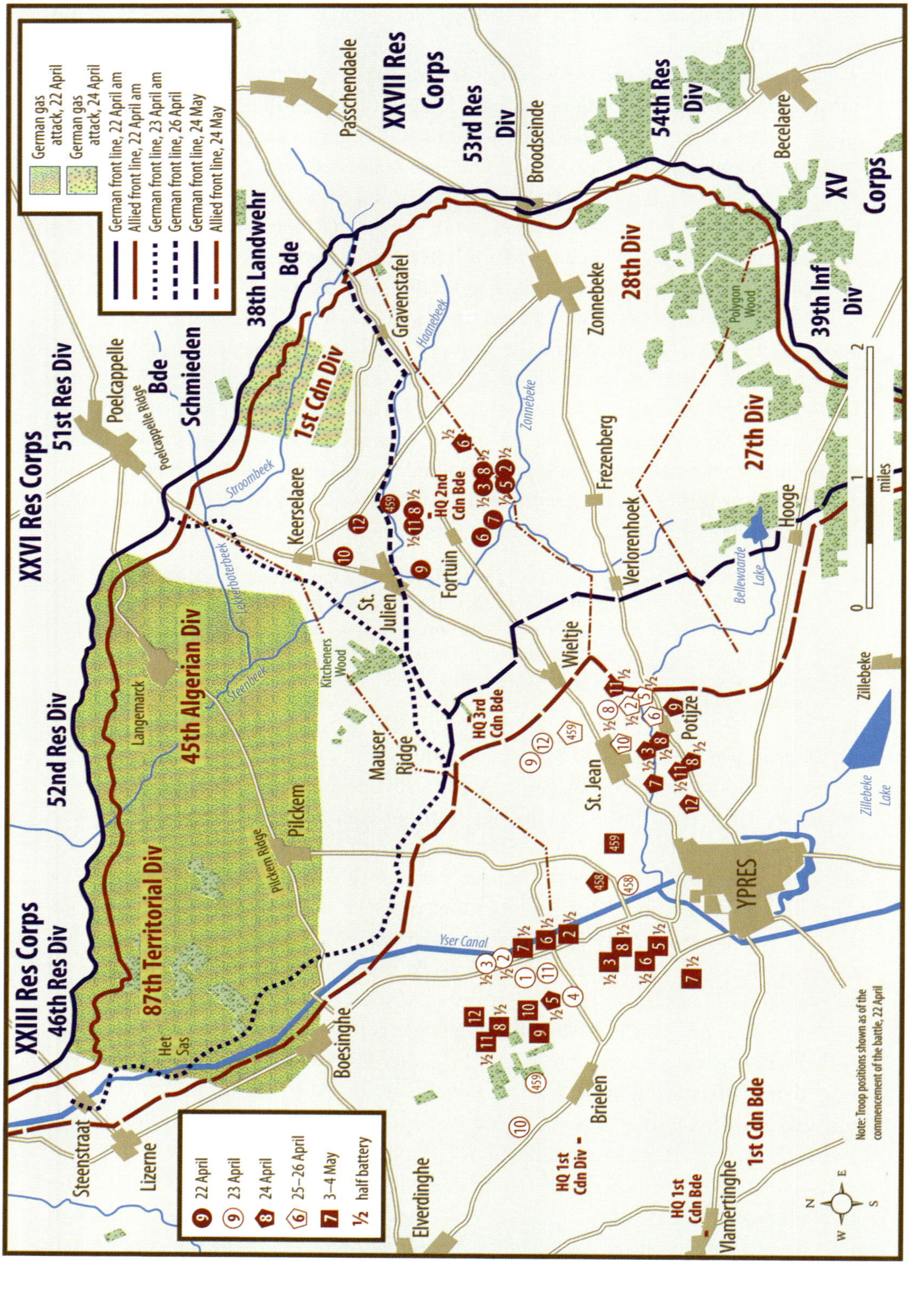

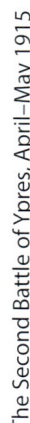

The Second Battle of Ypres, April–May 1915

gas victims, and under heavy artillery, machine-gun, and even rifle fire, the order made sense. Unfortunately, it was not received by 8th Battery's Right Section, which remained in place near St-Julien through the night. They finally got word to withdraw in the early morning hours and made it back to the new 3rd Field Brigade position at the chateau in St-Jean under duress. Afterwards, Corporal Ainsley Hicks of Jolicure, New Brunswick, was recommended for a gallantry award. "In the face of what seemed like certain death, Corporal Hicks saved a battery gun and retreated successfully."

Even while 3rd Field Brigade was abandoning its most exposed gun positions, 2nd Field Brigade's commander was having second thoughts about moving back. His guns had excellent firing positions behind Zonnebeke Ridge, 1,000 yards south of St-Julien, and they were secure behind Canadian infantry in trenches in front of Gravenstaffel Ridge. While 2nd Brigade withdrew its guns back to Wieltje in a night lit by fires, flares, and shell bursts, Lt.-Col. Creelman rode into Ypres to take up the matter of 2nd Brigade's withdrawal directly with Brigadier Burstall. Meanwhile, Canadian counter-attacks at Kitchener's Wood were stabilizing the open northern flank. Those attacks were supported by 3rd Field Brigade, including its Moncton section, before it withdrew. Encouraging reports from the northern flank helped Creelman convince Burstall that 2nd Brigade should return to its forward positions behind Zonnebeke Ridge. So before dawn on 23 April, 2nd Field Brigade limbered up again, braved enemy shells and small-arms fire, and redeployed in their old positions. Their determination helped save the day. When the sun came up, German infantry were seen massing to attack from the northeast. The 6th and 7th Batteries opened fire on the road behind the German front, while 5th and 8th Batteries raked the German front-line trench. They kept that fire up all day, disrupting German attempts to organize an assault.

The 2nd Brigade's decisive fire on 23 April was made possible by the previous night's efforts by 1st Division's Ammunition Column. Ten minutes after the initial attack stalled late on 22 April, orders came from Burstall's headquarters to "send up lots of ammunition." The column pushed up 2,800 shrapnel shells for the Canadian 18-pounders, 200 Lyddite high-explosive rounds for 118th Royal Field Artillery Brigade's 4.5-inch howitzers, and 600,000 rounds of rifle and machine-gun ammunition. Supply wagons circulated all night long. Two horses were injured by shellfire, and one wagon was smashed.

The main action on 23 April took place on the northern rim, where Canadian, British, and French counterattacks towards Mauser Ridge were stopped with bloody results. The problem was that the Allies did not have enough heavy guns or high-explosive shells to inflict damage on the German defenders, who were snug in freshly dug trenches behind newly laid barbed wire, or to respond against German long-range counter-batteries. The 8th Battery's FOO, Lieutenant Harvey Tingley, wrote home about his frustration: "So far as we know, no heavy artillery supported us. We could not get back at the Germans, who were pounding us, for we only had field artillery against the German heavy guns." Others, senior to Tingley, came to the same conclusion.

The worst was yet to come. Early on 24 April the winds blew a second German gas cloud directly at the apex of the Canadian front. Toronto's 15th Battalion and Winnipeg's 8th Battalion took the brunt of the gas, and of a furious fifteen-minute artillery and mortar barrage that followed. The 8th Battalion had anticipated trouble and laid extra telephone lines between the front and 2nd Field Brigade's guns. When German infantry emerged from their trenches to follow their gas and barrage, Lt.-Col. Lipsett called down pre-registered SOS fire from Creelman's guns. Bursting 18-pounder shrapnel shells and Winnipeg rifle fire "shredded" the German assault. The British Royal Artillery history credits 2nd Field Brigade with breaking up "attack after attack at ranges of 3500 yards."

The Toronto battalion manning the exposed northeastern apex on the Canadian front was less fortunate. Before dawn, 3rd Field Brigade was ordered to begin moving back yet again, to Ypres itself and comparative safety behind the Yser Canal. That put them out of range of the apex. Fighting in two directions without artillery support while choking on gas forced 15th Battalion survivors back towards reserve positions on Gravenstaffel Ridge. The morning's events reinforced what many Canadian soldiers already knew – that successful defence against infantry depended on good communications – that is, on good vantage points for FOOs connected by multiple communication links to strong artillery forces with ample stocks of ammunition.

At 0830 the German attack spread across the northeastern apex of the front, which was manned by 3rd Canadian Infantry Brigade. The attack was heralded by destructive artillery concentrations. Medium 5.9-inch and heavy 21 cm German high-explosive shells literally blew Canadian infantrymen out of their trenches or buried them alive. The Germans then attacked with three times the numbers of the exhausted Canadian defenders. Canadian infantry fought on, their Ross rifles jamming from the heat of constant firing, while gunners of 2nd and parts of 3rd Field Brigade ripped through the German battalions that were attempting to storm St-Julien through a cloud of shrapnel. The attack ground to a bloody halt, at least for a time. Battery Sgt.-Maj. Slader would remember that no one had expected to require so much ammunition on what was supposed to be "a relatively quiet front. Thanks to good planning and tremendous exertion on the part of all concerned the supply was maintained." The night before, the ammunition column had delivered 6,900 18-pounder rounds. Ammunition drivers had also brought up more than one million bullets and spare parts for the strained guns. Most of the newly dumped ammunition had been fired by 0945 hours. As the day wore on, 2nd Field Brigade hung on precariously, supporting the vicious battle for the commanding strongpoint known as Locality "C." They made their few remaining shells count on the

Unseen and unheralded work behind the front. A Canadian ammunition column winding its way through a ruined village. (LAC PA-001976)

target-rich front. By mid-afternoon "there appeared no sign of reinforcements or chance of getting more ammunition," so the beleaguered Canadian forward infantry companies withdrew to a shorter, more defensible line anchored on the village of St-Julien.

The morning German attack on 24 April caught 3rd Field Brigade in the process of pulling their guns westward behind Yser. The 8th Battery's Right Section, still attached to 3rd Field Brigade, had just arrived west of the canal at noon when they received counter-orders to ride back through Ypres and into the salient so that they could support the beleaguered 3rd Canadian Infantry Brigade. Captain Harry Crerar, 11th Battery's second-in-command, had the composite 8th and 11th Battery gallop in fifty-yard rushes through Ypres as it was torn apart by German long-range heavy artillery. "Bodies of dead soldiers and civilians, dead horses and dogs, shattered buildings and ripped up roads met the eye on every side," 11th Battery reported later. "High explosive and shrapnel are bursting at erratic intervals." An 8th Battery driver, William Curley from Woodstock, wrote that "the city was being shelled in such a desperate shape that no living thing could stay there, but we had to advance through there to regain our old position. We started through at the dead gallop with all our horses and guns, and very few of us expected to get through

Lt.-Col. S. Boyd Anderson. Major Boyd Anderson commanded 19th (Moncton) Battery before the war, mobilized it, took it overseas, fought with it in 1915–16 as 8th Battery, took command of 12th Field Brigade in 1916, and ended the war commanding 2nd Field Brigade – as one of NB's most distinguished field gunners.
(Moncton Museum)

alive. Only one man was lost, but half our horses were killed. I have a lovely team and thank goodness they were spared."

The 8th Battery's Right Section made it back to a new position behind the GHQ Line near Potijze, where Lt.-Col. Creelman had repositioned 7th Battery and the main body of Anderson's 8th Battery. They had precious few shells left, but a small convoy of three ammunition wagons reached them late in the afternoon. It was enough to hold the Germans at point-blank range at St-Julien and to cover 5th and 6th Batteries' withdrawal into 2nd Field Brigade's new position at Potijze. As darkness fell, Creelman reorganized 2nd Field Brigade to support a pre-dawn British counterattack around St-Julien planned for the morning of 25 April. The 2nd Brigade's log reported in frustration that it was "impossible for FOOs to observe correctly" in support of the hastily planned counterattack. Nor were there enough heavy guns or high-explosive ammunition to harm the newly entrenched German defenders or cut their wire. The result was predictable. Early that morning, British 10th Brigade was cut to ribbons by German machine-gun and artillery fire.

The 2nd Field Brigade won payback after the sun came up, when Creelman's FOOs spotted German troops massing to drive the faltering British infantry from St-Julien. At 0700 hours, 2nd Field Brigade gunners pumped ten minutes of rapid fire into the German ranks. The well-observed fire stopped the attack cold – for the moment. They even scrounged twenty rounds of rare 18-pounder high-explosive ammunition to blow apart a house sheltering a German machine gun. The Germans re-formed and pressed relentlessly south from St-Julien. By late afternoon, when the enemy attacked out of Kitchener's Wood west of St-Julien, 2nd Field Brigade fired everything they had at them. It was not much, for ammunition supplies throughout the Ypres salient were now almost exhausted.

German long-range heavy artillery fire, on the other hand, never seemed to slacken. Gunner George Patterson of Middle Coverdale, New Brunswick, wrote home that

> for days and nights we were hit by shells that would tear holes in the ground six to ten feet deep and ten feet in diameter. Motion pictures give but a slight idea of the terrible work done by the war machines used in this war. On our lines the air is full of bursting shells and here and there a heavier shell striking the ground and throwing mud and splinters of steel a distance of 75 yards and I will leave it to your own mind when there are many troops moving or standing about in the open. But thank providence so far I am still alive and unhurt.

Two other members of the Moncton Battery were not so lucky. Gunner Ira Mills wrote to his sister: "I never thought I would see human flesh cut up as it was in that scrap." That day, direct hits to 8th Battery's lines killed gunners Fred Popow and George Talbot. Talbot was an Irish immigrant working in Moncton when the war broke out. All four of his brothers had been killed in action in 1914. There was nothing left of Popow and Talbot to bury. Their names are commemorated on the Menin Gate in Ypres.

Long-range German 150 mm and 170 mm guns penetrated deep into the Canadian base areas around Ypres and everywhere in between. The enemy had even brought up gigantic, fortress-smashing 420 mm siege guns to fire 2000-pound shells into Ypres, taking the city apart building by building. The intense action over these three days placed an enormous strain on the guns themselves. Part of Ned Slader's job as a Battery Sergeant Major in the Ammunition Column was to keep the guns working. On the morning of 25 April, he brought parts through the maelstrom to 12th Battery, where two guns had been knocked out and two others needed overhauling. All four guns were brought back into action that day. Slader wrote: "I was in the saddle almost without rest or sleep for nearly six days checking up with Brigade Ammunition Columns and riding up with a haversack full of small parts. It was necessary to take to the fields as the roads were being heavily shelled."

Gas and enemy shelling were driving Belgian farm families westward. "All roads out of Ypres and Vlamertinghe were crowded with refugees, their former homes on fire or reduced to rubble." Vlamertinghe was under heavy fire when Slader left on the morning of 25 April, but seemed quiet on his return. "I had just cleared the western end when the Germans reopened fire. One shell struck the Church which was being used as a hospital. Right in front of the church was an old woman carrying a pack and trudging along the pavement. I looked back and a second shell burst on the road. The old woman was no more." No place was safe in or behind the Ypres Salient, and at this point in the war there was nothing that the Canadians – whose only heavy battery was still south of Armentières – could do about it.

The great peril abated somewhat on 26 April. The 1st Canadian Division became immediately famous in the Empire for standing firm in the eye of two gas attacks at Ypres. They gave ground but never broke, and in the end they played a key role in thwarting German plans. That day, on which 1st Division's infantry battalions were mostly relieved by British troops, marks the end of Canadian accounts of Second Ypres. But for British troops, the battle would go on for many weeks more, and the Canadian Divisional Artillery remained in action for another full week. New Brunswick gunners supported counterattacks by British, Indian, and French units as casualties in men and horses mounted. Exhaustion and death were ever present. From 26 April right through to 3 May, the Canadian artillery bastion around Potijze endured steady German counter-battery bombardment. By 27 April, 2nd Field Brigade was short three officers, fifty gunners, and eighty horses despite drawing in men – especially trained gunners – and animals from the Brigade and Division Ammunition Columns.

On 29 April, German heavy shells finally found their mark in 8th Battery Left Section's lines north of Potijze. Battery Sgt.-Maj. Noah Steeves was wounded. He wrote that evening from a field hospital about his experience.

> I saw one strike fair on a gun of another battery near us and part of the carriage flew 50 yards and came down fifteen feet from where I stood. The crew on that gun was badly cut up, three killed outright and three wounded. The Germans are still using the famous Jack Johnson shells [5.9-inch shell emitting black smoke]. Don't ever believe any of the yarns you hear or see in the papers about Germany being short of ammunition. They have both guns and men and ammunition.

2nd Field Brigade's war diary confirmed Steeves's assessment. On 29 April it recorded that "the enemy are superior to us in heavy guns and dominate our position with aeroplanes. We have no means of locating their batteries beyond the ridge which the enemy holds." One heavy shell landed three feet behind Gunner Leslie Miller of Newcastle, New Brunswick. Five separate white-hot shell splinters pierced his hips, and the blast sprained his back, but he survived. Gunners Gordon Turner of Moncton and Fred Gunn of Chatham were bringing up fresh rations to the gun positions when the fire came down. The blast tore Turner's hand off, and the right side of Gunn's torso was torn open. Gunn was a trained machinist and employed by Major Anderson as the battery artificer. "He was the greatest help to me, could test all the sights, buffer range drum, and kept the guns in the best condition." Boyd Anderson wrote home that "the team drivers ran out and brought Fred in and told me he was badly wounded. I could not go see him as I had gone through a lot there.

On his way to the dressing station he told the men not to tell his mother or father how badly he was wounded."

Fred Gunn died in a field hospital the next day. That same day, 8th Battery's Right Section on the west side of Potijze experienced its heaviest shelling so far. Sergeant Grant was severely wounded. Lt.-Col. Creelman himself was evacuated on 29 April with a high fever after too much exposure to gas and what he himself later described as shell shock.

On 1 May 1915, Canada's Divisional Artillery got word to retire behind the Yser Canal, where they could disperse batteries better. Their artillery fire base at Potijze had become too exposed to German shelling from three sides. Before the move commenced, word came from the front that the Germans were massing for something. The 8th Battery gunners joined a Canadian barrage against German forward assembly areas before commencing their withdrawal over the canal by sections. The withdrawal was half-complete at 0300 on 2 May when the Germans released another massive chlorine gas cloud. German guns pummelled the Allied trenches and the Potijze artillery position, where 2nd Field Brigade still had seven guns in action, including 8th Battery's Left Section. The 2nd Field Brigade gunners opened fire on SOS targets along the front, bursting shrapnel down on the attacking infantry. When the weight of German shot cut telephone connections between FOOs and the forward infantry, signalmen acted as runners to carry target information back to the gun line. Quick-thinking British infantry waited in support trenches until the wind carried the gas cloud onto them and then charged through it to reoccupy the front trench. German attackers following the gas cloud were caught between British rifle bullets and Canadian shrapnel bursts. French 75 mm guns added their weight from the northern flank. Lt.-Gen. Alderson reported that the "attack was repulsed with heavy [German] loss in spite of a considerable portion of our front having been incapacitated by gas." Gunners from all of the forward Canadian gun sections were among the gas casualties.

During this third major German gas attack on 2 May, Lieutenant Harvey Tingley and his telephone operator, Signaller Joseph Arthur Comeau, manned 8th Battery's observation post in a house south of the main road between St-Jean and Wieltje along the crown of St-Jean Ridge. From that commanding location they called down 8th Battery's guns on the northern wing of the German attack and their front-line trench, 350 yards from the house. All day the German barrage rained down around them, knocking down portions of the house they occupied. Tingley wrote afterwards: "Sig Comeau and I were sitting in a room in the back of the house downstairs. We were sitting close together – so close our elbows were touching. It was about 3 o'clock in the afternoon that we were struck. A shell burst through the top of the house, demolishing the roof and carrying away a portion of the front of the house." Tingley's leg was smashed. Comeau, formerly on the staff of the *Moncton Times*, was hit badly in the face and later died in an English hospital.

Lt.-Col. Beverley Armstrong, South African War veteran and son of another 3rd New Brunswick Regiment commanding officer. During the Great War, Armstrong defended Saint John harbour and trained some 2,000 New Brunswickers to serve with the Canadian heavy siege artillery overseas.
(Loyal Company Association Collection)

Despite these losses, the New Brunswick gunners had done their share to stop this third German gas attack at Ypres.

On the night of 3–4 May, the Canadian Divisional Artillery completed its move to well-dispersed positions on the west bank of the Yser Canal, near Brielen. Although much better spread out, Canadian batteries remained under heavy German counter-battery fire. Al Humphrey, 8th Battery Right Section's sergeant, wrote home about the day to Mrs. Fletcher Polleys, mother of Ned Polleys of Moncton. Humphrey's crew served their gun under heavy German shellfire all day. "At about 4:30pm, several shells came very close to our guns and one pitched about ten or fifteen feet away. After some time, Ned Polleys called out, 'Boys, I'm not hit, I'm paralyzed.' He was lifted from the gun seat and placed beside the wheel. All medical aid possible was rendered but he passed within minutes." As Humphreys explained to Mrs Polleys, "the whole battery, both officers and men, join me in expressing to you our most sincere regrets and deepest sympathy." Gunner Polleys was the last New Brunswick gunner to die at Second Ypres.

New Brunswick gunners – indeed, *all* Canadian gunners with 1st Division – had much to be proud of. As much as they felt the effects of wicked German counter-battery fire, their own shrapnel shells broke or blunted nearly every enemy lunge forward behind all three German gas attacks against Ypres. Later in May a flood of letters home from the front filled Canadians in about their little army's stand east of Ypres as well as about the losses suffered. On 25 May 1915, citizens of Moncton and all over southeastern New Brunswick gathered at Bend View Square to remember the first four members of "Anderson's Battery" killed during the Great War. It was, as the papers called it, a "solemn and impressive service in memory of Moncton's fallen heroes." Eleven other members of the battery had been wounded in April and at least that many more again in the first week of May. "I know where all the Moncton boys are buried," Major Anderson wrote to the *Moncton Times*, "and made a mark on the map so that anyone can locate them should anything happen to me."

The first Canadian actions at Ypres, and indeed the whole experience of the British Expeditionary Force on the Western Front since 1914, demonstrated the need to vastly expand the heavy and siege artillery of the field armies. Second Ypres convinced the British Army that the war could not be won until British and Dominion troops matched Germany in heavy artillery. In 1915 the British began forging hundreds of new heavy guns and howitzers. They would need thousands of trained gunners to serve them, and they called upon the Empire to help. New Brunswick answered the call.

Over the winter of 1914–15, 3rd New Brunswick Regiment's Lt.-Col. Beverley Armstrong had lobbied hard for more provincial representation in new Canadian contingents being raised for overseas service. He had also pushed hard for more concerted use of the skills of coast gunners. Ottawa paid little attention until Britain's appeal for more heavy guns arrived. The British were building the guns;

And so it begins. The 4th Canadian Overseas Siege Battery parades in Saint John before its departure. (NBM 4th Siege Battery-3)

what was urgently needed was trained heavy gunners. The 3rd NB Regiment finally received authority to raise its own overseas unit in October 1915, as a response to this appeal for "imperial" heavy batteries. By mid-December, 4th Overseas Siege Battery had been formed and was at full strength. Eighty-four men transferred from 3rd NB Regiment Composite Battery and Regimental Headquarters, and the regiment recruited 132 more, including fifteen from its Halifax Detachment. Major L.W. Barker took command, joined by Captain R.A. Ring and Lieutenants J.H.A. Fairweather, W.G. Kerr, and G.B. Wetmore. The 4th Battery shared garrison duties on Partridge Island until its departure at the end of March 1916.

Authorization to form a second overseas battery soon followed, thanks to the continued efforts of Lt.-Col. Armstrong. Still the OC of 3rd NB Regiment, since the outbreak of war Armstrong had also served as the New Brunswick representative at Militia District 6 Headquarters in Halifax, with special responsibility for organizing recruiting in the province. Early in March 1916 Armstrong moved to Halifax, where he was named Deputy Assistant Adjutant and Quartermaster General at MD 6 Headquarters. In that position he would be responsible for recruiting and equipping overseas drafts of troops and arranging their transport overseas. In the words of the history of the district staff, "his grasp of details was unusual, and his knowledge of shipping and business affairs was of great assistance, particularly in connection with the very important work of transporting, embarking and disembarking troops."

But administration was not Armstrong's real passion. He had been pushing for over a year for coast gunners to be employed at the front. Shortly after his arrival in Halifax, 3rd NB Regiment received authority to raise "7th Siege Battery," later renumbered the 6th. This was a further Canadian response to Kitchener's appeal for more siege artillery. On 20 April 1916, 105 other ranks from the Composite Battery on Partridge Island and fourteen from the regiment's Halifax Detachment were transferred to the new battery. Like 4th Battery, the 6th concentrated on Partridge Island, where it shared duties with the Composite Battery. By the time it departed the island for overseas at the beginning of June 1916, its strength included 146 other ranks, of whom no more than forty were new recruits. The commanding officer was Major L.T. Allen, who transferred to 6th Siege Battery together with Lieutenant H.A. West from the Halifax Detachment of 3rd NB Regiment.

The raising of 4th and 6th Siege Batteries was just the start. It seems that those old 4.7-inch guns on Partridge Island, and the expertise in using them gained between 1905 and 1910, were a solid foundation on which to build the heavy artillery of the Canadian Corps. That artillery would become the key to breaking the stalemate of the Western Front.

Chapter 3

Building the Corps Artillery, 1915–16

As the depleted batteries of 1st Canadian Division artillery drifted out of the line at Ypres in May 1915, units of the Second Canadian Contingent reached France. The 6th Canadian Field Brigade, which included 23rd and 24th Field Batteries assembled in Fredericton, arrived so early that it was redesignated the "Reserve Brigade, Canadian Field Artillery." Soon men and junior officers were being dispersed to fill gaps in 1st Canadian Division's batteries. The fate of 23rd and 24th Batteries was followed closely in New Brunswick; this was especially so for 23rd Battery, which included twenty students from the University of New Brunswick. Readers of the *Fredericton Daily Gleaner* learned from Sergeant Major Patchell of 23rd Battery that some of their "local men" were going to 8th Battery, which had specifically asked for New Brunswickers. Major Anderson's 8th Battery now represented the entire province.

It seems, however, that many New Brunswickers remained with the Reserve Brigade and were available to help form new 4.5-inch field howitzer batteries to beef up Canada's divisional field artillery. By January 1916, these new howitzer batteries in 1st Canadian Division had been grouped as 6th Howitzer Brigade, which included a new 23rd Howitzer Battery, Canadian Field Artillery. As a result, a large number of New Brunswickers ended up with the new howitzer brigade, and many in the new 23rd Battery. The howitzers brought the division a powerful new weapon capable of throwing a reasonably powerful high-explosive shell at high angles into German positions. It was a start.

The rest of 1915 was a frustrating one for Canadians on the Western Front. In May, 1st Canadian Divisional Artillery moved south as part of General Douglas Haig's British First Army spring offensive between Aubers Ridge and Festubert, which was intended to pin German units on that front while the French attacked just to the south towards Vimy Ridge. The move brought 1st Canadian Division close to their brothers in 1st Canadian Heavy Battery, who were still dug in near Neuve Chapelle. Major Magee's 60-pounders had been there since mid-April in the quiet shade of an orchard, but the intensity of their war was about to change. Cyrus Inches wrote: "We were in position just behind the village of La Couture. It was a beautiful orchard in blossom. Nothing disturbed our serenity until the unsuccessful attack on Aubers Ridge on May 9th when the men were called upon to fight their guns under fire for the first time." Magee's battery now formed part of an elite counter-battery task group of three 60-pounder batteries: twelve guns in all. Since the BEF had only thirty-three of the modern 60-pounders available for the attack, Magee's guns represented a critical portion of the heavies deployed for the assault. Most of the other eighty-eight British heavy pieces were obsolete 4.7-inch guns and 5-inch howitzers. Ammunition was also in short supply. By later standards, this was a pitifully small force of heavy artillery.

Major Magee and now Captain Inches prepared 1st Canadian Heavy Battery for the attack as best they could. They registered their guns with the help of Royal Flying Corps air observers, and the week before the attack fired counter-battery missions to protect assembling British troops. Ammunition shortages kept shoots to an average of twenty rounds until "Zero Day." On 5 May they fired an experimental shoot with four No. 65 fuses, combination time-percussion fuses intended to burst shrapnel rounds over an enemy observation post known as "the Little Grey Home in the West." Shelling on both sides intensified as the assault neared. Magee's battery retaliated wherever possible to temporarily "silence" German batteries if not destroy them outright.

The Germans had learned much about the lethality of massed British artillery during the battle at Neuve Chapelle and had greatly strengthened their defences. They had been ordered to hold in the west in 1915, and they did it in style. In the low, wet country barring the western approaches to Aubers Ridge, they had erected six-foot-high parapets between fifteen and twenty feet thick. The fortress system linked together reinforced machine-gun posts with overhead cover that could take all but direct hits by heavy high-explosive shells. They had also greatly widened their barbed wire fields to make them nearly impossible to cut with shellfire. And they had prepared reserve trenches with deep dugouts in belts behind the main front. The British at Neuve Chapelle in March had not encountered the kind of prepared defences that were stretched before them now at the foot of Aubers Ridge in the spring of 1915.

At dawn on 9 May, one Indian and two British divisions advanced across no man's land. Within hours, 11,000 men had fallen dead or wounded, with few getting past the German wire. The simple reality was that too many German machine guns were left covering too much intact wire. The 1st Canadian Heavy Battery fired 711 shells that day, their largest counter-battery mission of the war so far. What they hit remains unknown. The battery's forward observation post stayed connected to the gun line all day, enabling correction data to flow back. At least they could correct for the weather. Target registrations for most British batteries had been shot in the wet damp days before the attack. But 9 May had dawned with fine, clear weather, which meant that atmospheric conditions had changed and pre-registered barrages missed their targets. It is probable that 1st Heavy Battery prevented some German guns from firing and making the casualty lists even longer, but they and their British counterparts did not possess enough 60-pounders to silence all German guns. One of only two radios available in supporting observation aircraft also failed. According to the official Royal Artillery historian, Sir Martin Farndale, enough German guns were left in action to wreak havoc "on British trenches now packed with a confused mass of wounded men and support troops."

The battle for Aubers Ridge is little-known except as one in a string of disasters. But for British and Dominion artillery, it marked a critical point in the development of a war-winning attack doctrine. According to the Royal Artillery history, the battle drove home lessons about daily meteorological adjustment for every gun, as well as the need for long, destructive preparatory bombardments, "accurate information about the enemy's defences, the need for really accurate artillery fire, the urgent need for an accurate medium howitzer, and the need to be able to locate enemy guns accurately." These ideas eventually gave birth to Canada's own heavy artillery organization, and the Composite Battery on Partridge Island training gunners on 4.7-inch guns would prove instrumental in making that organization possible.

Fighting south of Aubers Ridge dragged on through May 1915 in some of the most dismal and seemingly pointless battles fought by Canadians in the Great War. Indeed, studied in isolation (as they usually are) from the events farther south on the eastern slopes of Vimy Ridge, these battles seem tragically futile. After taking a week to replenish artillery ammunition stocks and gather intelligence on enemy defences, and after a seventy-two-hour bombardment at Festubert, General Haig's offensive reopened in the early morning darkness of 13 May. Major Magee's 1st Canadian Heavy Battery launched part of that preparatory fire, in the form of short nighttime concentrations on known German observation posts and batteries. Captain Inches captured the mood in a letter home: "Picture to yourself two fat Deutchers retiring for a good old snooze among the draperies of one of these French creations termed a couche. Sixty pounds of Lyddite from one of our guns enters the window. Deutchers seek another billet." According to exhausted German prisoners, the harassing fire had an effect. On the night of the attack on 15 May, 1st Canadian Heavy Battery loosed off 562 rounds of both shrapnel and Lyddite. Similar numbers of shells were stacked to keep up that rate of counter-battery fire for two more days until 17 May.

The first assaults by British and Indian troops between 16 and 18 May were reasonably successful, forcing the Germans to bring in reserves from Ypres and Arras to stiffen their buckling front at Festubert. In a very real way, the attack eased pressure on the French Tenth Army's struggle for the Lorette Spur at the end of the Artois Heights overlooking Vimy Ridge. But General Haig needed to give German reserve units cause to stay at Festubert. His solution was to have 1st Canadian Division and 51st Highland Division press the attack against a now alert and reinforced enemy on 18 May. There was little time to gather information or properly plan an attack. Also, the Canadian Divisional Artillery was a week's march behind the infantry brigades, which had been in action steadily at Ypres. Unfamiliar British gunners and FOOs were assigned to support the Canadian attack on a series of German strongpoints in the second and third German support trench lines east

A Canadian 60-pounder on the move in France with its team of draft horses. (LAC PA-002470)

of Festubert. Ammunition for heavier guns was running short. The 1st Canadian Heavy Battery reduced its rate of fire by half as the battle went on: only 263 rounds on 20 May, 205 the next day, and 131 on 22 May. By that time, German heavy artillery were beginning to win the artillery duel, putting fire on 1st Canadian Heavy Battery billets and gun positions; one enemy shell landed a yard in front of the No. 4 gun. Major Magee had drivers ride the battery's horses out of danger under fire on 24 May.

Canadian infantry paid a heavy price in blood to keep the Germans pinned to the low ground along the La Bassee Canal in May 1915. Canadian field guns finally arrived on 23 May, in time to participate in the last Canadian local attack on German strongpoints the next day. That left them little time to prepare gun pits in the waterlogged ground or to lay telephone lines to observation posts. As it turned out, the FOOs could see almost nothing on the bullet-swept pancake of no man's land. Gun positions were exposed, ammunition grew very short, and phone lines were cut by German fire as gunners became frustrated at not being able to support their infantry properly. The 2nd Canadian Field Brigade, with New Brunswick's 8th Battery deployed on its southern flank, fired on German counterattacks and attempted to support Brigadier Arthur Currie's 2nd Infantry Brigade in its struggle for the infamous K5 strongpoint, for which they had been battling since 21 May. That fight petered out inconclusively, with the K5 strongpoint itself becoming the new no man's land. Mercifully, there were no fatal casualties in the three New Brunswick batteries at Festubert.

In the last frustrating days at Festubert, Captain Inches wrote home that "the Canadian Division, both infantry and artillery, are all in our vicinity again and some of the infantry are in the trenches ahead of us." Inches remained hopeful about General Burstall's rumoured request that 1st Canadian Heavy Battery be returned to the division. It was not to be. The brief co-location ended on 12 June, when Major Magee received orders to move 1st Canadian Heavy Battery back to the La Couture area to support the Indian Meerut Division.

The last Canadian operation in the La Bassee Canal sector as part of the French Second Battle of Artois was launched at Givenchy on 15 June. The action amounted to a limited attack by two Canadian battalions against a pair of German strongpoints shielding the flank of the main British 7th Division assault. The action is noteworthy for what it portended. The Canadians in particular, and the British in general, were learning quickly what was necessary to attack and defeat the German army. Unlike the rushed action at Festubert, Brigadier Burstall had three weeks to prepare at Givenchy, gather information, and lay telephone lines in triplicate. He also held the advantage of better ground, for the low southwest tip of Aubers Ridge was now in their control and forming a shield behind which to dig in guns and dump ammunition. Canadian field guns were supported by a British heavy artillery group of batteries and by some 155 mm French guns. Preparations were made under steady German harassing fire and had to be concealed from the eyes of probing German aircraft.

Gunner Harold McInerney from Richibucto, New Brunswick, one of the University of New Brunswick students who ended up in 8th Battery after Ypres, wrote home about those days of preparation. In early June he formed part of a thirty-man work party that had been sent forward quietly, carrying filled sandbags to strengthen 8th Battery's observation post, which was only eighty yards from the German forward trench. "Sometimes when you would be walking through a trench a sandbag would show above the parapet, and then you would hear a bullet hit the sand about a foot from your head. I tell you what, the snipers were right on their job." New, rudimentary British anti-aircraft batteries mounting 13-pounder horse artillery guns were set up behind Aubers Ridge to protect the divisional gun area from enemy air observation, which would most certainly lead to accurate German counter-battery fire. McInerney wrote about a German Taube observer plane poking its nose over their gun line. "She would get so far and then our anti-aircraft guns would open fire and drive her back. She tried all morning and then gave up in disgust."

The battle at Givenchy opened at 1500 hours on 15 June when 8th Battery and the whole Canadian Divisional Artillery began their twenty-seven-hour preparatory bombardment. The 3rd Canadian Field Brigade blasted assault lanes through German barbed wire in no man's land and then maintained fire on them to keep away German repair parties. The 2nd Canadian Field Brigade pounded the enemy front-line trench with a precious allotment of high-explosive ammunition to blow down the parapet. As daylight faded, 2nd Canadian Field Brigade FOOs reported that 75 per cent of rounds fired in the first five hours of the bombardment landed "in or very near trenches" and that the parapet was badly damaged. The guns stabbed the sky with fire nearly all night save for a ninety-minute pause at 2000 hours intended to keep the Germans on edge and unsure when an assault might begin.

At sunrise on 15 June, 6th Battery's FOO reported no signs of repairs to damaged parapets or strongpoints in 2nd Canadian Field Brigade's area. Daylight and a small but accurate and steady Canadian drizzle of shells kept German work parties away. The Germans responded by shelling Canadian rear areas and communication trenches heavily. Finally, at 1730 hours on 15 June, the main bombardment commenced with the FOOs carefully observing the fall of shot from dangerously close distances. "I tell you we made things hot for the Germans until 6 o'clock when the bombardment stopped to allow our infantry to charge," Gunner Launce O'Leary of Richibucto explained in a letter home. "During that two days you could not hear a locomotive whistle 25 yards from you." The concept of creeping barrages had not yet been developed, but when the infantry assault commenced, Canadian guns shifted their fire deeper into the German position to shield them from enemy positions and to prevent German reinforcements from reaching the trench.

Lieutenant Laurence Kelly commanded one of several Canadian 18-pounders in concealed firing positions in the front trenches. The New Brunswicker's gun lay quiet for the first ten minutes of the barrage, then unmasked and fired point blank at a German strongpoint. It was an innovative solution to the lack of heavy guns to destroy strong fortifications. Kelly's crew loosed off forty rounds before the striker malfunctioned. He and the crew were struggling to fix it when a large "Krupp" shell smashed into their position, wounding Kelly. Moments later, a Royal Engineers tunnelling company detonated a massive underground mine nearby, signalling the start of the infantry assault. The blast wrecked the German strongpoint but went off too close the Canadian jump-off position, killing or wounding fifty men. Kelly, already suffering from a shell splinter in his arm, had his left leg crushed by debris from the mine blast. He was later decorated for his actions.

The Canadian attack went well, but the gains were abandoned when the main British 7th Division attack faltered to the north due to insufficient bombardment. Gunner O'Leary showed little sympathy for the 7th British, explaining his frustrations in a letter home: "In the charge our Canucks in the trenches did gallant work, but I cannot say as much for those whom the Canadians relied on for support. However this is only one instance when our boys showed their superiority over their comrades as well as the Huns." So ended 1st Canadian Division's participation in the dismal British spring offensive of 1915. No New Brunswick infantry units were there, but the gunners were and the battles are commemorated on the provincial cenotaph in Fredericton.

A week after Givenchy the Canadians marched back to Ypres. In theory, Ypres was now a "quiet" sector. But Andrew Iarocci's work reveals how, after a year of bitter fighting, no live-and-let-live spirit existed between the BEF and their opponents in the fall of 1915. The Canadians understood that they might receive orders to reopen the offensive any day and likewise that the Germans might attack without warning. Bombardier Thomas Hennessy of Irishtown, New Brunswick, called it "the siege." He wrote to his father: "I think we're in for another winter of it." The New Brunswick gunners' siege warfare vigil in the trenches remained a deadly business, with snipers taking a toll of the careless and harassing shellfire adding to the "wastage" even on quiet fronts. Gunners practised their craft even if shell allotments remained low. They registered regularly to allow for weather corrections and shifting mud in gun positions, and they duelled steadily with their German counterparts. Casualties were not high, but the threat of death remained constant. Moncton Bombardier Edwin Lutes, an original from 23rd Field Battery assigned to 8th Battery as a replacement, was wounded by German shell fragments in late July 1915.

Ypres in mid-1916. The city had not yet been completely demolished by long-range German heavy artillery. Mount Sorrell provided enemy forward observers with excellent observation of the city. (LAC PA-000561)

In September 1915, 2nd Canadian Division finally arrived at the front. Its New Brunswick artillery component comprised 232 officers and men of Lt.-Col. Harry Harrison's 2nd Divisional Ammunition Column, including the Headquarters Group and Captain George Gamblin's 1st (NB) Section. A detachment of twenty gunners from 3rd New Brunswick Regiment also arrived with 2nd Canadian Heavy Battery, the start of a steady trickled of gunners from the Composite Battery on Partridge Island that would soon transform Canadian artillery on the Western Front. Like 1st Canadian Heavy Battery, 2nd Canadian Heavy Battery was immediately detached to the pool of British heavy artillery. Other New Brunswickers serving with Major Randolph Crocker's 28th Field Battery from Newcastle, New Brunswick, and 23rd Howitzer Battery forming in England from the old 23rd New Brunswick Field Battery, joined the division in the new year. The 2nd Canadian Division also contained the first dedicated NB infantry unit to reach the front: 26th (New Brunswick) Battalion of 5th Infantry Brigade. Roy Robinson from Marysville, New Brunswick, an 8th Battery veteran gunner, spotted 26th Battalion marching along the road, including his brother Private Jack Robinson. "The greeting was hearty," the *Moncton Times* reported, "the two brothers having not seen one another for upwards of a year."

Lt.-Col. Harrison's 2nd Canadian Divisional Ammunition Column, which landed at Le Havre on 17 September 1915, found itself alongside 1st Canadian Division in the Ploegstreet sector of the front south of Ypres. The union of the two divisions heralded the formation of the Canadian Corps under command of Lt.-Gen. E.A.H. Alderson, a regular British officer. Brigadier Burstall followed Alderson to the new Canadian Corps Headquarters as the GOC, Royal Artillery (GOCRA), Canadian Corps. The concept of a Corps Artillery Headquarters to direct heavy guns was just emerging in British practice. In time it would provide a place for Canadian heavy and siege artillery batteries to assemble under Canadian command. But for the time being the Canadians followed standard British practice: heavy artillery, like 1st and 2nd Canadian Heavy Batteries, were controlled centrally and assigned to corps only as required for specific operations.

As the Canadian Corps formed at Ypres, Major Magee's 1st Canadian Heavy Battery shifted to a new battlefield just north of Festubert, near the coal-mining town of Loos, north of Lens. There the British were attacking again in support of yet another French attempt to take Vimy Ridge and an even larger assault in the Champagne area, east of Paris. The assault at Loos would be the largest mounted by the BEF thus far. The British assembled six divisions opposite strong German positions at Loos and Hill 70, which barred the approaches to the major railway junction town of Lens. French and British commanders understood that German defences were growing ever stronger, deeper, and more complex with every battle. According to Royal Artillery veteran and historian Dominick Graham, because

A Great War "fuel" dump. Canadian Artillery drivers load fodder for draft animals. Drivers in the ammunition columns and field batteries relied on horse transport throughout the war.
(LAC PA-002545)

they lacked sufficient "heavy howitzers to destroy them in short intense bombardment, the French and British adopted long methodical ones." This time the British planned a four-day preparatory bombardment across a four-mile front, and for the first time planned to support the assault with the use of gas.

The 1st Canadian Heavy Battery moved its Right Section into the line at Bully-les-Mines in early September to make preparations for the Loos battle. The Left Section's two guns remained back below Aubers Ridge to help maintain the illusion that the British would be renewing the attack there instead. Finally, on 20 September, Captain Inches brought the Left Section south to rejoin the battery. Together with 48th Heavy Battery, Royal Garrison Artillery, they formed "Phip's Brigade." As they dug in, surveyed, and stocked gun pits, they also began locating the German artillery positions in the sector. They reported themselves ready for action by 0300 hours on 23 September. The next day they began their portion of the preparatory fire plan; their task was to cut barbed wire and conduct counter-battery shooting aided by the Royal Flying Corps. The flying conditions were good, but with a break in the weather there were too many artillery batteries in the sector suddenly trying to register guns, making it difficult for air observers and FOOs to determine which exploding shells were theirs. The action demonstrated to everyone that a more centrally directed target registration plan was necessary, especially when trying to conceal the strength of the assault until the last days. Ammunition remained in short supply: the battery had only 200 rounds for 24 September, the day before the assault.

Zero Day, 25 September, dawned cloudy and rainy again, with fitful wind. The gas, which the British hoped would make up for their lack of heavy artillery ammunition, was released, but shifting winds spread it evenly into German and British trenches alike. Nevertheless, the assault went in at 0530 hours. The 1st Canadian Heavy Battery did what it could to neutralize the German guns during and after the initial assault. They also smashed a brick wall at their FOO's request, which concealed a nest of German machine-guns. Officers from British 47th Division facing the strongpoint wrote a letter of thanks for the excellent shooting. The other job for Major Magee's battery that day came after the sun set. Experience had demonstrated how quickly the Germans responded to a break in any part of their defences. Reinforcements were certain to flow in from quiet sectors. So after the sun set, Magee's gunners turned their guns on the Lens central train station to smash the facility and catch unloading trains on the sidings. It was impossible to know the result without direct observation, but in principle both the counter-battery and the interdiction-of-reinforcements tasks assigned were sound. The problem was that only 354 rounds had been dumped at the battery for the job. Even at Festubert they had had 562 for the day of the attack. At Loos they had only 300 rounds to last for the two days after Zero Day against enemy batteries and the train station. The only upside was that good weather and Royal Flying Corps aircraft enabled 1st Canadian Heavy Battery to make those rounds count.

Small shell stocks forced rates of fire to drop to around 100 rounds per day for the battery in the last three days of September, and often less than that as the fighting dragged into October. By then, German reinforcing artillery had negated the small British firepower advantage and forced 1st Canadian Heavy Battery to relocate twice in the ruined mining suburbs north of Bully-les-Mines. During those days, Major Magee's battery was the BEF's right-most heavy battery, adjacent to the French Tenth Army gun positions in the southern half of Bully. Captain Inches wrote: "We were thus enabled to see much of the French gunners and compare with them the respective merits of British and French guns and gunnery." Such learning opportunities might be invaluable, but they offered little compensation for shell shortages. "I often wonder just how much damage we did with our daily shoots with aeroplane observation upon the batteries behind the Liévin Hills," Inches wrote. "Fifteen to twenty rounds without subsequent fire for effect was the limit that our supply of shells in those days could stand." Thankfully, around the Empire the design and manufacture of heavier guns and ammunition was now well under way.

So, too, was the mobilization and training of siege gunners. Prewar Canadian militia artillery units in port towns like Saint John, Halifax, Charlottetown, Quebec City, Victoria, and Vancouver were being trained to man medium and heavy long-range guns. That meant routinely addressing the unique problems associated with handling heavier ammunition and firing at "out-of-sight" targets. New Brunswick's long tradition of maintaining an effective coast defence artillery regiment and the happy coincidence of 4.7-inch guns on Partridge Island combined to give the province a central role in the growth of Canada's overseas siege artillery force. In 1915, 3rd New Brunswick Regiment's operational Composite Battery on Partridge Island manned these obsolete but still useful guns. The regiment had in fact been equipped with them for a brief period before the war, and the 4.7-inch remained in service in the BEF in France and Belgium alongside its modern replacement, the 60-pounder. The 4.7-inch may have been useless for coast defence, but the existence of a battery of them on Partridge Island, with their own ranges out over the bay, provided a unique and increasingly important opportunity to train heavy and siege gunners for the Western Front. By the end of the year, 3rd NB regiment had sent large drafts of skilled heavy gunners overseas. This was just the start.

These men would soon be needed. By the end of 1915 a wave of new Canadian "siege batteries" were on their way. While the "heavy" batteries operated 60-pounder guns designed for long-range counter-battery and interdiction fire, these new siege batteries were equipped with massive howitzers designed primarily for destroying field fortifications and smashing their German howitzer counterparts (which also operated close to the front). The 1st Overseas Siege Battery sailed to Britain in

Canada's Siege Artillery assembles. The newly arrived 131st, 165th, and 167th Siege Batteries parade under their "Imperial" numbers in Horsham England, June 1916. They were renumbered 4th, 5th, and 6th Canadian Siege Batteries and made part of the Canadian Corps. (NBM E.M. Slader 14809)

November 1915. Of its total complement of six officers and 151 men, two officers and 64 gunners were from New Brunswick. By then at least 200 more officers and men (also largely from 3rd New Brunswick Regiment's Composite Battery) for 4th Overseas Siege Battery had been recruited. The officers were almost all New Brunswickers: Major Louis Barker was in command, Captain Roy Ring was his second-in-command, and Lieutenants Gordon Kerr, J. Adams Bruce, Jack Fairweather, J.W. Prince, and Barton Wetmore were among the junior officers.

The raising of these batteries was a response to a request from the British Secretary of State for War, Lord Kitchener, for coastal gunners to man the new siege batteries. The War Office was looking for tall, healthy volunteers led by educated officers to serve new weapon systems intended to equal and ultimately better the German army's artillery. Kitchener knew that coast gunners possessed the skills needed to make the growing force of imperial heavy artillery work. His plea for trained coast gunners echoed the appeal then being made by Lt.-Col. Beverley Armstrong, the erstwhile commanding officer of 3rd NB Regiment, who by the spring of 1915 was on the district staff in Halifax, tasked with recruiting. With the Halifax fortress taken up by operational tasks, it made perfect sense to develop Partridge Island and 3rd NB Regiment as "force generators" for the Canadian Corps.

By late 1915 the guns, too, were on the way. The War Office began ordering medium and heavy howitzers in September 1914, including dozens of the new breech-loading 6-inch 26cwt howitzer. Howitzers delivered heavy high-explosive shells at a high angle, dropping them behind hills and buildings or down into trenches and dugouts (something the 60-pounder gun could not do). The first eight newly designed 6-inch medium howitzers to serve at the front proved their value in 1915: they were mobile, accurate, and hard-hitting and could fire a 100-pound shell 9,800 yards. This made the new howitzer a match for the German 5.9-inch howitzer, which fired a 90-pound shell 9,400 yards.

The British also needed heavier howitzers to match the German 21 cm "Mörser" and even heavier siege guns. These guns fired shells weighing 200 pounds or more, including large, deep-driving explosive warheads (some with armour-piercing caps) capable of destroying Western Front fortifications. Until they developed their own heavy howitzers, as a stopgap, the British fashioned 8-inch howitzers by cutting down and hollowing out decommissioned 6-inch coast artillery guns, with only rudimentary recoil systems. Meanwhile, Britain's famous Vickers armament works was commissioned to design and build new 8-inch howitzers with a recoil system that would allow sustained and accurate fire. The first of the new 8-inch BL (breech-loading) Mark VI howitzers were due in the spring of 1916. Other orders were placed for super-heavy 9.2-inch and 12-inch howitzers. Meanwhile, Royal Navy and Royal Marine long-range guns were prepared on a wide array of field mountings. The first of the new 6-inch BL howitzers arrived at the front in late 1915. These and other howitzers were slated to equip new siege batteries being raised by Kitchener in Britain and the dominions. Major Minden Cole's 1st Siege Battery was assigned to man the new mammoth 9.2-inch howitzers; Major Barker's 4th Siege Battery was to receive four brand-new 8-inch howitzers.

The 4th Siege Battery headed overseas in April 1916. Major Lawrence Allen's 6th Siege Battery followed in May. Even though the war was long into its second year, the departure of the two New Brunswick siege batteries drew huge crowds in Saint John. The 6th Siege Battery's history records that in May 1916, when it marched from Reeds Wharf to the train station, "the streets along the way were lined with people but the real crowd appeared when the station was approached. About this time, going away parcels appeared and in time some carried more parcels than they did equipment." Both 4th and 6th Siege Batteries crossed the Atlantic on RMS *Olympic*, now stripped of her finery so as to become a fast and efficient troopship. She needed to be fast. It was diverted to Newfoundland for several days because the German High Seas Fleet had engaged the Royal Navy in a great battle off Jutland on 31 May, and there had been fear that "German raiding cruisers might have taken the opportunity to break out into the Atlantic."

Then there were the U-boats. "I guess we had a pretty close call from a submarine," Gunner Charles Douglas wrote home about the passage. "We pretty nearly

The 4th and 6th Canadian Siege Batteries' new equipment, the breech-loading 8-inch Mark VI heavy howitzer. (LAC PA-002500)

ran over one in the Irish Sea. The submarine hadn't time to turn around and fire the torpedo. We had two torpedo boats as escorts but they couldn't get the submarine as it was too dark. A pretty close call though it wasn't it." When Major Allen's gunners disembarked on 8 June, they were told that Lord Kitchener, the very man responsible for the raising of siege batteries across the British Empire, had gone down with HMS *Hampshire* when she struck a mine en route to Russia. The advent of submarines as a long-range naval threat would soon give the gunners on Partridge Island a real operational task.

The 4th and 6th Siege Batteries arrived at Horsham Camp in Sussex, home of the Royal Garrison Artillery, and found no guns waiting. Other siege batteries, including 1st Canadian Siege Battery, were there waiting for guns, too. So they trained as best they could on late-nineteenth-century 6-inch 30cwt platform howitzers. The 1st Canadian Siege Battery finally got its "Big Mother" 9.2-inch superheavy howitzers in May and proceeded to France in June. Louis Barker's 4th Siege Battery received their 8-inch heavy howitzers, Holt Caterpillar gun tractors, and four-wheel-drive ammunition lorries a month later and made for France in August. Major Allen's 6th Siege Battery waited until late September for the next batch of 8-inch howitzers, tractors, and lorries. The word camouflage had yet to enter army language, but "protective colouring" was employed to break up the shape of large guns to confuse distant observers. The 6th Siege Battery gunners recalled how this consisted of painting the new guns with "dabs and streaks of several colours, none of them too adapted for the purpose but the only colours at hand. The result was quite striking."

All of the new heavy howitzer batteries figured in Field Marshal Haig's great plans for 1916. The vast majority of them went straight to the battlefield north of the River Somme, where a great offensive was planned. At the Allied conference in Chantilly in December 1915, Russian, Italian, French, and British military leaders agreed to launch a combined offensive against the Central Powers in 1916. The French and British would attack side by side astride the Somme. The Germans, of course, had their own plans, and launched a massive attack on the French army at Verdun in February 1916. They also sought to disrupt British plans for 1916 by launching local attacks in the Ypres sector, where the Canadian Corps still held a portion of the line, in the spring. So while Canadian heavy guns and gunners assembled in England, the Canadian Corps fought two major actions near Ypres.

The first came in April in the vicinity of the crossroads hamlet of St-Eloi, just south of Ypres. There, 2nd Canadian Division fought its first major battle of the war. The division supported British 3rd Division in an attack to evict the Germans from positions on a small piece of elevated ground where the front bent like an elbow southward to follow the Wytschaete–Messines Ridge. The objective was a slight rise in the low, wet ground in the gap between the north end of the Wytschaete–Messines Ridge and the Hollebeke "mound" of excavated earth from the Ypres–Comines Canal to the east. Essentially the area was a low pass through which ran the road to France.

The small operation coincided with tunnelling efforts under the German front by the Royal Engineers. On 27 March 1916, after six massive mine blasts obliterated the German defenders in the forward lines, British 3rd Division attacked the shattered hamlet of St-Eloi and forced a small salient into the enemy trench system. Chaotic, desperate fighting surged around the mine craters for a week before 2nd Canadian Division arrived on the night of 3 April. Its task was to relieve the British assault troops and hold the new gains against German counterattacks. The 2nd Canadian Divisional Artillery is normally included in this story only after they had relieved British 3rd Division's gunners on 10 April. However, 2nd Canadian Division's guns formed a critical part of the attack from the outset.

By the opening of the battle for the St-Eloi craters, 2nd Canadian Divisional Artillery was complete, and included the largely New Brunswick 23rd Howitzer Battery in 6th Canadian Howitzer Brigade and Major Randolph Crocker's 28th Newcastle Battery in 7th Canadian Field Brigade. Lt.-Col. Harrison's 2nd Divisional Ammunition Column delivered 13,000 shells to forward dumps in the last days of March, the largest amount they had ever handled. Much like at Vimy Ridge a year later, Harrison's gunners worked in darkness and behind great camouflage screens and nets strung along the roads. At the same time, 1st Canadian Divisional Artillery, farther south in the Ploegsteert sector, prepared to fire a deception barrage on the German front-line trenches along the southern end of the Wytschaete–Messines Ridge.

In late March, 2nd Canadian Division's gun positions lay east of Mount Kemmel, the great round hill southwest of Ypres that allowed observation over the Wytschaete–Messines Ridge. The 2nd Canadian Division's gunners were part of a carefully concealed buildup of artillery. When British 3rd Division's assault commenced on 27 March, signalled by the detonation of the mines, 2nd Canadian Division's observers and guns took on German guns shielded behind the northern end of the Wytschaete–Messines Ridge.

During the initial attack, the 4.5-inch field howitzers of 23rd New Brunswick Battery fired 35-pound high-explosive shells into enemy trenches around the west end of the line of craters. Meanwhile, Newcastle's 28th Battery and the rest of 2nd Canadian Division's artillery started a counter-battery shoot that lasted for six days, pounding any German battery that revealed itself. While the infantry fight degenerated into a brawl around the craters, the Canadian gunners did their best to prevent German artillery from interfering. Canadian observers high atop Mount Kemmel spotted the flashes and directed the Canadian batteries onto targets until the Germans ceased fire – for a time, at least.

But the 2nd Canadian Division gunners could do little to help the infantry in the confused, close-quarter grenade and trench mortar fight that raged in the cold mud around the craters. There were too few commanding points of observation to see and direct fire. Lt.-Col. William King's 6th Howitzer Brigade had good observation posts on Mount Kemmel, but this was not enough. On the fifth morning of the struggle, 1 April 1916, 28th Battery and all of 7th Canadian Field Brigade fired on every German muzzle flash and silenced them all. But the enemy guns benefited from aircraft observation and German domination of the sky, and before the German guns were silenced, their shells had crashed into 28th Battery's gun line. Gunner Samuel Regan was killed, and Gunner Frank Curry was wounded in the hip. The Newcastle battery had suffered its first losses.

By the time the exhausted British 3rd Division was relieved by 2nd Canadian Division's infantry on 3 April, they had only partial control of the ragged front line along the six massive craters. The 2nd Canadian Division's guns moved north to relieve British 3rd Division's artillery around Dickebusch to support their own division. Their new gun pits and forward observation posts behind St-Eloi held no advantage over the enemy, who could look down on the assault area. At the same time, 1st Canadian Division and its artillery took up position to the west of St-Eloi, around Hill 60 and Mount Sorrel at the tip of the salient. German artillery activity increased around the entire Canadian Corps sector in early April. Shells found 8th Battery's lines southeast of Ypres at a place along the rail line known as Railway Dugouts. Sergeant Noah Steeves, already wounded a year before at Second Ypres, was hit by shell fragments again, this time in the arm and back. Major Anderson wrote to Steeves's mother that Noah "commanded a subsection and it was one of the best. I hoped to see him get a commission before long. He was a close personal friend of mine." After Steeves was hit, the rest of his close-knit crew moved to get him on a stretcher and to a dressing station. As they did so, another German shell landed by their gun pit, wounding every man in the crew: Bombardiers F. Owens of Woodstock and Murray McAdam of Fredericton, and Gunners Henry Steeves, George Stone, and Jack Sewell, all of Moncton. Sergeant Steeves wrote to his sister Ethel about the incident: "Spoiled the best gun crew in the 8th Battery. I loved the boys and it almost makes me cry that we were wiped out like so much chaff. Thank God none of us were killed."

As time wore on, reinforcements to the German artillery negated the slight advantage held in the opening week of April. The hopeless action at the St-Eloi craters finally ended on 19 April at a cost of 1,373 Canadian casualties. Among them was Lieutenant James Hazen from Saint John. His brother Douglas Hazen was on Mount Kemmel, temporarily attached to 1st Canadian Divisional Artillery, when James was killed. Douglas was studying at the Royal Military College when the war broke out and had given up his place to go overseas with 25th Alberta Field Battery. His Saint John law partner, Captain Cyrus Inches, had persuaded him to transfer to 1st Canadian Heavy Battery in early 1916. Before the paperwork was processed, Douglas was killed when a shell exploded prematurely in an overworked gun. The Hazen boys' father, Sir Douglas Hazen, was a well-known Saint John lawyer and the federal Minister of Marine, Fisheries, and the Naval Service.

After the fighting ended at the St-Eloi craters, New Brunswick's artillery units found themselves caught up in the first of a series of changes in British and Canadian artillery organization that characterized the following year. These were spurred by a ceaseless review of practices, procedures, and organization after each phase of the war. Change was also stimulated by the massive expansion of British and Dominion forces and by preparations for the coming multinational offensive against the Central Powers planned for the summer of 1916. The 3rd Canadian Division arrived in France that spring, and the 4th was not far behind it. During this period, command of the Canadian Corps passed to Lt.-Gen. Sir Julian Byng, a quiet, competent officer who quickly learned to get the best out of his unruly Canadians. His respect and admiration for Canadian soldiers was reciprocated, and perpetuated after the war in Saint John by a veterans' group known as the Byng Boys.

One major change for the British and Canadian Divisional Artillery was that light howitzers were dispersed across the organization as more of those guns arrived at the front. At the end of May, 2nd Canadian Division carved up 6th Howitzer Brigade and sent a howitzer battery to each of its three field artillery brigades. It also moved several 18-pounder batteries – among them Major Crocker's 28th Battery – into the new, mixed 6th Canadian Field Brigade. As part of this shuffle, the New Brunswickers in Major Fred Geary's 23rd Howitzer Battery moved to 5th

Canadian Field Brigade. Similar reorganization was planned for 1st Canadian Division in June. The changes came with demands for experienced leaders to take over the new units. In 1st Canadian Division, Major Boyd Anderson was promoted to lieutenant-colonel to command the new 12th Canadian Field Brigade, including 8th Moncton Battery.

The demand for more trained and experienced artillery officers sparked a search for senior non-coms with command potential. Sergeant Steeves was one of those identified, but he was badly wounded before he could accept the promotion. The 23rd Battery's Sergeant Jack Hipwell, a Saint Johner and University of New Brunswick graduate, was another. So was Ned Slader, who had risen to become RSM in 1st Divisional Ammunition Column. General Burstall interviewed Slader personally and set out to commission him from the ranks and assign him to Major Magee's heavy battery. By then, Burstall and other Canadian senior gunners were working behind the scenes to grow a uniquely Canadian heavy artillery force and concentrate it under Canadian Corps command. Slader, Hipwell, and scores of other gunner non-coms were pulled from the front in the spring of 1916 and sent to the Canadian School of Gunnery at Shorncliffe in Kent. There they lived as tent mates during their three-week officers-conversion course. The experience may have taught them to behave and carry themselves as officers, but they learned little about the art of gunnery. Slader complained that there was "little up-to-date instruction" offered to these battle-experienced veterans. Hipwell and Slader were both commissioned as lieutenants in May 1916. Hipwell was posted to 5th Battery in 2nd Canadian Field Brigade, while Slader joined Magee in 1st Canadian Heavy Battery.

Lieutenants Hipwell and Slader returned to the Canadian Corps lines in the Ypres Salient in early June 1916 to find the British front alive with action. In late May 1916, the Germans on Vimy Ridge – with the benefit of overwhelming artillery superiority – had mounted a local attack against the British defenders holding former French positions north of Neuville-St-Vaast. The attack came after plans were already in place to move Major Magee's 1st Canadian Heavy Battery from the Aubers Ridge area south to the Somme, where the great British offensive of the year was building. In response to the German attack at Neuville-St-Vaast, Captain Inches took one section of the battery to the Vimy sector immediately. Inches established an observation post on the commanding heights of the Lorette Spur. From positions at Bully Grenay, his 60-pounders fired a small number of shells in support of British units fighting to seal off and counter the German penetration. But since Field Marshal Haig was reluctant to let the Germans divert his effort on the Somme, neither reinforcements nor many shells were spared to retaliate at Vimy Ridge in 1916.

The same was true two weeks later, when the Germans expanded their attempts to disrupt the Somme offensive east of Ypres. At 0800 on 2 June, German 13th Württemberg Corps, following behind the heaviest and densest artillery bombardment yet experienced by the British and the detonation of several mines, attacked the Canadian Corps at Hill 60, Mount Sorrel, and Sanctuary Wood. The 3rd Canadian Division bore the brunt of the attack. Two of its forward battalions were nearly wiped out. The Canadian official history records a German eyewitness description of the Canadian front following the denotation of the mines as a cloud of dust and dirt "into which timber, tree trunks, weapons and equipment were continuously hurled up, and occasionally human bodies." Major Magee's remaining two 60-pounder guns fired 875 shells between them, desperately trying to dampen the German artillery. But they were badly outgunned and, as always in the Ypres Salient, overlooked from three sides. Counter-battery fire crashed into their positions. Frank Magee was wounded, but 1st Canadian Heavy Battery escaped largely unscathed. The 2nd Canadian Heavy Battery was not so lucky: it was virtually destroyed, losing three of its four 60-pounder guns to German fire.

The German attack had caught 1st Canadian Divisional Artillery in the midst of its reorganization. The newly promoted Lt.-Col. Anderson was away organizing the new 12th Canadian Field Brigade, but his 8th Battery was still at the front. It was attached to 9th and 10th Batteries on the division's northern flank, directly adjacent to the German assault area. The fire of these and other Canadian guns brought the attack to a halt before it penetrated even closer to Ypres. That night they supported a hasty Canadian counterattack only to receive word that it had failed, with heavy losses. The next morning it was clear why. The Germans only wanted the high ground around Sanctuary Wood and Mount Sorrel, which offered a commanding view of Ypres just two miles away. German infantrymen had fortified their newly captured ground, from which their artillery observers could direct fire on virtually any place inside the salient. If the lost heights were not recaptured, the Ypres Salient might have to be abandoned. The BEF's commander, Field Marshal Haig, temporarily reinforced the Canadian Corps with three British Heavy Artillery Groups and released a substantial quantity of precious ammunition. The total number of guns in the Canadian sector rose to 218, more than 100 of which were howitzers ranging from 4.5-inch field to 6-inch medium and 12-inch superheavy. Ammunition supply columns had dumped 400 rounds per gun in the Canadian sector by 5 June in case the Germans pressed their attack further and as a buildup for a Canadian counterattack. The Germans struck first on 6 June, blowing four mines under Manitoba's 28th Battalion around Ypres–Menin road. But the survivors and flanking Canadian units stopped the attack in the ruins of the hamlet of Hooge.

The following week, British and South African heavy and siege artillery took up position behind the Canadian Corps and fired steadily. Concentrating artillery power and replacing losses from the attacks of 2 and 6 June placed demands on the Divisional Ammunition Column, not least their personnel, as their trained gunners came up as replacements. Captain George Gamblin formed a temporary battery from the New Brunswick Section in 2nd Divisional Ammunition Column. They went into action as "13th (Divisional Ammunition Column) Battery" to hold the front at St-Eloi and keep German batteries dispersed as much as possible.

Meanwhile, Canadian field gunners in front of Mount Sorrel watched as the heavy and siege guns prepared gun pits all around them. The 2nd Canadian Field Brigade's war diary recorded how there "are so many batteries on this front at present that some of them are firing all the time and it should not be much time before we get the Hun's goat." Finally, on 9 June, the Canadians struck back. The attack began with a general bombardment across the German-held ridge aimed at caving in newly dug trenches and knocking down new belts of barbed wire. For three full days the guns of the three Canadian divisional artilleries and the attached heavies pounded the German front, firing thousands of rounds per day. On 12 June they opened a full-scale bombardment, ratcheting up the rate to 2,000 to 3,000 rounds per battery per day. By this point, Lieutenant Slader had arrived in 1st Canadian Heavy Battery's Left Section, now under command of Lieutenant Dick Leach while Major Magee convalesced. Slader was sent forward to the section's observation post to direct fire. British reinforcing artillery had improved the situation since the first week of June, but the German heavy batteries were not outgunned. The best that 1st Canadian Heavy Battery's Left Section could do was draw German heavies into a duel while friendly field and siege batteries took apart the German trenches and wire. They were responsible for stirring up eleven German batteries. Slader recalled that "enemy retaliation was so swift that almost before we could take cover we were shelled in return. Fortunately our cover was good and enemy ammunition was poor quality with a large percentage of duds." Bad weather helped their cause, softening the ground with rain so that German duds buried themselves deep; also, poor visibility limited the German air and ground observation advantage. On the other side, British shell and fuse quality was improving. Also, the Germans did not seem to have a clear artillery plan to protect their new positions, instead scattering their shells evenly across the Canadian front with no decisive concentration at any one point. The Canadians had learned to dig deep to survive that kind of dispersed shelling.

In the late afternoon of 9 June the Canadian–British barrage ceased for a few moments to sow confusion in German command posts before resuming at a steady heavy rate until 2000 hours. Sweating gun crews then cranked up the intensity again, firing intensely for thirty minutes before stopping completely at 2030 hours. The Germans were left stewing anxiously in smashed trenches for over four hours, waiting for an attack that seemed like it would never come. Instead, not long past midnight on 13 June, Canadian, British, and South African gunners opened fire again for forty-five intense minutes. The German defenders along the ridge from Mount Sorrel and the Tor Top did not have the protection of fully developed field

Canadian Ammunition Column drivers watering horses behind the Somme front, 1916. (LAC PA-000849)

fortifications, as did their compatriots in other sections of the Western Front. The Württembergers were shattered by British and Canadian shellfire. Their front-line defenders were not in position to defend the top of the ridge, and the Canadians recaptured the position. German reserve battalions counterattacked at dawn and again on 14 June. Both times, Canadian and British artillery fired protective barrages, which caught the German infantrymen in the open. When the action finally died down, the Canadians, not the Germans, held Hill 60 and the Ypres Salient was secure. The Canadian achievement at Hill 60–Mount Sorrel is commemorated by one of Canada's six major Western Front monuments.

The real test of the British army came on the Somme in 1916. Between July and November of that year, a majority of British and Dominion units cycled through the killing fields there. The offensive was made possible because the mobilization of British and British imperial resources had by then begun to make itself felt on the Western Front. Dozens of new divisions arrived at the front that spring, including 3rd and 4th Canadian Divisions. New heavy and siege artillery batteries and new guns and howitzers arrived as well. Not everything was in place on 1 July, when the great offensive began, and many of the new formations were inexperienced and poorly trained.

One of the many: Gunner William Barker Wasson of 6th Siege Battery in September 1916. Wasson was badly affected by German gas at Passchendaele in November 1917.
(NBM Wasson & Turner-6)

But the war had its own logic. The German attack on the French at Verdun, which began in February, became the longest and bloodiest battle of the Great War. The German strategy was simple enough: to bleed France white. Verdun therefore formed the backdrop of everything that happened in 1916. By the summer the armies locked in mortal combat at Verdun were barely halfway through their nine months of hell, and the French had just begun a series of brutal counterattacks that would go until November. The British Empire could not stand idle while France suffered at Verdun.

At the end of June, as the preliminary bombardment along the Somme began, the Canadian Corps was still fighting at Ypres and New Brunswick's 4th and 6th Siege Batteries were still training at the Royal Garrison Artillery depot in Sussex. Both were still anxiously awaiting their new howitzers. On the very eve of the Somme offensive, 4th Siege Battery moved to the Lydd ranges on the Kentish coast to fire their first practice rounds on 18-pounders and a handful of newly built 6-inch medium howitzers. The 6th Siege Battery followed soon after. They also practised building dugouts and gun pits based on the latest lessons flowing back from the front. Finally, on 8 July – seven days after the Somme battle began – the first two brand-new 8-inch heavy howitzers arrived on the ranges at Lydd. Major

Barker directed a notional Battery Command Post while his officers cycled through practice directing the two-gun section and as observers. Gunner Donald Cummings wrote home about the new guns. "We received our 8 inch guns today; they are beauties I tell you. The boys had gunfire the last three days and have trimmed everything yet here; out of twelve shots made eight bulls eyes, a distance of two miles and two were in the inner ring." Camp staff complimented their shooting and gun drill, calling it "the best work seen in the camp for the past two years." Whether they knew that most of the gunners were already experienced on the old 4.7-inch gun is unclear, but the results speak for themselves: the Composite Battery on Partridge Island trained good heavy gunners. By late July both batteries were completely kitted out with guns and Caterpillar tractors. While they trained and waited their turn to go to France, other Canadian gunners were already busy on the Somme.

The opening phase of the Somme is not typically seen as a Canadian story, but the gunners were there. The first to arrive were 1st Canadian Heavy Battery's Right Section commanded by Captain Inches. He was ably assisted by Lieutenant Bill Vassie, another Saint John First Contingent gunner from the old 3rd New Brunswick Regiment, who had transferred in from 1st Divisional Ammunition Column. Inches had taken temporary command of the battery while Major Magee recovered in England from his wounds. The Right Section arrived on 10 June as the advance

Canadian Divisional Ammunition Column gunners and field gunners loading 18-pounder cartridges into field gun caissons along the Somme front, October 1916. (LAC PA-000937)

The 1st Canadian Heavy Battery's four 60-pounder guns near Mametz, on the Somme, July 1916, painted by E.M. Ned Slader as a gift for Cyrus Inches. (Loyal Company Association Collection)

party for the battery, and began work on elaborately concealed and protected pits and dugouts for all four guns. Their position lay beside a water-powered mill on the east bank of the Ancre River, shielded by the ruins of Albert's southern suburb of Méaulte. A week later, Lieutenants Leach and Slader brought the Left Section down from Ypres to the partly prepared pits. The 1st Canadian Heavy Battery was assigned to 23rd Heavy Artillery Group in support of General Sir Henry Horne's XV Corps. It was the small beginning of a long and major association between the Canadians and General Horne, himself a gunner.

Five hundred medium and heavy guns and howitzers were massed for the Somme battle, an impressive accomplishment for the BEF, but Lieutenant Ned Slader saw the weakness masked by the numbers. "I was astonished by the heterogeneous collection of heavy guns," he wrote, "everything from the old 4.7s to modern 60-pounders; 5 inch Howitzers vintage 1898 to the later 6 inch type, and many other converted guns I had never seen before." Among them were 6-inch naval guns cut down and bored out to serve as emergency 8-inch heavy howitzers until the purpose-built 8-inch heavies arrived. Although the guns were antiquated, the scale of logistic preparation and ammunition stockpiling exceeded anything yet done by the British on the Western Front. New supply roads and railways carried sandbags, angle iron, and corrugated steel to build shelters, food, water, and above all ammunition, all of which was scattered in dumps under and behind camouflage nets and screens.

On 19 June, Captain Inches started bringing 1st Canadian Heavy Battery into action; his 60-pounders registered datum points along the heights overlooking the Ancre River. After that the battery went quiet for three days as part of a wider plan to conceal how much artillery was massing behind the British front. At that point the battery's experience with the latest heavy gunnery techniques was not appreciated by their new 23rd Heavy Artillery Group counterparts. "We were an unknown quantity, and being colonials we were regarded as a joke," Inches wrote, "so much so that while one of the English batteries in the brigade had been detailed for the counter-battery work and to answer aeroplane calls, we were given easy targets and we were not asked to fire by night!"

The preparatory barrage to demolish the German defences opened two weeks before the scheduled start of the attack. During this preliminary period, 1st Canadian Heavy Battery fired high-explosive shells at German trenches, dugouts, and assembly areas around Fricourt. The Germans had fortified the tiny village, like all those along Thiepval Ridge, turning the area into an underground fortress. Fricourt and neighbouring Mametz commanded the approach up a ravine running to the crest of Thiepval Ridge called Caterpillar Valley. That week, Fricourt became the focus of 1st Canadian Heavy Battery's wrath. Captain Inches directed Charles Garland and Lieutenant Slader to set up an observation post on the slight rise of ground between Méaulte and Albert from which they could correct the fall of shot. They used the famous "Leaning Virgin of Albert," a Madonna statue hanging

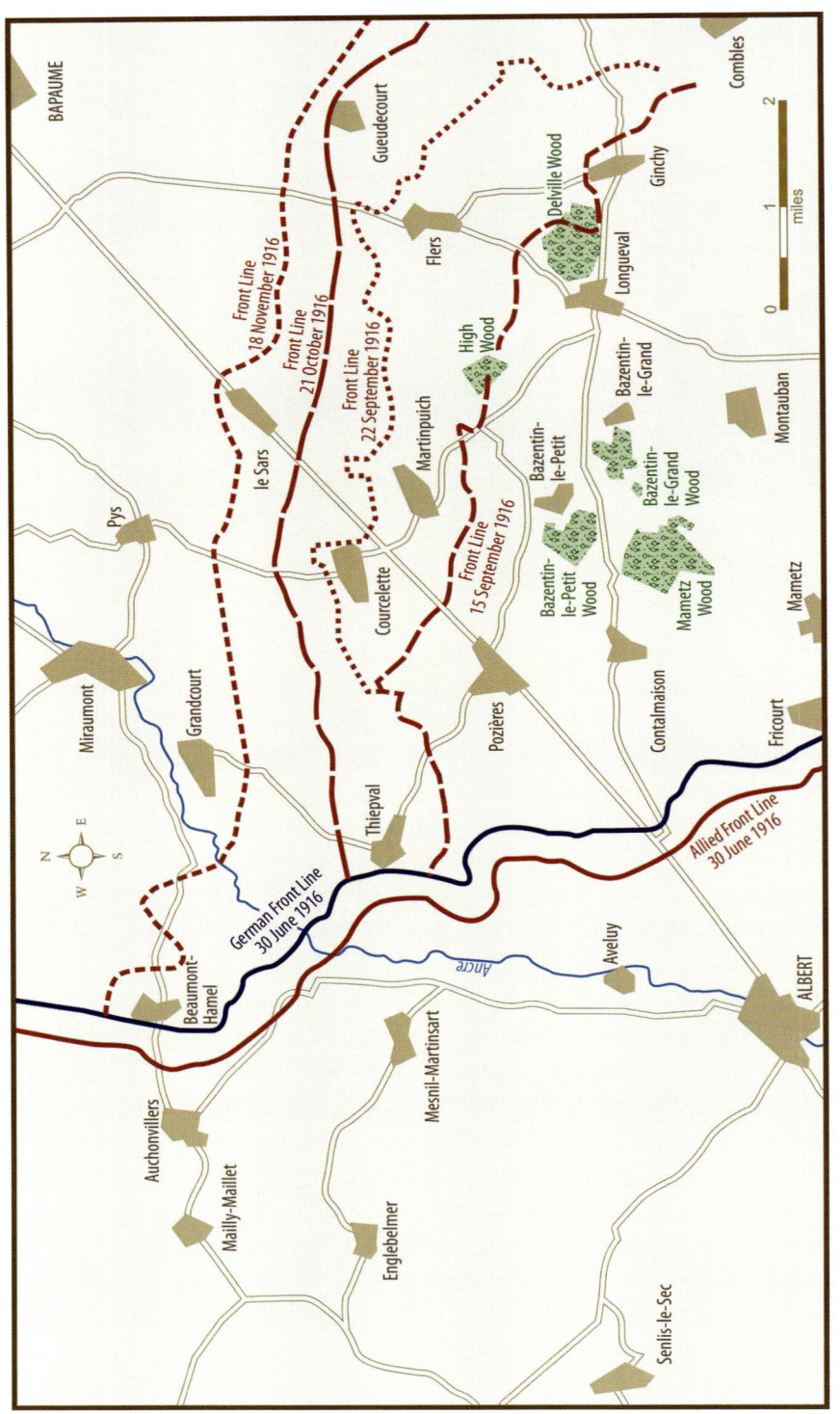

The Somme, July–November 1916

precariously off the top of the basilica, as a compass aligning point to correct the line of the battery. From their perch, Garland and Slader directed 1,080 shells per day into Fricourt and the trench system around it. Every one of those days, an old woman from Méaulte emerged from her cellar to cut grass, presumably for her livestock, right beneath the battery's blazing guns. Slader watched as "she paid no attention." She was but one "of thousands carrying on while their men fought. Witnessing the bravery of the French civilians was to me a morale builder."

On the last day of June the bombardment slackened as rain pummelled the men on both sides. At 0730 on 1 July, the weeks of steady hammering transformed into something different. The 1st Canadian Heavy Battery opened its assault barrage that day by heaving 200 high-explosive rounds into Fricourt at a rapid rate. At Zero Hour they then joined in one of the first large-scale creeping barrages of the Great War. General Horne's XV Corps was one of three to experiment with the new method that fateful day. Garland and Slader directed the battery as it laid 668 rounds along six successive lines in a barrage fired by field batteries in XV Corps and two Heavy Artillery Groups. The plan was to blast their own infantry forward across no man's land, then lift fire to German support trenches and strongpoints just as the first line of trenches was reached. In theory, the Germans who were not killed by the week-long preliminary bombardment would now be killed or neutralized by the creeping barrages.

The first day of the Somme was the most catastrophic day in British military history. Despite the best efforts of Cyrus Inches and thousands of other gunners, the two-week preliminary barrage had been largely a failure. On long stretches of the 22-kilometre front, the German wire was not cut, counter-battery fire was ineffective, and enemy dugouts, machine-gun positions, and road and communications junctions had not been struck. The creeping barrages marched away, leaving the attacking infantry stranded on the enemy wire. The cost of the first day was staggering: 56,000 casualties, including 22,000 dead. The BEF was so overwhelmed by wounded men that some were evacuated as far as Edinburgh, Scotland, still lying on the same stretchers, in the same mud-coated uniforms, and with the same bandages as when they were removed from the battlefield.

Only in the south, adjacent to the French and east of Albert, where 1st Canadian Heavy Battery laboured so hard, were worthwhile gains made. There, XV and XIII Corps employed rudimentary creeping barrages to successfully blast their infantry onto a toehold on the heights overlooking Albert. German units defending the fortified villages suffered heavily both during the attack and in desperate attempts to counterattack. Despite the stellar work by 1st Canadian Heavy Battery and scores of British guns, Fricourt did not fall on 1 July. In fact, the two weeks that followed are sometimes referred to as the Battle of Albert, as the British fought to capture the Ancre River heights overlooking the town.

Canadian gunners were fully engaged in the Battle of Albert, and they soon impressed their skeptical British commanders. Lieutenants Leach and Slader went forward to link up with British 7th Division infantry in Fricourt only to find that the Germans still clung doggedly to its cellars. As effective as the creeping barrage had been, there were not enough heavy howitzers to crack the reinforced cellars in the village. The enemy was finally driven out on 2 July after both sides suffered staggering losses. With the mouth of Caterpillar Valley and the heights overlooking the Ancre in the control of General Horne's XV Corps, 1st Canadian Heavy Battery moved its guns 3 kilometres forward to near the ruins of Bécourt. From there, their 60-pounders reached deep over the highest part of Thiepval–Pozières Ridge to engage German artillery on the reverse slope at Martinpuich. There was no direct line of sight, so the battery relied on the Royal Flying Corps, which had won local air superiority. On clear days, Royal Flying Corps observer aircraft and balloons directed 1st Canadian Heavy Battery's shooting at enemy batteries and at German infantry and carrying parties moving back and forth along roads deep in their second-line trench system. The fire of Captain Inches's battery slackened after the move to Brécourt to a few hundred rounds per day because of the difficulty getting ammunition forward. By then the battery had earned the praise of their British

A Canadian breech-loading 9.2-inch heavy howitzer, possibly from 1st Canadian Siege Battery during the last successful Canadian attacks along the Somme front, November 1916. (LAC PA-000917)

Heavy Group commander Lt.-Col. Pritchard, who declared himself "guilty of criminal negligence" in so misjudging the capabilities of his colonial heavy gunners.

On 13 July, 1st Canadian Heavy Battery ratcheted up their rate of fire in support of British Fourth Army's renewed assault on Thiepval–Pozières Ridge. For two days the NB gunners hammered the fortified villages of Contalmaison and Bazentin, where Caterpillar Valley rose up to the main ridge southeast of Pozières. They also fired on upwards of thirty-eight different German artillery battery positions along and behind the ridge. On the day of the attack they hitched up their guns and moved into Caterpillar Valley itself north of Mametz. General Horne wanted to ensure that as his infantry advanced, his counter-battery artillery advanced with them. Captain Inches moved the battery at 0900 and soon had them back in action to fire a deep barrage onto German reserves moving south to counterattack from Martinpuich. Lieutenant Slader moved the battery observation post to the captured German Pommiers strongpoint near Montauban at the head of Caterpillar Valley, where he could see Bazentin. They also made the rounds on seventeen different identified German batteries firing on or behind the ridge. For the rest of July, 1st Canadian Heavy Battery kept up their partnership with Royal Flying Corps and balloon observers to duel with German batteries.

The wear on guns and gunners took its toll on all of 23rd Heavy Group, but 1st Canadian Heavy Battery demonstrated their technical skill by keeping all four of their guns in action. Captain Inches proudly recalled that "on one day when only five out of twelve guns in the brigade were in action, four of them were ours." The New Brunswick gunners knew their business. That was certainly the case with 3rd New Brunswick Regiment veteran sergeant Jim Stackhouse, the No. 1 on a gun in Lieutenant Vassie's section. During the intense firing of July 1916, Stackhouse noticed a fuse already burning on a shrapnel round as it was rammed into the breech. The gun was pointed out over a mass of wagons heading towards the front, and premature detonation of the huge shell would have shredded the column. Stackhouse ordered every man out of the gun pit, then opened the breech and spun the elevation gears to depress the barrel as low as he could. When the shell burst inside the gun, the shrapnel blasted out harmlessly into the earth while the spent casing blew backwards out the open breech. No one was injured. Lieutenant Slader felt that Stackhouse's "cool assessment of the situation undoubtedly saved many lives. He was one of the best gunners I ever met." Sergeant Stackhouse won the Distinguished Conduct Medal for his actions.

As XV Corps penetrated farther up Thiepval–Pozières Ridge, 1st Canadian Heavy Battery came within range of more German guns. Aerial photographs and good weather in late July helped locate German batteries. So, too, did a strong link between Ned Slader's observation post and one particular Royal Flying Corps pilot observer, Captain Charles Portal, from No. 3 Squadron, who daringly guided the

Battlefield success depended on forward observation officers (FOOs) and their signallers maintaining telephone communications with the gun line behind the front. Keeping lines connected both along trenches and across open ground was the most dangerous job in any Canadian heavy or siege battery. (LAC PA-002444)

battery onto German muzzle flashes. Portal, later Viscount Portal of Hungerford, became a Marshal of the Royal Air Force and Chief of the Air Staff for much of the Second World War.

The fight for the plateau atop Thiepval–Pozières Ridge dragged on through the late summer, forcing the German army to break off its offensive at Verdun and shift units to the Somme. Meanwhile, the BEF rotated fresh divisions through the Somme meat grinder. Allied offensive actions and German counterattacks were punctuated by periods of buildup, unit reliefs, and information gathering. In mid-July the Australian–New Zealand Corps (ANZACs) arrived on the battlefield facing Pozières on the Albert–Bapaume road, while XV Corps to their south continued hammering their way towards High Wood on the highest part of the ridge. By this stage, ammunition was running low, and 1st Canadian Heavy Battery had only a couple of dozen 60-pounder shells available to supply each gun. Accuracy mattered, although they could do little more than temporarily silence enemy guns by driving their gunners below ground. To make matters worse, by the end of

July, German heavy artillery reinforcements had begun searching out Allied guns, including 1st Canadian Heavy Battery's position at Mametz. On 28 July a German concentration landed in their lines, wounding two gunners. Two days later, as British transport columns filled the upper stretch of Caterpillar Valley as part of a divisional relief, German artillery observers directed a wicked fire onto them. Part of the barrage landed in the 1st Canadian Heavy Battery lines at Mametz, inflicting five casualties. Gunner Arthur "Bunny" Cobham of Saint John was killed, Gunner William Hunter died the next day en route to the Canadian hospital at Étaples, and three others were wounded.

For much of August the Germans fought for every yard of the ridge from Pozières to High Wood, recognizing it as the key high ground barring the approaches to the vital road junction at Bapaume. The ANZACs finally captured Pozières, but it had been a brutal welcome to the Western Front. The Germans also clung tenaciously to the northernmost end of the ridge at Thiepval and Courcelette, and north of the Ancre Valley bend around Beaumont-Hamel in their original first line of strongpoints. The Ancre bend contained a labyrinth of interlocking German strongpoints and machine-gun nests shielded by a deep valley. Breaking the German divisions defending the ridge and the valley would require fresh troops, more

The 4th and 6th Canadian Siege Batteries fired their brand-new 8-inch heavy howitzers like these ones for the first time on the Somme sector. (LAC PA-002350)

and heavier guns, and more ammunition. Among the fresh troops arriving in late August were General Byng's Canadian Corps, who had been ordered to relieve the exhausted ANZACs at Pozières. The Canadians formed part of General Hubert Gough's newly created Reserve Army, which included British XIV Corps in the sector north of the Ancre bend facing Beaumont-Hamel. They would need all the heavy and siege artillery they could get to crack open German defences along the valley. Among the guns assigned to that job were the brand-new 8-inch Mark VI heavy howitzers of the imperial "131st Siege Battery," the short-lived name given to Major Barker's 4th Siege Battery. They took up station as part of the elite British 1st Heavy Artillery Group.

Major Barker's battery received its four howitzers and Caterpillar gun tractors just days before embarking for Boulogne. Their final advance from Raincheval, 25 kilometres northwest of Albert, to the front was one of the first mechanized columns in British military history. Holt tractors towed guns and limbers while four-wheel-drive lorries hauled ammunition and stores. The 4th Siege Battery relieved an Australian 6-inch battery in somewhat exposed positions in an orchard on the edge of Mailly-Maillet, 8 kilometres west of Beaumont-Hamel. Barker and his advance party arrived a day ahead of the tractors and guns and began enlarging the gun pits to fit the much larger 8-inch howitzers. Tractor drivers towed the guns into position in the early morning darkness on 6 August. That day was spent building overhead cover on the gun pits and digging fire trenches and dugouts to protect crews during counter-bombardments. This was time well spent. They also dug out a new control station for the battery command post and signals telephone exchange. The 4th Siege Battery signallers wired their telephone system between the gun pits, the command post, and their forward observation post in a trench outside Auchonvillers, looking down slightly over the former Newfoundland Regiment trenches opposite Beaumont-Hamel. The observation post allowed for observed fire in fair weather. Barker brought all four howitzers into action at 1500 hours on 7 August with a twenty-round registration shoot on a trench junction beside Beaumont-Hamel.

These were some of the first operational rounds in the whole British sector using the new 8-inch howitzer, so much work was done calculating actual range and effectiveness. These guns' 200-pound projectiles where propelled by 40-pound bags or "cartridges" of propellant. The new howitzers released extraordinary energy, placing great strain on the recoil recuperator and the carriage, not to mention driving the whole system down into the soft soil. After their first test shoot, the battery spent another day building a rock bed underneath each gun and building up the blocks at the end of each gun's trail, where the recoil shock pushed hardest at the earth. On 9 August, Major Barker's gunners fired again, this time taking on a German battery and section of trenches with the help of a Royal Flying Corps air observer. Heavy mist obscured the target, making it impossible for them to measure

Canadian Artillery drivers and horses on their way to water, behind the Somme front, 1916. (LAC PA-000864)

their success, but their shooting attracted German artillery, whose staff apparently had noticed that massive shells were being fired at them from close behind the front-line British trenches. According to 4th Siege Battery's history, "Fritz now began to pay some very undesirable attention to the orchard and to the village of Mailly-Maillet with the result that unit personnel soon learned how to take cover." The dugouts and fire trenches built with so much labour proved their worth immediately, and thus no one was hurt during this first taste of action.

Even so, the staff of XIV Corps Heavy Artillery decided that 4th Siege Battery's position was too exposed. By day's end an advance party had gone off to prepare new positions in a depression behind nearby Englebelmer. The new position, some 3 kilometres to the south, stood on about the same line as the previous one but offered better cover and flash concealment. It also linked into the "Continental" observation post in the tiny, shell-battered hamlet of Hamel, on the lip of the Ancre Valley bend with a view of the rear of the German strongpoint tucked into a reverse slope between Beaumont-Hamel and Beaucourt-sur-l'Ancre. After the sun set, tractors towed the heavy guns to the new position and the whole battery started from scratch in the darkness, undertaking all the construction necessary to operate their four guns in the siege warfare of the Somme. To their credit, 4th Siege Battery's howitzers were ready to fire by dawn. They would have plenty more time to get comfortable: the battery did not move again for two months.

By mid-August, preparations for the next round on the Somme were well under way. British XIV Corps and its heavy artillery were relieved in the Beaumont-Hamel sector by V Corps. Newly ensconced 4th Siege Battery stayed put and was placed under command of V Corps's 16th Heavy Artillery Group – all still part of General Gough's Reserve Army. In preparation, Major Barker had his gunners build a camp in a wood farther west, safe in the low ground behind Englebelmer so that they could sleep and eat in relative safety. He also had a second observation post built higher up the Ancre bank in an old French trench between Hamel and Mesnil-Martinsart. The 4th Siege Battery's historian recorded that from that higher ground they could see all the way "up the bend of the Ancre to Grandcourt and Miramount" over 10 kilometres to the east. "Once in the O.P. an observer could feel quite safe, but the approach there to through trenches and paths was not always so healthy." Lieutenants Bill Kerr and Jack Fairweather would use both observation posts to direct 4th Siege Battery's guns with great effect in the coming weeks. Unlike Captain Inches and 1st Canadian Heavy Battery farther south facing High Wood, 4th Siege Battery had a direct line of sight between their observation posts and the enemy's Beaumont-Hamel–Beaucourt strongpoint.

Meanwhile, on the south bank of the Ancre, the Canadian relief of the ANZACs on Pozières Ridge was under way by the end of August. That move was not yet complete when the offensive resumed on 3 September. On that day, 13th Australian and 3rd Canadian Infantry Brigades mounted a joint attack on the infamous Mouquet or "Monkey" Farm, a key strongpoint along the Pozières–Thiepval road. The attack was in support of a larger V Corps effort on the north side of the Ancre Valley, for which 4th Siege Battery fired its first major barrage of the war. Preparations had begun two days before the infantry attack with concentrations of twenty to fifty 200-pound heavy shells targeting German trenches and dugouts, directed by ground and air observation. The 1st Canadian Heavy Battery fired on German batteries farther south behind High Wood as part of the same assault in British Fourth Army's sector. The 1st Canadian Divisional Artillery took up position between Major Barker and Captain Inches, behind Pozières, taking over from Australian and British gunners. This included Lt.-Col. Anderson's newly formed 12th Canadian Field Brigade, built around Moncton's 8th Battery together with 47th and 49th Batteries. Anderson's gun positions lay in Mash Valley beside the captured German Usna Redoubt north of La Boisselle on the former 1 July German front line. The 4th Siege Battery's history recalled how the rain- and wind-swept ground was "so badly cut up it is almost impossible to distinguish anything but what looks like a ploughed field."

The main barrage for all Canadian batteries engaged on 3 September opened before dawn, at 0500 hours. The results were mixed. Lt.-Col. Anderson's FOOs spotted a German counterattack assembling on a road along Thiepval Ridge and managed to cut it up before it could advance, but that constituted one tiny success on a bloody day. Farther south, two French armies attacked successfully behind an effective counter-battery artillery fire plan, but the timing of the renewed offensive was ill-suited to the British Reserve Army: too many reliefs had either just completed or were not finished. More time was needed to prepare fire plans and gather information. By French (or German) standards, British staff work in the management of a huge and complex field force was still rudimentary, and it showed at the Somme. It is fair to say, too, that not enough of the newly available heavy artillery was committed to counter-battery work. German batteries responded violently, supporting fierce enemy counterattacks to retake lost trenches and strongpoints.

By 5 September the rest of 2nd and 3rd Canadian Divisions had arrived to complete the relief of the ANZACs. The next ten days were a time for careful preparations for a more coordinated and better supported push against the northern wing of the German line, whose defences now ran just behind the crest of the Thiepval–Pozières Ridge between Beaumont-Hamel and Flers. For the first time in the Great War, New Brunswick's artillery units all found themselves deployed within a few kilometres of one another. Lt.-Col. Harry Harrison's 2nd Canadian Divisional Ammunition Column had set up its dumps along the road to Doullens, just outside Albert, to feed 2nd Canadian Division's field batteries deployed on the Ancre below the great bend. Major Geary's 23rd Field Howitzer Battery had taken position on the bank of the Ancre east of Bouzincourt a few kilometres from 4th Siege Battery at Englebelmer. Major Crocker's 28th Field Battery had dug in a few kilometres south in the Albert Brickfields. Lt.-Col. Anderson's 12th Canadian Field Brigade had moved forward into the old German fortified ruins of La Boisselle, within walking distance of the 1st Canadian Heavy Battery positions at Mametz. The Canadian Corps had been assigned sixteen siege and heavy artillery batteries from the Corps Heavy Artillery for what would be remembered as the battle for Courcelette, but only one of those batteries was Canadian. For the time being all siege and heavy batteries remained part of the imperial heavy artillery park. It was the centrality of the Somme offensive, rather than nationality, that brought them together.

The new attack planned for 15 September saw a more standardized use of the creeping barrage on a concentrated 4,500-yard front. More imperial heavy batteries were assigned to join in the counter-battery plan, including Major Barker's 4th Siege Battery, which on Zero Day was to switch from caving in German trenches to hammering German gun positions hidden in the Ancre Valley. Ammunition supplies were replenished. Much had been learned in recent months about correcting the fire of all guns according to daily temperature and barometric pressure shifts. As a consequence, more shells could be delivered closer to the target than ever before. Field guns and howitzers made ready for the creeping barrage to commence at Zero

Panorama of an artillery barrage on the Somme front, October 1916. The creeping linear barrages made famous at Vimy in 1917 were first employed on the Somme by British and later Canadian gunners. (LAC PA-004426)

Hour, but only after a three-day destructive bombardment to cut barbed wire and "soften up" strongpoints. In addition to artillery firepower, forty-nine tanks had been assigned to support the attack, including six in the Canadian Corps area. The ground very much lay in the Canadians' favour, especially from an artillery standpoint. Their forward trenches and observation posts overlooked the German front at Courcelette. So long as the weather stayed clear, shells would find their targets.

At 0620 hours on 15 September, the Canadian field guns opened their first creeping barrage of the war, fired at an intense rate of four rounds per minute per gun. Meanwhile, field howitzers, including New Brunswick's 23rd Battery, hammered the main trench with 4.5-inch high-explosive. After one minute, as Canadian infantry came over the top, the field guns joined the effort to pin the enemy in their trenches and dugouts for three full minutes. That is how long the infantry had to rush across the kill zone before the Germans got their machine-guns into action. After that the barrage lifted 100 yards every three minutes, creating a curtain of exploding shells in front of the infantry to shield them from fire and from counter-attacks by enemy support trenches. Some medium and heavy howitzers fired standing concentrations on known enemy strongpoints and command posts deeper in the German position while others took on the enemy guns. The 4th Siege Battery hurled their 200-pound shells at four German batteries on the Canadian Corps left. On the right, 1st Canadian Heavy Battery planted 126 60-pound shells into a crossroads before switching to their now usual counter-battery mission, taking on twenty different German batteries behind High Wood with nearly 800 rounds.

The results revealed much about how the war could be won, at least so long as good weather allowed air and ground observation to correct the fall of shot. The debut of tanks on the Somme front was important, but 15 September was a day unequivocally decided by artillery guided on target by direct observation. The new heavy guns had finally made themselves felt, and on a deliberately concentrated

front to achieve maximum effect – indeed, twice the concentration employed on 1 July. Efforts by RFC fighter squadrons to hold air superiority over the battlefield paid off in September. The RFC fighters prevented all but a few German planes from making an appearance that month, and this enabled observer aircraft to fly boldly over the enemy front searching out muzzle flashes and smoke puffs. Balloon observers also aided in the effort, with some forty stretching across the front.

As a result of all this, Canadian infantry owned the front trench system fifteen minutes after the barrage opened. Canadian and supporting British artillery then lifted their fire to protect the newly won ground and shoot up German counterattacks that morning, especially at Courcelette itself. At 1540 hours, the gunners were warned to prepare a second barrage for the second major assault that day. A new barrage table arrived at Lt.-Col. Anderson's headquarters at 1730 hours, and his guns opened fire at 1800. This second barrage shot 5th Canadian Infantry Brigade, including 26th New Brunswick Battalion, into Courcelette itself and then ringed the village with fire during the bitter fight for its ruins and against German counterattacks. Moncton's 8th Battery set up its observation post with the infantry from Nova Scotia's 25th Battalion defending the northern rim of the ruins. From there they directed fire on the roads leading into town from the north, seeking out potential counterattacks before they could launch. By day's end the Canadian Corps had penetrated 1,000 yards through enemy support and reserve trenches. On their right, 1st Canadian Heavy Battery supported the main British Fourth Army battle to win control of Martinpuich, High Wood, and beyond to Flers. On the left, British II Corps clawed their way to the edge of heavily fortified Thiepval village. Compared to everything else experienced by British and Dominion troops on the Western Front, the victory at Courcelette and Flers stood out as a resounding success and as proof that a well-dug-in enemy force could be defeated at a manageable cost in casualties. Courcelette grew the Canadian Corps's reputation for skill at arms.

The action at Flers–Courcelette inflicted heavy losses on German front-line divisions, many of which had to be relieved by units transferred from Verdun and other sectors. In broad strokes, then, the renewed Somme offensive delivered results even if a "breakthrough" failed to materialize. German reinforcements and guns packed into the Thiepval–Beaumont-Hamel sector at the northern end of the Somme battlefield, determined to hold at all costs the bend in the Ancre River and the last high ground in front of the railhead at Bapaume. The northern defences connected to the new German front east of Courcelette along the last spur of Thiepval Ridge, barring access to the upper Ancre Valley. The Canadians named the trenches running east to west along its reverse slope "Regina" and "Desire." In front of them lay the Zollern Graben and Hessian trench systems, immediately across no man's land north and west of Courcelette. While follow-on attacks were being prepared to capture Thiepval and Regina Trench, the weather turned in Germany's favour. Grey skies and four straight days of heavy rain made everything difficult. Not least, it became harder to keep guns in continuous action and to haul heavy shells across the glutinous, crater-pitted landscape. September's victories had been decided by accurate and concentrated artillery fire delivered in clear weather under excellent observation. In October 1916, such days would be rare.

That fall the weather determined the timing of each lunge forward. The next concerted effort opened on 26 September after several clear days had dried the ground. That allowed the Canadian Corps field artillery to move up more batteries to the area around La Boiselle, where Lt.-Col. Anderson's 12th Canadian Field Brigade was already in action. Major Crocker's 28th Battery moved up into Sausage Valley south of La Boiselle. Lt.-Col. Harrison moved 2nd Divisional Ammunition Column's wagon lines up on the bald slope of Tara Hill, behind La Boiselle, and set up an ammunition dump on the main Albert–Bapaume Road. A massive artillery and transport park was assembled in the vicinity, numbering some 6,000 horses. This great mass of guns opened a harassing barrage on 23 September, focused mainly on trench destruction and wire cutting. The 23rd Howitzer Battery was specially allotted 1,000 rounds of 4.5-inch high-explosive per day for three days to obliterate a 300-yard section of Zollern Graben. While this was heavy compared to 1915 preparatory bombardments, ammunition was not as plentiful by October as it had been a month earlier, and the results were therefore not as good either.

At 1235 hours on 26 September, Canadian guns opened a creeping barrage in front of the Zollern Graben. FOOs could plainly see and correct their barrage as it pounded the depression north of Courcelette and then climbed the Thiepval Spur behind it, blasting the infantry into the German forward trenches. New Brunswick's field batteries from 1st and 2nd Canadian Divisional Artillery hammered Zollern Graben's eastern end in support of 2nd Canadian Infantry Brigade. On the other side of the Ancre, Major Barker's 4th Siege Battery pounded German trenches north of Thiepval. Twelve minutes after opening fire, Anderson's FOOs reported

The 6th Siege Battery experimented with cutting enemy barbed wire and caving in trenches in October 1916. The task was difficult, with too few 8-inch shells and modern fuses to go around, not to mention bad weather for observation. (LAC PA-000180)

"situation going splendidly – very little opposition." Thirty minutes into the assault the Germans opened a "back-barrage," a wall of exploding shells designed to strike Canadian infantry advancing behind their own creeping barrage. FOOs working with 2nd Canadian Infantry Brigade reported that the infantry were leaning in so close behind their own bursting shells that they were not being caught by the back-barrage. Nonetheless, it was clearly important to silence the enemy's artillery. The 4th Siege Battery switched to counter-battery shoots that afternoon. As they did, the forward infantry waves pressed beyond Zollern Trench and disappeared over the crest of the Thiepval Spur and into the Hessian trench system. On the Canadian right, closer to Courcelette, German machine-gunners evaded the creeping barrage by coming forward of it to craters in no man's land. By day's end, however, Canadian infantrymen had fought their way onto most of the crest.

But the Germans still held the reverse slope in Regina Trench, just out of sight of direct observation from anywhere except the front-line Canadian trenches on the crest itself. Exposure there meant instant death. It is difficult to imagine how the infantry from either side survived atop that shell-churned crest. The 4th Siege Battery FOOs reported that the "ground around Thiepval seemed to be pounded beyond description." Two days of heavy rain once again forced another pause. General Gough nonetheless pressed the Canadians to secure Regina Trench, which led to more fruitless attempts to penetrate an increasingly strong German position. Mist shrouded German artillery in the Ancre Valley from view and prevented effective counter-battery shooting. Infantry casualties from enemy shell and machine-gun fire mounted.

During the steady rain that followed the capture of Hessian Trench, Major Lawrence Allen's 6th Siege Battery arrived at Boulogne and made its way to the Somme. Gunner Keltie Kennedy wrote in his diary about his band of youthful, unbloodied gunners: "This bunch is the most cheerful bunch that ever came out I think, they joke over everything. The French people look at us with a sad look on their faces and some shake their heads as much to say 'poor boys.'" They arrived as the October rains began in earnest. The mud deepened as 6th Siege Battery dug in their 8-inch heavy howitzers at Ovillers-la-Boisselle, in the lee of a spur jutting southwest from Pozières. Heavy rain for four days turned the chalky soil into paste, coating everything it touched. Before guns could be dug in, the battery first had to bury bodies left in the open after the bitter summer fighting. Gunner Green wrote that "very little was left of them except the skeleton covered with shreds of uniform. The rats had cleaned up the bodies as thoroughly as vultures could have done." The dead were not the only legacy of earlier fighting. When someone's boot triggered an unexploded hand grenade, the Battery Sergeant Major was wounded by the blast, making him 6th Siege Battery's first casualty.

In the rush to get new heavy howitzers into the line, gunners arrived without warm clothing or even gloves to handle their 200-pound shells in the cold October rain. Eventually, tin helmets, leather jerkins, and woollen balaclavas offered some measure of protection from the elements. A plank road was laid across the mud from the road behind Ovillers-la-Boisselle to the gun pits so that the heavy shells could be rolled down to the guns. Once in position, 6th Siege Battery's 8-inch howitzers were assigned to help cut the great belt of barbed wire protecting Regina Trench. They were the first of New Brunswick's heavy artillery units to be officially placed under the command of the Canadian Corps Heavy Artillery. They fired their first registration rounds on 5 October and joined in the preparatory barrage the next day. Gunner Kennedy worked as a telephonist and linesman for one of 6th Siege Battery's FOOs, Lieutenant Herb MacDonald. "We started to bombard the enemy at 9am and kept it up steady until 8pm and then not a gun being fired along our part of the front." The dummy halt formed part of yet another deception. The 6th Siege Battery fired high-explosive shells fused to burst on contact with the earth. Needless to say, their 200-pound shells blew gaps through barbed wire entanglements far better than 18-pound shrapnel rounds.

Unfortunately, the Canadian Corps still had too few heavy howitzers, too few heavy shells, and not enough time to seek out and destroy enemy defences. Most

The 4th and 6th Siege Batteries learned that when observation was good and heavy shells plentiful, German trenches and earthen machine-gun posts could be destroyed. Somme front, 1916. (LAC PA-000287)

wire cutting for the 8 October attack on Regina Trench was left to 18-pounder shrapnel shells, which were firing on wire out that was of sight of most observation posts. Nor were there enough heavy guns to smash Regina Trench and its strongpoints. The Germans apparently recognized their sweet spot in the fold between two spurs branching northeast from Thiepval. They invested heavily in men and resources to make the position impregnable. German heavy guns gave back as good as they got. British and Canadian firepower superiority, held in September, had yet to be regained. A 9.2-inch heavy howitzer battery firing only 100 yards in front of 6th Siege Battery lost two guns to direct hits during the action. Gunner Kennedy and Lieutenant MacDonald worked from an observation post in the ruins of Pozières, where "there is only one wall left in the whole city, the rest of the place is nothing but shell holes."

When 1st and 3rd Canadian Division infantry reached the crest of the Thiepval Spur, too much. German wire remained intact. Lanes blasted through in daylight during the previous two days had been closed by the enemy at night. The few riflemen who made it through had neither the numbers nor the firepower to clear Regina Trench, let alone hold it. The result was another 1,364 casualties: many of them lie there still, amid the rolling fields above the Ancre in the remote and solemn Regina Trench cemetery. The attack on 8 October also marked the end of fighting on the Somme for the 1st, 2nd, and 3rd Canadian Division infantry. They were relieved by the new 4th Canadian Division, which did not yet have its own divisional artillery (until that was formed in June 1917, 4th Division was often supported by the Lahore Division Artillery, a remnant of the Indian army's presence on the Western Front). The divisional artillery of the three departing formations remained behind in mud-caked misery for another month. In the British Fourth Army sector south of the Albert–Bapaume Road, 1st Canadian Heavy Battery gunners built a dugout for Captain Inches and his Battery Command Post. It ran "forty feet long, eight feet wide and six feet high – roof of logs laid closely together with corrugated iron on top of that to keep out the rain" (although he complained about the "ominous trickle" inside). Inches dubbed "October and November as the muddiest in our history."

That October, General Gough's Reserve Army became the new British Fifth Army, tasked with destroying German defenders manning the Ancre River bend and its commanding heights. Canada's gunners – including all of New Brunswick's batteries – played a role in this next phase of the Somme battle. In the north, Major Barker's 4th Siege Battery secretly relocated to new positions southeast of Courselles-au-Bois; from there, they could deliver long-range fire on German batteries well behind the Beaumont-Hamel strongpoint at Puisieux and Grandcourt. Barker's men camouflaged each gun position to resemble a haystack, helped in this case by low visibility, rain, and cloud cover. This earned them praise from V Corps's senior artillery officer, who ordered other Royal Artillery officers to visit and study 4th Siege Battery's work.

South of the Ancre River, Canadian ammunition columns laboured in the mud to increase the flow of ammunition of all types. This time there would be "no limit to the number of rounds fired on each spot except that each section of trench must be completely obliterated." Instead of cutting lanes in the wire, medium and heavy howitzer batteries, including Major Allen's 6th Siege Battery, spent days blasting apart the entire barbed wire network. German guns tried to halt the destructive fire. Gunner Kennedy spent those days constantly moving back and forth from Lieutenant MacDonald's observation post and Major Allen's 6th Battery Command Post, repairing breaks in the telephone network blown by German shells. The Germans "did their best to get me, but luck was with me." Kennedy was hit numerous times by shrapnel, which thankfully only perforated his clothes. The most dangerous of all places was at the forward observation post in Kenora Trench, only 300 metres from Regina Trench. There Kennedy dug himself out several times after being buried alive by huge clods of mud thrown up by exploding heavy shells.

The British Fifth Army attack on the Ancre River heights was divided in two parts. On 21 October, 4th Canadian Division (backed by all of the Canadian field artillery) attacked the eastern end of Regina Trench as part of a British II Corps drive to clear the heights south of the Ancre. Events that day proved how much heavy artillery could accomplish when well prepared and matched with an effective creeping barrage. The 4th Canadian Division advanced behind the line of bursting shells that their war diary said was "like a wall," across flattened barbed wire, and lept into Regina Trench "less than 15 minutes after zero hour." Quite simply, the only way to destroy the enemy manning powerful defences was to invest time in intelligence gathering, ammunition stockpiling, and destruction. Anything less cost too high a price in blood.

After the success on 21 October, rain and mist settled in for much of the rest of the month. Aerial observation was impossible. As the Germans clung to their concealed fortress network in the Ancre Valley, Canadian and British gunners relied again on FOOs operating from exposed observation posts and connected by telephone lines running across constantly shell-churned mud. In order to move fast enough to get the work done, Gunner Kennedy "went up over ground as the trenches were too muddy for speed." On the surface he found "dead bodies everywhere both Canadian and German and the stench in this place is awful." The 6th Siege Battery's signallers all had multiple close calls that month as they kept the telephone lines operating to the forward observation posts. Only one, Bombardier H.D. Wetmore, was wounded. On the north side of the valley, 4th Siege Battery's observer teams were less lucky. On 25 October the Germans scored a direct hit on one of their observation posts. Lieutenant Gordon Kerr of Saint John and his telephonist, Gunner C.S. Ashwood of Sussex, were killed. These first combat deaths of two well-liked members a battery family that had been together for well over a year on Partridge Island and then overseas came as a shock. "Volunteers immediately started out from the battery position," the war diary records, "and the bodies were brought back amid general sorrow."

Payback for so much suffering in and around the Ancre Valley came in November. Early in the month the weather turned clear and cool. Good visibility and firmer ground allowed preparations for the final attack on the Beaumont-Hamel strongpoint. Artillery duelling intensified in the first days of the month as German counter-battery fire tried to stop Canadian and British guns from wrecking the German defence network. On 6 November, German long-range heavies found 6th Siege Battery's position at Orvillers and hammered them for a full hour, driving the men into dugouts and fire trenches. Major Allen called out in the din to locate Lieutenant Herb West and got a reply from a nearby fire trench: "I'm down here and it's a damn good hole, too." During those clear nights, German bombers and Zeppelins also searched out gun areas, and bombed Albert to disrupt resupply and repair. Artillery duelling and preparatory shooting intensified through early November. Four-wheel-drive lorries delivered shells every night for the next day's shooting, allowing almost no rest for the exhausted gunners. Finally, on 9 and 10 November, all the British Fifth Army siege and field batteries cranked up their rates of fire to support an assault on both sides of the Ancre Valley bend.

Pillboxes and dugouts in the last section of Regina Trench and the old Newfoundland killing ground at Beaumont-Hamel were finally given the weight of shot necessary to cave them in. The 4th Siege Battery lashed at German gun batteries in the valley. Canadian field artillery pounded the German trench network and helped deliver the creeping barrage. The 6th Siege Battery bombarded the Beaucourt strongpoint behind Beaumont-Hamel during the initial attack. No. 1 gun set a record by firing fifteen of its massive rounds in six minutes. Given the effort it took to manhandle each 200-pound shell and 40-pound charge bag into the breech, this rate of fire was truly extraordinary. On the night of 10–11 November, 4th Canadian Division surged behind a nighttime creeping barrage they described as perfect. All of 1st Canadian Division's fifteen batteries of field guns and howitzers concentrated solely on shooting 11th Canadian Infantry Brigade forward and then shielding it from two German counterattacks. Two days later, 51st Highland Division attacked on the north side of the river at dawn behind another barrage and a massive mine detonation. Gunner Green wrote that "there was some freezing snow that morning and the footing was treacherous. Once, when carrying a shell to the gun both carriers slipped and the fuzed shell skidded down on the gun trail. It had been reported that a fuze required a turning motion as well as impact in order to detonate. This incident proved that the story was true but it might have been demonstrated in a less than hair-raising way." Despite the slush, the Highlanders penetrated the toughest German defences on the Somme, after they had been blasted to piles of splinters and mud with the occupants buried alive underneath. Once the Highlanders were in, 6th Siege Battery hammered the fortified ruins of Serre all day long. Serre was among the most likely rearward bases from which the Germans could counterattack to retake Beaumont-Hamel, and 6th Siege Battery hit it with 127,600 pounds of high-explosive fire.

The successful capture of the Ancre River heights at the great bend around Beaumont-Hamel marked the end of the Battle of the Somme. These last actions further tested the new artillery methods made possible by increased numbers of heavy and siege artillery. The 4th and 6th Siege Batteries met the test of battle and lived up to the artillery standard set by field and heavy gunners in the Ypres Salient. What was needed now was a period of rest, recovery and new training to prepare for good weather in the new year. What remained unclear was whether Canada's "imperial" siege and heavy artillery would concentrate under General Byng's Canadian Corps.

Chapter 4

War on Two Fronts, 1917

By the end of the Somme battles in November 1916, New Brunswick gunners were well represented on the Western Front. One section (out of four) of 1st Divisional Ammunition Column, and the headquarters and one section of 2nd Divisional Ammunition Column and three field or howitzer batteries (8th, 23rd, and 28th) were with the Canadian Corps. More importantly, by the end of 1916 a growing number of Canada's heavy and siege artillery personnel came from the province as well. The 1st Canadian Heavy Battery (60-pounders) was commanded by Frank Magee from Saint John, and half of his 186 officers and men were from 3rd NB Regiment. The 2nd Canadian Heavy Battery, the other 60-pounder unit, from Prince Edward Island, was leavened with about twenty New Brunswickers. Of the six Canadian siege batteries in service (8-inch and 9.2-inch howitzers, each with a personnel strength of about 160), the 4th and the 6th were essentially New Brunswick batteries, while the 1st, 2nd, and 5th had notable contingents of both officers and men from the province. Only 3rd Siege Battery seems to have existed outside the orbit of New Brunswick gunners. This trend only strengthened as the war continued.

By the end of 1916 it was clear that the key to the development of Canada's heavy artillery was 3rd NB Regiment and its batteries on Partridge Island in Saint John harbour. By then the regiment's Composite Battery had trained more than 1,200 personnel and despatched them to the front. It had, in fact, become the de facto Depot Battery for the rapidly evolving Canadian heavy and siege artillery.

By the fall of 1916 the Composite Battery, led by Major Percy W. Wetmore, in acting command of 3rd NB Regiment while Lt.-Col. Armstrong served in Halifax from March 1916 until the end of the war, was recruiting and training 9th Siege Battery in expectation of its imminent transfer overseas. While the men trained on the island's 4.7-inch guns, officers and specialist personnel went on courses in Halifax, Quebec City, and Kingston. The 9th Battery's personnel, numbering 175 by the end of the year, followed a syllabus that included basic recruit training (marksmanship, physical conditioning, drill, etc.), but more importantly they were taught the skills of controlling and firing heavy guns at long range. Such skills included flag and telephone signalling (essential for transmitting target and fire correction data from FOOs to the guns), gun drill, and plotting of targets and fall of shot. Training was conducted by two gunnery instructors from the Royal Canadian Garrison Artillery. When officers from 3rd NB Regiment completed their qualifications at the permanent force schools, they took over the training program in 1917.

In January 1917, General Thomas Benson, Commander of MD 6, reported favourably on 9th Battery's progress. He noted its "esprit de corps," and successful efforts to develop specialist personnel, "having the following, not including those in the draft qualified at the Siege courses in Halifax, NS.: [Battery Commander] Assistants 9; Plotters 19; Layers 28; Signallers 25; while all the officers passed very high in the courses they took in Siege Artillery." General Benson urged that 9th Siege Battery be sent to the front as a unit, but without result. Instead, in January drafts of men began to leave Partridge Island for England, and when 100 personnel departed in March 1917, 9th Battery was effectively gutted. Lieutenant J.G. Rycroft, the respected gunnery instructor at Halifax, made an appeal through the artillery community that reached Brigadier General E.W.B. Morrison, General Officer Commanding of the Canadian Corps artillery, to send 9th Siege Battery and its sister Depot Battery in Halifax, the 10th, overseas as formed units. Morrison supported him, and General Benson, on a visit to Ottawa, lobbied for the batteries to be dispatched. Nothing happened. So throughout 1917, as 3rd NB Regiment's Composite Battery developed into an effective coast defence force focused on the rising submarine threat, 9th Siege Battery on Partridge Island evolved into a formal Depot Battery for overseas service, a producer of skilled and highly capable heavy gunners for the Western Front.

The decision to keep 9th Battery on Partridge Island was probably taken because the defence of Canada's east coast had suddenly become a priority. Recall that the establishment of the Composite Battery on the island in 1914 had been a political decision, not a military one: there was no threat from coal-fired surface warships on an ocean wholly dominated by British seapower. In 1915 the Germans had responded to that dominance by using diesel-electric-powered submarines to attack Allied merchant vessels. At first their U-boats lacked the range to operate beyond European waters. Then in early November 1916, *U-53*, a new long-range

U-boat, visited the United States and, after a courtesy call to New England, sank five British and Canadian merchant ships near Nantucket. The war had come to North America. Soon after, the captain of the British cruiser HMS *Isis*, escorting a valuable transport while it loaded at Saint John, was so worried about the port's vulnerability to submarine attack that he insisted that the harbour commissioners charter a tugboat for the cruiser's crew to operate as a lookout patrol until the big ships left.

The 4.7-inch guns on Partridge Island, while excellent for training gunners for the Western Front, were no match for a modern submarine. In any event they were deployed to fire out to sea, perhaps to catch a surface raider at a great distance; they could not bear on the inner harbour, where a submarine was most likely to appear. By early 1917, it seemed that it was only a matter of time before Germany's U-boats attacked eastern Canada, which was the only overseas operational area they could easily reach. The certainty of this threat became manifest on 31 January 1917 when the German chancellor, Bethmann-Hollweg, announced that Germany would commence unrestricted submarine warfare on all Allied shipping in European waters starting the next day. This meant that submarines would now be sinking ships on sight, ignoring the niceties of international law. For the moment the declaration was limited to European waters, partly as a sop to the Americans, whose protests had brought two previous unrestricted submarine campaigns in 1915 and 1916 to a halt. This time the Germans were resolved not to back down: they hoped to win the war before American manpower could be felt on the Western Front.

Everyone expected that this new phase of the war at sea would not be limited to European waters. So by early 1917 the gunners on Partridge Island had found an important role in harbour defence, and the resources to do that job soon arrived. The government sent to the island two additional 4.7-inch guns mounted on modern coast defence pedestals. These could traverse very rapidly and accurately to engage a submarine at close range. Two 25-inch searchlights from HMCS *Niobe* also arrived, that ship having been immobilized as a floating naval barracks at Halifax. The guns were mounted in a new concrete battery, comprising two semicircular gun platforms joined by a long concrete revetment (which survives at the northeast end of the island), overlooking the immediate entrance to the harbour. The personnel of the Composite and 9th Siege Batteries carried out much of this construction. The searchlights were installed in one of the hospital staff residences on the shore near the new battery. Not until November 1917 were the guns fully ready for operation, and work on the lights continued into the early part of 1918, just in time for the first U-boats of the 1918 season. Now the two batteries on the island had clearly defined – and important – roles.

Meanwhile, the batteries at the front underwent a significant reorganization prior to the opening of the great British offensive at Arras slated for the spring. Until early 1917, all British heavy and siege batteries on the Western Front had been army-level assets, and as previously noted, these huge batteries tended to remain in place while infantry formations shifted around them. Opportunities to build relationships, trust, and common procedure or to train together were limited. General Burstall, the CCRA of the fledgling Canadian Corps, wanted Canada's siege batteries to serve with Canadian divisions. But the Somme offensive had drawn every new gun and gunner to it, and the new siege batteries coming from Canada in 1916 were "imperial" resources. Major Barker's 4th Siege Battery, for example, was officially "131st Siege Battery," while Major Allen's 6th Siege Battery was "167th Siege Battery" of the BEF.

Getting Canadian heavy guns under Canadian command was a cause picked up by General Sir Julian Byng when he took command of the corps. In early 1917 he recommended that new siege batteries being raised in Canada and those already at the front be amalgamated into 1st and 2nd Canadian Heavy Artillery Groups, with plans for a third when men and guns arrived. That wish would take time to realize, but as a step forward, imperial army numbers assigned to Canadian siege batteries were dropped and all reverted to status as Canadian Garrison Artillery. Meanwhile, four more siege batteries were mobilizing at home. Most cycled through 9th Siege Battery on Partridge Island, and all contained a leavening of New Brunswick volunteers. Of the more than 2,000 officers and men in Canada's two heavy and eight siege batteries concentrated north of Arras in the winter of 1917, about one-third were New Brunswickers. Another third were Maritimers recruited through Saint John and Halifax.

When Canada's field, heavy, and siege batteries pulled off the Somme front and moved to Arras in early 1917, they all took a few well-earned days of rest while worn guns went to workshops. Captain Inches wrote that they needed it. The men of his battery "were beginning to show the results of the strain; some who were mere boys when we came to France are looking old beyond their years." Inches's battery got nearly a full month off after two years of service. The newer siege batteries got less time to relax: 4th Siege Battery just a few days at Bruay-la-Buissière southeast of Bethune, and 6th Siege Battery barely a week. The interlude proved memorable. Gunner Kennedy later recalled the French "estaminets," improvised pubs set up in many a farmhouse, often by women whose husbands were off at the front or dead. They provided a hot plate of eggs and chips and a pint of homemade beer, and some found other comforts.

Rest periods, reorganization, training, and firing at the front formed the winter routine. Front-line duty often involved supporting trench raids to gather information about enemy units and defences. The 6th Siege Battery helped shoot the Royal Canadian Regiment into German lines on Vimy Ridge just before Christmas, in a trench raid that bagged more than fifty prisoners and blew up an enemy ammunition dump. Lt.-Col. Harrison's 2nd Divisional Ammunition Column set up shop at the Canadian base and railhead area at Barlin, where it offloaded ammunition and hauled it east by wagon towards the front. The 23rd Howitzer Battery set to work shooting up German trench mortar positions on the north end of the sector.

Over the winter of 1917 all of Canada's artillery drifted into the Vimy sector, joining the massive British effort behind the Arras offensive. The 1st Canadian Heavy Battery's Left Section took position on the Lorette Ridge, with Lieutenant Slader in an observation post on the Lorette Spur overlooking the northwest end of Vimy Ridge. Battery Headquarters and the Right Section set up in familiar territory around Bully-les-Mines, near where they had fired during the Battle of Loos. The Right Section observation post was inside a shot-up mine building overlooking Liéven, close to the 26th NB Battalion sector. The 2nd Division's Ammunition Column, 23rd Howitzer Battery, and 28th Field Battery were nearby. The 4th Siege Battery took position in the same vicinity, and before long the New Brunswickers all found one another. The 6th Siege Battery was the odd unit out from this reunion. Major Allen's heavy howitzers deployed in the Arras suburb of Anzin-Saint Aubin behind the high bluff descending to the Scarpe River. A lime kiln operation next to the gun positions became relatively comfortable living quarters not far from a YMCA canteen.

Winter preparations for a great spring offensive proceeded apace. The French were massing for what came to be known as the Nivelle Offensive, after their new Chief of the General Staff, General Robert Nivelle. He had won fame at Verdun in 1916 and believed he had solved the problem of how to rupture the front – with sophisticated artillery preparations and overwhelming firepower. "I have the solution," he trumpeted. The British agreed to support him with a limited offensive at Arras timed to start just ahead of the French assault and thereby draw off German reserves. Canadian preparations to capture Vimy Ridge were part of this larger Arras offensive.

So in the late winter of 1917, the BEF's heavy artillery concentrated north and west of Arras. Since the Allies had lost control of the skies to the new German Albatross fighter, massing the guns, securing them against counter-battery fire, and using aerial observation to see and hit their targets was difficult. Not surprisingly, when 4th Siege Battery dug in, they prepared pits complete with overhead cover and protected ammunition storage. Every New Brunswick battery commented on the quality of billets in the Vimy sector; all found hard shelter and at least partly intact buildings as living quarters behind their gun positions. Gun pits, trenches, and observation posts were also in better condition, having decent drainage, more duckboards, and better-reinforced parapets; they were generally preferable to the fire-churned mud of the Somme. Field and heavy gunners and ammunition columns carried on the preparation work through the winter.

At the end of January, 4th and 6th Siege Batteries gave up their comfortable billets and shifted north to the Ypres front, where they joined a force of twelve Canadian and imperial heavy batteries to forestall a German spoiling attack. On

2 February 1917, New Brunswick's two heavy howitzer batteries were the first to fire the new, purpose-built 8-inch Mark VI heavy howitzers in the Ypres area. It was during this short stay in Ypres that 6th Siege Battery began calling itself the Rag-Time Battery, presumably for their musical prowess. Both batteries spent two weeks throwing heavy shells at fortified German batteries and machine-gun posts on the northern part of the salient before moving to the southern part at Mount Kemmel on Valentine's Day. Hours after they left their northern positions a massive German retaliatory barrage, including gas shells, lashed at their emptied gun pits.

In the Kemmel area, New Brunswick's siege batteries supported a limited attack against Messines Ridge. Both fired large quantities of ammunition in short periods in an attempt to deceive the Germans about the amount of heavy artillery massed in the area. It was at Kemmel that 6th Siege Battery learned to match 4th Siege Battery's ability to keep three 200-pound shells in the air at the same time: one about to land, one in mid-flight, and one exiting a muzzle. Doing so meant manning the ammunition cradle with two strong and well-drilled men rather than the textbook four, meaning that each loader handled 120 pounds every time their gun fired. The 6th Siege Battery also learned something from the 4th about camouflage – how to tie bits of burlap sack to chicken wire screens to conceal guns from German aerial observers. The 4th Siege Battery was also introduced to a new sound-ranging method for searching out German gun positions behind Messines Ridge, which involved taking compass bearings on enemy gun flashes and then counting the seconds until shell impact to determine the range. All of these lessons would come in handy in the months to come.

On 23 February, 4th and 6th Siege Batteries left Ypres to rejoin their Canadian comrades in the Vimy sector. By then, plans for the Arras offensive had matured. Vimy Ridge would form the northernmost wing of an Allied general spring offensive, which was to extend for over 100 miles of British and French sectors south to the Aisne River. British and Dominion forces were to mount diversionary attacks between Arras and the Somme to prevent German units from shifting south to meet Nivelle's attack in late April. The Canadians' capture of Vimy Ridge would shield the northern flank of British Third Army's attack from Arras eastward towards Cambrai. In the late winter, the urgency of achieving some kind of victory in 1917 was impressed on everyone. While shipping losses from Germany's unrestricted submarine assault skyrocketed, Russia was descending into revolution. Kerensky's new socialist government in St. Petersburg had agreed to continue the war against Germany, but few believed he could. Everything, it seemed, hinged on Nivelle, and on the success of the BEF's Arras offensive.

The Canadian task in the Arras offensive of defeating the well-dug-in Bavarian Corps on Vimy Ridge would not be easy. The story of systematic infantry rehearsals, concealed ammunition stockpiling, tunnelling, intelligence gathering, improved communications, and ultimately assembling the largest and densest concentration

War on Two Fronts, 1917 | 103

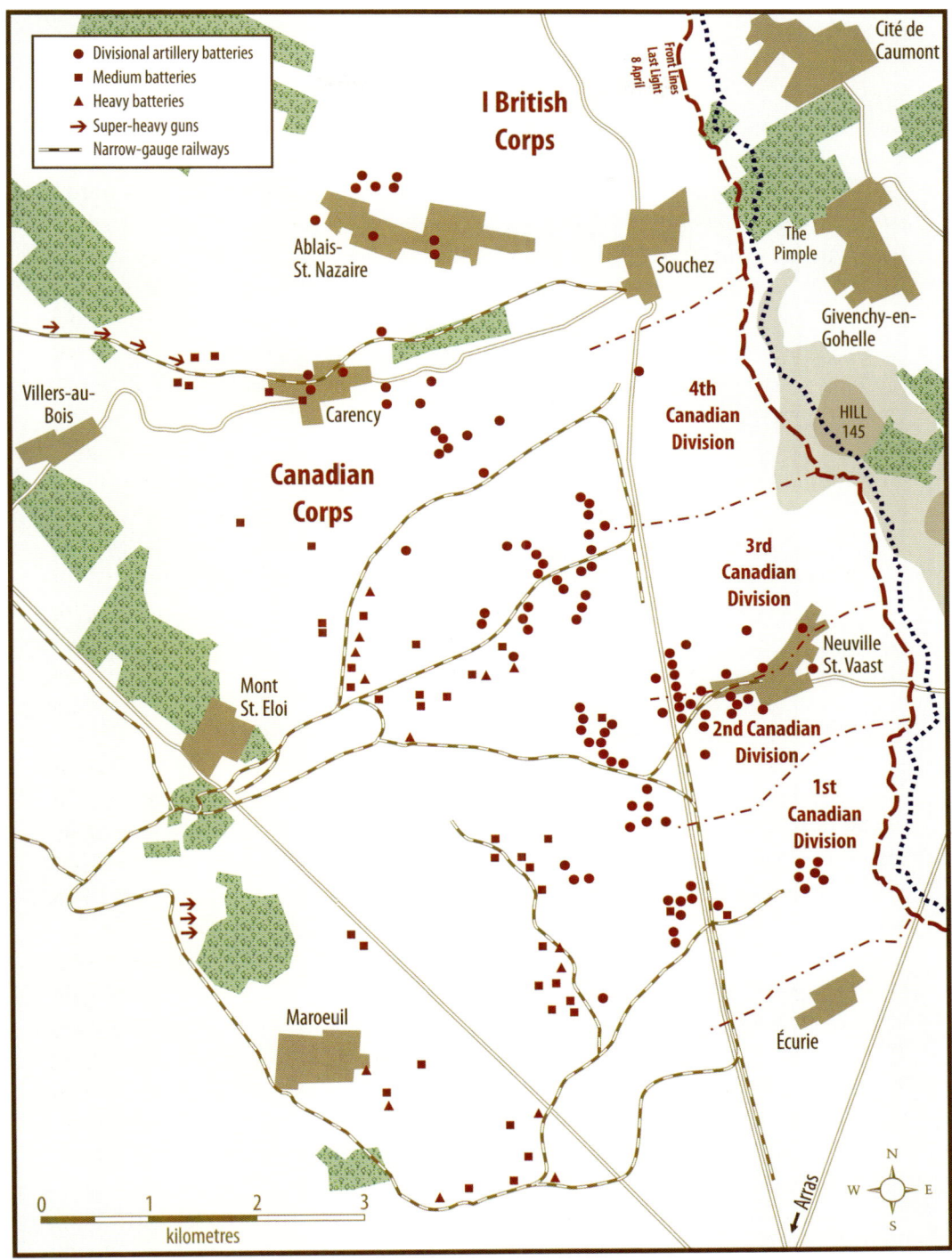

Vimy Ridge Artillery Positions, March–April 1917

A key element of success at Vimy was improved quantity and quality of Allied ammunition, especially in medium and heavy shells. These required immense manpower and infrastructure. (LAC PA-003803)

of artillery organized on any front in the Great War to date has long been part of the Vimy story. A closer look at New Brunswick's heavy artillery activity in March 1917 sheds light on how Canadian and British gunners made the plan work. On the Somme, British heavy gun batteries had gathered for some months before the assault opened, and pounded the enemy for two weeks before the attack began. At Vimy and Arras, plans centred on waiting until the last possible moment to mass the heavy guns, and then to silence the enemy with a crushing weight of fire.

When 4th and 6th Siege Batteries arrived back at Vimy, their 8-inch howitzers were sorely needed across the whole front. Major Barker took 4th Siege Battery's Right Section behind Mount St-Eloi (not to be confused with St-Eloi south of Ypres) as part of the newly formed 1st Canadian Heavy Group. Major Allen took 6th Siege Battery's Right Section to the same area, on the bank of the upper Scarpe River. There the two half-batteries prepared gun positions for all of their battery's guns. Meanwhile their Left Sections took up position in the northern part of British First Army's sector, facing Loos. Gunner Kennedy and half of 6th Siege Battery's signallers went with the Left Section to Mazingarbe, the next village north of Bully. There they set a record by getting their howitzers into action in twelve hours and then firing off a shoot accurate enough to score four direct hits on an enemy strongpoint. A Royal Garrison Battery coming into the line beside them took three days to get their first rounds off. The 4th Siege Battery's Left Section deployed farther north on the old Festubert battlefield at La Couture. From these positions, the heavy 8-inch howitzers of the two New Brunswick batteries made themselves look like full batteries. Every few days these sections laboriously winched their massive howitzers out of the mud and towed them to the next position with their Holt tractors. The Royal Garrison Artillery batteries they relieved in each case got their turn for a rest before moving south to join the artillery park massing behind Mount St-Eloi and Arras. At every new location, 4th and 6th Siege Batteries' Left Sections blasted off plenty of rounds to make two guns appear to be four. They fired at every kind of target: German command posts, machine-gun posts, artillery batteries, trench mortars, trench junctions, and even a distillery. On 4 March an RFC observer walked 6th Siege Battery directly onto a German gun position, on which it scored three direct hits. Kennedy remembered it as "the best Aeroplane shoot we ever had!" The 4th Siege Battery's Lieutenants Bruce and George Wetmore were both awarded the Military Cross for their actions in directing the Left Section guns during the deception shoots, which often invited heavy German retaliatory fire. Their signaller, Lance Bombardier W.A. Connell, won the Military Medal. The 1st Canadian Heavy Battery's Left Section kept working over German batteries at Lens.

Overall, the New Brunswick heavy gunners did everything possible to be seen and have their impact felt. The new 8-inch heavy howitzers remained a rare

Field gunners loading 18-pounder caissons at a Divisional Ammunition Column dump established safe in the folds behind Vimy Ridge. (LAC PA-001393)

commodity on the Western Front. Their presence offered a strong clue as to where the next British offensive might open. The old 1915 Aubers Ridge and Loos battlefields were a good choice for such a deception. That ground offered a way around Lens and posed a threat to the German base at Lille. Even the Canadian Field Artillery and infantry got in on the deception. The 8th Battery and 2nd Canadian Field Brigade took up positions in March in Bully Grenay behind Loos; from there, they supported Canadian trench raids and fed German concerns about what the future might hold in the sector north of Vimy Ridge. All the while, the Right Sections of 1st Canadian Heavy Battery and 4th and 6th Siege Batteries prepared guns positions, filled sandbags, and strung camouflage nets around Mount St-Eloi in the south for the real attack. Lt.-Col. Harrison's 2nd Divisional Ammunition Column hauled hundreds of thousands of shells from railheads to staging dumps. Those ammunition dumps had to move towards Vimy for the actual attack, but that move was timed for the last possible minute to avoid detection.

One final reorganization of Canadian artillery was completed just prior to Vimy, in March, and resulted in a further concentration of New Brunswick's gunners in the Canadian Corps's heavy artillery. Because of improvements in communications, it was decided to increase the size of field batteries from four to six guns and to shift the officers released by this move into key corps-level artillery staffs. This change eliminated one-quarter of Canada's field batteries, including New Brunswick's only two. One section of 8th Moncton Battery went to 5th Westmount Battery and the other to 7th Montreal Battery, which at least kept the sections in 2nd Canadian Field Brigade. The reorganization also eliminated Lt.-Col. Anderson's 12th Canadian Field Brigade, but he shifted to command of 2nd Canadian Field Brigade. The 28th Newcastle Battery suffered a similar fate: one section went to 15th Battery and the other to 16th Battery, all still in 6th Canadian Field Brigade. A large complement of New Brunswickers from 22nd Howitzer Battery also went to 6th Canadian Field Brigade. Only the notionally New Brunswick 23rd Howitzer Battery (raised in Fredericton but recruited throughout the region) of 5th Canadian Field Brigade remained intact, as did the province's presence in 1st and 2nd Divisional Ammunition Columns.

The reorganization of March 1917 raised questions about the politics of unit preservation, the influence of Montreal (whose infantry and artillery units at the front were maintained on the strength of recruits from Atlantic Canada), and perhaps the success of lobbying by Lt.-Col. Armstrong and others from Saint John regarding the central importance of coast gunners to the development of heavy artillery. The latter fight was by no means won as of the winter of 1917, and Armstrong travelled to Britain and France in the summer to continue it. In the meantime, the reorganization of field artillery in March 1917 shifted the focus of New Brunswick's gunner effort squarely onto the siege and heavy artillery. As evidence of that, in mid-March, Canada's heavy artillery was organized into 1st and 2nd

In preparation for the assault on Vimy Ridge, the 4th and 6th Siege Battery gunners built elaborately camouflaged, well-protected gun pits, much like the one depicted here, for their 8-inch heavy howitzers (LAC PA-002373)

Canadian "Heavy Artillery Groups." Major Frank Magee was promoted to Lieutenant-Colonel and given command of the new 2nd Canadian Heavy Artillery Group: its primary task was counter-battery work. Captain Inches was promoted to Major and took Magee's place in command of 1st Canadian Heavy Battery. The New Brunswick gunner mafia was moving up.

While the field artillery sorted itself out, the work of the heavy guns in front of Vimy Ridge went on. It was not without peril. The 60-pounders of 1st Canadian Heavy Battery were ordered forward for counter-battery shooting on 15 March. The new position was well camouflaged, but German airplanes attacked them with machine-guns. Fortunately, the planes failed to transmit an accurate location for the battery. Only once did German guns range in close, hitting the battery dispatch horse and rider. "A shell landed under his horse," Lieutenant Slader remembered, "blowing the beast to bits, one of its legs landed against our mess table, about 30 yards away. The rider, Gunner Doetzell, was shot into the air and lost one foot. He survived. A miracle."

By late March, Lt.-Col. Harrison's 2nd Divisional Ammunition Column had begun in earnest to move ammunition from behind Mount St-Eloi to forward dumps and gun pits behind Neuville-St-Vaast. Harrison's 600 gunners and 650

This concrete-protected German gun position behind Vimy Ridge received heavy and concentrated Canadian and British counter-battery attention in April 1917. (LAC PA-001132)

animals struggled through rain and snow, shifting their efforts into overdrive. The light railways helped, but superhuman effort and overexertion of the horses was still required. "The cold weather and heavy work caused considerable debility amongst the horses and mules," Captain Clark recalled. "Harness was exposed to the weather and therefore it was very difficult to prevent galls, even with the greatest care. The inevitable result was many deaths and the horse situation throughout the army became most serious." Altogether, some 50,000 horses supported preparations for the Vimy offensive. Keeping them fed and healthy was a major effort.

Illnesses, including trench fever, ran through the artillery lines as well, laying low gunners and officers alike. Severe cases were evacuated to England. At one point that March, 57 percent of 6th Siege Battery's gunners were out of commission. But the hard labour went on in deadly earnest. This work coincided with the opening of the preparatory barrage by half the guns assembled west of Vimy Ridge, including 1st Canadian Heavy Battery. The shells landed on the foremost German trenches and wire, and on working parties and well-travelled trenches in the rear. For the moment, German artillery batteries were being spared anything beyond "normal" counter-battery harassment.

The balance of Canadian and British heavy and super-heavy artillery packed into the assault area used the cover of the initial barrage to conceal their final deployments between Mount St-Eloi and Neuville-St-Vaast. This included reuniting 4th and 6th Siege Batteries, whose Left Sections slipped into their secretly prepared positions at the end of March. Each battery position was stocked with 2,800 heavy shells and propellant cartridges dug into protected magazines. "I have never seen so much traffic in my life as there is down here," Gunner Kennedy wrote about the arrival of 6th Siege Battery. "Motor Lorries are lined up along the roads for miles. Ammunition limbers are strung out for miles. The traffic is much larger than it ever was on the Somme ... Everywhere you look there are batteries, field, heavy and siege all side by side lying everywhere." The 4th Siege Battery, reassigned to Lt.-Col Minden Cole's 1st Canadian Heavy Artillery Group, found "fifteen heavy artillery batteries within ten minutes' walk." Cole's Canadians and two groups of heavy British guns were tasked with trench destruction.

The Canadian heavy artillery assembling at Vimy was given a boost in March with the arrival of three new siege batteries: 7th Siege Battery from Montreal equipped with 6-inch mediums; 8th Siege Battery, primarily from Charlottetown but with a contingent of New Brunswickers from 4th Siege Battery; and a new 9th Siege Battery. The latter was composed mostly of personnel from Halifax and some from Esquimalt, BC. The 9th Siege Battery, equipped with 6-inch 26cwt medium howitzers, arrived in front of Mount St-Eloi on 5 April 1917, just in time to register for the big day. In all, some 245 British and Canadian heavy guns were assembled in front of Vimy Ridge by early April, one for every 20 yards of front. Nearly 700 field guns and howitzers were packed in as well, one for every 10 yards. It was a massive concentration of firepower for a corps level attack.

The standard view of the German defences on the northern end of Vimy Ridge characterizes them as tightly packed and lacking in depth, with no room to fall back if the high point of Hill 145 was lost. However, fortified villages behind Vimy Ridge on the plain of Douai held command posts, gun positions, and counterattack reserves. To the south in front of 1st and 2nd Canadian Divisions, the ridge flattened completely and the German defences extended two miles deep across a plain. The New Brunswick siege batteries were deployed in the middle and so were able to influence the entire front, and reach deep into the German positions behind it. Both 4th and 6th Siege Batteries took position just forward of Mount St-Eloi. Major Inches's 1st Canadian Heavy Battery was nearby, at Berthonval Farm, as part of Lt.-Col. Magee's 2nd Canadian Heavy Artillery Group. Magee's headquarters and four other Canadian and British counter-batteries were in the centre as well. The 6th Siege Battery remained in the south, behind 2nd Canadian Division (and New Brunswick's 26th Battalion). From these central locations all three New Brunswick heavy batteries could reach targets 2 to 3 kilometres behind Vimy Ridge.

By early April, after ten days of bombardment, the German front line was already badly damaged. However, the zone between the German first- and second-line defences, and around Thélus on top of the ridge, as well as gun positions and

Thick belts of barbed wire were the most dangerous component of German defences. The highly sensitive British 106 fuses, introduced by early 1917, burst on the slightest contact, detonating shells above ground amidst wire entanglements and shredding them. The new shell also prevented cratering of the ground. This photograph shows 106-fused heavy trench mortar shells shredding a belt of barbed wire. (LAC PA-001907)

base areas in the villages of La Chaudière, Vimy, and Farbus behind the ridge, had yet to be fully attended to. These targets were being spared for the last week of bombardment, again to conceal Canadian intentions.

On 1 April, 4th and 6th Siege Batteries fired five or six rounds per gun from their secret forward positions in order to register, then for two days they fired only a few rounds each day to register on other datum points within their range. Finally, on 3 April, they opened fire in earnest for a week of preparatory bombardment, remembered by the Germans as "the Week of Suffering." They hammered the villages of Thélus, Farbus, Givenchy, and La Chaudière, as well as trench junctions, gun batteries, dugouts, and strongpoints, including those on the lips of craters near La Folie Farm. The 6th Siege Battery spent most of that week taking Thélus apart, brick by brick. The village, with its deep stone basements, stood as a fortress in the second German line in the 1st and 2nd Canadian Division sector. The 1st Canadian Heavy Battery, meanwhile, was tasked with counter-battery work, and fired just enough to compel the German gunners to take cover, but not enough to encourage them to move. Intelligence had located an estimated 83 percent of enemy batteries, and the Canadian Corps Artillery Commander, Brigadier General Morrison, did not want any counter-battery shooting beyond what looked like normal retaliation shooting until Zero Hour.

During the Week of Suffering, heavy batteries pulverized the area between the first and second lines, caving in communications trenches and making it extremely difficult for the Germans to bring water and food up to the front and the wounded back. German records later revealed this "breakdown in the food supply as a major cause of weakness in the defence." In the final two days before the attack, 6th Siege Battery switched its focus to the large belt of barbed wire covering the second German line behind Thélus. In two days the battery fired 1,000 rounds, each capped with new No. 106 fuses designed to burst on graze. The shells ripped apart the barbed wire with terrific new efficiency, opening routes for 2nd Canadian Infantry Division.

The standard Vimy story contends that most German artillery had been neutralized by the time the attack began, but this was not strictly true. British and Canadian counter-battery fire was very restricted in that last week before Zero Day, and New Brunswick's batteries experienced plenty of German retaliation. The 6th Siege Battery's forward observers were repeatedly blasted out of their observation posts, and their gun positions were raked with shellfire. Part of the problem was

This caved-in German concrete bunker behind Vimy Ridge illustrates the impact of concentrated, heavy shells, fired in quantity based on accurate target intelligence and good observation. All of these were in too short supply in early battles in 1916. (LAC PA-001295)

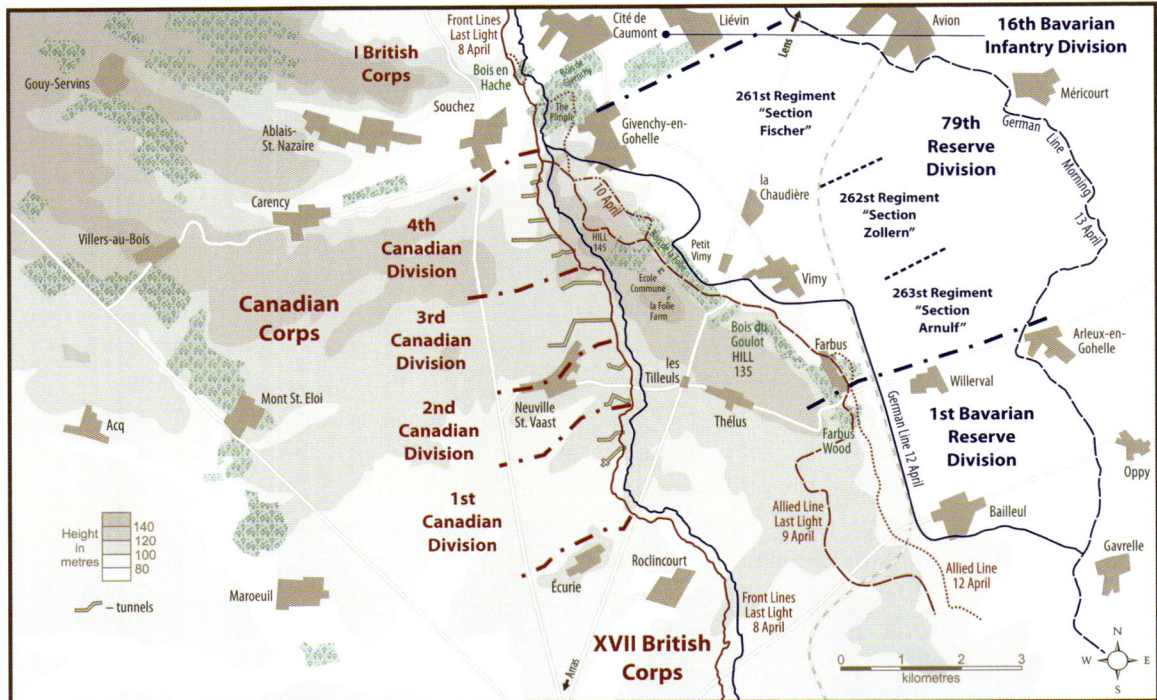

The Battle of Vimy Ridge, 9–12 April 1917

that the Allies did not hold air superiority over Vimy Ridge. No. 16 Squadron of the RFC lost a large number of air observer planes to enemy fighter planes while doing their best to spot the fall of shot and locate German batteries. Just as important, the RFC was unable to deny aerial reconnaissance to the Germans. As a result, German gunners returned heavy fire all during the Week of Suffering, tearing up telephone and signal cable and keeping battery signallers busy reconnecting the forward observation posts. Sergeant Wallace of 6th Siege Battery's Signal Section took fragments in the head while working on the lines. He survived, and his section managed to reconnect the battery to the "CANADA Observation Post" at Écurie just fifteen scant minutes before Zero Hour. Brigadier General Morrison's plan to hold off the main counter-battery shooting until Zero Hour had its costs.

Finally, before dawn at 0530 on 9 April, the steady rain of German shells along Vimy Ridge ended abruptly. "A split second before 5:30 am a single gun beat the schedule and fired but the flash was still visible when all guns opened up," wrote 6th Siege Battery's Gunner Steve Green. "All along the line and behind the Battery gun flashes could be seen so close together that there was a continuous pulsating light." Gunner Kennedy recalled that as soon as the full barrage opened, "the Germans kept the sky full of flares and their SOS signals could be seen from one end of the line to the other." The 1st Canadian Heavy Battery joined the massive counter-battery neutralization shoot, while the siege batteries revealed their full power. The 4th Siege Battery fired standing concentrations in support of 3rd Canadian Division, while 6th Siege Battery did the same for 2nd Canadian Division; both sent shells crashing down on German support trenches and second-line strongpoints in depth so that they could not challenge Canadian infantry surging into the first-line trenches. Then, after fifteen minutes, the 4th and 6th shifted their fire deep into the German positions, joining 1st Canadian Heavy Battery in the counter-battery shoot while also catching counterattack reserves moving up. The tidal wave of fire obliterated most of the German defences and powered the Canadian Corps to the top of almost all of Vimy Ridge that day.

Only Hill 145, where the Canadian National Great War Monument stands today, held out for another day. Lieutenant Slader was caught up in the middle of the struggle for Hill 145. He and his signaller, Sergeant Jim Robertson, followed behind 11th Canadian Infantry Brigade through their chalk tunnel up to Hill 145. They emerged into a shell-torn morass "and crawled the last few hundred yards through slime and water to avoid enemy machine gun fire." They connected their cable into the telephone network and linked up with 1st Canadian Heavy Battery's command post, but could not see to fire. German strongpoints on Hill 145 remained lethal. Slader and Robertson waited behind 85th Canadian Infantry

The notorious 5.9-inch or 15 cm German medium howitzer. This one was neutralized and captured in its concrete gun position in Farbus village, behind Vimy Ridge, April 1917. (LAC PA-000978)

Battalion (Cape Breton Highlanders) until the Nova Scotians could mount a night attack to take control of the heights by dawn.

Reports from New Brunswick gunners suggest that German artillery continued firing most of the day on 9 April and was particularly fierce in the first hour of the attack. German artillery was never fully silenced. It is worth remembering that for all the ammunition expended and all the Germans killed or dazed by the barrage, enough of them and their weapons remained in action on 9 April to kill or wound more Canadians in a single day than on any other in this nation's history. Between 9 and 10 April the Canadian Corps suffered 7,707 casualties, including almost 3,000 dead. Many of those casualties were inflicted by German shellfire, and it was fortunate that casualties among New Brunswick's heavy and siege gunners were mercifully light: only a dozen of them were wounded. But it was clear that more counter-battery effort was necessary. The ideal balance between devoting heavy guns to cutting wire and destroying defences versus attacking enemy guns had yet to be found. Canada could not afford too many victories like 9 April 1917.

The battle did not end when Vimy Ridge fell into Canadian hands. The Germans wanted it back, and the superb observation from the ridge over the Douai Plain was a gunner's dream. So as the Canadian guns moved closer to the ridge in order to reach deep into German positions, the Germans had a good idea where Canadians guns would deploy, and enemy fire became more lethal. At the same time, the amount of firepower west of the ridge declined, as British heavy artillery shifted south to support British Third Army's drive towards Cambrai. Ironically,

A Canadian Artillery Forward Observer and his signaller on the southeast slope of Vimy Ridge correcting the fall of shot on Arleux. New Brunswick FOOs made great use of the heights around Vimy from April 1917 through to August 1918. (LAC PA-001189)

Canadian gunners making use of an early-model German 10.5cm field howitzer, captured intact at Vimy Ridge in April 1917. (LAC PA-001156)

therefore, it was after Vimy fell that the Canadian Corps Heavy Artillery suffered its heaviest casualties.

The essential task was to use the commanding height of Vimy Ridge to dominate the Douai Plain to the northeast. At dawn on 10 April, Lieutenant Slader got his first glimpse of what the Canadian Corps had paid for with its blood. Visitors to the magnificent monument atop Hill 145 have a similar reaction. Slader could plainly see German batteries firing from the outlying villages south of Lens and thus direct fire onto their positions. On 11 April, Slader called in a destructive shoot on a German 5.9-inch battery firing from well-protected concrete positions. His own 1st Canadian Heavy Battery 60-pounders and the 8-inch howitzers of 4th Siege Battery cracked open the overhead cover and destroyed three of the four German guns. The commanding officer of 11th Canadian Infantry Brigade visited Slader's observation post to watch the show and commented, "You must be having a good time."

On the flat south end of the ridge, things were less rosy and good observation posts were hard to come by. Lieutenant MacDonald and Gunner Kennedy of 6th Siege Battery worked their way through the smashed ruins at Thélus, which was still under too much German fire for them to lay telephone cable but also too far away for signal flags. They needed to put fire on the new enemy front between

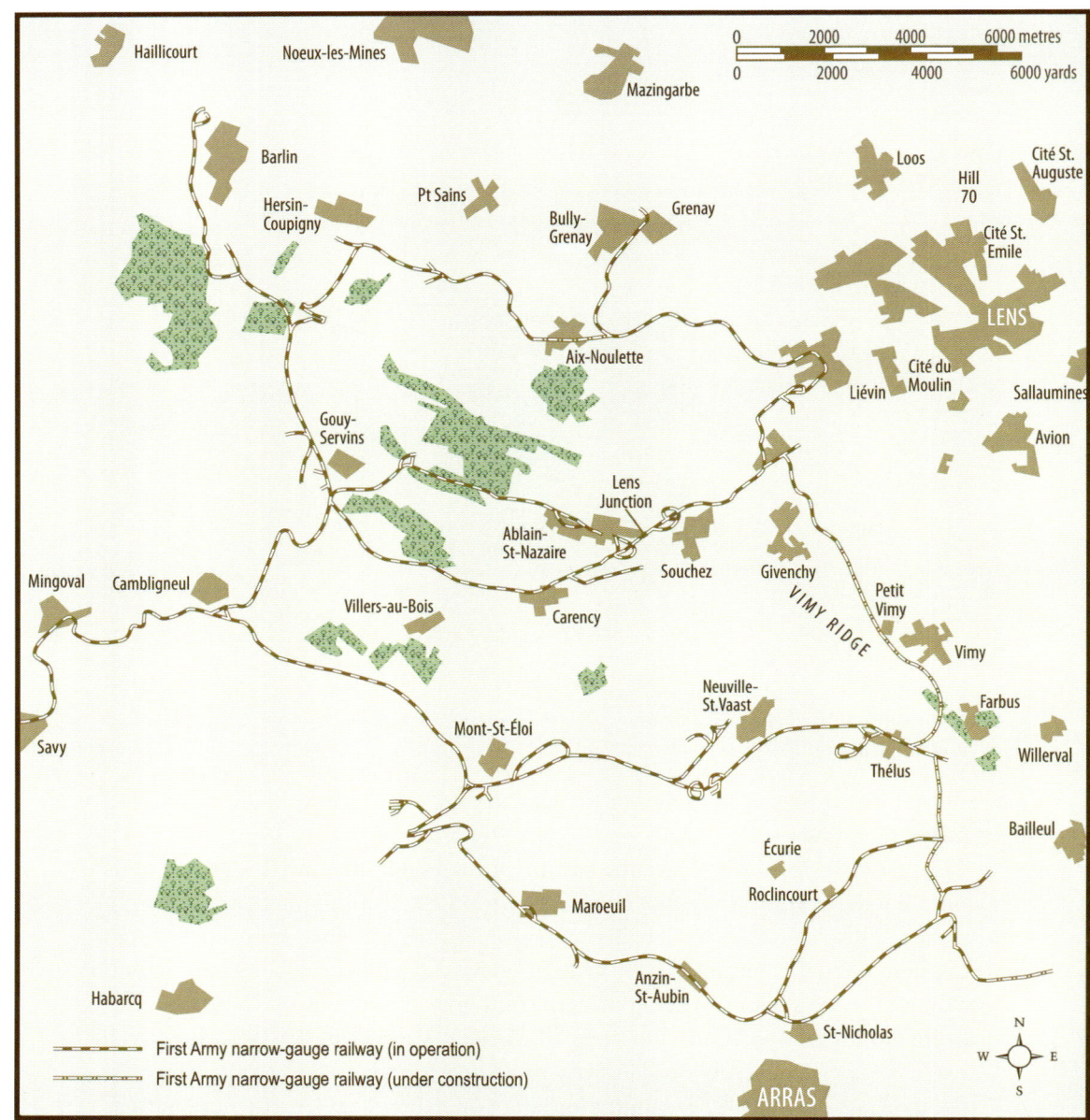

The Arras–Vimy–Lens–Hill 70 Sector

Farbus and Arleux, a low knob out on the Douai plain to the east. Snow and sleet impeded observation, at least for the Canadians. When the snow cleared, the Germans spotted the observer team. Kennedy wrote that they "shelled the hell out of our OP." Farther west, in the centre of the ridge, 4th Battery's Lieutenant John Bruce tried to get an OP set up near La Folie Farm. German shell fragments struck his arm and jaw, sending him back down the friendly side of the ridge. Lieutenant Jack

Fairweather went up after him. The 4th Siege Battery's historian recorded Fairweather's description. "The state of the country we went over was almost beyond description; simply a waste with no distinguishable marks. Shell hole upon shell hole, – some big enough to put a small house in, and most filled with water and mud. A tangled mass of old wire, iron, pit props, equipment, and here and there, the bodies of friend and foe, – a ghastly sight." Fairweather strung line to his new observation post in Bur Trench on the ridge and from there directed fire from 4th Siege Battery's 8-inch howitzers as well as the 6-inch medium howitzers of 72nd South African Siege Battery.

In the week after Vimy fell, the Germans on the Douai plain offered Canadian heavy gunners plenty of targets. Reserve troops marching south to recapture the ridge were smashed by heavy shells before they could assemble. Other Germans were caught in the open by Canadian fire while pulling back guns and equipment to a new line northeast of Vimy, farther away from the Canadian observers firmly in control of Vimy Ridge.

The Canadian Corps remained in control of Vimy Ridge for most of the next eighteen months. Guns moved forward onto or just behind the ridge so that their fire could reach the new German front running from Lens and Avion to Arleux and Oppy and southwards into British Third Army's sector east of Arras. The 1st Canadian Heavy Battery dragged its guns onto the ridge behind La Folie Farm. The mud was impassable to horses, so each 60-pounder was pulled into position by ninety gunners with ropes. The 4th Siege Battery moved their 8-inch howitzers northward into the deep cleft of the Souchez Valley behind the northern end of Vimy Ridge. They had spent only a day there when a German shell aimed at a British observation balloon damaged their No. 4 gun. The broken heavy howitzer shifted when its crew pulled it out of position to move it to a workshop, crushing to death Gunner William Harper when it slid.

The 6th Siege Battery's 8-inch howitzers moved twice in April to new positions near the Arras–Lens road a mile and a half south of Thélus. From there, Major Allen's howitzers could hit the German front-line-fortified village of Arleux and targets identified by Lieutenant MacDonald's observation post above Farbus. As always, forward observation work was the most dangerous task in the battery. The observers had installed themselves in an abandoned bunker that received regular German artillery attention, forcing them to the floor inside. Before the local battle for Arleux began, Gunner Kennedy had observed how the ground east of Vimy Ridge was lush, green, and "very pretty as it had not been shelled yet." That was about to change. The 6th Siege Battery took part in a vicious local artillery duel tied to a limited 1st Canadian Division attack that captured Arleux on 28 April. That day, Lieutenant MacDonald and a detachment of signallers moved forward to set up a new observation post in order to see behind the Arleux rise. A German 5.9-inch shell landed among them. Gunner A.T. White from Campbellton, New

Canadian gunners building a new fortified gun pit in the Souchez Valley within reach of Lens. Moving heavy siege howitzers around the battlefield to mass guns and deceive the enemy required enormous labour. Tramlines helped when they were available. (LAC PA-003808)

Brunswick, was killed outright, and MacDonald died minutes later from loss of blood. Kennedy and Gunner Browning were both badly hit in the legs. The observation post had been destroyed.

More than a few times in April and May, German batteries scored hits on ammunition dumps, despite the best efforts of Lt.-Col. Harrison's men of 2nd Divisional Ammunition Column to disperse, protect, and camouflage them. Bringing ammunition forward remained a perilous business. On the night of 9 May a detachment from Major Gamblin's New Brunswick Section with pack horses and mules bound for 22nd Field Howitzer Battery was struck by a German heavy shell outside Willerval. Gunner Percy Allaby of Saint John, along with Gunners P. Beach, Michael Harpell, and Herbert Robertson, were killed instantly. Three more were wounded. The animals, of course, also suffered. The only unwounded man, Driver Frank Hamm of Saint John, was awarded the Military Medal for his gallantry that night. "By his promptitude in carrying the wounded to a dressing station and caring for the animals, even to the point of bringing his own wounded mule four miles back to the Divisional Ammunition Column camp, he saved what was left of the party."

Gun batteries pushing forward to support local attacks also suffered casualties. On 14 May, Major Allen got word to take 6th Siege Battery into the danger zone at Thélus so as to extend their range enough to support Canadian attacks around Fresnoy. For the next four nights, officers and men dug and camouflaged new positions. After dark on 20 May, their Caterpillar tractors pulled the first two heavy howitzers into Thélus. Just after midnight, Lieutenant David MacLaren's section was dragging No. 89 gun into position when a German heavy shell crashed directly on the gun, smashing it. The blast tore off MacLaren's leg and killed Bombardier Spencer Howard and Gunner T.B. Bryce. Three more gunners, J.F. MacRae, H.O. Winslow, and R.W. Secord, were wounded. So was MacLaren's No. 1, Corporal James Hart. The very able Hart was later commissioned and returned to 6th Siege Battery as a lieutenant.

So the heaviest casualties to New Brunswick gunners occurred in the weeks that followed the capture of Vimy Ridge. Apart from its commanding height, Vimy was important because it lay opposite an important junction between German positions protecting Lens and Lille to the north and the new Hindenburg Line extending southward. The German army, especially its artillery units, spared no effort to reinforce the sector and contain the Canadian penetration. Of course, drawing German strength northward had been one of the intended goals of the Canadian

A 4th Siege Battery 8-inch Mark VI howitzer in a rather exposed position, but shielded by high ground west of Lens, September 1917. Note the thick-planked firing platform for stability and to increase the elevation, the camouflage net for the gunners to conceal themselves from enemy aircraft, and the ammunition tram line. (LAC PA-003822)

operation. The price for this successful diversion was that Vimy Ridge remained a dangerous place during the spring and summer of 1917. Barely a week after the disastrous hit on Lieutenant MacLaren's section, German counter-battery fire on 6th Siege Battery's new very forward position killed Gunner J.A. Wheaton.

At the north end of Vimy Ridge, 4th Siege Battery had also moved farther forward in May. By then they were part of Lt.-Col. Magee's 2nd Canadian Heavy Artillery Group, located directly alongside 1st Canadian Heavy Battery for the counter-battery effort. The 4th Siege Battery's Left and Right Sections deployed about a mile apart in the Souchez Valley, behind the mining hamlet of Cité de Caumont, somewhat shielded by the sharp relief of the northernmost tip of Vimy Ridge. A little farther south, on the Pimple, Lieutenant Barker set up his observation post. The weather improved, and so did the effectiveness of the RFC support. The deployment of the Sopwith Triplanes of No. 10 Squadron, Royal Naval Air Service, commanded by Canadian Raymond Collishaw and piloted largely by Canadians, tipped the balance. On 21 May 1917, good visibility and air observation allowed 4th Siege Battery to put 100 shells on a single German battery. This was the first in a series of

Two 21cm German Mörser 10 heavy howitzers at Vimy Ridge, turned to face their former owners. Their German crews had abandoned them intact, in part due to "neutralizing" by counter-battery fire, which opened in earnest on 9 April. The shell-churned earth around them illustrates the effect of Canadian and British artillery. (LAC PA-001222)

Major Louis Barker held a 4th Siege Battery funeral for four members killed in an artillery duel near Souchez behind Vimy Ridge in May 1917. The 4th Battery members prepared special crosses and flowers like these at the grave of Gunner Leigh Alexander Northrup. (LAC PA-001442)

counter-battery experimental shoots. The 4th Siege Battery's fire invited retaliation, and two days later German guns found the battery's billet in the Souchez Valley. One massive shell killed four men instantly: Gunners Cyrus Gaskin, C.W. Boyd, Vernon McClaskey, and Leigh Northrup, all original members of the unit. It was the single worst day of the war so far for Major Barker's battery. Barker held a formal funeral for them at what is now Caberet-Rouge Commonwealth War Graves Cemetery on the Souchez–Arras road so that the survivors could grieve. The steady artillery duelling continued for the rest of spring as the ground dried, the countryside behind the front blossomed, and the skies cleared.

In June the Canadian Corps, now commanded by General Arthur Currie, received orders to capture Lens as a diversion for the pending Third Ypres offensive. Haig wanted the Canadians to attack into the ruins of the city and into a saddle overlooked by two German-controlled hills, Hill 70 to the north and Salumines to the south. Currie refused to do it, but offered Haig an alternative: capture the hills and then kill Germans in large numbers when they counter-attacked to recapture

Canadian siege batteries levelling coal-mining hamlets and blowing down German defences around Hill 70 and Lens in July 1917. Note the belts of barbed wire and chalk spoil marking trench lines in the foreground. (LAC PA-001430)

them. The Canadian Corps's heavy guns and howitzers were central to Currie's remarkable plan.

The Canadian attack was to coincide with the shift of heavy artillery northward to Ypres during the summer. This would allow a number of British batteries to participate while en route to Ypres. In the meantime a few Canadian and British batteries inched closer to Lens and Hill 70 so that they could strike deep behind the front at enemy gun positions. Among these early arrivals were 1st Canadian Heavy Battery and 4th Siege Battery of Lt.-Col. Magee's 2nd Canadian Heavy Group, which deployed in the hills southwest of Lens. In June, 4th Siege Battery manhandled two guns of their Right Section onto the back side of a steep, shell-torn hill overlooking Cité de Caumont and Lens, using a combination of the engineers' light railway, jacks, ropes, planks, and brute strength. "The guns had to be jacked off the truck, the truck pulled away, and then, the gun jacked down to the ground, plank by plank, turned around, hauled over a bridge, spanning a wide trench, and manhandled up the hill and over a road, hastily made between shell holes." So recorded the battery's war diarist. "[Moving] Eight-Inch howitzers up a hill is almost too much for manpower." Almost, but they managed it. The work put Right Section's guns forward of most field artillery batteries and only a few hundred yards behind the infantry. It also gave them deep reach into German gun positions around Lens. A day after the second gun was dragged into position, King George visited the Canadian front.

According to 4th Siege Battery's history, the king spotted their position on the hill and asked, "Since when have guns had wings?"

Major Inches's 1st Canadian Heavy Battery had sprouted wings too. By now it had also grown to six guns. Inches and his men manhandled their 60-pounders onto the back of Hill 145 at the north end of Vimy Ridge. This safe reverse-crest position was to be their fire base for the coming attack. Getting them there was no easy task, since the slope was too steep for horses. Inches wrote: "Probably no 60-pounder battery has been in a similar position on the Western Front. It was Alpine Warfare with a vengeance." The effort was well worth it. The 1st Canadian Heavy Battery and 4th Siege Battery would remain in their high-country fire positions for the rest of the summer.

Both batteries went to work in June and July trading fire with German guns, making no attempt to conceal their unique – and almost untouchable – positions. On every day clear enough to observe the fall of shot, they opened up on German guns, carefully applying fire in proportion to the degree they could adjust the fire accurately. If no aircraft were available, only twenty rounds might be fired, enough to adjust guns for line and range and send German crews diving for cover. If an airplane or balloon was available, they might fire anywhere from 100 to 200 rounds, testing to see just how many heavy shells it took to destroy an enemy gun position. That summer, Canadian heavy gunners came to realize that almost no

Canadian Artillery FOO and his telephonist taking advantage of the height offered by this shell-scarred two-storey house in the coal-mining hamlets west of Lens.
(LAC PA-003806)

A Canadian 6-inch medium howitzer battery fortified with rubble from a shattered coal-mining hamlet north of Vimy, near Lens. Note the location next to a hard-packed road for ammunition resupply, and the enemy counter-battery fire exploding nearby. (LAC PA-001954)

amount of heavy shelling could completely destroy an enemy gun position that was well dug into the earth and had overhead protection. However, they learned that if the fire accurately fell on the battery position itself, it would at least "neutralize" those German guns by preventing crews from standing beside them. And at times, lucky strikes would damage guns and ammunition. So harassing German gunners, reducing their fire and thereby saving Canadian infantry, was the most important result the heavy guns and howitzers could achieve.

Major Allen's 6th Siege Battery at Farbus had a much rougher summer. In June, while operating with 78th Heavy Group on a counter-battery mission, they moved into former concrete German gun positions on the enemy side of the ridge, facing Arleux and the eastern suburbs of Lens. Before bringing their own guns into action, they turned around several German Mörser 21 cm heavy howitzers, the enemy's equivalent of their own equipment, that lay abandoned in the position. They fired the Mörsers until all the ammunition had been expended, then moved their own howitzers into the concrete gun emplacements. They also lived inside the German bunker complex, on rows of bunk beds dug deep into Vimy Ridge. The Germans knew precisely where they were, and their action invited retaliation, especially large, aircraft-directed shoots. A few hours after a 200-round shoot on 7 July, German guns hammered 6th Siege Battery's concrete positions, wounding Gunner H.A. Grant. As a rule, 6th Siege Battery tended to fire shorter bursts of ten or twenty rounds at a time, prompting a German counter-battery response. They also moved guns to new positions frequently, as soon as it was clear that the

Germans had identified the old ones. Life in 6th Siege Battery's series of exposed but well-concreted former German gun pits was strange. Gunner Green wrote: "The surprising thing is that for all this weight of shelling the Germans did very little real damage," at least physically. Gunner E.C. Moller was killed and R.S. Black was wounded. Major Allen's war diary openly admits that weeks of it broke two of his men. Gunners E.A. Hopper and H.M. Warneford were evacuated on 17 July with shell shock.

In August, more 60-pounder and 8-inch shells arrived through the supply chain and more British reinforcing artillery arrived in readiness for the Hill 70 operation. Canadian heavy batteries, firing at Hill 70 from two directions, concealed their intentions in the first two weeks of August by firing harassing concentrations of one round per gun on visible enemy batteries, command posts, trenches, and road junctions behind the front. This was both to correct guns for line, range, and atmosphere and to generally keep the enemy awake, alert, and pressed. The Canadian Corps Counter-Battery Office, led by now Lt.-Col. A.G.L. McNaughton, had prepared detailed maps identifying all known and suspected enemy gun positions, each with a letter and number code. On 12 August, 4th Siege Battery ramped up the pressure with larger shoots, including 200-round airplane-directed missions. The 1st Canadian Heavy Battery fire roamed the German gun area with thirty- to sixty-round bursts on batteries. Farther south, 6th Siege Battery took it

Signallers of 9th Overseas Siege Battery on Partridge Island, late 1917. Gunner Kenneth Wills (standing, fourth from left) and most of the New Brunswickers pictured here volunteered for an overseas draft that formed 12th Canadian Siege Battery in France in early 1918. (Shirley Wills MacCallum and Kenneth Wills Collection).

on the chin for the rest of them. A German 21 cm Mörser battery plastered them with 450 armour-piercing rounds in an attempt to crack their concrete bunkers. Incredibly, no damage was done to guns, ammunition, or men. The next day, 6th Siege Battery resumed a long series of ten-round bursts of fire with shorter bursts at enemy batteries.

When Zero Day for Hill 70 arrived on 15 August, the New Brunswick heavy and siege guns of Lt.-Col. Magee's 2nd Canadian Heavy Group fired for two hours steadily on German gun positions, with increased weight and tempo. The 6th Siege Battery kept up the pressure from the south with ten-round bursts. The method of delivering accurate, pre-registered bursts in varying sizes worked as hoped. German guns were not destroyed, but their crews were frustrated and largely rendered unable to fire on Zero Day. Some of the Canadian medium and heavy shells contained gas to make life even more difficult for enemy gunners. The Germans gave plenty of gas shells back, so gas alarms and labouring in respirators was part of life for Canadian gunners in the summer of 1917.

Canadian and supporting British heavy guns enabled Canadian infantrymen to capture most of Hill 70 and Salumines, and helped to hold them. While the infantry lined their forward positions with light machine-guns and used their heavy, water-cooled Vickers machine-guns in an indirect role as light artillery, and while the field batteries maintained a shield of fire in front of the forward lines, the Canadian Corps heavy and siege artillery searched German rear areas for targets. The 4th and 6th Siege Batteries' role remained counter-battery work, while 1st Canadian Heavy Battery from its commanding position on Vimy Ridge watched for enemy counterattacks. Lieutenant Slader ranged his "60 pounders on one target of opportunity after another." A German 77 mm field battery galloping up from the reserve area was destroyed with air-bursting shrapnel rounds. "I could see frantic efforts made to scatter." Slader recalled. "Fire was continued. Bursting shells, riderless horses and overturned gun carriages." Later in the day, Slader spotted an enemy infantry battalion marching to the front, with its commanding officer on horseback. He was not the only Canadian observer to see it. As the enemy battalion marched into the mining hamlet of Sallaumines, southeast of Lens, "every gun that could reach the target area opened fire on this confined area with terrible effect." When the smoke lifted, no movement was observed. For several days, more German units arriving to counterattack walked into well-registered kill zones. Early in the morning of 22 August, 4th Battery's command received a call from Lieutenant Hugh Lawson about a fleeting target of enemy infantry in the open. Within minutes, two 200-pound 8-inch howitzer shells with ground burst No. 6 fuses landed among them, to create an effect reported in the war diary as "very disastrous to the enemy."

The Germans tried to retaliate, but the ground was not in their favour. At the end of August they tried once more to evict 6th Siege Battery from their German-built pits at Farbus, firing 600 21 cm armour-piercing rounds on the battery. Shells

A Canadian FOO team sets up shop in an abandoned German gun position overlooking Lens, after the Battle for Hill 70, September 1917. (LAC PA-001895)

fell so densely that one landed directly in No. 1 gun's pit. The round broke the concrete floor, lifted the howitzer into the air, and spun it in the other direction. Another round caught the lip of another concrete pit, breaking off a half-ton piece of masonry and damaging some ammunition. Once again, the concrete saved all of Major Allen's men.

There was time for most in the Canadian Corps to take leave in September, to replace worn equipment, and generally to recover from six solid months of intense activity. The 8-inch Mark VI howitzers of 4th and 6th Siege Batteries, for example, had fired some 6,200 rounds at maximum charge for long range, and their barrels were worn and carriages buckled: so they were replaced with new guns.

The Hill 70 operation demonstrated to the Allies how to destroy the German army while keeping losses to a minimum. Part of that solution involved refinements in counter-battery tactics, which confirmed that accurate information and precision firing of a limited number of shells per day could render enemy guns largely ineffective. This also enabled the infantry to capture ground and kill the enemy when they counterattacked. The war-winning combined arms system was coming into its own.

A Canadian 6-inch 26cwt medium howitzer with traction pads during the Battle for Hill 70. By then, 9th Overseas Siege Battery at Partridge Island had provided drafts to form new Canadian 6-inch batteries. It sent several more that winter to crew these versatile, powerful, and highly mobile howitzers. (LAC PA-003716)

But to do this properly the Canadian Corps needed more heavy and siege batteries, and those batteries needed to be under corps command as well as more nimble. This was well on the way to being accomplished, but not all gunners were yet part of the solution. When in August 1917 word arrived in Saint John from headquarters in Ottawa that additional drafts were needed to establish two additional siege batteries overseas, Major Percy W. Wetmore made a personal appeal through the chain of command pointing out that 3rd New Brunswick Regiment already had men – especially well-trained officers – ready to go, including himself:

> I beg to point out that Number 9 Siege Battery was raised in June 1916 and has already sent overseas three Lieutenants and 150 other ranks and it is sincerely hope[d] that now that the personnel of two Batteries is required that the Officers who have worked so long and faithfully in Canada recruiting and training the men may be given an opportunity to do their bit at the Front. In view of the recent call for Officers who have had Siege courses to volunteer for service in the Imperial Forces it is not understood why there is not a chance for us to do some good in the fighting line, as there is evidently a scarcity of siege Artillery officers.
>
> Personally I have been on Active Service since March 1915 and have recruited during that time No. 4 and No. 7 [6th] Siege Batteries who have gone to the front as

well as sending the full strength of a Siege Battery from No. 9 with the exception of the Officers. Until March 1916 I was A[cting]/Ad[j]utant of the 3rd Regiment Canadian Garrison Artillery which is on active service and upon the commanding officer being seconded to Headquarters M.D. 6, I was left in command of that Regiment, through which all Siege Batteries from New Brunswick have been raised and I have not been permitted to go overseas while I have seen nearly all Officers of the above mentioned Batteries overseas who are junior to myself, and I sincerely hope that after having sent the drafts forward that I would be permitted to recruit to strength and have the honour to take No. 9 over myself.

Lt.-Col. Armstrong, by then overseas on a six-week tour of duty, was pursuing the issue of front-line employment of trained siege artillery officers from the Maritime provinces. Armstrong had extraordinary access. He met artillery staff at the British War Office, and in the Canadian Ministry of Overseas Military Forces in London. He visited Canadian heavy artillery at the front in France, and talked with General Arthur Currie, who encouraged him in his campaign to raise additional Canadian siege units. Armstrong also went outside the chain of command with his reports, sending them to F.B. McCurdy, the parliamentary secretary of the Department of Militia and Defence. This speaks to Armstrong's stature, but also to the continuing importance of politicians in decisions about who got to serve at the front.

Lt.-Col. Armstrong's main difficulty was the legacy of the former Minister of Militia and Defence, Sir Sam Hughes, who had been fired in November 1916. Hughes had politicized the army by authorizing patriotic civic leaders to recruit complete units, with full slates of officers, promising that they would see front-line service. Most of these units had been broken up in England to reinforce units at the front. By 1917 there were thousands of unemployed and unqualified officers in England. Currie and the Canadian Corps wanted little to do with them. Meanwhile, the Canadian staff in London were making appointments to siege units from their large surplus of field artillery officers (after the reorganization from four- to six-gun batteries) and endeavouring to train them in the science of modern gunnery. As Armstrong wrote to McCurdy in September:

> This lack of appreciation of Siege Artillery conditions is also accentuated by the fact that Senior Artillery Officers are largely Officers belonging to the Field portion of the Artillery Branch. The reason for this is that the Field Artillery are much the more numerous. It is a well-known fact that Field Artillery Officers, who naturally consider there is nothing like their own particular kind of Artillery, are inclined to give a small amount of attention to Siege Artillery even though the latter sub-division has developed to an enormous extent in this War.
>
> [T]he training of Field Artillery Officers does not fit them for Siege artillery. In the training of Field artillery Officers in Canada no attention whatever is paid to the working out of the Battery commander's initial correction, nor to the working of the slide rule, and very little, if any, attention to these points in training of Canadian Field Artillery Officers in England. These two matters are very essential for Siege Artillery

work … In brief, a Siege Artillery Officer must be mathematically inclined, and have a good mathematical [education?] – Civil Engineers being the best class form which appointment to Siege Artillery can be made.

The result of Lt.-Col. Armstrong's efforts was disappointing: a few billets for junior officers of 3rd NB Regiment in combat units, including in the British Army. By the fall of 1917, Canadian heavy and siege artillery had enough officers for the two heavy and nine siege batteries then in action. This may be because the final reorganization of heavy and siege artillery had generated a small surplus of skilled heavy gunners. In the fall of 1917 the nine siege batteries at the front were each expanded from four to six guns (the two heavy batteries had done this earlier). The first incarnations of 10th and 11th Batteries, created in the spring of 1917 with drafts from Canada (all of which had been trained at either Partridge Island or Halifax), and still waiting in England, were broken up to form the new sections of the batteries at the front.

The expansion of heavy and siege batteries to six guns in the fall of 1917 proved to be just one more step in the final creation of a Canadian Corps heavy artillery. For the moment there were two Canadian Heavy Artillery Groups. But not all the guns in them were Canadian, and not all Canadian batteries were in the Canadian Heavy Artillery Groups. Moreover, plans were still in place to create a 3rd Canadian Heavy Artillery Group. In all of this, perhaps because of Lt.-Col. Armstrong's persistent lobbying, New Brunswick gunners retained a critical role, with a steady 30 to 35 percent of the men in Canadian heavy and siege artillery coming from that province and with an increasingly critical role for New Brunswick officers. The 3rd New Brunswick Regiment may not have been in the field, but by 1918 it was exerting a powerful influence at the front. Gunner Kenneth Wills was part of it. Born in Saint John, Wills had studied civil engineering at the University of New Brunswick for over two years before dropping out to join 9th Battery on Partridge Island a week after the capture of Vimy Ridge. A number of his UNB classmates and dozens of others from around the province joined him, perhaps in response to extensive press coverage about Vimy. Wills first learned basic soldiering and then advanced to heavy gunnery, practising on the island's venerable 4.7s. By the end of 1917, he and 153 others had formed a third draft of 9th Battery volunteers bound for the Canadian Siege Artillery Depot at Whitley Camp in England. Major Wetmore's 9th "Overseas" Battery never deployed together as he had pleaded, but it continued to function as a Depot Battery, feeding a large pool of trained heavy gunners to the expanding Canadian siege artillery in Europe.

Before the Canadian Corps's heavy artillery achieved its final form, several key battles remained to be fought. The most gruelling of these was Third Ypres, popularly known as Passchendaele. It was authorized as a series of limited attacks to relieve pressure on the French, whose army had descended into mutiny after the Nivelle Offensive proved a disaster in the spring, and as a possible strike for

Belgium's channel ports to disrupt U-boat bases. By the late summer, Third Ypres had become yet another seemingly endless battle of attrition, fought under increasingly appalling conditions. By September and early October, the BEF – led by the ANZACs – had launched a series of bite-and-hold assaults, clawing its way towards the well-drained high ground of Passchendaele Ridge. The Canadians' turn came in October.

The first Canadians to arrive in the Ypres Salient, in the fall of 1917, were 6th Siege Battery, who arrived without guns. The autumn mud and the long distance made it not worth moving their brand-new weapons – besides, they expected to return soon to the Vimy sector. What was needed around Ypres were fresh gunners to replace exhausted ones. Major Barker's experienced 4th Siege Battery stayed on guard in the Vimy sector, well positioned on its hillside opposite Lens. There they took a lead role within British 42nd Heavy Group, which had taken over the sector from Lt.-Col. Magee's 2nd Canadian Heavy Group. In late October, Magee's Group Headquarters along with 1st and 2nd Canadian Heavy Batteries relieved Australian and New Zealand gunners around the old 1915 front line near Mount Sorrel.

The Canadians found the guns at Ypres as worn as the men who had operated them. When Major Allen's men took over a British 8-inch Mark VI battery, only one gun was operational. All six were sitting on the new Vickers firing platform developed to stabilize the gun in muddy conditions, but five of the six platforms had been pounded crooked, making the guns virtually useless. Much work was needed to get the guns ready and to get new telephone lines laid to the front. The same was true for Major Inches and 1st Canadian Heavy Battery. When they took over from a British 60-pounder battery in a bog behind Frezenberg Ridge only three of its six guns were in place; the other three were parked in their wagon lines. Inches secured a heavy gun transporter tank – which was designed specifically to carry 60-pounders forward across shell-scarred ground – to move the other three guns to their patch of good ground at the foot of Frezenberg Ridge. One gun was delivered before the transporter was knocked out. Inches found a spot of ground big enough for two guns alongside the light railway that brought ammunition to the position, and the last two guns were sited there. "It was impossible to do justice to the description of this position," he wrote later. The 6th Siege Battery's Gunner Green wrote that "the country had to be seen to be believed." The torn-up earth combined with a ruined drainage system had produced vast, impassible lakes filled with water "variously coloured green, red, or just muddy. Above the surface could be seen odd bits of equipment, dead mules, occasionally dead soldiers and such grisly displays as a separated foot with part of a puttee spiraling off of it."

Both 1st Canadian Heavy Battery and 6th Siege Battery were in position to support the Canadian Corps second-phase attack on Passchendaele Ridge on 30 October 1917. Canadian heavy gunners possessed none of the advantages they had at Vimy – no concealment, no good road and rail service, and no clear oversight of

A Canadian 6-inch medium howitzer on its way to the front by tramline towards Passchendaele, November 1917. The 6th Canadian Siege Battery fired its last 8-inch heavy shells there before converting to this mobile howitzer for following month. (LAC PA-003670)

the battle. In fact, as the attack drove for the high ground around Passchendaele the Canadians pushed deeper into a narrowing salient, exposed to German artillery fire from three directions. Moreover, the muddy salient had too few passible roads or light railways to feed shells forward in order to win the counter-battery fight. To top it off, the Germans were using Gotha bombers to strike at British and Dominion batteries from the air. Perhaps that is why New Brunswick artillery veterans of Passchendaele wrote so bitterly about the experience. They certainly tried their best. The 6th Siege Battery fired on German batteries and strongpoints without benefit of ground or air observation. The 1st Canadian Heavy Battery's position farther east was little better, but with the latest-generation 60-pounder shell they could reach German gun positions around Moorslede, the next major town east of Passchendaele.

With the Germans arrayed on three sides of the Ypres Salient, the struggle for Passchendaele Ridge become a gunner's duel. For the first three days of November, 6th Siege Battery's position was pounded mercilessly with shrapnel and gas shells. The battery cookhouse was blown up, three gunners were wounded by shell fragments, and thirteen were gassed. During the last Canadian attack to secure the crest of Passchendaele Ridge and the town on 6 November, German shells killed

Gunners William Goldsworth, G.T. Tambling, and Stanley Wainwright. Wainwright was from Cambridge, Massachusetts, and had dropped out of Harvard to join 6th Siege Battery. More than a dozen were wounded, including Gunner W.J. O'Neill, who died the next day. After the town was captured, the battery set up its observation post in a former German bunker beside the ruins of the church and not far from 26th NB Battalion's sector. The bunker became a refuge for anyone trying to survive the storm of German fire, and it quickly filled up with about forty-odd infantrymen. The roof cracked under the weight of shot until finally an armour-piercing shell demolished it, killing most of the men inside. A 6th Siege Battery signaller, Gunner J.H. Lawson, simply disappeared in the explosion; his name is carved on Ypres's Menin Gate. Miraculously, 6th Siege Battery's FOO and another signaller escaped. Elsewhere, Gunners Allen Wetmore, Walter MacAdam, Alfred Plummer, E.H. Landry, and W.J. Alexander, from Barker's 4th Siege Battery, were also killed that day. They were all together on a gun with Lieutenant Roy Ring, serving on loan with 8th Siege Battery to help fill positions after that unit had taken a direct hit near Hill 70.

Passchendaele was the deadliest battle of the war for British and Canadian gunners. In the first three days the 2nd Divisional Ammunition Column lost three men killed and twenty-one wounded, along with sixty-one animals killed and fifty more wounded. By the time they were relieved, they had lost 123 men – their worst losses of the war in any sector. The same went for 6th Siege Battery. Passchendaele left deep scars. Lieutenant Slader wrote afterwards that "the Passchendaele battles were hell without respite and should never have been launched in such unsuitable terrain … and it was nonsense that the enemy suffered more than we did." In December, New Brunswick's gunners packed their gear and went "home" to the Vimy sector.

While New Brunswick gunners in France and Belgium fought the German army in 1917, 3rd New Brunswick Regiment of the Canadian Garrison Artillery at home in Saint John prepared to fight the German navy. The threat of submarine attack in 1917 was real, and it grew as the war went on. As a result, the regiment kept the Composite Battery on Partridge Island close to its full establishment of five officers and ninety-five other ranks during the last half of the year, and it never stopped recruiting. By the end of 1917 the two 4.7-inch guns on coast defence mountings at the north end of the island were ready for service, bringing personnel strength to eight officers and 179 other ranks. This was a substantial increase, because the new anti-submarine guns were manned night and day, while the two naval searchlights installed near the battery needed crews at night, too. In contrast, the four mobile 4.7-inch howitzers on the south end were crewed only by day, and they continued to train 9th Overseas Battery drafts of men for overseas.

Conscription had been introduced in the summer of 1917, and recruiting offices had been closed; even so, 3rd New Brunswick Regiment actively recruited throughout the province. The regiment specifically targeted recruits below the minimum age for overseas service (or, now, for the draft), and presented Partridge Island as a wholesome place for personal development. When a worried mother asked about her seventeen-year-old son, the recruiting officer was reassuring: "You need not be uneasy about him. The quarters are very comfortable, and the food first class. Regular hours and discipline are good for a lad of his age, and I think you will find he will be benefited by his time here." The arrival of more than seventy recruits between January and March 1918 (and smaller numbers thereafter) allowed older men to transfer to 9th Overseas Siege Depot Battery, and then on to the Canadian Siege Artillery Depot in England in preparation for active service overseas. The need to keep the Composite Battery on Partridge Island up to strength did not abate until the war ended, but – as events in 1918 would reveal – recruiting was not the primary reason.

Chapter 5

The Guns of Victory, 1918

In November 1917 the BEF fought a new kind of battle at Cambrai, one that would set the standard for the final year of the war. It consisted of a massive assault by combined arms teams – tanks and infantry – along a five-mile front. It had been organized in complete secrecy. Special care had been taken to hide all the battle preparations. There was no preliminary bombardment, no massive ammunition dumping program, no construction of new rail lines and roads to support the movement of heavy guns and shells, no pre-registration of targets that would reveal British intent. Tanks and guns were moved at night, the sounds of engines masked by overflights of aircraft. Artillery positions were surveyed in, guns arrived and were completely hidden. German gun positions were mapped using sound location and registered "silently." It was the first time that the BEF had strived for both operational and tactical surprise, and it worked.

When the attack commenced on 20 November it was preceded by a thirty-minute "hurricane" bombardment based on "predicted" shooting, making extensive use of the No. 106 fuse so as not to crater the ground. This was followed by an attack of 437 tanks, supported by infantry trained to fight and move alongside them. The attack was a stunning success, smashing through the German front lines and penetrating to a depth of three miles. More was accomplished in a day than the BEF had been able to achieve in weeks of brutal fighting at Passchendaele. But the British were unprepared for such success – there were no reserves to exploit the victory, and the tanks quickly broke down. Then the Germans counterattacked, launching their own hurricane bombardments and employing elite assault units that had been specially equipped and trained in fire and movement. Within two weeks the British had been driven back to their start line of 20 November. But the pattern had been set for 1918: a new kind of battle had come to the Western Front.

Cambrai had been a portent, and over the winter of 1917–18 everyone on the Western Front prepared for the much-anticipated German spring offensive. The strategic situation made it a certainty that it was coming. A second revolution in Russia in October had overthrown the Socialist government and replaced it with a Communist one, which immediately sued for peace. By December 1917, Russia was out of the war and Germany was free to shift enormous forces westward. By the end of the year it was not a question of *if* the Germans would attack, but when. The winter of 1917–1918 therefore became a period of reorganization, re-equipping, and training, and that effort included the Canadian Corps Heavy Artillery.

That winter, 6th Siege Battery was officially assigned to Lt.-Col. Magee's formation, now renamed 2nd Brigade, Canadian Garrison Artillery. Magee now commanded all of the clearly New Brunswick heavy and siege batteries, including 1st Canadian Heavy Battery and 4th and 6th Siege Batteries. The brigade was rounded out with the joint Prince Edward Island–New Brunswick 2nd Canadian Heavy Battery, Prince Edward Island's 2nd Siege Battery, and Vancouver's 5th Siege Battery. Canada's port-town siege batteries shared a great many officers around 2nd

The 6th Siege Battery gunners at an advance canteen taking a moment off the gun line for "a spot of beer." (NBM Humphrey-F5-64)

Garrison Brigade, and New Brunswickers were prominent in every battery. Captain "Big" Doug White had long served with Prince Edward Island's 2nd Siege Battery, and by 1918, Norm MacLeod had risen to take command of the 9.2-inch superheavy howitzers of Vancouver's 5th Siege Battery. One of MacLeod's section commanders was another New Brunswicker, Lieutenant Eber H. Turnbull. All in all, the New Brunswick heavy artillery mafia held sway in Magee's 2nd Garrison Brigade. New Brunswickers also maintained a strong presence in what was now 1st Brigade, Canadian Garrison Artillery. By early 1918, all that remained to be established was 3rd Brigade, Canadian Garrison Brigade, and that would come in the summer.

In January and February, all Canadian field and garrison artillery units enjoyed a period of rest and adjustment to the new circumstances. Everyone expected the front to rupture in 1918, resulting in a more open and fluid kind of combat. So even the gunners got back to basics: foot drill, small-arms training, gun drill, physical training, and route marches. Refresher courses on rifles and Lewis light machineguns were given by a detachment of Princess Patricia's Canadian Light Infantry, as the whole BEF adapted to open warfare. In this new environment, heavy and siege artillery needed to turn their battery positions into fortresses capable of all-round defence; this would entail the use of barbed wire and trenches to fight off infantry. Canadian gunners also built fall-back fortified gun positions well behind the front.

This training would be equally applicable when the tide turned against Germany. Allied planners anticipated that at a certain point in 1918, German strength would ebb and American units would enter the line, reversing the anticipated open warfare eastwards towards Germany. In fluid conditions, gunners would again need to use small arms to protect convoys and battery positions as they leapfrogged forward. Perhaps the most important value of rifle and Lewis machine-gun training was for anti-aircraft defence. German air forces had been the bane of British and Canadian gunners for years, and never more so than in 1917, when their new Gotha bombers attacked gun positions behind the front regularly. In 1917, experiments proved that if half the battery stood to the guns and the other half manned two Lewis guns and fifty rifles, they could put enough fire into the air to drive off or even bring down marauding planes. Divisional ammunition columns trained on small arms for the same reasons.

The winter training period allowed 2nd Garrison Brigade's batteries to get comfortable with the six-gun organization, and for 6th Siege Battery to convert from 8-inch heavy howitzers to new 6-inch 26cwt medium howitzers. This change was part of a broader plan to ensure that each new garrison artillery brigade had guns suitable for every task: mobile 60-pounders and 6-inch medium howitzers for long-range heavy fire in mobile battles, in addition to the less mobile heavy and super-heavy howitzer batteries for whenever the enemy chose to stand and fight from fixed positions. The 4th Siege Battery thus cannibalized the best of 6th Siege Battery's old 8-inch heavies to become, along with Major MacLeod's 9.2s in 5th

A well-protected 6th Canadian Siege Battery emplacement at Vimy Ridge, after they were re-equipped with new 6-inch medium howitzers. These are firing wire-cutting missions against the Hindenburg Line, February 1918. (LAC PA-002492)

Siege Battery, 2nd Garrison Brigade's heavy hitters. The 8-inch batteries were the optimum of the two heavy types, for their Holt Caterpillar tractors enabled them to follow an advance fully assembled and go into action far more quickly than the cumbersome super-heavies.

In March, 2nd Garrison Brigade was back on station at the foot of Vimy Ridge. The 1st Canadian Heavy Battery deployed three 60-pounders in Petit Vimy facing northeast into Lens and three more on the western outskirts of Lens near Liéven. The 4th Battery's 8-inch howitzers went into pits at Angres not far from their 1917 positions and just behind Major Inches's northern section. Major Allen's 6th Siege Battery, having converted to the new 6-inch howitzer, went through a winter training period in England. They finally deployed four of their new guns in the village of Vimy itself and the remaining section in a silent position at Angres close to the other New Brunswick heavy guns. In late February, Captain Cyrus MacMillan, former second-in-command of 7th "McGill University" Siege Battery and a McGill faculty member who had joined with his students, took command of 6th Siege Battery. All batteries settled back into a counter-battery duelling routine and prepared to meet the German attack. Then, as Lieutenant Slader remembered, on 21 March, "it came."

The German spring offensive, Operation Michael, struck British Fifth Army in the Somme area in an attempt to split the British and French armies. It began with a hurricane of explosions and gas across a vast front, deep into the British positions. British Fifth Army and the twenty miles of front it held disappeared within hours. The rupture was complete, and German reserves poured through the breech. On 25 March the Germans spread the attack northwards, striking at the right flank of British Third Army east of Arras. When the attack along the Somme faltered in early April, the Germans switched north to the Ypres Salient. The British position there collapsed as well. All that had been won in four years of fighting had been swept away as German troops surged to the gates of Ypres itself, lapping around the bastion of Mount Kemmel before stopping. Desperate fighting and the final dispatch of Britain's home reserves saved the day.

While all of this was unfolding, Lieutenant Slader was promoted to captain and posted to 4th Siege Battery as Major Barker's second-in-command. "I will never forget the anxious time looking out from the O.P. on Vimy Ridge," he recalled after the war, "and seeing the encircling Verey lights in the south creeping farther and farther back on our right and rear and on our left, the same thing going on. I wondered what our fate might be if the two lines met." He was not alone. For the first time in the war, Lt.-Col. Harrison's ammunition column gunners and drivers were hauling ammunition west, evacuating forward dumps under shellfire. Through it all, the Canadian Corps held steadfast behind their Vimy bastion, playing baseball beside gun pits and tending vast vegetable gardens to help feed the British Expeditionary Force. In the end, their strength was not tested. The Germans thought better than to try the steep eastern slopes of Vimy.

But they were also not willing to give the Canadians a complete free pass. German long-range guns and heavy howitzers duelled with Canadian heavy batteries in the Vimy sector and shelled front-line trenches, as if they knew the Canadians were coiling in readiness to strike. When Captain Slader went on an inspection visit of 4th Siege Battery's gun positions at dawn on 27 May, the morning light revealed a new German observer balloon overlooking the Souchez Valley. Slader called out for all hands to take cover just minutes before the first 5.9-inch German shell landed on their position. Slader rushed into the Battery Command Post and directed a counter-battery shoot from 1st Canadian Heavy Battery's 60-pounders. The enemy battery stopped, but when darkness returned the enemy medium battery began pounding them heavily. Slader was blown out of his cot that night. Gunner Harold Craig and Corporal George Gamble, both old Saint John originals, were mortally wounded. Slader went to see Gamble at a nearby dressing station before he died. The two were old schoolmates and had served together in 3rd New Brunswick Regiment before the war. Heavy German counter-battery fire also found 6th Siege Battery's positions farther south that same day, killing Sergeant Graham Duff. The

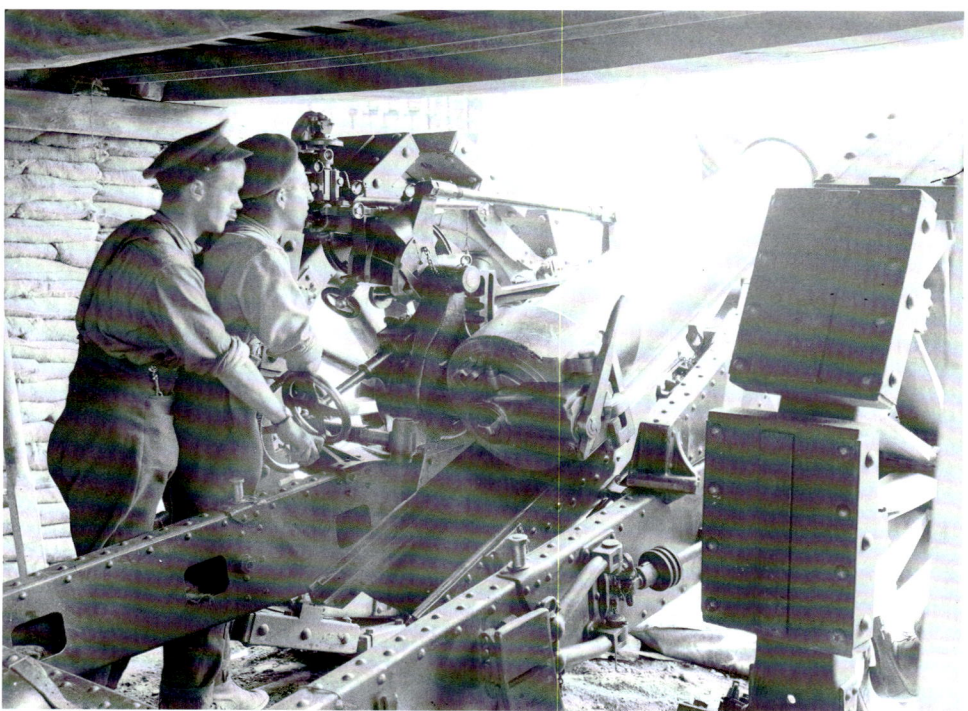

A brand-new Canadian 6-inch medium howitzer being laid on target inside a strongly fortified emplacement near Vimy Ridge. Note the new paint and clean traction pads. By June 1918, 10th, 11th and 12th Siege Batteries had arrived in the Vimy Sector, where they joined 8th Battery to form the New Brunswick-affiliated 3rd Brigade, completing the Canadian Garrison Artillery expansion. (LAC PA-002194)

next day, 6th Siege Battery traded guns and positions with 2nd Siege Battery, bringing them alongside 4th Siege Battery facing Liéven. The wind, the terrain, and the north–south alignment of the front there encouraged German heavy gunners to use plenty of gas, and it soon saturated 6th Siege Battery's area. Three gunners did not find shelter or their respirators in time. One of them, C.L. McCutcheon, took five painful months to die in hospital in England.

In May the weight of German attacks shifted south, in three successive smaller offensives against the French. The French line buckled, too, but it did not break, and the Germans finally exhausted their supplies and manpower. In the late spring and summer the Canadian Corps along with the rest of the Allies prepared to open the offensive that would ultimately end the war.

While New Brunswick gunners in France waited anxiously to strike back, their colleagues at home waited for the Germans to attack. Decryptions of German radio signals by British naval intelligence had revealed that the Germans were converting several large freight-carrying submarines into long-range fighting vessels, and building new classes of submarines for distant operations. About the time Ned

Slader was diving for cover in the Souchez Valley in May 1918, the big submarines began to sink ships and lay mines along the US coast. The volume of food and munitions shipped through Saint John skyrocketed in 1918 because of new demands on US ports. Saint John was Canada's major east coast winter commercial port; furthermore, it had much better rail connections to the west than Halifax. Taking charge of the port's defences, the Navy and Militia Headquarters created a Committee of Public Safety at Saint John, responsible to the Minister of Militia and Defence. It oversaw security personnel at the docks and other transportation facilities, watched for enemy saboteurs (a perennial fear throughout the war), and ensured the safe handling of munitions, including the movement of rail traffic through the city.

The new Militia District No. 7 Headquarters at Saint John took a further step in April 1918 by drafting a defence scheme for the city in which 3rd New Brunswick Regiment would play a key role. That scheme laid out the measures to be taken by military and civil authorities, including police and hospitals, in the event of an attack on the port. For in addition to the submarine threat, there was now an increased danger that new enemy oil-fired cruisers might break out from the North Sea and make a fast run on the short Great Circle route to Canadian ports. Both surface warships and submarines, which carried powerful deck guns, were capable of bombarding port facilities, while subs might torpedo ships in harbour or land agents or parties of saboteurs. American, Canadian, and British naval forces operating from Halifax, or from the new American base at Shelburne, Nova Scotia, would be crucial in dealing with seaborne attacks. The guns on Partridge Island were critically important to the defence of Canada's overseas trade and its war effort. New Brunswick's gunners were now fighting on two fronts.

The first alarm came on 27 June when the navy reported a submarine off Digby, Nova Scotia, and Saint John's defences were mobilized. Infantry guarding the West Saint John docks deployed four machine-guns, and 9th Siege Battery dispatched thirty men to Partridge Island to reinforce the Composite Battery, while engineers manned the searchlights. The mayor turned off all street lights, and sixty infantrymen helped the police keep order during the blackout. It was a false alarm – there was no U-boat in the Bay of Fundy … yet. The only excitement that night was flickering lights from the Acadia sugar refinery, which appeared to be an attempt to send signals. Investigation revealed torchlights carried by the refinery employees engaged in their regular duties. At 0515 on 28 June the street lights came back on and the troops returned to barracks.

The second alarm was genuine. On 3 August, news arrived that the day before, *U-156*, one of the large submarines, had stopped, searched, and burned the four-masted sailing ship *Dornfontein* off Gannet Rock near Grand Manan Island. *Dornfontein* had been built in Saint John over the previous winter, and the city had watched her departure on her maiden voyage just days earlier. When news of the attack arrived, Saint John again went to full readiness, while American and Canadian anti-submarine vessels rushed to the Bay of Fundy. In the event, *U-156* crossed to southwestern Nova Scotia and continued on to the Halifax approaches. It finished its Canadian sojourn with a rampage through the fishing fleet off Cape Breton. A second submarine, *U-117*, hunted seaward of Nova Scotia and Newfoundland at the end of August and beginning of September, and a third, *U-155*, lingered off Halifax in September. *Dornfontein*'s crew survived to tell their tale of capture by German pirates. The ship itself burned to the water line, but was later salvaged. Not surprisingly, naval vessels appeared more frequently at Saint John during the last months of the war to escort merchant ships to their assembly points, reflecting a new system of trans-Atlantic convoys under anti-submarine escort.

The sinking of the *Dornfontein* was as close as the war ever came to Saint John, but no one could know that at the time. At the end of August 1918, Ottawa authorized further improvements on Partridge Island, including new concrete gun positions on the high ground on the southwestern part of the island to give the guns better all-around coverage. The two travelling guns on the improvised pivots on the

Charles Ballantyne, Canadian Minister of the Naval Service, watches an 8-inch heavy howitzer in full recoil, firing from a well-prepared gun pit in the Vimy sector, July 1918. Although more difficult to move than the 6-inch, the 8-inch batteries with their Holt tractors remained the most mobile of the Canadian heavy guns, earning them a place in the coming war of movement. (LAC PA-002809)

southeastern coast of the island, whose arc of fire was now covered by the north-end battery completed in 1917, were to shift to new positions, too, although the concrete work was not completed before the war ended.

While the garrison on Partridge Island prepared for U-boat attacks, it continued to train and push gunners overseas. Their last major contribution was to the establishment of 3rd Brigade, Canadian Garrison Artillery, the final part of the Canadian Corps Heavy Artillery plan. Its new batteries included gunners from all over Canada, including 8th Siege Battery (now commanded by 4th Siege Battery's Captain Ring) and the newly formed 10th, 11th, and 12th Siege Batteries. The 10th and 12th, in particular, contained a number of New Brunswick officers and men from the last Partridge Island drafts, and all three new siege batteries were assigned experienced officers and non-commissioned officers from seasoned batteries. Saint John's Doug White was promoted to Major to take command of 10th Siege Battery. Another prominent Saint John gunner, Major Colin MacKay, took command of the new 12th Siege Battery. Gunner Kenneth Wills and dozens of other volunteers from 9th Overseas Battery in Saint John trained through the spring of 1918 on 6-inch howitzers before receiving their own brand-new guns to fill out White's and Mackay's batteries. But perhaps the greatest contribution from New Brunswick was the new Brigade Headquarters. It was formed on Partridge Island (under Lt.-Col. William Beeman) from the one of the last large drafts dispatched overseas from New Brunswick. The new, aptly named 3rd Brigade arrived in the field around Vimy Ridge in June 1918 to begin practising their craft.

By high summer of 1918 the heavy artillery of the Canadian Corps was complete. Roughly one-third of its personnel were New Brunswickers, and about another third were Maritimers. The corps itself still relied heavily on British heavy and siege artillery in its major operations, but the flexibility and innovation of the corps's own garrison brigades paved the way for its ultimate success in the final push of the war. The vast majority of those gunners, perhaps 60 percent of them, had been trained and sent overseas by 3rd New Brunswick Regiment's establishment on Partridge Island. In many ways, the rocky little island at the entrance to Saint John harbour was the home of Canada's heavy artillery.

When summer arrived and the German offensive waned, most of the Canadian Corps pulled out of Vimy and travelled south to Amiens, where the German March offensive had penetrated deepest. The Germans there were well beyond their Hindenburg Line fortifications and were vulnerable because of their overextended supply lines. Only 2nd Garrison Brigade, which contained New Brunswick's veteran batteries, was left behind. The commander of the British Corps relieving the Canadians at Vimy wanted at least one garrison brigade with intimate knowledge of the ground and the enemy's guns to stay there to help. Lt.-Col. Magee's gunners were the logical choice.

Canadian heavy battery gunners manhandling their 60-pounder gun into a firing position barely 1,000 yards from the enemy near Amiens, August 1918. Note the comparatively scar-free battlefield with grass and intact trees. (LAC PA-040174)

Meanwhile, the rest of the Canadian Corps artillery, including 2nd Divisional Ammunition Column and the new 3rd Garrison Brigade, moved to Amiens. They joined in the great British, French, Canadian, and Australian attack of 8 August 1918, which marked the start of the Allies' Hundred Days offensive. There was little preparatory bombardment, and the landscape was little marked by war. The attack opened with a hurricane bombardment to carry assaulting infantry and tanks through the Germans' front and into their field gun line. The 3rd Garrison Brigade's batteries, in their first offensive action, had taken up position and piled ammunition only two days before Zero Day. Even then, not all of the ammunition available was fired on 8 August. At day's end, Captain Gamblin's 1st New Brunswick Section of 2nd Divisional Ammunition Column collected unused shells and ferried them forward to the next fire base as the Canadian Corps pressed their attack.

The plan worked. The Amiens front was ruptured, and Canadian and Australian troops drove deep over verdant countryside. General Erich Ludendorff, Quartermaster General (and de facto commander) of the Imperial German Army, famously described it as "the Black Day of the German Army." More than 400 enemy guns were captured or destroyed on that first day, the first of a series of rolling hammer blows against the Germans. Lt.-Col. Harrison's drivers and gunners strained to keep the attack fed with ammunition as the enemy reacted violently. German air raids against Canadian supply columns and dumps were some of the most intense since Passchendaele. Within days, German reinforcements and Allied exhaustion had slowed the advance. The 2nd Divisional Ammunition Column felt the shift, as German long-range guns searched out their dumps and wagon lines. On 17 August, as 1st and 2nd Sections were getting ready to move out of Caix, a

The Guns of Victory, 1918 | 145

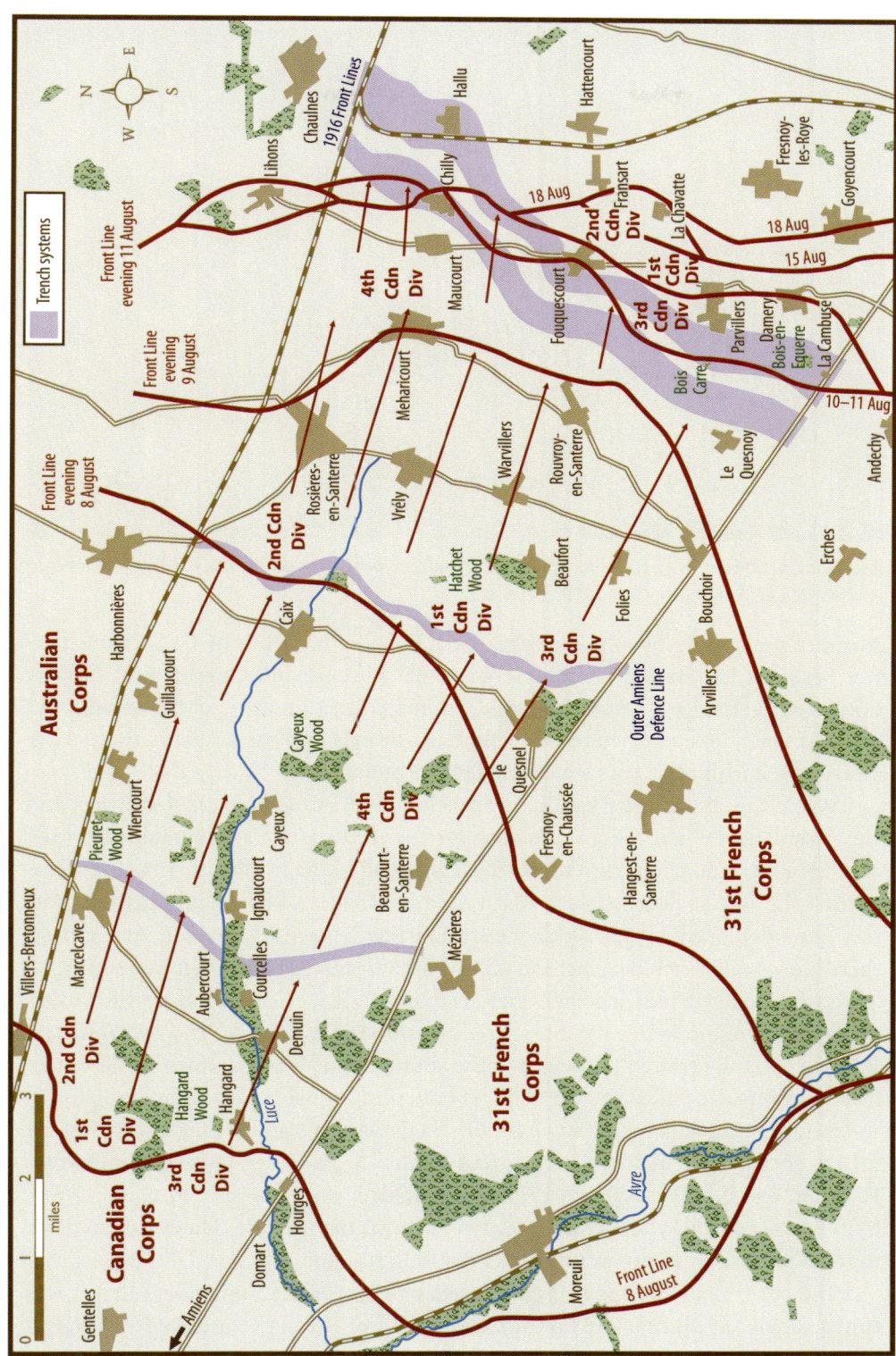

Amiens, August 1918

A Canadian 60-pounder, caisson, and crew in action out in open country during the surge eastward from Amiens, August 1918. (LAC PA-002999)

storm of fire struck down men and horses. The cool reactions of 1st Section's Farrier Sergeant J.S. Starkey, Acting Sergeant J.S. Pitman, and Gunner E.A. Callum mitigated the damage. Under Captain Gamblin's direction they got the column out of the impact zone and tended to wounded animals and men. Gamblin was later awarded the Military Cross for his leadership under fire.

While the rest of the Canadian Corps fought at Amiens, Lt.-Col. Magee's 2nd Garrison Brigade laid the groundwork for the next corps battle by taking on the stretch of German front from the Arras–Lens road to the northeast corner of Arras in the valley of the Scarpe River. All of the 1st Canadian Heavy and 6th Siege Battery guns deployed around Roclincourt, halfway between Vimy and Arras; from there, they could reach deep behind the German front, especially with supercharged loads of propellant pushing each shell. Half of 4th Siege Battery's heavy howitzers deployed there too, while its other three guns waited in reserve. The 2nd Garrison Brigade carefully shifted its weight to the south end of Vimy; meanwhile, German heavy batteries pounded the Lens–Arras road position with gas and high-explosive shells. On 4 August a mixed salvo hit 6th Siege Battery's area. Gunner J.R. Stewart took a shell fragment in the hand. Bombardier D.H. Daley, Acting Bombardier H. Ryan, and Gunner William Winsor all inhaled too much gas. Winsor, a Newfoundlander from Wesleyville, took two painful days to die. Daley suffered for months until sadly but mercifully his breathing stopped.

The success at Amiens had convinced senior Allied commanders that it was time to abandon caution and hit the Germans hard. The plan conceived by Marshal

Ferdinand Foch, now the Allied Supreme Commander, involved a series of attacks all along the Western Front. Each was designed to last just a few days, until the momentum was lost and casualties began to mount. The intent was to break the German army with a series of hammer blows by rupturing their front at numerous places, exhausting their reserves, and threatening their rail system at two critical hubs – Cambrai and Sedan – as well as along the key laterals. It was a brilliantly conceived and executed plan, and it ended the war.

To achieve Foch's vision, much hard fighting remained. As part of the general Allied offensive, the Canadian Corps moved back to the Arras–Vimy sector, this time to attack east towards Cambrai. Barring their path were some of the most formidable Hindenburg Line defences, including a series of fully developed lines and "switch" lines extending to a depth of some 30 kilometres across the rolling plain between Arras and Cambrai. This was the widest and strongest hinge in the German defences on the Western Front, which defended the critical northern rail hub at Cambrai. The Germans hoped to make any advance into the Hindenburg Line costly enough to force the Allies to accept German peace terms.

The Canadian Corps had done the staff work for this attack during their long quiet period at Vimy in the spring of 1918, so when it took command of the front east of Arras on 25 August the operation was already on the move. That day, 2nd Garrison Brigade fired a heavy counter-battery shoot down the north bank of the

Belts of German wire protecting the Hindenburg Line, east of Arras. Canadian 6- and 8-inch howitzer batteries had much wire-cutting work to do in August and September 1918 to open the way to Cambrai. (LAC PA-003280)

A Canadian 6-inch medium howitzer in full recoil near the Arras–Cambrai Road, September 1918. The open position and exposed shell stacks illustrate the transition to more open warfare in the last months of the war. (LAC PA-003133)

Scarpe River and Sensée stream east of Vimy, on enemy guns that could fire into the flank of the main Canadian attack. The 2nd Garrison Brigade also fired on German bridges over the Scarpe to help isolate the battlefield. This was only the first of the several critical roles that 2nd Garrison Brigade would play in the next two months' events.

The first German position to be attacked was the old British front line anchored at Monchy-le-Preux, which had been captured by the Newfoundland Regiment in the 1917 but then lost during the German spring offensive. Behind it lay a nebula of old German trench networks and wire belts from battles past. Lt.-Col. Magee's gunners had been gathering information on the Monchy battlefield since July. When the time came to strike, 4th and 6th Siege Batteries mixed their tactics. They fired 40-round bursts on some German batteries and then 200-round shoots directed by airplane observers on others. Overall accuracy had improved tremendously since Passchendaele thanks to new methods for surveying the precise location of each gun and then using aiming stakes to keep them on target in smoke, darkness, and fire. All of this was coupled with better knowledge of the difference between true north and magnetic north. The 1st Canadian Heavy Battery's 60-pounders and 6th Siege Battery's new 6-inch medium howitzers also fired more gas shells than ever before, especially at night. Night was normally a time for gunners at the front to rest, handle ammunition, and repair positions. Dousing German gun areas with gas forced the enemy to carry out that work in gas masks, which increased fatigue and casualty rates.

The main attack of the Battle of Arras began at 0300 on 26 August with enormous artillery support. Lt.-Col. Magee's 2nd Garrison Brigade continued to focus on the north bank of the Scarpe, thus protecting the Canadian Corps flank in concert with 51st Highland Division. The 6th Siege Battery fired an incredible 2,000 rounds (each weighing 100 pounds) through their 6-inch howitzers that day – more than 300 per gun. The 1st Canadian Heavy Battery opened the morning by shooting up enemy batteries, then switched to roads and tracks leading to the front to catch counterattack reserves on their way forward. They too fired nearly 2,000 rounds. The ammunition quality and supply problems of earlier battles were no longer an issue. The 4th Siege Battery brought three guns into action against German batteries, each gun tasked with striking one enemy battery steadily through the pre-dawn attack and well into the morning. That day Major Barker moved his remaining three guns of 4th Siege Battery forward into Roclincourt as preparation for moving the entire battery up behind the Canadian advance.

A Canadian 60-pounder heavy battery in action against German artillery near the Drocourt–Quéant Line. During the intense Hundred Days campaign, medium and heavy battery positions were sited adjacent to roads so that trucks could easily find and resupply the constantly moving guns. (LAC PA-003029)

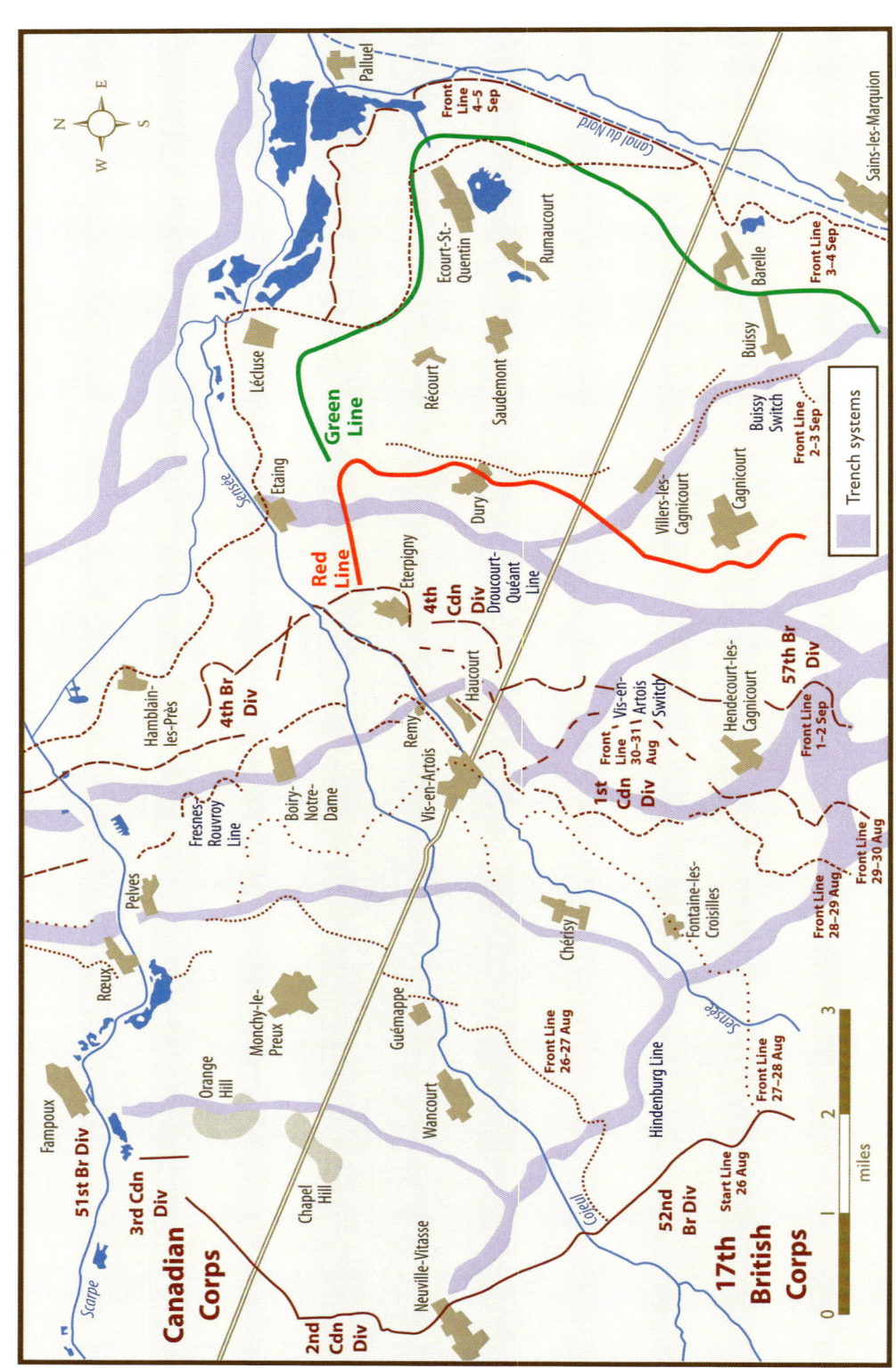

Arras, 26 August–5 September 1918

While 2nd Garrison Brigade had weeks to prepare for its role on the northern flank, the rest of the Canadian Corps rushed into the assault on the defensive belts between Monchy and the main Drocourt–Queant Line, virtually off the line of march from Amiens. To move an entire corps and launch a major attack in a matter of days was an exceptional feat by Great War standards, one that speaks to the professionalism of the corps and its staff, who were now almost entirely Canadian. The job, however, remained tough. The 3rd and especially 2nd Canadian Divisions paid for the rush, taking 5,800 casualties over three days. The Germans suffered, too, not least in that more than 3,000 went into prisoner cages. It is not clear how many more were killed or wounded. Lt.-Gen. Arthur Currie and his First Army commander, General Henry Horne, agreed that the next phase, the assault on the main Drocourt–Queant Line, required time for preparation. Brig.-Gen. McNaughton, the Corps Counter-Battery Commander, issued orders accordingly. The heavy guns would have to redeploy while intelligence officers located their targets.

Lt.-Col. Magee's 2nd Garrison Brigade moved eastward into range of the Drocourt–Queant Line. The 60-pounders went first into the new gun area between Athies and Fampoux, sheltered on the north bank of the Scarpe flood plain. The 1st Canadian Heavy Battery moved four guns there on the night of 27 August in driving rain. The 4th Siege Battery brought two of its 8-inch heavy howitzers in under cover of darkness on the night of 29 August; it was followed by all of 6th Siege Battery. Other batteries of the brigade, especially the heavies, deployed nearby. They spent the next four days hitting the Drocourt–Queant Line and its outer works the old-fashioned way, for it was a well-prepared German position, with deep dugouts as well as strong machine-gun posts behind belts of barbed wire. Arguably, the Drocourt–Queant Line was the strongest German position left on the Western Front. The 2nd Garrison Brigade split its fire between searching out German guns, smashing positions, and cutting wire. They continued mixing plenty of gas shells into their counter-battery missions. The 4th Siege Battery's 8-inch heavies obliterated one German strongpoint with help from a balloon observer, who made the powerful shells fall in a tight grouping. The Germans also put balloons in the air, to see down into the valleys cut by the Scarpe, the Sensée, and their feeder streams. Major Inches and 1st Canadian Heavy Battery used their massive 60-pounders as anti-aircraft guns, bursting shrapnel around the balloon and forcing the Germans to haul it down, thus blinding the German artillery on the northern flank. German gunners retaliated with heavy gas concentrations. Inches's battery stayed in action wearing respirators for eight full hours. Even then, twenty of his gunners and a number of non-coms fell victim to the gas. German guns in the fortified village of Sailly-en-Ostrevent remained particularly dangerous to the Canadian left flank for the attack on the Drocourt–Queant Line and therefore continued to get 2nd Garrison Brigade's attention.

The attack on the Drocourt–Queant Line opened at dawn on 2 September 1918. The Canadians carried the day, but not without heavy loss of life. Many Canadian infantry were killed by German shellfire after false reports that Canadian armoured cars had penetrated well beyond the Drocourt–Queant Line brought counter-battery fire to a halt for fear of hitting friendly troops. In fact, German artillery (and their machine-gunners) remained lethal in the face of collapse. Nonetheless, the most powerful Hindenburg Line defences in the northern sector were ruptured. As they collapsed, the enemy rushed reserves up to hold the interim Marquion Line along the Canal du Nord, the last line protecting their Cambrai hinge and base. Pushing through the Marquion Line was a tall order, and pulling it off was the Canadian Corps' greatest triumph of the Great War. New Brunswick heavy gunners played a starring role.

First the gunners of 2nd Garrison Brigade had to cross the Scarpe and close up behind forward Canadian infantry. Instead of moving guns and tractors across the river during the pause after the Drocourt–Queant Line fell, 2nd Garrison Brigade swapped guns and positions with British 53rd Garrison Brigade, which had been behind the main Canadian Corps attack along the Arras–Cambrai road. The trade brought Lt.-Col. Magee's brigade into position around Cagnicourt, south of Dury,

Trucks supplied ammunition for heavy and siege batteries, but field batteries and the infantry still relied on the horses of the Divisional Ammunition Columns, depicted here during the drive towards Cambrai. Note the artillery observation balloon in the distance. (LAC PA-003098)

in what had been the field gun zone of the shattered Droucout–Queant defences. The 4th Siege Battery's heavy howitzers took up station in Cagnicourt, registered, and went silent. The 6th Siege Battery took position slightly north at Villers-les-Cagnicourt not far from the Arras–Cambrai highway. The battery's command post set up in the town cemetery along the highway behind the last rise overlooking the Canal du Nord. The 1st Canadian Heavy Battery took position between 4th and 6th Siege Batteries.

It was a logical place to put guns, and therefore German guns gave them due attention. Around this time, 3rd Brigade Canadian Garrison Artillery arrived from the Amiens area and took up position with 8th, 10th, 11th, and 12th Siege Batteries, the last three engaging in only their second action of the war. The 8th Siege Battery was their strength. It had been in theatre longest and was commanded by Major Ring, a veteran of 3rd NB Regiment and a 4th Siege Battery original who had proved his mettle under Major Barker's leadership. Lieutenant John Bruce joined him there after recovering from wounds he had received in his Vimy Ridge observation post. The new brigade also benefited from Major White's long experience with 6-inch howitzers while serving with Prince Edward Island's 2nd Siege Battery: he now commanded 10th Siege Battery. The 3rd Garrison Brigade came into action in line with 2nd Garrison Brigade, on the north side of the Arras–Cambrai road at Dury. All went into action, duelling with German heavy batteries that were struggling to stabilize a new front along the Canal du Nord, which the Canadians made ready to attack.

The Marquion Line along the Canal du Nord, some 10 kilometres east of the Drocourt–Queant Line, was too strong and too well manned for a hasty attack. So another set-piece attack was necessary, but this was entirely in keeping with Foch's concept of operations. In early September he ordered a series of attacks to begin later in the month, to include the Belgians north of Ypres, the Canadians and British at the Canal du Nord, British and French armies farther south, and the new First American Army in the Muese–Argonne region. The pause in mid-September allowed the Allies, including the Canadian Corps, time to build up strength and to gather information.

The Germans obliged by mounting counterattacks on the new Canadian front and keeping up a steady fire from their guns, revealing their locations. Lt.-Col. Magee's headquarters reported German artillery behaviour in mid-September as "nervous." The 2nd Garrison Brigade responded at night by dousing German gun areas with gas. By day they fired short ten- to fourteen-round bursts spotted by (now) Royal Air Force observers to mark the new German gun positions and temporarily shut them down without forcing them to move. Counter-battery tactics were indeed a black art, and Canadian gunners paid a price too. During this pre-battle gunnery duel before the Canal du Nord, German guns hit back hard. The 6th Siege Battery's command post team took macabre shelter in a deep family

An oblique aerial photograph of the Canal du Nord at Inchy-en-Artois, where New Brunswick's heavy and siege gunners pulled off their most daring and important contributions of the First World War in late September 1918. Note the trees and houses still intact. (NBM C.H. Cochrane 1957.89.18)

mausoleum in the Villers-les-Cagnicourt cemetery. Gunner Green wrote that "at times the vault structure rocked like a boat and the candles on the switchboard table were blown out." The gun line itself took direct hits, including one on a pile of 6-inch gas shells, cracking several and forcing a gas alarm. The 3rd Garrison Brigade went into action during the duel around Villers-les-Cagnicourt, where Major MacKay's new 12th Battery suffered its first losses of the war. Heavy firing resulted in a pre-mature explosion in one of their 6-inch medium howitzers. Hot metal gun parts and fragments badly wounded Kenneth Wills and four others, including Gunners Turner, McCallum, Glanville, and Brewer, bringing an end to their short war. The remainder carried on pounding the German gun line.

General Currie's plan for breaching the Canal du Nord was daring. It required squeezing the entire corps through the dry, 3,000-yard uncompleted portion of the canal between Marquion and Inchy-en-Artois, then having it fan out across a wide plain on a front of 10,000 yards while attacking east. A few tanks and the Canadian Independent Force, comprising two brigades of motorized machine-gun battalions, would support the advance. All of this required a complex and exquisitely timed fire and movement plan, effective wire-cutting, and perfect counter-battery work. Then the corps would swing northeast to hook around Cambrai rather than attacking the heavily fortified city directly. The bold plan depended on Canadian units of all arms pulling off the extraordinary. When the commanding officer of Third Army, General Sir Julian Byng, reviewed Currie's plan he was astounded by its boldness and complexity, and he challenged Currie directly on his ability to pull it off. When Currie assured him that it would work, Byng accepted the plan but warned Currie quietly that "if you fail it means home for you."

Sustaining the attack once across the canal and across the plain to the gates of Cambrai was a critical issue. The corps planned to use "galloping batteries" of field guns to leap-frog fire support forward as the front moved, with brigaded trench mortars and heavy machine-guns in support. Lt.-Col. Magee's 2nd Garrison Brigade would play a key role in solving that problem, especially in the opening phase. It was to secretly move guns to the very bank of the Canal du Nord so that they could immediately open counter-battery fire on German guns that tried to stop the Canadian expansion on the other side. That meant neutralizing the commanding hill opposite the crossing point at Bourlon, about 4 kilometres east of the canal.

Magee's gun crews went forward at night to quietly dig and camouflage gun pits on the slope descending to the canal bank. The 6th Siege Battery built theirs in front of Buissy, shielded by a railway embankment overlooking Sains-les-Marquion.

Canadian Garrison Artillery four-wheel-drive trucks towing caissons and 6-inch medium howitzers during the drive towards Cambrai. The 6th Siege Battery was the first Canadian Corps Heavy Artillery unit to cross the Canal du Nord to take new positions at Bourlon Wood and open the attack on Cambrai, 27 September 1918. (LAC PA-003103)

Their forward positions were right under the noses of a German machine-gun crew and a field gun detachment dug in on the west bank of the canal. Meanwhile, 4th Siege Battery and 1st Canadian Heavy Battery built their forward positions farther south at Inchy-in-Artois; from there, they could fire on the heights at Bourlon. Moving 4th Siege Battery's 8-inch howitzers and their weighty shells was the biggest challenge and took the longest. On each of five nights, a single gun or a few lorry loads of ammunition came forward.

While 2nd Garrison Brigade slipped secretly into place, the rest of the Canadian Corps Heavy Artillery, including 3rd Garrison Brigade, fired a steady harassing and preparatory barrage of high-explosive, shrapnel, and gas every night for a week. This noise, coupled with German retaliatory fire, concealed the sounds of 2nd Garrison Brigade's trucks, Caterpillar tractors, and shovels. The 4th Siege Battery alone brought up nineteen lorry loads with some 200 shells per gun. Captain Ned Slader wrote that "all this was accomplished under more or less heavy night firing, through country reeking with gas, over shell torn roads." The 1st and 6th Siege Batteries planned to move their more mobile guns into position on the night of 25 September and the last guns the night before the attack. In the end, all of 2nd Garrison Brigade's forward positions lay within plain view of the enemy. Yet the

A German second-generation 21cm Mörser 16, counterpart to 4th Battery's 8-inch heavy howitzers, neutralized and captured intact during the fight for the Canal du Nord and Cambrai, October 1918. (LAC PA-003276)

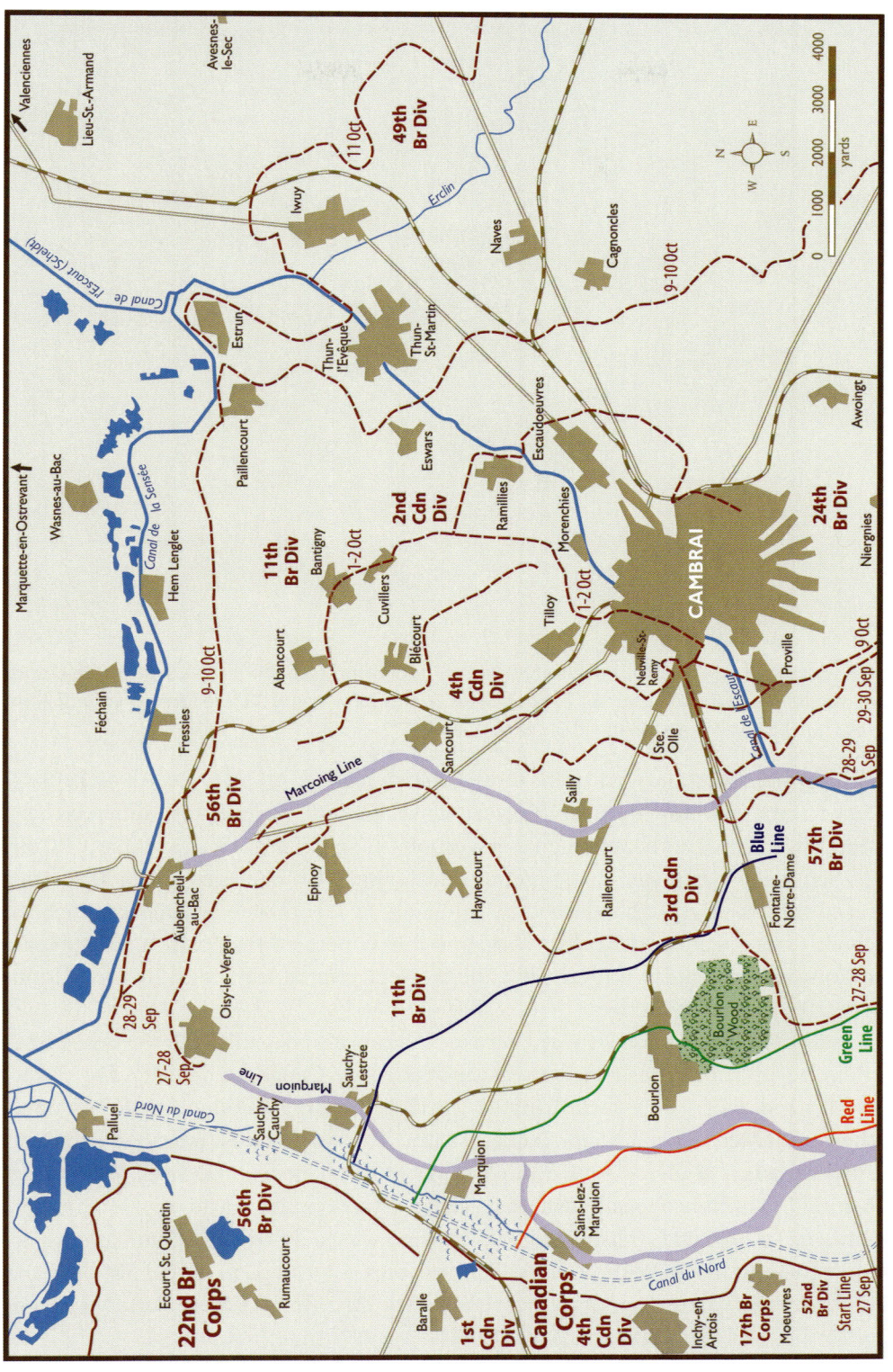

Canal du Nord and Cambrai, 27 September–11 October 1918

Proof of effective Canadian counter-battery fire during the battles for the Canal du Nord and Cambrai. This seven-ton German 21 cm Mörser 16 was blown onto its side after its ammunition supply exploded from a direct hit. (LAC PA-003418)

stealthy construction work went more or less unnoticed. Only one 4th Siege Battery tractor was blown up, on its return drive. The 6th Siege Battery suffered their last fatal casualty of the war, Signaller Vernon Clark. Zero Hour was set for 0520 on 27 September. That night, the crews went forward to man their guns. They laid on to targets using lights flashed by signallers in identifiable landmarks (such as church towers) along the canal. Wind and rain concealed their last-minute preparations in the pre-dawn hours, but the weather cleared for the 0520 Zero Hour. Then they went into action.

As Canadian infantry surged across the canal and began to fan out across the plain beyond, Bourlon Heights was smothered by Canadian artillery fire. "Tree trunks and debris were seen flying up through the air. This pounding lasted until the woods were taken," Major Inches wrote. "The enemy must have had an awful surprise when at Zero Hour all this heavy stuff opened up on him, from close behind the front in a locality where no sane person would ever think of looking for artillery." Now, 2nd Garrison Brigade's mission was to destroy German batteries or force them to move. Without the concrete overhead protection of the middle years of the war, Germans gunners either retreated or died. The 6th Siege Battery applied

1,100 6-inch rounds to six German batteries, concentrating more shells more accurately on fewer targets than they had since Vimy Ridge. The 4th Siege Battery had fewer heavy shells to work with in their forward positions, but they made 463 of them count. Carefully allowing for barometric pressure and temperature measured against their carefully surveyed gun pits, their 200-pound 8-inch shells hit the mark on sixteen hastily dug-in German batteries in and near Bourlon Wood. The 1st Canadian Heavy Battery fired counter-battery plans as well, loosing 1,000 rounds at nine enemy batteries around Boulon Wood. When that was done, Inches's gunners increased their propellant to supercharge to throw 130 more at four German batteries at Haynecourt, behind the section of the Canal du Nord not to be assaulted directly. North of the Arras–Cambrai road, 3rd Garrison Brigade fired over the flooded part of the Canal du Nord, taking on German batteries behind Sauchy-Cauchy and towards Haynecourt.

General Currie's bold plan and 2nd Garrison Brigade's carefully concealed preparations paid off on 27 September 1918. As Canadian troops poured over the canal and fanned out, complex and highly effective supporting fire plans from heavy machine-guns and field and medium artillery supported them in three directions. It was an astonishing piece of work. By late morning, German units holding the Canal du Nord directly in front of the Canadian Corps were wrecked. Major Barker's 4th Siege Battery reported: "Enemy prisoners and our own walking wounded came streaming back by the gun positions." By late morning, 2nd Garrison Brigade had a new kind of target to fire on – enemy troops, trucks, and horse-drawn wagons escaping east in broad daylight, pursued by Canadian infantry, the

More proof of effective counter-battery fire. German trench mortars and field, medium, and heavy artillery abandoned by enemy gunners on battlefields between Arras and Cambrai. Note the particularly abundant and dangerous 10 cm Kanone 14s and 17s on the back row left and the 15 cm field howitzer 13s on the back row right, nemesis for Canadian heavy gunners. (LAC PA-003168)

The 6th Canadian Siege Battery firing their 6-inch medium howitzers against German gun positions during the drive towards Cambrai while German prisoners help wounded Canadians to the rear. (NBM Humphrey-F5-36)

Canadian Independent Force, and British tanks. This exodus was anticipated. Each New Brunswick battery had a target list that included road and track junctions to switch their fire to when the Germans started to fall back. Many retreating Germans fell victim to medium and heavy shells.

By noon on 27 September the Germans had retreated out of range. But that, too, had been anticipated, and by then 2nd Garrison Brigade was on the move. The 6th Siege Battery had the honour of being the first battery in the Canadian Corps Heavy Artillery to cross the Canal du Nord. The popular Canadian Corps Padre Canon F.G. Scott rode past them in a motorcycle sidecar calling, "We have them on the run boys, we have them on the run now." Hundreds of miles to the southeast, in the Meuse–Argonne sector, the American Expeditionary Force opened their greatest attack of the war, while the British and French pushed hard all along the line. The end was indeed near, but the pressure had to be kept on the wavering enemy a little longer yet to finish the job.

The objective of 2nd Garrison Brigade on 27 September was the commanding height of Bourlon Wood. From there, Lt.-Col. Magee's observers could look down on Cambrai and 10 kilometres of the battlefield to the north and northeast. So far in this war, Canadian heavy guns had never bounded forward on the first day of a major assault. The New Brunswickers and their colleagues in 2nd Garrison Brigade now accomplished that unheard-of feat. Moving heavy guns across any obstacle and into a fluid battlefield came with risks. General Currie accepted those risks and pushed 2nd Garrison Brigade forward. Advance parties from 4th and 6th Siege Batteries suffered accordingly, but perhaps not unduly, given the payoff. Captain Slader and Lieutenant Lawson went ahead to find positions for 4th Siege Battery near Bourlon. The two had finished the job when a cluster of German shells landed. Fragments cut into both of them, one snapping Slader's leg and another grazing his head. Apparently, despite surviving the whole war so far, mostly as a FOO in the most dangerous places, Ned Slader had not yet used up all his luck. The blast threw him into an abandoned German gun pit. While he was lying there, an empty wagon came by from 1st Divisional Ammunition Column. The driver was Yank Wiley, one of the few old Saint John originals still in the unit. Despite the dust, blood, and soot, Wiley recognized his old Sergeant Major. Wiley loaded Slader and Lawson in his wagon and drove them to a casualty clearing station. The 6th Siege Battery's advance party also took fire. Lieutenant Reed Sinclair was hit in the arm. Gunners M. Shephard and J.W. Holden were both hit in the legs. All three survived, and not long after, their guns and battery mates arrived to set up.

From Bourlon Wood, 2nd Garrison Brigade's guns and howitzers could reach the last German fall-back position, the Marcoing Line, and the villages a few miles behind it where surviving German batteries were attempting to stand. On the plain below, Canadian infantry supported by galloping batteries of 18-pounders from the field artillery crept relentlessly towards and through the Marcoing Line, where the Germans mounted desperate last-ditch counterattacks. New Brunswick's batteries also drove 10 kilometres farther north to Haynecourt; from there, they could reach the Sensée and L'Escaut Canals, which boxed in the ground north of Cambrai. The Haynecourt flats, now home to a French air force base, was the last gun position in the Great War that 1st Canadian Heavy, 4th, and 6th Siege Batteries fought from for a prolonged period. The 3rd Garrison Brigade set up behind them.

The German army clung tenaciously to Cambrai for the first nine days of October. Gotha bombers pounded the Haynecourt gun positions by night. German guns struck back too, even though the end was in sight. On the second day in the position, Gunner Walter Geoffrey Bidlake, an old original from 4th Siege Battery, was one of many feeding ammunition to hungry guns. He had joined New Brunswick's Garrison Artillery in 1915 and become fast friends with fellow 4th Siege Battery Gunner Cyrus Gaskin. Bidlake fell in love with and married Gaskin's sister before 4th Siege Battery departed overseas in 1916. Mrs. Bidlake lost her brother Cyrus in the Souchez Valley in May 1917. On 2 October 1918, her husband Geoff was killed by a German shell. The news would not reach her for some time. Geoff Bidlake still

Cambrai to Mons, 12 October–11 November 1918

The one heavy and three medium howitzer batteries of 3rd Canadian Garrison Brigade parade victoriously past General Sir Arthur Currie after the armistice of November 1918. The 3rd Brigade, including Captain Roy Ring's 8th Siege Battery with 8-inch Mark VI heavy howitzers, was formed overseas in 1918 largely from drafts of New Brunswickers and other eastern Canadians who trained with 9th Siege Battery on Partridge Island. (LAC PA-003502)

lies in a small Commonwealth War Graves Cemetery beside his Haynecourt gun position.

Fighting intensified in early October north of Cambrai, as the Germans rushed troops from more than a dozen divisions to block the Canadian advance as well as four other major Allied thrusts across the Western Front. In early October, Canadian gunners were still smashing German counterattacks and firing counter-battery shoots. Their Haynecourt gun position still drew German counter-battery fire. On 5 October a German shell killed Gunner William Davison, one of 6th Siege Battery's originals from the Mount Allison University contingent. Infantry casualties piled up on both sides in the dramatic climax until Cambrai fell on 9 October. The 3rd Garrison Brigade suffered worse in the Haynecourt sector. Ring's 8th Battery lost no men, but a direct hit on his headquarters blew apart his war diary. Doug White's 10th Battery lost two men killed and nine wounded, while 11th Battery suffered five wounded. Colin MacKay's 12th Battery was hardest hit by German gas and high-explosive shells, loosing 39 men killed and wounded during the intense struggle in front of Cambrai.

After a pause to reorganize, the Canadian Corps drove hard towards Valenciennes in a fluid mobile advance. On 17 October, German units along the Canadian front began withdrawing behind a screen of demolitions and booby traps, foreshadowing a future war. The 4th Siege Battery's 8-inch heavy howitzers fired until the enemy retreated out of their range on 19 October. Since the engineer bridges over the Sensée could not carry the 8-inch guns, it fell to 1st Canadian Heavy Battery's horse-drawn 60-pounders and especially to 6th Siege Battery's four-wheel-drive-towed 6-inch medium howitzers to support the pursuit. Magee's 2nd Garrison Brigade continued advancing along the north bank of the L'Escaut Canal behind 2nd Canadian Division, with 2nd Divisional Ammunition Column wagons hauling shells up behind them. For the first time in the war, the Canadians began liberating French villages and towns that had not yet been smashed by the years of fighting. They found the inhabitants destitute after years of German occupation, and hungry after retreating Germans pilfered their food. The 6th Siege Battery's Gunner Green wrote that "the country had been robbed bare of everything." Major Inches observed that "the civilians have an intense loathing of the Hun, who seemingly treated them without much consideration." He was impressed by "arriving in a town full of civilians to have them greet you with flags and other tokens of enthusiasm."

The 1st Canadian Heavy and 6th Siege Batteries dove headlong into the pursuit, moving to new firing positions every day or two, keeping a continuous harassing fire on the roads along which the Germans were retreating. They fired from Hem Lenglet along the Sensée for a night, then on through much more rolling countryside to Marquette-en-Ostrevant and then Bellaing outside Valenciennes, where the Germans turned to fight briefly. The 2nd Garrison Brigade's firing positions were at the northwest corner of Valenciennes, within range of the main roads leading east to Mons in Belgium. The main German defences were on heights south of the town, which were the only dry approach across a landscape that had been deliberately flooded by the enemy. On 31 October and 1 November, 2nd Garrison Brigade fired southward from their positions west of town, into the rear of the German batteries that formed the main German defences. The stiff battle raged for four days as the Germans counterattacked. Shells from 1st Canadian Heavy Battery and 6th Siege Battery silenced German guns and crashed among their counterattacks in response to calls for help from 4th Canadian Division and directions from air observers. The same batteries watched carefully from their own ground observation post for signs of enemy movement. At that point, to 6th Siege Battery "came the chance that every artilleryman dreams about." They caught a full battalion of German infantry massing to counterattack and shattered it. Finally, on 5 November, 2nd Garrison Brigade moved east to support the Canadian drive over the Belgian border towards Mons.

That day – 5 November 1918 – 6th Siege Battery fired its last rounds of the war. The 1st Canadian Heavy Battery fired their last on 9 November. The German army was ruined and in retreat across the entire front. By then a new German government, formed in October in response to shattering defeats, was in talks with the Allies about ending the war. Even so, for the men at the front the end came unexpectedly. Gunner Green wrote: "It is hard to describe that day. There were no outward demonstrations of jubilation. For over two years the Battery had never been beyond the range of German shells. For months past, life after the war had only been a dream. Had there been anything to drink it might have been a more festive occasion." If they only knew, it would take six more months to get home.

The armistice ending the fighting came into effect on 11 November 1918. The details of the peace remained to be settled, and at the time it was not clear that the war was actually over. Under the terms of the armistice, Allied forces advanced to and crossed the Rhine, occupying a small bridgehead. Two Canadian divisions participated in the occupation, marching through a Belgian countryside that had been smashed and stripped by retreating Germans. The 1st and 6th Batteries were both part of the Canadian occupation force during the winter of 1918–19. They went ready to fight, and deployed their guns around the city of Cologne as Germany descended into chaos and near civil war. By January 1919 the Canadian contingent in the occupation force had been withdrawn. The two batteries were back in England by April.

It was not until 4 May 1919 that most of New Brunswick's gunners assembled on the SS *Mauretania* for passage to Halifax. Major Inches and 1st Canadian Heavy

Lt.-Col. Frank Magee (front centre), perhaps Canada's most distinguished heavy gunner, and his officers of 2nd Brigade, Canadian Garrison Artillery headquarters at Mehlem on the Rhine as part of the Canadian Occupation Force in Germany, January 1919. (LAC PA-003880)

6th Siege Battery gunners stand watch on the Rhine as part of the Canadian Occupation Force in Germany, January 1919. (NBM Humphrey –F5-35)

Battery, being a mixed provincial unit, demobilized at Montreal before Inches brought the New Brunswick contingent home to Saint John by rail. The 4th and 6th Siege Batteries travelled home together by rail under Major Barker and Captain MacMillan to Saint John. With them were packets of other New Brunswick gunners from other units. Both batteries marched downtown to King Square for a formal city welcome and then to the armouries, where many had first enlisted a lifetime before in 3rd New Brunswick Regiment.

Chapter 6
The Long Armistice, 1919–39

As the guns fell silent across western Europe in November 1918, some New Brunswick gunners were on their way to a new war far to the north. A year earlier the Russian Bolsheviks under Vladimir Lenin had seized power in St. Petersburg. That new regime had bought its way out of the war in early 1918 by ceding vast tracts of the western Russian empire, including Poland and most of Ukraine, to Germany. Since then, Russia had descended into civil war, and European states now braced themselves for communist insurrections at home. In June 1918 the Allies started sending troops to Russia to prevent the ports of Murmansk and Archangel from falling into German or Red Army hands. Among them were some 600 Canadians, including 16th Brigade, Canadian Field Artillery, consisting of 67th and 68th Batteries of the Siberian Field Force.

Gunners from 65th Depot Battery in Woodstock joined the Siberian Field Force, and other New Brunswickers joined from units overseas. Among the latter was Captain Oliver Mowat of Campbellton. He had received his lieutenant's commission and enlisted in 24th Field Battery in Fredericton when it was mobilized in 1915, and had been slightly wounded at Ypres in July 1916. Then in June 1917 he was seriously wounded, and in August was sent home to convalesce. In March 1918 Mowat returned to Britain, where he soon joined 68th Battery as its adjutant and then second-in-command. His luck ran out in Siberia.

The 16th Brigade departed Dundee, Scotland, on 20 August 1918, leaving half of 68th Battery's guns on the wharf in order to load onions, which were in short supply in Archangel. Once settled, the Allied Expeditionary Force moved south

Right at home in the bush. Gunners of 68th Battery of the Canadian North Russia force, grouped around their camouflaged 18-pounder, Mala Beresnik, along the Dvina River, May 1919, about the time they fought their most intense action of the campaign. (LAC PA-037395)

from Archangel to defend the railway and to secure the line of the Dvina River. Force levels were low, and the front was porous, so every gunner carried a rifle and every crew a light machine-gun. They would need them. On 13 October, 67th Battery was nearly overrun by the Red Army at Seletskoye, and saved itself and the Allied position only by firing shrapnel set to burst at seventy-five yards. The 68th Battery's first major action was supporting the Franco-American attack on Kadish on 30–31 December, which was successful. The defence of Shenkursk on the frozen Vaga River, which followed on 19 January 1919, was not. The Red Army invested the town, and 68th Battery and the Allied garrison withdrew in the nick of time. Mowat was wounded in that action and later died. His body was returned to Britain along with the rest of the contingent. His remains were later repatriated to New Brunswick, and in 1919 he was buried in the Campbellton Rural Cemetery.

While Mowat is now largely forgotten, another New Brunswick artillery officer with the Siberian Field Force is not. Captain John D. Winslow from Woodstock, New Brunswick, was recovering from wounds received at Passchendaele in late 1917 when he volunteered for service in northern Russia. Winslow survived 68th Battery's sojourn, including its "gallant" role in defence of Vystavka on the Vaga River in early March, and the fighting along the Dvina at Tulgas in the spring of 1919. The latter was probably the battery's most intense fighting – it fired almost daily between 1 and 12 May. Effective and resilient gunners made up for the general weakness of the force in northern Russia. General W.E. Ironside, commander of the force, later wrote: "The Canadians out here, especially the gunners, have been

Return of 26th (NB) Battalion, CEF, and 2nd Division Ammunition Column, Saint John railway station, May 1919. (PANB P551/50)

Gunners of 4th Overseas Siege Battery on their return to Saint John, 19 May 1919. (PANB P551/44)

the backbone of the expedition." When they paraded prior to boarding their ships for home in June, the Russian governor made the unprecedented gesture of awarding twenty St. George Crosses – the Russian equivalent of the Victoria Cross – to officers and men of 16th Brigade, Canadian Field Artillery. Winslow received the Military Cross for his efforts, and in 1993 the armoury in Woodstock was renamed the Major John Douglas Winslow M.C. Armoury in his honour.

Major Winslow was one of thousands of New Brunswickers who returned home from war in 1918–19. Many – indeed, perhaps most – were suffering from physical or psychological trauma. The worst cases were invalided home, and many casualties of the Western Front died quiet, lingering deaths in the province's veterans' hospitals years after the war. Many others coped with what we now call post-traumatic stress disorder, which psychologists of the day called neurasthenia, and which the veterans themselves called shell shock. There was no cure for them; they either got over it or drank themselves into oblivion. Fortunately, most men made a successful transition back to civilian life. No doubt, wartime training and experience contributed to postwar success for many of them. An example is Kenneth Wills, who had been wounded at the Canal du Nord. After returning home, Wills completed his engineering degree at the University of New Brunswick, where he was valedictorian in the Class of 1921. He went on to lead a full life serving in prominent engineering posts with the New Brunswick Department of Transportation. Many other returned men stayed active in their local Militia units, and it was this core of committed Canadians who kept gunnery skills alive in the interwar period.

Among those who built successful postwar careers and stayed active in the Militia artillery was Major Cyrus Inches, who joined King Hazen in one of the most respected law practices in the province. Captain Ned Slader, who like Inches survived four years of fighting on the Western Front, rose to prominence in the Saint John Police. Albert Dodge, who spent most of the war as the RSM of 2nd Division Ammunition Column, went back to engineering – and to Militia service. The veterans who stayed in uniform trained the new generation of volunteer gunners. Many still served in the late 1930s as the threat of war returned at the end of what some members of the regiment called "the Long Armistice." Some, like Dodge, returned to active service in the Second World War. Even those who were too old to head overseas a second time played a critical role in readying the next generation and maintaining a coherent structure that ultimately mobilized and rapidly grew the Canadian army for the next world war.

During the Great War, the old Militia had continued to exist as a distinct entity from the Canadian Expeditionary Force. Officers and men, overage, underage, or physically unfit, kept their units going. A few units, like 3rd NB Regiment, had played an active operational role at home during the war. The biggest problem facing the Canadian Militia by 1919, therefore, was how to reconcile the accomplishments and battle honours of the enormously successful artillery of the Canadian Corps with the identity, traditions, and personnel of the old Militia at home. Never before had the Militia been faced with such a daunting challenge. By 1919 there were vastly more highly proficient, decorated, and experienced officers and men returning from Flanders than their hometown Militia units could absorb. Moreover, many Captains and Majors found that the only vacancies available for them were at the rank of Second Lieutenant – that is, the rank in which they had initially been gazetted. And there was the even more vexing question of how to perpetuate the accomplishments and battle honours of overseas units – of all types. The links between overseas units and the home Militia were by no means clear. It was obvious something had to be done. On 23 April 1919, Maj.-Gen. Sir W.D. Otter was charged with forming a committee to investigate and make recommendations as to the best method of reorganizing the whole Canadian Militia to reconcile these issues and many more besides. Also sitting on the Otter Commission were Maj.-Gen. Sir E.W.B. Morrison, Maj.-Gen. W.G. Gwatkin, and Brig.-Gen. A.G.L. McNaughton.

McNaughton, the brilliant former Counter-Battery Commander of the Canadian Corps and the architect of so many of its gunnery accomplishments, was an obvious choice for the Otter Commission. One might have expected his sentiments to lay entirely with the old 3rd (Montreal) Field Battery, which he had taken overseas in the fall of 1914. New Brunswick gunners knew better. They had, after all, played a very dominant role in the Corps heavy and medium artillery during the war, and many of the senior gunners in the province knew him well. They also thought of him as a native son, and with good reason. His father, Robert Duncan McNaughton, had been born and raised in the city and had owned a ship chandlery in partnership with a Mr. Andrew Gray. The Great Fire of 1877 had wiped them out, and the lure of the west, which the railway had helped create in the 1880s, attracted Robert McNaughton to Moosamin, Saskatchewan. There he settled, married, and raised his two sons, one of whom he named Andrew after his old friend in Saint John. The Grays and the McNaughtons remained close, and it was quite natural that young Andrew would visit the Grays in Saint John, as he did in the spring of 1895 as a boy of seven for his first holiday by the sea. And it was there that young Andrew was introduced to the wonders of gunnery.

On 18 May 1895, Andrew Gray took his namesake to Fort Dufferin to witness the Loyalist Day salute fired by 3rd Regiment's No. 2 (Carleton) Company. The company was unable to muster a full gun detachment, and McNaughton, whose eagerness was apparent, was "pressed into service" running charges from the magazine to the gun platform. "It was the General's first association with guns and gunners," Alward wrote in his draft of the regimental history, "and it is more than likely that as he sat in the Saint John Armoury on that November day in 1920 [when the

Otter Commission met in the city], he reflected upon that other day, when, as a 'powder monkey' he served the guns of the 3rd Regiment."

The Otter Commission began its work in Ottawa by reviewing the petitions forwarded by CEF units desiring perpetuation. It quickly became apparent that the commission would not be able to please everyone. Old Militia regiments did not wish to lose their identity by changing their titles or dropping their numerals to perpetuate overseas units. They had their own traditions, and pardonable pride in the numbers of officers and men whom they had furnished for active service. On the other hand, a large number of CEF units disclaimed any connection with existing Militia regiments. They wished to be added to the Militia establishment as they were then constituted and in that way preserve their individual existence. There was no happy meeting ground, and as it turned out, practically all the old Militia units lost their numerals – 3rd (New Brunswick) Regiment being one of a very few permitted to retain its old title.

The plan for reorganization was based on a Militia strength of eleven infantry divisions, four cavalry divisions, and the appropriate number of supporting arms and services. The requirement for such a large force was based on Defence Scheme No. 1, which had been prepared by Colonel Sutherland-Brown, the Director of Military Operations and Planning. The only reason Sutherland-Brown could think of for a Militia on this scale was the threat of a direct invasion of Canada by the United States. Certainly no one in Sir Robert Borden's Union Government saw any further need for an overseas expeditionary force, especially after the successful conclusion of "the war to end all wars." But postwar relations between Britain and the United States remained uneasy after 1918, not least because Britain remained allied to Japan and the Japanese and Americans were great rivals in the Pacific. This was even more the case after mid-1919, when the new League of Nations awarded the Japanese stewardship of Germany's vast holdings in the south Pacific, especially the Marshall and Caroline Islands. As bizarre as it now sounds, a war in the Pacific between Japan and the United States over control of those islands might well have resulted in an American invasion of Canada.

Sutherland-Brown's scheme envisaged that fifteen Canadian divisions could hold back the "American Tide" until Britain and the rest of the Commonwealth mobilized and sent assistance. Later variants called for a Canadian strike into New England to forestall American thrusts into Canada and to provide a bargaining chip to recover the west, which could not be defended. Brown's plan found little favour among politicians and was never fully developed, but it was the basis for the Militia reorganization of 1920.

Between September and December 1919, the Otter Commission toured the country. They held seventeen meetings in Canada's principal cities and in each case dealt solely with the problems concerning the perpetuation and redesignation of units. They arrived in Saint John on 17 November 1919 to meet the province's key

Militia officers. Lt.-Col. W.H. Harrison spoke on behalf of 3rd Regiment, and his address made plain the wishes of the officers: "There is a keen desire here to perpetuate the name of the 3rd (New Brunswick) Regiment, not simply on account of the one hundred and twenty-five years of history behind it, but also because of its war record." As Harrison told the commissioners,

> the 3rd Regiment sent overseas more than two thousand officers and men. At the time of the Armistice, one-half of all the heavy and siege batteries in the Canadian Corps were commanded by officers who originally came from this regiment.
>
> Thus we feel that the "3rd" has a strong claim for having its name perpetuated in the Canadian Corps … The regiment also wishes to be converted to a heavy brigade, that is, from a regiment of garrison artillery with three companies, to a brigade of heavy artillery with three batteries – one heavy and two siege. It is further felt that the 4th and 6th Siege Batteries should be continued and perpetuated in the Regiment and that the third battery should be styled the 1st Heavy, to perpetuate the 1st Heavy Battery of the Canadian Expeditionary Force, which was commanded throughout the war by an officer of the 3rd Regiment and very largely manned by personnel of this unit.

The Otter Commission agreed to all of Lt.-Col. Harrison's requests, save one. The brigade would have a heavy battery, but the original 1st Canadian Heavy Battery was part of the old Montreal Heavy Brigade and one of the few Militia units to have a counterpart in the CEF with the same title. The 3rd NB Regiment's claim was not

Men of C Subsection, mostly New Brunswickers, of 10th Overseas Siege Battery, photographed around their 6-inch medium howitzer, Boussu, Belgium, 19 December 1918. These guns came home and equipped two batteries of 3rd NB Medium Regiment during the interwar years. (PANB P551/35)

strong enough to take it away from Montreal. Instead, an entirely new creation, with no prewar or Great War connections, would be formed: 15th Heavy Battery. The new 15th would replace No. 1 Company on the new regimental slate; as such, it would take over its traditional links and become a part of the thread leading back to The Loyal Company.

By General Order No. 13, dated 2 February 1920, 3rd NB Regiment was reorganized and redesignated as 3rd (New Brunswick) Heavy Brigade, Canadian Garrison Artillery, composed of 15th Heavy Battery, Canadian Artillery (formerly No. 1 Company), 4th Siege Battery, Canadian Artillery (formerly No. 2 Company), and 6th Siege Battery, Canadian Artillery (formerly No. 3 Company). The regiment could well be pleased with its new organization and its new role. During the Great War, 3rd Regiment had devoted much of its effort to building and sustaining the heavy and medium artillery of the Canadian Corps. And although it had done increasingly important work in securing the port of Saint John in its coast defence role, the magnificent accomplishments of Saint John and New Brunswick gunners on the Western Front overshadowed everything else. Ned Slader, Cyrus Inches, Frank Magee, Lawrence Allen, Louis Barker, D. King Hazen, Colin MacKay, J.I. McGowan, Roy Ring, William Vassie, Albert Dodge, P.W. Wetmore, W.A.I. Anglin, John Bruce, Herb A. West, H.C. Alward, Wallace Alward, I.F. Archibald, W.L. Caldow, W.C, Ewing, G.C.L. Foster, F.P. Gutelius, R.D. Magee, J.B. McNair (who would become premier of the province), and scores of others had won great battles and great honour in the service of their country and had become some of the most proficient and successful gunners in the world. Indeed, the quality of their work in the Hundred Days campaign was unsurpassed; they knew it, and so did the Otter Commission. For the next two decades, 3rd (New Brunswick) Heavy Brigade would honour that legacy. It is unfortunate that Lt.-Col. Colonel B.R. Armstrong, the man who had built that legacy, had retired on 15 January 1920, just a month before the new brigade was formally established.

The first task facing the new commanding officer, Lt.-Col. William H. Harrison, D.S.O., was the preparation of a new slate of officers. The 3rd Brigade's problems were a reflection of larger issues regarding the reintegration of wartime officers into the existing Militia establishments. By 1918 there were some eighty-four officers holding commissions in the regiment, the vast majority of these just home from overseas. Harrison needed only twenty-two, including himself. To make possible free action in creating new appointments and adjusting seniority, Militia Headquarters officially disbanded and then reactivated all brigades and batteries on the same day. This ensured continuity of service; it also cleared the slate for immediate reappointments and enlistments regardless of seniority. Nonetheless, Harrison had to make some agonizing choices. Officers who did not receive appointments in the reorganized unit were obliged to transfer to another one, take an appointment on the unit's reserve list, or retire.

By General Order No. 130, 3rd (New Brunswick) Heavy Brigade was disbanded and reorganized, with effect from 15 June 1920. It was the only second Militia unit in Canada to accomplish this so far, which suggests a level of harmony in the Saint John gunner community that contrasts with units where there was much bitterness, and where officer slates were neither produced nor approved for many months.

As of June 1920, the Brigade Headquarters consisted of Lt.-Col. Harrison, D.S.O., as Commanding Officer; Major William A. Harrison, M.C., as Quartermaster, and Captain E.M. "Ned" Slader, CdeG, as Adjutant. The 15th Heavy Battery was commanded by none other than Major Cyrus Inches, D.S.O., M.C., with Captain J.H.A.L. Fairweather, M.C., and Lieutenants R.H. Bruce, and R.K. Jones, K.A. Brown, and Provisional Lieutenant E.R. Puddington. The 4th Siege Battery was commanded by Major Norm MacLeod, M.C., who had commanded 5th Siege Battery in the war. He was helped by Captain Doug White, M.C. (formerly CO of 10th Siege Battery) and Lieutenants C.S. Bennett, H.F. Bennett, and A.A. Dodge. The 6th Siege Battery belonged to Major George Gamblin, M.C., with Captain R. St. C. Hayes, M.C., and Lieutenants E.H. Turnbull, H.A. Bridges, and I.N.M. MacLaren, M.C., and Provisional Lieutenants A.E. Brown and B.W. Turnbull. Of the twenty-two officers in 3rd Brigade, two had D.S.O.s and eight had M.C.s; this was probably a common phenomenon across the country.

In addition to the "active officers" list, a Corps Reserve was authorized for each artillery brigade. This was merely a list of names of those officers who wished to continue their association but who, for various reasons, did not desire to serve actively or were unable to do so. In most cases, civilian life interfered, and many moved away after the war to pursue their education or to take jobs. Some of these officers would again serve the brigade in an active capacity, and one of them would command it during the Second World War. Meanwhile, a large number of men who had initially enlisted "for the duration" re-enlisted in the new medium brigade, thereby enhancing the continuity of the overseas batteries. This was particularly true of 4th Siege Battery, due in large measure to the fact that most of the men were neighbours on the west side of Saint John. Major Inches's 15th Heavy Battery, on the other hand, was composed largely of younger men who took pride in their youth and keenness. The 6th Siege Battery, it seems, was a blend of both old and new gunners. The peacetime strength for a Siege or Heavy Battery was 120 all ranks, while the total establishment for a Heavy Brigade was 24 officers and 379 all ranks. The Annual Inspection Reports for 1923 show that the brigade had recruited about 60 percent of its allowable strength.

The brigade's ordnance initially consisted of four 6-inch 26cwt howitzers and the four quick-firing 4.7-inch guns left on Partridge Island. The 6-inch howitzer, with a maximum elevation of 45 degrees and an all-up weight of roughly five tons, could fire an 85-pound projectile to a maximum distance of 11,400 yards and was well suited for siege work. The 4.7-inch gun – as these experienced heavy gunners knew – was obsolete by 1914 and not suitable for use with the Heavy Battery. Despite persistent urging that they be replaced by modern 60-pounders, as late as 1938 the 15th Heavy Battery was still nursing its antiquated 4.7s.

In other parts of New Brunswick it is unclear just how many veteran field gunners returned from the front and rejoined the Militia in traditional gunner towns like Woodstock, Moncton, and Newcastle. Lt.-Col. Boyd Anderson returned to Moncton and to the colours, taking command of all three New Brunswick field batteries grouped into a new 4th Field Brigade. Anderson had enough veterans and enough clout to convince the Otter Commission in 1920 to renumber 4th Field Brigade as 12th Field Brigade, in homage to the wartime unit he had commanded. Moncton's old Militia 19th Battery, which had soldiered on during the war on the home front, was also renumbered to perpetuate 8th Battery, which had fought so well from 1915 to 1917. By the time the dust had settled from the Otter Commission Militia reorganization in June, the 12th Brigade, CFA, had been sorted out. Major Arthur Barton, who had served with 1st Field Brigade during the war, commanded Moncton's 8th Battery; Major R.V. Jones led 10th Battery in Woodstock; and Major J.W. Lawlor commanded what was now 90th Battery in Newcastle. They took their respective batteries to Camp Petawawa for the annual summer training camp that year. For that first decade after the war, when Permanent Force and Militia units remained full of combat veteran gunners, summer training standards were set high. The 12th Field Brigade's three batteries went through their paces hauling the ubiquitous 18-pounders behind teams of horses into firing positions and live-firing on practice ranges.

That same year, plans to commemorate Moncton's war dead were well in train, led by Lt.-Col. Anderson and 12th Field Brigade. His wartime prominence as Moncton's most famous veteran encouraged the local chapter of the Imperial Order Daughters of the Empire to attach his name to theirs and to enlist Anderson's wife in the organization. Both therefore became involved in IODE efforts to build the Soldiers Memorial in Moncton's Victoria Park, unveiled in on Armistice Day 1922. The 8th Battery under Major Barton formed an honour guard for the ceremony. The parade included a mounted detachment hauling gun and limber draped with 2nd Field Brigade's wartime flag. Anderson acted as master of ceremonies, and one of his former gunners, Stanley Steeves, who had been wounded on the Somme, unveiled the new monument along with Peter Legere, who had lost an arm serving with 79th Battalion. Anderson's prestige as a distinguished gunner earned him the job of president of the Canadian Artillery Association in 1923, giving New Brunswick a strong voice in that important national organization.

Veterans in Newcastle were not so fortunate. They lobbied for their unit to be renumbered after another successful front-line battery, the 28th. They failed to persuade the Otter Commission and ended up as 90th Battery. This was not a happy outcome, but it was not the end of the story. Randolph Crocker, who had commanded the Newcastle battery before the war and commanded it as 28th Battery on the Western Front, and others continued lobbying and got their wish some seven years later when the 90th was renumbered 28th Battery. Woodstock gunners likewise wanted to renumber their 10th Battery the 65th, to perpetuate their Depot Battery during the war and the unit from which a great number of New Brunswick gunners had gone off to war. But that number was already designated for a Saskatchewan battery. Therefore, during the 1920 reorganization Woodstock's old 10th Battery officially became 89th Field Battery.

Unlike 3rd (NB) Heavy Brigade, which was concentrated in Saint John, Lt.-Col. Anderson's 12th Field Brigade was spread across the province. That did not stop him from travelling the railways and the province's early road network to visit them regularly in Newcastle and Woodstock. Ironically, in the coming years his batteries would spend more time concentrated as 12th Brigade during summer training camps at Petawawa than in their own province.

The life of a Militia gunner in the 1920s and 1930s consisted of two things: training, and social and ceremonial events. Training revolved around local training at headquarters, sometimes combined with Provisional Schools of Instruction. The units mustered in their armouries in the fall, winter, and spring, doing routine training, drill, and basic courses. In late June the militia normally concentrated at Camp Sussex for about two weeks to conduct unit and formation training in the field. The gunners then spent evenings and weekends in July in feverish preparation for the trip to Petawawa, where 3rd and 12th Brigades concentrated for their annual program of firing.

The ceremonial role for NB gunners – indeed for all Militia units – was no less important because it demonstrated the army's presence in the community. The first major postwar ceremony for 3rd Brigade took place on Monday, 12 July 1920, when the HMS *Calcutta*, flagship of the Royal Navy's 8th Light Cruiser Squadron, arrived in Saint John. The official landing of Rear Admiral Sir Allen Everett, Royal Navy, took place on Monday, 12 July, with 6th Siege Battery under command of Lieutenant Albert Dodge firing a salute of thirteen guns from Reeds Point. The first major inspection of the new brigade followed early in 1921, when Lt.-Gen. Sir Henry Burstall, KCB, KCMG, then Inspector General of the Canadian Forces, arrived for a visit. General Burstall had a distinguished career in France as the first GOC of the Canadian Corps' Divisional Artillery and was one of the most noted gunners of the time. The 3rd (NB) Heavy Brigade was called to attention by Lt.-Col. Harrison, and the three batteries had every available man on parade. General Burstall noted that the brigade was progressing satisfactorily. The inspection ended with the presentation of the Colonial Forces Long Service Medal to Lt.-Col. Colonel Harrison and Major McGowan.

During the winter of 1921–22 a number of changes took place in the senior appointments of 3rd (NB) Heavy Brigade. Lt.-Col. Harrison transferred to the

Corps Reserve, and Major MacLeod was promoted to take command. Major Inches and Captain Fairweather also transferred to Corps Reserve, and Captains White and Slader were promoted to command 15th and 4th Batteries respectively. Captain Turnbull's appointment as adjutant completed the major substitutions, which would remain unaltered, with one exception, until 1926. Also during this period, two future commanding officers joined the brigade: Lieutenant Henry Morrisey, posted to 6th Siege Battery, and Lieutenant J.G. Hart, now fully recovered from wounds suffered at Vimy in 1917, who became a member of the 4th.

Annual inspections by the District Officer Commanding provide the best measure of the state of the Militia from this era, and a review of the Inspection Reports gives some insight into the training problems that confronted 3rd (NB) Heavy Brigade. A major one was qualifying non-commissioned officers, gun layers, and signallers – especially the latter – within the limited time allotted. It was customary to have an intensive six-day training period at Local Headquarters just prior to attending summer camp, but this was hardly enough without qualified instructors and proper training material. Furthermore, with the advent of field telephones and wireless, the need to site observation posts so that they could be seen from the gun positions was gone, so signalling had taken on a different and more complex form. Fire discipline, concealment, and message handling now became of primary importance, and it took many months to train a good signaller. In 1921 the brigade had only three qualified telephonists and ten signallers, and the situation improved little as the years went by. In most of his reports, Lt.-Col. MacLeod advocated longer training periods at Local Headquarters under the supervision of Permanent Force instructors.

Lt.-Col. MacLeod was also concerned about the complete lack of training in mobile operations and pleaded that some practice be provided in moving the heavy guns during the summer camp. His advice went unheeded, and it was a sign of the times that nothing could or would be done. There was little enough money to send the batteries to camp, let alone increase the training period or hire horses so that the brigade could practise moving guns around. This lack of mobility, and especially the inability to practise the critical art of mobile warfare, must have been particularly frustrating for gunners with wartime experience. The remarkable contributions of 4th and 6th Siege Batteries to the Hundred Days campaign in 1918 had been predicated on their mobility. The brigade would have to make do with what it had and what could be improvised, but apart from summer gun camps, training in the armoury could consist of little more than courses and drill on guns parked inside or in the yard.

The first postwar practice camp took place at Petawawa in 1922. All the batteries of 3rd Brigade and 12th Brigade attended. The 4th Siege Battery, composed largely of veterans, took all honours for medium batteries. It proved to be the most efficient in 3rd (NB) Heavy Brigade; indeed, it took first place in the Canadian

Artillery Association competitions for general efficiency (the Governor General's Cup) and gun practice (the Wilson Smith Challenge Cup). It was unusual for one battery to win both competitions. This was Major MacLeod's last tour of duty as Battery Commander. The success of 4th Siege Battery suggested that the choice of MacLeod as commanding officer had been a wise one. He and his battery officers (Captain Dodge, Lieutenant Hart, and Lieutenant Simonds) could well feel proud when Lt.-Col. C.F. Constantine, the Camp Commandant, described the 4th as "a good battery, well balanced throughout and considerably above average." Later on, the Chief of the General Staff, Maj.-Gen. J.H. MacBrien, sent a letter to the New Brunswick District Officer Commanding requesting him to "please convey congratulations [to the 4th Siege Battery] from the Honorable Minister of Defence and the members of the Militia Council on the excellent results achieved."

By contrast, 15th Heavy Battery did not fare well in 1922. Out of the eight batteries competing, it took seventh place in the general efficiency competition and last place in the gun practice – exactly opposite the results of 4th Siege Battery. Except for Major White, however, the battery had no qualified officers at the Practice Camp, and as previously mentioned, all the men were new recruits. In the years to come they would more than redeem themselves. As might be expected, Major Gamblin's 6th Siege Battery, with its balance of experienced gunners and new recruits, held the middle ground between the wartime artillerymen of the 4th and the new men of the 15th. In the signalling competitions, Gunner E.D. Walsh, a future officer in the brigade, took first-prize money for 6th Siege Battery, and Corporals E. Earle and J.A. Ricketts, along with Bombardiers E.J. Fournier, G.A. Ricketts, L.J. Strang, and Gunners J.E. Doane, and J.B. Pemberton, gained "pocket cash" for excellence in gun laying.

In 1923, the three batteries again attended summer camp. The "West Saint-Johners" of the 4th still stood out as one of the best siege batteries in Canada, while Major White's 15th Heavy Battery showed "much improvement." Lieutenant H.C. Alward, a medical student at McGill, was home on vacation and took a call-out with 15th Heavy Battery. It was noted that he was keen and receptive and would probably make a good officer. The following year, Alward's medical practice took him to California, but he would be back. It was a frequent occurrence for officers to transfer from the Corps Reserve to the active list, remain with the brigade for a short time, then return again to the reserve list when their civilian occupations compelled them to move away.

The 1924 Annual Inspection, made by Colonel Boyd Anderson, CMG, D.S.O., now District Officer Commanding of the New Brunswick Militia District, was held at the armoury on 14 November. Although 3rd (NB) Heavy Brigade could muster only fourteen officers and seventy-eight men, Anderson found a good and efficient unit. He was less happy with the brigade's administration. "As usual with City Corps," Anderson commented, "the battery orderly rooms were not well organized, nor the books well kept." Only three gun detachments attended camp at Petawawa that year. Six days' training at Local Headquarters were authorized, and all three batteries were termed efficient at standing gun drill – 4th Siege Battery, once again, being especially commended.

By the time of Colonel Anderson's inspection, Canada's artillery units were on the verge of yet another change in nomenclature. The British army had already departed from the standard Great War practice of differentiating field and garrison branches of artillery, and many officers felt that Canada must conform as all training was based on the Royal Artillery manuals. As a result, under General Order No. 82 of July 1925, the titles "Field" and "Garrison" artillery were replaced by the single generic title "Canadian Artillery," and the nature of the unit was now reflected in its individual title: "siege" and "garrison" artillery became "medium" and "coast," while "field" unit titles remained unchanged. Finally, the old term "company" disappeared forever from artillery usage in the British Empire and Commonwealth. These changes brought forth yet another iteration of 3rd Regiment's name, this time to "3rd (New Brunswick) Medium Brigade, Canadian Artillery." The name of the New Brunswick's other artillery unit, 12th Field Brigade, remained unchanged.

These changes took place in 1925, but the year is better remembered by 3rd Regiment for the laying up of its colours. Traditionally, an artillery unit's colours are its guns, and it is not customary for artillery regiments to have their own regimental flag. The notion of distinctive artillery colours, however, is not unknown. In the eighteenth century, artillery colours were carried on a "Flag Gun," typically the heaviest piece of ordnance in the field. However, by the twentieth century only two regiments in the British Empire were authorized to carry their own colours: the Honorable Artillery Company of London, and 3rd Regiment of Saint John. How The Loyal Company got their colours is still not clear. Alward, writing about the problem in the mid-twentieth century, assumed that Colonel Richard Hayne, the NB Brigade's commanding officer in the mid-nineteenth century, knew of this precedent, and he very likely gave assistance to the project. He had many contacts in England and may have known personally the Adjutant General or the Inspector of Regimental Colours. Both these gentlemen would have had to be involved if official sanction was sought and given.

What *is* known is that through the efforts of a Lieutenant Deacon, the flags were made in England of the "heaviest and most costly silk" and arrived by packet in Saint John in early December 1861. Both standards closely conformed to the regulations of the day. The "Queen's Colour" was a Union Jack with a garter star at its centre enclosed by a wreath. The wreath, in turn, was surmounted by Queen Victoria's crown, while underneath stood the date "1793" with the numerals worked in gold. The "Regimental Colour" to be absolutely correct should have been based on the facing colour of the brigade's uniforms at the time, which was red. Instead, the Regimental Colour was made as a blue ensign (blue being associated with artillery), with the garter star at its centre enclosing the words "New Brunswick" and the whole being encircled by a wreath of leaves. Once again, Victoria's crown was placed above the wreath, and the date "1793" below – a reminder that the 3rd was the oldest artillery unit in Canada. These colours were presented to the brigade by the women of the City and County of Saint John in 1861.

By 1925, 3rd Brigade – and its antecedents – had had the colours for sixty-four years, and they clearly pre-dated the establishment of the Dominion of Canada in 1867. The distinguishing feature of colours of the British Commonwealth (outside the British isles) is that the central wreath is composed of the leaves from a national tree or plant. In Canada, wreaths are traditionally composed of red autumnal maple leaves. The leaves on the colours of 3rd (NB) Medium Regiment in 1925 were – and are – willow, reflecting the unit's pre-Confederation New Brunswick lineage. That, apart from age and the fact that the regiment was unique in having its own colours, may well have been reason enough to retire them in 1925.

On Sunday, 13 September 1925, the colours were laid up in the Saint John's Stone Church for safekeeping. The event was a solemn occasion, with 3rd (NB) Medium Brigade parading from the armoury along Carmarthen, Mecklenburg, and Sydney Streets to King's Square, then down King and along Germain, Union, Peel, and Carleton Streets to the church. Lt.-Col. MacLeod was in charge of the parade, and all but one the brigade's officers marched. Lieutenant Merritt carried the Queen's Colour and Lieutenant Fowler the Regimental Colour, with a guard consisting of the three senior sergeants of the brigade: H. Pike, M.M.; W.J. Peters; and C.W. Walton. The Colours were laid on the altar and blessed by the bishop. Then the drummers and buglers sounded the Last Post, the Soldiers' Hymn (used particularly at the laying up of Colours) was sung, and the service ended. In the special seats, reserved in the body of the church, were many former officers of the old brigade, including Lt.-Col. J.B.M. Baxter, the Premier Designate of New Brunswick, and Lt.-Col. Beverley R. Armstrong, along with Colonels W.W. White, T.E.G. Armstrong, and Colonel Anderson, who represented the Permanent Force. Thus, the only artillery unit in modern times to possess a stand of colours, laid them up.

Lt.-Col. MacLeod retired on 20 May 1926, leaving newly promoted Lt.-Col. Gamblin in command. Life and training went on. All three batteries attended camp in Petawawa, with Captain Dodge holding command of 6th Battery briefly before his retirement in 1927. With war stocks of ammunition from the Canadian Corps now depleted, particularly in the larger calibres, training began to drift away from serious war-fighting skills. With what was left of the 6-inch howitzer and 60-pounder ammunition retained for emergency use, medium batteries were introduced to field guns – the 4.5-inch howitzer and the 18-pounder. And so it would remain for the next decade.

The Otter Commission had resolved the basic structure of the postwar Militia in the early 1920s, but the more vexing issue of battle honours and perpetuation of overseas units lingered through the decade. Much thought had been given to the problem, and it was earnestly hoped that the traditions and sacrifices of the Great War batteries would be kept alive and would help foster esprit de corps in the young militiamen. When the Otter Commission was so drastically revising the old prewar Militia, they had the perpetuation of CEF units in mind. However, many of the brigades and batteries in the reorganized Militia still had neither territorial nor historical associations with their numbered counterparts in the CEF, and it was considered important that the numbers of both be the same. In any event, it was decided that perpetuation would be on a territorial basis – as far as possible – and that only those CEF brigades and batteries that had actually fought in France, Belgium, and northern Russia would be perpetuated.

There was no dispute, of course, that 4th and 6th Medium Batteries would perpetuate their overseas counterparts. The 3rd (NB) Medium Brigade itself was to carry on the traditions of 3rd Canadian Heavy Brigade, Canadian Garrison Artillery, which had formed on 12 March 1918. Of the four batteries in this overseas brigade, three had been commanded by Saint John officers: 8th Siege by Major King; 10th Siege by Captain White, M.C.; and 12th Siege by Major MacKay, M.C. So it was fitting that the "3rd" should perpetuate the "3rd." General Order No. 83, dated October 1927, gave official sanction to the brigade to have its CEF connections

An 18-pounder of 28th Newcastle Battery at full recoil, Petawawa, ca. 1930. This photo indicates clearly how the single trail of the gun prevented the barrel from elevating, thus limiting the range of the gun. (NPL, Reid Collection)

perpetuated and recorded, as follows: 3rd (New Brunswick) Medium Brigade, Canadian Artillery, to perpetuate 3rd Canadian Heavy Brigade, CEF; 4th Medium Battery, Canadian Artillery (Howitzer), to perpetuate 4th Canadian Siege Battery, CEF: and 6th Medium Battery, Canadian Artillery (Howitzer), to perpetuate 6th Canadian Siege Battery, CEF. Battle honours came along with this connection. As the CEF's siege batteries were numbered from 1 to 12, and the heavy batteries from 1 to 2, 15th Medium Battery of 3rd (NB) Medium Brigade perpetuated nothing.

Some changes were in order for the names of New Brunswick field batteries in order to connect overseas batteries with their proper regional affiliations. The gunners of Newcastle had sought to have their old prewar 12th (Newcastle) Field Battery renumbered by the Otter Commission as 28th (Newcastle) Battery. Its Battery Commander in the 1920s, Major R. Crocker, had not only commanded 12th Battery before the war but also raised from it 28th Overseas Field Battery and then commanded the 28th in France. In 1927, Crocker won his long fight to have the battery renamed the 28th so that the Newcastle Battery could perpetuate its own CEF traditions. The number 90 was reassigned to a new Militia field battery authorized to form in Fredericton in 1928.

In 1927, Saint John's 15th Battery won the Archangel Cup at gun camp. The cup had been given to the Canadian Artillery Association by 16th Field Brigade of the North Russian Expeditionary Force to honour the battery with the greatest number of men attending who had been to previous practice camps. The 15th Battery beat fifty-six others to bring the cup back to Saint John. The year before, 4th Battery had won the distinction, and in 1928, 6th Battery had won the general efficiency competition under Major Anglin. Lt.-Col. MacLeod, now president of the Canadian Artillery Association, must have been well satisfied to see the high standing of his former brigade in all the competitions. This level of skill and enthusiasm would be hard to sustain in the coming decade.

By the late 1920s there was a general belief that another major war was a very remote possibility, and with cuts to training budgets it was increasingly hard to sustain morale and recruiting. The lack of funds to modernize Canada's artillery had an impact on all this too. The Great War had demonstrated clearly the possibilities of mechanical transport, and much thought was given to mechanization in the 1920s. The Canadian Corps's swift concentration in front of Amiens made possible by bus columns and by tractors for towing heavy artillery in the Hundred Days campaign was but one example of the mobility and surprise that motor transport offered. A major challenge was to develop a vehicle with good cross-country capability; the Great War vehicles had been strictly road-bound, with their rear axles rigidly fixed to the chassis. British designers overcame the problem by articulating the two rear axles about a common point so that they could overcome obstacles without affecting the vehicle's longitudinal stability. This opened up new horizons in mobile warfare, and limited production of prototypes of a medium six-wheeled

New Brunswick's 12th Field Brigade, motorized and assembled, Petawawa, ca. 1930. Note that the guns and limbers still have wooden wheels: suitable for the speed of draught horses but not motorized vehicles. (NPL, Reid Collection)

vehicle was begun by Thornycroft and (a lighter vehicle) by Morris. And in 1929 an artillery tractor, named the "Dragon," was issued as a trial to one British Field Brigade.

Staff officers in Ottawa avidly watched this progress, and accepted an offer made by the Gotfredson Motor Company of Walkerville, Quebec, to produce – at the company's own expense – a Canadian prototype heavy six-wheeled vehicle for military purposes. A trial was conducted at Rockcliffe, outside Ottawa, in 1928 between the Gotfredson "heavy," the Thornycroft "medium," and the Morris "light." The Gotfredson did not match the performances of the two British vehicles in any of the tests and was never heard of again. The trials did demonstrate, however, the suitability of the medium six-wheeler as an artillery tractor under all circumstances, and the value of the light six-wheeler for Militia training, where circumstances would be more favourable. It was also conclusively shown that with four vehicles (even of the "light" type), a battery could move more quickly and more efficiently than with horses.

Such conclusions appear obvious today, but many planners in the late 1920s were not convinced that motor transport should supplant horses, and they regarded with caution "the captivating blandishments of the apostles of Mechanization." It was found, however, that two objectives could be reached through mechanization. First and foremost, as far as the government was concerned, it offered a way to reduce expenses incurred through hiring horses and maintaining large establishments for horse brigades and batteries. And from the military point of view, mechanization offered a way of training the Militia artillery under modern conditions. This was one of the rare cases where the government and the military were in accord – albeit for different reasons – and in 1929, authority was granted to equip the three permanent force batteries at Kingston with mechanical transport. These were "A" and "B" Batteries of the Royal Canadian Horse Artillery and the regular army's 3rd Medium Battery. The following year, eight Militia artillery brigades from Ontario and Quebec were placed on the Militia Establishment as mechanized. As was typical, the mechanized transportation was not forthcoming for these Militia units, but the designation nicely reduced their allowable strength in personnel, thus permitting a savings. As for 3rd (NB) Medium Brigade, their only vehicle training would be the one-week summer camp at Petawawa, where they would receive instruction on mechanical transport from the Permanent Force.

On the eve of the Great Depression, New Brunswick's two artillery brigades were in good shape. The enthusiasm of new gunners was still leavened by combat-experienced NCOs and officers, and this showed in their annual inspection and summer camp reports. In 1929, 3rd (NB) Medium Brigade paraded 143 all ranks out of a total strength of 214 for annual inspection, and Brig.-Gen. Hill's remarks were again complimentary: the headquarters was very efficient, and the esprit de corps throughout the brigade was excellent. At Petawawa, the brigade stood sixth

The officers of New Brunswick's field batteries and the headquarters staff of 12th Field Brigade at Petawawa in 1933. (NPL, Reid Collection)

out of twenty-one in general efficiency, and at the battery level, 6th Battery placed fourth out of twelve competitors.

The 12th Field Brigade was doing well too. Its new four-battery organization was finally filled out with the newly formed 90th Field Battery (Howitzer) from Fredericton, and all four batteries made the trek to Petawawa. As usual, they spent weeks preparing for the camp, training intensely on their guns and going through their drills. Then the brigade made its way to Ontario on special troop trains organized to move the Militia units. The Moncton and Newcastle batteries travelled by CNR line through the Gaspé and along the St. Lawrence River, while batteries on the Saint John River took the CPR troop train through Maine. They all assembled in Montreal for the final train to Petawawa, the only place where New Brunswick's 12th Field Brigade was ever fully assembled as a unit.

The 1929 Practice Camp was 90th Field Battery's first summer field exercise, but they were well prepared. While 8th Moncton, 28th Newcastle, and 89th Woodstock Field Batteries practised with 18-pounders, 90th Battery drilled on the 4.5-inch field howitzer. All batteries had a day of practice shooting from fixed positions, followed by a half-day of field manoeuvring and a half-day of predicted map shooting and air-directed shooting. After that they fired instructional shoots as part of battery tactical training. Then on the final day came Canadian Artillery Association competitive firing practice.

The 28th Newcastle Battery staff work out a fire solution, Petawawa, ca. 1933. (NPL, Reid Collection)

Training was rigorous, inspired by wartime experience as well as by the latest technological developments. Permanent Force instructors placed special emphasis at the 1929 camp on operating around gas-saturated areas and selecting battery positions for protection against enemy tanks. Their standards were high, their criticism sharp. The 12th Field Brigade's batteries generally performed well given the mixture of veteran gunners and new militiamen. The 8th and 89th Field Batteries were the best in their brigade that summer. The 28th and 90th took the criticisms levelled at them to heart, and they arrived at the 1930 summer camp determined to improve their record, which they did. That was the summer when experimental mechanized training spread to Militia field batteries. The 90th Field Battery was among the first to exercise with motor lorries at that camp.

By the time 3rd (NB) Medium Brigade returned to Petawawa in 1930 it had a new name, again. General Order No. 33 of March 1930 restored some of the brigade's heritage, ordering that it now be called "3rd (New Brunswick) Medium Brigade, Canadian Artillery (The Loyal Company of Artillery)." Here was official recognition of the links to the past and to Captain Colville's Company of 1793. The title was unwieldy, and as the next twenty years would show, the restoration was by no means permanent.

Both New Brunswick brigades got new commanding officers in 1930. Lt.-Col. Ned Slader, previously in command of 4th Siege Battery, became the new CO of 3rd (NB) Medium Brigade. His was a fairy-tale story. He had joined the regiment as a gunner, served as the Regimental Sergeant Major, fought overseas for four years, was severely wounded, and served nearly nine continuous years as a Battery Commander. Under his guiding hand, 4th Battery twice won the Governor General's Cup. It was now Slader's chance to guide the regiment, and it would need his steady and fearless hand through the next few years, as the Western world plunged into the Great Depression. The field gunners of 12th Brigade also got a new commanding officer in 1930: Major H.H. Ritchie, who had previously commanded the Newcastle Battery.

By the time Slader and Ritchie took command of New Brunswick's artillery brigades, the Great Depression had begun. In the coming times of uncertainty, it was good that New Brunswick's gunners were well connected. In 1929, Lt.-Col. Gamblin had been elected one of the four vice-presidents of the Canadian Artillery Association. He would be followed by the next three commanding officers of 3rd (NB) Medium Brigade: Lt.-Cols. Slader, Morrisey, and Hart. The 3rd Brigade maintained a strong interest in the Artillery Association, and at many of the annual meetings it was not unusual to find five or six senior New Brunswick gunners in attendance. Their interest is the more remarkable in that they had to pay their own transportation and expenses; in the Depression years, this was not a lightly considered matter.

The Canadian Artillery Association's meetings provided a venue where problems and views could be aired, and where recommendations could be drafted that were based on Dominion-wide discussions rather than individual opinion. The Governor General, the Minister of National Defence, and the Chief of the General Staff, along with the Adjutant General and the Quartermaster General, often attended. The association sponsored the annual brigade and battery competitions held at Petawawa, and other Militia camps. It was also the venue where lobbying about the fate of Militia units could be most effective. During the Depression years, New Brunswick's gunners would need political connections and influence to preserve their units in the face of cutbacks and change.

By the time Lt.-Col. Slader took over, the shortages of the late 1920s and the dwindling of Great War influences were beginning to seriously affect the war skills of his brigade. The commandant of the 1930 Practice Camp observed that "most of the officers are inclined to be too deliberate and do not give the time factor as much consideration as they should." Firing needed to be faster and more urgent. As Alward concluded in his draft history, "the remark deserves attention but it might have been more valid had adequate supplies of ammunitions been available." With only ten rounds allocated for firing practice during its week at camp, each shoot was planned, and grave responsibility attended every fire order sent to the battery when only one projectile was permitted for each set of orders.

By 1931, Canada was fully in the grip of the Great Depression. Only $1,606,000 had been allotted for Militia training that year, so Practice Camps were suspended. There was just enough money to permit the city brigades four or five days' training at their own local armouries, providing they attended without pay. The Canadian Artillery Association evolved a plan to continue their competitions, and while training at Local Headquarters, the brigades and batteries competed as usual. The 15th Battery under Major Morrisey won the Association Challenge Cup for general efficiency, and also the Mercier Challenge Trophy for gun practice. The 4th Battery under Major Hart was close behind in each of these competitions.

It is sometimes wondered how the Militia survived the early 1930s. In the face of great economic adversity, which did not allow for equipment, clothing, or ammunition, training only continued because of the dedication, imagination, and resourcefulness of the officers and men of each unit. James Eayrs in his book *In Defence of Canada* described it as "malnutrition in the Militia." A few of the quotations he compiled provide insight into the difficulties of the period:

> We got no pay. We waived our pay into the regimental fund – every cent of it … When we enlisted a soldier, he signed a waiver of pay along with his attestation card, or he wasn't accepted … We had an MT [motor transport] unit but from 1926 until the outbreak of war we never had one item of motor transport issued to us – not a motor cycle, a van or a truck … Since the withdrawal of harness – our guns have become completely immobile. No adapters [for the gun hitch] have been issued, which makes it impossible to move them even if we had trucks. As a result, the guns almost assume the role of garrison pieces … In a memorandum circulated in 1935, General McNaughton gave

dramatic illustrations of existing deficiencies. As regards reserves of equipment and ammunition the matter is shortly disposed of – there are none. As regards equipment the situation is almost as serious …

   (i) There is not a single modern anti-aircraft gun of any sort in Canada,

   (ii) The stocks of ammunition on hand represent 90 minutes' fire at normal rates for the field guns inherited from the Great War, and which are now obsolescent …

   (iii) The Coast Defence armament is obsolete … as a number are defective and not considered capable of firing more than a dozen rounds … we have not dared for some years to indulge in any firing practice.

   (iv) About the only article which we have in abundance, is harness, and this is practically useless …

Those who kept their units together did so at great personal cost in time and money, and in the face of much public jeering at "the after-supper soldier." As one officer put it, "I used to pay out of my pocket about seven hundred dollars a year to keep a little Company of thirty men going … During the period of worst unemployment I had to provide carfare to get my men out on parade … It became our hobby … I don't know why we did it." Maj.-Gen. A.G.L. McNaughton, Chief of the General Staff during these trying years, may have provided a partial answer. "They bent their energies – perhaps unconsciously – to making Canada's defences as secure as possible," he wrote later, "for most of them had had experience and knew something of war's real misery. They also knew that it was highly improbable that the Great War would be the last one." Lt.-Col. Slader certainly believed in the early 1930s that another major war was likely. He saw "that the German ulcer was a cancerous growth." He also foresaw a rapid German mechanized thrust through Belgium putting a quick end to a campaign in continental Europe, and that "our next problem would be defending the shores of the United Kingdom itself." The men of 3rd Brigade – and indeed the Canadian Militia in general – probably shared that belief. Certainly, the loyalty and dedication of New Brunswick gunners to their skills is well amplified in the Canadian Artillery Association's prize lists of the 1930s.

The allotment of training funds improved in 1932, to $1,837,400. This was a modest increase of only $200,000 over the 1931 figure; even so, it permitted the central Practice Camps to open again. That summer, 15th Battery won the Governor General's Cup for efficiency and the Wilson Smith Challenge Cup for gun practice. Not since 1922 had a 3rd Brigade battery brought back both these high honours. The 15th Battery would nearly duplicate the feat again, in 1935, when, under the command of Major A.B. Gilbert, it came first in general efficiency and took the Wilson Smith Challenge Trophy for second place in the gun practice competitions. This time, the Governor General himself presented his cup to Gilbert at

Lt.-Col. E.M. "Ned" Slader, as commanding officer of 3rd (New Brunswick) Medium Brigade in Saint John. Slader joined the regiment in 1904 and served for four years overseas during the First World War first as a battery sergeant major and then as an officer and skilled FOO. He commanded batteries in the 1920s and took command of the brigade in 1930. (Loyal Company Association)

the annual meeting of the Artillery Association. Practice reports for the years 1933 to 1935 show that the brigade stood well to the front among the Canadian Artillery.

In 1933, Lt.-Col. Slader took 3rd Brigade through their first fully mechanized exercise at Petawawa. "I conducted the predicted shoot working out the lines of fire on the map beforehand," he recalled, "and applying weather corrections on the day of the shoot. Brigade HQ staffs moved by car to the firing position and the guns followed drawn by Leyland trucks. Everything was done at speed." No doubt a tribute to his Great War experience, despite the speed of deployment Slader's first salvo landed on target. Under Slader's leadership the overall efficiency of 3rd (NB) Medium Brigade remained high throughout the 1930s, even with obsolescent equipment and lack of training money. It placed eighth in 1933, seventh in 1934, and eighth in 1935, out of the twenty-four medium brigades from across the Dominion. All three of its batteries journeyed to Petawawa each summer. Reviewing the brigade in 1934, Brig.-Gen. Parsons remarked on its excellent esprit de corps, noting also that "all personnel were of a superior type." The 1934 Practice Camp was Lt.-Col. Slader's last as commanding officer. He had guided the brigade safely through the darkest days of the Great Depression – in itself a great tribute to his leadership and dedication.

There was no question that 3rd (NB) Medium Brigade gunners needed to be proficient. In theory they were medium gunners, and their regiment was still equipped with Great War vintage 6-inch howitzer and even older 4.7-inch guns. As they answered questions during their proficiency tests, they had to know all the specs and firing characteristics of the 6-inch howitzer and the 60-pounder gun (both were theoretically part of their order of battle) and their ammunition; at the same time, they had to know all about the lighter field guns which they were required to fire during their range practices. It is a measure of their devotion to service and of the dedication of their officers and NCOs that Canada's interwar gunners were so good. They would soon have cause to use those skills again.

As the 1930s drew on, further changes awaited Canada's Militia gunners. In 1935, battery ammunition columns were disbanded and – again following British practice – the duty of resupply to batteries was transferred to the Royal Canadian Army Service Corps. Also, the Canadian Artillery got their own "Royal" prefix that year. In commemoration of King George V's Silver Jubilee, the title "Royal" was conferred on all Militia artillery units. The Permanent Force batteries already used the title, so in 1935 all of Canada's gunners became part of the RCA. To distinguish between the two, the Militia units would henceforth carry the notation "N.P." – for "Non-Permanent" – on all official correspondence. The 3rd Brigade's full title now read: The 3rd (New Brunswick) Medium Brigade, Royal Canadian

Mechanization in the late 1930s required that 18-pounders be refitted with pneumatic tires, as seen on this gun being fired by 28th Newcastle Battery gun at Petawawa. Note that the trail has been dug in. This simple adaptation, common during the Great War, provided an additional 1,000 yards of range from the gun. (NPL, Reid Collection)

Artillery (The Loyal Company of Artillery) (N.P.). As the international situation darkened in Europe and the Far East between 1936 and 1938, the Militia was also thoroughly reorganized, resulting in what some called a "revolution by consent." The origins of this revolution go back to a memorandum of December 1931 from Maj.-Gen. McNaughton to the Minister of National Defence. The memorandum surveyed developments that, in McNaughton's view, removed the need to maintain a Militia organization based on the maximum available manpower in the Dominion. "A Militia establishment of four Cavalry and eleven Infantry Divisions had been recommended in 1919 because of a possible war with the United States," he wrote. "International developments since then have made such an eventuality most unlikely, and the need for such a large Militia has disappeared." Quite apart from the declining likelihood of a war with the United States, McNaughton felt that the existing establishment was unbalanced, being over strength in cavalry and infantry and ancillary arms and too light in firepower. He also felt that it was too large a force to be trained with current appropriations, and that if this circumstance continued, the result would be weak units and an overabundance of senior officers. With this as his background, McNaughton then proposed a force of one cavalry and six infantry divisions.

The real purpose of McNaughton's scheme of organization was to generate expeditionary forces for overseas service, or for rapid response at home. In many ways his ideas were visionary. He understood that Canadian membership in international organizations like the British Commonwealth and the League of Nations carried obligations. Moreover, in the increasing likelihood of a war between the United States and Japan, it would be necessary to maintain Canadian neutrality by ensuring that neither belligerent could use Canadian territory to attack the other.

In 1931 the Canadian government responded favourably to these proposals. In the depths of the Great Depression, McNaughton's proposed cutbacks dovetailed nicely with austerity measures, and also with the Disarmament Conference at Geneva. Not surprisingly, the Militia's response was cooler, especially among the Cavalry and Infantry Corps. McNaughton outlined his reasoning at the meeting of the Conference of Defence Associations in Ottawa in November 1932. Lt.-Col. G.A. Drew, then president of the Artillery Association, made a resolution in favour of McNaughton's proposed reorganization. The artillery, of course, was naturally in favour, for it stood to benefit. Cavalry and infantry representatives were not immediately persuaded, but in the end, the resolution passed with no dissenting votes.

Striking eight divisions – nearly half – of the Militia from the order of battle was a complex and politically fraught process, and finding the balance took years of planning. Work went ahead at a steady but gradual pace between 1933 and 1936. Throughout those years the wisdom of McNaughton's proposals became increasingly apparent. Although Canada did little – if anything – to support the League of Nations or to embrace defence planning in the Commonwealth, the prospect of

The Militia reorganization of 1936 created a second field brigade in New Brunswick, the 23rd, composed of 18-pounder batteries from Moncton, Newcastle, and Campbellton and a howitzer battery from Saint John. This photograph, taken in 1938, shows the brigade staff with their commander, Lt.-Col. A.T. Mclean, VD, of Moncton, in the front row, centre-left, and the officers of the four batteries. Captain Robert Reid, the 28th Battery officer who left a remarkable collection of photographs of the Newcastle battery training in Petawawa, is seated in the front row, second from the right. Major J. Campbell, who mobilized the Newcastle Battery in 1939, is to Reid's right.
(NPL, Reid Collection)

war grew with every passing year. In 1931 the Japanese had invaded China, starting a prolonged war that eventually would spill over into a much larger Pacific war in 1941. The Nazis' seizure of power in Germany in 1933 began a six-year period of increasing tensions in Europe that would culminate in a major European war. In 1936 one member of the League of Nations, Italy, attacked another, Ethiopia, in a blatant war of aggression and conquest, which the league was powerless to stop. International bodies fared no better when Fascist forces led by Spain's colonial army rebelled against the democratically elected leftist government in Madrid and started a brutal three-year civil war. Democratic governments, wedded to the notion of non-interference, stood by while Italy crushed Ethiopia and while German, Italian, and Soviet forces supported factions in Spain. The world seemed to be headed for a catastrophic collision. By the late 1930s it was no longer a case of "if" a major war would happen again – it was simply a matter of when.

McNaughton and many of his Permanent Force and Militia officers understood that Canada needed a smaller, more modern and balanced force, one that emphasized mechanization, armour, and firepower. With the planning principles envisaged, it was determined that the Cavalry Corps were surplus twenty-three regiments and the Infantry Corps fifty-one battalions. By the same token, the artillery was short sixty-eight batteries, and there were also serious deficiencies among engineers, signallers, and services. Some surplus cavalry and infantry units were to be converted to new artillery and armoured units. The reorganization called for more field artillery units organized on the successful Great War model of four batteries: three field and one field howitzer.

This scheme resulted in a major shuffling of New Brunswick Militia units, the outlines of which were clear by the fall of 1936. The NB Dragoons and the NB Machine Gun Battalion were both struck off the order of battle, and the Carleton Light Infantry and the York Regiment were amalgamated. Out of this emerged the province's third artillery brigade. The new 23rd Field Brigade included Moncton's 8th Battery, 28th Newcastle Battery, and the newly established 103rd Field Battery in Campbellton (remustered from "A" Squadron of the now-defunct New Brunswick Dragoons). The 23th Brigade's howitzer battery was formed by plucking 6th Battery from 3rd (NB) Medium Brigade and converting it to 106th Field Battery

The 105th Battery at Petawawa, 1938, just after its conversion from C Squadron, NB Dragoons. In the front row, centre-left is Lt.-Col. Albert A. Dodge, the 12th Field Brigade Commander, and to his left Lt.-Col J.O. Spinney, the battery commander. Spinney had risen through the ranks of the NB Dragoons and achieved command of the regiment at the moment it was struck from strength. To Spinney's left is Captain Walter Love, also late of the NB Dragoons, just back from his gunnery conversion course in Kingston, and to Love's left Lt. Gordon Coffey. Three of the gunners behind them died in action just a few years later. (Courtesy Bruce Jackson)

Church Parade, Petawawa, late 1930s, probably 12th Field Brigade. (Walter Love Collection)

(Howitzer). So the new 23rd Field Brigade, commanded by Lt.-Col. A.T. Mclean, V.D., with headquarters in Moncton, stretched in a great arc from Saint John around the eastern part of the province to the north shore. New Brunswick's original 12th Field Brigade, which had shifted its headquarters to Fredericton in 1930, retained 89th Woodstock Field Battery and 90th Fredericton Field Battery (Howitzer). It now added 104th Fredericton Battery, formed from the New Brunswick Dragoons "B" Squadron and men from the NB Machine Gun Battalion in Fredericton, and 105th St. George Battery remustered from "C" Squadron of the Dragoons. The 12th Field Brigade was therefore tightly grouped in the lower Saint John River area. Lt.-Col. Albert A. Dodge was recalled from retirement to command it.

Many of the officers, NCOs, and men from cavalry squadrons and the machine-gun battalion, already well qualified in those branches of service, now learned to become gunners. This started locally, with basic conversion courses and then special camps of instruction held to help qualify the troops in their new branch. Among those to make the transition was Captain Walter Love, of C Squadron, NB Dragoons. The son of a Great War veteran, Love had spent the 1920s in the York Regiment, leaving in 1929 as Acting RSM to join the Dragoons. He had just qualified as a cavalry captain in 1936 when his unit became an artillery battery; now he had to retrain all over again in a third branch of service. By 1938 he had completed the special course laid on in Kingston, Ontario, and earned his full qualifications as a gunnery officer. Love would later earn further distinction as the only prewar New Brunswick gunner to command his new battery, the 105th, in action overseas. His dedication and adaptability were not unique. New Brunswick militiamen across the province, who had carried on through the uncertainty and the penury of the 1930s, would still be there – trained, qualified, and ready – when Canada needed them in 1939.

The great question mark in the reorganization of 1936 was the fate of 3rd (NB) Medium Brigade. The transfer of 6th Siege Battery to the field artillery had reduced 3rd Brigade to two batteries, and in late 1936 there was talk of amalgamation with the Prince Edward Island medium unit to form one regiment. By the end of the year, that fate had been staved off. But in an age of increasing air power and of expectations that much of what heavy artillery had done in the Great War would now be done by bombers, there seemed little need for a medium regiment as part of a mobilization plan. In fact, Canada possessed no modern medium or heavy artillery at all, and units like 3rd (NB) Medium were still using the same guns they had two decades before.

So it was a much reduced and rather uncertain 3rd (NB) Medium Brigade that travelled to Petawawa – for the last time – in 1937. Brig.-Gen. L.F. Page, D.S.O., conducted the annual inspection on 2 August 1937, just prior to the brigade's departure. Without 6th Battery, its strength was reduced to 20 officers and 118 other ranks, and only 14 officers and 70 men were on parade for Page's inspection. Lt.-Col. Morrisey was singled out for his exceptional abilities in guiding the technical training of his officers and men, but Page noted – as Colonel Anderson had many years before – that the administration was below par. At Practice Camp, attended by all of New Brunswick's artillery batteries at the same time, 3rd (NB) Medium Brigade came seventh out of twenty-six in general efficiency. This was the Artillery Association's number one competition, and it must be remembered that it included all of the Dominion's field, medium, and heavy brigades. The 15th Battery, in particular, maintained its standard of the past five years, placing very high in the various competitions for general efficiency and gun drill.

While the army prepared for expeditionary war overseas, the Mackenzie King government had other ideas. Canada had the right to determine its own contribution if Britain and the Commonwealth became involved in another war, but King and his cabinet colleagues believed that the Canadian contribution would be mainly economic and that conscription for overseas service should never be adopted. A controversial defence program that might arouse tensions between English and French Canada or regional animosities was to be avoided at all costs. This meant that the defence program, to secure general acceptance, would have to be, in the first instance, a program of home defence. With this in mind, military planners revised Defence Scheme No. 3, which had emphasized sending an expeditionary force overseas. Also, a chapter on "Local Defence and Internal Security" was now added to that scheme. It laid down the responsibilities for District Officers Commanding for the protection of their districts, against such risks as attacks on Canadian coastal ports, damage to vulnerable points, raids by enemy sympathizers from across the border, and civil unrest.

The problems of coast defence were increasingly pressing. During the Great War, the ability of enemy warships to attack Canada's coast had been severely restricted by their reliance on coal-fired engines. That was why coast defence for Saint John had been seen as a political but not a military necessity in 1914. Diesel-electric-propelled submarines had changed that calculation by 1917–18, giving the batteries on Partridge Island a clear and important operational role in the final stages of the Great War. The expansion of large, oil-fired warship fleets throughout the 1920s and 1930s, and the construction in Germany of large, very-long-range oil-fired raiders, totally changed the coast defence scenario throughout the British Commonwealth. Moreover, the Germans were known to be working on a fleet of refuelling tankers, which could simply pump fuel oil through a hose to warships at sea. The operational capabilities of oil-fired raiders were not limitless, but changes in marine propulsion did make the North Atlantic an easy cruising ground. Certainly Canada could no longer take such a cavalier attitude towards the defence of its critical ports.

In September 1936 it was decided to make provisions for the undefended ports of Sydney, Saint John, Vancouver, and Prince Rupert. The "garrison towns" of Halifax, Quebec City, and Victoria had maintained Coast Brigades throughout the 1920s, but they too were woefully unprepared with regard to ordnance and ammunition. The British War Office was therefore asked to send out an expert to review Canada's coast defences. The Royal Artillery sent Major B.D.C. Treatt, M.C., a gunnery instructor from the coast artillery school at Shoeburyness. His report, based on the anticipated scales of attack as prepared in advance by Canadian military authorities, provided a comprehensive survey of the requirements for each of the ports selected for defence, and was the basis for future planning.

Major Treatt's report had a strong impact on the fortunes of 3rd (NB) Medium Brigade. There was no question that Saint John needed to be properly defended. It was still Canada's main cargo port between November and May each year, when the St. Lawrence was closed by ice. Halifax still handled most of the high-value – and high-profile – passenger traffic, but Saint John had more alongside cargo-handling capacity and better rail connections. Moreover, the Saint John dry dock, constructed in the 1920s on Courtenay Bay, was among the largest in the world. Its design and construction had been coordinated and subsidized by the British government to ensure that it could handle the largest warships planned for the Royal Navy. Similar dry docks had been built around the Empire. If nothing else, the dry dock – the closest one to Britain – needed to be secured against bombardment and damaging raids.

With the rapid expansion of the German navy, by late 1938 the probable scales of attack envisaged for Saint John included bombardment by an 8-inch gun cruiser or an armed merchant vessel. Also considered was the risk of attack by motor torpedo boats, one or two modern submarines, or a landing party of up to 250 all ranks. Treatt in his report recommended that a modern fortress system be constructed to protect the port of Saint John and the Canadian staff augmented his proposals to deal with increasing German capabilities. This included both counter-bombardment and close defence batteries, the latter sited at the southern end of Partridge Island and the former at Mispec, on the outer reaches of the harbour.

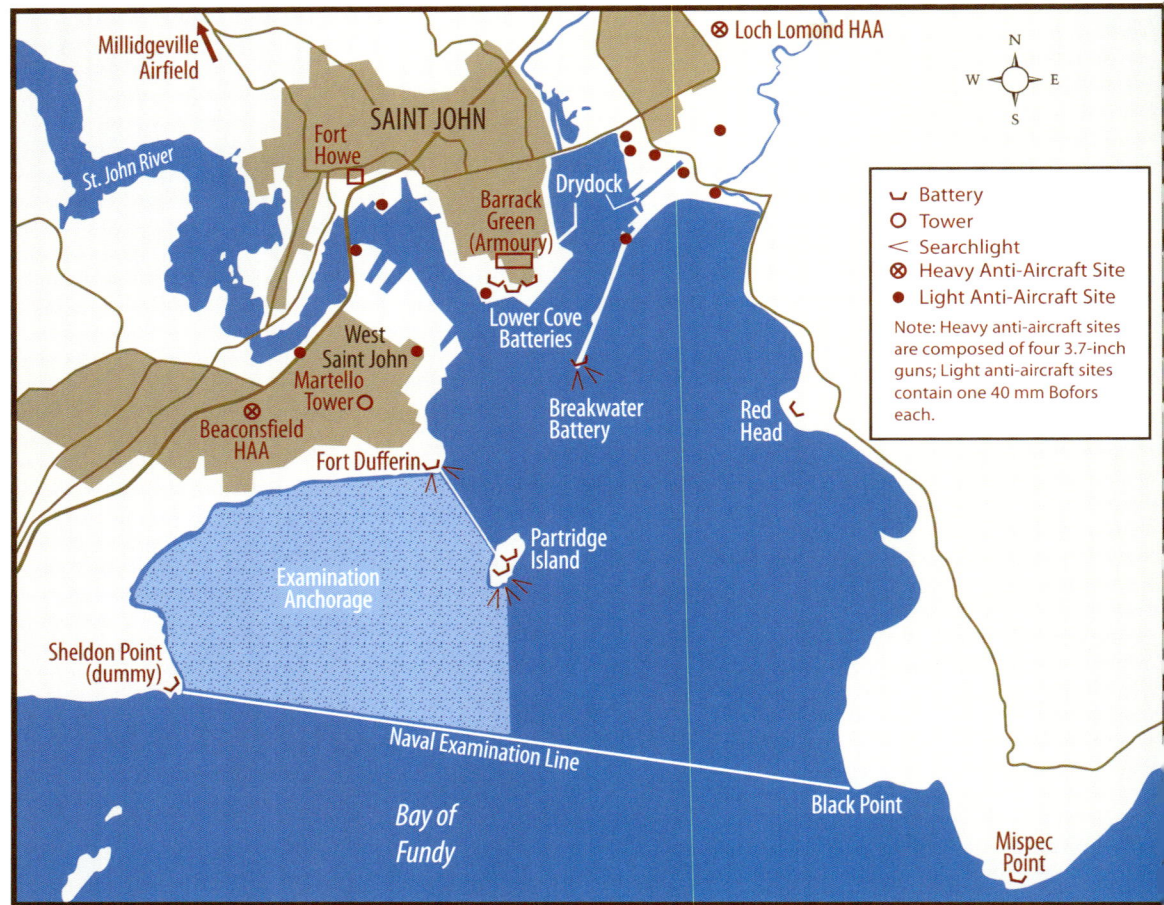

Fortress Saint John, 1880–1956

To guard against motor torpedo boats inside the harbour it was recommended that two 12-pounders be installed at Fort Dufferin and two near the end of the Courtenay Bay breakwater. In addition, a substantial garrison of infantry would be required to handle possible raiding parties.

It was one thing to develop plans for a coast defence program, but quite another to get the ordnance required. In late 1937, a tabulation was made of the requirements for coast guns together with the estimated dates of delivery if orders were placed immediately. It was found that the armament of most defended ports could not be completed before 1942–43. In view of the deteriorating international situation, it was rightfully assumed that this would be too late. So an "interim plan" was drawn up that made use of the ordnance already available in Canada and of guns that could quickly be provided by the British. Plans were made to erect a counter-bombardment battery of three 7.5-inch naval guns at Mispec, and orders were sent to the British Admiralty which had a reserve of these guns from warships scrapped after the First World War. Even so, on the eve of the Second World War, no fixed defences of any description had been installed at Saint John (or Sydney, or on the Strait of Canso).

Along with the problems of supply and construction went the problem of manning the coast defences. For reasons of training, availability in emergency, and cost, it was felt that the Militia units manning the coast and anti-aircraft defences should be localized at or near their war stations. So it was natural that the brigade based in Saint John should be converted to a coast defence role to defend its own city. This duly occurred on 14 April 1938, when 3rd (NB) Medium Brigade became "3rd (New Brunswick) Coast Brigade." This was, of course, a return to a role that the regiment had played at the beginning of the century. The 15th Medium Battery – still manning its antiquated 4.7-inch guns – became 15th Heavy Battery, but for the moment, 4th Medium Battery and its 6-inch howitzers remained "attached" to 3rd Brigade for administrative purposes.

In the early months of 1938, a course of instruction in the new coast defence role was held at the Saint John Armoury to instruct the officers and senior NCOs. Conducted by D. McCarthy, a Permanent Force Warrant Officer of the Halifax Garrison, with Sergeant Horwell as his assistant, the course was designed to qualify personnel in Part One (i.e., the technical portion) of coast gunnery training. Part Two, the practical portion of the course, would run concurrently with the annual training at Practice Camp. It would seem that the personnel of 3rd (NB) Coast Brigade embraced their new duties with enthusiasm. Part One of the course was well attended and took the place of the customary spring training period.

That summer for the first time ever, Saint John gunners went east for their practice camp. On 15 August 1938, officers and men of the brigade set off for Halifax via Digby to undergo training in coastal gunnery. It would have been quite normal for 4th Battery, which had not yet been formally converted to a coastal role, to have trained at Petawawa. Authority was granted, however, for it to go with the brigade to Halifax as well. Headquarters and both batteries (the 4th and 15th) were quartered at Sandwich Battery on the approaches to Halifax harbour, and were joined by the newly converted 16th Coast Brigade from Sydney, Nova Scotia. All of the brigade's officers and thirteen other ranks completed their Part Two Coast Gunnery Qualification. There was no competitive firing, nor was there any signalling competition. Rather, gun laying and the basics of coastal gunnery were the focus. When Brig.-Gen. Page returned for the annual inspection on 2 December 1938, he observed that the brigade was functioning in a satisfactory manner and that the new commanding officer had faced the changes with cheerfulness and energy.

The regiment took its final, prewar form in March 1939. On 1 March, 4th Battery was redesignated 4th Heavy Battery and formally allocated to its mother unit.

Also, a new element was added to the brigade that month when 1st Searchlight Battery, Royal Canadian Artillery (Coast Defence), was authorized, ordered to recruit immediately, and attached to 3rd (NB) Coast Brigade.

A general feeling of insecurity prevailed throughout the world in 1938. The Anti-Comintern Pact between Japan, Germany, and Italy had been signed, and British Prime Minister Neville Chamberlain went to Munich to placate Hitler. The Nazi leader had already remilitarized the Rhineland, begun a massive rearmament of Germany, and annexed Austria. Now he claimed that all he wanted was Czechoslovakia and peace would be assured. Britain and France gave him a peaceful entry. The nation in question was not even at the conference. As one British source said, "it was like standing around a table in a mortuary and dissecting a body that wasn't there." Chamberlain returned to Britain waving the Munich agreement and proclaiming "Peace in our time," telling his countrymen go home and "sleep quietly in your beds." Not everyone was convinced. By the summer of 1939, Hitler was sabre-rattling again, this time over Poland and lingering German grievances over territory that had once been part of Prussia. In truth, Hitler needed no provocation, and it was increasingly evident he was bent on a major war.

A reunion dinner for 6th Overseas Siege Battery, Admiral Beatty Hotel, Saint John, October 1938.
(NBM, G.W. Humphrey Collection)

A general gloom, therefore, hung over 3rd (NB) Coast Brigade's "at home" in the Georgian Ballroom of the Admiral Beatty Hotel in August 1939. About 300 guests were present. They were received by Honorary Lt.-Col. and Mrs. Harrison, and by the Brigade Commanding Officer, Lt.-Col. Hart, and his wife. On the centre of the ballroom's east wall, placed between two Union Jacks, stood a chart tracing the brigade's history from 1793 to 1938. Supper was served at 11 p.m., and the guests enjoyed dancing to the strains of Bruce Holder's orchestra. Many thought they were close to the end of the "Long Armistice."

On 19 August the brigade departed for Halifax for what was to be its second – and last – Practice Camp at Sandwich Battery. The officers and men paraded at the Saint John Armoury at 0700 hours and marched to Reeds Point, where they embarked on the CPS *Princess Helene* for the trip across the Bay of Fundy, and then travelled by train to Halifax. They were joined by the new 8th Anti-Aircraft Battery and No. 1 Fortress Company, Royal Canadian Engineers, both of which were critical to the developing plan for the Saint John Fortress. The entire body of thirty officers and 230 other ranks composed what was thought to be the largest Saint John contingent to embark from the city since the Great War.

Meanwhile, events overseas were moving with alarming rapidity, and the newspaper headlines told the story for all who watched anxiously. On 23 August, Germany was told that Britain would stand by her pledge to Poland, even as Hitler insisted that Poland simply capitulate in the face of his demands. France reaffirmed her guarantee to Poland as well; for Hitler, the line in the sand was clear. It mattered not at all. Hitler had already hatched a plan with his new friends, the Soviet Union, to carve up Poland, and he would fabricate the necessary provocation. On 26 August all Permanent Force leaves were cancelled, and 3rd (NB) Coast Brigade (still training in Halifax) was called out for active service. So the summer Practice Camp of 1939 quickly assumed an operational role, helping man the Sandwich Battery. Four days later, as New Brunswick's field batteries were called to active duty, 3rd (NB) Coast Brigade returned home to defend Canada's most important east coast cargo port and one of the largest dry docks in the world. Hitler invaded Poland on 1 September, and two days later Britain and France declared war on Germany. Canada waited another week before formalizing her entry into the war, but by then, thousands of its men – including thousands of gunners – were already on the march.

Chapter 7

War on the Home Front, 1939–45

In the early hours of 1 September 1939, Germany invaded Poland. The news was hardly a surprise. The sabre-rattling and apprehension of war had led the Canadian government to prepare for mobilization through August, including units and formations for home defence and for an expeditionary force in the event of a general European war. The mobilization of fifty-six batteries (fifty-one of them Militia) for general service was approved on 24 August. Two days later, 3rd (NB) Coast Brigade, in Halifax for its annual training, went on active service, and prepared to return to Saint John to take charge of the fortress guarding that key port. Sixteen hours after German forces crossed the Polish border on 1 September the "mobilization telegram" went out, which called up four New Brunswick field batteries for war. The 8th Field Battery in Moncton and 90th Field Howitzer Battery in Fredericton were assigned to 1st Canadian Division, while 28th Field Battery in Newcastle and 89th Field Battery in Woodstock joined 2nd Canadian Division. For the men of these units – and for tens of thousands of men across Canada – the Second World War started a full ten days before Canada declared war on Germany. No one could have anticipated then how long the road to war would be or where it would ultimately take them.

In August 1939 only the officers and men of 3rd (NB) Coast Brigade knew with certainty where they were going: home. Unlike in 1914, when the government hastily dispatched four obsolescent 4.7-inch guns on field carriages to Saint John

The armed merchant cruiser (AMC) *Laconia* undergoing repairs in dry dock, June 1940. This was the start of a wave of repair work that would keep the dockyard and dry dock busy for the whole war. The AMC *Jervis Bay* followed in the dry dock in July and August, then steamed out to her destruction by the German pocket battleship *Scheer* off Newfoundland in November – proof, if it was needed, that the enemy was out there. (Milner Collection)

in an entirely symbolic gesture to placate local anxiety, in 1939 the government scrambled to meet a real and present danger. During the interwar years Germany had built a fleet of powerful long-range oil-fired raiders, along with a small flotilla of large tankers to support them in the broad reaches of the North Atlantic. Naval and air forces were supposed to keep these ships at arm's length, but weather conditions off Canada's coasts meant that the only sure defence against them – night and day, good weather and bad – were coastal gunners. In this second world war in a generation, New Brunswick's heavy gunners had a vital role to play in defence of the port of Saint John. Indeed, over the next three years they would become the heart and soul of one of Canada's most complex and sophisticated fortress systems, guarding Canada's most important all-season east coast cargo port.

When Saint John's gunners converted from a medium artillery role to coast defence in 1936–37, the government's plans for defending Saint John were still modest. Initially these were limited to a single three-gun 6-inch battery on Partridge Island, with supporting batteries of light quick-fire guns at Fort Dufferin and on the Courtenay Bay breakwater. The Partridge Island 6-inch guns were to have the latest "high-angle" coast defence mountings, with a range of approximately 20,000 metres, ample to match the guns of an armed merchant ship attempting long-range bombardment, and with a high-volume fire at shorter ranges to stop attempts to rush into the harbour. By 1938, the Germans' emphasis on building heavy warships well suited to long cruises had increased the possibility that major warships might strike at Canada's east coast ports. In the case of Saint John, the military chiefs now anticipated bombardment by a heavy armoured warship from distances of over 30,000 metres. Consequently, in 1938 the militia general staff revised the plans for Saint John to include a battery of three 9.2-inch guns on modern high-angle mountings. These weapons fired a 360-pound projectile (compared to 100 pounds for the 6-inch) to a range of 30,000 metres.

Surveys concluded that Mispec Point was the best location for this specialized long-range counter-bombardment battery. The ground was high and gave a wide arc of fire that covered the whole of the approaches to the harbour. The proposed battery at Mispec made it unnecessary for the Partridge Island battery to have long-range capability, and the militia staff changed the armament there to three 6-inch guns on low-angle mountings, which were adequate for close defence. In short, the revised plans of 1938 – for a counter-bombardment battery at Mispec and a close defence battery on Partridge Island, with supporting quick-fire batteries at the mouth of the inner harbour – laid the foundations for the development of the modern coast defence fortress that 3rd NB Coast Brigade was destined to man.

The 3rd Brigade and 8th AA were still at Halifax when, during the night of 25–26 August, the Canadian government received a "precautionary" telegram from Britain to begin security measures in anticipation of war. At Saint John, volunteers from the local infantry unit, the Saint John Fusiliers, came out on active service to guard the armouries at Lower Cove, the dry dock, and the government radio station at Red Head. By the time 3rd Brigade disembarked from the *Princess Helene* on 1 September, military engineers of 1st Fortress Company, RCE, were at work at the southern end of Partridge Island, pouring concrete platforms into which were imbedded mounting bolts for the two 6-inch low-angle naval guns of the "interim" armament. These came from the navy's first cruiser, HMCS *Niobe*, and had been held in reserve after she was decommissioned in 1920. Three days later the brigade, at a peacetime strength of 171 officers and men, including 4th and 15th Heavy Batteries and 1st Searchlight Battery, moved out to the island and took up residence in the quarantine station buildings, as they had in 1914. By 10 September – the day Canada declared war – Permanent Force artillery technical personnel from Halifax, with assistance from the brigade, had mounted both guns, and ammunition for them had arrived. The Saint John fortress was now operating.

Delivery of the big naval guns for Mispec – the 7.5-inch guns that were to serve until still heavier army 9.2-inch guns could be procured – was some months away, but work on the substantial fortifications required for the naval guns was also well in hand. By the time war broke out, as part of the accelerated program for the battery that the government approved in the spring of 1939, the engineers in Ottawa had nearly completed the design for the fortifications. Just as mobilization began, headquarters authorized the New Brunswick military district to let contracts to industry for construction of the new battery.

The "interim plan" developed for Saint John included only the Partridge Island and Mispec batteries. However, the district staff in New Brunswick had made plans in 1938 to augment the defences with guns on field carriages drawn from stocks available in the province. In the latter part of September 1939, four of the venerable 4.7-inch guns and four 18-pounders dating from the Great War were emplaced at Fort Dufferin. The 4th Heavy Battery moved from Partridge Island to the fort on the mainland, where wooden barracks were under construction, and brought the guns into action. Dufferin's guns and the two 6-inch guns on Partridge Island covered the primary channel into the harbour (which is now blocked off by the breakwater linking the island to the mainland). The wheeled carriages at Fort Dufferin limited the ability of the guns they carried to engage fast-moving vessels that might be expected at the harbour mouth, but eight guns firing as a battery could generate a considerable volume of fire. In any event, they were useful for training new personnel – just as they had been a generation before.

In October, 4th Heavy Battery at Fort Dufferin moved one of its 18-pounders to the Courtenay Bay breakwater to serve as interim armament until the quick-firing battery planned for that site was built. The unit used its own funds to rig a platform that would allow the field gun to be swung around more quickly. In October as well,

SS *Urla* entering Saint John harbour, August 1940. The main cargo docks are to the right: Saint John had more alongside cargo-handling capability than Halifax. This part of the harbour was assigned primarily to 15th Battery of 3rd NB Coast Regiment. The headland on the right, at the foot of the breakwater, is Fort Dufferin, with Partridge Island in the background. (LAC PA-104135)

National Defence Headquarters arranged for the supply of two commercial searchlights, which the engineers set up on the shoreline at the southern end of Partridge Island, below the gun positions. Operating these became the task of 1st Searchlight Battery. Their "concentrated beam" projected a narrow fan of light to a range of 4,000 to 5,000 metres to track incoming vessels. To provide area lighting closer to the harbour mouth, the fortress engineers also rigged up automotive spotlights at Courtenay Bay breakwater.

The 3rd Brigade, in having to master coast defence from almost a standing start with utterly inadequate equipment, was in fact repeating the experience of the Composite Battery during the Great War. The brigade had converted to the coast defence role only in 1938 (and 4th Battery only later in the year), so the only experience the brigade had had was in the two short summer sessions at Halifax, in which the training strength had been limited to only fifty-five personnel per battery. During the first weeks of the war, two Permanent Force non-commissioned instructors in gunnery arrived from Halifax to help. They had a weekly training syllabus, which paid particular attention to the training of specialists such as range takers, gun layers, and signallers. Unlike during the Great War, Saint John was now classed as a defended port, on a scale comparable to Halifax, as well as to Sydney in Cape Breton (the other newly designated "defended port"). For that reason, 3rd Brigade was to receive further assistance from the Permanent Force artillery at Halifax: about a dozen specialist personnel to serve at Partridge Island. Their arrival, one officer and ten other ranks, was delayed by personnel shortages at Halifax until 25 January 1940. The officer was former Regimental Sergeant Major Nicks, a highly experienced instructor in gunnery, who was commissioned as a lieutenant to meet Saint John's needs; he was particularly helpful in instructing and advising the brigade's officers.

When the army's Inspector General, Maj.-Gen. E.C. Ashton, formerly Chief of the General Staff, visited 3rd (NB) Coast Brigade in March 1940, he was impressed by the keenness and efficiency of the officers and the quality of the men in all three batteries. The brigade's strength had grown to 270 all ranks. "Recruiting was good," Ashton commented. "Units proceeded slowly in order to select suitable personnel." Important for the technical work of coast defence, "a fair selection of tradesmen was obtained." Ashton thought the unit had done well with training, but emphasized that it could not be considered effective until it had carried out gun practice. Here was a Catch-22: the brigade had guns, but it was improvised armament, and the fortress's still nearly non-existent fire control equipment raised doubts about how useful gunnery practice would be. Ashton urged haste in improvements, such as mounting the 4.7-inch guns on improvised coast defence pedestals (as in fact had been done in the Great War).

While 3rd (NB) Coast Brigade struggled to meet the standards expected, the strength of the Saint John garrison continued to grow. By early March 1940 it was already at 1,389 personnel of all ranks. The 8th Anti-Aircraft Battery (198 all ranks) was in barracks recently completed at the "K" Grounds, and provided detachments to crew machine-guns on high-angle mounts at the dry dock and other key facilities that might be the target of air attack. The Fortress Headquarters and main encampment were at the Barrack Green Armories, which housed the engineers, signallers, service corps, and medical corps, together with the infantry (at this stage the New Brunswick Rangers and Saint John Fusiliers, with 322 all ranks each). The Saint John Fusiliers provided guard detachments and additional machine-gun posts at the dry dock and the West Saint John ocean terminals, while the New Brunswick Rangers carried out shore patrols to the east and west of the city. The main role of both units, however, was to be ready quickly to move large bodies of troops in response to landing parties in the vicinity of the port or along the adjacent coasts. Lt.-Col. Hart, commander of 3rd NB Coast Brigade, was double-hatted as the commander of the garrison; thus the headquarters of 3rd Brigade in the Barrack Green Armories also served as the headquarters of the defended port.

The army garrison was not expected to defend Saint John alone: both the navy and the air force were part of the larger scheme. In September 1939 the main east coast naval forces, based at Halifax, included all six modern destroyers of the Royal Canadian Navy and, for a time, two cruisers of the Royal Navy's America and West Indies Squadron – the first of many British and Allied warships that would carry out shipping defence from Halifax all through the war. The main base for the RCAF's long-range reconnaissance and bombing aircraft was also in the Halifax area, and a new airfield was under construction at RCAF Station Dartmouth. Their main job was to work with the navy in securing the ocean shipping routes off the Maritime provinces and Newfoundland, and keep watch for enemy vessels headed towards the Canadian coast. Work was also under way on new airfields for heavy aircraft at Sydney and Yarmouth, Nova Scotia, so that bombing and reconnaissance aircraft would be immediately available for long-range coverage of the approaches to the Gulf of St. Lawrence and the Bay of Fundy.

Saint John was well inside this outer ring of defences, so its air and naval requirements remained modest: light aircraft were needed in support of the coast guns, while the navy needed the apparatus of naval control of shipping for the port. The air force component of the Saint John defences included the headquarters and one "flight" (out of two) of No. 2 (Army Co-operation) Squadron, a Permanent Force unit of the RCAF. The squadron, whose peacetime base was Trenton, Ontario, moved to Halifax during the initial precautionary mobilization in late August 1939. On 31 August, RCAF ground personnel arrived at Saint John, and the following day, four Armstrong-Whitworth "Atlases" flew in to the municipal airport at Millidgeville. The Atlas, which the RCAF had purchased from Britain in 1929, was

The west side of the port of Saint John, ca. 1942, with two Lysanders of 1st Coast Artillery Co-operation flight RCAF, over Courtney Bay. This part of the harbour defences fell largely to 4th Battery, 3rd NB Coast Regiment, along with various anti-aircraft units. The Saint John Drydock and Shipbuilding Company, with one of the largest graving docks in the world along with building slips, lies at the base of the Courtenay Bay breakwater; downtown Saint John and Partridge Island are on the right. Mispec Point, site of the counter-bombardment battery manned by 4th Battery, lies just around the headland at the top left.

a large, slow biplane, with open cockpits for a pilot and an observer. It had been designed for "army cooperation," to spot fall of shot for the artillery and to report the location and movements of enemy troops. But by 1939 the aircraft were too old and undependable for extended over-water operations, especially in the sudden fogs so prevalent on the east coast. Nevertheless, the airmen embarked enthusiastically on their new role – spotting and correcting long-range coast artillery fire at fast-moving ships was especially challenging – and established close ties with 3rd NB Coast Brigade for combined training. During the fall of 1939, as work began on a hangar and other buildings for the air force at Millidgeville, RCAF headquarters reassigned No. 2 Squadron to its previous role of support for mobile army forces, and replaced it at Saint John with a new unit, No. 118 (Coast Artillery Co-operation) Squadron. This was largely a paper change, as many of the personnel at Saint John were transferred to the new unit. A similar reorganization in September 1940 changed the designation to No. 1 (Coast Artillery Co-operation) Detachment,

Infrastructure of global significance: Saint John's Drydock and Shipbuilding facilities bustling with construction and ship repairs and the graving dock in the centre. (LAC PA-197028)

the name under which the unit would serve until late in the war. In the winter of 1939, the capabilities of the RCAF unit supporting the fortress greatly increased after the antiquated Atlases were replaced by four modern Westland Lysanders. The Lysander was a dependable all-metal monoplane that was highly manoeuvrable at low speeds to facilitate close, accurate observation of events on the ground or at sea. The Lysander was available so promptly only because this was one of the few major items of modern equipment whose manufacture in Canada the defence department had been able to organize in the late 1930s.

Meanwhile, retired naval personnel who had agreed to come out on active service in the event of war began arriving on 31 August at Saint John, where the RCN soon established a base organization called HMCS *Captor II*. In their efforts to organize naval services at the port they had the assistance of the city's naval reserve division, HMCS *Brunswicker*. On 5 September, two RCMP patrol boats arrived from Halifax, and soon after, both the vessels and their crews were formally transferred to the navy.

Small boats and cooperation with the navy were essential for the port's examination service, which began on 19 September 1939, when the 6-inch guns on

Partridge Island were ready for use. All ships entering a defended port were obliged to stop at an "examination anchorage" (which at Saint John was south of Partridge Island) under the muzzles of the examination battery. While the army's gunners kept their ordnance pointed at the ship, a boat put naval officers aboard the vessel to check its cargo and manifests to ensure that the ship was what it claimed to be and that no sabotage was intended. Only then was the vessel cleared to pass into the harbour. The examination boats were in constant communication by signal flags, lights, and, after early 1940, by radio telephone. Also, a naval signals detachment was housed with the Partridge Island battery, whose guns were ready to deliver supporting fire in the event a merchant ship did not comply with entry instructions. This vital task would be carried out for nearly six full years. During the winter of 1939, the patrol boats often had difficulty keeping station in the rough seas, so early in 1940 they were replaced by two large tugs, which continued to carry out the examination role until late in the war.

The navy signals detachment on Partridge Island also exchanged recognition signals with incoming warships during the first eighteen months of the war until a proper Port War Signal Station was built. Contracts were let for this work immediately, and in December 1939 the station – a wooden building with an observation deck on the roof – was completed on the high ground behind Mispec Point. This commanding position, however, was too far removed from the ship channel at the

Mispec Point counter-bombardment battery under construction, with the three gun positions nearly complete. This was the principle war station for 4th Battery, 3rd NB Coast Regiment. (DND Photo)

The easternmost 7.5-inch gun at Mispec Point, complete and camouflaged, ca. 1943. (DND photograph)

southern approaches to Partridge Island for the use of signal flags, and the required high-powered signal light and electrical generator – both of which were in very short supply – were not installed until early 1941.

At the beginning of 1940 the navy augmented its support for the port by assigning to Saint John the old Canadian government hydrographic survey ship *Cartier*, now commissioned into service, armed with one small gun and a rudimentary anti-submarine outfit. She was the sole seaward patrol vessel to keep regular watch in the approaches to the port and out into the Bay of Fundy until January 1941, when the armed trawlers HMCS *Vernoe* and *Venosta* arrived. These, too, were old ships that had done service with the Royal Navy during the Great War, and then been sold for commercial use. In theory – and it turned out, in practice – with a large naval base at Halifax this was all Saint John needed for naval defence.

The 3rd NB Coast Brigade finally got its hands on big guns again in 1940, when the major components of the fortress system were completed. Mountings for the 7.5-inch guns for Mispec arrived by sea from Britain in March, and the barrels on 1 April. They were unloaded at the Courtenay Bay dry dock, a secure location guarded by strong infantry detachments, where there were the facilities to unpack, examine, and chip and repaint the heavy components. The gun barrel, mounting, and shields (to protect the crew) for each 7.5-inch gun weighed some 45 tonnes. Mounting them at Mispec was well beyond the capability of 3rd Brigade or its local engineers. So in late June a "gun-bucking" party of Permanent Force artillerymen from Halifax arrived to move the components to Mispec and to install them. This took weeks of arduous labour. The guns fired proof rounds successfully on 5 August.

The installation of guns at Mispec occasioned a reorganization of 3rd NB Coast Brigade, with 15th Battery assuming responsibility for the west side of the harbour and 4th Heavy Battery for the east side. The plan had always been that 4th Heavy Battery, trained in the arts of using the 4.7-inch guns at long range, would crew the counter-bombardment battery. The first group of thirty-two personnel from 4th Battery abandoned their Great War–vintage artillery at Fort Dufferin and moved to Mispec on 25 June 1940. On 20 September the remaining personnel moved to the east side, and 15th Heavy Battery sent a detachment to take over Dufferin. The 4th Heavy Battery detachment on the gun at the end of the Courtenay Bay breakwater remained in place.

The 4th Heavy Battery got the best job in the fortress: counter-bombardment. Although the 7.5-inch battery was an "interim" structure, it was heavily built and the guns were big and powerful. The scale of the works was partly dictated by the size of the guns and partly by the exposed site: the battery was (and remains) on the forward slope of Mispec Point looking directly out to sea. It was placed in this shoreline position because of uncertainty about whether the naval guns could readily be adapted to army coast artillery fire control systems. Naval guns were normally fired in batteries in a direct role from waterline positions, and naval gunners often saw their targets. In contrast, the army system for heavy coastal guns resembled the one for batteries in the field – that is, they fired indirect from hidden positions, it was not expected that the men at the guns would see their targets. Firing data from multiple observation posts on high points hundreds of metres from the guns (essentially FOOs) was transmitted instantly to the battery, which fired onto a grid or map reference. Moreover, counter-bombardment batteries – like the one at Mispec – were often tucked into ground back from the shoreline, safe from direct naval fire. This was something that the Great War gunners of 3rd Brigade understood well. This "counter-battery" work was virtually identical to that which 4th Heavy Battery's predecessor, 4th Siege Battery, had carried out on the Western Front a generation earlier.

None of this army gunnery control apparatus and procedure was in place by 1940, and there was a desperate shortage in Canada of fire control instruments. So the Mispec's 7.5-inch guns were emplaced so that they could be controlled from the battery position. The intention at that time was that the 7.5-inch battery would be superseded when 9.2-inch high-angle equipment became available. Entirely new fortifications would be required for these very large guns, and they would be located well inland. One of the basic principles of the coast artillery plan was that interim positions should be located well clear of the sites for the "ultimate" batteries. Putting them very close to the sea ensured that and at the same time gave the 7.5-inch batteries a clear view of the bay from the gun positions themselves.

The 7.5-inch guns were naval, not army, and although their role in counter-bombardment was familiar, the guns were quite unlike anything that 3rd (NB)

Brigade had fired since the Composite Battery's service on Partridge Island in the Great War. Mountings turned on a central pivot set into a heavy foundation ring. The emplacements, therefore, were similar to the circular "barbette" emplacements that had become standard in coastal fortresses since the 1890s. The ones at Mispec were the first ones to be built in the Saint John area. The foundation ring was bolted at the bottom of a large circular pit, approximately 2 metres deep, whose sides were of massive, steel-reinforced concrete. The gun itself sat on a mounting at ground level under an armoured gun shield. A deck of steel plates surrounded the gun, closing off the top of the barbette to protect the equipment within it and to serve as a platform for the gun's crew. The whole effect was very much like a naval gun mounted in a ship, which was appropriate since the 7.5-inch guns had previously been on British cruisers.

There were other elements about the Mispec battery that reflected its interim role. Normally in a British or Canadian heavy battery, ammunition was stored in underground magazines beneath the working area and connected to it by elevator shafts. In the case of an interim work, however, as many structures as possible were built on the surface for speed and economy of construction; the solid rock of the Mispec site left little alternative anyway. For these reasons the magazines and gun equipment stores at Mispec were located in surface buildings set back from the gun positions. The site's exposure dictated the heavy reinforced concrete structure of these buildings; the crew transported ammunition from the magazines to the guns on wheeled trolleys.

To coordinate the battery's fire, a concrete battery observation post was built atop an 80 metre hill behind Mispec Point. It was completed in November 1940. Until that time, the artillery had used the Port War Signal Station nearby, which – because of communications problems – had not yet been occupied by the navy. Initially only simple line-of-bearing instruments were available for fire control. To range on distant targets, the Mispec observation post took a bearing and, by telephone, obtained a bearing from Partridge Island; where the two bearings intersected on the plotting chart in the observation post gave the position of the target. The time consumed in telephoning between Mispec Point and Partridge Island, manually calculating the data, and then telephoning it to the guns made the system ponderous and difficult. In January 1941, 4th Heavy Battery received a nine-foot-long naval coincidence range finder to speed things up, but an instrument of this size was not accurate for long ranges. Finally, in June 1941, the National Research Council of Canada completed extensive modifications to an old coast artillery "position finder" to adapt it to long-range firing with the naval pattern equipment. Position finders triangulated the distance to targets, much like a surveying instrument. Accuracy depended on how high the instrument was above sea level, and the great height of the Mispec battery observation post was an important asset. The advantage of the position finder was that it automatically converted firing data

Gunners of 4th Battery training on their 7.5-inch gun, Mispec Point, ca. 1943. (DND Photo)

and transmitted it by electric cable to bearing and range dials on the guns; the crew had only to traverse and elevate the barrel until the settings matched those on the dials. Among the early trials, the position finder followed air force Lysanders from Millidgeville as they flew towards targets not visible from the battery, thus allowing quick adjustments of fire on the basis of corrections radioed by the air crew to the observation post.

The completion of the Mispec battery's guns in the fall of 1940 came none too soon. By the time the first proof rounds landed in the Bay of Fundy, German submarines were operating from their new bases in France along the open Atlantic coast, and German bases were developing quickly in Norway. Major surface units of the German navy were already loose in the North and South Atlantic, and more were sure to follow. Moreover, Britain faced imminent invasion, and there was every likelihood that the naval war in the Atlantic was about to spill over to Canada.

All of this immediately injected urgency into the Canadian coast defence program. The ruling assumption had always been that the Royal Navy would continue to serve as the strategic shield for Canada, as it had done since the eighteenth century. There was now a real chance that Britain might fall, and even if the navy survived in something like fighting form, it would have to withdraw to the nearest secure imperial ports – that is, to Canada's east coast. This stark realization

Lt.-Col J.G. Hart, commanding officer of 3rd NB Coast Regiment and, for much of the war, commander of the Saint John fortress. (3rd Field Collection)

transformed Canadian war policy and highlighted the vital role of 3rd (NB) Coast Brigade in the defence of Saint John, its port facilities and the massive drydock on Courtenay Bay.

One of the first measures taken after the fall of France in June 1940 was to build up the units already on coast defence duty to full war establishment. By mid-September, 3rd (NB) Brigade had grown to 496 all ranks, mainly the result of the expansion of 4th Heavy Battery to provide the 190 personnel required for Mispec. Meanwhile, the New Brunswick Rangers had reached a strength of some 770, and the Saint John Fusiliers 690 all ranks. Overall the Saint John garrison comprised 2,538 personnel by mid-September 1940, and with the expansion came a change in command arrangements. On 15 October, word arrived from Military District 7 that Lt.-Col. Hart had been promoted full colonel, with command of the "Defended Port of Saint John" his full-time appointment. His headquarters staff at the armouries at that time consisted of just three officers and twelve other ranks.

Hart's promotion to overall command of the fortress opened the way for Major Wallace Alward, commander of 15th Heavy Battery, to take command of 3rd (NB) Coast Brigade. Alward had been associated with the regiment for most of his adult life. A native of Saint John (born in 1892), he had studied architecture, ultimately earning a master's degree in architecture from Harvard University in 1916. He then joined 9th Siege Depot Battery and went overseas in charge of the March 1917 reinforcement draft that laid the foundations for the growth of the Canadian Corps Heavy Artillery. Perhaps thanks to Colonel Beverley Armstrong's efforts, Alward was one of the garrison artillery officers who secured a British appointment, and in November 1917 he went to the front with the Royal Garrison Artillery. After he was injured on 6 August 1918, he returned to the Canadian forces in England, where he evidently made a full recovery. On demobilization in 1919 he entered architectural practice with firms in Montreal. Then in 1926 he opened his own office in Saint John, and later founded the Architects Association of New Brunswick. Except for one short interval, Lt.-Col. Alward would command 3rd (NB) Coast Brigade for the balance of the war.

When General Ashton's successor as Inspector General, Maj.-Gen. T.V. Anderson, visited Saint John in August 1940 to review progress at all the forts, and hurry along the work, it seemed that Canada might soon become the front line. The German air assault on Great Britain was beginning, and the Germans were assembling an invasion force along the French and Belgian coasts. Given the desperate shortage of equipment in Canada, and the pressing needs of all defended ports, Anderson had little to offer other than encouragement.

The immediate outer ring of Saint John's defences was being provided mainly by the RCAF's Eastern Air Command, whose mission was to operate long-range maritime patrol aircraft from Yarmouth, Nova Scotia (in part to screen the Bay of Fundy), Halifax, Sydney, and Newfoundland. To some extent, this compensated for the withdrawal of British and Canadian warships from Canadian waters to the defence of Britain in 1940. The RCAF, however, had only two squadrons of long-range aircraft, enough only to undertake patrols from Newfoundland and Halifax. The airfield at Yarmouth, Saint John's forward bastion, was just nearing completion, and the aircraft available, Canadian-built Bristol Bolingbrokes, were just entering service. But the Bolingbrokes lacked the range that was proving essential for effective maritime reconnaissance. In short, the long-range air and naval defences that were supposed to provide the main defence of the Atlantic coast were very thin indeed in 1940, which meant that the port defences formed the first rather than the third line of protection. The future looked grimmer still, for Britain was under heavy bombing attack by the German air force, which was now able to operate from bases in France. During the last half of 1940 and the beginning of 1941 there was a real possibility that Germany might mount a full-fledged invasion of Britain. If Britain fell, the Canadian coast would face much greater danger than the hit-and-run raids that the defences had been designed to counter.

In 1940 and 1941 there was, then, some urgency about completing the Saint John fortress. Coastal defence mountings of a simplified type for field pieces were now being manufactured in Canada, and between May and July 1940, two of 15th Battery's 4.7-inch mobile guns at Fort Dufferin were shifted to these mountings.

The mountings were much more effective than their Great War equivalent. The new designs were complete mounts on low pedestals – similar to the 6-inch naval guns at Partridge Island – so they could be emplaced on flat concrete platforms. The engineers constructed two of these, surrounded by earth banks revetted by low concrete walls, at the northwest end of Fort Dufferin. During the fall, the engineers installed a depression rangefinder at the battery, complete with range and bearing dial transmission systems that delivered the data to dials at each of the gun positions. The engineers also fitted up the old brick-and-stone magazines with electric heat and light sufficient to keep them in service until the end of the war. The 15th Battery's other two 4.7-inch travelling guns from Fort Dufferin were now removed for training and coast defences elsewhere in the country.

The situation for 1st Searchlight Battery and 15th Battery on Partridge Island had also improved by early April of 1940, when civilian contractors began work on the permanent fortifications. The first part of this large project completed that summer was three box-like concrete searchlight structures along the southern shore. Their seaward walls bowed out on a semi-circular trace and featured tall embrasures extending around the whole semi-circle like a huge, curved picture windows. These positions for the searchlights of the ultimate armament replaced the interim commercial lights that had been set up in the fall of 1939. The reflectors of the new lights were 60 inches in diameter and produced 800 million candlepower. They were one of the few items of coast artillery equipment that could be produced in Canada, and orders had been placed shortly before the war. Canadian General Electric in Peterborough, Ontario, began delivery early in 1940, with Partridge Island being one of the sites with priority for the first production. The big lights were traversed to follow a target by means of remote control equipment in 15th Battery's observation post so that the Battery Commander could coordinate the movements of the lights with the training and firing of his guns. The wide embrasures on the seaward face of the emplacements were covered by curved steel shutters on rollers that could be rapidly opened when the Battery Commander called for a sweep of the harbour approaches, and quickly closed if the beam detected nothing; this reduced the danger that an undetected enemy could home on the light beam. The low, heavy concrete building behind the central searchlight emplacement contained the diesel engines and generators that powered the lights.

After the special efforts to complete the equipment of the batteries, the first full-scale gun-firing practices for 15th Battery took place during the first two weeks of October 1940. The Royal Canadian Army Service Corps steamer *Alfreda* came from Halifax to tow wood and canvas targets, a duty she had been carrying out at the Nova Scotia fortress since the last years of the British garrison early in the century. There were shoots on nine days, from the 6-inch guns at Partridge and from the 4.7-inch and 18-pounders at Dufferin and 4th Battery detachment on Courtenay Bay breakwater. Because ammunition was expensive, and each round eroded the barrel, the initial shoots from Partridge used 3-pounder sub-calibre guns that had recently been fitted. These were smaller barrels fitted into the bore of the gun, which fired light rounds with minimal expense and no barrel wear. The gunsights could be adjusted to allow for the smaller round. (Subsequently, 1-inch aiming rifles were fitted to the 4.7-inch; again, a small tube allowed firing without wear to the barrel.) One virtue of 15th Battery's 18-pounder field guns at Dufferin, which did not have a primary defence role, was that they could be fired more freely, although even in this case the gunners used reduced propelling charges to save barrel wear. The climax of the annual shooting was "battle practice," in which Partridge Island, Dufferin, and the breakwater battery were all engaged, firing a total of ten rounds of 4.7-inch, six full-charge rounds of 6-inch, and ten rounds of 18-pounder reduced charge. The war diary noted: "One target destroyed by A-1 [6-inch at Partridge]." There was also a shoot of eight full-charge 6-inch rounds with fire corrected by one of the RCAF's Lysanders, and a night shoot using the 6-inch 3-pounder sub-calibre guns.

A notable feature of the shoots was the testing of the recently completed "auto-sights" for the Partridge Island guns. An auto-sight, like a depression rangefinder, used the angle of depression from the gun mount to the target on the water to calculate the range, but it also automatically adjusted the elevation of the barrel to shoot to that range. It was accurate only to moderate distances, but because of its speed it was valuable for defence against near targets; the gunners of 15th Battery just had to keep the sight on the target. The extreme tides of the Bay of Fundy created a challenge when it came to making similarly large adjustments to the sight through the day. The sight installed on the guns at Partridge had been designed by General A.G.L. McNaughton, the soldier-scientist who now commanded Canada's army in England, and built by National Research Council staff, who were at Partridge Island during the October 1940 shoot to adjust the equipment.

By February 1941, work on the fortifications on Partridge Island was complete, and the 6-inch naval guns and other equipment had been installed in the new battery. Unlike the interim battery at Mispec, these works were fully dug into the terrain and featured high standards of protection throughout despite the difficulties of construction on the sheet rock that lay close to the surface. The reason for these efforts was that the 6-inch naval guns closely enough resembled the 6-inch coast artillery types designated for the "ultimate" armament that they could be readily adapted to the works. The intention of the coast fortification program launched in the 1930s had not been merely to meet the existing international crisis, but to provide long-term security to the country's ports – including Saint John.

Because the "ultimate" plan was for three 6-inch guns, the new works included three emplacements, one facing south and the other two oriented to the east, directly covering the main channel into the port and the examination anchorage. Like the Mispec positions, they were widely spaced – each position was about 30 metres from its neighbour – so that a hit on one emplacement would not disable the others. Unlike at Mispec, the positions were connected by deep, concrete-lined trenches to allow personnel to move from one to another while under cover. The emplacements were fully developed coast artillery barbettes, with semi-circular reinforced concrete shields of some five metres in thickness on the seaward face. The rear part of the barbettes were broad structures, which provided working platforms for the ammunition handlers of the guns' crews. The magazines were 10 metres underground, behind the emplacements; elevator shaft openings were in concrete revetted walls on the flanks of the gun positions. On the flanks of each gun position were bunkers that served as shelters for the guns' crews and as equipment stores.

The two 6-inch guns available in 1941 were mounted in the southernmost positions, leaving the northern one vacant. The barbettes, designed as they were for standard coast guns mounted on pedestals, were too deep for the naval 6-inch mountings, which were of a type that bolted directly to a ship's deck. In the central emplacement, a heavy steel framework raised the bolt-down ring to the level of the platform at the rear of the barbette. Clearly, it was necessary to improvise to protect Canada's ports during the critical first years of the Second World War.

The control centre of 15th Battery's position on Partridge Island was the observation post, a long, narrow, stepped-up building with four view slits on the seaward front, on the hill immediately behind the gun positions. When completed in early 1941, there were only the first three levels. Here were the remote controls for the searchlights, the line-of-bearing instrument that took readings on distant targets to give cross-bearings to Mispec Battery, and the depression rangefinder that fed ranges to the Partridge Island battery's own guns. The depression rangefinder, like the depression position finder, calculated ranges on the basis of the instrument's height above sea level, but unlike the position finder it was not equipped to plot the position of the target and estimate its rate of movement to allow predicted fire of the type necessary for long-range shooting, when the shell would be in flight for thirty seconds or more.

In March 1941, Captain C.P.H.E. Huxford, Royal Artillery, visited Saint John, spending a full week at Mispec and then a second week on Partridge Island. He was a coast artillery specialist of considerable experience, having worked on the Singapore defences before the war, and most recently on emergency defences in the Thames Estuary, the approach to the great port of London. Huxford advised 3rd (NB) Coast Brigade on how to set up the equipment and charts in the Battery Observation Posts for efficient operations; the construction of simple training equipment, such as dummy loaders (a wooden structure that reproduced the key features of a gun's breech for practising fast and accurate lifting and positioning of projectiles); the siting and construction of local defences such as machine-gun positions; and camouflage schemes to protect the works against aerial observation and attack. "He also lectured to all ranks, or to officers and sergeants, each evening," commented the brigade's war diary. "His visit was a good example of the value to be obtained from an exchange of officers between R.A. and R.C.A."

When Huxford returned in the early summer of 1941, he was impressed by the progress. "The condition of things in this port appeared to be good," he wrote. Both Colonel Hart and Lt.-Col Alward had done a superb job of building the fortress and training and motivating their personnel. As Huxford observed, "there is a feeling that everyone has confidence in his ability to do the job, and there is sufficient drive and initiative amongst all ranks to see a job through thoroughly. Where equipment is lacking makeshifts have been constructed locally and have worked well. The standard of technical training amongst officers is quite good." By the spring and early summer of 1941 the batteries of 3rd (NB) Coast Brigade had been made as effective as possible with the equipment available in Canada, and 4th Battery's 7.5-inch gun position at Mispec was the most modern in the country.

Having reached something of a mature state by 1941, the Saint John fortress and 3rd (NB) Coast Brigade once again became "force generators" for a rapidly expanding Canadian artillery. In 1941 there were two critical needs: garrisons for new defended ports on the Atlantic coast, and more anti-aircraft gunners in general. During the grim summer of 1940, the army had begun to build fortifications at Gaspé, Quebec, and Shelburne, Nova Scotia, as well as local coast defences at St. John's and Botwood (the port that serviced the transatlantic airport at Gander), both in Newfoundland. Each of these required a garrison of some 250 artillery troops, organized as a single large heavy battery for each port. The army also now needed several thousand trained anti-aircraft gunners. In the summer of 1940, with the Luftwaffe striking heavily at British cities from its new bases in France, it had become clear that there was no hope of deliveries from Britain of the anti-aircraft armament ordered for the defence of Canada – and now Newfoundland as well. Canada's needs were large enough, therefore, that production was begun in Canada of the two main guns, the 40 mm Bofors light gun and the 3.7-inch heavy gun. Deliveries from Canadian manufacturers would begin in late 1941, and gunners would be needed to man the equipment.

The model for expedited training of large numbers of artillery personnel was the British "anti-aircraft training regiments." At Halifax, the army's Atlantic Command (set up in August 1940 under Maj.-Gen. W.H.P. Elkins to coordinate the defences in the whole of the region, including Newfoundland) used this British concept to consolidate and expand the training staff and facilities in the fortress. Thus was born, in April 1941, in Halifax, the Coast and Anti-Aircraft Artillery Training Centre, later designated A-23 Training Centre. Its initial mission was to provide the coast artillery personnel for the new defended ports and then, as equipment became available, to build up a still larger anti-aircraft force. The senior staff were Permanent Force training specialists, and in this sense the centre was an expanded version of the old Royal Canadian School of Artillery at Halifax.

The Saint John fortress played a key role in these expansion plans. To help provide the large numbers of personnel needed for the new coast artillery defences, at least 156 trained infantry reinforcements were dispatched to the Saint John forts in early May 1941 for a three-week artillery course under a cadre of twelve instructors from the new centre in Halifax. These personnel, together with some 124 experienced personnel from 3rd (NB) Brigade, then went into camp at the Bedford Ranges outside Halifax to help form the four heavy batteries required for the new defended ports at Shelburne and Gaspé and in Newfoundland.

This was the beginning of significant change in the personnel of 3rd (NB) Coast Brigade. In May 1941 the unit ran a special basic training course for 107 new recruits directly into the brigade, but thereafter personnel came from the new training centre in Halifax, including a draft of ninety-one other ranks on 27 August. In time the practice of sending drafts of experienced personnel away and receiving drafts of recruits from Halifax would profoundly alter the nature of 3rd (NB) Coast Brigade, making it less local and more national in character. Despite the loss of the personnel transferred to the new coast batteries, the strength of 3rd NB Brigade grew to twenty-two officers and 524 other ranks by mid-September 1941. The establishment to man the new equipment and fortifications at both Mispec and Partridge Island was completed in the spring and summer of that year.

Among the newcomers was Lt.-Col. K.J.B. ("Ken") Partington, who on 25 September 1941 succeeded Colonel Alward as commanding officer of 3rd (NB) Coast Brigade. Alward moved to Sydney, Cape Breton, where he took command of 16th Coast Brigade. Partington had recently been promoted from command of 9th Heavy Battery at Halifax, a unit equipped with mobile 8-inch siege guns from the Great War. They had deployed in 1939 in Halifax as an emergency effort to provide long-range fire pending the arrival of modern 9.2-inch coast guns. A dozen years younger than Alward, Partington was only a boy of fourteen at the end of the Great War. He had become an accountant in civilian life and was also a devoted member of the Militia artillery at Halifax, having taken and passed the Militia staff course, and had qualified as a Brigade Major of Artillery before the outbreak of war. Partington would remain in Saint John for just eleven months. On 14 August 1942 the regiment held a farewell dinner for him on Partridge Island as he prepared to move to Sydney to replace Lt.-Col. Alward, who would return to Saint John to resume command of 3rd NB Coast Brigade until the end of the war.

While work continued in the fall of 1941 to complete the fitting out of the Mispec and Partridge batteries, there was significant progress with the inner harbour defences despite limits to what could be done because of equipment shortages. The breakwater site was designated for a modern, twin-barrelled, semi-automatic 6-pounder that had been ordered from Britain. But deliveries of this type of gun – which by 1940 was the state-of-the-art British anti-tank gun as well – would not begin until late 1942 at the earliest, and other ports had priority. Fort Dufferin was supposed to have two of the older 12-pounder quick-fire guns, but delays in the supply of the twin 6-pounders meant that all the 12-pounders in the country were tied up as interim armament at other sites on both coasts, leaving Saint John without any efficient quick-fire coast defence guns early in the war.

The weakness of defences in the inner harbour was slightly reduced in the fall of 1941 by improvements at Fort Dufferin. When a 4.7-inch on a proper coast defence mounting became available, the engineers constructed a full barbette position at Dufferin, including a thick concrete shield on the seaward side and a platform in the rear. In addition, a searchlight system was installed on the bluff below the fort. These two searchlight emplacements, nearly identical to those on Partridge Island, were revetted with concrete because of the loose soil. The lights were the standard 60-inch type, but with reflectors that projected a broad, 45-degree beam to create an illuminated area off the fort and across the harbour entrance. Any hostile vessel trying to rush into the harbour at night would have to cross the illuminated area in the face of rapid fire from 15th Battery's guns at Fort Dufferin and a detachment of 4th Battery on the Courtenay breakwater. The Fort Dufferin lights began to operate in October 1941. In November two more of these "dispersed beam" lights began to operate from the Courtenay breakwater, one at a standard emplacement at the very tip, the other on the seaward face to illuminate the whole approach to Courtenay Bay.

The staff in Ottawa understood from the outset of planning for the Saint John fortress that a Fire Command Post, separate from the fortress headquarters at Barrack Green Armories, would be needed to coordinate its guns. The best position, with a commanding view of the whole of the seaward approaches, was the Carleton Martello Tower. Apart from service as an observation post, the Martello tower had lost its importance as a fortification in the late nineteenth century. Its commanding position and robust construction made it ideal as a Fire Command Post for the fortress, and the staff approved construction of a modern observation post atop the old structure. Because of the shortage of fire control equipment of the type needed, and the crush of other demands, work on the two-storey steel-and-concrete command and observation post atop the tower did not begin until late 1940. By August 1941, work was sufficiently advanced for the senior staff of 3rd (NB) Coast Brigade to move there from Partridge Island. The Fortress Command Post atop the Martello tower was the hub of a complex network of telephone and telegraph communications linking the post to all the batteries – both coast and anti-aircraft – and to the air force and the navy.

Considering the paucity of resources available in August 1939, the armed forces and the civilian construction industry did remarkable work in completing the main elements of the Saint John fortress by 1941. This was an important achievement because from the very first days of the war, Canada's ports had proven more vital than anticipated to the Allied cause. The first report of the naval commander of the port of Saint John, Captain J.E.W. Oland, DSC, RCNVR, submitted on 29 February 1940, listed 1,187 vessels entering the port since 1 September 1939. Most were local coastal and fishing vessels, but the examination service had boarded 299 foreign ships, and Oland's staff had routed 197 ships to their destinations – including seventy-three to Halifax for trans-Atlantic convoys.

In January 1940, Saint John also became a major centre for support of defensively equipped merchant ships (DEMSs). DEMSs were commercial vessels equipped with some form of defensive equipment, from guns, to armour plating around the bridge, to barrage balloons, degaussing equipment (to protect against magnetic mines), other anti-mine equipment, and small arms. Thirty-seven DEMS inspections were done that first month, and the work remained unrelenting during the war. In the early years, much of the DEMS work focused on large liners, which called at Saint John to refit in the huge dry dock. These included not only fast troop transports, but also liners converted into auxiliary naval cruisers, dubbed armed

Mayor Fred Story of Moncton speaking during the commissioning of the corvette HMCS *Moncton* at Saint John on 25 April 1942. Three corvettes – the first ever ordered by the RCN – were built at Saint John Shipbuilding and Drydock – *Amherst*, *Sackville*, and *Moncton* – before the yard was overwhelmed by repair work. Later the yard built 4,700-ton merchant ships. (LAC C-025305)

merchant cruisers (AMCs). The most famous AMC to refit at Saint John in 1940 was HMS *Jervis Bay*. She spent July and August in the dry dock and was sunk the following November by a German pocket battleship while valiantly defending convoy HX 84 in the North Atlantic.

The weight of winter shipping fell heavily on the port, as the St. Lawrence closed and cargoes shifted to Saint John. Sixty foreign vessels visited the port in March 1940, fifty-four in April. The coming of spring that year did not ease the work. When Germany invaded Denmark, Norway, the Low Counties, and France in the spring of 1940, ships from all of these countries sought refuge, replenishment, and repair in Saint John. Not all of them were eager to continue the war effort. The examination battery on Partridge Island brought a couple of these ships to a stop by firing blank charges, while trouble with foreign crews kept Saint John authorities busy (the local jail became know as the merchant seamen's "manning pool").

There was some expectation early in the war that Saint John would also be a major shipbuilding yard for merchant and naval vessels. And indeed, in May 1940 Saint John Shipbuilding and Drydock received the first of three contracts for a new class of patrol vessels for the RCN. This was the very beginning of Canada's corvette-building program. Almost immediately, however, the collapse of Europe and the bombing of British yards burdened Saint John with repair work, and only a modest program of shipbuilding (primarily small merchant ships) had been completed by the end of the war. And in November, as traffic in the St. Lawrence River and its gulf dwindled for the winter, traffic once again increased in Saint John. The winter of 1940–41 proved to be perhaps the busiest yet. A steady stream of AMCs and warships used the dry dock, including the battleship HMS *Ramilles* in late winter. Meanwhile, from December 1940 through to May 1941 an average of seventy ocean-going ships per month called at the port. About half of these were routed to Halifax or Sydney for transatlantic convoys. If the men in 3rd (NB) Coast Brigade ever wondered about the value of their work, they needed only look around at the scale and importance of the traffic flowing into their city.

Some measure of Britain's – and Canada's – vulnerability was revealed by the loss of the *Jervis Bay* to a powerful German pocket battleship in the mid-Atlantic in November 1940. A more terrifying demonstration of the danger to Canada was the sudden appearance of two German battle cruisers *Gneisenau* and *Scharnhorst* within less than twenty-four hours' steaming of Newfoundland on 22 February 1941. They sank five merchant vessels on the Grand Banks that day, and sixteen more on 15–16 March. They evaded the best efforts of British battleships and cruisers operating from Halifax and British bases to catch them. *Gneisenau* and *Scharnhorst* escaped into safe harbours in France, along with the heavy cruiser *Admiral Hipper*. By May 1941 the Germans were forming a powerful long-range squadron in the Atlantic, and they dispatched their new super-battleship *Bismarck* and another heavy cruiser to join it. The British trapped and destroyed the *Bismarck* when it attempted to repeat the battle cruisers' attacks on the North Atlantic convoys, but the threat remained. The next great battleship, *Tirpitz*, would be ready to sortie into the Atlantic by the fall. Coast gunners had every reason to be anxious and diligent.

The Germans posed a multiple threat in the Second World War. While powerful warships seemed to cruise at will, long-range patrol aircraft from France and Norway roamed the North Atlantic and the U-boat fleet expanded rapidly, to more than 100 submarines by the fall of 1941. In June of that year, shortly after the destruction of the *Bismarck*, groups of U-boats appeared on the Grand Banks, immediately east and south of Newfoundland. The submarines did not proceed even farther west only because Hitler was being careful not to give the United States a pretext for entering the war. Their operations in the Western Atlantic were supported by a small fleet of auxiliary tankers, which the British systematically destroyed in 1940–41. Even so, the prospects for extensive German surface and submarine patrols in the North Atlantic remained.

The war took another fateful turn on 7 December 1941, when Japan attacked American and European possessions in the Pacific and Southeast Asia. Hitler used the occasion to declare war on the United States, and within weeks U-boats were on their way to Canadian and US waters. During the last two weeks of January 1942 and the first two weeks of February, the U-boats sank some fifty merchant ships off the coast of Newfoundland and Nova Scotia. Most of these vessels were sailing alone, without escort. The Canadian navy responded effectively by organizing convoys between Canadian ports and by helping the Royal Navy improve the organization and protection of ocean convoys.

Saint John's importance now grew in two respects. It was a secure anchorage where ships could be assembled into coastal convoys bound either for US ports or for Halifax, and its role as a repair centre burgeoned along with the RCN's escort fleet. Most of the latter were Canadian-built corvettes and minesweepers that, although simple by naval standards, required a high standard of support services.

The enemy finally arrived off Saint John in early 1942, in an action very reminiscent of the *Dornfontein* incident of 1918. On 17 May, *U-588* sank the Norwegian steamer SS *Skottland* sixty miles southwest of Yarmouth. Twenty-three survivors were sighted the next day by the RCAF, rescued by the Canadian fishing boat *O.K.Service IV*, and taken to Boston. The U-boat had less luck with its next target, the SS *Fort Binger*, operated by the Free French Navy. On the night of 17 May a torpedo thumped into the side of the ship just south of Yarmouth and failed to explode, alerting *Fort Binger*'s crew, who manned their guns. A surface battle ensued in which *U-588*'s deck gunners fired at least seven shells into the ship without serious effect. The crew of *Fort Binger*'s single 4-inch gun placed four rounds close enough to force *U-588* to submerge. *Fort Binger* landed one dead and four wounded crewmen in Yarmouth the next day.

The navy's operational history describes this as a "wild encounter that marked the end of U 588's adventures on the fringes of the Canadian zone." That may be strictly true: the Gulf of Maine was the southern edge of the Canadian coastal zone of operations. For their part, all Germans who operated in the area also described it of marginal importance, complaining of constant fog and a lack of targets. But Canadian historians have been too willing to take the Germans at their word: there were lots of targets. That month, May 1942, Saint John cleared 112 ships for other ports and ran nine convoys to Halifax. In the winter months the Bay of Fundy was Canada's major commercial artery.

The German notion that Saint John was unimportant probably stems from two patrols off the port in May 1942. The first to arrive was *U-213*, commanded by Kapitanleutnant von Varendorf, which had orders to land a spy along the Fundy coast of New Brunswick and "where possible knock-off a steamer near Saint John before departure." *U-213* entered the bay on 12 May near Grand Manan Island, guided by inadequate charts and facing both fog and powerful tides, all of which made Varendorf anxious to complete his task and get out. The submarine reported navigation lights and markers, which still functioned as in peacetime, and the sweeping of searchlights off Saint John. *U-213* landed "Lieutenant A. Langbein" at Salmon River. Langbein eventually made his way to Montreal, where it took him a year to spend all the cash he was carrying before surrendering to the RCMP. After landing the spy, Varendorf cleared the Bay of Fundy as quickly as he could, signalling the successful completion of his mission on 16 May. But Varendorf had been only partly successful: he had attacked no shipping in the bay. He blamed persistent poor weather for his inability to find a target.

The other submarine off Saint John in May 1942 posed a much greater threat, and its failure to encounter any shipping probably had long-term positive implications for the security of the port and the bay. In late May, *U-553*, fresh from sinking the first ships in the St. Lawrence River – which shocked Canadians – entered the Bay of Fundy specifically in search of ships using Saint John. The Germans knew that Saint John had a large harbour, with deep water alongside, and a dry dock. But that was about it. German radio propaganda was already trumpeting Korvettenleutnant Karl Thurmann's success in the St. Lawrence when he arrived off Saint John harbour in the early hours of 27 May. So unlike Varendorf of *U-213*, Thurmann was no shrinking violet.

Thurmann immediately surfaced in full moonlight six miles off Partridge Island to have a look. "Radio and navigation beacons as in peacetime," *U-553*'s war diary records. "Barrage at harbour entrance with a powerful search light which apparently is tested a couple of times at the outset of darkness. Lay stopped on the surface." Thurmann patrolled off Saint John for several days, watching the port and signalling his observations. It seems likely that Thurmann's brazen use of his wireless every night revealed his presence. During his stay off Saint John no ships or convoys sailed, but direction-finding stations never got a good fix on *U-553* either.

Certainly there was nothing – however tenuous – for 4th Battery at Mispec to fire at, and it seems that Thurman never got close enough to Partridge Island for 15th Battery to engage him. In the approaches to Saint John the only threats to *U-553* were a few aircraft and naval vessels, which came close once. In the dark hours of the morning of 29 May, *U-553* lay on the surface as aircraft flew overhead and escorts steamed to within 1,000 yards without ever spotting it. Thurmann put these efforts down as an exercise, but they were probably hunting for him. At this stage of the war, few Canadian small ships or aircraft had radar, and finding *U-553* in the darkness would have been a stroke of luck. In the event, Thurmann reported – completely erroneously – that Saint John "is not used as a loading terminal for convoys." The "lively coming and going" of small escort vessels suggested to him that Saint John was a support base for escorts, used to "take the pressure off the convoy assembly ports." *U-553* sank several ships off Nova Scotia and in the Gulf of Maine before heading home.

U-553 was the last U-boat to enter the Bay of Fundy and the last to hunt off Saint John. Thurmann's reports were probably the cause of abiding German disinterest. Certainly there were targets aplenty, especially in the winter. It seems that the Germans had no idea of the seasonal fluctuations in Canadian shipping and the importance of Saint John. The completion of the naval high-frequency direction finding station at Coverdale, NB, in 1943 helped solve the problem of accurate fixes on radio transmissions in the Bay of Fundy area.

By the time the U-boats were operating off Saint John in May 1942, the fortress was largely complete and was evolving into a key part of Canada's east-coast defence infrastructure as well as a mobilization base for the army itself. The buildup of Canada's coast defences continued through 1942 and early 1943, but in the face of growing demands for military manpower. The Mackenzie King government had pledged never to send conscripts abroad, for this would divide the country along language lines, just as had occurred in 1917–18. In August 1940, at the height of the crisis over the collapse of Western Europe, the Canadian government had passed the National Resources Mobilization Act (NRMA), which allowed for the conscription of men of military age for service in Canada. At the time, the NRMA was largely a political response to demands from English Canadians that the country prepare to give all possible assistance to Britain. But not until the summer of 1941, with strains on the manpower pool becoming evident with the rapid expansion of the overseas army in England, did the Department of National Defence began to call up conscripts for full-time home service. In the coming months, NRMA or "Home Defence" personnel – in contrast to the "General Service" volunteers – would become the main intake for the Coast and Anti-Aircraft Artillery Training Centre in Halifax, which fed home defence artillery units in eastern Canada. This in turn would allow home defence units to release some of their General Service personnel for overseas units or reinforcement drafts. By the end of January 1942, 145 of 3rd Brigade's 507 other ranks were NRMA conscripts – that is, nearly 30 percent. The new system inaugurated in late 1941 of posting personnel to all units from the Halifax training centre marked the beginning of the end of the brigade's "homegrown" nature; the personnel, conscripts and General Service alike, were now coming from all parts of the country. As part of this process, individual Saint John officers and gunners now began to join artillery units overseas. The unit also received a new designation mid-war. Effective 19 May 1942 it became 3rd (New Brunswick) Coast Regiment, RCA, comprising 4th and 15th Coast Batteries. This was the result of a general updating of nomenclature in the RCA that applied to all coast artillery units.

The main new element in the mid-war buildup of the army's coast defences was modern anti-aircraft artillery – guns were now pouring from Canadian factories. There was always the fear that even a few aircraft launched from an enemy ship could inflict grievous damage on port facilities essential to sustaining the war effort. In the case of Saint John, there was particular worry that a single aircraft could easily put a torpedo into the gates of the dry dock and disable them. That was why 106th Field Battery, converted from 3rd (NB) Medium Brigade's 6th Battery as part of the general expansion of militia artillery in the 1930s, had been converted again into 8th AA Battery in 1938, and dispatched cadres (only thirty-three all ranks) to Halifax in that year and the summer of 1939 for basic training in their new duties. The plan was that the battery would expand to a wartime establishment of more than 300 all ranks to crew modern anti-aircraft artillery ordered from Britain. The battery mobilized on 8 September 1939, and recruited to a strength of over 270 all ranks that fall. The men endured wet, cold weather in tents on the East End Grounds until wooden barracks could be completed at the K Grounds. The battery gratefully moved into its new accommodation on 30 November 1939. (Exactly one year later, at the end of November 1940, the battery returned to the East End Grounds, where barracks had just been completed.)

The 8th Battery initially had to make do with light machine-guns, which it mounted in sandbagged positions around the city. For artillery training, the battery joined in courses run by 3rd (NB) Brigade. It also provided detachments of men for duty in the forts when the brigade was short-handed. For a time, the anti-aircraft battery even used one of the brigade's 18-pounders for basic artillery training.

The equipment situation improved, but only slightly, in the summer of 1940 when 8th Battery received two 13-pounder anti-aircraft guns from Halifax. These were Great War equipment, a modification of a field artillery piece that had been the first specialized anti-aircraft gun produced in the British army. Although obsolescent by 1939, it was still useful for training. The 8th Battery constructed earth, timber, and sandbag gun positions at Fort Howe, whose heights commanded the harbour. The engineers built a large hut for the duty crews, and the location became a well-developed anti-aircraft site, fully equipped for training while also assigned to an operational role. Sometime later, 8th Battery acquired four .5-inch heavy machine-guns, which were placed in sandbagged positions to cover the approaches to the dry dock; one of the positions was on the Courtenay Bay breakwater.

The peacetime commanding officer of 8th Battery, Major E.D. Walsh, who brought the unit out on active service in 1939, remained in command until August 1941, when he was succeeded by Captain H.G.E. Ellis. Ellis was another of the unit's peacetime officers who had come out on active service, and had been posted to Newfoundland as part of the Canadian garrison that had begun to deploy there in the summer of 1940. Walsh was in turn posted to Newfoundland, to command 7th AA Battery at the Gander air base.

Ellis took over Saint John's key anti-aircraft battery (there were others in the fortress) during a period of upheaval, as trained people were transferred to help build up new units in anticipation of the delivery of anti-aircraft guns from Canadian factories. Replacements, always fewer than the people posted out, came from the Coast and Anti-Aircraft Artillery Training Centre in Halifax, and many were conscripts. By the time Ellis arrived, the strength of the unit had fallen to its lowest level, only ninety all ranks, and people were frequently away on course. Captain Phillip Oland, a prewar Militia officer from 3rd (NB) Coast Brigade, was assigned as Ellis's second-in-command in 1940. In December 1941, shortly after Ellis assumed command, the unit got word that it had been designated a "Type H" battery, for heavy armament, to be equipped with 3.7-inch guns. These did not begin to arrive until July 1942, when the first four were quickly brought into action at a temporary site, Smith's Farm, to the east of the city. At this point, 8th Battery's 13-pounder battery at Fort Howe was dismantled. Early in October the guns and crews moved to a new camp, farther east of the city at Loch Lomond. In December 1942, when four more 3.7-inch guns arrived, the unit brought a second site into action at Beaconsfield in West Saint John, completing the "ultimate" plan for heavy anti-aircraft artillery in the fortress. By the end of December, 8th Battery had reached strength of 261 all ranks, of whom 176 were conscripts.

It speaks to the importance of Saint John in the Second World War that a large number of units from other provinces were assigned to its fortress as well. One of the new units (supported by a draft of 8th Battery's trained people) was 25th Light Anti-Aircraft Battery, which completed its organization at Debert, Nova Scotia, in the spring of 1942. The battery arrived in Saint John on 1 June 1942 and by the end of the month had four 40 mm Bofors light anti-aircraft guns in action at four posts (including one on the breakwater) that covered the gate to the dry dock. In August the battery brought four more Bofors into action at four sites in West Saint John that covered the ocean terminals. Drafts from the training centre in Halifax during the summer and fall of 1942 doubled the strength of the battery to 159 all ranks, of whom eighty-five were NRMA personnel.

The arrival of 25th Battery to augment 8th Battery led to the establishment of a proper anti-aircraft regiment in the city in the fall of 1942. Major G.L. Kent, promoted to Lieutenant-Colonel, took command of the new 22nd Anti-Aircraft Regiment, RCA, on 1 January 1943. The Regimental Headquarters, whose establishment was forty-three all ranks, was located, along with the headquarters of 8th and 25th batteries, on the East End Grounds. These barracks had been the main camp of 8th Battery, most of whose personnel were now accommodated in huts at the large gun sites at Loch Lomond and Beaconsfield. Similarly, the crews of 25th Battery were accommodated in new huts at each of the eight Bofors gun sites. Although no one knew it at the time, the establishment of 22nd Anti-Aircraft Regiment portended the future for Saint John gunners in the post-1945 era.

The new anti-aircraft guns were all on mobile mountings – platforms that provided a stable firing base to which wheels could readily be attached. This allowed the guns from each site to be moved periodically to the Saints Rest beach area west of Saint John for firing practice. Such was the barrel wear from the powerful charges required for these very high-velocity weapons that spare barrels were installed specifically for practice. As had been the case since the installation of the 13-pounders at Fort Howe in 1940, the RCAF towed target drones for realistic training.

At the heart of the anti-aircraft defence system was another new unit, No. 8 Anti-Aircraft Gun Operations Room, which also came into operation on 1 January 1943. It had been organized at the armouries adjacent to the Fortress Headquarters offices in the fall of 1942. The main operations room at the armoury had large wall maps of the Saint John area on which plotting staff, members of the Canadian Women's Army Corps, tracked the flights of all aircraft around the clock. Officers from the two anti-aircraft batteries took turns standing watch in the operations room. Basic information came by landline from the RCAF's Eastern Air Command Headquarters in Halifax, which controlled all flying operations in eastern Canada and Newfoundland and over the Northwest Atlantic. The operations room in turn had direct telephone communications with all of 22nd Regiment's gun sites, both to receive information about sightings of any suspicious aircraft, and to coordinate fire.

Development of the anti-aircraft defences continued throughout 1943. The main improvement in equipment was delivery of state-of-the-art "predictors" to the gun sites starting in the spring. These sophisticated analogue computers tracked the speed, altitude, and course of an aerial target and calculated deflection – in three dimensions – so as to allow for the movement of the aircraft while the artillery shell was in flight. In October 1943, "G.L." (gun-laying) radar equipment was installed at both the heavy anti-aircraft sites; it could track unseen targets at night and in foggy daytime conditions. Work by that time was under way on command post buildings at both sites, together with cable communications systems to the guns that integrated the fire control equipment and allowed the guns' crews just to "follow the pointers" on height and bearing dials. During the fall of 1943, work was also under way on four new Bofors positions in East Saint John to strengthen protection of the dry dock and other port facilities. By this time, 25th LAA Battery had switched places (in July) with 30th LAA Battery from the remote new airfield at Goose Bay, Labrador. The war diary of the 25th noted, with evident relief: "Men seem well satisfied with the new station [Goose Bay], according to letters being censored by Officers. Everything is much better than they expected and all seem quite content."

By the time the war was over, more than fifty units from across eastern Canada had served in the Saint John fortress. Among them were various Royal Canadian Engineer companies, including 1st (Brighton) Fortress Company from Carleton Country, NB; eight different coast and anti-aircraft batteries; 1st Aerodrome Defence Battalion (Regiment de Chateauguay); three Highland battalions (PEI, Pictou, and Cape Breton Highlanders); three Ontario infantry battalions (the Midland Regiment, the Lake Superior Regiment, and the Canadian Grenadier Guards); the Royal Rifles of Canada from Quebec City; and the Regiment de St. Hyacinthe; as well as the Saint John Fusiliers and the NB Rangers. About a score of Ordnance, Provost Corps, Canadian Women's Army Corps, Fortress, and Radio detachments had served there, as well as various RCAF detachments, holding depots, and various elements of the RCN's Examination and Naval Boarding Services and auxiliary vessel establishments. At its peak, the Saint John garrison (army, navy, and air force) probably numbered well over 3,000 personnel.

By 1943 the tide of the war had turned. Although this had no impact on the ongoing construction of the fortress, the declining threat had important consequences for the level of manning in Saint John. By 1943 the enemy was less able, and less likely, to mount raids in strength on the North American coast. Moreover, as the Canadian army entered combat in Italy and the landings in France loomed in early 1944, the 73,900 trained men in the home defence establishments in Canada and Newfoundland were an obvious pool of reinforcements to replace casualties overseas. The first round of cuts in the fall of 1943 reduced the army garrison of Saint John from its peak strength of around 2,600 army personnel to around 1,800. The largest reduction was in the infantry component. The full battalion and a half that had formed a key part of the garrison by 1943 was replaced – for the moment – by three companies of the Pictou Highlanders.

Coast artillery was also trimmed back, and this had a major impact on 3rd NB Coast Regiment. The 15th Battery's 4.7-inch guns at Fort Dufferin were no longer manned, although the searchlights associated with them remained in operation. The 4th Battery at Mispec was cut back as well, so that only two of their three 7.5-inch guns were still manned. The air force began to cut its establishment across

Canada, and No. 1 (Coast Artillery Co-operation) Detachment at Milledgeville was slated for disbanding on 1 April 1944.

The changes in the summer and fall of 1943 brought the strength of 3rd (NB) Regiment from a peak of over 600 all ranks in the spring of 1943 to around 500 by the end of the year. More important was the accelerating departure of medically fit General Service personnel for overseas service and their replacement by conscripts and General Service personnel of a lower medical category. Once it was clear that the threat to Saint John had passed, fit, keen members transferred out to units bound for overseas service in a steady stream. Among them were Captain Phillip Oland and Lieutenants James Turnbull and Neil McKelvey, who transferred to field artillery batteries overseas. Bombardier Arthur Pottle became a sergeant with the elite Canadian–American First Special Service Force. The report of Maj.-Gen. T.L. Tremblay, the Inspector General for Eastern Canada, who visited Saint John in June 1944, provides a telling sketch. The heart of 3rd (NB) Regiment were the senior NCOs (eight warrant officers and twenty-four sergeants), who were "qualified[,] dependable and have been with the Regt a long time." Of the 425 junior NCOs and gunners, only 110 were General Service, and of those, only forty-six qualified for overseas service. The remainder of 3rd NB Coast Regiment by 1943 were NRMA conscripts, and "out of these a large percentage are from Western Canada, and of foreign extraction." With a high turnover of personnel, keeping the regiment trained therefore remained an ongoing task. Personnel to replace those who left for overseas were rushed direct from the basic training centres, and it fell to the old hands to carry out advanced and specialist instruction with detailed syllabi provided by Atlantic Command. Tremblay reported that the "situation in instructors and senior N.C.Os. is satisfactory."

Much larger reductions came to the Saint John fortress in the summer and fall of 1944. By that time, the German navy's surface fleet had been virtually wiped out, and the Allies were ashore in France. On 6 June, the day of the Normandy landings, Lt.-Col. Alward addressed personnel of 4th Battery at the Mispec Battery to urge the conscripts to volunteer for General Service. Many of them did, and the regiment could handle the reduction. Further cuts soon stripped the Saint John garrison to cadre strength of approximately 350 personnel by removing the last infantry, all of the anti-aircraft organization except for the group of 40 mm Bofors around the dry dock (this last detachment disappeared early in 1945), and all of the coast artillery personnel except for the garrison on Partridge Island and small caretaking detachments for the other forts. The reduction of the Mispec Battery to caretaker status also meant striking 4th Battery from active service, ending that battery's association with big guns that dated back to 1916. After 1 September 1944, only 15th Battery on Partridge Island remained on active service, under the command of Major J.F. Shaw. He was at that time forty years of age, an old Militia hand, and a barrister in civilian life; General Tremblay reported on his technical

The Courtenay Bay breakwater position, 1943. The observation post has been camouflaged as a lighthouse. The 4th Battery's 18-pounder is visible on top of the white structure (the newly completed position for the twin automatic 6-pounder mount that arrived in 1944). Crew shelter (E) is in the foreground. (DND Photo)

knowledge and efficiency in glowing terms. Shaw had been in command of 15th Battery in September 1942, when he moved to 4th Battery, and now returned to his original unit.

The reason why it was not possible to shut down the coast defences entirely, even as Germany was in a last-ditch defence against crushing Allied armies and air forces, was that the U-boat force, against all odds, was still able to strike in North American waters in the last year of the war. In 1944 the Germans had equipped their submarines with snorkel-breathing masts that allowed them to run their diesels while submerged, showing only a small tube above the surface, and to do so nearly indefinitely. Most Allied air and naval radar, which had been decisive in turning the tide against the U-boats in 1943, was not able to detect the small snorkel heads, and sonar was not effective for long-range searches, and often almost blind in the complex conditions of coastal waters. The installation of a field of six anti-submarine indicator loops (cables lying on the seabed that detected changes in magnetic fields cause by ships passing over them) in the approaches to Saint John facilitated anti-submarine defence in the final year of the war. The loops were monitored from a control station at Mispec and could alert the harbour's defences to the approach of a submerged U-boat. It was expected that the combination of large and strong tides and comparatively shallow waters in the inner harbour would restrict any actual attack there by a U-boat to one on the surface.

Further improvements were made to the defences of the inner harbour in 1944. Contractors built a heavy concrete "gantry" near the tip of the Courtenay Bay breakwater, just behind the temporary 18-pounder gun position. The gantry structure contained space for a magazine, and on top was a platform for the gun itself. The "ultimate" armament, a twin 6-pounder semi-automatic gun, finally arrived in the spring of 1944: the guns could fire sixty to seventy projectiles per minute, finally giving the inner harbour defences a potent weapon. After the wooden observation post for the breakwater battery burned down in 1944, the engineers rebuilt it in steel-reinforced concrete. It, too, was designed to look like a lighthouse, and by 1944 it carried the navigation beacon light that marks the east side of the entry to Courtenay Bay.

The delivery of the twin 6-pounders to Canadian ports in 1943–44 freed two 12-pounders to provide the "ultimate" armament of Fort Dufferin. In September 1944, engineers built concrete platforms at the northeastern extremity of Fort Dufferin, and artillery technical personnel mounted the guns. Artillery maintenance crews kept this armament, and all of the other equipment that had been taken out of operation at other forts, ready quickly to re-enter service in the event that an unexpected setback in the war at sea increased the danger of attack.

The decision to retain rudimentary inshore defences proved prudent. Beginning in the summer of 1944, snorkel-equipped U-boats returned in strength to Canadian waters. Although too slow while submerged to locate and sink large numbers of ships, they achieved some notable successes. Among them was the destruction of the Canadian steamer *Cornwallis* off Mount Desert Rock, on the northern coast of Maine, by *U-1230* on the night of 30 November 1944. It was entirely possible for the snorkel boats to enter the mouths of ports (outside the range of indicator loops) without being detected. *U-1232* did precisely that off Halifax harbour in December 1944 and January 1945. So it was necessary to maintain searchlights and close defence guns to guard against attempts at a fast surface run for a close-range torpedo attack against moored shipping and port facilities, and to support small harbour patrol craft in the event they succeeded in forcing a snorkel boat to the surface. Partridge Island was one of a handful of batteries on the Atlantic coast kept in full operation until 31 May 1945, three weeks after the German capitulation on 8 May, as a safeguard against any effort by a snorkel-equipped submarine still in North American waters to defy the surrender orders and attempt a final blow against the enemy.

The reduction in manning of the Saint John fortress did not, for the moment, reflect any change in policy towards building a modern defensive system to guard the port. During 1944–45, work continued to improve the coastal fortifications as equipment arrived from Britain, or from Canada's now substantial armaments industry. The coast artillery plan of the late 1930s had not been made purely in anticipation of the war; it was also intended to provide long-term security for Canada's ports. The one "ultimate" project for Saint John that the Ottawa headquarters staff cancelled, in December 1942, was the 9.2-inch counter-bombardment battery for Mispec. Delivery of these guns from Britain could not be forecast, so the project was abandoned.

The largest late-war changes in the fortress took place at Partridge Island and reflected long-term planning for postwar defences. Canadian-built twin-barrelled, high-angle 4-inch naval guns, which came on stream in 1942, provided an alternative armament for close defence batteries that was much more effective than the low-angle 6-inch guns then in service. Although the twin 4-inch fired a round of

Partridge Island, looking north, 1943. The left-hand gun position has steel and concrete overhead, and a similar protective roof is half-finished at the position to the right. (DHH)

Partridge Island looking south in 1943, with at least eight steamers in the examination anchorage waiting to enter the harbour. In the foreground are the permanent buildings of the immigration hospital that housed the 3rd Regiment garrison during both world wars, and to the right are the additional barracks built in 1939–40. (LAC PA-108409)

only 35 pounds as compared to the 100-pound projectile of the 6-inch, the two barrels gave a formidable rate of fire of some thirty rounds per minute, and the maximum range was about 18,000 metres, nearly double that of the older armament. Installation of the navy deck-type mountings required considerable reconstruction of the coast artillery barbette emplacements. Work began in the fall of 1943, and in April 1944 the garrison moved the southernmost 6-inch gun out to a temporary gun platform so that the fort's full armament could remain in operation while construction continued. In May the first 4-inch twin was installed in the southern emplacement, and in July the second went into the previously unused northern emplacement.

The 4-inch twin was a dual-purpose anti-aircraft and surface weapon, and Partridge Island was the trial site for its employment as coast artillery. The trial was not a complete success. The mountings, which together with the twin barrels weighed fifteen tons, were not sufficiently level and stable. National Defence Headquarters therefore had to order the manufacture of heavier bed plates for seating the mountings on the concrete platforms. Given the reduced scales of attack, the project seems not to have had a high priority, and the old 6-inch guns from HMCS *Niobe* remained in action on Partridge Island until the end of the war. It is fitting that one of these guns stands in front of the armouries today. The improvements and corrections to the naval 4-inch installations were finally completed in July 1945. By that time, work was well advanced on a large, four-storey concrete tower north of the battery. This would be an observation post for the battery designed to accommodate the latest radar fire control equipment, the CDX that had been developed by the National Research Council of Canada. All of this work suggested that 3rd NB Coast Regiment had a clear role in coastal artillery in the future.

The victory in Europe, announced in a radio broadcast on 7 May 1945, scarcely interrupted 15th Battery's routine on Partridge Island. There was a holiday the next day, VE-Day, as far as essential duties allowed, and a movie night in the recreation hall. Also, a detachment of personnel went into town to march in the victory parade. Then the garrison went back to work, assisting in the installation work at the new 4-inch gun positions, dismantled the interim 6-inch naval guns, pulled down camouflage from the installations, removed ammunition from the magazines for shipment to central storage facilities, and placed equipment in maintenance. On 14 August 1945 the war diary reported the surrender of Japan. Then, on 15 August, came the final entry: "The 15th Coast Battery, R.C.A., was to-day reduced to 'NIL STRENGTH.'" With 4th Battery already struck off strength, 3rd NB Regiment – surrounded by the most complex fortress system ever constructed in Canada for a commercial port – reverted to Militia status.

Chapter 8

The Long Road to Combat in Europe, 1939–44

The Second World War was supposed to be a war of movement, characterized not only by the rise of the tank and the airplane, but also by sophisticated and supple modern field artillery. The great weeks-long barrages of the Great War were to be replaced by quick and accurate radio-controlled artillery fire. On a fluid battlefield, medium and heavy artillery were considered almost redundant, for their tasks would be handled easily by aircraft. But there were also new types of artillery, such as anti-tank and anti-aircraft, that would spread gunners across the operational area, from the rear echelon to the very forward edges of the battle lines. As in the Great War, New Brunswick's gunners found themselves thrust into these new forms of artillery. Between 1939 and 1945, four batteries from the province served in the anti-tank role, two had distinguished service as field batteries, and one saw action as an anti-aircraft battery.

The RCA during the Second World War functioned in ways that submerged the story of local batteries in a much larger context, so the story of New Brunswick gunners overseas in that war is much less focused and distinct than that of the Great War. Field batteries, like New Brunswick's 8th from Moncton and 28th from Newcastle, operated within larger field regiments, which were typically composed of three batteries and a Regimental Headquarters. As in the Great War, field artillery provided indirect fire support to movement elements (infantry and armour) on the battlefield using gun-howitzers. Ideally, field regiments deployed far enough behind the front to avoid being struck by direct enemy fire, and if possible, they remained concealed from enemy observation and counter-battery fire. Their fire was controlled by a Forward Observation Officer (FOO) in the front lines, linked to the Battery and Regimental Headquarters by telephone lines or radios. To be effective, field batteries remained concentrated, often firing in unison with other regiments, hundreds of guns at a time. The fire of field regiments was therefore usually delivered en masse, making it a form of area weapon. Unlike the NB's medium batteries of the Great War with their designated counter-battery roles, field batteries had little independent role in Second World War battles, and their story is largely submerged in that of their parent regiments and higher formations. In short, field artillery was all about the regiment.

Also, the stories of anti-tank batteries are less distinct than those of the heavy and siege batteries of the Great War, but for precisely the opposite reason: they were too dispersed. Anti-tank batteries, too, belonged to operational regiments, but that is about where the similarity with field artillery ends. Anti-tank regiments usually consisted of four batteries (not three) and a Regimental Headquarters. However, because anti-tank guns were a direct-fire weapon, they were deployed on the front lines so that the gunners could see and engage their targets. Anti-tank batteries typically operated twelve guns organized into three four-gun troops, each in turn divided into two-gun sections. In action the guns of divisional anti-tank regiments normally deployed in two-gun sections with the forward infantry companies within 1,000 metres of the enemy. Heavier anti-tank units, belonging to a Corps Headquarters and armed with massive 17-pounder anti-tank guns and self-propelled guns like the American M-10 or the British Archer, formed a powerful mobile reserve. They either covered ground in depth behind the front and did so at much greater ranges, typically 2,000 to 3,000 metres, or used their self-propelled guns to respond to crises. These guns, too, generally deployed as two-gun sections or perhaps four-gun troops. Either way, at the front or deployed to handle an enemy breakthrough, anti-tank guns normally fought dispersed among the infantry and armour at the front. There was no formal reporting system for the actions of sections, troops, or (once integrated into operational regiments) even batteries, so there is seldom a specific record of what anti-tank gunners did. Moreover, since division or corps level anti-tank gunners usually deployed alongside the anti-tank guns of infantry battalions, or in the case of self-propelled anti-tank guns alongside tanks, their story is often indistinguishable in the larger narrative of a given action.

Finally, unlike the Great War experience in which the time from mobilization to battle was short, it took a long time for these New Brunswick artillery units to see action in the Second World War – in the case of 28th Field Battery, nearly five long years. In the interim, the men of artillery batteries, typically few in numbers (120 to 150 all ranks) to start with, were constantly on the move. The Royal Regiment of Canadian Artillery was (and remains) a single "regiment," and its officers and men were extremely mobile within their larger regiment. The tribalism and tight regional affiliation of Canadian infantry or armoured units, as often evidenced by their very names, such as the North Shore (New Brunswick) Regiment or the 8th (New Brunswick) Hussars, does not generally exist in artillery units. Personnel shifted, through promotions and advanced training, from battery to battery, regiment to regiment, with ease. So nothing like the corporate memory of the Carleton and York Regiment, or the 8th Hussars, survives for the artillery batteries raised in New Brunswick between 1939 and 1945. In the end, New Brunswick gunners in the Second World War were, as their regimental motto says, ubiquitous. And so too were their batteries. As a result, their story is the story of Canada's gunners at war.

At 1545 hours on 1 September 1939, 89th Field Battery's orderly room in Woodstock received Telegram "Typhoon," the code word requesting voluntary mobilization of Canada's Non-Permanent Active Militia for the defence of Canada. Nearly every member of the battery answered the call. The next day the 89th began recruiting to full war establishment as part of the Canadian Active Service Force. By 4 September, a day after Britain declared war on Germany, 89th Battery numbered some 127 all ranks and had begun training. Woodstock was not alone. The same orders and process occurred at 8th Field Battery's armoury on Church Street in Moncton, 28th Battery in Newcastle, and 90th Field Howitzer Battery at their armoury on Queen Street in Fredericton. On 6 September, 89th Field Battery assembled for roll call in Woodstock's Old Vogue Theatre before boarding trucks for Fredericton. By the time Canada declared war on Germany on 10 September, 89th Field Battery had joined 90th Field Howitzer Battery at New Brunswick's 12th Field Brigade's training area on Fredericton's exhibition grounds, much as their fathers had done in the last war.

But unlike in 1914, when the First Contingent was concentrated quickly at Valcartier, Quebec, mobilized units in 1939 remained quartered at local facilities during the initial phase. That said, some NB gunners quickly learned whom they would be deploying with. A week after mobilization, 8th Field Battery joined familiar partners, Montreal's old 7th Battery and St. Catharine's 10th Battery, to once again form 2nd Canadian Field Brigade (soon redesignated a field regiment). Just as in the last war, these three famous batteries made up part of the artillery for 1st Canadian Infantry Division. They were joined briefly by Sherbrooke, Quebec's, 35th Howitzer Battery, as the RCA adjusted to the British concept of four-battery combined gun/howitzer field regiments. Meanwhile, Fredericton's 90th Field Howitzer Battery was at first assigned to 1st Canadian Army Field Brigade, along with Montreal's 27th Battery, Ottawa's 51st, and Quebec City's 57th. Despite the new assignment, 90th Field Howitzer Battery carried on at the Fredericton Exhibition Grounds alongside 89th Field Battery, which – along with 28th Field Battery – had yet to be assigned.

Those early weeks of combining batteries from different regions into field regiments started a trend towards reassigning officers away from their home units. As a rule, New Brunswick's Militia artillery officers were not destined to command their own units in action in this new war. The Great War veterans who had raised batteries were deemed too old to take them into battle – or in some cases even overseas. Changes started early. The 8th Field Battery's Major J.R. Dickie was replaced by Major Edward McCordick, a Royal Military College graduate and former member of St. Catharine's 10th Battery. The 90th Field Howitzer Battery's Major Barker was replaced by Major J.L.W. Harris. Veteran gunners who mobilized batteries in the subsequent waves fared better, but only one New Brunswicker survived the long years of training and change to command his battery in action. That said, the experience and organizational skills of Great War veterans were not tossed away. The 6th Siege Battery veteran Gunner Keltie Kennedy was a Lieutenant-Colonel by 1939 commanding 8th Hussars. His old Vimy Ridge leg wound prevented him from taking the Hussars overseas, but not from being appointed as officer commanding all Canadian Active Service Force units assembling and training in Fredericton.

While the First Contingent assembled, everyone followed news reports from Europe with concern. The quick defeat of Poland in September 1939 raised the alarm about the danger posed by tank columns breaking through and then pressing deep behind forward defence lines. British and Canadian Army planners understood that their infantry, tank, and artillery units alone could not stop a concentrated German tank column backed by air power. Clearly, a substantial anti-tank capability manned by trained gunners was essential in modern war. In October 1939, 90th Field Howitzer Battery and the whole 1st Canadian Army Field Brigade were re-roled as an anti-tank unit, and then in November formally designated as 1st Anti-Tank Regiment, RCA. This was just the start.

Because of their assignment to 1st Canadian Division, 8th and 90th Batteries had priority in November and December 1939 for new uniforms and equipment in preparation for departure for England. In early December, 8th Field Battery loaded its aging 18-pounders on flatcars and left Moncton by rail for Halifax. There they joined the rest of 2nd Field Regiment and the rest of 1st Canadian Division to board their troopship at Pier 22. As had happened in 1914, their liner, Canadian Pacific's *Empress of Britain*, had yet to be reconfigured as a troopship and still possessed her full complement of service staff "to make the gunners beds, stewards to serve their slightest desire at tables covered in spotless napery and serviced with the finest silver and glassware; superb meals were served and whiskey, ale and beer were not rationed." Their enjoyable cruise ended in the mouth of the Clyde on 17 December. The 90th Anti-Tank Battery and the rest of 1st Anti-Tank Regiment were not so fortunate. They sailed on 22 December aboard *Reina del Pacifico*, which had already stripped down for wartime duty, and the crossing in heavy seas turned many stomachs. By early January 1940, all of 1st Canadian Division had arrived

The 8th Field Battery gunners manhandle their 18/25pdr on exercise in England, 1941. (DHH 112.3P1-713-30)

and begun collective training in earnest in British Army barracks towns in Surrey in and around the Aldershot training area.

In 1914, 8th Battery had gone to war with modern equipment. That was not the case twenty-five years later. The well-designed, first-class new 25-pounder field gun–howitzer was in full production in Britain, along with four-wheel-drive field artillery tractors designed to pull it, but it would be months before 1st Canadian Divisional Artillery was fully equipped. For the moment, Canadian artillery was caught in the transition from a field gun and howitzer combination – the Great War 18-pounder and 4.5-inch howitzer – to the new gun-howitzer, and therefore operated the two types of guns in amalgamated batteries. That winter of 1939–40, in keeping with the latest British thinking, 8th Field Battery combined with a howitzer troop of 10th St. Catharine's Battery. By March 1940 the combined 8th/10th Battery was fully equipped with converted 18/25-pounders (essentially an 18-pounder able to fire a 25-pounder shell), although they still used a hodgepodge of civilian vans to tow them.

The officers and men of 90th Battery had to soldier on during that first winter in England without any guns at all. They and the rest of 1st Light Anti-Tank Regiment made the best of their training time, practising basic gun drills and maintenance with old field guns, firing .50-calibre Boyes anti-tank rifles, and borrowing British anti-tank guns whenever possible. They also sent off men to British anti-tank, driver-maintenance, and signals courses. In this new war every gun crew

The 1st Anti-Tank Regiment 2-pounder crew training in England in 1941. The guns were already obsolete; even so, they provided 90th Battery and the rest of New Brunswick's anti-tank gunners with a system to train with that closely resembled the guns they took into action. (DHH 112.3P1-720-7)

would eventually get its own radio and four-wheel-drive vehicles. Doing their jobs now meant dispersing batteries over wider spaces while integrating their fire into a divisional plan. Then of course each battery and section had to be able to defend its battery positions. So skill at arms with rifles and light machine-guns and digging fighting positions were all part of the training scheme. In March 1940, 90th Anti-Tank Battery and 1st Anti-Tank Regiment began receiving their first 2-pounder anti-tank guns. This was an effective gun capable of taking on most German tanks of the day. Gun tractors began arriving later in the spring.

The 1st Canadian Division's artillery units were still inadequately trained and only partly equipped when the German army crashed into Belgium and France in May 1940. Germany's "Blitzkreig" had radically changed the nature of war. The 2nd Field and 1st Anti-Tank Regiments made emergency plans to combine each battery's incomplete equipment to form half-regiments to sail immediately for the Western Front. Mercifully, these drastic plans were scuttled by the speed of France's collapse. By the end of June, France had capitulated and what was left of the British Expeditionary Force had been evacuated from the continent. What would happen next was anyone's guess, but one thing was painfully clear: Germany's combination of massed tank forces and motorized divisions covered by bombers providing a kind of airborne heavy artillery seemed to all to be the war-winning formula. More anti-tank and anti-aircraft artillery forces would be required to combat this new German war machine.

Over the next three years, Canada's overseas army would grow from one division to five, organized into two corps and a field army. Two of those divisions were equipped with tanks to form "armoured divisions," and two armoured brigades were raised to support the three infantry divisions. The RCA grew and evolved to meet these new challenges. The loss of France and an active Western Front was a curse in many ways, but it meant that Canada's field force could grow and train out of the firing line. After the British army's evacuation from France in 1940 at a cost of so much equipment abandoned, 1st Canadian Division found itself in the unusual position of being among the best-equipped formations available to meet a potential German invasion of Britain in the summer of 1940. The Canadians travelled around southeast England from one assembly area to another during the dark days of mid-1940, ready to meet a German landing.

In the meantime, new units and formations formed in Canada. Fredericton's 104th Field Battery mobilized for active service on 15 July 1940 at the Queen Street Armoury. They had recruited to full strength by the end of the month and moved to the Experimental Farm on the outskirts of the city to begin training. Their ultimate role in the artillery expansion was uncertain until October 1940, when 104th

If the guns cannot stop them! 90th Battery Gunner E.P. Jarvis of Stanley, NB, practices throwing an anti-tank grenade in England, while Gunner L.C. Pond of Ludlow, NB, waits his turn, April 1942.
(DHH 112.3P1-669-8)

Major P.S.A. Todd, commanding officer 28th (Newcastle) Battery from July 1940 to December 1941. Todd is roundly considered the best Canadian gunner of the Second World War. He was the CRA of 3rd Canadian Division during the planning and execution of the Normandy landings in 1944. (NPL, Reid Collection).

Battery was assigned an anti-tank role and transferred to Kingston, Ontario, to train for it. They sailed for Britain in April 1941.

By 1940, the RCA had reorganized itself into operational regiments rather than brigades (as in the Great War) and the units mobilized the previous September had all found homes. Both 28th Newcastle and 89th Woodstock Field Batteries joined the newly formed 5th Field Regiment, RCA, of 2nd Canadian Infantry Division, which concentrated in Petawawa, Ontario, at the end of April 1940. The two New Brunswick batteries arrived in good form and by all accounts at full strength. The 28th Field Battery had trained in Newcastle since its mobilization the previous September. Much of this was very basic: parade and rifle drill, first aid, basic engineering, vehicle maintenance, and camouflage. When Lt.-Col. R.E.G. Roome, the designated commander of 5th Field Regiment, a prewar professional gunner from Dartmouth, Nova Scotia, visited the battery in late April, he described the state of the 28th under Major S.J. Campbell as very "favourable." The situation with 89th Field Battery, commanded by Major J.M. Boyer, which had moved to Toronto in late winter, was much the same. But the two Quebec batteries of 5th Field Regiment, 5th Battery from Westmount and 73rd (Howitzer) Battery from Magog, were seriously understrength. They were amalgamated into 5th/73rd Battery at the end of April, in keeping with the contemporary practice of pairing batteries in order to distribute the regiment's gun (flat trajectory) and howitzer (indirect) capability. After much discussion it was agreed that the two New Brunswick batteries would be amalgamated too. On 29 May 1940, 28th/89th Field Battery was officially formed. The 5th Field Regiment was formally established on 1 June 1940.

Considering the urgency of the situation in the spring of 1940, the training 5th Field Regiment received over the next six weeks at Petawawa was good even by the standards of the day. There were never enough guns to go around, and the 5th only had about a dozen vintage Great War 18-pounders. But they fired them, limbed them to trucks, and moved them around. It was while at Petawawa on 4 July that command of 28/89th Field Battery was taken over by Major P.A.S. Todd, a Great War veteran. He proved to be one of the finest gunners in the Canadian army, and in 1944, as a Brigadier General, he would command all the artillery – some 300 guns – assigned to the Canadian division assaulting France on D-Day. For the next eighteen months, until December 1941, Todd commanded the New Brunswickers of 28th/89th Field Battery.

The alert for overseas service was received on 17 July, and for the next three weeks, 5th Field Regiment prepared for departure. On 12 August the regiment fired all day on the ranges at Petawawa; then three days later the men of 28th/89th Field Battery were granted leave to travel home and visit their families. They would rejoin 5th Field Regiment in Halifax just prior to departure. By 21 August the convoy carrying 2nd Canadian Division – six large liners and 10,000 troops – was ready to sail. The 5th Field Regiment was aboard the *Empress of Australia* along with 4th Field Regiment, the headquarters of 2nd Canadian Division, and several infantry battalions. The convoy departed on 27 August and took nine days to reach Greenock. They were arriving at an anxious time. The Battle of Britain was building to its climax, and a German invasion of Britain might follow any day. In September 1940 no one in 5th Field Regiment could possibly have suspected that they would wait nearly four long years – forty-seven months – before they met the enemy in battle.

The 5th Field Regiment moved south immediately, to Leipzig Barracks in Camp Aldershot. By the end of September, armed only with rifles, it reported itself ready to meet an invasion. None came, of course, and by the end of the month the men had been granted leave. A few ancient French 75 mm guns arrived in October, one barrel stamped 1878. The first experience with modern guns came at the School of Gunnery at Larkhill, where in October, 5th Field Regiment fired the new 25-pounders for the first time. Intense training and firing on the ranges at Larkhill allowed the war diary to claim by early December that 5th Field Regiment was

Canadian anti-aircraft gunners studying friendly and enemy aircraft recognition. The 89th Battery formed part of 1st Light Anti-Aircraft Regiment and played a role in the air defence of Britain. (DHH 112.3P1-248-13R)

"Complete" and presumably ready for war. That was an ambitious claim: the regiment was still short of guns, and all of those in its inventory were either ex-French 75 mm or antiquated British guns of the same calibre.

In October, word was received that 5th Field Regiment would be reorganized into a three-battery regiment – 5th, 28/89th, and 73rd – in accordance with new British practice for field regiments equipped with 25-pounder gun-howitzers. The new 25-pounder eliminated the need for a dedicated howitzer battery in field regiments, and the "triangular" organization of infantry brigades (composed of three battalions), made a three-battery regimental organization logical. The 28/89th Field Battery was still strong at nearly 300 officers and men, and during the six months the 28th and 89th were amalgamated they had remained largely distinct entities. If the 28/89th was to be reduced, it made sense to simply send one battery off to the anti-aircraft business in early 1941. So 89th Battery left with most of the Woodstock Battery's original personnel to join the new 1st Canadian Light Anti-Aircraft Regiment.

The new anti-aircraft regiment was formed in March 1941 when 89th Field Battery joined 35th Battery from Sherbrooke, Quebec, and the 109th from Trail, British Columbia. The new pan-Canadian unit, under command of Lt.-Col. Walter Huckvale, became the light anti-aircraft regiment for the new I Canadian Corps, formed when 2nd Canadian Division arrived. The 1st Light Anti-Aircraft Regiment spent March and April 1941 on an intense conversion course, being readied for immediate service in the air defence of Great Britain. Experienced Royal Artillery instructors trained them on the new Swedish-designed 40 mm Bofors medium anti-aircraft gun. By May 1941, the whole of 1st Light Anti-Aircraft Regiment was manning gun positions at Clacton-On-Sea on the Essex coast north of the mouth of the Thames. In the high summer they moved to Somerset to practise firing their 40 mm guns before returning to southern Essex in October 1941 to man guns at critical locations at the Tilbury docks on the mouth of the Thames and nearby RAF airfields at Hornchurch and Rochford. These were the first operational deployments of NB gunners in the Second World War.

Canadian military personnel who spent time in England during the early years of the Second World War experienced the reality of the Blitz and its consequences for civilians. During this period much of the Canadian overseas force was spread around Croydon and surrounding communities southeast of London. The 90th Anti-Tank Battery captured their first prisoner of the war when the pilot of a crippled German bomber parachuted into their area in the fall of 1940. These Canadians endured the Blitz with the English people, dousing fires, digging out the wounded and dead, and cleaning up the aftermath. In late 1940, 100 personnel from 2nd Field Regiment, including men from 8th Field Battery, failed to turn up at the 2300 hour curfew check. Next morning they straggled in, "clothes, helmets and often skin burned," having spent the night helping the Croydon fire department cope with a raid. All were duly charged with being absent without leave but exonerated, especially after letters of praise arrived from the town council.

Canadian light anti-aircraft gunners training to strip, clean, and reassemble their 40 mm Bofors anti-aircraft gun, England 1941. (DHH 112.3P1-162-9)

Teatime. A group from 28th Newcastle Battery pause along an English roadside for a mug-up, a scene very familiar to those who spent years in garrison and training across southern England. (NPL Reid Collection)

The 1st Canadian Division gunners suffered casualties along with the English people. Indeed, 90th Anti-Tank Battery's single worst day of the war came not on a land front, but during the Blitz on 16 April 1941. That night the Luftwaffe struck Greater London heavily, including the little village of Shirley, near Croydon. German planes arrived in waves all night long, dropping a mixture of high-explosive bombs to blast open roofs and incendiary bombs to set fires. Major D.S. Harkness ordered 90th Anti-Tank Battery into action to help put out fires. The work was not without risk. One bomb landed squarely on a gun tractor as it raced through the maelstrom to help. Sergeant Harry Olive and his entire section were wiped out in a moment: Lance Bombardier Clarence Green and Gunners J. Stanley Chase, Bertram Clarke, Roy Warman, Harold Wheeler, and Edgar Richard. Gunners D. Critchlow and A.A. Forbes survived their injuries. The raid carried on till near dawn the next day, when the all-clear klaxon finally sounded. It had been a bitter night for 90th Anti-Tank Battery. Their convoy exercise scheduled for the next day was cancelled. Instead, the 1st Canadian Division commander, Maj.-Gen. Pearkes, a decorated combat leader from the last war, visited 90th Anti-Tank Battery to help rally their spirits. Two days later the whole regiment organized a funeral at the Brookwood Commonwealth Cemetery. Each battery in the regiment sent a detachment; 90th Anti-Tank Battery formed the firing party.

The bitter spring of 1941 gave way to a busy summer. By then, batteries in England, especially in 1st Canadian Division, were well advanced in individual training and had enough equipment to take to the field on exercise alongside infantry brigades and engineer companies. At the time, 8th Field Battery still operated converted 18/25-pounders, but at least there were enough for all eight crews. That summer, 1st Anti-Tank Regiment reorganized itself to attach one twelve-gun battery to protect each infantry brigade from enemy armour, and field gunners fired live barrages to shoot the infantry onto their objectives. Anti-tank gunners then towed their guns on to newly captured ground to hold it against counter-attacks. When the divisional guns were not on exercise that summer, they went to the ranges to practice, or they did garrison duty along England's south coast.

It was in that summer of 1941 that 90th Anti-Tank Battery received a new commanding officer, Major Arthur George Welsh. They could not have done better. The New Brunswickers formed a strong bond with the native of Sunderland, Ontario. Welsh had flown fighter planes with the RFC during the Great War, and the Western Front had convinced him, like so many others, that he wanted no more of military life. That was until Japan's attack on Manchuria and Italy's invasion of Ethiopia in the 1930s. He then joined the local Militia as he had "a feeling inside me something terrible was coming to the world." Together, Welsh and 90th Anti-Tank Battery were destined for greatness.

For 5th Field Regiment, the great event of 1941 was the arrival of its first 25-pounder gun-howitzers in June. This allowed 28th Field Battery and its colleagues to begin training in modern gunnery. The first regimental barrages were fired at Larkhill on 24 June; this was followed by a week of firing and then garrison

The 8th Field Battery gunners practise gun drills in a camouflaged position on exercise in England, 1941. Gunner Charles Little of Moncton, holding the 25-pounder shell in the centre, was later killed in action in Italy in September 1944. (DHH 112.3P1-713-27R)

A three-gun battery of 5th Field Regiment on exercise with their new 25-pounders at Glynleigh (near Eastbourne), England, 29 January 1942. (DHH 112.3P1-515R)

duty near Eastbourne. During anti-invasion duty along the English Channel it was customary to deploy the regiment's guns in prepared defensive positions at night, then pull them out for training during the day. The ranges at Allfriston, near Eastbourne, were used in August, and then troops helped with the harvest. The 28th Field Battery represented the regiment during a division gun camp and competition at Larkhill in late September, which ended with a week-long field exercise. Garrison duty was resumed in October and November, and a small firing program took place in early December. That month, Major Todd left command of 28th Field Battery to become Brigade Major of 2nd Canadian Division before moving on to command 4th Field Regiment. It would be fair to say that by the end of 1941, both 28th Field Battery and all of 5th Field Regiment were ready for war. Their equipment was complete, their training had been excellent, the exercise and gun camp reports were generally good.

Meanwhile, more New Brunswick gunners were on their way to Britain. The expansion of the war in 1940 had forced the Canadian government to reconsider its army plans. What had begun as a limited European war changed dramatically in 1940 into a fight for survival. Two divisions were not going to be enough. In addition to sending 2nd Canadian Division overseas, in May 1940 the government decided to form 3rd and 4th Canadian Infantry Divisions. It was not clear, at the time, if and when 3rd Canadian Division would go to England. For the moment the decision was moot anyway, for everything that was available had been swept up in the mobilization and dispatch of the first two divisions. It would be months, perhaps a year, before a 3rd Canadian Division could be raised and trained, let alone equipped.

All of these problems lay in the future on 25 May when 105th Field Battery, RCA, at St. George, was notified for mobilization as part of 3rd Canadian Infantry Division. The commander of 12th Field Brigade, RCA, Lt.-Col. Albert A. Dodge, E.D., took a reduction in rank to Major to command the battery. Dodge had served for four years on the Western Front as the RQMS and RSM of 2nd Division Ammunition Column and had briefly commanded a battery of 3rd NB Medium Brigade before retiring in 1926. The first person Dodge recruited for 105th Battery was one of its own officers, Captain Walter K. Love, a former cavalryman who had made the transition to qualified gunner when the St. George squadron of the NB Dragoons converted to artillery in 1936. Love was a thirty-year-old St. Stephen native, son of a Great War veteran, and was married with three children. Like Dodge, he took a demotion in rank to "go active." Dodge clearly knew his man: by 1943, Love was in command of the battery, and he would remain in that role until the end of the war.

The early days of the new 105th Anti-Tank Battery are well recorded, and they provide a glimpse into the long road to war experienced by most units. On the last day of May 1940, now-Major Dodge and Second Lieutenant G.W. Coffey, another 105th Battery militiaman and St. Stephen native, established a temporary recruiting office and unit stores in the Masonic Building in St. George. On 3 June, Dodge travelled to St. Stephen to inspect the old Clark Shoe Factory (the Quartermain Building). It was found to be "most satisfactory," with 29,000 square feet of space, enough to house the battery and with room for a .22-calibre rifle range.

Meanwhile, recruiting began in earnest. The battery had an authorized strength of three officers and 125 other ranks and could afford to be selective. Men were passed in small groups through a medical examining board led by Dr. S.H. Calnek, and by 14 June the battery had three officers (Dodge, Love, and Coffey) and 100 other ranks on strength. Two days later the medical board was discontinued. Authorization for the move to St. Stephen came on 17 June, the same day that three other ranks from 4th Heavy Battery in Saint John, who apparently had joined the 105th for the chance to get overseas, were sent back under guard. The move to St. Stephen was completed on 18 June. Dodge now went off to Kingston for a command course while the critical NCO positions were filled. The first issue of battle dress arrived on 22 June, and the next day the battery held its first church parade. The following Monday the cook was sent on course; apparently he needed to learn his trade.

In the summer of 1940 all that 105th Battery had was about 130 men, a few rifles, and lots of time. The summer was spent in parade ground drill and rifle, gas, and infantry training: "hardening," as Love described it. Three twenty-mile route marches were part of the weekly routine. Reveille was at 0600 hours, followed by physical training from 0645 to 0715, then breakfast at 0730. Roll call and inspection were at 0815, and the day's training began at 0900. Dinner – in the Maritime tradition – was at noon. There was another roll call at 1345 and two and a half hours of training from 1400 to 1630. Supper was at 1715 and lights out at 2200.

The only break in the monotony of this routine was the panic caused by the total collapse of France at the end of June and the fear of Nazis turning up everywhere. On the day Major Dodge returned from Kingston, 17 July, the battery was assigned coast observation duty along the rugged shoreline of Charlotte County between Blacks Harbour and L'Étaing. Major Dodge and Lieutenant Love motored out the next day for reconnaissance. They settled on L'Etaing as the most useful vantage point for the coast watchers, and for the next ten days a detail of one NCO and three gunners manned the observation post. On 19 July, Dodge and Love scouted roads from the Passamaquoddy area to Fredericton looking for blocking positions. This was followed on 6 August by an "alert" in which armed patrols from the battery watched the coast, manned the blocking positions on roads out of the bay area, and conducted patrols. On 12 August they were warned of a possible enemy raid, and on 14 August the battery built a sandbag wall in front of their barracks.

By Friday, 27 August, with the final arrival of greatcoats and 1937 pattern webbing equipment, the 105th was able to have its first route march in full kit. They were carried along by the music of the Calais–St. Stephen Band, an international ensemble. The *St-Croix Courier* reported that they "moved with a smartness that reflected great credit upon the officers and men alike." At least two more noteworthy parades were held in September. October 1940 was a month of intense infantry training, with route marches and rifle, gas, and bayonet drills. There was not much else that the 105th could do – it still had no vehicles and no guns. When the first seven Chevrolet 15cwt trucks arrived on 6 November – dirty, damaged, and much abused, with over 600 miles on their odometers – training began on driving and vehicle maintenance. One 15cwt four-wheel-drive and a car augmented the fleet on 20 November, the day the first Bren machine-guns also arrived; classes on the Bren started the next day.

The first artillery pieces arrived by train, along with two carloads of equipment, on 2 December 1940. The guns, apparently shipped from Vancouver, were four Mk II 18-pounder quick-firing guns of Great War vintage; two more arrived on Christmas Eve. Nothing was done with the guns, except perhaps routine maintenance, before the New Year. Winter caps and overboots arrived on 5 December, a day when twelve inches of snow fell. The next day, Maj.-Gen. Ernest W. Sansom, the General Officer Commanding of 3rd Canadian Division, which was assembling at Camp Debert, Nova Scotia, inspected the battery. By the middle of December, a combination of influenza and Christmas leave had reduced the battery to inactivity.

Even Lieutenant Love had to be recalled from his leave when Major Dodge took ill, and the church parade of 15 December was cancelled because so many men were sick.

The new year of 1941 ushered in training on the battery's six 18-pounders. This was all elementary: basic loading and firing drills, laying, and "firing." There is no suggestion of tactical training by troops or sections, and there was no place where the guns could actually be fired. But Walter Love recalled that the training was very good; the officers and NCOs learned their skills quickly and well and passed them along to the men, who were eager to learn, too. Brig.-Gen. H.O.N. Brownfield, the Commander, Royal Artillery, of 3rd Division, visited the 105th on 27 January. Ten days later, he ordered the battery to move to Camp Debert. The guns left St. Stephen by train and the motor transport section left by road on 11 February. The next day the remaining officers and men of 105th Anti-Tank Battery boarded a train at 0700 hours and headed east. After a brief stop and parade in Moncton, the battery arrived at Debert at 2100 hours. If the enemy wanted details of the move, they simply had to buy a copy of the *St-Croix Courier* – it was all laid out there.

The battery's vehicles and guns arrived at Debert on 14 February, and from 15 to 17 February the 105th's Chevy trucks were used to move their own guns as well as those of 4th Anti-Tank Battery and 94th Anti-Tank Battery from the rail siding to the camp. The 52nd Battery from Weymouth, Nova Scotia, was already there. When the Weymouth gunners arrived the previous fall, Debert had been little more than a poorly cleared patch of wilderness. Walter Love, arriving in February 1941, found it "still a bare and cheerless place." But it now had canteens and two cinemas and was well on its way to becoming a major concentration base for Canadian formations headed overseas.

The 3rd Anti-Tank Regiment, RCA, was one of the first anti-tank regiments in the Canadian army. Its composition of four batteries – the 4th from Peterborough, Ontario; the 52nd from Weymouth, Nova Scotia; the 94th from Quebec City; and the 105th from St George, New Brunswick – remained unchanged for the duration of the war. Each battery was composed of three or four "troops," each with three or four guns (the state of equipment and organization of the batteries changed quite frequently). In 1940–41 each battery was, in theory, organized into three troops of four 2-pounder guns each. Of course, there were no anti-tank guns, so 3rd Anti-Tank Regiment trained on its 18-pounder field pieces. The Regimental Headquarters was raised in Toronto, and the new commanding officer, Lt.-Col. Mackenzie Waters, M.C., E.D., chose the officers and NCOs who formed it.

Once the snow disappeared in May 1941 the regiment took to the back roads of Cumberland County, dragging their guns along, sleeping under canvas and requalifying in small arms. As the regimental history notes, "a simple form of deployment was practised during battery exercises at Debert," and the regiment trained in selecting suitable gun positions. Men were taught to "develop an eye for country and to take up gun positions and come in and out of them with the maximum of concealment." But overall, the results were "not very satisfactory." The regiment had no modern equipment, and the officers were reluctant to teach "habits which would later have to be unlearned." Physical fitness, basic infantry tactics, and small-arms proficiency, as well as communications and principles of command and control, were all that could be usefully taught. It was at Debert in the spring of 1941 that Major Dodge relinquished command of 105th Anti-Tank Battery to become second-in-command of the regiment. Command of the battery passed to Major J.A. Blackey, M.C. 2 Bars, formerly the Regimental Quartermaster. Captain Walter Love now became the new RQM.

In June 1941 the 105th and its sister batteries finally fired their guns. They were among the first to use the new range at Tracadie, in northeastern New Brunswick. This was 3rd Anti-Tank Regiment's first major road move, and it took two exhausting days of travel to get the whole regiment and its guns north, along 350 kilometres of winding roads. Apart from the mosquitoes ("as large as dive bombers and just as deadly," in Love's words) and the heat, the most distinguishing thing about the gun camp was that the firing – using 18-pounders as anti-tank guns – was "surprisingly good." Basic gun drills "presented no problem."

While 3rd Anti-Tank Regiment fired on the Tracadie range, Major Dodge and a rear party in Debert prepared for imminent departure for Britain. When the batteries returned from Tracadie they packed frantically for overseas. Then the embarkation orders were cancelled. With everything packed and ready to go, and 3rd Canadian Division on notice to move soon, 3rd Anti-Tank Regiment spent the summer and early fall doing route marches lasting several days. Finally, on 5 October, 3rd Anti-Tank Regiment embarked on the SS *Andes*. They sailed for England on 9 October and reached Liverpool without incident – except for the loss of the regiment's band instruments – on the 17th.

When 3rd Canadian Division arrived in Britain in the fall of 1941, the Canadian Army overseas was just starting to equip and organize itself for modern war. In July 1941, the Canadian Corps got its own anti-tank regiment. Conceptually, this corps-level regiment would reinforce the infantry divisions as necessary, or deploy in the corps area to coordinate a deep anti-tank defence zone that could absorb the weight of a German armoured thrust and grind it to dust. Until then, Major P.J. "Paddy" Kennedy's 104th Anti-Tank Battery from Fredericton had trained as a surplus battery under command of 4th Canadian Division's Anti-Tank Regiment. In July they were ordered to form the core of the new 7th Anti-Tank Regiment. They were joined by 15th Battery from Toronto, 111th Battery from Nelson, British Columbia, and 113th Battery from Regina. All had mobilized in 1939 or 1940 and had yet to get final assignments. Lt.-Col. L.A. Devine took command of the new regiment. In the new organization 104th Anti-Tank Battery comprised J, K, and L Troops, each with four guns.

The 1st Canadian Anti-Tank Regiment officers on exercise in England, 1942, laying out their scheme for protecting 1st Canadian Division from enemy armoured counterattacks. Then Captain Hugh Burnett, kneeling third from the left, later earned the Military Cross serving as 90th Battery's second-in-command before succeeding Major George "Tiger" Welsh in command. (DHH 112.3P1-720-3)

The 104th Anti-Tank Battery was the best established of the lot, having been re-formed for anti-tank service for a nearly a year. The others of 7th Anti-Tank had been trained as field batteries, so the new marriage went through a rough opening patch. According to 7th Anti-Tank Regiment's war diary, part of the problem was "strife between men of the 104th Battery which had been an organized, tight unit for a long time, and other batteries in the unit which were as yet rather polyglot outfits. The 104th resented the advent of the Regiment into Colchester [Essex, England] and in turn the others resented the superior attitude of the 104th." RSM Al Pugh attacked the related discipline problems with vigour. Perhaps more importantly, much of the trouble dissipated when 7th Anti-Tank Regiment took to the field together in Wales to train as a forty-eight-gun 2-pounder regiment in the fall of 1941.

By then, 3rd Anti-Tank Regiment and the gunners of 105th Anti-Tank Battery had received the first dozen 2-pounder anti-tank guns as well. These were the first "modern" anti-tank weapons the Canadians received, although the tiny 2-pounder was now obsolete. The 3rd Anti-Tank Regiment got its first chance to fire them, using blanks, at moving tanks in early November 1941 in a series of limited battery exercises; 105th Battery was the first to fire. It was good training, if nothing else.

8th Battery's Command Post Troop on exercise in Sussex England, April 1942. (DHH 112.3P1-713-8)

From 10 to 12 December the 2-pounders were fired in earnest for the first time on a range in Sennybridge, Wales. Then, after a quiet Christmas at Caterham, the regiment paid the first of many visits to the ranges at Lydd, on the Romney Marshes of Kent southwest of Folkstone, for the first of a long series of regimental shoots. The results, according to the Commander, Royal Artillery, of 3rd Canadian Division, were not very satisfactory.

The year 1942 brought a further expansion of the army in Britain, as well as new equipment, new personnel, and updated training. Lessons learned from the Mediterranean Theatre, especially from the Western Desert where Commonwealth troops in British Eighth Army were experimenting under fire with how best to coordinate modern mobile forces connected by radio, were especially important. Experience in North Africa confirmed that the 2-pounder anti-tank gun was too small to defeat the latest German Panzers and that its lack of a high-explosive shell made it useless against anything but tanks. A new 6-pounder anti-tank gun was on the way. It could reach out to over 1,500 yards with a flat-trajectory high-velocity armour-piercing shot; it could also fire a high-explosive shell out to nearly 5,000 yards against soft-skin targets or infantry. Even then, plans were in train to build even bigger, longer-ranged anti-tank guns.

In January 1942, 7th Anti-Tank Regiment became the first Canadian unit to receive the 6-pounder, which they reported to be "a very workmanlike weapon and very easy to camouflage." As more came available, the divisional anti-tank regiments were also re-equipped. The 90th Anti-Tank Battery got their new 6-pounders in September 1942. The 1st Anti-Tank Regiment of 1st Canadian Division set up a school to train infantry anti-tank gunners on their now surplus 2-pounder guns. When enough 6-pounders rolled off assembly lines, the anti-tank "platoon" infantry battalions would get the 6-pounder, too.

In 1942, Canada's divisions then in England rotated between field exercises and operational coast defence duty stations along England's south coast. During those periods of coast defence duty, 90th Anti-Tank Battery manned Royal Navy 6-pounder guns from the last war, which were mounted in fortified concrete strongpoints along the south coast. The danger of invasion had begun to dissipate by 1942, but the threat from the Luftwaffe never went away. In August 1942, 104th Anti-Tank Battery and all of 7th Anti-Tank Regiment were going through their paces at battle school on the South Downs when the Luftwaffe struck the nearby village of Petworth in a surprise daylight raid. The town's school was hard hit. The whole regiment was pressed into service to rescue survivors and recover remains. When the task was complete, 7th Anti-Tank Regiment used their vehicles to assist the town with a mass funeral for the thirty-two children killed in the raid. No matter what their reasons for first enlisting, those days spent living and dying alongside the British people while facing the Luftwaffe's wrath fostered a strong sense of purpose in the minds of many about why the war must be fought and won.

Vehicles of 7th Anti-Tank Regiment laden with children's coffins and flowers at the cemetery outside the Parish Church of Saint Mary in Petworth, Sussex August 1942. The truck in the foreground, K2, is from 104th Fredericton Battery. (PANB P543-2)

Training and equipping continued through 1942. At Burwash, inland from Hastings, 8th Field Battery finally received its complement of eight newly forged 25-pounder gun-howitzers. The 2nd Field Regiment's history records how "the new gun was received with enthusiasm and liked from the very start." Around the same time, 7th Anti-Tank Regiment's 104th Battery was assigned a new commanding officer, Major S.B. Smith, who would lead them into action. The new equipment and lessons from the front stimulated ever larger and more sophisticated field exercises in 1942. The New Brunswick field and anti-tank batteries alternated between training and coast defence tasks from 1941 into 1942; meanwhile, 89th Anti-Aircraft Battery remained on constant operational service protecting southern Essex from the Luftwaffe until April 1942. That spring, 1st Canadian Light Anti-Aircraft Regiment pulled out of fixed defences and moved to the field to begin mobile warfare training. By then, they had mustered enough artillery tractors and trucks to tow their guns and equipment. From then on, 1st Light Anti-Aircraft Regiment formed part of the I Canadian Corps artillery. For the rest of 1942 and into the winter, they alternated between open warfare training in the field and joining the rest of the Canadian army in England on guard along the coast between Hastings and Eastborne. In 1942, the regiment maintained only twenty-eight 40 mm Bofors guns, which were divided among the three batteries. Given the worldwide Allied demand for new 40 mm Bofors guns aboard ships, to protect airfields and other fixed points as well as to provide mobile guns for the field armies, it took until March 1943 for the regiment to acquire all fifty-four guns.

The spring of 1942 brought an intense cycle of exercises, moves, and training, and the year as a whole saw a marked shift into combined arms and some amphibious training. By the time Lt.-Gen. McNaughton, then commander of I Canadian Corps, visited 3rd Anti-Tank Regiment in mid-April, he felt compelled to comment "how tough the men of the 105th [St George] Battery looked." The men from southern New Brunswick might have taken that as a compliment. Exercise Beaver, which followed in May, found the batteries of 3rd Anti-Tank Regiment assigned to their respective brigades of 3rd Canadian Division for the first time: 4th Battery with 7th Brigade, 94th Battery with 9th Brigade, and 105th Battery with 8th Brigade (which contained the North Shore (New Brunswick) Regiment); 52nd Battery was in divisional reserve. This was "the usual breakdown," according to the 3rd Anti-Tank Regiment history, but in fact such assignments varied over time. As that history records, by this stage 3rd Anti-Tank Regiment was "fully trained on the 2 pdr gun, well equipped and morale was high. It could have gone into action at any time and given a good account of itself."

As it turned out, 3rd Anti-Tank Regiment would never take the 2-pounder into action. When the first 6-pounders arrived in the regimental lines in July, 3rd Anti-Tank Regiment went back to Lydd to fire the new guns. By August they were billeted near Steyning, West Sussex, northwest of Brighton, with 105th Anti-Tank

Battery along the coast at Worthing. It was there that the St. George battery suffered its first fatal casualties when a Heinkel German bomber crashed into the house where the men of 105th Battery's K Troop were lodged. The resulting fire badly wounded four men, three of whom later died of their burns. It might have been worse. The whole troop would probably have perished had the bombs gone off. The balance of the year was spent operating out of Haywards Heath due north of Brighton, with yet another visit to Lydd to fire their 6-pounders and a short trip to Poole to practise loading guns onto landing craft. By January 1943, 3rd Anti-Tank Regiment was back in Steyning, where once again the regiment was attacked by German bombers – with no ill results this time.

Personnel continued to move throughout the Royal Regiment of Canadian Artillery in 1942, as the strain of training and wartime service weeded out those who were not up to the challenge. Among the first to go in 3rd Anti-Tank Regiment in February was Major Albert Dodge, the Great War veteran who had raised 105th Anti-Tank Battery and had come overseas as second-in-command of 3rd Anti-Tank Regiment. He was sent home. The commanding officer of 105th Anti-Tank Battery, Major Blackey, was also sent home, but in his case he was promoted to Lieutenant-Colonel and sent back to mobilize and command 6th Anti-Tank Regiment, RCA. That regiment, which was being raised for Home Defence, would eventually bring another New Brunswick anti-tank battery to northwest Europe. Captain Walter Love, the first person – officer or man – selected by Dodge upon mobilization of the 105th, was promoted to Major and assumed command of 105th

Six-pounders on a beach range in southern England, probably Lydd. (RCA Museum)

Battery. Love was to remain in that position until the end of the war. Despite these and other changes, the 105th remained primarily a New Brunswick battery. Love's meticulous notes from this period reveal that by the fall of 1942, five of its nine officers were still from that province, and its NCO cadre (Sergeants, Lance Sergeants, Bombardiers, and Lance Bombardiers) was overwhelmingly New Brunswickers, roughly 83 percent. Moreover, the vast majority of 105th Battery's NCOs (31 of 54) were still from Charlotte and Saint John counties.

The unit that Lt.-Col. Blackey went home to command, 6th Anti-Tank Regiment, was part of 6th Canadian Division. The Canadian government planned to use 6th Division, which had been raised for Home Defence following the Japanese attack in the Pacific in December 1941, to secure the west coast. Its manpower came primarily from men conscripted for Home Defence under the new National Resources Mobilization Act. The 6th Anti-Tank Regiment itself was raised in April 1942.

Lt.-Col. Blackey arrived home to find his new regiment was little more than a shell. Three of his batteries – the 56th from Lindsay, Ontario; the 33rd from Simcoe, Ontario; and the 74th from Rock Island, Quebec – were either seriously understrength or had only recently enlisted NRMA conscripts. As 6th Anti-Tank Regiment's history records, only 103rd Battery from Campbellton, NB "was almost up the strength with basically trained General Service men and it was the only battery in the Regt to arrive 'ready-made.'" The 103rd Battery had worked hard to achieve that level of readiness. As a Militia unit under Major A.A. Gillis, M.C., it had been active in recruiting and training, attending camps at Petawawa in 1940 and firing on the Tracadie ranges in 1941. In March 1942, in anticipation of going active, the battery was allowed to recruit to full strength, and by the end of April it comprised seven officers and 151 men. On 29 April, command passed to Major L.C.D. Ottey from Dalhousie, where he was the pulp mill superintendent. Ottey was another member of New Brunswick's Great War gunnery mafia, having served overseas with 6th Siege Battery before taking a commission and joining a field brigade.

Not surprisingly, 6th Anti-Tank Regiment spent much of the summer of 1942 in basic training while integrating new personnel. Their "guns" consisted of "tree trunks and trestles," but these allowed for instruction in basic gun drills until the first 2-pounders arrived in August. Firing began on 24 August and continued throughout the fall. Gun detachments were sorted out, and in November the regiment began a conversion to the more powerful and modern 6-pounder guns.

That same month, 6th Anti-Tank Regiment was officially passed to the command of 6th Canadian Infantry Division and readied for service on the Pacific coast. Within weeks, however, the regiment was told that it would be deploying to Europe, where the formation of II Canadian Corps had created a need for another corps-level heavy anti-tank regiment. As the regimental history noted, this was a "prospect which was acclaimed by all those who joined to fight" – a calculated swipe at the NRMA conscripts, who still made up about 40 percent of the regiment's personnel. With the decision to send the regiment to war, these men – concentrated in the three Ontario and Quebec batteries – had to be replaced. As a result, a high proportion of the original cadre of 6th Anti-Tank Regiment that went overseas came from 103rd Campbellton Battery. As events in Normandy would later reveal, the 103rd had indeed come to fight. The changeover in personnel was completed in February 1943, and as the regimental history observed, "at long last a fighting unit began to appear and morale rose to the highest peak."

Meanwhile, the Canadians stationed in Britain finally got into action in 1942, during the tragic landings at Dieppe. There was little role for gunners in the attack, and there was only one battery from New Brunswick (28th Newcastle) in the division involved. The raid on 18 August by 2nd Canadian Division involved only one of its anti-aircraft units, while the attacking infantry battalions had FOOs from various regiments attached to control naval fire support. Apparently no personnel from 5th Field Regiment were involved. Sixteen officers and 256 men of 2nd Canadian Division's artillery took part; forty-eight were killed in action.

For most Canadians in England, 1942 was just another long year of training, waiting, and frustration. Life for gunners alternated between coastal garrison duties, firing on ranges in the south of England and in Wales, and major field exercises. The big news for 5th Field Regiment in February was the arrival of Lt.-Col. E.D. Nighswander, a regular gunner from Toronto, to assume command. This was part of a broad pattern of pushing out the old and incompetent and replacing them with the young and – everyone hoped – gifted that rippled through units in the late winter of 1942. Nighswander would see 5th Field Regiment through most of the northwest Europe campaign. A series of battery shoots in March followed by a regimental gun camp in April gave him the measure of his challenge. The results were disappointing. As the war diary recorded, good results were mixed with "some dismal" firing, with rounds falling all over the place. Things improved for 28th Field Battery in June, when Major J.F. Morlock from Toronto assumed command. He would stay with them through the long and increasingly intense years of training, and finally took 28th Battery into Normandy in July 1944.

New key personnel and an intense summer of exercises and shooting followed for all of Canada's artillery units in Britain, and they got much better at their job. The 5th Field Regiment was on the ranges every month for the rest of the year, and their gunnery improved noticeably. The regiment had no sooner moved to its winter quarters at Selsey, on the West Sussex coast south of Chichester, in October when it departed for a ten-day gun camp at Builth Wells, Wales. This was, in many ways, 5th Field Regiment's first serious and complex shooting, and their experience speaks to the ways in which the years of training and exercises layered experience and skill onto increasingly proficient gunners. At Builth there were exercises in movement and chemical warfare, punctuated by barrages, night shoots, and troop and battery concentrations. By all accounts the standard of shooting was now very good.

The 8th Field Battery and other 2nd Field Regiment gunners taking a break from training to queue up for a hot lunch, England, 1941. (DHH 112.3P1-713-18)

A month later, just prior to an inspection by the senior officers of 2nd Canadian Division, and by the artillery commander of II Canadian Corps, the skill of 5th Field Regiment was put to the test. On the Alfriston ranges in East Sussex, the personnel of the regiment marched behind a barrage fired by 28th Newcastle Field Battery. Everything went according to plan, and the men who braved the fire of Major Morlock's battery were said to be "quite impressed" by the skill of the New Brunswick gunners. They would not be the last to say so. The division's artillery commander returned in early January 1943 to commend 5th Field Regiment for the excellence of its firing in November.

The regiment may have believed that it was ready for war at the end of 1942, but there was much yet to learn. Artillery weapons, equipment, and techniques were evolving rapidly, so for units left behind in Britain, 1943 was characterized by increasing sophistication and variety in both training and equipment. And while the gunners were busy mastering their trade, many of the exercises in 1943 were now designed to train the division, corps, and Army Group Royal Artillery staffs in proper handling and coordination of massed formations and fire support. For others, 1943 brought an end to the long road to war and the start of an even more arduous road to victory in the field.

The great test of 1st Canadian Army's readiness for war came in the late winter of 1943 in Exercise Spartan. Canada's Second World War army had been created for a major role in the return to France, when all five Canadian divisions and two armoured brigades would fight together for the first time as a single, national field army. Its task would be to break out of a beachhead created by British forces and commence a war of movement that would culminate in Germany's defeat. For 1st Canadian Army's commander, Lt.-Gen. A.G.L. McNaughton, and indeed for some of his fellow general officers like Lt.-Gen. Harry Crerar, who also had served on the gunnery staff of the Canadian Corps in the Great War, the Canadian Army was to reprise its role in the Hundred Days campaign: it was to smash the key enemy defences in the west at the culminating point of a long war. Exercise Spartan in the late winter of 1943 was designed to test 1st Canadian Army's ability to break out and conduct a campaign of movement.

Almost all Canadian formations and units in England participated in Spartan. The 89th Anti-Aircraft Battery and the rest of 1st Light Anti-Aircraft Regiment practised the mobile air defence of I Canadian Corps Headquarters, gun areas, and key choke points along roads whenever the corps moved. Partway through the exercise, Major Keller, the 89th Battery commander, became 1st Light Anti-Aircraft Regiment's second-in-command; later that month, Major G. Wright would replace him in command of the 89th. The 7th Anti-Tank Regiment, including 104th Battery

A 6-pounder crew from 7th Anti-Tank Regiment with included New Brunswick's 104th Battery. Note that the detachment trained to deploy a Bren gunner for close infantry protection of the gun detachment. England, 1942. (LAC PA-131550)

Working for the cameraman. Gunners of 5th RCA manhandle their 25-pounder, February 1943. Typically they would wear coveralls over their uniforms to save them from the mud. (DHH 112.3P1-5507R)

from Fredericton, also tested out its role as I Canadian Corps's anti-tank regiment. The task of coordinating the corps's anti-tank plan fell to Lt.-Col. "Long" John Gillies, the new commanding officer of 7th Anti-Tank Regiment.

The gunners of Newcastle's 28th Field Battery endured Spartan as well. They joined the rest of 2nd Canadian Division after calibrating their guns in January 1943 and after an anti-tank shoot at Beachy Head over the British Channel. The two-week-long manoeuvre exercise by two armies simulated something that 5th Field Regiment and 3rd Anti-Tank Regiment would try to accomplish fifteen months later in Normandy. Only 1st Canadian Division, along with 8th Field and 90th Anti-Tank Batteries – then in the highest state of readiness in the Canadian Army overseas – missed Spartan. They stood on guard in southeast England so that the exercise could proceed in safety.

After Exercise Spartan, 89th Anti-Aircraft Battery slipped back into a local air defence role at Eastbourne. On 3 April, Major Wright was warned that the Luftwaffe might attack the town that day. The intelligence report proved correct. Twelve German Focke-Wolfe 190 fighter-bombers swept in over the English Channel that day and down over 89th Anti-Aircraft Battery Headquarters. The Battery Fitter, Sergeant J.J. Parker, narrowly escaped the strafing, as a German machine-gun bullet pierced his hat. D and E Troop's 40 mm guns opened fire on the low-flying German fighters, spitting out shells as fast as crews could feed the guns. Bombardier L.J. Henry's gun in D Troop claimed one FW-190 brought down. Other D Troop guns all claimed hits. Overall, the attack amounted to a mere nuisance raid, but 89th Anti-Aircraft Battery did its job that day. As a result of that raid of 3 April 1943, 89th Anti-Aircraft Battery from Woodstock was the first New Brunswick artillery unit to engage the enemy in combat in the Second World War.

In April, 90th Anti-Tank Battery fired their 6-pounders at the Cooden Beach ranges in Sussex and proved that they, too, could hit their targets. The regiment averaged a 65.9 percent hit rate, including against moving targets, the highest score of any anti-tank regiment to shoot there. Meanwhile, new and improved field artillery tractors as well as new trucks were arriving in 2nd Field Regiment, bringing that regiment up to War Office standard. In April, Captain Frank Fullerton of Moncton was promoted to Major and took command of 8th Field Battery. Officers had come and gone over three years, but the battery spirit remained in Moncton's old 8th. Indeed, Fullerton's appointment buoyed the gunners' confidence and readied them for action. That spring, they and all the gunners of 1st Canadian Division felt as ready as they could ever be for war.

In the summer of 1943, 1st Canadian Division, and with it 8th Field Battery, 89th Anti-Aircraft Battery, and 90th Anti-Tank Battery, finally went off to war. But it was not where most Canadians expected them to go. The focus of Canadian planning, and indeed the expectation held by most Canadians at home and abroad, had been that their army would deploy in France and retrace the steps of their forefathers in the Great War. The Canadian government had other plans. In the spring of 1943, the tide of public opinion was running strongly against Mackenzie King's Liberal government. Mackenzie King had tried to fight a low-casualty war, content to leave the army idle in Britain while Canadian naval and air forces carried the burden of the fighting and war industry kept civilians working and busy. But most Canadians identified war fighting with the army, and by early 1943 they were increasingly restless about Canada's combat record. Everyone else, even the Americans, were fighting while Canada continued to garrison the British Isles. In the spring of 1943, Mackenzie King's government needed headlines about Canadian troops in the fight. So his government lobbied successfully to have 1st Canadian Division included in the invasion of Sicily slated for July 1943.

In time, most New Brunswick units – infantry, armour, and artillery – sent overseas would serve in Italy. The deeds performed by the Carleton and York Regiment in 1st Canadian Division and by the 8th Hussars in 5th Canadian Armoured Division are well known, not least because both units produced popular regimental histories after the war. Those two regiments also suffered heavy losses in Italy that affected families across the province. But New Brunswick also sent four of its seven overseas artillery batteries to Sicily and Italy. In fact, gunners collectively outnumbered their infantry and armoured brethren overseas, reflecting the Canadian army's emphasis on firepower in this war. On average, about 15 percent of 1st Canadian Infantry Division's fighting troops served in the rifle companies at any

A Canadian rapid-firing 40 mm Bofors gun on guard at Brighton Beach, March 1943. On 3 April 1943, 89th Battery gunners brought down a German Focke-Wulf 190 fighter off the coast at Eastbourne, east of Brighton, becoming the first New Brunswick gunners to engage the enemy in the Second World War. (LAC PA-154973)

one time, while 17 percent served in its artillery batteries. The gunner story is virtually unknown, not least because New Brunswick batteries in Italy were dispersed among four separate artillery regiments engaged in three different tasks.

New Brunswick batteries deployed to Italy in two waves. The first to go were 8th Field and 90th Anti-Tank Batteries as part of 1st Canadian Infantry Division. Their journey began in late April 1943 when 2nd Field and 1st Anti-Tank Regiments moved to Scotland for what amounted to pre-deployment training for their role in the coming invasion of Sicily. The 1st Anti-Tank Regiment assigned its batteries to each brigade in 1st Canadian Division to train their infantry anti-tank platoons with the 6-pounder gun. That same month, new, longer Mark IV barrels arrived for the anti-tank regiment's own 6-pounders. These increased range and improved accuracy. At the same time, the regiment received twelve brand-new long-range 17-pounder heavy anti-tank guns. The initial plan was to re-equip 27th Battery entirely as the regiment's heavy anti-tank battery. Just a few weeks later, that plan changed, and one troop in each battery was equipped with 17-pounders. In 90th Battery, J Troop got the 17-pounders. At the time, the gun's tremendous high-velocity power and muzzle blast were not yet legendary. J Troop's Sergeant A.B. Clynick found out the hard way. The 1st Anti-tank Regiment's unpublished history recorded that "Clynick, who will be remembered for his large and flowing moustache, made the mistake of peering over the shield as the first round fired. It was some time before he could once again twirl his moustache."

In mid-June, 2nd Field Regiment, now commanded by Lt.-Col. Harry Hague, another Great War veteran, boarded the SS *Benedict* for amphibious landing Exercise Stymie. The anti-tank batteries boarded a variety of transports and "landing ships, tank" (LSTs), divided up to land with the infantry they were assigned to support. The weather made things impossible, and time ran out. On 24 June 1943 the transports and LSTs carrying both regiments got under way again, this time for a destination unknown. "The future promised to be far from dull and it looked like the years of training in England would be put into practical use at last." After a week in the mid-Atlantic, the convoy passed through the Strait of Gibraltar and into the Mediterranean. There the men were issued tropical uniforms and told that 1st Canadian Division was now part of Field Marshal Montgomery's famous Eighth Army. Their mission was to land on Italian home territory in Sicily, defeat the Axis forces, and convince the Italian people to topple Mussolini's Fascist government. With luck, that might remove Italy from the war. If they succeeded, nearly 2 million Italian soldiers, sailors, and aircrew defending Europe's Mediterranean coast would have to be replaced by German troops, tanks, planes, and ships. Such a diversion and dispersion of German military power would help the Soviet Union on the Eastern Front and help guarantee success for the much-anticipated return to France sometime in 1944.

The trouble was that in July 1943, control of Mediterranean was still heavily contested. En route to Sicily, U-boats attacked the Canadian convoy, sinking three transports. One carried part of 1st Anti-Tank Regiment's headquarters and the 17-pounder troops of 27th and 57th Batteries. Another carried a troop from 10th St. Catharines Battery in 2nd Field Regiment. Given the long supply lines and shipping shortages the Allies still faced in 1943, it would take months to get replacement guns and gunners. Major Welsh's 90th Battery and 51st Battery were now the only two fully equipped anti-tank batteries in 1st Canadian Division. Likewise, Montreal's 7th and Moncton's 8th Field Batteries were the only two full eight-gun batteries in 2nd Field Regiment. Much work would fall on them in the coming days during what became known as Operation Husky.

A 25-pounder of 5th Field Regiment, RCA, and its new Canadian Military Pattern field artillery tractor (FAT), England 1943. (LAC R112-5504-2)

While 1st Canadian Division sailed off to war, the men, units, and formations left in England carried on with their preparations. In April 1943, 5th Field Regiment fired its first smoke screen at Sennybridge; then at Larkhill in June the regiment trained on the new time and graze-action Type 222 fuse, which could be used for airburst. Then the regiment practised loading and off-loading its guns on "landing craft, tanks" (LCTs) – an encouraging sign that they might soon be going somewhere. The busy summer and fall for the field gunners of 2nd Canadian Division culminated in Exercise Blast in October – a full-scale division artillery exercise. At the end of it, 5th Field Regiment reported in its war diary that "the regt was really clicking." Then in December, as if to prove the point, the regiment fired 3,000 rounds over the heads of advancing infantry in Exercise Crescendo, ending 1943 on a high note.

The anti-tank gunners, too, were making their final preparations throughout 1943 for real soldiering. On 15 March, command of 3rd Anti-Tank Regiment passed from Lt.-Col. Waters to Lt.-Col. J.P. Phin. Phin was relieved in the Fall of 1944. It also fell to Phin and the staff of 3rd Anti-Tank Regiment to coordinate the anti-tank plan for 3rd Canadian Division's beachhead in France. In the event, that included not just Phin's own regiment, but also by 1944 the anti-tank reserve of British I Corps, under whose direction the Canadians would land. It seemed fitting, therefore, to provide 17-pounder guns to 3rd Anti-Tank Regiment as well in the spring of 1943. In April, 52nd Battery was converted to the powerful gun, leaving 4th, 94th, and 105th Batteries equipped with 6-pounders.

Lt.-Col. Phin's first major outing with 3rd Anti-Tank Regiment came in May, when the regiment spent two weeks in Wales training and firing on ranges at Harlech and Burling Gap. In late May, 3rd Anti-Tank Regiment returned to Sussex, to Denne Park, where it spent the summer. Lydd was only a short drive away, and a week there in June helped 52nd Battery learn the intricacies of their new guns. As things turned out, mastering the 17-pounder proved to be premature. Over the summer, 3rd Anti-Tank Regiment, along with the rest of 3rd Canadian Division, began training for Operation Overlord, and it was soon determined that the regiment would need more nimble guns for the assault in France than the towed 17-pounder.

As 1st Canadian Division stormed ashore in Sicily and 3rd Canadian Division began to train in earnest for the assault on France, one final NB anti-tank battery was en route to England. By the spring of 1943, Lt.-Col. Blackey's 6th Anti-Tank Regiment was training hard at Petawawa, and on 24 May it boarded trains for Debert. As usual, the initial move to the east coast was followed by long weeks of waiting, with days filled by route marches and occasional forays into Truro. Only the Campbellton gunners of 103rd Anti-Tank Battery were within easy range of home leave. By the high summer, morale was faltering just as orders arrived to

Tank killer extrordinaire. The size and latent power of the 17-pounder anti-tank gun show well in this photo of one on a range in western Canada. (RCA Museum)

embark. The initial move on 9 August 1943 was by 380 men and twenty officers to Halifax to guard the great liner *Queen Mary*, which had just brought Winston Churchill to Canada for the first Quebec Conference. That conference finally settled the date for Operation Overlord: May 1944. The rest of the regiment departed Debert three weeks later, when *Queen Mary*, carrying 6th Anti-Tank Regiment and 17,000 other Canadian troops, finally left for Britain. By 1 September 1943 the regiment's advanced party was in their billets at Chobham Common, Surrey. The 6th Anti-Tank Regiment would be the last Canadian-trained unit to see action during the war.

One of the first tasks for Lt.-Col. Blackey was to get his regiment in line with the war establishment for anti-tank units. This meant four batteries of three troops each, rather than the four-by-four organization that 6th Anti-Tank Regiment had arrived with. So six officers and 104 other ranks were sent off to No. 2 Canadian Army Replacement Unit for reassignment in late September. In typical army fashion, this change in establishment was followed almost immediately in October by the designation of 6th Anti-Tank Regiment as the anti-tank reserve of II Canadian Corps, to be re-equipped with towed 17-pounders and self-propelled American 3-inch gunned M-10s. This new tasking required an increase in personnel by almost precisely the number of men recently struck off strength. As things turned out, many of the original surplus personnel from 6th Anti-Tank Regiment were still unassigned and simply came back. How much of 103rd Anti-Tank Battery remained New Brunswick through this process is unclear.

In the meantime, 6th Anti-Tank Regiment hit the ranges in October with a full complement of 6-pounders, and fired regularly two or three times a month for the balance of the year. As the artillery official history observed, 6th Anti-Tank's arrival in September 1943 was "skirting very close to the deadline" for Operation Overlord, and much strenuous training remained to be done. And while rumours abounded about the final equipment of the regiment, the assignment of personnel to courses for driving tracked vehicles substantiated at least those suggesting M-10s. In fact, it was learned by the end of the year that 6th Anti-Tank Regiment would be composed of two batteries of M-10s (33rd and 56th Batteries) and two batteries of towed 17-pounders (74th and 103rd Batteries). The latter would be pulled by Canadian-built Ram tanks, with their turrets removed. The Rams were being discarded by the armoured regiments as they converted to the new US Sherman tank, and they made superb gun tractors.

All of this proved to be true, although the new equipment came slowly and the organization changed. The first sixteen Ram gun tractors arrived in January, but the M-10s – twenty-five of them, rather beaten up and worn from previous use – did not arrive until 2 March 1944. The regiment's 17-pounders were picked up a week later. Even so, when the King George inspected 6th Anti-Tank Regiment on 9 March, he was told that the regiment was equipped with an amalgam of 6- and 17-pounders and M-10s. The equipment issue was resolved by the end of the month, with 33rd and 56th Batteries on the ranges with their refurbished M-10s, and 74th and 103rd Batteries firing their 17-pounders for the first time on 30 March.

By the spring, just a few equipment problems remained. On 10 April, twenty-four 25-pounder ammunition limbers arrived for the 17-pounder towed batteries; 6th Anti-Tank Regiment spent the next two months experimenting with storing 17-pounder ammunition in them. The final piece, the remaining Ram gun tractors, arrived on 13 May so that by the time General Dwight D. Eisenhower inspected the regiment at Sandling Park, in Kent (where II Corps had gone as part of its role in the D-Day deception, Operation Fortitude), 6th Anti-Tank Regiment was fully equipped and ready for war.

As 1944 dawned, everyone knew that the invasion of northwest Europe was imminent. The 3rd Canadian Division was tasked with an assault role in Operation Overlord in July 1943, at which time 3rd Anti-Tank Regiment began an intense program of combined arms training that would eventually lead them to Juno Beach nearly a year later. Training for the assault commenced immediately alongside the Regina Rifle Regiment of 7th Brigade. Lt.-Col. Phin was "quite put out" when he had to crawl up a scramble net (used on the sides of assault ships to allow the men to get down into assault craft) into the Reginas' headquarters during an exercise that month. In August, three of the regiment's batteries went off on combined arms training exercises in Scotland, while some personnel were sent to the US army's 803rd Tank Battalion to learn to drive M-10s – an indication of how the regiment's equipment needed to change for an assault landing.

The first of the new American self-propelled 3-inch guns finally arrived in late September and, as the war diary commented, "considerably enhanced the potency of the regiment." A close relationship was established with the Americans, who helped 3rd Anti-Tank Regiment make the transition to the American gun and its tracked carrier. After a demonstration of US M-10s on the Kimmeridge Range, which produced "impressive results," the Americans were invited for dinner in the 3rd Anti-Tank Regiment lines amid toasts and cross-border friendship that the New Brunswickers of the regiment would have understood perfectly.

Through the fall of 1943, as the regiment's batteries dispersed to train with the units they would be supporting in the forthcoming landings, new equipment continued to arrive. The new establishment was confirmed in November: each battery would consist of two troops of 6-pounders and one of M-10s. The war diary expressed hope that this would be the last of what had been "an extremely long series" of equipment changes. That proved to be a false hope.

The long period of dispersion finally came to an end after Christmas, when 3rd Anti-Tank Regiment assembled on the range at Lydd for a nine-day gun camp. The Lydd ranges faced seaward, across the channel, so exercises depended on good visibility and the absence of shipping. This was particularly important for the regiment's first night-firing exercise. While at Lydd in early January, 3rd Anti-Tank Regiment received delivery of four 20 mm anti-aircraft guns for its own use, which prompted the war diarist to observe that it did look like "every man is to be provided with a 6-pounder and a vehicle." The comment reflected the priority given the assault formations for the completion of their equipment. In late January this included the new Mk IV "invasion" helmets. These arrived along with a supply of the new "Canadian Volunteer Service Medal," which was quickly dubbed – with intentional irony, after the years spent waiting and training – as either the "Sussex Star" or the "Order of the Mild and Bitter".

In February, 3rd Anti-Tank Regiment moved to the 3rd Canadian Division concentration area around Southampton, in preparation for the assault on France. At nearby Beachy Head the 6-pounders were zeroed for the new discarding sabot ammunition, which made these little guns especially lethal to German tanks. Apparently the shooting was "very good." That month, the regiment's band instruments – forgotten in a locker aboard the SS *Andes* for over two years – finally turned up.

The final major change in equipment came in April. Up to this point the 6-pounders had been towed by trucks, but it was not clear that these could easily cross a fire-swept beach during the initial assault. The plan for all British and Canadian formations landing on 6 June was to have their guns either self-propelled or pulled by tracked vehicles. So in mid-April, 3rd Anti-Tank Regiment received its first issue of Bren gun carriers, officially "Universal Carriers," to use as gun tractors. Loading trials were conducted on 21 April. The results were mixed, but the issues were quickly worked out, and reports from the next day were "better than expected."

April also brought a significant reorganization of the regiment for the assault, one that would shape it for the first month ashore. According to British and Canadian military doctrine of the time, the task of the tanks of the armoured brigade supporting 3rd Canadian Division in Operation Overlord was primarily to attack and exploit gaps made in the enemy's line, or to counterattack enemy armour that penetrated the front. It was not precisely the cavalry role of earlier days, but the doctrine for the armoured brigade did reflect an independence and mobility free from the plodding infantry and artillery of the standard Canadian division in the line. Providing close anti-tank support for defensive battles was the job of anti-tank guns, be they self-propelled or towed. So it fell to Lt.-Col. Phin, commanding officer of 3rd Anti-Tank Regiment, to develop and implement the anti-tank defences of 3rd Canadian Infantry Division. This included the 6-pounders held by the division's infantry battalions, as well as the heavier guns of the corps anti-tank reserve in his area (in Phin's case, 62nd Anti-Tank Regiment, Royal Artillery, from British I Corps). Thus the infantry brigades got tank support as and when necessary, but close anti-tank support was always there from the division's own anti-tank regiment.

Overlord, then, called for 3rd Anti-Tank Regiment to directly support the three infantry brigades of 3rd Canadian Infantry Division. This was normally done by assigning a battery to each brigade and keeping one in reserve to strengthen the front as required. In the run-up to D-Day, 4th Battery had normally worked with 7th Brigade, 94th Battery with 9th Brigade, and 52nd Battery with 8th Brigade, leaving 105th Battery as the reserve. Each of those batteries was organized the same: two troops (four guns each) of 6-pounders and one (four guns) of M-10s. The troops were numbered alphabetically, starting with the lowest-numbered battery, with the last troop of each battery equipped with M-10s:

4th Battery: A, B, and C troops

52nd Battery: D, E, and F troops

94th Battery: G, H and I troops

105th Battery: J, K, and L troops

This basic organization was completely changed for D-Day. The three infantry brigades that comprised the Canadian assault now each had different tasks, and 3rd Anti-Tank Regiment was reorganized to support them. All of the 6-pounders were grouped into 4th, 52nd, and 94th Batteries, and all the M-10s into 105th Battery. The batteries supporting the assaulting brigades (52nd Battery with 8th Brigade, and 94th Battery with 7th Brigade), were strengthened by the 6-pounder troops from 105th Battery, while 4th Battery, reduced to its two troops of 6-pounders, acted as the reserve. 3rd Anti-Tank Regiment was to retain this order of battle until early July. It speaks well of Major Love and his command team that the mobile firepower of 3rd Anti-Tank Regiment was placed in the hands of 105th Battery for Operation Overlord. Its task was to support the inland thrust by 9th Brigade to the Carpiquet airfield.

Anti-tank units were vital not just to the success of the Canadian landings but to the overall success of Operation Overlord itself. The 3rd Canadian Division had perhaps the single most important task of any Allied formation landing on 6 June 1944 – to defeat the primary counterattack by German Panzer divisions that was intended to throw the Allies – as a whole – back into the sea. Since the summer of 1943, Allied planners had identified the plains running down to the sea on either side of the Mue River, west of Caen, as crucial. If the British could take and hold Caen, or even mask its northern perimeter, and if they could occupy Bayeux to the west, there would be no other place on the whole landing front where Panzer divisions could launch a decisive armoured counterstroke. The Germans knew this too. The commander of Army Group B (North Sea to the Biscay), Field Marshal Erwin Rommel, wanted four Panzer divisions on this key ground in May; he got one, with another close by, and two more within a day's drive.

The Canadian task on D-Day was, therefore, to get inland and secure the division "covering position" astride the Caen–Bayeux highway at Putot, Brettville, and

Carpiquet, defend the critical corridors to the sea, and defeat "the" counterattack. The forward edge of that position would be secured by infantry battalions and their 6-pounder guns, which would be backed by the guns of 3rd Anti-Tank Regiment, the 17-pounders of 62nd Anti-Tank Regiment, Royal Artillery, the tanks of 2nd Canadian Armoured Brigade, and nearly 200 field and medium artillery guns – all under Canadian control. The trick would be to get ashore and dug in before Rommel's vaunted Panzers could arrive in strength to crush the landings. Allied planners expected something to happen within the first five days ashore. They were right on all counts. As part of this plan, Major Walter Love and the staff of 105th St. George Battery were given command of 3rd Canadian Division's mobile anti-tank force. Their job, and that of 9th Brigade, was to block easy German access to the great plain north and west of Caen by seizing a fortress position around Carpiquet on D-Day.

While 3rd Canadian Division and its 3rd Anti-Tank Regiment prepared to land on D-Day, 2nd Canadian Division and II Canadian Corps (to which 28th Field Battery and 103rd Anti-Tank Battery belonged) were tasked with a follow-on role. Both would deploy to France sometime in July for the break-out battles as part of 1st Canadian Army. In the meantime, they were anything but idle. Intense training continued, and as it turned out, 1st Canadian Army would have a critical role to play in Operation Fortitude, the massive and highly successful deception operation designed to keep German forces fixed in the Pas de Calais and well away from the Normandy beachhead farther south.

The channel coast was swarming with invasion troops by early 1944, and they had priority on local ranges. So in February, 5th Field Regiment made a nearly 400-mile road move to the large artillery practice camp at Otterburn, near Redesdale, Northumberland (on the border with Scotland), for a week of firing. They returned to their billets in Rottingdean at the end of the month, where they were inspected by General Bernard L. Montgomery, Overlord's ground force commander. The regiment was on various ranges through March and April, which became available as assault units moved to their concentration areas, doing final checks on a whole gamut of capabilities: anti-aircraft guns were fired on the Kithurst range, a regimental shoot took place at Alfriston, anti-tank gunnery was practised at Beachy Head, and in Exercise Step in early April "the last big ex before D-Day" brought five days of firing in support of infantry. In May, 5th Field Regiment shifted its billets to Waldershire Park, seven miles north of Dover. On 1 May the regiment received the order, issued by 1st Canadian Army on 11 April to all units headed to France, to paint white American stars on their vehicles for identification purposes. Many Canadians were not too happy with this order, and painted the stars on upside down in protest; they had to be ordered to do it properly. Three weeks later the first issue of berets was made, and orders came down to wear them. "They look O.K." the war diary lamented, "if worn properly."

Waiting for action. A group from D Troop, 28th (Newcastle) Battery, at Westenhangar Race Course, 27 May 1944. Front row, L–R: Troop Sergeant Major F.J. Gillin from Hartland, Bombardier C.L. Cole from Woodstock, Gunner R.J. Aiken from Breadalban, PEI. Back row, L–R: Gunner H.J. Porter from Woodstock, Gunner W. Murray from Tabusintac, Gunner M.D. Dunbar from Fredericton, Lance Bombardier S.C. Delaney from Albany, PEI, Sergeant J.A. Troy from Woodstock, and Lieutenant E.O. Steeves from Moncton. (NPL, Reid Collection)

In May, 2nd Canadian Division, II Canadian Corps, and 1st Canadian Army shifted their weight to Kent in support of Operation Fortitude. The 1st Canadian Army was part of a fictional First US Army Group, which included 3rd US Army. The US formation was still in the embryonic stage, and its formations and units were concentrated far to the west, around Liverpool. It was therefore the job of the Canadians to rattle the sabre along the Kent coast, to help sustain the fiction that an Allied landing in the Pas de Calais was imminent. The guns got back to the ranges at Alfriston and Lydd briefly during the month. The cryptic lament in the war diary for 5th Field Regiment on 11 May that the regiment was undertaking a reconnaissance for the "coming sigs exercise" belies its operational role in Fortitude. The signals exercise, Operation Quicksilver, was intended to mimic radio traffic for First US Army Group, including that of 3rd Canadian Division, in order to convince the Germans that all of 1st Canadian Army was in Kent waiting to land near Calais. Although 6th Anti-Tank and the other units of II Canadian Corps were not assigned to the initial assault in Normandy, the two weeks following D-Day were marked by frantic – and quite deliberate – preparations for imminent embarkation. On 2–3 June all the vehicles of 5th Field Regiment were waterproofed, which

Gunners of 5th Field Regiment silhouetted against a sunset, England, 1942. (DHH)

effectively reduced the regiment to idleness. These activities, including a warning for immediate notice of departure on 8 June, must have seemed mindless to many. But they were all part of an elaborate, and ultimately successful, ruse designed to keep German forces fixed in the Pas de Calais while the battle raged farther south.

Operation Overlord began on 6 June 1944, with 3rd Canadian Division (along with 105th Anti-Tank Battery) in the assault wave. Everyone in 5th Field Regiment was "electrified by the news" of the landings in France; "we will be in action shortly," the war diary speculated. The alert on 8 June, putting the regiment on six hours' notice to move starting at 0800 on 10 June, also caused a wave of anticipation that the long wait was over. But that warning order was just a ruse to convince the Germans that a landing in the Pas de Calais was likely on 10 June: two Panzer divisions en route to the Canadian front in Normandy were diverted northward as a result. The men never knew. On 15 June the war diary of 5th Field Regiment lamented, "still waiting with baited breath for our marching orders." Indeed, they had been for nearly five years.

All of that was about to change. By 3 July 1944 the artillery of 2nd Canadian Division was concentrated in east London near the Albert Docks, waiting under a rain of V-1 bombs to embark on transports. The next day, 5th Field Regiment boarded four separate ships and then – along with the rest of their convoy – moved down the Thames to an anchorage at Gravesend. The convoy departed for France on 6 July, arriving off Gold Beach the next day. It took two full days to land the regiment and all its equipment at St-Come-de-Fresne, east of Arromanche. By end of 9 July, 5th Field Regiment was concentrated at Ryes and ready for war. Nearly five full years after it was mobilized for active service, New Brunswick's 28th Field Battery was about to become the last of the province's artillery units to go into action.

Chapter 9
Sicily and Italy: New Brunswick's Batteries in I Canadian Corps, 1943–45

Italy was not where Canadians were supposed to be, but it turned out to be Canada's longest land campaign of the Second World War. Their initial task as part of Operation Husky, the invasion of Sicily in July 1943, was to gain some desperately needed combat experience and to placate an angry electorate at home: Canadians expected their army to fight, and it had been in garrison far too long. The jump to the Italian mainland in September, and the concurrent commitment of a second Canadian division and Corps Headquarters, served slightly different purposes. If the Allies could drive the Italians from the war, Germany would have to find nearly 2 million troops plus tanks, planes, and ships to replace them. When that happened in September 1943, Italy became a massive containment operation to keep German troops away from the Eastern Front and, by the spring of 1944, away from Operation Overlord.

In the final eighteen months of the war, Allied troops toiled in Italy's rugged landscape without enough men, weapons, and supplies to overwhelm the enemy in what became a massive holding action reminiscent of the last war. These circumstances shaped the way Canadian gunners fought in Italy, making them innovative,

Sicily, July–August 1943

aggressive, and determined. For nearly two years they wrestled their guns into extraordinary firing positions, adapted continuously to make up for the perpetual shortage of Allied infantry, and consistently beat a skilful and ruthless enemy.

New Brunswick batteries deployed to the Mediterranean Theatre in two waves. The 8th Field and 90th Anti-Tank Batteries were first to go as part of 1st Canadian Infantry Division. Lt.-Col. Harry Hague, another Great War veteran, led 2nd Field Regiment into Sicily, with Major Fullerton's 8th Battery from Moncton in tow. Lt.-Col. G.O. Hutchison returned in June 1943 to take command of 1st Anti-Tank Regiment just in time for the landings at Pachino. By this stage only one New Brunswick officer remained in Fredericton's 90th Battery, Lieutenant Gerald Charles Evans from McAdam, who led L Troop. But most of the senior NCOs of the battery were still New Brunswickers. These included Battery Sergeant Major J.W. Frank Lofstrom from Kingsclear.

In July 1943 no one was sure how the enemy would react when Allied troops waded ashore on Sicily, the first Axis home territory to be invaded. Italian units had fought well in Tunisia in the spring, revealing signs of improvement in equipment, supply, and combat effectiveness. The Royal Italian Army had not yet fought on its own soil, so no one took them lightly. Also, it was impossible to predict how many enemy divisions might shift to Sicily if the Axis chose to make a stand there. So Allied commanders concentrated the landings in southeastern Sicily for mutual protection and security. The plan was to deliver the assault force safely to the beaches, grab Axis air bases nearby, and then prepare to receive the expected counteroffensive. Beyond that, it was difficult to make plans until the enemy showed his hand.

The Husky plan assigned three British divisions, air assault troops, and commandos to the capture of the ancient port of Syracuse. The 1st Canadian Division was to guard their left wing by landing on the Pachino Peninsula and capturing the airfield there. The 7th US Army's three assault divisions, along with Ranger and parachute units, would land farther west across the Gulf of Gela on the south coast. Their main mission was to seize airfields in the broad Gela and Acate valleys and the commanding heights above them, where General George Patton planned to meet the enemy counterstrike. After winning the beachhead battle, General Montgomery expected his three British divisions to turn north and drive on Catania and the neighbouring Gerbini airbase complex before carrying on to Messina and cutting the Axis link to mainland Italy. General Patton would land a fourth US division and advance to central Sicily to engage Axis forces left intact after the opening battles, including those in western Sicily. The Canadians were to guard the British inland shoulder and provide a link with the Americans in the most remote part of the assault area; they were considered the least likely to see an Axis counterattack.

The 1st Canadian Division landed with 1st Canadian Infantry Brigade on the right and 2nd Canadian Infantry Brigade on the left – the most exposed flank.

Major Frank Fullerton (right), 8th Battery Commander, his signaller Gunner Orville Brown, and Lt.-Col. Harry Hague, 2nd Field Regiment's commanding officer, at an observation post directing fire on Monte della Forma in Sicily, 18 July 1943. Two weeks later Fullerton was wounded and Brown killed at Regalbuto. Fullerton, a skilful forward observer, later returned to the unit and brought 8th Battery home to Moncton in 1945. (DHH 112.3P1-21904)

Major Welsh's 90th Anti-Tank Battery had the task of helping secure that exposed far left flank of the whole British–Canadian landing zone. They came ashore with 2nd Canadian Brigade, putting J Troop's 17-pounders ashore alongside the Princess Patricia's Canadian Light Infantry, while K Troop went ashore with the Seaforth Highlanders of Canada. L Troop landed farther west in support of the Royal Marine Commandos of 2nd Special Service Brigade, which was tasked with capturing Castelazzo Point, the headland commanding the west end of the Canadian beach. The 2nd Field Regiment, including Moncton's 8th Battery, supported the battalions of 1st Canadian Brigade on the Canadian right.

Operation Husky commenced well before dawn on 10 July in the Canadian zone. Assaulting infantry stormed the beach under cover of darkness, supported by naval fire. The job for 1st Canadian Division's gunners was to get ashore at dawn and harden the beachhead. In the event, the main Axis counterattacks crashed against American and British units on either side of the Canadians. In the Pachino area, the local Sicilian Coastal Defence Regiment area was largely anti-Fascist, poorly supported by mobile reserves, and ready to quit Mussolini's war. A few holdouts resisted on D-Day, mostly around Pachino Airfield, and were quickly overcome. An Italian Blackshirt Legion counterattack on the left was destroyed by Royal Marines and Canadian heavy mortars in the morning. By afternoon, 1st Canadian Division had begun driving inland towards Ispica and Rosolini to secure a deep, defensible beachhead. On the way there, K Troop of 90th Battery drew first blood for Canadian gunners in Italy, when Italian mortar and artillery fire hit the Seaforth Highlanders. Sergeant William Upton spotted one of the mortar positions, unhitched his 6-pounder, wheeled it around, and destroyed the mortar, killing the crew and their six-horse team. It was not the protective anti-tank role envisaged for the divisional anti-tank batteries, but 90th Battery proved that skilled gunners could deliver direct fire support to infantry when tanks were not available. The incident set the tone for the campaign ahead.

Meanwhile, 8th Battery struggled to pull their 25-pounders and gun limbers through the sand dunes and onto firm ground below Pachino (a lesson not lost on Overlord planners). The guns were in action by evening, but "targets were lacking." However, "in short time contact was made with 'vino,' a contact never lost in the months of the Sicilian and Italian campaigns that followed." Over the next five days, Italian and German forces retreated north from the Anglo-Canadian landings to a more defensible line in the northeast corner of the island. Luftwaffe and Regia Aeronautica fighters and bombers strafed the Allied convoys travelling dusty roads in daylight. The 8th Battery's convoy was attacked more than once, but mercifully suffered no loss. Others were not so lucky.

The 1st Canadian Division and the closest American formation, 1st US Division, drove deep into Sicily to cut the island in half before Axis forces could mount a solid defence around the base of the great Mount Etna volcano. Meanwhile, most of 7th US Army pushed west to Palermo, and the British on the right drew the bulk of local Axis forces into battle on the Catania plain. As the Canadians pushed north, Axis troops from western Sicily drove east to join in the fight against the British. This put the Axis force on a collision course with 1st Canadian and 1st US Divisions, which were moving towards Enna. The Canadians' drive north, along narrow, winding roads connecting hilltop towns, was led by a motorized vanguard with an infantry battalion in trucks, a tank squadron, and a towed anti-tank battery. The whole divisional artillery followed behind the vanguard. On 16 July it was 2nd Canadian Brigade's turn to lead. The Loyal Edmonton Regiment was backed by Lieutenant Evans's L Troop from 90th Battery and a Three Rivers Regiment tank squadron. They bumped into a battlegroup from 15th Panzer Grenadier Division at a depression in the ridge south of Piazza Armerina.

The Germans announced their presence with machine-guns and mortars. Canadians returned the fire, with the Loyal Edmonton Regiment charging into the attack. Farther back in the column, 8th Battery went into crash action and fired their first rounds in anger. The Germans responded with mortar and artillery fire. German shells landed farther back in the column as well. One landed on Sergeant Upton's K1 gun tractor. The blast wounded Gunner C. Clark and filled Upton's arm and head with shell fragments. Upton died two days later and thus was the first New Brunswick gunner lost in action in Europe during the Second World War. Sergeant John Towe's crew, whose gun had broken its trail three days earlier and had to be abandoned, hitched their Quad to Upton's gun, loaded up the unwounded members of his crew, and carried on.

The infantry from Edmonton defeated the German blocking force, which fell back and set up a stronger delay battle position south of Valguarnera. There they needed to slow the Canadians down and buy time for German reinforcements from the mainland to arrive in Sicily and establish a main defence line across the broad Dittaino Valley, north of Valguarnera. The main line would be anchored on a steep, rocky feature capped by the towns of Leonforte and Assoro. When General G.G. Simonds, the divisional commander realized the size of the German blocking force assembled south of Valguarnera, he responded by bringing up the whole of 1st Canadian Division to swarm and destroy it. Simonds's chief gunner, Brigadier Bruce Matthews, called observers forward from all three field regiments to join in the first divisional fire plan of the war. Lt.-Col. Harry Hague went forward personally for 2nd Field Regiment, bringing along Major Fullerton and his signaller, Gunner Orville Brown from 8th Battery. The three set up on a hill overlooking the Grottacalda crossroads commanding the highway fork carrying both key routes to the centre of Sicily. From there they could observe the fall of shot on Monte Della Forma, where most of the German blocking force had dug in to stop the Canadian advance. At midday on 18 July they helped direct a storm of shot and shell down on the main enemy position while 3rd Canadian Brigade – including fellow Maritimers from the Carleton and York and West Nova Scotia Regiments along with the Royal 22e Régiment – both fixed and flanked the Panzer-Grenadiers. At the same time, 1st Canadian Infantry Brigade attacked Valguarnera directly after a gruelling cross-country night march. Collectively the Canadians encircled and nearly destroyed the large German and Italian force at Valguarnera. The effort came off less than perfectly. Rocky Sicilian hills, ranging from 2,000 to 3,000 feet high, often blocked radio signals, cutting off the 1st Brigade infiltrators from their supporting guns as they ambushed German rear areas and reinforcements around Valguarnera. This war was bringing new challenges.

Canadian shells landing on Monte della Forma, the main German position barring the approaches to Enna and Valguarnera in central Sicily, 18 July 1943. The 8th Battery and all of 1st Canadian Division's artillery hammered the hill while Canadian infantry encircled and infiltrated it from both directions. (DHH 112.3P1-21903)

By 19 and 20 July, 1st Canadian Division was hot on the heels of the Germans and Italians, spreading out to press the full divisional attack. A great race developed to seize the Leonforte–Assoro feature, which controlled a highway junction that was critical to the long-term defence of Sicily. For anyone standing on floor of the Dittaino Valley, the 2,300-foot-high ridge complex on which are perched Leonforte and Assoro looks like a titanic mountain fortress. The capture of that ground is the stuff of legend; Canadian infantry performed feats of climbing that the Germans thought impossible. But the dramatic victory won on those heights between 21 and 23 July 1943 would have been impossible without the artillery. Major Welsh's 90th Battery formed part of the 2nd Canadian Brigade column driving towards

Leonforte. Major Fullerton's 8th Battery and the rest of 2nd Field Regiment supported 1st Brigade's assault on Assoro.

On the left, the 2nd Canadian Brigade column benefited from the early capture of a low hill on the floor of the Dittaino Valley, which gave them a well-covered base of fire, behind which they placed two regiments of field artillery. Farther east, 2nd Field Regiment's guns took up positions concealed in the folds of the valley's floor, 200 yards from a large Italian ammunition dump and in the midst of grass fires ignited by tracer fire. When night fell on 20 July, the Hastings and Prince Edward Regiment scaled the high terraces and gained the castle-topped peak overlooking Assoro. They brought with them a powerful radio set strapped to a mule – another carried the batteries. The Hastings and Prince Edward Regiment's second-in-command, Major A.A. "Bert" Kennedy, had been a militia gunner before the war and now acted as FOO, directing 2nd Field Regiment's batteries down onto the wealth of targets: mortar, rocket, and gun positions, truck convoys, and infantry counterattacking in the open. The whole 1st Canadian Divisional Artillery joined in the shoot. German batteries out of range of the 25-pounder field guns got a dose from a British medium regiment attached to the Canadian Division. The Germans reacted violently to the presence of the Canadians on the high plateau. The small-arms ammunition carried by the infantry during their arduous climb was quickly expended, making the curtain of 25-pounder shells protecting their perimeter critical. It was during this fight for Assoro on 21 July that a timed or command-detonated enemy demolition charge exploded in the ammunition dump beside 2nd Field Regiment's gun pits, "sending masses of shrapnel, mud, flames and smoke hundreds of feet in the air." The concussion could be felt 1,000 yards away. Careful selection of gun pits in lower ground saved most of the regiment, although 10th Battery lost one man killed and three wounded. The blast did not stop 2nd Field Regiment from keeping the Hastings and Prince Edward Regiment alive on top of Assoro. Indeed, midway through the morning they took up new positions a few miles north to extend their range well beyond Leonforte and Assoro to secure the Canadian hold on that vital ground.

A few thousand yards west and within sight of Assoro, by dawn on 21 July the Seaforth Highlanders had grabbed a toehold on the high feature looking down on Leonforte. The Loyal Edmonton Regiment relieved the Seaforth Highlanders after German shells scored a direct hit on the Battalion Command Post and inflicted heavy losses on its leadership. The Loyal Edmonton Regiment then infiltrated along Highway 121 into Leonforte across a steep gully cut by a small stream where German engineers had blown the bridge. As darkness fell, the Germans surrounded the lightly equipped Canadians in the village. A confusing night fight erupted in which neither side could fully control the streets. Radios failed again, cutting off contact with the Loyal Eddies inside the town. Meanwhile, the Canadians knew that a German tank company was on its way to Leonforte. It was now critical to

Lieutenant Gerald Charles Evans of McAdam, NB, being decorated with a Military Cross by Eighth Army's General Sir Bernard Law Montgomery. Evans earned his MC for his daring leadership of 90th Battery's L Troop in the desperate fighting for Leonforte in Sicily, 20–23 July 1943. Four other 90th Battery members were decorated at that ceremony, including Major "Tiger" Welsh, who earned the Distinguished Service Order.
(DHH 112.3P1-24244)

bridge the gully under the cover of darkness in order to reinforce and resupply the Loyal Edmonton Regiment before the enemy tanks swung the battle in the enemy's favour.

A flying column prepared to rush in as soon as a bridge was built. It was based on a Princess Patricia's Canadian Light Infantry rifle company, a Three Rivers Regiment tank squadron, and 90th Battery anti-tank guns. As the engineers built the bridge, German and Italian shells burst among the 2nd Brigade column. One shell struck 90th Battery, wounding Bombardier Nelson Amos and Gunners Zamer and Alexander. Lance Bombardier David Bemrose courageously carried Amos to an ambulance while shells burst around them. Bemrose himself was hit by fragments in the arm, but helped a wounded infantryman into his truck before going to an aid post. Bemrose was one of six members of his Fredericton family serving in uniform, including two sisters serving in the Canadian Women's Army Corps.

As Canadian engineers worked on the bridge, Major Welsh deployed L Troop's 6-pounders and J Troop's 17-pounders close to the bridging site, and then scrambled across the gully to the Leonforte side to see how to get his guns in. Lieutenants Evans and Murdoch went with him. Welsh spotted a German tank and some infantry forming up, and watched the engineer company in Leonforte stop work to fight off a counterattack. Welsh recrossed the gully and told Evans to manhandle two of his 6-pounders to fire on the Germans threatening the bridging site. The ravine and the wildly winding Highway 121 traversing it must be seen and driven to appreciate what Welsh had asked Evans's L Troop Sergeants Morehouse and Swift and their crews to do. They pushed their 6-pounders to the edge of the ravine and opened fire from exposed positions at 900-yards range. They scored direct hits on the German tank and nearby machine-gun posts, which allowed the engineers to go back to work.

At dawn on 22 July, the 2nd Canadian Brigade flying column launched over the new bridge with machine-guns blazing. Evans's L Troop rode their Quads, limbers, and guns in behind the Three Rivers tanks. Each Quad had Princess Patricia's Canadian Light Infantry hanging off it, firing at German rooftop snipers as they went. The column fought its way to the town centre, where a close-quarter tank battle ensued. The Shermans hunted the German tank platoon in the streets of Leonforte while Evans's gunners deployed in and around main piazza. L Troop guns blasted German machine-guns out of upper-storey windows and off of the heights above town, helping the Loyal Edmonton Regiment and the PPCLI win control. Lieutenant Murdoch brought up the 17-pounders to seal off the northern end of the town along with an infantry company, shutting the door on any more enemy tanks. The fight raged all day as three German battalions and parts of several Italian units backed into Leonforte after being driven from the heights around Assoro. By day's end the disorganized remnants of 104th Panzer-Grenadier Regiment had quit the Leonforte–Assoro feature completely, dragging their wounded and dead north and eastward.

The action on both sides of the Leonforte–Assoro heights demonstrated courage and skill at arms in all the Canadian units involved, but 90th Battery won more decorations for valour than any other. Lieutenants Murdoch and Evans both won the Military Cross. Sergeant Towe and Bombardier Bennett both won the Military Medal. Major Welsh became the first RCA officer to win the Distinguished Service Order in the Italian Campaign, and he earned the nickname "Tiger" from Brig.-Gen. Chris Vokes, commander of 2nd Brigade. Their deeds made national headlines. The *Ottawa Citizen*'s Ross Munro described Welsh as "a short, unassuming man past the age of most battery commanders," yet "he led his anti-tank battery with amazing dash at Leonforte and is known throughout the division now for his front line exploits. He goes around wearing a sun helmet which seems to crowd him still closer to the ground. When you meet this artillery dynamo he will probably not talk about the war but first impress upon you he is the postmaster of Sunderland."

The battle for Leonforte–Assoro unhinged the Axis defence of Sicily by securing a foothold at the critical corner of the mountain chain they had planned to defend indefinitely. For the next week, German reinforcements piled into central

Sicily to stop 1st Canadian and 1st US Infantry Divisions from rolling up their flank. They massed on the western approaches to Agira and Troina, backed by heavy 150 mm and 170 mm long-range guns. The enemy supported their new defences with heavy air attacks. On 23 July, German planes caught 90th Battery on the move north of Leonforte at the Highway 121–117 junction. No one was injured. The next day, German artillery fire was more effective. Heavy German shells crashed down around 90th Battery's K Troop, wounding Sergeant Thornton and Gunner Breen. As the anti-tank gunners moved forward, the Moncton gunners of 8th Battery and the rest of 2nd Field Regiment moved up to Leonforte, thereby extending their reach all the way to Nissoria Ridge, where 1st Canadian Brigade crashed headlong into the new Axis line.

For the first time in Sicily, German and Italian ground forces were massing in sufficient density to warrant a major divisional fire plan. On 25 July, 2nd Field Regiment moved up again, just behind the ruins of Nissoria, dug gun pits, and dumped ammunition. The rest of 1st Canadian Divisional Artillery massed there, too: 3rd Field (composed of western batteries) and the Regular Force gunners of 1st Regiment, Royal Canadian Horse Artillery, reinforced by British field and medium regiments. Brig.-Gen. Bruce Matthews, the "Commander, Royal Artillery (CRA)," of 1st Canadian Division, and his artillery staff prepared a massive fire plan to support 2nd Infantry Brigade in a deliberate attack against the enemy's new main line of resistance, which was set to commence later that evening. The 90th Battery followed 2nd Canadian Brigade into the forming-up areas. Before the barrage, Lieutenant Charles Waterous and Gunner James Gordon Clarke climbed the ridge in search of forward positions for their anti-tank guns and came face to face with a camouflaged German tank concealed among the rocks. Both were killed before they could escape.

The 8th Battery got payback for Clarke and Waterous after the sun went down. The Moncton gunners joined in a thunderous barrage, firing 300 rounds per gun that night alongside eight other field and two medium batteries in the largest Canadian barrage of the Second World War so far. Attacking infantry reported that "the barrage was so even and so steady that the infantry closed right up on it and were on the enemy before they recovered from the shock of the barrage." The effect on German and Italian infantry was devastating. The rocky surface of Nissoria Ridge made it impossible for them to dig in, so they sheltered above ground in "sangers" made by piling rocks in a surface pit. Few of those sangers or the Axis troops inside survived the barrage. War correspondent Ross Munro reported that "captured Germans asserted that Canadian artillery fire was the equal to anything they had undergone on the Russian or Tunisian fronts."

But heavy fighting continued around and beyond Agira as fresh German troops rushed to plug the gap. The Germans, reinforced by Italian infantry and heavy weapons, fought desperately to prevent the Canadians from reaching Mount

Gunners of 7th Battery, sister battery to 8th Battery in two world wars, within 2nd Field Regiment, preparing to fire their 25-pounder gun-howitzer during the Battle for Agira, 28 July 1943. Days before, all Canadian guns in Sicily had fired the largest Canadian artillery barrage of the war to that point, inflicting heavy losses on the large German force defending Nissoria Ridge. (LAC PA-177113)

Etna and cutting their line in half. Major Welsh pushed 90th Battery hard to provide direct fire support for 2nd Canadian Brigade's drive eastward while staying on guard against the tank threat. Most of the German tanks in Sicily were already destroyed, but Axis artillery remained a menace. Shells struck a 90th Battery tractor and gun on 28 July, severely wounding Gunner W.L. Dunn. Agira fell later that day.

At the beginning of August, 1st Canadian Division closed in on Regalbuto and Catenanuova, setting up the start line for an Allied general offensive in Sicily. The 1st Canadian and 1st US Divisions attacked together towards Mount Etna, screening the arrival of two fresh reserve divisions, one British and one American, brought in to break the Axis main line when it became clear they intended to stand

and fight. The Canadian task was to keep attacking the strong German force spread between Regalbuto and Catenanuova, after which 78th British Division would take over. "The Germans are fighting desperately to prevent a breakthrough in this sector," Ross Munro reported. "Canadian and British artillery fire here is becoming a nightly tempest with shells flashing and roaring over the whole front. There are numerous artillery actions during the day too, and the Allies' air blitz is being stepped up." To make up for his shortage of long-range heavy artillery, General Montgomery employed Allied medium bombers to strike deep at German heavy batteries, staging areas, and road junctions.

German reinforcements from Herman Goering Division fought stubbornly to hang on to Regalbuto. On 1 August, Major Frank Fullerton of 8th Battery and his signaller, Gunner Orville Brown, were supporting the combined efforts of 231st Malta Brigade and the Royal Canadian Regiment from a battery observation post overlooking Regalbuto. The Germans plastered it with mortar fire, killing Brown and wounding Fullerton. The loss was deeply felt, as the two were already forging a reputation for ably supporting the Ontario infantry battalions in 1st Brigade. A few days later as Regalbuto fell, the very able Major G.A. Rankin took command of 8th Battery, but Fullerton's wounds were not too severe. He would be back.

From Regalbuto the Canadians drove eastward towards Adrano, at the foot of Mount Etna, which was to be their finish line in Sicily. British and American troops, including freshly landed reserves, carried on the task of clearing Sicily. On the second-last day of Canadian artillery action, 2nd Field Regiment and 8th Battery in particular suffered their worst casualties of the campaign, when a crippled US Army Air Force Mitchell bomber crashed into their positions. A great ball of fire roared up between 2nd Field Regiment's headquarters and 8th Battery's lines, fed by an apparently near full load of fuel. The inferno incinerated the Regimental Command Post and badly burned twenty-eight officers and men. One man died outright. The 8th Battery's Lieutenant Laurier Joncas pulled charred men away from the fire in spite of his own burns. Over the next three days, seven more gunners died from their injuries, among them 8th Battery's Joncas, Sergeant Leonard Trites, Bombardier Joseph Attis, and Gunners Frank Downing, Joseph Amirault, and Clifford Steeves. As the war diary concluded, the crash formed "a gruesome epitaph to a four week battle that an accident should, in a few seconds, kill and wound more men than the battle itself."

Despite losses, morale in both New Brunswick batteries remained high when they reached the rest and training camp at Scordia on 9 August 1943. Those who came through unscathed took justifiable pride in a job well done. The 8th Battery had performed every kind of mission, from roadside crash action and observed shoots on call, to predicted barrages against fixed enemy positions and even counter-battery fire. The 90th Battery had proved that the 6- and 17-pounder guns were useful for more than just shooting up tanks. Overall, Canadian infantry had learned just how critical their divisional guns were to keeping them alive on the modern, highly lethal battlefield by destroying or at least neutralizing enemy heavy weapons. New Brunswick gunners felt proud to be part of General Montgomery's Eighth Army and heartily cheered him when he visited their camp. Montgomery told the Canadians publicly that victory in Sicily had depended on Canada's great inland wheeling movement. "If you had failed, we should still be fighting on this island. But you handled yourselves according to the best and highest standards of my army in this very short, model little 39-day campaign."

In the event, Sicily was just the start of Canada's Mediterranean adventure. By August, plans were under way to nearly triple the size of Canada's "Central Mediterranean Force" by adding 5th Canadian Armoured Division and I Canadian Corps Headquarters along with supporting corps and army troops. The August 1943 Quebec Conference finalized Allied plans to press on to the Italian mainland in return for Italy joining the Allied cause. It remained unclear whether the Germans would make a stand in Italy, but they clearly anticipated an Italian collapse. By August they had shifted dozens of divisions to southern France, the Italian peninsula, and the Balkans. It seemed likely that if the Allies pushed on to the mainland, Italy would capitulate and even more German forces would be drawn into the area. Also, having bomber bases on the Foggia plains would allow the Allies to strike targets in southern Germany. All of this began a chain of events that added two more New Brunswick artillery batteries to the Italian Campaign: 89th Anti-Aircraft Battery from Woodstock, and 104th Anti-Tank Battery from Fredericton, both elements of I Canadian Corps.

In the meantime, on 3 September 1943, New Brunswick's Carleton and York Regiment and the West Nova Scotia Regiment of 3rd Canadian Brigade made history. When they crossed the Strait of Messina and landed at Reggio di Calabria in Operation Baytown, they became the first Allied soldiers to return to Europe's mainland with the intention of staying. The landings were unopposed, not least because the mountainous Calabria region, hemmed in tightly by the sea on both sides, offered no opportunity for rapid explotation. Moncton's 8th Battery came ashore in the afternoon and had all guns ready to fire by 1700, but there was no resistance. The 90th battery landed two days later as part of the follow-on force, and the long trek began. Winston Churchill had complained that he did not want the Allies to crawl up the boot of Italy like a bug, but there was a clear purpose to these Canadian landings on the toe of the boot.

Operation Baytown was actually a feint in support of the main British and American landings at Salerno (south of Naples), and a British landing at Taranto on the heel of Italy. The main fighting in September raged around Salerno, where German Panzer and Panzer-Grenadier divisions tried to throw the British and American troops back into the sea. As that desperate fight went on, the Canadians crawled northward from Calabria along 300 kilometres of rugged countryside and blasted roads. As the Germans retreated they left a trail of devastation and explosive traps behind. So the Royal Canadian Engineers led the way, building diversions around demolitions, lifting mines, disarming booby traps, and clearing a path. There was little for gunners to do except help with the manual labour of road repair. Only a few Canadians saw a German in September, but their presence was felt. On 12 September 1943, 8th Battery's Forward Observer's universal carrier struck a mine in Calabria. The blast wounded Sergeant W. Spottiswood and Gunner E. Hope and killed Gunner Lynd Piers of Moncton. The good news that month was that Italy did surrender – in fact, most of it switched sides. This, too, had unexpected consequences.

In October the German retreat from Calabria slowed and turned into sharp rearguard actions. Allied intelligence suggested that the Germans planned a fighting withdrawal all the way to northern Italy. Stiffening German resistance in October, however, offered the first clues that they had decided to stand firm south of Rome along a belt of permanent defences under construction across the narrowest part of the Italian peninsula. This played into Allied strategy: Axis troops, guns,

In addition to destroying German tanks, 90th Battery and 1st Anti-Tank Regiment provided highly accurate, direct fire support to 1st Canadian Division infantry in the Italian campaign. Here, a 6-pounder gun takes on German fortified houses in Campobasso province, October 1943. The open, rolling country shown here is typical of Italy's southern regions. (DHH 112.3P1-25684N)

tanks, and other military resources were pouring into Italy from Western Europe and the Russian Front.

German resistance stiffened the closer the Allies got to the German Winter Line defences between Ortona and Cassino, but the Canadians slogged their way forward and were never far from their guns. When the Royal Canadian Regiment met a strong German force at Motta Montecorvino, however, complete with a troop of vaunted 88 mm dual-purpose anti-aircraft/anti-tank guns, which guarded the mountain road leading up from the Foggia Plain, the eight guns of 10th Battery were not enough. Tight concentrations from the whole regiment, 10th, 7th, and 8th Batteries, were needed to shoot the Royal Canadian Regiment into Motta and open the drive to Campobasso.

During the isolated hilltop actions in October, the guns of Major Welsh's 90th Battery were frequently called upon to give direct fire support for 2nd Canadian Brigade's infantry. Lightweight 6-pounders were often pushed by hand into precarious hilltop positions, from which they could reach German machine-gun posts in old stone Italian houses. At San Bartolomeo in Galdo, J Troop's venerable Sergeant Clynick, his great moustache restored, climbed up to lay a 6-pounder of the Loyal Edmonton Regiment on German machine-gun posts across the deep upper Fotore Valley at Baselice. The accurate fire stirred the ire of a German 105 mm field battery, but also enabled the Loyal Edmonton Regiment to cross the valley and take the town in darkness. The 90th Battery also proved they could manhandle J Troop's 17-pounders – three tons of bone-crushing steel – into hilltop long-range sniping positions. The 17-pounder gun's accuracy, weight of shot, and high muzzle velocity made it a superb tool for punching holes in thick stone walls with a single round. Sergeant Markey on J-2 (the second gun of J Troop) and Sergeant Foster on J-3 were particularly successful at blasting fortified houses identified by Loyal Edmonton Regiment scouts.

The summer experience in Sicily and the October–November drive through the lower Apennines had prepared New Brunswick's two batteries for the challenge awaiting them. Both 8th and 90th Batteries took a short, well-earned rest in Campobasso in late November before shifting over to the Adriatic coast in time to join in British Eighth Army's drive on the coastal road junction towns of Ortona and Pescara.

Meanwhile, 89th and 104th Batteries prepared to move to the front, although they had no idea which front it would be. The firepower of 7th Anti-Tank Regiment hugely increased in the months before departure from Britain as new weapons systems became available. The 15th Toronto Battery and 111th Nelson Battery received the new American-built M-10 self-propelled tank destroyer, which mounted a high-velocity 3-inch naval gun. The 113th Regina and 104th New Brunswick Batteries each got a troop's worth of 17-pounders to go with their 6-pounders, making them equivalent in organization to the division-level anti-tank batteries already in

A 1st Anti-Tank Regiment 17-pounder in action in Campobasso province, October 1943. The 90th Battery's "J" Troop operated four of these heavy anti-tank guns. Their long range, great accuracy, and powerful anti-tank shells enabled them to crack open the Italian farmhouses, whose thick stone and masonry walls were employed by the Germans to shield machine-gun posts and other defences. (DHH 112.3P1-26013N)

Italy. After training up on the new equipment, they left it all behind and sailed from Bristol on 15 November 1943. "Rumours of where we are bound for are running all the way from home in Canada to Egypt and even Burma," the war diary of 7th Anti-Tank Regiment noted. "Only time will tell." The 89th Battery and the rest of 1st Light Anti-Aircraft Regiment had left Bristol two weeks earlier. They, too, had sailed without guns and equipment under the assumption they would take over equipment already in theatre. When, on 6 November 1943, twelve German torpedo-bomber aircraft attacked their convoy, a few 1st Light Anti-Aircraft Regiment gunners helped man their ship's 3-inch heavy anti-aircraft guns. Those who got the chance "thoroughly enjoyed this taste of action on the high seas." After a brief stay

A 2nd Field Regiment 25-pounder crew engaging German targets from positions near Torella in the upper Biferno Valley, 30 October 1943. (LAC PA-115916)

at a transit camp in Algiers, I Canadian Corps's artillery units – including 89th and 104th Batteries – all moved to Messina, Sicily. There, 1st Light Anti-Aircraft and 7th Anti-Tank Regiments spent the rest of 1943 training – without guns. As fighting along the Winter Line south of Rome intensified in November and December, shipping priorities shifted to ammunition and replacements for Allied units already in action. So 5th Canadian Armoured Division and I Canadian Corps troops spent a frustrating winter cooling their heels waiting for equipment and the chance to reach the front. The wait was especially exasperating given reports that 1st Canadian Division was heavily engaged.

In the first days of December 1943, 1st Canadian Division and its guns crossed over to British Eighth Army's bridgehead across the Sangro River for the drive up the Adriatic coast. The battle there had started in November when British and Indian troops, including 166th (Newfoundland) Field Regiment, attacked a heavily defended German line anchored along the Sangro. Eighth Army's attack was at first aimed at Pescara, where a major highway crossed to Rome. If General Montgomery's army reached Pescara, it would threaten German forces defending Rome's southern approaches on Italy's western coast. Eighth Army's Sangro River attack encountered the Adriatic wing of a powerful German defensive zone, and managed to do little more than force a crossing of the Sangro itself. Over the next weeks, Allied commanders realized that Hitler had changed his mind about holding Italy south of Rome and that German 10th Army had new orders to stand "permanently"' along what was dubbed the Gustav Line.

German intentions were still unclear in Allied Headquarters in early December, when 1st Canadian Division crossed the Sangro and arrived on the heights above the Moro River to relieve 78th British Division. The relief marked the beginning of the battles for the Moro River and Ortona, arguably the best-known chapter of Canada's Italian campaign. The story is well told elsewhere, but as is usually the case, the gunner part is less familiar. At first, Canadian infantry battalions probed over the Moro River without an artillery barrage, testing reports that suggested only delaying forces were present. In fact, the German 90th Panzer-Grenadier Division was dug in on the north bank in great strength, backed by mortars, tanks, and artillery of every type. The first barrages were fired on 6 December after the initial Canadian probes met powerful German strongpoints and counterattacks. Those attacks were shot up with Canadian shellfire, but not before 2nd Field Regiment's Captain T. Le M. Carter was wounded in the legs while observing for the Seaforth Highlanders during their first run on San Leonardo. Carter refused evacuation and stayed to cover the Seaforth withdrawal, earning a Military Cross in the process.

The 6 December probes demonstrated that the Germans were resolved to stand firm at the Moro River. The problem for them was that the Hastings and Prince Edward Regiment (the Hasty Ps) had established a small bridgehead across the river in the steepest part of the Moro River valley, close to its mouth. The location was poor for fording or bridging to get tanks and anti-tank guns across. The Hasty Ps' survival depended famously on two of their own 6-pounder anti-tank guns, which they had manhandled onto the tiny bridgehead. More importantly, they depended on 2nd Field Regiment's guns answering their FOOs' calls for fire on German counterattacks. Major Frank Fullerton had recovered from the wounds he had taken in Sicily and was one of those FOOs. By now 2nd Field Regiment had cemented its partnership with 1st Canadian Infantry Brigade. Within that brigade all-arms team, 8th Battery most usually found itself shooting for the Hasting Ps. But during the struggle for the Moro River, all twenty-four guns in 2nd Field Regiment delivered hot fire to defend the Hasty Ps' toehold.

A more deliberate attack covered by a substantial artillery barrage was planned for 8 December. Unfortunately, a Luftwaffe air raid on the port of Bari a few nights earlier and bridge washouts at the Sangro River limited ammunition supplies. Service Corps truckers laboured against odds to get the necessary ammunition dumped at 2nd Field Regiment's gun pits. The new assault would use the Hasty P bridgehead as a base to launch one part of a two-pronged attack on the main

Italy, July 1943–February 1945

highway crossing over the Moro at San Leonardo. The 8th Battery's mission was to protect the Hasty Ps' bridgehead and to support a daring Royal Canadian Regiment attack farther up the Moro River towards the San Leonardo crossing.

Major Welsh and 90th Battery arrived south of the Moro River on the night of 6 December, too late to support the first rush across the river. Lieutenant Murdoch's J Troop 17-pounders deployed on the heights along the south bank, where they could fire across the valley at San Leonardo. The Germans welcomed J Troop with heavy shell and mortar fire. Gunner Flagle was hit badly in the leg, and a small piece of shrapnel struck the venerable Sergeant Clynick in the face. The unit medical officer plucked the jagged piece out, and he plunged immediately back into the fight. That same night, Welsh, his second-in-command Captain Hugh Burnett, and

L Troop Leader Lieutenant Evans crept down to the valley floor to survey potential fording sites. All three were pinned down by thick enemy machine-gun fire, which also stopped all engineering work to build a ford near the blown bridge below San Leonardo. The Germans knew full well that the Canadians must open a crossing site there along the main two-way paved road leading northwest to Ortona. The enemy had turned the village of San Leonardo into a fortress guarding the bridging site.

The deliberate two-pronged attack planned for 8 December included 90th Battery. Once the right prong pressed out of the Hasty Ps' bridgehead downstream, 90th Battery was to follow 2nd Canadian Brigade's assault directly on San Leonardo, after the engineers opened a crossing near the blown main highway bridge. Their mission was to defend their bridgehead against anticipated counterattacks from 26th Panzer Division tanks and possibly 90th Panzer-Grenadier Division's tank battalion. On 8 December, Lieutenant Evans moved two L Troop 6-pounders down into the valley to cover the engineers working on the crossing site. That night, German shellfire set L-4's Quad on fire. Sergeant Warrell pulled a case of

A 1st Anti-Tank Regiment Field Artillery tractor towing a 17-pounder about to descend into the Moro River Valley. The 90th Battery's 17-pounder troop crossed the Moro River on 9 December 1943, stiffening the Canadian bridgehead at San Leonardo against repeated German counterattacks. (LAC PA-107933)

high-explosive ammunition and burning duffle bags out of the vehicle to save it. It was difficult to replace equipment in the Italian campaign: if L Troop lost their truck, there was no telling when they might get another. K Troop was not so fortunate: one of their Quads had its driveshaft smashed by a shell.

Vehicle losses south of the Moro offer a small clue to how fiercely the Germans contested the second Canadian attack on 8 and 9 December. In the hours before dawn on 9 December, Major Welsh, Captain Burnett, and Battery Sergeant Major Frank Lofstrom were at J Troop's fire base covering the crossing site, impatient to get 90th Battery guns across and into San Leonardo to meet counterattacking German tanks. Once the Seaforth Highlanders and Calgary tanks won control of the village, work on the fording site proceeded apace. Finally, by evening, L Troop got over the river to site two guns each on the northern and western approaches to San Leonardo. K Troop took position with all four guns covering the eastern approach. The 90th Panzer-Grenadiers mounted strong counterattacks, backed by substantial artillery fire against the original Hasty P bridgehead, San Leonardo, and all points in between. Instead of surging on towards Ortona after the Moro had finally been bridged, the Canadians fought a stubborn three-day defensive battle to hold what had been the German side of the Moro. The German attacks foundered against the now protected Canadian bridgehead, suffering crippling losses, especially on the Canadian right in the Hasty P area, where Fullerton and the other 2nd Field Regiment FOOs called down thousands of shells. The battle proved the 25-pounder gun-howitzer to be a lethal counterattack killer. Its range, accuracy, rate of fire, and capacity for high-angle fire enabled field regiments to deliver concentrations of shells close to Canadian positions. So long as an FOO remained alive, could see the enemy, and work his radio, Canadian troops could hold almost any ground.

The Germans threw back plenty of shells, including heavy counter-battery fire. One tore off Lt.-Col. Hague's arm while he was forward with his observation posts from 2nd Field Regiment. Hague was popular in both 90th Battery and 8th Battery, having previously commanded 1st Anti-Tank Regiment: the wound ended his war. Two more 2nd Field FOOs were also wounded. During the night of 9–10 December, Major Welsh moved 90th Battery's 17-pounders across the Moro to guard the bridge directly while other batteries from 1st Anti-Tank Regiment stiffened the bridgehead. It was a tense night. Battery Sergeant Major Lofstrom broke an ankle while dodging exploding shells. German machine-gun bullets struck Lance Bombardier R.J. Upton just above his heart and in his arm. A German infantry patrol closed in on Sergeant James Bailey's gun. He and his crew, with the help of some Seaforth Highlanders infantry, nabbed the German officer leading the patrol and two German panzer-grenadiers. Counterattacks raged on around San Leonardo through to 11 December. The 90th Battery guns met no enemy tanks but stayed forward in the infantry fight. Meanwhile the division's artillery, including 8th Battery, rained shells down around the bridgehead in response to defensive fire calls.

The 90th Panzer-Grenadier Division was wrecked in the process. Farley Mowat, the great Canadian literary figure and a Hastings and Prince Edward Regiment veteran, captured the sentiments of his fellow infantrymen in that unit's history, *The Regiment*. "The Massacre of the attacking Germans was due in large part due to the assistance of the FOOs and the gunners of the Second Field Regiment." Frank Fullerton and his comrades "wore the artillery badges, but their loyalties belonged equally to the Regiment [Hasty Ps]. After the Moro River the Regiment thought of the Second Field as its good foster brother whose strong hand could always be called upon to smite the Hun."

A Canadian infantryman looks on as a 90th Battery 15cwt truck tows a 6-pounder into the shell-battered ruins of San Leonardo during the Battle for the Moro River, 9 December 1943. The battery arrived in time to help defeat the counterattacking 90th Panzer Grenadier Division. (DHH 112.3P1-27361N)

Crossing the Moro and Ortona, December 1943–January 1944

The reality of the new Italian campaign materialized along the Moro River. The Germans had decided to hold a fortified line across the middle of Italy in depth and at all costs. When the 90th Panzer-Grenadier Division's counterattacks were defeated on the north side of the Moro, they did not break contact and withdraw as they had done through southern Italy. Instead, the survivors fought for every farm, every ditch, every ravine, and every piece of defensible ground in an effort to stop what looked to be an Allied breakthrough. And they were reinforced in the Moro sector by the elite 1st Parachute Division, which had been sent to the Adriatic sector to stop the Canadians. Thus the Germans were doing what the Allies had hoped – transferring troops and weapons to the sector from more important fronts. This "good news" would not have been welcomed by the Canadian troops who were struggling to expand their Moro River bridgehead. They and their Allies were now fighting a brutal war of attrition.

After enemy counterattacks ceased around San Leonardo, 90th Battery remained in position while 1st Canadian Division pressed the attack northward. The Germans, appreciating the importance of the village as a base, hammered San Leonardo incessantly with mortar and shellfire. Major Welsh's men dug deep to survive. They worked above ground only at night, but even that was dangerous. A heavy stonk of German mortar bombs struck J Troop in the darkness of 12–13 December. Gunners Elwood Sleep and Rufus Hooper were killed. Meanwhile, 8th Battery crossed to the Moro bridgehead and took new positions near San Leonardo from which they could reach forward troops from 1st Canadian Division and neighbouring 8th Indian Division attacking across Vino Ridge towards the gully in front of Ortona.

The ammunition supply improved in mid-December, dramatically increasing 2nd Field Regiment's rate of fire and ability to blast 1st Canadian Division forward. Fighting south of Ortona reached a climax along the deep, stream-cut ravine called The Gully and at the crossroads beyond it code-named "Cider." By mid-December, 90th Battery had evacuated its first three "nervous exhaustion" casualties of the war, the result of a continuous hail of enemy fire for ten straight days. After 9 December, wet weather made the ground too soft for tanks to help infantry with enemy machine-guns or even to push 6-pounder guns off road. The weather also grounded the most important Allied counter-battery resource, fighter-bombers, thus enabling the German artillery to fire at will with little likelihood of retribution. In such conditions it became impossible to keep soft-skin vehicles safe, and 90th Battery "vehicle" casualties piled up. The only good news was the long-overdue arrival of mail, a batch of eighteen replacements, and confirmation of Gerald Evans's promotion to Captain. Otherwise "the common saying was, only seven shelling days till Christmas".

In mid-December, 1st Canadian Division's field regiments fired their largest concentrations of the war so far. They made first use of the "Uncle" target, which

A 2nd Field Regiment Forward Observation Post near Ortona, December 1943, helping direct 8th Field Battery's fire. Italian stone buildings were valuable to both sides for shelter, protection, and observation. This made them targets. (DHH 112.3P1-28866N)

involved massing all seventy-two field guns in the division, with a single FOO calling them down on one priority target. Modernized fire control and radios made such coordination possible with awesome effect against well-protected German strongpoints and counterattacks caught in the open. But constant firing at high rates strained 8th Battery's guns and gunners. On 15 December a premature round blew an 8th Battery 25-pounder to pieces, killing Lance Bombardier Robert Van Buskirk and Gunners E. Ross MacDonald, Adrien Howe, and Douglas Campbell. MacDonald had lied about his age (sixteen at the time) in 1939 to join the original battery. Both MacDonald and Van Buskirk were well known in Moncton. Lance Bombardier Art Boudreau was nearby when it happened. "I could hear the command post officer hollering 'why isn't number one gun firing? Why isn't number one gun firing?' Later on I found out why." Word reached all four families back home at Christmas.

It took the largest Canadian artillery barrages of the war to date, on 18 and 19 December, along with bitter infantry and tank action, to finally defeat the German units clinging to the north side of the Gully and Cider crossroads blocking the approach to Ortona. On 21 December, 2nd Canadian Infantry Brigade fought their way into Ortona's southern edge. Meanwhile, 1st Canadian Brigade's infantry worked their way around on the inland flank. Intelligence reports and experience again suggested that the Germans might abandon Ortona and fall back. War correspondent Ross Munro reflected that optimism in Saint John's *Telegraph-Journal*. The previous "eight days' fighting have virtually wiped out the German 90th Panzer Grenadier Division and its place has been taken up by the German 1st Parachute

Gunners of 8th Battery and other members of 2nd Field Regiment, warming up around a fireplace in a damaged Italian farmhouse along the static Ortona–Arielli front in February 1944. (LAC PA-134531)

Canadian 40mm Bofors position protecting the supply route from Eighth Army's base to the Ortona Front. 89th Battery took up their first positions in Italy along this line in February 1944.
(DHH 112.3P1-30824-N)

Division. The Canadians also hit the paratroopers heavy blows, particularly with a massive artillery barrage." But instead of abandoning Ortona, the German paras dug in and contested every inch. Wet weather denied the air support vital for neutralizing German heavy batteries, while German shellfire and mud thoroughly blocked 1st Canadian Brigade's attempts to envelop the city from the west. Ortona would have to be won building by building, street by street.

The papers back home (and subsequent historians) wrote about the "Western Canada troops" who fought their way into the town backed by tanks and anti-tank guns: most of the anti-tank guns were from New Brunswick's 90th Battery. K and L Troops manhandled their 6-pounders down Ortona's streets right behind the

Seaforth Highlanders and Loyal Edmonton Regiment, respectively, and alongside Three Rivers Regiment Sherman tanks, and used them at close range as assault guns. It was dangerous work but devastatingly effective.

At the edge of town the Canadian all-arms combat team encountered large piles of rubble that had been blown down by German engineers to block the main street to Canadian tanks. Enemy machine-gun, sniper, and mortar fire was too thick for engineers to clear the obstacles. So Major Welsh pushed his 90th Battery 6-pounders into range and blew the rubble piles down low enough for tanks to crawl over. Once in the town centre, Captain Evans took L Troop straight down the Corso Vittorio Emmanuelle with the Loyal Eddies, and Lieutenant R.B. Ferguson took K Troop to the west end to support the Seaforths. Each infantry battalion in the town

Sergeant F.V. MacDougall and Battery Sergeant Major J.H. Ferguson of 2nd Field Regiment emerging from their dugout northwest of Ortona, February 1944. Life for 8th and 90th Battery gunners along this static front reminded First World War veterans of 1914–18. Newly arrived 89th and 104th Battery members got their first taste of action in conditions like these. (LAC PA-193899)

also had its own anti-tank platoon. All of them learned how to cave-in clay-tile roofs onto German snipers with a single well-placed 6-pounder shell. When it was discovered that the 6-pounder's solid shot could not penetrate the thick stone and masonry of Italian row houses, they fired high-explosive rounds through windows and doors to burst inside in their own version of room-clearing tactics. Upper-storey windows were too high for tank main guns to elevate, so the 6-pounders were rolled up rubble ramps. Their accuracy meant that 90th Battery guns could fire "in close proximity to our leading troops" as infantrymen marked targets with tracer fire from their Brens. Welsh's after-action report described "the effect of 6 pounder high-explosive in buildings" as "devastating." The Germans seemed to agree with Welsh's assessment. As the war diary recorded, "from the evidence of enemy prisoners interrogated, the effect on the enemy was most detrimental."

The 17-pounders were too big and too heavy to heave around easily in an urban battle, so 90th Battery parked two J Troop 17-pounders alongside a troop of Three Rivers Regiment Sherman tanks on a headland southeast of town. From there they shot up buildings and defences along the cliffside promenade 1,500 yards away, where German paratroopers were contesting the advance. Captain Burnett of J Troop eventually brought the other two 17-pounders downtown to join L Troop. At that time in the war, the 17-pounder had no high-explosive round, and the super-high-velocity armour-piercing shot often passed clean through a building with little effect. The exception was soon discovered: if the armour-piercing shot struck structural steel, the building would come down. On Christmas Eve, J Troop gave the Loyal Edmonton Regiment a special gift. Armour-piercing rounds from a 17-pounder shattered the iron girders holding up a large building, bringing it tumbling down on German paratroopers.

By then, the fighting in Ortona had taken a gruesome turn. As often as not, 90th Battery guns, and the infantry's own 6-pounders, were blowing the corners off buildings to bring them down instead of risking infantrymen to clear them. Major Welsh wrote that "this was achieved on several occasions within a few minutes, with the expenditure of comparatively few rounds." In fact, the anti-tank gunners decided the downtown battle this way, by blowing down two large blocks in Ortona. Christmas Day 1943 counted among 90th Battery's most intense days of combat in the whole war. All guns inside and outside Ortona fired hundreds of rounds, blowing Germans out of buildings and/or just knocking buildings down. Bombardier William Joseph Doucette of Marysville, New Brunswick, distinguished himself:

> On December 25 1943, during the street fighting in Ortona, the advance of "D" Company of an infantry regiment was held up by intense fire coming from a house dominating the axis of advance. Tanks were unable to bring fire to bear on the house because of a pile of rubble which blocked the street. Bdr Doucette was in charge of an anti-tank gun supporting the advance of the infantry. Seeing the difficulty he, with his crew, man-handled the gun up to the pile of rubble and although under heavy fire

In early May 1944 all three of 1st Canadian Division's field regiments moved in behind Monte Trocchio facing the Gustav Line and Cassino. The razor-backed ridge at the mouth of the Liri Valley formed a great shield for Allied artillery massing in elaborately protected and camouflaged positions like this Canadian artillery regimental headquarters. (LAC PA-140133)

> from machine guns and mortars, destroyed the house, and thus enabled the infantry to move forward. This NCO's courage, determination and initiative were of the highest order and made a valuable contribution to the final success of the operation.

Doucette won the Military Medal. Fighting on Boxing Day 1943 grew even more intense as the Germans reinforced their garrison. Sergeant M.A. Fallon and Gunner Ray Adamson went forward to scout a new position for their gun and were cut down by machine-gun fire. Fallon made it back; Adamson's body was found two days later, riddled with bullets.

The dramatic fighting around Ortona continued to the end of December. Losses to 8th and 90th Batteries were remarkably low given the intensity of fighting. Captain Burnett won the Military Cross, and Major Welsh earned a Bar for his Distinguished Service Order and a rest. Word came that he was to return to Canada to help with a Victory Loan drive. The *Toronto Globe and Mail* interviewed him when he got home, and as might be expected of a great leader, he spoke not of himself but about his battery: "We had the finest spirit in Italy. We had not one neurosis before Ortona, though we slept in slit trenches and were blasted night and day for 21 days of steady rain." Under normal conditions the battery numbered

174 officers and men, but at Ortona "we went into the assault with 91 men." Major A.H. Warr came from 4th Anti-Tank Regiment to take Welsh's place. Captain Evans also needed a rest and was transferred to Regimental Headquarters as Quartermaster Captain. Lieutenant Murdoch transferred to 51st Battery to help fill leadership vacancies there. A number of NCOs were promoted based on their outstanding service and leadership to date, including Sergeant Clynick as J Troop Sergeant and Sergeant John Towe as K Troop Sergeant. Bombardier David Bemrose was named Acting Lance Sergeant to command the J-1 crew. Up to that point, 90th Battery's service in Sicily and south Italy had proved that their light, versatile guns filled a crucial assault artillery roll when tanks were unavailable, or when weather, terrain, and Old World European architecture blocked their path. Indeed, the battery had fired thousands of rounds in direct support of infantry attacks compared to only a few hundred against enemy tanks.

As the New Year dawned in January 1944, 1st Canadian Division settled into a long period of Great War–style static trench warfare, while the weight of the fighting shifted to the western side around Monte Cassino and Anzio. The 1st Anti-Tank Regiment spent the winter "subjected to more hardship than ever before." Their war diary went on to complain that "the weather was cold and wet with numerous snow storms, and due to the constant shelling, habitable houses were very scarce. Movement was kept to a minimum as the enemy possessed several O.P.s observing our area." The 90th Battery deployed two 6-pounder troops up and the 17-pounders in depth. They rotated personnel to give them a bit of a rest, as forward gun positions were the target for enemy fighting patrols. The 8th Battery and 2nd Field Regiment had less to do and little to do it with: 25-pounder ammunition was once again in short supply in Italy, and most of it went to the active front. Nonetheless, the 8th Battery gunners could not leave their guns for long, so they spent their time building elaborate dugouts and gun pits. The alternative was a visit to rest stations in Ortona for a movie, a hot meal, and a beer or some "vino."

In January 1944, Canada's Second Mediterranean Contingent moved from Sicily to the mainland. None of the artillery units, including 89th and 104th Batteries in 1st Light Anti-Aircraft and 7th Anti-Tank Regiments, yet had guns, tractors, or trucks. While they lived in tents near Altamura in southern Italy, the guns and vehicles dribbled in through January and February. The delay was well used: officers and NCOs of 104th Battery went forward at the end of January to do observation post duty with 1st Anti-Tank Regiment north of Ortona, where they gained firsthand experience with recent Italian campaign lessons. Among the first equipment to arrive around that time were six self-propelled 40 mm guns mounted on Morris truck beds, enough to equip one troop of 89th Battery. Not long after this, the whole of 89th Battery went forward to relieve a British regiment protecting Eighth Army's base area near Ortona. During their stay, Major Wright ran a training and demonstration program for the regiment to practise using their 40 mm guns in a ground

A busy Canadian artillery signals exchange deep in a protected bunker behind Monte Trocchio, 12 May 1944. That day 8th Field Battery was assigned to smoke off the infamous Abbey of Monte Cassino ruins and blind German artillery observers during offensive that broke the infamous Gustav Line. (LAC PA-143895)

role, including firing indirectly controlled by radio and telephones connected to forward observation posts. This was a portend for the Woodstock gunners. By then the Luftwaffe threat had been much reduced, and some began to wonder whether the manpower and equipment tied up in anti-aircraft units was justified. In February, 89th Battery's E Troop fired another test shoot against ground targets conducted by 1st Canadian Survey Regiment. The aim was to get results out to 4,000 yards. They discovered that with 12-second tracer, they could track 40 mm fire out to 7,000 yards. However, at that range the 40 mm anti-aircraft gun was not as effective against ground targets as other weapon systems already at the front. The shell was too small compared to the 57 mm 6-pounder high-explosive round for direct fire, and much smaller than the 25-pounder field gun shell or the 92-pound 5.5-inch medium round in the indirect role. For the anti-aircraft gunners, change was in the wind.

A long column of Royal Canadian Army Service Corps trucks ferries ammunition and supplies across the Gari River and the former German Gustav Line to new Canadian positions facing the Adolf Hitler Line on 21 May 1944. 89th Light Anti-Aircraft Battery's protected these bridges and the steady traffic across them as the battle surged up the Liri River Valley. The Luftwaffe frequently attacked the bridges and packed crossroads at last light. (LAC PA-151180)

Major S.B. Smith's 104th Battery of 7th Anti-Tank Regiment, the I Canadian Corps's anti-tank reserve, finally received guns and trucks in mid-February. On 22 February they and 113th Regina Battery relieved 1st Anti-Tank Regiment's 27th and 90th Batteries on the Ortona front. The 90th Battery won no rest for the relief. The deployment of 7th Anti-Tank Regiment to the front was part of a plan to thin out the British Eighth Army's lines on the Adriatic side and shift forces to the Cassino front. The plan had 1st Anti-Tank Regiment build fortified strongpoints behind the main Canadian front, capable of all-round defence. If a German counteroffensive penetrated the thinly held front, it would meet these fortified posts in depth manned by anti-tank gunners and engineers. "Guns were dug into elaborate pits reminiscent of the last war," the war diary commented. So while 104th and others held the front, 90th Battery built its fortress at Caldari on the old Moro River battlefield.

The German threat on the Ortona front was real, but they never tried their luck. Instead, heavy fighting around Cassino in February and March 1944 captured everyone's attention, and resources. Everyone understood that the quickest – if not the easiest – route to Rome lay up the Liri Valley. So by the end of winter the Allies were preparing a great spring offensive to destroy that German force around Cassino. Secretly, the Allies concentrated divisions along Italy's western coast to build temporary local superiority. In March and April, then, Canadian units began pulling out of the Ortona sector and disappearing into the Campobasso hills.

The 104th Battery was among the first to leave the Ortona sector. After only three relatively uneventful weeks in the line, they drove to a secret camp in the Biferno Valley at Montecilfone on 7 March 1944. Battery Sergeant Major Jim Thompson was directing their convoy into the unit's temporary gun park when a 17-pounder set off a stack of anti-tank mines. The blast threw the three-ton gun into the air and down onto Jim Thompson. The former regimental hockey-team captain was rushed to an Eighth Army base hospital at Termoli. By the time Major Smith and Thompson's brother, another sergeant in the battery, reached him, Thompson was dead. The 7th Anti-Tank Regiment's war diary records how he had been a "standout amongst any rank in the Regiment and certainly one of the best BSMs in the Army."

The 7th Anti-Tank Regiment came out of the line early to train on new equipment in time for the spring offensive. The self-propelled batteries received new M-10 tank destroyers, and 104th Battery drew four new M-3 half-tracks to pull their 17-pounders. Units of 5th Canadian Armoured Division also moved into the rear for more training. Among them were now over 100 New Brunswick gunners, both officers and men. Some were from the Saint John fortress, which was increasingly staffed by NRMA conscripts. Among those who requested transfers overseas was Gunner James Turnbull, who ended up in 8th Field Regiment (Self-Propelled). Turnbull would play a prominent role in the fate of New Brunswick artillery units many years later.

In April the last Canadian units left the Ortona front to join the rest of I Canadian Corps assembling for the spring offensive. Just before leaving, German shells struck 8th Battery's gun line, killing Gunner Charles Barnes. The battery buried him at the main Canadian cemetery at Ortona. Outside Caserta, on the Cassino front, New Brunswick's four artillery batteries drove into their designated areas by night, then used brush to "sweep up" and conceal wheel tracks. Camouflage nets strung between olive trees completed their concealment, and minimal movement was permitted in daylight. Still, dust-caked gunners had a chance to clean equipment and themselves in the warm April sunshine in nearby rivers.

Preparations for the great spring offensive, code-named Operation Diadem, were well in train. British Eighth Army formations would attack the Gustav Line

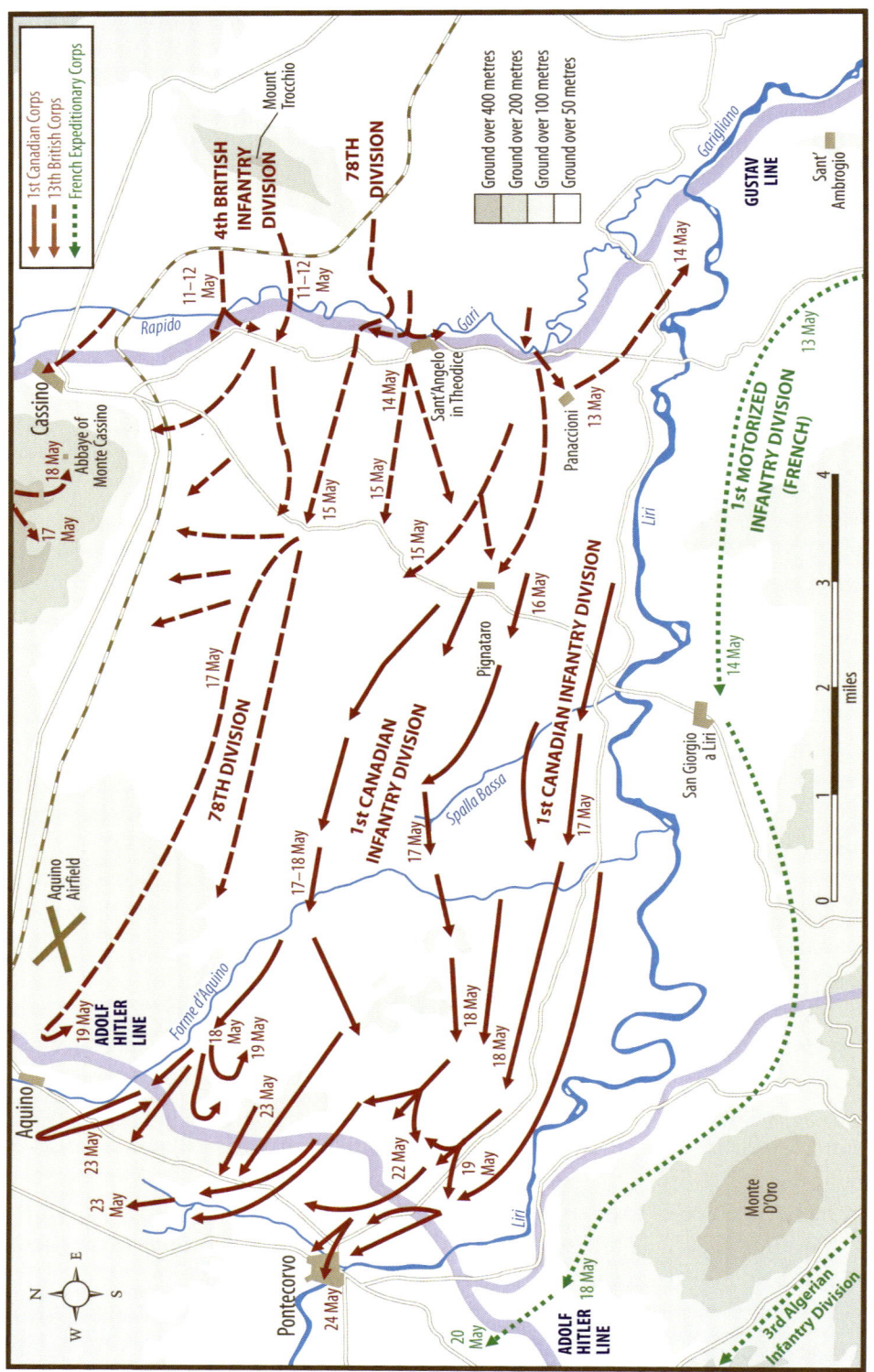

The Gustav and Hitler Lines, May 1944

at Cassino after the skies cleared and the ground dried in May. Once that line was breeched, I Canadian Corps was to pass through into the Liri Valley, break the German Hitler Line farther up, and crush any counterattack. Breaking the Hitler Line would be the signal for 5th US Army to break out of the Anzio beachhead to the west and threaten the Germans with encirclement south of Rome. The aim was to kill or capture as many Germans as possible, forcing Hitler to either reinforce Italy or abandon the country entirely. Given Germany's recent tendency to hold ground at all costs, the plan would convince Berlin to send large reinforcements to Italy just weeks before D-Day in Normandy.

For Operation Diadem to work would require a vast artillery concentration behind the shelter of Monte Trocchio, a long, knife-edged ridge. It lay across the face of the Liri Valley like a giant shield, within range of Monte Cassino and the main Gustav Line and well serviced by Highway 6. In April, 104th Battery sent work parties forward to dig gun pits and pile ammunition behind Mount Trocchio. On 20 April, Captain G.E. Screeton's D Troop of 89th Anti-Aircraft Battery reinforced air defences around the medium and heavy gun pits of what was now known as 1st Canadian Army Group, Royal Artillery. E and F Troops of the Woodstock gunners and the balance of 1st Light Anti-Aircraft Regiment provided air defence for the Canadian Corps Headquarters, which was hidden to the rear.

The grand concentration of Allied military power near Cassino, including troops from twenty-seven different countries, proved somewhat anti-climactic for New Brunswick's artillery batteries. The 8th Battery played the most significant role. On 9 May 1944 it moved into well-protected, sandbagged gun pits behind Monte Trocchio, barely two miles from the Gustav Line and three from the famous Abbey of Monte Cassino itself. For three days the Moncton guns lay silent, enduring searching enemy fire, which scored frequent near misses. But Monte Trocchio served its purpose as a shield: most enemy artillery shells exploded on its face or well behind it, creating a tiny artillery sanctuary at the mouth of the Liri Valley.

The 8th Battery's eight 25-pounders formed a small part of the 1,500 British, Indian, Canadian, Polish, French, Italian, and New Zealand field, medium, and heavy guns assembled to fire the opening barrage. At 2300 hours on 11 May 1944, "the entire area burst into life with thunder and lightning. The whole hillside trembled with the shock and the night was alight as from a flickering super-powered arc lamp." The 2nd Field Regiment joined the nighttime barrage to shoot 4th British Division across the Gari River and into the Liri Valley. At dawn, 7th and 10th Batteries switched fire to German mortar positions. At that point, Major Rankin's 8th Battery began their primary daytime job of blinding German artillery observers and fighting positions on Monastery Ridge (just below the abbey), and the Abbey itself, with a mixture of high-explosive and smoke. At key times in the fire plan, the whole regiment joined them. Blinding observers on those heights served both 4th

Well-prepared and concealed Canadian 25-pounder position behind Mount Trocchio, with ammunition stacked ready for the opening barrage of Operation Diadem. (DHH 112.3P1-32766-N)

British Division in the valley below, and 2nd Polish Corps, which attacked Monastery Ridge from nearby mountaintop positions.

The Germans did not give up easily. At noon on 12 May, local reserves launched a major counterattack against the bridgehead over the Gari. Canadian and British forward observers on Monte Trocchio cried "Uncle," directing all guns assigned to 4th British Division to rapid-fire on the enemy counterattack for ten full minutes. Uncle targets were called several times over the next two days whenever the Germans shifted troops in the open to contain the Allied attack. When not otherwise engaged with Uncle targets, 8th Battery kept firing on Monastery Ridge until 15 May, when Polish troops closed in on it. By then the Gustav Line had been well and truly breached, signalling the time for 1st Canadian Division to pass into the Liri Valley and drive on the Hitler Line. That day, 2nd Field Regiment reverted to Canadian command and began shooting 1st Canadian Infantry Brigade through German rearguards towards the Hitler Line. The 8th Battery once again took up position to support the Hastings and Prince Edward Regiment.

German fighter and bomber squadrons had by then been transferred to Italy to help stop the Allied offensive. They made their presence felt on the night of 15 May by dropping flares and then bombs at the Gari River crossing sites to disrupt Allied traffic flowing into the Liri Valley. It seemed that 89th Battery still had an anti-aircraft role to play after all. On 17 May, D Troop set up its six guns to bolster 35th

A/A Battery's eighteen guns protecting the two bridges over the Gari, while E and F Troops moved their twelve guns to protect 1st Canadian Army Group, Royal Artillery's, gun area behind Monte Trocchio. The next day, Canadian infantry units reached the Hitler Line and found it at least partly manned. At that point the whole Canadian Corps artillery needed to shift seven miles into the Liri Valley to get within range of the Hitler Line. German gunners did what they could to slow the move. On 20 May, 89th Battery suffered a direct hit on one truck, killing Lance Bombardier Kenneth Foster MacFarlane of Nashwaaksis. Gunner Kenneth Alexander Fraser was severely injured. Two nights later the Luftwaffe struck the Gari bridges again. It was a busy night for 89th Battery's D Troop. Splinters from exploding bombs wounded Bombardier C.J. Barry, but the bridges and the Allied lines of communication were too well protected for the Luftwaffe to do serious damage.

As 1st Canadian Division closed up on the Hitler Line, 2nd Field Regiment stayed close behind, covering 1st Canadian Brigade's drive on the left towards Pontecorvo. The 90th Anti-Tank Battery came up with 2nd Canadian Brigade, the divisional reserve. With Major Hugh Burnett now in command, the 90th deployed two composite troops of two 6- and two 17-pounder guns each to support their old friends the Loyal Edmonton Regiment and Seaforth Highlanders during the attack on the Hitler Line. Burnett also controlled a troop of four M-10 tank destroyers from 111th Nelson Battery. He was going to need all that firepower.

On 23 May, 1st Canadian Division, backed by 810 guns, opened its attack on the Hitler Line, code-named Operation Chesterfield. The 8th Battery's role was to pound the heavily fortified town of Pontecorvo itself, which formed the southern linchpin in the German defence and was strongest portion of the Hitler line. The 1st Canadian Brigade's infantry kept Pontecorvo's defenders' attention fixed while farther north, New Brunswick's Carleton and York Regiment cracked open the Hitler Line. Meanwhile, on the Canadian right, the battalions of 2nd Canadian Brigade were decimated by crossfire coming from their front and right flanks, and then were struck by German counterattacks. In the face of wicked German artillery and rocket fire, Major Burnett had no luck getting his guns forward to join the desperate struggle on the right flank. Fire from Panther tank turrets mounted on steel-reinforced concrete bunkers, towed anti-tank guns, and tanks wiped out the supporting British Churchill tanks. The shell-raked front was clearly no place for towed anti-tank guns. So Burnett kept 90th Battery back. Contact was intermittent to non-existent with the forward infantry. Reports from runners and walking wounded painted a grim picture of the Canadian front. On his own initiative, Burnett set up an anti-tank gun line in case German counterattacks penetrated past the small parties of Seaforth Highlanders and Princess Patricia's Canadian Light Infantry holding them near the town of Aquino. One gun and tower were lost to direct hits, thankfully with no loss of life. Burnett also set up an "anti-tank" report centre drawing on the radios of 90th Battery, which eventually became the only ones functioning in 2nd Canadian Brigade's forward area. This net became crucial for passing information from the surviving infantry back to the rear. The 90th Battery's passage of information resulted in a number of Uncle and Yoke (all the guns in the corps) targets fired on the fortified town of Aquino, and ultimately a William Target – all guns within range – for the first time in Commonwealth history. For that brief moment, every gun in the Eighth Army turned its attention to the 2nd Canadian Brigade front. In less than thirty minutes, nineteen field, nine medium, and two heavy regiments turned their attention to Aquino. In a matter of minutes they hurled seventy-four tons of high-explosive onto the target, reducing most of the heavily fortified ancient town to rubble, and convincing the German 1st Parachute Division survivors to abandon it.

The 1st Canadian Brigade, backed by 2nd Field's guns, kept the strong German force defending the Pontecorvo fortress pinned down and fighting for its life, powerless to intervene when 3rd Canadian Brigade tore open the Hitler line. By the end of 23 May, Canada's old enemy, 90th Panzer-Grenadier Division, had been soundly beaten. Survivors fled northwestward to link up with reinforcements coming from Rome. Farley Mowat remembers the aftermath of the Hastings and Prince Edward struggle for the north edge of Pontecorvo. "The 8th Battery of Second Field Regiment, which had for so long and so well supported the battalion, now fired a twenty-one gun salute in its honour."

The story of mobile warfare on the road to Rome in late May and early June 1944 belongs mostly to the infantry and tanks of 1st and 5th Canadian Divisions and to the gunners in the self-propelled anti-tank and field batteries. There was little more call on the towed guns. In fact, much to their disappointment, 104th Battery – the unit from central New Brunswick that was the I Canadian Corps heavy anti-tank asset – was never called forward to fire. The busiest New Brunswick battery during the pursuit was the 89th with its 40 mm Bofors. They followed the advance closely, setting up their guns at key bridge sites along the road to Rome. They took on German planes more nights than not, keeping them away from the road junctions at Pontecorvo, the Melfa River crossings near Roccasecca, and the main Liri River crossings at Ceprano. Beyond those bridges the towed field and anti-tank regiments moved from new position to new position, but by that time, the German 10th and 14th Armies – under attack now from the Anzio beachhead as well – were on the run north. Meanwhile, German divisions and replacements were being rushed to Italy to stop the Allied break-out, just as the Allied invasion armada touched down in Normandy. The Allied mission to draw German strength to Italy and away from vital fronts had worked better than any had hoped.

The I Canadian Corps moved into rest camps back near Caserta in early June 1944. No one in 104th Battery was particularly happy about that: they wanted to finish the job. But New Brunswick gunners were destined to play a key role in keeping the Germans pinned in Italy for the rest of 1944. The new task facing the Allied

The 2nd Field Regiment's command post and plotting board in a house south of the Gothic Line prior to the main assault, 30–31 August 1944.
(LAC PA-185003)

armies in Italy was to convince all the Germans who had rushed in to respond to the May 1944 emergency to stay there. The task was made especially difficult after four French and three US divisions were pulled out for landings in southern France: those that remained now had to work much harder to pose a real threat. The Canadian rest period in June and July 1944 nonetheless formed part of the Allied containment plan. The I Canadian Corps had proved itself tenacious in action against fixed German defences. As German forces once again mounted rearguard and covering battles in Italy through the summer of 1944, Allied senior planners knew they would eventually stop to make a determined stand on the Gothic Line, anchored on the northern Apennines. That summer the Canadian Corps trained and reorganized to breach the Gothic Line.

By the summer of 1944 all Commonwealth units in Italy faced serious shortages of infantry, tanks, self-propelled guns, engineers, and military police; at the same time, they were perhaps too rich in towed anti-tank and light anti-aircraft batteries. German reinforcements in Italy coupled with US and French withdrawals had equalized strength in Italy. If the Allies were to keep German units pinned in Italy for the rest of 1944, they would need to scrounge more infantry and keep the pressure on the enemy. The Germans had to be fooled into believing that the Allied forces were far larger than they were. The German believed that the Allies had mustered some thirty-six assault divisions (nearly double the actual figure of twenty) and enough amphibious lift to strike anywhere on Europe's south coast. This false information convinced Field Marshal Kesselring to spread his twenty-six divisions along a thin perimeter across northern Italy and its coast. The other way to keep the Germans pinned in Italy was to attack violently and relentlessly with the twenty Allied divisions available. This reality brought great change to 89th and 104th Batteries.

Fighting around the Gustav and Hitler Lines had demonstrated that the M-10 tank destroyer was the best way to get anti-tank guns into position rapidly. The M-10's 3-inch naval gun had longer range and greater hitting power than the lower-velocity 75 mm guns on the Sherman tanks. The 15th Toronto Battery's M-10s had proved at the Hitler Line that they could deliver hard-hitting direct fire support to infantry units. There was still a role for towed 6- and 17-pounders, but there were already enough of them in the divisional anti-tank regiments. The solution was to reduce the size of the corps's 7th Anti-Tank Regiment and motorize what was left. The 113th Regina Battery drew the short straw and was converted to engineers; 104th Fredericton Battery converted partly to M-10s. The quick conversion was effected by transferring in five experienced M-10 crews from 7th Anti-Tank Regiment's existing self-propelled batteries. The change was welcomed by the New Brunswicker gunners, who had yet to fire in anger.

The bigger shock came to 1st Canadian Light Anti-Aircraft Regiment in July 1944. Many had sensed their fate in June, when 35th Battery from Sherbrooke, Quebec, was retasked as a traffic control unit. What happened next, however, was unprecedented. On 11 July, officers were ordered to quietly survey personnel who might be suitable for service as infantrymen. Those physically unsuitable, as well as seasoned, well-trained artillery officers and NCOs, were assigned to the Canadian Base Reinforcement Depot at Avellino for reassignment to replace casualties in other artillery units. Some more went into the replacement gunner pool. Then on 13 July "1st Canadian LAA ceased to exist" officially, and two days later the remnant of the regiment – Woodstock's 89th Battery and 109th Battery from Trail, BC – was temporarily renamed "89th/109th Infantry Battalion" pending a decision on a proper infantry unit name. The new unit became the third battalion of the recently formed 12th Canadian Infantry Brigade in 5th Canadian Armoured Division. They were in good company in their new brigade: the Westminster Regiment, which had long been the divisional motorized infantry battalion, and 4th Princess Louise Dragoon Guards from eastern Ontario (amalgamated units from Ottawa, Kingston, and Prescott), had served as 1st Division's armoured reconnaissance regiment and had often carried out dismounted infantry-type operations. On 20 July the infantry-experienced Major W.C. Dick was promoted Acting Lieutenant-Colonel and assigned as the new commanding officer. The next day, eleven officers from the Saskatoon Light Infantry replacement company arrived from Avellino with 156 trained infantry replacements to bolster the new battalion.

The re-roling scattered many original 89th Battery officers and NCOs throughout I Canadian Corps. But a few New Brunswick gunners stayed on as infantry, including at least one 89th Battery Troop Leader, Captain V.G. Sinclair, who was named Acting Major and a company commander. A few found their way into the new battalion's support company, including Gunner A.G. Melanson and Lance Bombardier A.H. Scott, who joined the battalion's anti-tank platoon. There were also places for drivers and fitters in the battalion echelon. The remaining 89th Battery personnel joined the rifle companies. On 24 July their charismatic division commander, Maj.-Gen. Bert Hoffmeister, visited for a pep talk and to tell the new riflemen about plans to designate them as a highland regiment. Intense practice with small arms, Bren light machine-guns, PIAT anti-tank launchers, light mortars, hand grenades, and land mines followed.

While the new infantry battalion trained and built unit cohesion through July and into August, 1st Canadian Division headed north to Florence. Early plans for the Gothic Line envisaged the Canadians attacking from Florence through the high Apennine passes towards Bologna. But even as 8th and 90th Batteries relieved South African and New Zealand units on the Arno River's south bank in early August, Allied plans changed. The Canadian Corps and most of British Eighth Army secretly crossed the Apennines to the Adriatic end of the Gothic Line. There, in the rolling hill country of the Marche region, many felt that Eighth Army's experience fighting large-scale tank and artillery battles could better achieve the Allied mission. The 8th and 90th Batteries spent only a few days overlooking the great Renaissance city of Florence, long enough to experience German attempts to bait the Allies into firing into the city's world-famous historic centre. The Germans goaded the Canadians with machine-guns, mortars, and artillery as Italian fascist agents helped German shells find their mark. Canadian infantry and Italian partisans together cleared those observers out of southern Florence in a nasty little episode of a civil war that by then was raging within the Italian campaign. The 90th Battery was taunted repeatedly by their German counterparts, which fired 75 mm and 88 mm anti-tank shells that "came too close for comfort." No Canadians took that bait. They confined themselves to returning sniper fire and kept the heavy guns quiet, even after German shells hit 8th Battery's observation post vehicle on 8 August, killing Gunner Gordon Reeves and seriously wounding Gunner Knowlan. That same day, tension resulting from living between friendly partisans and Blackshirt infiltrators took its toll on 90th Battery. Bombardier Keith Kimball was shot dead by a Canadian sentry while returning to the unit in the dark. A day later, both batteries got word to pull back to Perugia.

The I Canadian Corps units shifted to the Adriatic in mid-August 1944, exercising for the coming attack on the Gothic Line even while on the move. Training time was especially critical for the "89th/109th Battalion" and for 104th Battery's new M-10 crews. Both units joined in 5th Division combined arms exercises alongside tank, engineer, and infantry units. Meanwhile, there was encouraging news from other fronts. In August word came that the Allies had broken out of Normandy and were driving hard for the German border. They also heard that Bulgaria had quit the war and declared neutrality, while the Russians had crushed a whole German army group and were deep into Poland. Real hope grew that the war might soon be over. Nevertheless, the Allied containment mission in Italy remained the same. The Gothic Line attack must proceed so that German forces in Italy could not be transferred to stop the Allied drive out of Normandy.

Operation Olive opened at 2300 hours on 25 August 1944. The 8th Battery, taken over four days before by Major J.M. Sinclair, joined the barrage covering engineer detachments bridging the Metauro River. Then 2nd Field Regiment's 25-pounders supported the Royal Canadian Regiment and the Hastings and Prince Edward Regiment as they swarmed the German outpost zone. The 90th Battery surrendered one of its troops to strengthen the engineer work parties. Major Burnett organized his remaining guns as D and E composite troops with two 6- and two 17-pounders each. He had other familiar help. Major Welsh could not stay out of the war for long, demanding to return to Italy after his Victory Bond drive. He was given command of 111th Nelson Self-Propelled Battery in 7th Anti-Tank Regiment, which worked closely with 90th Battery through the steep, semi-mountainous country of the Red Line.

On 28 August a Loyal Eddie rifle company reached the tiny hilltop village of Monteciccardo. They deployed in the village just moments before a German infantry battalion and tank platoon arrived to occupy this last high ground south of the Foglia River and the main Green Line I defence belt. A furious close-quarter battle broke out around a small convent at the village centre. The German infantry were soon driven inside an old stone convent with a deep basement while the enemy tank platoon lurked on the north edge of the hill. The Loyal Edmonton Regiment called Major Burnett for help. The 90th Battery found a flat and open spot big enough for a 17-pounder on the next wooded ridge south of Monteciccardo and opened fire. Ten carefully aimed shots fired from nearly 2,000 yards away brought down the convent's bell tower. Thirty more blew down its southern wall. The Loyal Eddies then fought their way inside by evening. The German Red Line outpost zone that was supposed to hold the Allies until the Germans fully manned the main Green Line I defences along the Foglia River Valley had fallen in three days. It took a day to bring up 5th Canadian Division to mount a deliberate attack against Green Line I. All hands now sensed that the main enemy defences could be "bounced." Vanguard infantry and tank units from both 1st and 5th Canadian Divisions therefore rushed Green Line I late on 30 August 1944.

While the infantry and armour cut their way through, 8th Field and 90th Batteries displaced several times a day to keep their guns in range of the fast-moving battle. The 8th Battery fired concentrations against 1st German Parachute Division

Sergeant John Hatt and his crew pose in front of their 104th Battery M-10 self-propelled 3-inch anti-tank gun near the Lamone River in northern Italy, December 1944. The open top and thinner armour made these vehicles more vulnerable than Sherman tanks, but their powerful and mobile high-velocity guns made them popular. The 104th Battery crewed M-10s from August 1944 to the end of the Italian campaign. (PANB P543-2)

troops manning elaborate bunker complexes around Pozzo Alto and Borgo Santa Maria while 1st Division infantry cleared them with rifles and grenades. They also joined in several massed shoots on German counterattacks. The Germans tried desperately to stop the Canadian thrust between the German paratroopers and the newly arrived 26th Panzer Division. Meanwhile, 89th/109th Battalion and 104th Anti-Tank Battery waited in reserve for their chance to join the fray.

By 1 September 1944 it seemed to many that the time had come to pursue a beaten enemy. The following day, the Woodstock gunners went into their first action as infantry and discovered that the enemy was far from broken. German rearguards backed by strong artillery units remained lethal. The 89th/109th Battalion lost eleven killed and twenty wounded in that first day of infantry combat. The losses reflected the much different scale of death between infantry and artillery units in both world wars. And 2 September was also the first day of an ugly clash between the Canadians breaking through the Gothic Line and German reinforcements arriving to establish a new main line of defence. Casualties mounted for the next two days in 89th/109th Battalion as a new front solidified along Coriano Ridge. At times their companies became isolated and surrounded, but they all stuck to their new task.

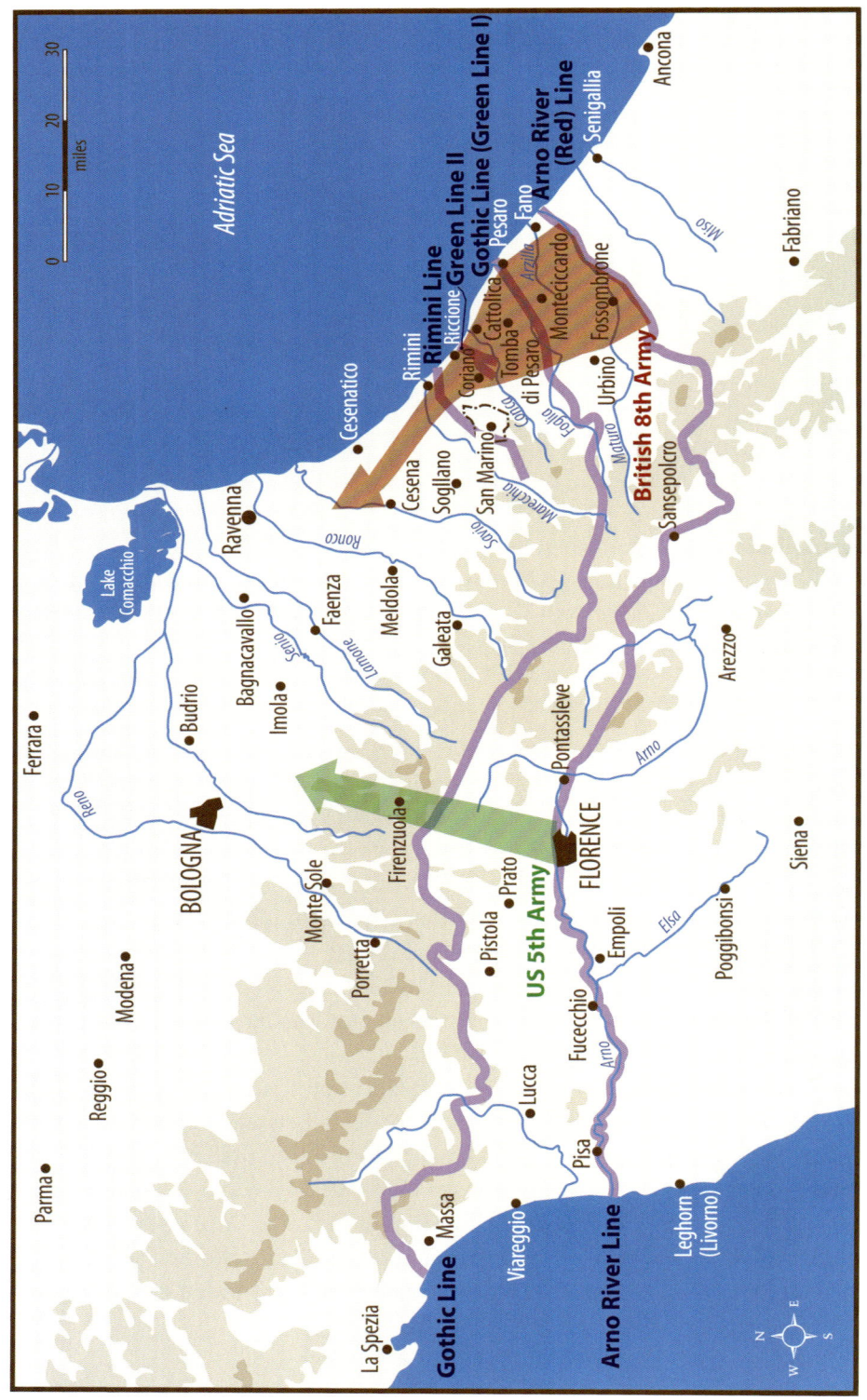

Operation Olive, August–October 1944

Relief came, in part, from Major Smith's 104th Battery, which had finally entered their first battle. The Fredericton gunners, manning their new M-10s, joined 89th/109th Battalion on the drive to Coriano Ridge. They fought alongside each other along Graveyard Hill facing Coriano Ridge on 5 and 6 September against one of the most powerful formations in the German Army, 29th Panzer-Grenadier Division. Behind the Grenadiers and the Gemmano–Coriano Ridge was the largest and most concentrated force of German artillery ever assembled in the Italian Campaign. Fed by ammunition drawn directly from factories in northern Italy run by the Fascist Salo Republic, German gunners faced no shortage of shells. Their fire, directed from dominating heights inland at Gemmano and Montefiore, gave Graveyard Hill its name. As 104th Battery manoeuvered their M-10s into good firing positions there, bursting shells inflicted the battery's first casualties. Gunner Chester Munro and Lance Bombardier Earle Fawcett were killed, and Gunners Schmidt and Kennedy wounded. M-10 armour provided some protection from bullets and shell fragments, but crews still had to expose themselves outside the vehicle when guiding it into firing positions, and the open-top turret made the gun numbers vulnerable to air bursts. Considering the sharp increase in German fire from Green Line I to Graveyard Hill, 104th Battery fared well. In contrast, 89th/109th Battalion's first four days in action cost them sixty-nine all ranks killed and wounded.

A mile to the east, 1st Canadian Division pressed up the coastal highway against the 1st German Parachute Division, which was backing into prepared coast defences and drawing on the same German artillery as had massed behind Coriano Ridge. The Luftwaffe also returned, reflecting Berlin's concern that the Allies, having breached the main Gothic Line, were now threatening to break through into agricultural and industrial areas vital to Germany's war effort. In early September, 8th Field Battery and 2nd Field Regiment shifted daily behind 1st Canadian Brigade's fight past the castle at Gradara and onto Misano Ridge. German 1st Parachute Division, settling into coastal defences south of Riccione, had been reinforced by parts of 162nd Turcoman Division. On 4 September, 8th Battery's Major Sinclair served as 2nd Field Regiment's FOO supporting the fight along the coastal shelf being carried out by the Royal Canadian Regiment and the 48th Highlanders. A direct hit blew Sinclair's moving jeep out from under him, mortally wounding his batman, Gunner James Wright. The next night, German planes dove on 8th Battery's muzzle flashes. Blasts and fragments killed Gunners Charles Little and Clayton Shackleton. German bombers also hit the coastal resort town of Cattolica, where 90th Battery and 2nd Canadian Brigade were resting in reserve.

Over the next week, I Canadian Corps drew up its administrative tail and prepared for an assault on Coriano Ridge and on towards Rimini, the last high ground before the vast plains of the Po Valley and the great industrial cities of northern Italy. The attack was part of a general Allied offensive that included American units attacking north from Florence. The intent was to wade into the wave of German divisions flowing towards the Gothic Line and cripple them a few at a time. To make it work, British Eighth Army stacked assault troops in depth so that exhausted units could be relieved for short rest periods by fresh ones. The I Canadian Corps, which already included Greeks, was reinforced with 4th British and 2nd New Zealand Divisions. The Canadian attack was aimed at the bend in the German line from Coriano and along the ridge to where the enemy line turned east to follow the Marano River to the Adriatic. The 5th Canadian Division would open the attack by capturing Coriano Ridge. The 4th British Division would wait behind them to push the assault. On the right, 1st Canadian Division, backed by 3rd Greek Mountain Brigade, was to cross the Marano and seize the low ridges overlooking Rimini. The 2nd New Zealand Division waited behind them to take up the baton.

The 8th Battery took up a tiny piece of real estate behind the cover of Graveyard Hill alongside more than 400 other Canadian Corps guns, including those of the 4th British and 2nd New Zealand Divisions. The 90th Battery waited to cross the Marano with 1st Canadian Division. The 104th Battery was assigned to 4th British Division to support it beyond Coriano Ridge. The 89th/109th Battalion sat this one

A Canadian 25-pounder firing from a well dug-in pit north of the Gothic Line, September 1944. During the fighting at Coriano heavy German shells scored direct hits on two 8th Battery gun pits shielded behind Graveyard Hill. (LAC ZK-860-11)

out. Word now finally arrived that they would receive a proper infantry name – the "Lanark and Renfrew Scottish," borrowing the title of an Ottawa Valley militia unit. It seemed to most that the end of the war was within reach. In early September, British and Canadian units had liberated most of Belgium and the Americans were closing up to the German border. Many hoped that more all-out effort to press through to the Rimini heights would drive the Germans across the floor of the Po Valley. But Allied commanders remained concerned that strong German units might escape Italy to fight in Germany. The Allies had to prevent that at any cost.

So for the tired "D-Day Dodgers in Sunny Italy" the war went on. The renewed Allied offensive opened before midnight on 12 September with a massive artillery duel. The 2nd Field Regiment had dumped 22,000 high-explosive and 2,000 smoke rounds at their positions in readiness. Two hours before midnight, 8th Battery opened fire in support of 5th Canadian Division's attack on Coriano. A British 155 mm "Long Tom" heavy battery beside them drew the ire of German long-range 170 mm guns. Commonwealth guns were so densely packed in the limited sheltered space behind Graveyard Hill that it was nigh impossible for German shells to miss. Two heavy enemy shells landed inside 8th Battery gun pits. One caved in the pit and filled a 25-pounder barrel with earth. Another landed directly on a ready ammunition pile beside a second pit, blowing it sky high. Gunner Joseph Jaillet of 8th Battery was wounded and died on a stretcher en route to a field dressing station; 7th and 10th Batteries also lost men that night.

As the sun rose on 13 September, Royal Navy destroyers and gunboats along with Allied medium and fighter bombers won the counter-battery duel, at least for the seven days of clear weather in the third week of September. This was the most intense week of combat for I Canadian Corps in the whole campaign. The Germans clung to every ridge and every day mounted counterattacks with fresh units. Fredericton's 104th Battery followed 4th British Division beyond Coriano and over the Marano River towards Ospedaletto. During that action a heavy German shell landed beside Sergeant Stewart's M-10, manned by a New Brunswick crew. Gunners Wallace MacCafferty and James MacFarlane, both Marysville originals in 104th Battery, were killed. Stewart and Bombardier LeBlanc were wounded and escaped. The battery spent eight hellish days exposed on both sides of Marano. But they helped break up German counterattacks coming down from the hills near the Republic of San Marino against 4th British Division's inland flank.

Farther east, 8th Battery shot 1st Canadian Division on to San Lorenzo–San Martino Ridge and poured fire onto German counterattacks intended to take it back. They did the same a few days later on San Fortunato Ridge. The 2nd Field Regiment reported that guns were blazing hot as "firing was continuous and our only respite was due to the fact that the Boche artillery was not shelling our positions" anymore. The 90th Battery anti-tank guns worked with Major Welsh's 111th Battery to hold open a corridor between the Marano River and San Martino against marauding German Tiger tanks, assault guns, and infantry patrols. By 18 September, Burnett's 17-pounders were dug in on San Martino Ridge; from there, they could reach San Fortunato. Two days later they followed the Seaforth Highlanders, Loyal Edmonton Regiment, and Welsh's 111th Battery M-10s onto San Fortunato Ridge for the climactic capture of that last piece of high ground. Major Welsh was wounded while searching the steep ridge for unblocked paths to get anti-tank weapons through. By the end of 20 September, San Fortunato Ridge was firmly in Canadian hands. What many hoped was the finish line had been reached; beyond it, the broad Po Valley and Romagna Plains beckoned. Nearly every German division in Italy had been committed to the bloody fight to hold on to the back reaches of the Gothic Line, and expended themselves in the process.

Until late September no one was sure what the Germans might do once the Allies reached the Po Valley and Romagna Plain. Allied senior leaders feared the enemy might cut and run to the Alps, where he could hold the Allies at bay with a fraction of the twenty-six divisions then fighting in Italy. Instead, surviving German units once again dug in firmly wherever they stood, backed by four more reinforcing divisions that had been rushed to Italy and 20,000 replacements to rebuild gutted units. Few seemed to realize at the time that the rump of Fascist Italy, the heavily industrialized region around Milan, Turin, and Bologna called the Salo Republic, had been fully integrated into the Germany industrial economy and could not be given up without a fight. The Germans made use of autumn rains and swollen rivers to thicken their defences. The result was another manifestation of the great paradox of the Italian Campaign. In late 1944, the Allied grand strategy was succeeding better than expected: even with the Allies near the German border, the Germans had chosen to dig in in Italy. For Allied fighting troops in Italy, including New Brunswick's four artillery batteries, this meant another morale-sapping winter in the wet dykelands of the Romagna. Now thirty German divisions had to be kept occupied, condemning I Canadian Corps to a series of waterlogged assault river crossings to maintain the pressure against them.

The last months of the Italian Campaign were all about perseverance as the end of the war flickered in and out of sight. It was also a time of innovation in the anti-tank regiments, which found new roles in the flat country of the Romagna plain. There were no more mountains and ridges for planting observers and shielding gun positions. In the Romagna, rivers drained out of the Apennines from southwest to northeast across the Canadian front. Over the centuries the Italians had built great dykes to contain them, some of them thirty feet above ground level. When it rained, the rivers swelled to torrents and the dykes grew soft, making them difficult to bridge. Dyke banks and two- and three-storey buildings, church belfries, and town hall clock towers were the new commanding high ground.

New Brunswick's four batteries in Italy had important roles to play in meeting this new challenge. For starters, the Lanark and Renfrew Scottish thickened

2nd Field Regiment gunners fire their Canadian-made 25-pounder from positions along the Lamone River against German targets along the Senio River west of Lake Commachio, February 1945. The flat, wet, dyke- and river-strewn country of the Romagna Plain made artillery observation difficult. (LAC PA-173594)

Canada's infantry numbers on the wide-open ground. Second, 8th Battery's long experience was put to the test because in the autumn of 1944, a shortage of 25-pounder ammunition once again plagued the Italian Campaign. They took great care to make available rounds count by securing the best tall buildings for observation posts. Third, 104th Battery's M-10s' long-range hitting power and comparatively abundant high-velocity 75 mm ammunition supplies made them a key tool for denying enemy observation, because they could knock down church towers and tall buildings behind the German front with accurate high-velocity fire.

The skilled old hands of 90th Battery tackled an especially difficult problem. The first dyke/river crossings in the late September rains made it obvious that getting heavy anti-tank weapons across to protect shallow infantry bridgeheads was among the biggest challenges that lay ahead. Just a few German tanks and self-propelled guns closing in on hard-packed roads could spell the end for Canadian infantry companies cut off from their heavy weapons by a swollen river. Part of the solution involved forming specially trained light infantry anti-tank platoons carrying as many PIAT launchers, PIAT bombs, and Hawkins anti-tank mines as they could carry. The other solution was the old 2-pounder anti-tank gun. That gun weighed under a ton and could therefore be towed by a jeep and rafted fairly easily. By 1944 some had been fitted with a "Littlejohn" adapter that tapered the bore from 40 mm at the breech to 30 mm at the muzzle. The gun fired a special round with a tungsten core covered with a softer metal coating. When fired, the gas pressure built up behind the round drove it through the narrowing bore, compressing and stripping away the soft metal and giving the tungsten core a velocity from about 800 to 1,100 metres per second. At that speed the new tungsten round could penetrate tanks as well as a 6-pounder provided the crew got close enough. Major Burnett organized and retrained 90th Battery to operate these Littlejohns.

These four elements were used to successfully cross the Rubicon River in early October and the Savio River later that month. In December all units took part in Operation Chuckle to cross the Montone and Lamone Rivers to reach the Senio to secure a good start line for a spring 1945 offensive to end the war in Italy. This last major offensive in Italy by I Canadian Corps tested everyone's resolve. The Germans fought stubbornly on the Lamone. The 8th Battery's FOO party worked its way up the south bank, helping the infantry by directing tight concentrations down on stubborn German defenders in fortified houses and dug-in posts along the high river dyke. German counter-battery fire reached back to the battery's newly occupied positions on 3 December, killing Sergeant Butler and offering some clue as to German intentions. Over the next two days the leading elements of the Royal Canadian Regiment tried to bounce the Lamone and were nearly annihilated by a large German counterattack supported by self-propelled guns. The Royals who survived owed much to a 90th Battery "Littlejohn" Section led by Sergeant James Bailey, who brought two guns into the bridgehead. Bailey left one to cover the crossing site and took the other forward to support the Royals as they fought to stem the tide. Bailey and the forward crew fought their way back to the remaining gun, where the whole section fought to hold open the crossing point until the survivors evacuated: only nine men of the Royal's A Company returned. Bailey was awarded the Military Medal for his courage, leadership, and devotion to duty.

The Royals were supposed to have the Hastings and Prince Edward Regiment on their right during that first attempt at the Lamone, but compounding errors resulting from rushed planning led the Hasty Ps to form up along the river dyke rather than 300 yards behind it. When the preparatory barrage opened, one of their sergeants yelled "Get down, for Christ's sake boys, they're falling short!" Half the men in one of the assault companies were killed or wounded and the whole force was stunned. Survivors attempted to cross and join the Royals, but in small numbers. Farley Mowat wrote extensively about the events on the Lamone, which left deep scars in the minds of Hasty P survivors, who until then had rarely known defeat. "It is revealing in fact that at no time was the artillery blamed. It seems to have been understood by every man that the gunners had no fault. Indeed [Lieutenant-Colonel] Cameron [the Hasty Ps' commanding officer] himself later visited the artillery units concerned and carried this message to them from the Regiment. But the gunners were sick at heart at what had happened, even though they were guiltless." The 8th Battery's iron relationship with their infantry brothers endured this trial and perhaps grew stronger because of it.

The second, deliberate attack by I Canadian Corps across the Lamone on 10–11 December involved almost all of New Brunswick's units in Italy. The 8th Battery crossed the Lamone behind their fellow New Brunswickers in the Carleton and York Regiment. When the Germans counterattacked this time, 8th Battery brought down defensive fire shoots in front of the Carleton and York trenches only 1,000 yards in front of their new pits. During the bitter fight for Bagnacavallo, 90th Battery's "Littlejohns" also moved up with the Carleton and York Regiment, where "it was not unusual for machine gun bullets to bounce off the gun shield." There, 90th Battery's mini anti-tank guns – the smallest in Allied service by that time – helped fight off counterattacking Tiger tanks. During that action, Gunner Ralph Amos became the last 90th Battery gunner and old original killed during the Second World War. The 104th Battery's M-10s also crossed the Lamone, providing direct fire support in attacks against fortified houses around Bagnacavallo. As the battery's war diary records, "104 did more shooting than ever before during this time." They usually deployed with two troops up and one back in depth: they stayed in action for sixty days straight.

The old hands of 89th Battery also crossed the Lamone, with the Lanark and Renfrew Scottish, to the northeast in 5th Canadian Division's area. They fought their most significant infantry action of the war along the Naviglio Canal, meeting German counterattacks at Osteria. The regiment suffered 100 casualties between 12 and 15 December, their heaviest losses of the campaign. Among them was Gunner Malcolm Manderville, one of 89th Battery's originals. The last major I Canadian Corps offensive in Italy wrapped up on 21 December 1944 after reaching the Senio canal bank opposite Fusignano. Anti-tank gunners took turns manning the front and rotating to quieter villages in the rear to celebrate what most hoped would be their last Christmas overseas. Captain Ross Zavitz, M.C., transferred in to take command of 8th Battery at the end of the Lamone fighting. Zavitz was well known and respected in the regiment as a daring and dependable FOO. The 2nd Field Regiment stayed in action, although each battery rotated back for a twenty-four-hour rest and a turkey dinner. As if to remind them that nowhere was safe in Italy,

8th Battery's Sergeant Walter Hogbin stepped on a mine on Christmas Eve. The blast killed him and wounded Lieutenant Besley.

After that, New Brunswick's batteries fought in one more small action to strengthen the Allied hold along the Senio after the ground froze in early January 1945. The 8th Battery played a key role. While 2nd Field Regiment's 7th and 10th Batteries supported 1st Canadian Division action south of Bagnacavallo, Captain Zavitz had orders to keep 8th Battery constantly firing from each of the regiment's three gun positions. They were meant to appear to be the whole regiment, firing on German mortar positions north of the Senio dyke. Farther to the north, on 6 January 1945, on the banks of the Senio, Leo Malley was killed during a raid by the Lanark and Renfrew Scottish Regiment opposite Fusignano. He was the last New Brunswick gunner killed in the Italian campaign.

In the final analysis, New Brunswick's artillery batteries in Italy had much to take pride in. They had pushed themselves and their guns to their physical limits and beyond in a campaign defined by difficult terrain and weather. They had proved themselves tremendously versatile and adaptable. They had contributed to every major Canadian victory in Italy, often decisively. Their determination and their fire saved unknown numbers of Canadian infantrymen. The 8th and 90th Batteries in particular counted as two of the most continuously engaged units in the RCA during the Second World War. But their war was not yet over.

In February 1945, I Canadian Corps began pulling off the Senio River line to start a long move to the Netherlands. New Brunswick's gunners were cheered at the prospect of invading Germany, especially if it might come with a chance for leave in United Kingdom. But neither was in the cards. The I Canadian Corps moved to Livorno and Naples, where they boarded ships to Marseille. In early March they travelled by train up the Rhône Valley to staging areas located on the old Great War battlefields at Cambrai and Passchendaele. There the Lanark and Renfrew Scottish Regiment and 104th Battery received bitter news. Orders had arrived that 5th Canadian Armoured Division was to revert to its former status to conform with the 21st British Army Group structure. Gunners-turned-infantrymen could hardly believe their ears on 10 March when the call came for those remaining in the unit qualified on the 40 mm Bofors gun to come forward: 1st Light Anti-Aircraft Regiment was to be reformed. It took three weeks to get guns and trucks back so that they could requalify. The regiment then needed weeks to retrain. By the time they were again ready for action, Germany had surrendered.

The venerable and adaptable old 90th Anti-Tank Battery was ordered in March to re-equip and retrain on the new Valentine self-propelled 17-pounder. They dropped out of the I Canadian Corps column and were not finally ready until 2 May. By then, 1st Canadian Division combat operations were largely over and Dutch humanitarian relief efforts were under way. The 104th Battery was also re-equipped, giving up their M-10s for towed 17-pounders. Other anti-tank units in II Canadian Corps were also upgrading to heavier guns as the war ended. For most, this last-minute reorganization and re-equipping made little sense. Certainly the Luftwaffe was a spent force, and there were few enemy tanks left to shoot. The most logical explanation is that Allied planners were thinking about what might happen after Germany was defeated and they faced massive Soviet tank armies and airpower along some ill-defined front.

What was really needed in April 1945 were more infantry to help with the liberation campaign in the Netherlands. Indeed, during that month, 7th Anti-Tank Regiment became a provisional infantry battalion: 104th, 111th, and 113th Batteries all took up rifles and Bren guns and took over sections of the front in the suburbs of Arnhem, relieving other Canadian and British battalions for the final attack on the German garrison in the central Netherlands. There they played a critical role in diversion operations around Arnhem that enabled the great humanitarian operation to liberate the western Netherlands and deliver food to starving Dutch families cut off in large urban centres from Rotterdam and Utrecht to Amsterdam. Only 15th Battery kept their new 17-pounder "Achilles" M-10s, to serve as the battlegroup's supporting armour. On 12 April, 7th Anti-Tank Regiment crossed west over Neder Rijn to Elst Island and took up position facing the infamous abandoned 1944 airborne bridgehead to form a blocking screen facing Arnhem. On 19 April, Major Smith took his 104th Battery "company," two troops of M-10s from 15th Battery, and several Dutch resistance companies, all organized together as "Smith Force," to block the Waal River front near Druten facing a German garrison that was still holding out. That was where 104th Battery heard the news that Germany had surrendered.

Only the field artillery maintained a clear role in the final phase of the war, although artillery fire was applied carefully in what was more of a humanitarian rescue mission than full-scale combat operations. Of the four New Brunswick batteries in I Canadian Corps, 8th Moncton Battery played the most significant artillery role in the Netherlands. All of 2nd Field Regiment crossed into the Netherlands in early April and fired smoke to cover 3rd Canadian Division's attack at Deventer. They then swung west on 11 April to support 1st Canadian Division's attack across the Ijssel River towards Apeldoorn. Shortly after that, they crossed west over the Ijssel, covering 1st Canadian Division's advance, 8th Battery gunners fired steadily, but carefully, avoiding unnecessary harm to Dutch civilians or critical infrastructure. Their mission within I Canadian Corps was to save the Dutch people. Although the war was all but over, fighting raged intensely for seven straight days. "Men were out on their feet," according to the war diary, "but there was a breath of victory in the air." German resistance in the western Netherlands largely collapsed after the fall of Apeldoorn. From then on the primary task was to negotiate with local German commanders to get relief supplies into the densely populated urban areas still in German control.

In May 1945, 8th Battery was joined in the province of Holland by the 89th, 90th, and 104th. All were tasked with disarming the German garrison, arresting SS troops, returning stolen property, and distributing food to the starving – and grateful – Dutch population. The 89th Battery drove to Den Helder on the northern tip of the Netherlands. There they distributed food and, on 12 May, mounted a raid on German barracks, where they arrested forty Dutch SS, who were placed under guard with other collaborators. The 104th Battery moved to Bussum on outskirts of Amsterdam. They were "welcomed in Bussum in such a way as to embarrass every man. Hailed as liberators all ranks were treated as heroes." The 8th Battery went to the city of Dordrecht to help the Dutch Underground with policing duties. The 90th Battery moved near Leiden, between The Hague and Amsterdam, to round up German troops and lock up their weapons and ammunition. The people of Leiden, too, treated them as heroes. Their war diary records the mood, "The reactions to victory of a people who never doubted that their day of liberation would come were a sight that will not soon be forgotten."

Chapter 10

Northwest Europe, 1944–45

Between 6 June 1944 and the end of the war in Europe on 8 May 1945, three New Brunswick batteries served in northwest Europe as part of II Canadian Corps. They included 105th Anti-Tank Battery from St. George, which was part of 3rd Anti-Tank Regiment of 3rd Canadian Infantry Division. The 105th came ashore on D-Day and witnessed some of the heaviest fighting of the campaign. The other New Brunswick batteries that fought exclusively in northwest Europe came ashore in Normandy on 9–10 July, with the landing of 2nd Canadian Infantry Division and the establishment of II Canadian Corps as an operational formation. With 2nd Canadian Division came 5th Field Regiment, which included 28th Newcastle Battery, while II Canadian Corps' heavy anti-tank unit, 6th Anti-Tank Regiment, included the Campbellton gunners of 103rd Anti-Tank Battery. Each of these batteries had quite different experiences over the next eleven months, and they continued to evolve in organization and equipment. But they all shared one thing: Normandy was their greatest test.

The Canadians' job on D-Day was to get inland and secure the division "covering position" astride the Caen–Bayeux highway at Putot, Brettville, and Carpiquet, to defend the critical corridors to the sea. The trick was to dig-in before Rommel's vaunted Panzers could arrive in strength to crush the landings and then defeat "the" Panzer counterattack when it came. Allied planners expected something to happen within the first five days ashore. They were right.

The forty-eight guns of 3rd Anti-Tank Regiment were therefore critical to Overlord. As Stan Medland, commander of 52nd Battery from Yarmouth, recalled:

A 6-pounder crew from 3rd Anti-Tank Regiment on the eve of D-Day drilling for quick action against expected enemy armoured counter-attacks, April 1944. (LAC e011083971)

"The role of the 6-pounder was unique. To be effective, they needed to be moved up quickly into each new area taken by the infantry to prepare for a counter attack." The key attribute of the 6-pounder was its new "armored-piercing, discarding sabot" ammunition. Developed by the French and carried to England by escaping engineers, the round consisted of a small tungsten dart embedded in a full-bore "shoe" (hence the French word *sabot*), which fell away once the round left the barrel. That allowed the full charge to propel the dart at 4,050 feet per second and penetrate 143 millimetres of armour plate. The dart had just enough kinetic energy to penetrate a tank but usually not enough to escape out the other side – with results that can only be imagined. Because the 6-pounder was low, small, and easily handled, it was usually fired within 900 hundred yards or less – in fact, seldom more than 500 yards. At that distance the tungsten dart reached its target in about an eighth of a second. No German armour could stop it.

When infantry and armour surged ashore along Juno Beach on the morning of 6 June, sea conditions – especially the powerful wave action at the height of the tide – prevented most of 3rd Canadian Division's anti-tank guns from landing. The first slated to land were the M-10s of Major Love's composite 105th Battery, at Bernières. Because of the storm they were unable to land directly from their landing craft. So two troops of 105th Battery made a perilous transfer to a Rhino ferry (a large, flat barge propelled by outboard motors) at sea around noon and managed to come ashore at 1600 hours. The first to land on French soil were the guns of L Troop of the St. George battery. I Troop came ashore and was drawn east in support of Royal Marines clearing the beach defences at St-Aubin. It seems that C and F Troops of Major Love's M-10 battery did not land until the next morning.

A worse fate befell 3rd Anti-Tank Regiment's towed 6-pounders: the sea was simply too rough to get most of them ashore. The first craft to try foundered and sank. By late morning the surf was running so high that it was impossible to put a towed 6-pounder gun ashore from a large landing craft because the Bren carrier pulling it – despite raised sides to help keep it out the surf – would run off the ramp and disappear in the sea. So it was decided to transfer them, too, onto Rhino ferries at sea and transship them to the beach.

This perilous undertaking was carried out only once, at Courseulles, in an attempt to get 94th Battery ashore. The Rhino met the landing craft carrying Lieutenant Jones's H Troop beyond the line of breaking surf. The ramp was lowered onto the ferry's deck; then four guns towed by steel-tracked Bren carriers skittered onto the ferry, followed by their crews in steel-shod boots. En route to the beach,

Small but mighty: loading a 6-pounder of 3rd Anti-Tank Regiment, Normandy, June 1944. The 6-pounder's discarding sabot ammunition, used in Normandy for the first time, proved lethal. (LAC e011083974)

one of the Rhino's engines quit, leaving the ferry slowly turning in circles. A combination of cursing by the gunners and, as Medland recalled, "the REs calling for the wrath of God brought it back to life." The guns drove off as soon as the ferry touched the beach, leaving their crews scrambling after them through the surf. No one was willing to try this again. As a result, the four guns of H Troop and the eight M-10s of 105th Battery were the only guns of 3rd Anti-Tank Regiment to land on D-Day. The rest of the regiment had to wait for 7 June and calmer seas.

The corps heavy anti-tank regiment with whom 3rd Anti-Tank Regiment was to work, 62nd Anti-Tank Regiment, fared no better: only eight guns got ashore on D-Day, all of them at Courseulles, all of them self-propelled. None of 62nd Anti-Tank Regiment's towed guns arrived until the afternoon of D+1. The tardy arrival of these guns, and those of 3rd Anti-Tank Regiment, was one of the costs of landing in bad weather.

As a result of losses, heavy fighting, and delays and confusion along Juno Beach, 3rd Canadian Division advanced only half the way to their final objectives on D-Day. Most of the M-10s ashore were soon acting as assault guns, supporting the mopping up of beach defences. By the morning of 7 June, as 9th Brigade prepared once again to make its dash for Carpiquet airfield, none of the 17-pounders of 62nd Anti-Tank Regiment assigned to 9th Brigade vanguard were yet ashore. Meanwhile the M-10s of Major Love's C and F Troops also failed to show. As they hustled forward after landing that morning, they were mistakenly engaged by Canadian tanks at Villons-les-Buissons and four were destroyed. So instead of having more than twenty anti-tank guns (self-propelled and towed) in support on the morning of 7 June, 9th Brigade had only the four M-10s of New Brunswick's L Troop.

The vanguard force of 9th Brigade consisted of the North Nova Scotia Highlanders (a battalion), fifty Sherman tanks of the Sherbrooke Fusiliers, four Vickers machine-guns of No. 11 Platoon of the Cameron Highlanders of Ottawa, two FOOs from 14th Field Regiment, RCA, a naval "Forward Officer, Bombardment" carrying a radio link to two cruisers offshore, and Major Love's four M-10s. Also, the vanguard had only two of its allotted four FOOs because half its field artillery had been taken away to support an attack on the Douvres radar station by the North Shore (NB) Regiment. In the early morning hours of 7 June 1944, these seemed minor problems.

The vanguard deployed in a wide arrow formation with the road through Buisson, Buron, and Authie and down to Carpiquet forming the shaft, with companies and squadrons on either side. The advance went well as far as Authie, as the vanguard fought its way through a battlegroup of 21st Panzer Division and elements of 716th Coastal Division. Just what the four M-10s of L troop did in this action remains largely unknown, although we know that around noon several engaged targets around St-Contest in the British sector on the vanguard's eastern flank. This was necessary when communications with 14th Field Regiment and the British cruisers failed and no indirect fire support was available. In fact, the vanguard fought through the whole afternoon and early evening without supporting artillery fire.

The Germans, in contrast, had plenty of artillery. And as the vanguard pushed south of Authie it bumped into elements of 12th SS Panzer Division that were preparing to attack. By the afternoon the Panzers of the 12th SS and the Shermans of the Sherbrookes were engaged in a swirling tank battle, one in which German anti-tank guns repeatedly destroyed Canadian tanks at long range. At this stage the 9th Brigade vanguard desperately needed its anti-tank guns. The scope and scale of the action seems to have left little for the four guns of L Troop to do.

A Canadian M-10 self-propelled anti-tank gun pressing inland from Juno Beach on D-Day. Rough seas on 6 June delayed the landing of many Canadian heavy anti-tank weapons. Nonetheless eight M-10s landed by Rhino Ferry by late afternoon in time to prepare for the expected Panzer onslaught. All came under command of Major Walter Love's 105th Battery. (LAC ZK-860-11)

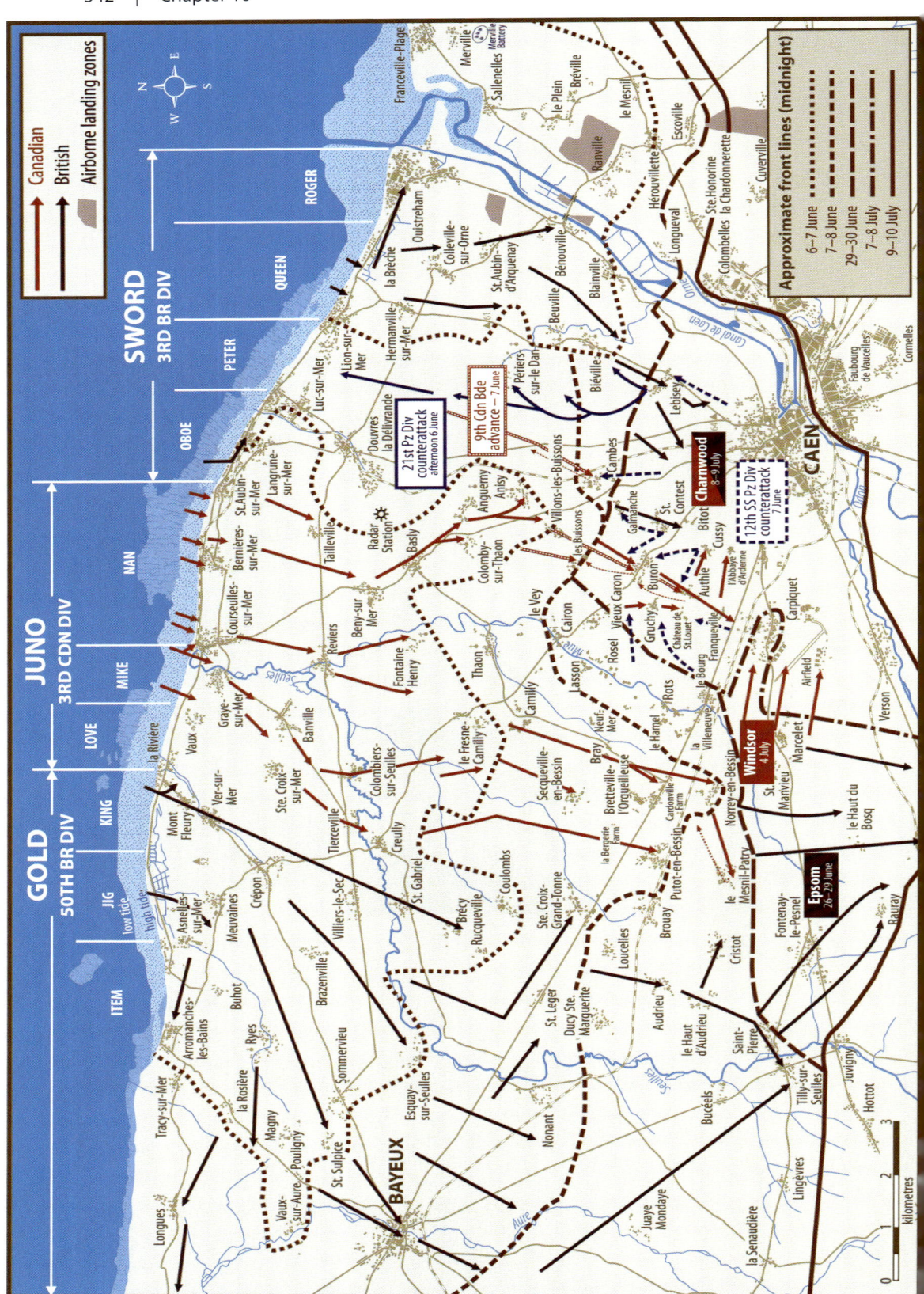

Eventually the forward companies of the North Nova Scotia Highlanders were overwhelmed. By about 1900 hours on 7 June 1944, what remained of them stood to around the anti-tank ditch halfway between Buron and Buissons. They were supported by two mortars and two Vickers machine-guns of the Cameron Highlanders of Ottawa, two 6-pounders of the North Nova Scotia Highlanders, about a dozen tanks of the Sherbrooke Fusiliers, and – according to Major Love – the four M-10s of L Troop. Behind them around the hamlet of Buissons, the Stormont, Dundas, and Glengarry Highlanders and a few recently arrived 17-pounders of 247th Battery, 62nd Anti-Tank Regiment, RA, were ready to support the last desperate stand of the vanguard. Contact had also been made with 14th Field Regiment. Together they stopped the German attack. Through it all, 105th Battery was extremely fortunate: the war diary lists just two wounded lieutenants, including W.T. Purkis, who commanded L Troop and was able to remain in action.

While 9th Brigade fought for its very existence, 7th Brigade got a free pass to its D-Day objectives at Bretteville, Putot, and Norrey on the western side of the Mue River. They arrived on their objectives around noon and had a day to settle in. Thus Lt.-Col. Phin had time to lay out his anti-tank defences properly. By the afternoon, the 6-pounders from 94th Battery had arrived, along with the 17-pounders of 62nd Anti-Tank Regiment assigned to the 7th Brigade front. Phin deployed G and K Troops (K Troop were St. George gunners attached to 94th Battery), eight guns in all, overlooking the eastern approaches to Bretteville; he also sent H troop to Putot to help the Royal Winnipeg Rifles secure the western sector of the brigade front. D Troop of 62nd Anti-Tank Regiment, RA, deployed its four towed 17-pounders in Bretteville. The 6-pounders of the infantry battalions covered other approaches within their sectors, especially south of Norrey, between Norrey and Bretteville, and at the Brouay railway crossing west of Putot.

Lt.-Col. Phin used the remainder of his 17-pounders, 246th (towed) and 248th (M-10 Achilles) Batteries, to cover wider arcs of fire on the open west flank, especially on the plain between Putot and Secqueville. Some of these powerful long-range tank killers deployed with the Canadian Scottish Regiment near Secqueville. Others settled into a copse of trees in the middle of the plain near La Bergerie farm; from there, the 17-pounders could dominate the whole area. A number of 6-pounders from 3rd Anti-Tank Regiment also deployed in the copse near the farm.

The first attacks on the 7th Brigade fortress by 12th SS Panzer Division began in the small hours of 8 June; they would continue throughout the day. These were largely infantry attacks, but a number of armoured vehicles also probed the brigade flank west of Putot. These overran H Troop of 3rd Anti-Tank Regiment, then smashed into the heavily defended copse near La Bergerie farm. There they were stopped by fire from the 3rd Regiment's 6-pounders and the 17-pounders of 62nd Anti-Tank Regiment.

The test for the batteries guarding the eastern approaches to Bretteville came later that night, when the Germans launched the first attack in Normandy by their vaunted Panthers, a forty-seven-ton tank generally reckoned to be the best of the war. "We were surprised by the violent anti-tank fire," Lieutenant Fuss, an SS infantry platoon commander, observed shortly afterward. "A great number of anti-tank guns seemed to be in positions along the edge of town." The anti-tank fire came from the eight 6-pounders of G and K Troops along the eastern edge of Bretteville supporting B Company of the Regina Rifle Regiment. The New Brunswickers of K Troop from St. George were almost immediately overrun, but G Troop fired effectively. Sergeant Herman Dumas manhandled his 6-pounder along a hedgerow, striking at least four Panthers at short range with the new discarding sabot round. The effort earned him a Military Medal. Meanwhile, Bombardier Cyril Askin stuck to his disabled gun got it working again and hit three more Panthers. He too was nominated for a Military Medal but was killed in action before it could be awarded.

At some point in the action the M-10s of Walter Love's L Troop arrived to help out. All that is known of their effort is that Sergeant C.B. Scullin of St Stephen was wounded and that Sergeant Don Walker, a twenty-three-year-old also from St. Stephen, became the first member of the St. George battery to be killed in action. Lieutenant L. Ray won a Mention in Despatches for his efforts, and Gunner Bill Riddell a French Croix de Guerre for sticking to the radio in his disabled M-10 and reporting on the enemy "swarming around him." In the end, 3rd Anti-Tank Regiment claimed at least seven Panthers on the eastern edge of Bretteville. The claim was inflated, but the regiment did kill several. Sergeant T.V. Wood of the Regina Rifles' No. 11 Platoon saw three Panthers hit by guns from G and K Troops and watched their crews bail out. When the Panthers returned in daylight the next day, seven more were destroyed by tank fire. These actions in early June cost 3rd Anti-Tank Regiment twenty-eight casualties, including five known dead and eighteen missing. Among the latter, six members of H Troop were later found murdered (alongside scores of other Canadians) by the SS at the Chateau d'Adurieux.

On 10 June, having defeated the Panzer counterattacks, 3rd Canadian Division made one futile and costly effort to push out of its lodgement – an ill-fated attack on the village of Le Mesnil-Patry. It then spent the rest of June holding the line and nursing its wounds. During this period the 6-pounder batteries of 3rd Anti-Tank Regiment were deployed forward, with the infantry brigades, supported in depth by guns from 62nd Anti-Tank Regiment. The locations varied according to circumstance and threat. Through most of this early period, however, the M-10s of Major Love's 105th Battery remained concentrated around Thaon under command of 2nd Canadian Armoured Brigade as part of the armoured reserve. By 13 June, the war diary reported that the front was stabilizing; by 18 June, it reported that things were generally quiet.

Late in June, as the Americans captured Cherbourg and then turned their efforts southwards towards St-Lô and Avranches, the British advanced to the Canadians' right, across the Odon River and onto the heights southwest of Caen, which swung the Canadian front east as well. As they did so, a danger arose that the Germans might strike out of the Caen area, across Carpiquet airfield and west towards Putot. So 105th Battery and an Achilles 17-pounder battery from 62nd Anti-Tank Regiment slipped in behind the front to provide a mobile anti-tank reserve. In the event, the German counterattack came from the west, into the flank of Operation Epsom, a major British attack across the Odon River and south to Pt. 112. The German counterattack, launched by 2nd SS Panzer Corps, was crushed by British anti-tank guns and artillery. By the time Epsom ended in late June, the 6-pounder batteries of 3rd Anti-Tank Regiment were all forward, with three brigades holding the front; meanwhile, the M-10s of Major Love's composite 105th Battery were back in reserve around Barbière.

On 1 July, 3rd Anti-Tank Regiment commenced a reversion to its proper organization, shifting M-10 troops out of the 105th and back to their original batteries, while J and K Troops of 6-pounders returned to Major Love's battery. The changeover was completed by the next day, just in time for the capture of Carpiquet by 8th Brigade in Operation Windsor. The operation called for a three-battalion attack across two kilometres of open farmland to capture the village and the airport. The 8th Brigade would plunge straight into the village, with the North Shore (New Brunswick) Regiment on the left and the Regiment de la Chaudière on the right. The Queen's Own Rifles of Canada would pass through them and take the control buildings east of the airfield. Meanwhile the Royal Winnipeg Rifles, of 7th Brigade, took the hangers on the south side of the airfield. The 52nd Battery was tasked to support the main attack into Carpiquet village, augmented by the M-10s of L Troop of the St. George battery under Lieutenant W.T. Purkis of Toronto. The advance was covered by a massive artillery barrage that would carry the troops in and secure them on the objective.

The attack commenced in the very early hours of 4 July with an artillery barrage that ripped apart the quiet of a summer morning. By midday, Carpiquet was secure, although under intense enemy artillery and rocket fire. Captain Philip Oland, a FOO from 12th Field Regiment, raced across the 2 kilometres of open ground into Carpiquet that afternoon to help direct fire. Oland had struggled hard to get overseas, and in early 1944 finally escaped the grip of the home army. At the time of the D-Day landings, he was waiting in England for his chance to join the fighting. Casualties among the FOOs of 12th Field during the first week ashore provided that opportunity, and he joined the regiment north of Putot on 17 June 1944. He would see plenty of action during his time with 12th Field Regiment in northwest Europe.

A 6-pounder of 3rd Anti-Tank Regiment rolls through Carpiquet, July 1944: 105th Battery's L Troop M-10s destroyed two Panthers just down the road from this spot. (LAC PA-132873)

By evening, the Winnipegs were back at their start line after two failed attempts to winkle the Germans out of the bunkers on the south side of the airfield. The Queen's Own, too, had given up trying to take their objective and were settled in the west end of Carpiquet as a reserve. The 8th Brigade now held a narrow two-kilometre-deep salient in the German lines, with Carpiquet at the tip. The Chaudières held the southern side of the village and main airfield buildings, leaving the North Shore Regiment and the four M-10s of Lieutenant Purkis's L Troop from 105th Battery holding the north and east faces of Carpiquet. The whole position was being pounded incessantly by German artillery, rocket, and mortar fire; the North Shores were also being snipped at by the 88 mm guns of Tiger tanks in hull-down positions to the north. Major Ralph Daughney of the North Shores asked Captain Oland, an old UNB classmate, to take out the Tigers with artillery fire. None of it worked. The tanks constantly jockeyed into new positions: all Oland could do was harass them.

However, artillery fire helped preserve the precarious Canadian foothold in Carpiquet. During the night of 4–5 July, five major counterattacks were launched against Carpiquet by 1st SS Panzer Division, four of which fell entirely on the North Shores. They were seen off smartly. Prearranged artillery fire was called down by Captains Nixon and Oland on the Germans, who were met by fire from every available weapon – including L Troop's M-10s – as they closed. During the most intense attack, at about 0200 hours on the morning of 5 July, Captain Oland called down three "SOS" barrages right in front of the New Brunswickers' positions just as it appeared that they were about to be overrun. By dawn the field in front of the North Shores was covered with dead and dying SS. Lt. Purkis's men were now short of ammunition for the machine-guns of their M-10s, and one gun had been completely burned out from non-stop firing.

The fifth German attack, launched in the early hours of daylight on 5 July, was the most dangerous. It was supported by six Panthers and hit the seam between the North Shores and the Chaudières on the south side of the village. The Chaudières' forward company buckled, exposing the southern flank of Major Daughney's C Company. Daughney ordered his last surviving officer, Lieutenant Chester MacRae of Fredericton, and his remaining forty-one men to hold while he went for help. He managed to find two of Purkis's M-10s, and then met with Oland to arrange supporting artillery fire. Then – as Oland recalled – Daughney "grabbed a PIAT gun and said that he would try to get one of the tanks."

The M-10s beat him to it. When four Panthers emerged from the dust and smoke, they blasted the hasty defences set up by Lieutenant MacRae's small band of North Shores along the main road. MacRae was blown off his feet and seriously wounded, and C Company was about to be overrun when Sergeant W.S. Edgar and Sergeant R. Waddingham of L Troop took on the Panthers. Edgar was a forty-year-old labourer from Three Brooks, Victoria County. His age and experience showed as he coolly killed one Panther with a single shot. Waddingham, a truck driver from Fredericton just a month shy of his twenty-fourth birthday, was a little less sure of himself. He unleashed no less than six 3-inch rounds at his target. One might have done it: Waddingham's shots were all found grouped "within the circumference of a dinner plate." As the two Panthers burst into flame, the other two and their supporting infantry beat a hasty retreat under a shower of shells called down by Oland. Carpiquet had been held. In the process, the Canadians had destroyed the tactical reserve for the Caen front and, just as importantly, secured observation into the Caen defences. Sadly, Lieutenant Purkis had little opportunity to savour his troop's accomplishment: he was killed a few days later when his carrier drove over a mine. Sergeant M.L. Burns of Hampton was also killed during the fighting at Carpiquet.

Field artillery battery command post, snug underground but with only canvas over the top, Normandy, summer 1944. (LAC PA-191014)

While 8th Brigade held on to Carpiquet, the rest of 3rd Canadian Division prepared for a direct assault on Caen from the west, through Buron, Authie, and the Abbey d'Ardennes. Major Love's 105th Battery had fought over this ground a month before, with less than happy results. This time would be different: the anti-tank guns were ready. The initial attack was made by 9th Brigade, supported by 94th and 105th Anti-Tank Batteries (less L Troop, which was still in Carpiquet), and reinforced by the self-propelled 17-pounders of 245th Battery, 62nd Anti-Tank Regiment, RA. Once Buron and Authie were cleared, 7th Brigade supported by 4th Anti-Tank Battery and one troop from 62nd Anti-Tank Regiment would pass through and carry the attack eastward.

Operation Charnwood commenced in the early hours of 8 July, and the initial fighting was intense, especially around Buron. Once the village was taken, Major Love moved his Battery Headquarters and two 6-pounder troops in. While J Troop deployed on the outskirts of Gruchy, Love and his men tried to deploy K Troop on the eastern edge of Buron, but as Love recalled in his memoir, "the enemy raised very serious objections in the form of heavy fire every time the guns tried to get into position." Attempts by tanks and flame-throwers to drive the enemy off failed. At that point Love called in his reserve – two troops of self-propelled Achilles from 245th Battery, 62nd Anti-Tank Regiment – to defend the forward edge of Buron. These eight British 17-pounder guns bore the brunt of the German counterattack on 8 July; in a heavy-weight duel, they destroyed thirteen enemy tanks but were all themselves destroyed. Terry Copp described 245th Battery's work at Buron as one of the finest anti-tank actions of the Normandy Campaign. The 7th Brigade passed through around 1600 hours to carry out its phase of Charnwood, and most of Caen fell to the Canadians the next day. That night, Love was able to deploy his 6-pounders on the outskirts of Buron; the next morning, he discovered that the enemy occupied trenches only twenty-five yards away. The Germans soon surrendered.

After the fall of Caen, much of 3rd Anti-Tank Regiment slipped into reserve, its first downtime since 6 June. As they did, two more New Brunswick batteries joined the fray. They were part of 2nd Canadian Division and II Canadian Corps, which had begun to land during the second week of July. The Newcastle gunners of 28th Battery came ashore west of Courseulles on 9–10 July and by late on 10 July had assembled with the rest of 5th Field Regiment at Ryes, northeast of Bayeux. The next day, while temporarily under command of 3rd Canadian Division, the regiment moved to a gun position west of Caen and fired its first rounds in anger. Caen had just fallen, and the shoot was called by FOOs of 12th Field perched in the steeple of Caen cathedral. Firing began at 1430 hours with ranging rounds from 5th Battery, followed ten minutes later by the entire regiment. It had been four years and 314 days since the units of 5th Field Regiment mobilized: their long road to war was finally over.

The next day, 12 July, 5th Field fired in support of 4th Canadian Brigade as the infantry of 2nd Canadian Division went into action for the first time since Dieppe in August 1942. Then, following a quiet day, the enemy found them. Counter-battery fire landed around 5th Field Regiment for an hour around sunrise on the morning of 15 July, then at 1000 hours it started again. The second wave struck the Regimental Air Post, wounding two gunners. It also killed Major John Forbes Morlock, the Toronto gunner who had commanded 28th Battery since June 1942: his war had lasted barely five days. Major N.D. Campbell moved in from 4th Field Regiment to take over. This proved to be just the start of the busiest two-week period of action in the history of 5th Field Regiment.

The arrival of 2nd Canadian Infantry Division alongside 3rd Canadian Division in Normandy allowed II Canadian Corps to become operational. The transfer of 3rd Canadian Division from British I Corps also meant a realignment of anti-tank forces, one that brought the two New Brunswick anti-tank batteries of that corps into close association until the end of the war. Up to this point, 3rd Anti-Tank

Regiment had worked closely with 62nd Anti-Tank Regiment, the heavy anti-tank regiment of British I Corps. The anti-tank regiment of II Canadian Corps was 6th Anti-Tank Regiment, RCA, which included Major H.R. Slater and 103rd Battery from Campbellton. It was one of two of 6th Anti-Tank Regiment's batteries (the 74th was the other) equipped with towed 17-pounders drawn by Ram tractors; the other two, 33rd and 56th Batteries, were outfitted with M-10s with 3-inch guns. For 3rd Anti-Tank Regiment the switch to working with 6th Anti-Tank Regiment came 24 July, when 74th and 103rd Batteries were deployed under command of 3rd Anti-Tank Regiment in support of the 3rd Canadian Division front around Caen.

The fall of the northern portion of Caen in early July marked the start of six weeks of the most sustained and intense fighting the Canadians experienced during the campaign in northwest Europe. Through the middle of July, while the Americans slogged their way through the bocage west of Bayeux, British and Canadian forces crossed the Orne River and the Caen Canal and enveloped Caen from both east and west. While the British and 3rd Canadian Division cleared the eastern outskirts of Caen and drove onto what the British called Bourguébus Ridge southeast of the city, 2nd Canadian Division clawed its way south of Caen from the west and up onto the high ground, reaching Point 67 overlooking St-André-sur-Orne and Verrières Ridge by 20 July.

Lavish use of artillery made all this possible. Starting on 16 July, 5th Field Regiment, operating from positions west of the Carpiquet airfield, fired a staggering amount of 25-pounder ammunition, starting with 7,459 rounds that day (over 300 rounds per gun) to help a Scottish division take the town of Version west of Caen. The gunners toiled just as hard the next day, supporting battles across a wide front. Barrages, defensive fire tasks, and regimental shoots kept them busy from midnight until noon, and then "Victor" targets – corps-level shoots – filled the afternoon. All the while, counter-battery fire landed around the regiment. On 18 July the regiment supported 3rd Canadian Division fighting in the eastern Caen suburb of Faubourg de Vaucelles, and 2nd Canadian Division's attack on Louvigny. The latter set up the major Canadian assault south of Caen called Operation Atlantic, intended to rupture the German line and open the road to Falaise. Four of the busiest days of the war followed for the gunners of 2nd Canadian Division. The 5th Field Regiment fired 8,302 high-explosive shells on 19 July, 11,644 the next day, and an unknown amount on 21 July. It received seventy-five truckloads – 15,000 rounds – of ammunition on 22 July alone.

That was not the end of it. Operation Atlantic faltered on the high ground south of Caen, and two quiet days followed. This was simply the lull before the storm. With the Americans poised to break out of the Normandy lodgement north of St-Lô, it was imperative that the weight of German armour be held in the Caen sector. The task of doing that fell to the Canadians, who attacked again across the high ground south of Caen on 25 July in Operation Spring. On that day alone,

Forward Observation Officer, with his supporting staff, at work in Normandy. (LAC PA-719239)

5th Field Regiment fired 13,636 rounds of high-explosives (about 568 rounds per gun) – more than its monthly average for most of the rest of the war. The next day, 11,056 rounds were fired. Despite this prodigious effort, Operation Spring secured virtually none of its objectives – except perhaps to hold the German armour long enough for the Americans to break out and change the tempo of the campaign. To help make all that happen, 5th Field Regiment fired 83,180 rounds in the first three weeks it was ashore – a rate of fire it would never surpass.

For both 3rd and 6th Anti-Tank Regiments, the stories of Operations Atlantic and Spring are largely ones of shifting forward under enemy fire and waiting for targets that – as a rule – never came. Most of the anti-tank action was on the 2nd Canadian Division front east of Highway 158, where 2nd Anti-Tank Regiment fought close actions with enemy tanks. The most notable came on 21 July, when 2nd Anti-Tank Regiment brought forward a lone 17-pounder to the high ground north of St-André-sur-Orne to snipe at Panthers beyond the range of their 6-pounder guns. Three Panthers were knocked out before the 17-pounder was hit and its crew wounded. That was not the end, however. Bombardier G.A. Grassick crawled over from his disabled 6-pounder, got the heavier gun working again, and single-handedly knocked out a fourth Panther. Nicholson's comment that "the whole episode was a striking demonstration of what could be accomplished by courageous and determined well-trained gunners" could be said of all of them in Normandy and beyond.

Meanwhile, the New Brunswick batteries were involved in the failed attempt to take the village of Tilley-la-Campagne on the other side of the Caen–Falaise road. The 17-pounders of Slater's 103rd Battery and 6-pounders of 4th Battery provided flank support for 7th Brigade, while 9th Brigade (supported by 94th and 74th Anti-Tank Batteries) conducted the assault. The 8th Brigade (52nd Battery) provided flank security on the other side, and Love's 105th Battery was in reserve. None of these attacks succeeded, and when the battalion commanders of 9th Brigade refused to try again, they were all sacked.

Following this attack on Tilley and a momentary counterattack scare, 3rd Anti-Tank Regiment slipped out of the line again for the first week of August. They had been at the front more or less continuously for fifty-six days. An inspection by the commander of 3rd Canadian Division on 3 August prompted the war diary to reflect on the regiment's accomplishments:

> There is a great feeling of pride in the Regiment tonight, but it is pride tempered by wisdom and sorrow. We have passed milestones in history, history that we helped make. But we have learned that the HUN is a cunning and determined enemy. We recall with pride the part we played at BURON and CARPIQUET and every engagement since D-Day. We look to the future determined to profit by passed [sic] experiences and pray that we may serve with the courage and dedication of those who have given their lives in this campaign.

While the tired gunners of 3rd Anti-Tank Regiment enjoyed a well-deserved pause, 6th Anti-Tank Regiment, including the 17-pounders of 103rd Battery, remained in the area east of the Caen–Falaise road. Initially they supported newly arrived 4th Canadian Armoured Division as it went into the line for the first time, and by 3 August the regiment was operating with British 51st Highland Division. By now, 51st Highland Division – indeed, all of British I Corps – was under command of 1st Canadian Army. It had become operational on 23 July and assumed control of the whole left flank of the Allied position, including the British Corps and the Polish Armoured Division.

The first major operation of the new 1st Canadian Army was a massive mechanized thrust to the south on either side of the Caen–Falaise highway to finally break the impasse. Operation Totalize, planned for 8 August, was to be conducted in three parts using innovative tactics. Two divisions carried in improvised armoured

A towed Canadian 17-pounder anti-tank gun in full recoil, engaging a French water tower across the field. The 17-pounders' high muzzle velocity and great range turned open spaces into tank kill zones and enabled crews to deliver precision fire on troublesome enemy positions. (LAC PA-137312)

personnel carriers would strike deep into the German positions along the highway; meanwhile, marching infantry would secure villages on the flanks just beyond the start line. Once the divisions astride the highway reached their objectives on the high ground around Cintheaux, a huge carpet of bombs dropped by the air force would clear the way for 4th Canadian and the Polish Armoured Divisions to plunge even deeper into the German position and perhaps rupture it. With luck, the German position around Caen would become completely unhinged and the whole front would start to move.

The task of the anti-tank batteries in Totalize was security of the start line and consolidation of the objectives once achieved. The 17-pounders of Major Slater's 103rd Battery were deployed behind British 51st Highland Division on the east side of the highway around Four, Soliers, and Bourguébus "to form a firm base for the advance." Most of 3rd Anti-Tank Regiment was held back initially as well, concentrated around Cormelles just south of Caen, with only 94th Battery forward on the high ground (Point 67) north of St-Martin-de-Fontenay.

Operation Totalize began just before midnight on 7 August when, as 5th Field Regiment's war diary records, eighteen field regiments opened up and "made quite a racket." As the armoured columns began to move in the early hours of 8 August, three batteries of 6th Anti-Tank Regiment moved in support. Two of these, 56th and 74th Batteries, worked with 2nd Canadian Division west of the highway while the M-10s of 33rd Battery supported 156th British Brigade to the east; 103rd Battery remained in reserve. The first phase went well, but delays, confusion, and a strong enemy response stalled Totalize late in the day. The advance in Phase 2 of Totalize, when the armoured divisions were supposed to ride a carpet of bomb-shattered enemy positions deep into the German rear, was complicated by a dreadful error in the bombing support. Things started well enough, but dust and the adoption of yellow target indicators that were the same colour as the army's recognition colours resulted in creep-back through the Canadian lines. Allied soldiers were killed and wounded by "friendly" bombs as far back as Caen. Among the casualties was the headquarters of 3rd Canadian Division, which was guarded by the M-10s of L Troop of 105th Battery. The division commander, Maj.-Gen. R. Keller, was seriously wounded. Casualties to 3rd Anti-Tank Regiment were not serious. The positions of 5th Field Regiment were accidentally bombed as well, without reported causalities. That regiment moved forward late in the day, to new gun positions south of Roquancourt. There, on 9 and 10 August, 5th Field Regiment was shelled from behind.

By 9 August it was clear that the breakthrough had failed to materialize. The 3rd Anti-Tank Regiment was warned on that day to prepare to deploy forward, and by the end of the day, all of the guns, except for 105th Battery, were in the front lines on either side of the highway around Grainville-Langannerie. Through all this, the St. George battery remained in reserve around Verrières, alongside the Regimental Headquarters. The 105th Battery and 6th Anti-Tank Regimental Headquarters moved forward to Lorguichon on 12 August and were joined there the next day by Major Slater's 103rd Battery, in preparation for the next big push, Operation Tractable. For a brief moment, then, on 13 August at Lorguichon on the Caen–Falaise highway, the St. George and Campbellton gunners deployed side by side.

As the armoured divisions, along with 3rd Canadian Division, prepared for a big mechanized thrust over open ground east of the Caen–Falaise highway, 2nd Canadian Division fought its way towards Falaise west of the road, along the Laise River valley. To support them, 5th Field Regiment moved into new gun positions east of Cintheaux. Two days of intense fighting on 12–13 August broke the German position around Bretteville-sur-Laise and opened the way. The commander of 6th Brigade, Brig.-Gen. W.J. Megill, thanked the gunners for the quality of their work on those days. "We got exactly the fire we wanted," he told 5th Field Regiment, "when we wanted it."

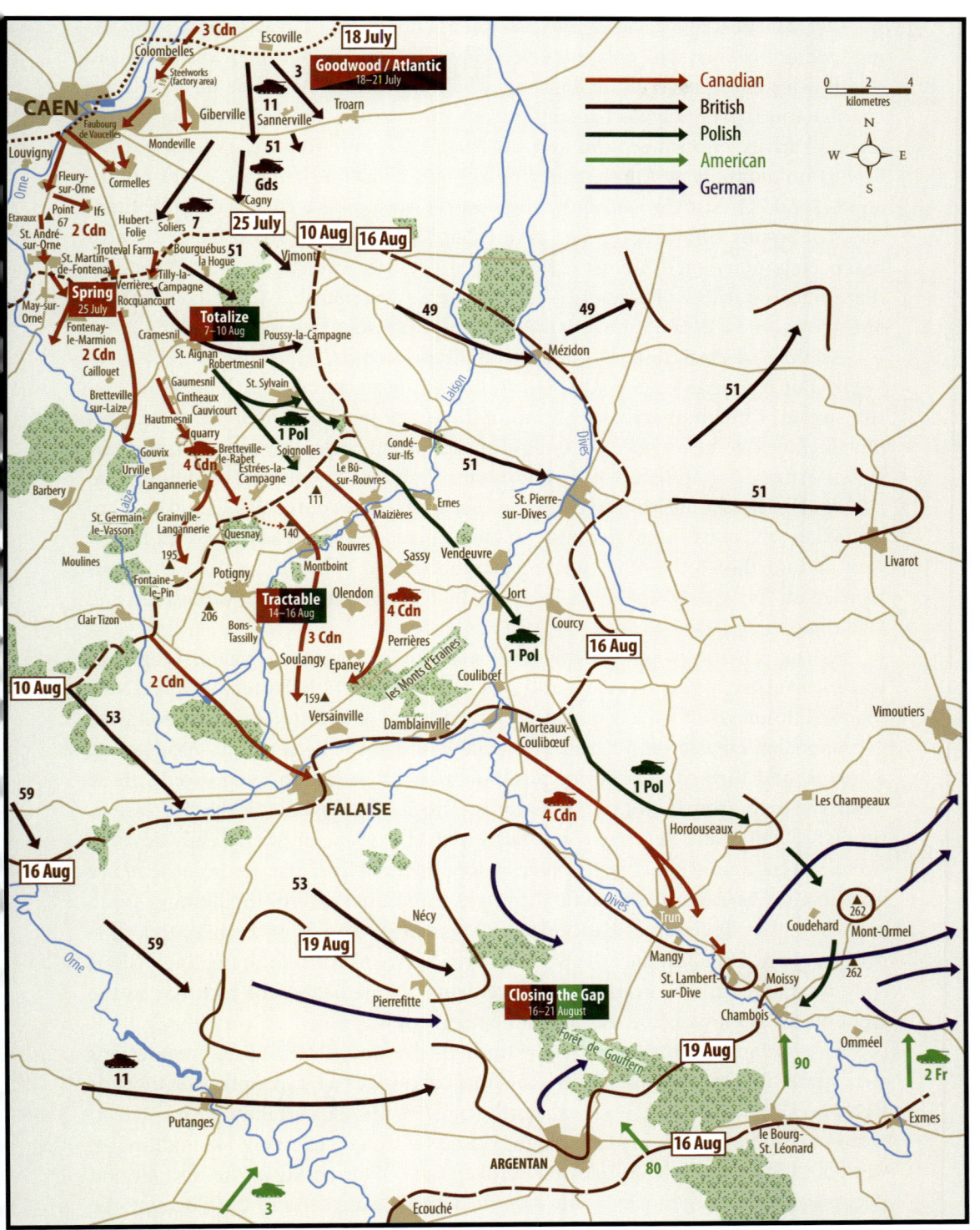

Normandy: Caen to Argentan, 18 July– 21 August 1944

Over the next few days, 5th Field Regiment put much of its effort into supporting Operation Tractable, a daytime version of Totalize with a slight twist. Instead of following the Caen–Falaise highway, which moves up an incline through close country south of Grainville-Langannerie, the mechanized assault would swing east through an arc of open ground towards Falaise. As with Totalize, Tractable relied heavily on bombing by Allied strategic air forces. Tractable launched on 14 August amid clouds of dust thrown up by the massive armoured columns and the thousands of bombs falling along the Caen–Falaise highway. The 105th Battery, which had been bombed on 8 August at the start of Totalize, was caught again. This time there were a number of casualties, among them Lieutenant L.N. Ray, commander of L Troop, and a dozen men at 3rd Anti-Tank Regiment Headquarters.

As the 3rd Anti-Tank Regiment war diary records, Tractable initially went "well." But reconnaissance had failed to notice the steep sides of the narrow Laison stream, which ran across the front of the attack just a few miles from the start line. It proved to be an effective tank obstacle, which broke the momentum of the attack. After delay to secure crossing points, Tractable regained momentum, and two distinct thrust lines emerged in the Canadian drive south. While 2nd and 3rd Canadian Divisions closed in on the shattered remains of Falaise from both northwest and northeast, the 4th Canadian Armoured and Polish Armoured Divisions focused on the wide plain east of Falaise, which runs southward towards Trun and Chambois.

As the scheme of movement developed, 2nd Canadian Division fought its way into Falaise, where its role – and that of 28th Newcastle Battery – in the Normandy Campaign effectively ended. Meanwhile, 3rd Anti-Tank Regiment followed 3rd Canadian Division in Phase 2 of Tractable across the Laison at Montbiont and Rouvres, and through a series of positions until the division overlooked Falaise along the high ground east of the highway. This battle moved quickly, and casualties in 3rd Anti-Tank Regiment were fairly high. The regiment was already down in overall strength and short twelve men at Regimental Headquarters because of the bombing on 14 August; now a further eighteen gunners fell in the fighting south of Laison. The Regimental Headquarters was bombed again that night, this time by the enemy. On 17 August the war diary reported 3rd Anti-Tank Regiment short sixty men and "in dire need of reinforcements." Nonetheless, the next day as the front began to move again, morale in the regiment was noted as "very high."

By 17 August, as infantry fought through the streets of Falaise, preparations were under way for the thrust down the final corridor of open countryside towards Chambois. What followed was perhaps the most hectic and certainly the most decisive week of the Normandy Campaign. While 1st Canadian Army was fighting its way south of Caen, 3rd US Army had broken out of Normandy in the west around the coastal city of Avranches. The Americans were supposed to then occupy the Brittany peninsula and secure ports for the buildup that was intended to support a thrust into Germany in 1945. Instead it was decided to swing 3rd US Army east, towards Paris, where resistance was virtually non-existent. The Germans responded by moving much of what remained of their armour in Normandy west and launching it at Avranches, in an ill-fated attempt to cut off the American spearhead. With the best of German 7th Army and Panzer Group West now in the bottom of the bag, it was logical to turn 3rd US Army north, towards Argentan and Falaise, meet the Canadians, and tie it off. This was the origin of the envelopment movement that would culminate in the Falaise Pocket, which trapped and virtually annihilated the German armies in Normandy.

This was easier said than done. The 3rd US Army turned north, but it stopped at Argentan at an arbitrary boundary established between British and Canadian forces pushing south and American forces pushing north. This left primarily the Canadians and the Poles the task of closing the gap. The situation had not been lost on German commanders. By 18 August what was left of their Normandy armies were moving east to escape, while forces were mustering outside the closing neck of the pocket to counterattack and keep an escape route open. What followed between 19 and 22 August was a collision of forces from all directions of the compass in the area between Trun and Chambois.

The thrust line of 1st Canadian Army into this maelstrom lay along two axes. The primary push was by 3rd and 4th Canadian Divisions and Polish armour along a network of secondary roads southeast of Jort that runs through and along the edge of rolling woodland. This targeted a series of high features: Hill 259, Hill 258, Hill 240, and finally Hill 262. The 3rd Anti-Tank Regiment followed this thrust. Moves were frequent, tensions were high, ranges were short, and the enemy was primarily infantry: the regiment records little action. While all these formations were fighting a confused battle against Germans trying to hold the gap or trying to break out, elements of 2nd SS Panzer Corps attacked from the east to help keep the gap open. Meanwhile, units of the Polish Armoured Division drove from high point to high point until they reached Hill 262 above Coudehard north of Chambois on 19 August. There they dug in and for the next three days acted like a cork in a bottle, defying all attempts to throw them off the hill, and killing or capturing thousands of their enemies.

Taking and holding the high ground seems to have been 1st Canadian Army's plan. While this was being done, the direct route across the rolling plain southeast of Falaise, through Trun to St-Lambert and Chambois and the wooded country beyond, was held firmly by Canadians only as far south as Trun. Beyond that, only patrols from 4th Canadian Armoured Division probed towards St-Lambert and Chambois.

The main avenue for escaping German troops lay between the little village of St-Lambert-sur-Dives in the west and Chambois two kilometres farther southeast. Bridges to both places over the Dives River were strong enough to take tanks and were on a good road link to the east via Vimoutiers. A reconnaissance unit of 4th Canadian Armoured Division composed of a tank squadron from the South Alberta Regiment and a company of infantry from the Argyle and Sutherland Highlanders of Canada probed St-Lambert on 18 August. This small force under Major David Currie tried to hold St-Lambert the next day but was forced back to the high ground (Point 117) immediately north of the village. Currie's force was later reinforced by more infantry, and then on 20 August two troops of 17-pounders from Campbellton's 103rd Battery of 6th Anti-Tank Regiment stumbled into his position. What followed was the most intense and successful engagement of the war for the battery, and probably for all of 6th Anti-Tank Regiment.

The arrival of the Campbellton gunners in St-Lambert on 20 August was entirely fortuitous. They were supposed to be supporting 9th Brigade, which was moving along a secondary road along the base of the high ground farther north where the main Canadian thrust lay. The battery passed safely through Trun, but the situation south of the town was still fluid, with no clear front lines and waves of Germans pushing eastwards to escape the closing net. So the gunners, tucked inside their Ram tractors and moving in the dark, travelled under German machine-gun fire all the way. When, in the confusion and darkness, K Troop, Major Slater, and the headquarters turned northward towards 9th Brigade, Lieutenant J.R. Flowers and Lieutenant McKinnon with J and L Troops carried on down the road towards Chambois. At some point during the night the battery's second-in-command was captured by the enemy. Flowers, McKinnon, and their men were more fortunate: a fortuitous encounter with the Argyles just west of St-Lambert kept them from driving straight into an ambush or captivity.

After overcoming their mystification at not finding 9th Brigade, Lieutenants Flowers and McKinnon contented themselves with supporting Major Currie, who no doubt welcomed the sudden arrival of eight 17-pounders at St-Lambert. Flowers deployed his guns of L Troop "for crash action" along the road into St-Lambert, with their muzzles pointed at the enemy in and around the village. One 17-pounder of L Troop was pointed back up the D13 towards Trun just in case. McKinnon's J Troop covered the southern and southeastern approaches from high ground on either side of the road. Among those laying out the anti-tank plan was Sergeant D.G. Firlotte, Troop Sergeant of L Troop. Firlotte was one of 103rd Battery's old hands, having joined in Campbellton in April 1942 as a bombardier. He reported afterwards that once the guns were in place, most of their crews were deployed "in all-around protection as infantry working in cooperation with the Argylls." Even the Browning machine-guns on the Ram gun tractors were removed and deployed alongside the infantry. Don Graves noted that "the gunners provided a much-needed boost" to Currie and his men.

Over the next two days the gunners from Campbellton fired everything they had, and there were plenty of targets. As the 6th Anti-Tank Regiment war diary for 20 August reported, the gunners "engaged enemy infantry with rifle, Bren and Browning fire." The diary continued: "This fire was effective and casualties were caused," with one brace of machine-guns killing or wounded over 200 of the enemy in a single incident. Meanwhile, the 17-pounders fired at armoured cars, houses, self-propelled guns, mortar positions, machine-gun nests, and of course tanks. The highlight was probably the destruction of a Panther tank (contemporary evidence says it was a Tiger) by L-1 gun of L Troop, which was pointed straight down the road into the village. When the tank appeared at the road junction in the centre of St-Lambert about 800 yards away, the crew of L-1 hit it with an armour-piercing round. That stopped the tank, then the gunners "fired a round of high-explosive hitting the same hole enlarging it to about two feet in diameter. You could see right through the tank."

Despite the success of Major Currie and his men, the situation at St-Lambert remained volatile and very fluid for several days, as fleeing Germans surged around, over, and through their positions. By the time Major H.R. Slater arrived at Hill 117 in the centre of Major Currie's embattled position in search of his guns, the entire command element of J and L Troops of 103rd Battery was nowhere to be found. In fact, they had all been captured. In the early hours of 21 August, Lieutenants Flowers and Mckinnon and their troop sergeants Firlotte and Burgess set off in the dark to figure out where they were supposed to be and to try to reconnect with 9th Brigade. They had just returned from making contact with the Algonquin Regiment when their observation post was overrun. Flowers, McKinnon, and Burgess were quickly captured, while Firlotte grabbed a rifle and tried to make a stand in the loft of a barn. The Germans drove him out with grenades. The first one hit Firlotte in the face, and he was able to roll away before it exploded. Then two went off behind him, wounding his shoulder and leg; at that point he surrendered. The Germans put him on a self-propelled gun, and the group, with Flowers, MacKinnon, Burgess, and other Canadians in tow, walked across fields until about 1000 hours, when they were pinned down by machine-gun and mortar fire from Canadians on their left and Poles to their front. After some debate among the Germans over what to do with their Canadian POWs – which ranged from surrender to them to drive them into their own machine-gun fire – a party of wounded Canadians and Germans, helped by Canadian POWs, reached the Canadian lines around 1330 hours. All of the 103rd Battery command team except Burgess managed to escape that day. (Burgess escaped on 10 September as he was being taken across the Rhine.)

All that Major Slater knew of his battery in the early hours of 21 August was that the two lost troops were forward, somewhere in the darkness, engaged with the enemy. He eventually found them, commanded by their sergeants, and ordered them to rendezvous around Hill 117, just as the leading elements of 9th Brigade arrived to relieve Currie's tired men.

The pursuit from Normandy: a Universal Carrier towing a 6-pounder anti-tank gun of the 3rd Anti-Tank Regiment, Gouy, along the Seine River, France, 30 August 1944. (PA-132421)

J and K Troops of 103rd Battery stayed on, firing from positions on Hill 117 on 21 August. Sergeant Dineen of J-2 killed a Panther with one shot, then destroyed a half-track and a mortar section attempting to set up behind a haystack. Hits on a wheeled vehicle and a Mk IV tank were unconfirmed. By 22 August, when J Troop moved into St-Lambert in support of the Highland Light Infantry, it had accounted for another Mk IV tank, an assault gun, and a self-propelled gun, as well as machine-gun positions. So in one short forty-eight-hour period, the Campbellton gunners of 103rd Battery had claimed one Tiger, one Panther, three Mk IV tanks, one self-propelled gun, one half-track, one armoured car, and "a very large number" of enemy infantry. It proved to be the best and most intense shooting in the brief history of 6th Anti-Tank Regiment. The cost to it for its part in closing the Falaise Gap was also its heaviest for any single action: one officer and twenty-two men killed, sixty-one wounded, and six missing. Six M-10s, one 17-pounder, and four Bren carriers had been destroyed. The two troops of 103rd Battery at St-Lambert in particular had done yeoman service with big towed guns in a situation that would normally have been handled by self-propelled guns or perhaps the smaller, more nimble 6-pounders of 3rd Anti-Tank Regiment.

By 23 August, 1st Canadian Army was on the move. The Falaise Pocket had been closed, and German forces were on the run for the Franco-German border. The war diary of 3rd Anti-Tank Regiment records the first day of the pursuit as "miserable," with heavy rain turning the roads into mud. The next day the skies cleared, and in bright sunshine the Allies raced for the Seine River against "very little opposition." The roads towards the Canadian crossing point at Elbeuf were littered with the detritus of a routed army. On 26 August, 3rd Anti-Tank Regiment reported that its batteries "are moving large numbers of infantry, even hanging onto the shields of their guns and sitting on the trails." The forward elements of 3rd Anti-Tank Regiment reached Le Mare Tassell just southwest of Elbeuf that day. The heavier guns of 6th Anti-Tank Regiment followed, travelling north towards Lisieux, through Livarot, then to Le Planquay before turning eastwards towards Elbeuf and settling in at Le Gros-Theil, just behind 3rd Anti-Tank Regiment. En route, 6th Anti-Tank Regiment received the first of its 17-pounder self-propelled guns, in this case mounted on a Valentine tank chassis (known as the "Archer"), to replace the M-10s. It also began an experiment with Crusader tanks as tractors to replace some of the aging and damaged Rams. The Crusader gun tractors proved mechanically unreliable, and the experiment was soon abandoned.

The Newcastle field battery, along the other elements of 2nd Canadian Division, joined in the pursuit, converging on Elbeuf. From 26 August until it crossed the Seine on 30 August, 5th Field Regiment fired in support of efforts to clear the Germans from the southern bank in the Forêt de la Londe, and then in support of units operating on the northern bank. Close anti-tank support for the crossing was provided by 3rd Anti-Tank Regiment, augmented by M-10s of 56th Battery from 6th Anti-Tank Regiment. The first anti-tank guns to cross were a troop from 94th Battery of 3rd Anti-Tank Regiment late on 27 August. The rest of the regiment crossed on 28 August, and by 30 August, 3rd Anti-Tank Regiment was concentrated north of the Seine around the town of Gouy.

A triumphant entry into the ancient city of Rouen followed on 31 August. The war diary of 5th Field Regiment reported that "the trip through the centre of Rouen was quite an experience … It was quite an ovation." From 3rd Anti-Tank Regiment's war diary: "The crowd lined the streets cheering, waving, showering us with fruit and flowers. All troops wished they could stop to express their appreciation." They could not, of course. Now that 1st Canadian Army was across the Seine, pursuit of the fleeing enemy was imperative. Five days later, 3rd Anti-Tank Regiment, along with 3rd Canadian Division, was enveloping the heavily fortified coastal city of Boulogne. The advance north was fast, with some of the M-10s from 56th Battery (still attached to 3rd Anti-Tank Regiment) covering 150 miles in less than a day, catching "the enemy completely by surprise." They shot-up roadblocks, enemy convoys, vehicles, and whatever lay in their path.

2nd Canadian Division gun positions along the Scheldt River fire on German positions two miles away, north of Antwerp, Belgium, 2 Oct. 1944. (PA-131239)

While the M-10s of 56th Battery supported the dash north of the Seine, the rest of 6th Anti-Tank Regiment and the gunners from Campbellton had a much less glamorous time. The regiment concentrated at Wisques, halfway between Boulogne and the Belgian border. There, "it was grounded and all men and vehicles made available for whatever purpose Corps might require." Until 2 October the men worked as labourers, guarded prisoners, drove supplies for the Service Corps, and secured captured supply dumps. Only the M-10s of 56th Battery, still with 3rd Anti-Tank Regiment during the attack on Boulogne, and one troop from 33rd Battery working with 2nd Canadian Division near Antwerp, remained in action.

While 3rd Canadian Division invested Boulogne, 2nd Canadian Division had a score to settle at Dieppe. By 1 September, 5th Field Regiment was outside the town near Offranville, poised to support 4th Brigade in the much anticipated assault. It never came, since the Germans wisely capitulated. On 3 September, all of 2nd Canadian Division, six abreast, marched through Dieppe to a "tremendous ovation" from its citizens. Then it was off to tackle a really tough nut: Dunkerque. The 2nd Canadian Division probed and pounded Dunkerque for a week between 7 and 14 September, to no avail. The 5th Field Regiment war diary recorded on 12 September that "the results were more or less negative as the place was very heavily fortified, even 17-pdrs didn't dent it." The 28th Battery had better luck a little distance away from the main show, supporting the Calgary Highlanders attacking the coastal town of Loon-Plage. Eventually the whole of 5th Field Regiment joined in the fight for this seaside town, which the Calgary Highlanders finally took on 9 September with superb artillery support. In fact, by this stage 5th Field Regiment and 5th Brigade had a special relationship, with Lt.-Col. Nighswander, the gunner commanding officer, virtually acting as Brig.-Gen. Megill's second-in-command. In the end the Canadians gave up trying to take Dunkerque and the Belgian White Brigade simply invested the town until the war ended in May 1945.

Boulogne was a different story. While 7th Brigade, supported by 4th Battery of 3rd Anti-Tank Regiment, masked the gun positions to the north around Cap Gris Nez, the rest of 3rd Canadian Division laid siege to Boulogne and prepared for an assault. The weight of the attack came in the centre, launched by 9th Brigade with 94th Battery in support, with a supporting attack to the north towards the village of Wimeraux by 8th Brigade backed by 52nd Battery. There were not enough infantry formations to fully encircle Boulogne, so the southern part of the city was contained by the Cameron Highlanders of Ottawa, a machine-gun unit acting as infantry, supported by Major Love's 105th Battery. The 6-pounders of the 105th snipped at targets from the Forêt de Boulogne, taking out some mortar positions, leaving the M-10s of L Troop free to join in the main attack by 9th Brigade. They acted like assault guns, providing close support for the infantry as they fought through layers of wire and pillboxes. Eventually what was left of the Boulogne garrison was cornered on a narrow peninsula across the river from the main part of the city. An appeal to the garrison commander to surrender or face death "by flame" – the

Guns of 28th (Newcastle) Battery in action from hastily dug gunpits, northwest Europe fall 1944. (NPL, Reid Collection)

Normandy to the Scheldt, September–November 1944

Canadians found flame-throwers a powerful and intimidating weapons in close fighting – persuaded the final remnant to surrender.

After Boulogne, 3rd Anti-Tank Regiment shifted north to help in the capture of Calais and the large coastal batteries around Cap Gris Nez. While 94th Battery helped at Cap Gris Nez, the rest of 3rd Anti-Tank Regiment participated in the attack on Calais. Once again the Cameron Highlanders of Ottawa were in the front lines as infantry, this time east of the city, supported again by Major Love's 105th Battery. Much of the gunners' time was again spent snipping at targets, while the M-10 troop "took over the job of drawing fire by lighting fires, moving about at night and firing with small arms." Calais was bombed extensively before the final assault went in, conducted over flooded polder in amphibious craft. The garrison surrendered without much of a fight.

After dealing with the channel ports, 3rd Canadian Division shifted northeast to join the rest of II Canadian Corps to tackle German positions along the Scheldt River estuary, which blocked access to the port of Antwerp. With British and Canadian troops already north of Antwerp to the east, the German enclave south of the Scheldt became the "Breskens Pocket," named for the major town in the area. While 3rd Canadian Division prepared to eliminate the pocket, 2nd Canadian Division fought its way northeast of Antwerp to close off the escape route of

2nd Canadian Division's gun line behind Woensdrecht Ridge at Ossendrecht, Netherlands, 21 Oct. 1944. 28th Newcastle Battery was hotly engaged there during heavy fighting for the approaches to the South Beveland peninsula. (LAC PA-142108)

Canadian M-10 self-propelled guns at Knokke, Belgium after helping to engage bunkers and fortified houses in the Breskens Pocket, 3 Nov. 1944. Powerful German defences there controlled the Scheldt River and the approaches to Antwerp. (LAC PA-137208)

Germans holding the northern side of the Scheldt on the South Beveland Peninsula and the island of Walcheren.

Between 20 September and 5 November, 2nd Canadian Division and 5th Field Regiment engaged in a relentless and bloody drive across canals and flooded polder against a determined and well-equipped enemy. They thought they had the Germans beaten by 7 October and that their way was open northwards to the eastern end of the Beveland Peninsula. But the Germans committed their reserve, "Battle Group Chill," named after its commander, Lt.-Gen. Kurt Chill, whom the Canadian army official history described as "an officer of great skill and uncommon energy." Battlegroup Chill contained elements of three German divisions, the Herman Göring Division's training replacement regiment, and 6th Parachute Regiment. It was an exceptional force, well-led, motivated, well-equipped, and supported by armour. Their job was to stop 2nd Canadian Division at Antwerp. As a result, four more intense weeks of bloody fighting followed. The 5th Field Regiment felt the effect almost immediately, when heavy counterattacks suddenly struck 5th Infantry Brigade's advance near the Dutch town of Hoogerheide. In one six-hour period between 1830 and 2400 hours on 8 October, the regiment fired eighty-two rounds per gun: the commanding officer of the Calgary Highlanders sent his personal thanks back to the gunners.

The next two days were characterized by intense firing as 2nd Canadian Division fought its way forward. The gunners seldom stopped firing. On 11 October, when 4th Brigade attacked, it was so short of infantry that one of the division's anti-tank batteries was sent forward as infantry to help. That same day, Major Campbell, who had commanded Newcastle's 28th Battery since the death of Major Morlock on 15 July, left to become Brigade Major, Royal Artillery, of 4th Canadian Armoured Division. His replacement, Major F.S.C. MacMillan, was seriously wounded almost immediately and evacuated. A week later, Major R.A. Harrison – the fourth commander since D-Day – arrived to take over 28th Battery.

Even without a commander, 28th Battery and the whole of 5th Field Regiment never missed a beat. The day after Major MacMillan was wounded, the division's guns saved a company of the South Saskatchewan Regiment from annihilation when it was cut off and surrounded. The 5th Field Regiment fired "a great number of DF tasks and M targets" to help save the trapped company; as the war diary reported, "they said it was all due to the grand job and quick response of the guns." Then on 13 October, 5th Field Regiment gunners helped extract the Black Watch (Royal Highland Regiment) of Canada from a near calamity, when they were trapped on open polder and nearly wiped out south of Woensdrecht. And on 16 October, they provided excellent fire support for the Royal Hamilton Light Infantry's attack on "Bloody Woensdrecht." The capture of Woensdrecht was a key to sealing off the Beveland Peninsula and preventing the easy escape or reinforcement of the garrison holding the northern bank of the Scheldt. The 5th Field Regiment fired 244 rounds per gun that day, and received the congratulations of both the division commanding officer and the division artillery commander. The peninsula was finally pinched off on 24 October, a day in which each gun of 5th Field Regiment fired no fewer than 398 rounds – just short of 10,000 for the whole regiment that month.

While 2nd Canadian Division was fighting north of Antwerp, 3rd Canadian Division reduced the Breskens Pocket south of the Scheldt in Operation Switchback. The assault began on 7 October with 7th Brigade crossing the Leopold Canal near the Dutch town of Eede and drawing the attention of German defenders south. Then late on 8 October, 9th Brigade launched a daring amphibious assault from the Scheldt on the northeast corner of the pocket, which was soon reinforced by 8th Brigade. Massive amounts of artillery ringing the pocket provided fire support from all directions. There was little for anti-tank gunners to do in this battle, but someone had to hold the western line where the Leopold Canal ran north to the sea. So 3rd Anti-Tank Regiment was drawn into front-line infantry duty for two weeks along the banks of the Leopold Canal north of Bruges.

The duty was not onerous, but it was challenging for gunners. As a rule, men of the towed batteries served as infantry, while the M-10 troops provided fire support, smashing enemy positions, pillboxes, guns, and strongpoints. The most dramatic moment of the front-line duty was probably a skirmish between 105th Battery and

The 17-pounders of J Troop from Campbellton's 103th Battery, towed by their Ram tractors and guided by American liaison personnel, arrive to support of 104th US "Timberwolf" Division, in the Netherlands, Oct. 1944. (Clive Law, Service Publications)

a German patrol. Men were wounded on both sides, and some German prisoners were taken. When one group of the enemy retreated to a dugout along the canal and refused to come out, an M-10 from L Troop was brought up and fired point-blank into the entrance. A couple of weeks along the Leopold Canal was followed by a short break, then 3rd Anti-Tank Regiment went back into the line a little farther north, opposite the ancient Dutch city of Sluis.

By then, 8th Brigade had landed along the Scheldt and pushed westward, clearing most of the Breskens Pocket. By late October all that lay between 3rd Anti-Tank Regiment and the advancing North Shore (NB) Regiment was Sluis itself. The North Shore Regiment was tasked with the main assault on the city from the east, but 3rd Anti-Tank Regiment supported it by attacking from the west and south, primarily as infantry. The preliminary advance on Sluis was made by 94th Battery on 29 October, when a patrol supported by its M-10s got into St. Joseph's College at the southern end of the town. They were soon joined by Germans in an adjacent wing of the building. The M-10s were kept at bay by strong enemy fire and a minefield, and the men of 94th Battery were stuck in the college for three days. However, jeeps and Bren carriers got through, bringing back wounded and bringing in reinforcements, food, water, and ammunition.

By 31 October a full-scale attack on Sluis was ready. The main assault was delivered by the North Shore Regiment, supported by Captain Philip Oland and 12th

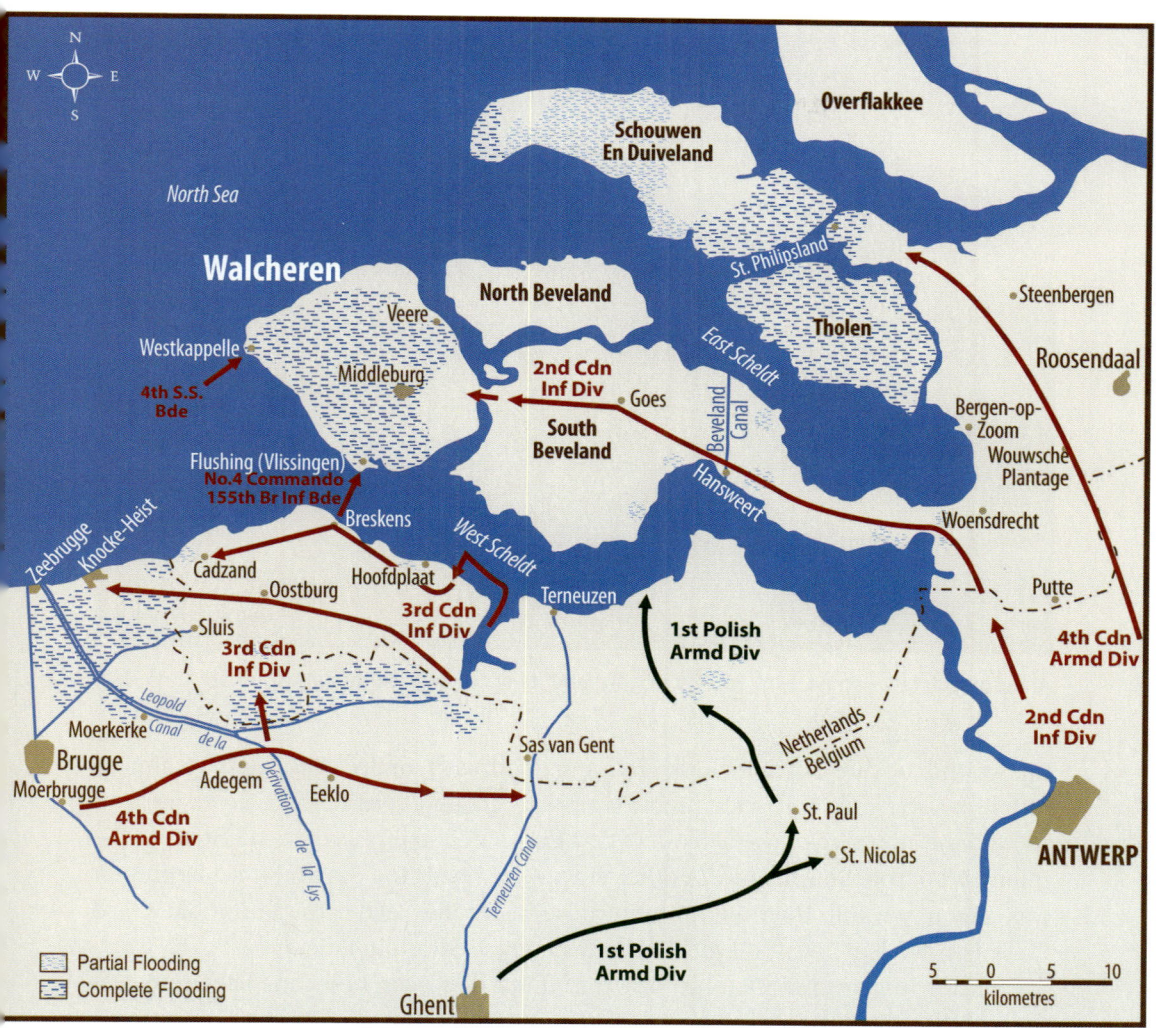

The Scheldt, October–November 1944

Field Regiment. Meanwhile, the rest of 3rd Anti-Tank Regiment launched its own attack from the west. Men of Major Love's J and K troops fought their way into the town as infantry along the canal, with the M-10s of L Troop supporting them. As the regiment's history observed, the operation was well controlled by Major Love, who kept L Troop "as a mobile reserve sent to quell points of resistance as required." The St. George gunners actually entered Sluis ahead of the North Shore Regiment; they "captured fifty prisoners and, as a result of carefully thought out battery tactics, casualties were much less than they might have been." The 4th Battery, however, ran into trouble, drawing heavy fire and suffering nine casualties, including a troop commander and his sergeant. Sergeant A.E. Dunphy from Mill Cove, NB, the Troop Sergeant of K Troop, covered the stretcher parties with fire as

An appropriately named 28th Battery dugout and its occupants, Netherlands, winter 1945. (NPL, Reid Collection)

the wounded were evacuated. Overall, the good work of 3rd Anti-Tank Regiment in its first and only full-scale infantry assault "created considerable diversion and so held the attention of the defenders that they failed to give proper attention to the infantry approaching from the other side. As a result the North Shore Regiment was able to get into town with a minimum of trouble." After the fall of Sluis, 3rd Canadian Division went off for a well-earned rest period in Ghent.

Meanwhile, in mid-October, 6th Anti-Tank Regiment had gone back into battle, with the 33rd Battery working with 8th and 9th Brigades of 3rd Canadian Division on the flooded polder of the Breskens Pocket, and with 56th Battery securing the back of 2nd Canadian Division as it turned west to attack along the South Beveland Peninsula. Campbellton's 103rd Battery went even farther afield, to 104th US "Timberwolf" Division's 414th Regimental Combat Team near Wuustwezel, east of Antwerp. Both 56th and 103rd Batteries were deployed in anticipation of an attack that did not develop. Neither battery saw any tanks, but 103rd Battery fired its machine-guns with effect while serving with the Americans.

As 3rd Canadian Division's assault on the Breskens Pocket developed in late October, 2nd Canadian Division began an arduous struggle westward along the South Beveland Peninsula towards the island of Walcheren. The 5th Field Regiment followed, supporting the assault across the Beveland Canal (just a few miles west of Woensdrecht) and then, after a brief rest, deploying in South Beveland near the city of Goes. The area was packed with troops from two divisions, and finding good gun areas on the flooded polder was a major problem. So 2nd Canadian Division's other field artillery regiments, the 4th and the 6th, withdrew to positions south of the river, in the just-cleared Breskens Pocket, leaving 28th Battery and the rest of 5th Field Regiment – along with the guns of 51st Highland Division – in South Beveland.

By 31 October the Canadians had reached the kilometre-long causeway connecting South Beveland with the island of Walcheren. Several attempts by infantry to force their way across the causeway ended in failure. In part these were diversions for the amphibious assault that hit Walcheren on 1 November. This was followed by one final attempt to cross the causeway the next day that ended unsuccessfully after severe and sustained fighting. The Calgary Highlanders then took over the final phase of the liberation of Walcheren, and 2nd Canadian Division went into a quiet sector southeast of Antwerp for a much needed rest. Through it all, 5th Field Regiment endured some of the worse conditions of the war, fighting below sea level in deep mud, suffering constant counter-battery fire and casualties from mines.

The II Canadian Corps slipped into front-line garrison duty in November. The 2nd Canadian Division held the line near s'Hertogenbosch, well within range of Germany for the gunners of 5th Field Regiment, who grew a little "exasperated" at the delay in opening fire on the Fatherland. On 14 November, 28th Battery finally

Archers of J Troop, 105th (St. George) Battery, waiting for the parade, Leiden, Netherlands, May 1945. The driver's hatch is open on the front glacis, while the gun points backwards, over the engine compartment. (Leiden Archives Collection)

Winter on the Nijmegen front: Gunners of the 5th Field Regiment, in their dugout with Judy, an Alsatian dog adopted by the regiment in France and now the mother of six pups, Netherlands, 1 Feb. 1945. (LAC PA-183989)

received a new permanent commanding officer. When Major MacMillan was wounded on 11 October, Captain W.C. Norman had taken over briefly, and was then replaced temporarily by Major R.A. Harrison. He relinquished command on 14 November to Major A.B. Nixon. As things turned out, Nixon would not be the last of 28th Battery's ill-starred commanding officers.

The months that followed were generally quiet. By early December most of the 17-pounders of 6th Anti-Tank Regiment were under control of 3rd Anti-Tank Regiment, as they held the line in the Nijmegen Salient. When 3rd Anti-Tank entered the line east of Nijmegen on 13 November they took over positions from US 82nd Airborne Division, which was still in place after the failed attempt to bounce all the rivers in September, Operation Market Garden. Major Love had reconnoitred his battery position two days earlier, and took the occasion – along with his troop sergeants – of slipping briefly across the border into Germany, thereby laying claim to be the first Canadian soldiers to enter the Reich. The Germans welcomed them for the next few days with heavy shelling, hitting the Battery HQ several times and forcing it to move.

During this deployment outside Nijmegen, Lt.-Col. Phin, who had commanded 3rd Anti-Tank Regiment with such distinction since March 1943, went on a well-earned leave, and command of the regiment devolved to its second-in-command, Major W.F. MacMullen. One of MacMullen's first tasks was to handle the alert resulting from the hugely successful German attack on the Americans holding the line in the Ardennes in Belgium. By early January, as the "Battle of the Bulge" peaked, the guns of 6th Anti-Tank Regiment were deployed in depth behind the front to forestall any local offensive.

Meanwhile, the organization and equipment of the anti-tank regiments continued to evolve. The big news for 3rd Anti-Tank Regiment in mid-January was the arrival of new 17-pounders. These came in both forms: towed and self-propelled. All of the regiment's American M-10s were replaced with the British "Archer" 17-pounder self-propelled gun, a curious hybrid of a Valentine tank chassis and a huge gun. To make it all work, the gun was mounted in a fixed position in the front of the chassis but pointing back over the engine compartment. That reduced the overall length of the vehicle. The arrangement was particularly good in "shoot and scoot" situations. The Archer was also significantly lower in profile than an M-10. The real improvement was to the gun itself: the new 17-pounder was more powerful and effective than the 3-inch on the M-10. L Troop of 105th Battery was the first in the regiment to receive the Archer, on 7 January 1945. The men were sorry to see the M-10s go. The battery fitter who had kept them going, Sergeant Roy Sypher of

A 5th Field Regiment 25-pounder in action, in this case 5th Battery, the Netherlands, winter of 1945. (LAC PA-168908)

The Final Months, February–May 1945

St. Stephen, received permission to drive them across the line briefly into Germany before they were handed in. The M-10s were all gone by 14 January. The war diary noted that when 105th Battery zeroed in their new guns on 19 January after several days of firing, "the men have become more enthusiastic about the new gun especially the self-propelled Valentine." A week later, Major Love's battery was the first to take them into the line.

The second troop of each battery of 3rd Anti-Tank Regiment surrendered its four 6-pounders. These were replaced with three 17-pounders, which required the same number of men to handle them as four of the smaller guns. However, unlike 6th Anti-Tank Regiment, which used Rams to tow 17-pounders, 3rd Anti-Tank Regiment was given "field artillery tractors," the same large trucks used to pull the 25-pounders of the field artillery.

While the Archer was a good anti-tank system, its weight and narrow track virtually eliminated it from the next major Canadian operation, code-named Veritable, in mid-February. Veritable was the largest operation of war ever conducted and controlled by Canadians, with virtually all the forces in 21st Army Group under Canadian command. The task was to break out of the winter position around Nijmegen and clear the west bank of the Rhine as far south as Xanten to facilitate a British assault across the Rhine itself. This required 1st Canadian Army and its attached British formations to break through the heavily fortified Reichswald, just inside the German border, then clear a sodden rolling plain through a series of heavily prepared and defended lines. Finally, in Operation Blockbuster, 1st Canadian Army was to breech the Hochwald Forest and capture Xanten. As originally conceived, Veritable/Blockbuster was to travel over frozen ground. But by the time it was launched, the first rains of spring had come and the approach to the Hochwald lay across miles of muddy terrain laden with wire, minefields, trenches, and machine-gun nests. Moreover, the German positions were well supported by artillery on the east side of the Rhine, which was able to operate effectively in the poor weather that characterized Veritable and Blockbuster, and the key road on the Canadian eastern flank was flooded and under observation. The operation was, in many ways, a mechanized version of Passchendaele.

Veritable was launched on 8 February 1945, but the preparatory firing had begun over a week earlier. The 5th Field Regiment was part of that essential work. During the opening phase of Veritable, 5th Field Regiment was attached to 3rd Canadian Division, and fired intensely in support of the North Shore Regiment on the first day. The Reichswald was pierced quickly, but the attack was slowed measurably by flooding and by mud. The 5th Field Regiment did little firing over the next week as 3rd Canadian Division fought its way over the plain towards the Hochwald. The gunners of 5th Field Regiment finally moved onto German soil on 19 February, to gun positions near Calcar. There they fired a series of barrages in support of 2nd and 3rd Canadian Division troops. Two days later, after another forward leap, the regiment operated in support of 9th Brigade's fight to reach the Hochwald, then on 23 February in support of 15th Scottish Division to their south.

Operation Blockbuster, the final push through the Hochwald to Xanten, commenced on 26 February. The 5th Field Regiment fired all day as part of a massive artillery plan in support of the attacking forces. The next day, as the regiment moved to provide support for its old friends in 5th Brigade, one of its FOOs was killed in action and Major Nixon, the sixth officer to command 28th Battery since D-Day, was seriously wounded. Nixon was evacuated but died the next day, as did another FOO at the front. Nixon was the third commander of 28th Battery either killed by enemy action or to die of his wounds.

The grim battle for the Hochwald went on for another week, under low, grey skies, torrents of rain, and occasional snow, all of which sheltered German artillery from attacking Allied aircraft and allowed it to fire effectively on the attacking troops and their supporting gunners. On 4 March, as 5th Field Regiment moved to Udem, it was raining steadily and "very muddy." The next day was dull and drizzly, with heavy rain off and on. As the regiment moved towards Xanten, the rain relented, but it remained dull and cold. On 8 March, Xanten fell to 4th Brigade, supported by 422 rounds per gun from 5th Field Regiment alone. The dreary weather allowed enemy counter-battery fire to strike 28th Battery again, wounding two gunners and killing a third on 9 March. The regiment's war diary did not record a quiet day – or good weather – until 11 March.

While the field gunners toiled against the weather and enemy fire to carry the infantry and tanks forward, there was not much for anti-tank gunners to do in Veritable and Blockbuster. One M-10 battery from 6th Anti-Tank Regiment fought a bitter action on the British front to the south with 53rd Welsh Division at the outset, but there was little call for anti-tank guns for the first week on the Canadian front. When the anti-tank regiments finally began to move forward again on 15 and 16 February, to take defensive positions around Cleve prior to Blockbuster, the mud was their worst enemy. Towed 6- and 17-pounders, with their small wheels, bogged easily, while 3rd Anti-Tank Regiment's new Archers – heavier than the M-10s and with a much narrower track – found the going almost impossible. Under heavy overcast, German artillery fire was virtually impossible to suppress, and one new Archer, commanded by Sergeant Waddingham (who had killed a Panther at Carpiquet) was destroyed. Waddingham escaped with wounds, but his bombardier was killed. Conditions were so difficult that M-10s from 6th Anti-Tank Regiment had to be called in to handle some tasks. It was an inauspicious start for 3rd Anti-Tank Regiment's new and much heavier guns.

The only real shooting done by 3rd Anti-Tank Regiment in the first days of Veritable, apart from potting at enemy gun emplacements, was firing indirect barrages of high-explosives in support of the infantry. This was done often enough to encourage the fitting of clinometres on the 17-pounders to allow more accurate

Gunners of "J-3" of 105th Battery, waiting for the parade, Leiden, Netherlands, May 1945. (Leiden Archives Collection)

indirect fire in the future. Both 105th and 103rd Batteries and their regiments also had a largely uneventful role in Blockbuster, the assault on the Hochwald. When that operation closed down on 9 March, 3rd Anti-Tank Regiment rallied at Cleve for a two-week rest. The experience of 6th Anti-Tank Regiment in Blockbuster was similar: not much shooting done. However, the Ram gun tractors of 103rd Battery and 74th Battery were used as armoured personnel carriers to ferry the Lincoln and Welland Regiment into battle. Once the infantry dismounted on the objectives, the Rams supported them with machine-gun fire, which, according to the 6th Anti-Tank Regiment history, "accounted for many of the enemy and materially assisted the infantry in their task." The Rams then carried out the wounded and towed some twenty Sherman tanks and 150 other vehicles out of the mud. This work is generally associated with 1st Canadian Armoured Personnel Carrier Regiment, but the Ram towers from 6th Anti-Tank Regiment – including those from the Campbellton Battery – continued to do this work for the balance of the war.

The Rhineland battles were the last attempt to deploy 1st Canadian Army's anti-tank regiments on a large scale in their intended role. When 56th Battery of 6th Anti-Tank Regiment went into reserve on 10 March it was "never really deployed again." By this stage there was very little need for heavy anti-tank guns. The regiment spent much of the rest of the month primarily in an infantry role, garrisoning the west bank of the Rhine, before shifting north into the Netherlands for April, while its Ram towers carried infantry into battle.

The smaller and lighter 6-pounders proved better suited to the final phase of the war in northwest Europe. While 1st Canadian Army reoriented itself for the final liberation of the Netherlands, 3rd Canadian Division represented Canada in Operation Plunder: the assault across the Rhine by British Second Army. The 9th Brigade, supported by 94th Battery, was in the initial assault, and they were soon followed by the rest of the division on the northern flank of the bridgehead, supported by 52nd and 105th Batteries of 3rd Anti-Tank Regiment. Their task was to screen the main British assault from the only Panzer reserve in the area, so for the final time in the war there was plenty for anti-tank gunners to do. In these battles the Archer self-propelled guns proved their worth, as they were "practically the only anti-tank guns that could be used because of mortar and machine guns and shell fire caused casualties to the FATs towing the 17-pounders." It was on the north flank of Plunder, around Emmerich, that Walter Love's 105th Battery scored some of its final hits on enemy armour.

On 30 March, 7th Brigade made its push towards Emmerich itself, with the Archers of L Troop of 105th Battery supporting the Royal Winnipeg Rifles. When D Company of the Winnipegs was held up by the enemy and a self-propelled gun, Sergeant D. Gomez (from Vancouver) manoeuvred his Archer into position and destroyed the gun with three direct hits. An hour later he moved boldly into the open to fire at another that was holding up the advance: it was disabled with a single shot. Later that day, Gomez and his crew "beat up a German patrol attempting to escape and captured six prisoners." Gomez was awarded the Distinguished Conduct Medal. While all of this was going on, 5th Field Regiment fired across the Rhine in support, primarily at the promontory of Hoch Elten, which provided the Germans with excellent observation. The gunners were busy, but the 44,136 shells fired by the regiment in these final major battles was barely half that fired in the last two weeks of July 1944 outside Caen.

In early April the Canadian divisions moved north, into the Netherlands again. It was there, near the town of Zutphen, on 7 April, that 105th Battery fought its last action of the war. By this stage the fighting remained intense at the local level. Some Germans still resisted tenaciously, but the German army was largely a spent force. It simply remained to fight through the last diehards with as much force and caution as circumstances allowed. In these conditions, the actions of a single well-dug-in enemy tank could delay movement for some time. Such was the case with an old French Somma tank sited in the approaches to Zutphen. It was engaged by a Sherman from 2nd Armoured Brigade on 6 April without a hit being recorded. L Troop of the 105th Battery arrived the next day with its 17-pounders and peppered the Somma with thirty-three rounds from 1,400 yards before it burst into flame. The battery then moved on with 7th Brigade to attack Deventer, and the war diary records no incidents.

The 105th Battery was withdrawn from the line on 14 April to fully re-equip with Archers, becoming an entirely self-propelled battery by early May. By 3 May it was well into Germany, supporting attacks on Aurich and Emden. The war in the Netherlands and northwest Germany ended on 5 May. The next day, Major Love's 105th Battery was selected to represent 3rd Anti-Tank Regiment in the Allied victory parade in Berlin: a fitting tribute to the exceptional work of the St. George Battery. It is unclear that it made that trek, but it was shiny and clean for the liberation parade in Lieden in mid-May.

Campbellton's 103rd Battery ended its war inauspiciously as infantry. They started working as infantry along the Ijssel River in central Netherlands, then shifted north as II Canadian Corps moved into Germany along the Ems estuary. The ground was low, wet, and problematic for the placement of large guns, and shelling was continuous. But 74th Battery managed to get one 17-pounder into position overlooking the Ems River, and became the only Canadian anti-tank battery to sink ships. Its claim was remarkable, according to the war diary: "one large tug, three smaller tugs and a motor launch were sunk and one ship of probably 8,000 tons set on fire." While the towed batteries were thus engaged, their Ram tractors were used constantly to carry infantry around northern Holland, cleaning up the last elements of the German army, and covering some 450 miles in the process. In May, 33rd and 103rd Batteries of 6th Anti-Tank Regiment moved into Germany in support of the Canadian advance. Campbellton's 103rd Battery ended at the war at Midlum.

Meanwhile, 28th Battery – mobilized even before the war had started and destined to wait the longest to get into action – spent the last six weeks on a "tour of Holland" that by all accounts went well. They moved north to support the attack across the Twente Canal in rain and hail. By 8 April, as they deployed near Holten, it was bright and quite warm, and the next day there was "much shirtless basking in the sun." There was firing too, about twenty-five to thirty rounds per gun per day until they reached Holten, at which point firing dropped to a dozen rounds per gun per day. The attack on Groningen on 15 April was the toughest battle in this final phase. The "opposition is strong and Jerry is putting up a good fight," 5th Field Regiment's war diary recorded that day. Even so, the regiment fired less than 600 rounds on 15 April. In total, during the final month of fighting in the Netherlands, 5th Field Regiment fired just 660 rounds per gun.

The campaign in northwest Europe ended at 0800 on 5 May 1945. The 5th Field Regiment was north of Oldenburg, poised to move in "the old Jock column system" of brigades and supporting batteries attached, when news arrived that the war would end. The war diary entry for 5 May notes the end of the fighting by recording that the Commander, Royal Artillery, decided to celebrate by having the artillery of 2nd Canadian Division fire one round of coloured smoke per gun at 0755 hours. In the days after, New Brunswick's three batteries with II Canadian Corps joined the four from Italy, and indeed the whole of 1st Canadian Army, in security, aid delivery, and reconstruction work across the Netherlands.

Chapter 11

Cold War and Turbulent Peace, 1946–2001

With the Second World War won, the Canadian army regrouped in the Netherlands and sorted out drafts for transport home. While infantry and armoured units with local affiliations often came back to welcoming parades, the RCA mustered its gunners by region – regardless of unit – and sent them home to local depots for demobilization. The result was a quiet return and quick release. Gunner William C. Milner from Sackville, who had served throughout northwest Europe with 13th Field, RCA, was supposed to demobilize in Moncton. When the train from Halifax slowed down in his hometown, Milner simply threw his kitbag out, jumped onto the platform, and walked home. He did the paperwork in Moncton a few days later. Milner reflected the general mood of Canada's field army: they had had enough. The government was eager to get back to normal, too. Equipment overseas was sold or disposed of, budgets were slashed, and the army once again scrambled to figure out what its new peacetime status would be.

As they had done a generation earlier, New Brunswick's gunners – volunteers to a man – brought home with them a combination of wounds to heal, memories to preserve (and forget), and an enormous wealth of experience and skills. Once again, returning veterans committed themselves to building not just a new life, but better communities – and to preserving and passing along the hard-earned lessons of war to the next generation of militiamen. An especially dedicated cadre of New Brunswick gunners went back to university and pursued careers in survey engineering, which derived from their commitment as gunners to knowing precisely where they were on the face of the earth – and where their shells might land. That particular group helped forge the Survey Engineering Department at the University of New Brunswick, which became a world leader in the development of the modern global information systems (including global positioning systems [GPS]) on which the twenty-first century depends. Others used their skills and organizational abilities for more prosaic purposes, such as building communities, raising families, operating successful businesses, and modernizing the province. They also saw New Brunswick's artillery units through their postwar heyday of growth, followed by their most perilous period of existence since the near extinction of The Loyal Company a century earlier.

Indeed, veterans – including a number of Great War senior officers – dominated New Brunswick's artillery for more than twenty years after 1945, some in uniform and others as community advocates. The difference between the 1920s and the late 1940s, however, was the advent of the Cold War, which very quickly pulled the army out of the uncertainties of immediate postwar planning and into preparations for a Third World War. Starting in 1947 with the international crises that led to the founding of the North Atlantic Treaty Organization in 1949 and carrying through to the late 1950s, the Canadian armed forces, including the militia, went through their largest ever peacetime expansion. It helped that there was a clear and present danger from the Soviet Union, that nuclear weapons had not yet fully rendered conventional forces obsolete, and that there was a surfeit of surplus wartime equipment. In fact, for the first time in its history Canada was maintaining and deploying overseas a large standing army as part of a NATO deterrent force, and as the cadre of a much larger force based on Militia mobilization in Canada. The impact of all this on New Brunswick was profound. For the first time since the British garrison left in 1871, regular troops and units were based in the province. The government had consolidated its east coast army bases into one new, massive training and concentration base near Oromocto named Camp Gagetown. The new base had accommodation for a full division and direct rail links to Saint John to facilitate deployment overseas. The combination of the Cold War and the presence of Canada's largest army base completely changed the landscape for Militia in New Brunswick, and for its gunners.

For about a decade, from 1947 to 1957, batteries and regiments of artillery – of all types except coastal – proliferated in New Brunswick. At its peak in 1952, New Brunswick fielded four and a half artillery regiments composed of fifteen batteries. These glory days lasted just a few years. Conventional war with a few hundred atomic weapons might well have been "winnable" in the early 1950s, but the advent of thermonuclear weapons – fusion weapons that released the power of the sun and had no theoretical limit in size – threatened to end all higher life on earth. The threat of imminent global thermonuclear war reversed Canada's militia expansion, and the advent of missile-borne thermonuclear weapons by the 1960s seemed to have rendered conventional ground forces utterly redundant. The Canadian government surmised that the mobilization of army reserve forces would not be necessary in a looming nuclear Armageddon: by the 1960s, future war would be "come as you are."

In the new era of mutually assured destruction (MAD) from intercontinental ballistic missiles carrying thermonuclear weapons, all of Canada's Militia gunners fought an intense and often bitter political battle for survival. At a time when the strategy was to avoid war at all costs, it seemed that the new, large regular army was all Canada really needed. Certainly, it was difficult to demonstrate the relevance of Canada's reserve army to society, and to convince senior military leaders and the politicians in Ottawa that maintaining the combat readiness of a reserve artillery force was of any value whatever. In the second decade after the war, Canada's Reserve Forces were slashed in size, and defence funds were reassigned to an increasingly expensive Regular Force. In the process, civilian and military officials in the Department of National Defence repeatedly reorganized the militia, eliminating units across Canada by the dozen. In this struggle for survival, almost all of New Brunswick's artillery regiments and batteries were swept away. Within a decade, NB's four and a half artillery regiments had been reduced to just one: 3rd Field Artillery Regiment (The Loyal Company).

That 3rd Field Regiment remained on the order of battle at all was due almost entirely to the efforts of three influential Second World War veterans: Philip Oland, James Turnbull, and Martin O'Leary. They had returned from the battlefields of Italy and northwest Europe to successful civilian careers. All three had risen to command 3rd Regiment and had served long years after as honorary colonels, mentors, and volunteers. Oland, Turnbull, and O'Leary were paragons of community leadership and had the political connections necessary to keep the regiment alive.

It was well they did. For within a decade of the advent of MAD and the apparent obsolescence of conventional military forces, the poor state of NATO conventional deterrence highlighted the need for an effective military response to Soviet aggression short of a full-scale nuclear duel. In the 1970s, Canadian army units stationed in Europe needed to maintain a high state of readiness; a rapid reaction force would go to Norway, and reinforcements – at least on a small scale – might head to Europe in time of crisis. Conventional forces provided a capability for measured response, and such forces needed gunners. By the 1980s, 3rd Field Regiment had a clear role: it might never go overseas as a formed unit, but its trained gunners would. Their new mission of augmenting Regular Force units was reminiscent of the situation in the Great War and was therefore not entirely new. The pattern established in the latter half of the Cold War helped the Canadian army respond to the explosion of foreign missions that began at the end of the twentieth century.

The struggle to adapt to a rapidly changing security environment began in 1946, when the Canadian government adopted plans to maintain a large peacetime standing army, backed by a strong Militia. This was a new and totally unexpected development. The plan emerged under Brooke Claxton, the Minister of National Defence, who had been a Battery Sergeant Major in the Great War. The Regular Force would be built around an immediately deployable brigade group, with appropriate artillery (one field regiment and one battery each of medium, anti-tank, and heavy and light anti-aircraft guns). At the same time, the Militia would be structured to "reflect the military potential of the country" as part of a mobilization plan. The Militia was organized into six divisions and four independent brigades with enough corps- and army-level troops to field two corps under one Field Army Headquarters – a mirror of its wartime structure in 1945 prior to demobilization. For the Militia gunners this meant eight medium regiments, twenty field regiments, eight anti-tank regiments, nine heavy and eighteen light anti-aircraft regiments, and five coast artillery regiments. Never before had the Canadian Militia been organized on this scale.

In this ambitious scheme, New Brunswick was to be the home for an entire Army Group, Royal Artillery (AGRA). The AGRA centred on what was known just after the war – rather awkwardly – as 3rd (Reserve) (New Brunswick) Coast Brigade (The Loyal Company of Artillery). In April 1946 the unit's name was changed to the 3rd (New Brunswick) Coast Regiment (Reserve). The removal of the "Loyal Company" from the name, on the grounds that including it and the words "New Brunswick" as well was too cumbersome, did not sit well with the Saint John gunners, who never faltered in referring to themselves by their historic title.

The 1946 organization also kept alive the old 12th Field Brigade, which dated from the pre-1914 reorganization of the Canadian Militia, now as 12th Field Regiment (Militia). It consisted of two NB batteries with storied field artillery legacies – Moncton's 8th Battery and Newcastle's 28th – along with Fredericton's 90th, which was converted from its Second World War role as an anti-tank battery back to its field battery origins. New Brunswick's pre-1939 23rd Field Regiment reformed in 1946 as 23rd Heavy Anti-Aircraft Regiment, based largely at Saint John. The wartime 8th Anti-Aircraft Battery, descended from the old 6th Medium and the guardian of Saint John's air space between 1939 and 1945, shifted into this new 23rd HAA Regiment as 124th Battery. The 23rd also included 104th (now in Saint John) and 105th (St. George) Batteries, now converted to the new air defence role.

A second anti-aircraft regiment, 64th Light Anti-Aircraft (New Brunswick) Regiment, was also formed in 1946. It was almost completely new. It drew on the rump of the disbanded New Brunswick Tank Regiment and formed three totally new batteries, the 190th, 191st, and 192nd, centred on Moncton and Fredericton. Apart from medium artillery, the only thing NB lacked was its own anti-tank regiment, but it did have two anti-tank batteries in the 1946 organization. Woodstock's venerable 89th Battery – field artillery, then light anti-aircraft early in the Second World War, then absorbed into the infantry as part of the Lanark and Renfrew

The 3rd (NB) Heavy Anti-Aircraft Regiment's band performing in front of Saint John's Barrack Green Armoury under the direction of the talented Bruce Holder (senior). The band first formed in 1949 after Major Philip Oland asked Holder to take charge. It is still one of Atlantic Canada's best-known bands. (Loyal Company Association Collection)

Scottish – now became an anti-tank battery. The 103rd Battery, in the process of moving its armoury from Campbellton to Dalhousie, retained its well-earned anti-tank role. The other two batteries of 47th Anti-Tank – 88th and 146th Batteries – were from the Annapolis Valley, and they all belonged to a new Maritime regional 47th Anti-Tank Regiment headquartered in Wolfville, Nova Scotia. None of these gunners had far to go for training. A Regular Force artillery school, formed at the wartime Camp Utopia in Charlotte County, served for a time as the Canadian Army Eastern Command training base.

Many of these Militia batteries and regiments had their own bands. This was one of the few initiatives that allowed local communities to show extra pride in their units. By 1947 both 12th Field and 23rd Anti-Aircraft Regiments maintained active bands in Moncton and Saint John, to provide music for ceremonial occasions and parades. Even 89th Battery maintained its own band, in Woodstock. By tradition, bandsmen provided medical and stretchers parties for army units, and so the personnel could be borne on strength. The extras, such as special uniforms, instruments, and other paraphernalia, had to be funded locally. A combination of peacetime reorganizations and wartime demands left 3rd (New Brunswick) Coast

Regiment without a band, much to the displeasure of then-Major Philip Oland. While marching with the regiment in the 1948 Remembrance Day parade, Major Oland spotted Bruce Holder (senior) directing traffic. Holder was a well-known musician and bandleader, but also a volunteer with the Saint John Salvage Corps, an auxiliary force that supported the city's Police and Fire Departments. So he was a man with a sense of duty to his community. As soon as he returned to the armoury and was dismissed, Oland jumped into his car and raced back to King's Square. Regimental legend has it that Oland pulled up alongside Holder, rolled down the window, and said "I want a band and you are going to make it happen." Before the end of the year, the band had been formed and instruments had been found, and early in the new year, 3rd (New Brunswick) Regiment Band held is first rehearsal under the newly commissioned Lieutenant Bruce Holder. It has been going strong ever since.

As the 1940s drew to a close and NATO came into being to confront the Soviet threat, winds of change were blowing over the 1946 Militia gunner scheme. The first to feel those winds were those along Canada's east coast. Defence planners had surmised that in the new Jet Age, the Royal Canadian Navy and Air Force would be able to meet well offshore any direct threat to Canada's coasts from enemy naval vessels, long before they came within range of coast defence artillery. In any event, the Soviet Union lacked an ocean-going fleet and bases along the Atlantic littoral and so was considered a negligible maritime threat.

Given the lack of any definable Soviet threat at sea, Canada quickly abandoned all its coastal fortifications. Most were dismantled in 1946–47. The first of the Saint John elements to go was Fort Mispec, in June–July 1946. That fort had been an emergency interim project any way: construction on permanent positions for much heavier guns had never been started, and the risk of bombardment by an enemy warship was now virtually nil. The army had intended to keep the other three Saint John forts equipped, but the government imposed severe economies that made that impossible. In 1947 the Saint John forts were stripped, and the equipment and ammunition was carefully stored at central depots in Nova Scotia and New Brunswick, ready for rapid reinstallation in the event of war.

The danger of an early, major conflict greatly increased in 1948–49, when the Soviets seized control of Czechoslovakia and blockaded the sectors of Berlin occupied by the Western powers. It was clear by then that the Soviets had an increasingly strong submarine force based on the latest snorkel-equipped German submarines of 1944–45. Rapid-firing guns like the twin automatic 6-pounders in storage for Saint John had to be ready to support the navy's light coastal patrol vessels. As part of efforts to improve preparedness, in 1951 militiamen from Saint John began to travel to Halifax each summer to conduct practice-firing at the coastal forts that were still active. The army's role in harbour defence soon declined again, however, this time for good. Soviet submarines were beginning to carry long-range missiles

Gunners of 3rd (NB) Heavy Anti-Aircraft Regiment pose in front of a 3.7-inch gun. The later versions fired a 28-pound high-explosive shell upwards of 45,000 feet. (Loyal Company Association Collection)

that would make it unnecessary for them to come close to the coast, and the RCN and RCAF were expanding and acquiring new equipment to provide defence against submarines far offshore. At the end of 1956 the Militia coast artillery unit at Saint John disbanded, and the Partridge Island battery, which since 1950 had been the only site at Saint John designated for rearmament in the event of war, was finally struck off the mobilization plans.

By then, 3rd NB Coast Brigade had found a new role, adapting once again to the changing requirements of the age. The real danger to Canada's coasts – and indeed to all major urban and communication centres – was now considered to be enemy aircraft. It is true that even long-range Soviet bombers would have to fly one-way missions to reach North America, but few doubted that dedicated communists would attempt such attacks. On 29 April 1948, therefore, 3rd (New Brunswick) Coast Regiment changed its name and its role to 3rd (New Brunswick) Heavy Anti-Aircraft Regiment, with Great War veteran Lt.-Col. Wallace Alward in command. The local 104th Battery transferred from 23rd HAA Regiment as part of the reorganization. The change of role for 3rd Regiment gave New Brunswick two heavy A/A regiments, opening a seventeen-year period of large-scale air defence artillery presence in the province. Meanwhile, 5th Anti-Aircraft Operations Room was stood up in Saint John to direct the air defence of the port city.

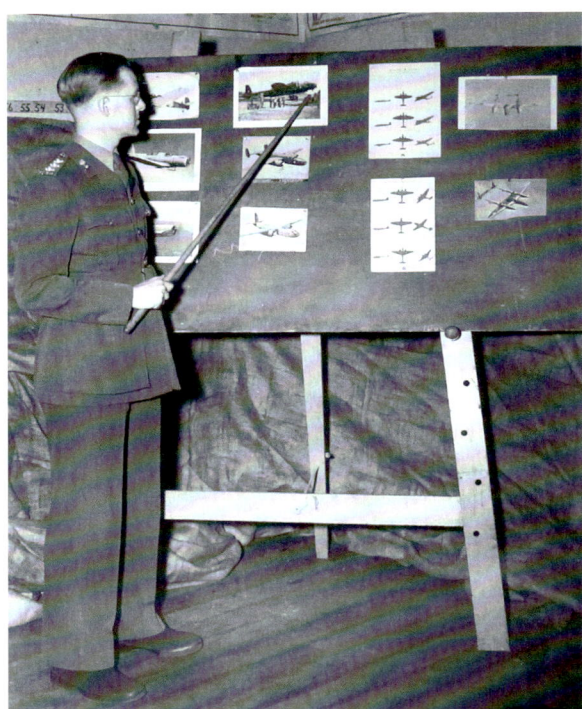

Aircraft recognition training for gunners with 3rd (NB) and 23rd Heavy Anti-Aircraft Regiments. The threat posed by Soviet bombers to Saint John harbour in the early Cold War added urgency and realism to Militia training. (Loyal Company Association Collection)

Organizing and equipping three air defence artillery regiments (3rd, 23rd, and 64th), a field regiment (12th), and two anti-tank batteries within the province was all possible due to surplus but still serviceable 3.7-inch heavy and 40 mm light anti-aircraft, 25-pounder field, and 6-pounder and 17-pounder anti-tank guns and ammunition available in Canada. The 89th Battery even maintained a 17-pounder Achilles self-propelled anti-tank gun at their Woodstock armoury to qualify crewmen and maintain skills. Other familiar patterns remained, including field artillery summer camps in Petawawa for 12th Field Regiment. The 89th and 103rd Anti-tank batteries joined them there at times, but also made use of the Tracadie–Sheila firing range on New Brunswick's Acadian Peninsula. The new 3rd (New Brunswick) Heavy Anti-Aircraft Regiment and 23rd HAA and 64th LAA Regiments all made use of the new Royal Canadian Artillery School (Anti-Aircraft) set up in the late 1940s at Picton, Ontario. The new facility became home to the Regular Force 127th HAA Battery, which in part was tasked to assist with militia training. The Picton camp was the site of the former British Commonwealth Air Training Plan airfield south of today's RCAF base at Trenton. Firing ranges were set up a few kilometres farther south at Point Petre. There, 3.7-inch and 40 mm guns could explode airburst shells somewhat harmlessly into Lake Ontario, near the now-popular Sand Banks Provincial Park. Postwar modernization also meant that civilian passenger aircraft soon replaced trains for conveying gunners to summer training camp at Picton.

In the postwar decade, 3rd (NB) and 23rd Heavy AA Regiments trained primarily to protect critical sites and infrastructure around the port of Saint John. Training focused on the finer points of radar-directed high-altitude air defence gunnery as part of a network directed by 5th AA Operations Room, all for local home defence. New Brunswick's remaining batteries in 12th Field Regiment, 64th Light AA Regiment, and 89th and 103rd Anti-Tank Batteries trained to form part of a mobile field army either to defend Canada or to deploy overseas. Second World War veteran officers and senior NCOs trained new members in basic gunnery skills, then battery and regimental tactics as well as the capability to manoeuvre and maintain guns, tractors, and transport vehicles as part of a large field formation. The ubiquitous wartime quad field artillery tractors were found in armoury vehicle parks in Woodstock, Campbellton (later Dalhousie), Newcastle, Fredericton, and Moncton. In many respects, little had changed since the war.

Philip Oland, newly promoted to Lieutenant-Colonel, took over from Lt.-Col. Alward during those first heady years of heavy anti-aircraft service in 1948. Lt.-Col. J.M. Crosby commanded the neighbouring 23rd Heavy AA Regiment in Saint John. Lt.-Col. M.Y. MacLean led 12th Field Regiment from Fredericton, and Lt.-Col. W.T. Cooper commanded 64th Light AA Regiment from Moncton. Lt.-Col.

The officers of 3rd (NB) Regiment, ca. 1950. Lieutenant-Colonel Philip Oland sits in the front row, sixth from the left. Also in the front, second from the right, is a young Captain James Turnbull.
(Loyal Company Association Collection)

Oland also became the eastern Canadian representative for the Royal Canadian Artillery Association, and therefore also within the Conference of Defence Associations. The CDA was (and remains) a not-for-profit advocacy group composed of scores of military and defence associations, devoted to defence and security issues. Those two agencies – the RCAA and the CDA – proved essential in having New Brunswick's voice heard in Ottawa in the coming decades.

By 1950 the advent of NATO and the deepening Cold War with the Soviet Union further changed the nature of Canadian defence planning. A shift had begun away from a small professional army as a cadre to mobilize the "military potential of the country" (as had been the case in 1914 and 1939) towards a standing professional army of long-serving regulars with its own operational tasks. By the spring of 1950, even before the outbreak of war in Korea, plans were under way to raise a permanent Canadian brigade with supporting troops for service in Germany as part of NATO. When the Korean War broke out that June, the government began to recruit a second Regular Force infantry brigade, along with 2nd, 3rd, and 4th Regiments, Royal Canadian Horse Artillery, to meet Canadian obligations in Germany and a new combat mission in Korea. Several recruiting drives in Atlantic Canada drew substantial numbers of veteran and newly trained reserve gunners, especially

Veteran members of 3rd (NB) Heavy Anti-Aircraft Regiment train new gunners on the 3.7-inch gun ca. 1950. (89th Battery Museum)

for 27th Canadian Infantry Brigade and its attached regiments, which took station in Germany in 1951.

In the early 1950s, concerns that hostilities in Korea foreshadowed a global war between the West and the communists (now including mainland China) brought renewed earnestness to the training of 3rd (NB) and 23rd Heavy Anti-Aircraft Regiments. In those strange days between war and peace in 1951, 3rd (NB) HAA Regiment carried on as good Militia units always had to maintain tradition and community spirit in Saint John. The grand celebration of the regiment's 158th birthday, which occurred during May's Loyalist Days, highlighted its pride in its status as Canada's oldest serving artillery unit. Lt.-Col. Oland marched the regiment on parade past Lieutenant Governor Donald McLaren. Also on the reviewing stand were legendary past commanding officers and Great War veterans, including Lt.-Cols. Wallace Alward, George Gamblin, E.M. "Ned" Slader, and William Harrison. Behind them stood other former officers and Great War veterans, including Colin MacKay (senior) and J.G. "Gil" Hart, who had also commanded the Saint John fortress during the Second World War. The splendid march past was set to music by Lieutenant Bruce Holder's 3rd (NB) Regiment's Brass and Reed Band. A service in the Stone Church, where the regiment's colours are laid up, followed.

The following February, Canadians grieved the death of King George VI, who had kept up the morale of many in the Commonwealth during the recent war. New Brunswick gunners turned out on parade across the province with black armbands to lead mourning processions. Second World War veterans, who still dominated the ranks of New Brunswick's four artillery regiments, especially among officers and NCOs, had fond memories of King George's many Royal Visits to their units in Britain and at the various fronts in Italy, Normandy, and northwest Europe. They turned out in similar strength in June 1953 to celebrate the coronation of Queen Elizabeth II.

New Brunswick's Militia artillery regiments formed a central part of communities all over the province. Combat veteran officers and NCOs offered discipline and training in the use of modern technology along with employment and comradeship to a new generation of young men. In 1951, Donald Cox was drawn to the always bustling Woodstock armoury, which was shared by 89th Battery and a company of the Carleton and York Regiment. The very popular Major Gerald Clark, who had served with 28th Field Battery in Normandy and northwest Europe, then commanded 89th Battery. Under Clark's direction, Cox became part of the next generation of postwar junior officers. He remembered learning to master anti-tank direct fire gunnery skills on the 6- and 17-pounders, at least until the blast wave of dramatic change swept across the world in 1954.

On 1 March 1954 the United States detonated the world's first weaponized thermonuclear device in the Bravo test on Bikini Atoll in the South Pacific. The Americans had proven the concept two years earlier on the island of Elugalab, with a deuterium bomb set off by a large atomic trigger: Elugalab had simply disappeared, replaced by an enormous crater in the sea. But the Bravo test was of a deliverable weapon, one that used a small atomic fission bomb to trigger a fusion explosion of lithium. The yield of this first thermonuclear weapon was fifteen megatons, twice what the scientists had estimated and nearly 1,000 times more powerful than the bombs that had destroyed Hiroshima and Nagasaki in 1945. This was, in fact, the power of the sun, now transformed into a weapon of war. Even before the Bravo tests, the world's powers had possessed enough atomic weapons to shatter the major cities of the industrialized world: now, a decade later, they wielded enough thermonuclear weapons to destroy almost all life on the planet.

Also in 1954, 4th Regiment, Royal Canadian Horse Artillery, was assigned to duty in New Brunswick, having returned from the last active combat rotation in Korea. It was posted to Camp Utopia. This marked the first time that a Regular Force RCA unit had been garrisoned in the province. When most of what became "4th Royal Canadian Horse Artillery" (the distinction RCHA now denoting a Regular Force artillery unit) moved to Germany in 1958, it left behind "W" Battery, which fired the last 25-pounder round in Canadian service at Camp Utopia that year. "W" Battery later moved to the new east coast concentration and training facilities at the new Camp Gagetown, east of Fredericton, which opened in 1956. Gagetown had been established as part of the early NATO planning for a large-scale conventional Third World War in Europe; such a war would once again require the mobilization of forces in North America for service in Europe. In previous major wars, the army had used a series of training bases and staging points for expeditionary forces moving through eastern Canada to operations overseas. These staging points included Camp Debert, Nova Scotia, and two NB bases – the venerable Militia base of Camp Sussex and, after 1942, the infantry training centre at Camp Utopia. Gagetown was designed to do it all: to accommodate a full division, with extensive firing and manoeuvring areas and easy access to the sea by rail through the port of Saint John. It would also become home for Regular Force lodger units, including a force of gunners.

As the Regular Force grew in size and stature, and the nature of full-scale war shifted from conventional to thermonuclear, the Reserve Force began an unprecedented existential struggle. After the Korean War ended, the Canadian government launched the first in a series of hearings chaired by Maj.-Gen. Howard Kennedy followed by reorganizations to adapt to evolving Cold War circumstances and technological developments. In 1953 the Kennedy Commission toured the country studying Canada's reserve army in light of operations in Korea and other Cold War trends. Among other things, the commission recommended that the Canadian Army Active and Reserve Force formally return to the prewar distinction between the Permanent Force (or now "Regular Force") and the Militia. Divisions were done away with, and the old prewar Militia District system returned. As part of these early changes, Philip Oland was promoted to full Colonel and assigned to command New Brunswick Militia District 6 in the southwestern part of the province, which included the two heavy anti-aircraft regiments. Lt.-Col. D.B. Armstrong took his place in command of 3rd NB Regiment, the third member of his gunner family to do so. District 5 took in the northern and eastern parts of the province, including 12th Field Regiment and 64th LAA Regiment, then led by Lt.-Cols. W.F. Roberts in Fredericton and F.C. Judd in Moncton.

The Kennedy Commission also recommended changes in the army's order of battle. The advent of theatre-level surface-to-surface and surface-to-air guided missiles marked the end of Regular Force light anti-aircraft units, even if the capability was retained in the Militia for the time being. The commission sought also to reduce the number of types of artillery units. Anti-Tank batteries were disbanded or re-roled, with the anti-tank function taken over by armoured regiments. As a result, in the spring of 1954, 89th Woodstock Battery returned to its traditional field artillery role and to its traditional home unit of 12th Field Regiment. By then, Lieutenant Donald Cox was a troop leader in 89th Battery, responsible for converting anti-tank gunners and training new recruits on the 25-pounder gun in the field artillery role.

The impact of the Kennedy Commission on northern New Brunswick was much greater: it lost both its artillery units. The 103rd Battery from Campbellton–Dalhousie was disbanded and transferred its lineage to 89th Battery, along with any members willing to travel. The venerable 28th Newcastle Battery, which had fought with distinction in two world wars, was also struck off the order of battle. Its lineage and personnel were swept into the changes that were coming to NB's infantry units at the same time. These did away with locally affiliated infantry regiments, such as the North Shore Regiment and the Carleton and York, and the short-lived New Brunswick Scottish (an earlier amalgamation of the Saint John Fusiliers and the NB Rangers) and combined them all into a new "Royal New Brunswick Regiment." The idea was not new, but the infantry arrangement was bitterly opposed throughout the province. It was finally "sold" at least partly on the basis that this would be the model for the rest of Canada and that other provinces would soon follow (which never happened). The result was that the gunners of northern NB were largely absorbed into 2nd Battalion, Royal New Brunswick Regiment (North Shore). This marked the first in a long series of New Brunswick militia artillery reductions and amalgamations.

The core message in the Kennedy Commission's report was that the next war would happen quickly, like Korea, and would be fought by the forces-in-being; this placed a premium on the Regular Force and a much lower priority on the Militia. The Militia, then, was to lose its revered status as the basis for mobilizing Canadian expeditionary forces abroad; instead, it would hold to a lower readiness standard of partly trained and partly equipped forces that could be mobilized in the unlikely

Members of 115th Radar Battery with their new, American-built M33c Radar system to direct new 90 mm anti-aircraft guns received in 1955. (Loyal Company Association Collection)

event of a long war. Indeed, many argued at the time that the Kennedy Commission did not go far enough. Among those who believed that the Militia was no longer relevant was the Canadian Army Chief of the General Staff, Lt.-Gen. Howard Graham, who had been appointed to the post in 1955 and was himself a former Militia officer. Graham argued that any future war "must be fought by forces in being and *in situ* and will be of short duration. The other battle will be in this country to assist in restoring order out of the dreadful chaos and state of anarchy that may exist as the result of enemy attacks with long range nuclear weapons." Not surprisingly, Graham led the charge to refocus the Militia on civil defence training in support of emergency measures organizations. The new assignment and shift away from its traditional role did not go over well with Militia units and with the Conference of Defence Associations.

In 1955 the exception to the new Militia civil defence concept was home air defence. In the mid-1950s, before the age of ballistic missiles, heavy anti-aircraft guns remained relevant although they had received a curious redesignation to "medium." The Kennedy Commission recommended retaining and modernizing the equipment for eight medium anti-aircraft regiments for static home defence at critical places to protect against Soviet bombers. The port of Saint John was designated one of those critical places, not least because the army's new expeditionary concentration base at Gagetown was tied to it by rail. So began the reinvigoration of the newly named 3rd (NB) and 23rd Medium Anti-Aircraft Regiments. They continued to form the backbone of 3rd New Brunswick "Army Group, Royal Artillery," along with 12th Field and 64th Light Anti-Aircraft Regiments. Other modernized MAA Regiments were retained at Vancouver, Sault St. Marie, Montreal, and Halifax.

The 3rd (NB) Regiment modernized their "Medium" anti-aircraft organization in the summer of 1955 when they replaced their obsolete 3.7-inch guns with more powerful and longer-range – and brand-new – American-built 90 mm guns. They also received new M33c target acquisition radar to kit out 115th Battery, which now became the regiment's Radar Battery. Lt.-Col. Armstrong's slate of officers included Major J. Craig as his second-in-command, and Captains James Turnbull and Neil McKelvey. Both captains had served as 3rd (NB) Coast Regiment gunners early in the war, and both had gone overseas: Turnbull with 8th Self-Propelled Field Regiment, McKelvey with 4th Anti-Tank Regiment. Both had benefited from education programs for demobilizing soldiers. Turnbull had graduated from Canada's so-called Khaki University while awaiting passage home to Canada. McKelvey had returned to complete his studies at Dalhousie Law School. Turnbull had entered the insurance business in Saint John after the war; McKelvey had established a well-known law practice. Both had taken commissions and become active members of 3rd (NB) Regiment in 1946 and had risen to prominence by the time the regiment received its new guns in 1955. By then, Turnbull was in command of 104th (West Side) Battery. Their balance between civilian and military service and community leadership epitomized what the militia had always been in Canada. Nearly all of the unit's officers and senior NCOs continued to be Second World War veterans who had served some kind of field, medium, anti-tank, or anti-aircraft gun in action. All were accustomed to changing up equipment and training to meet the evolving threat to Canadian security.

Also in 1955, the Royal Regiment of Canadian Artillery celebrated the centennial of the 1855 Canadian Militia Act. That legislation was an act of the Province of Canada, a union of the colonies of Upper and Lower Canada formed in 1841. The celebrations rather typically conflated the history of the "Canadas" with the history of the nation born in 1867. Constitutionally, the Dominion of Canada was an entirely new nation, not a continuation of the Canadas with the addition of New Brunswick and Nova Scotia (as is so often assumed). This was clearly understood outside of central Canada, if not by those in Ontario and Quebec. The "centennial" celebrations, which privileged the traditions of Ontario and Quebec units, therefore rang hollow in a province that routinely celebrated founding of The Loyal Company of Artillery in 1793 as the beginnings of artillery service in what was, after 1867, the Dominion of Canada. Needless to say, the 1955 RCA centennial was celebrated with something less than enthusiasm in New Brunswick.

Despite the first wave of Militia cuts in 1954–55, the summer training camps in 1956 were the largest and most elaborate since the end of the Second World War. The 3rd (NB) and 23rd Medium Anti-Aircraft Regiments travelled to the anti-aircraft school at Picton and fired their new 90 mm guns for the first time, directed by M33c radar. The 12th Field Regiment travelled to Petawawa to practise-fire the new, American-built 105 mm howitzers. The 89th Battery had only got 25-pounders back in the Woodstock armoury for two years before the new 105 mm guns arrived. In time these American guns were replaced by Canadian-built 105 mm guns that proved remarkably durable. Ironically, as New Brunswick artillery regiments travelled west for summer training in 1956, Regular Force units came east for a large divisional field exercise at Camp Gagetown. The next year, 3rd (NB) and 23rd Medium Anti-Aircraft Regiments returned to Picton and Point Petre for summer camp. The 3rd (NB) Regiment won first place for general efficiency among all medium AA regiments in Canada in the first competition of its kind sponsored by the RCAA. At the time, Lt.-Col. W.N. Anderson was serving as commanding officer, with Major James Turnbull commanding 104th (West Side) Battery, Major F.E. Devenne commanding 117th (City Road) Battery, and Major K.J. Brown commanding 115th Radar Battery. Competition was fierce among strong contenders. Second place went to Sault St. Marie's 49th MAA Regiment and third place to 1st MAA Regiment in Halifax.

Despite the accolades, the new equipment, and corresponding purposeful training in the medium AA regiments, more Militia artillery reorganization and cuts lay on the horizon. In 1957, General Graham's plan to re-role the Militia as a civil defence corps to assist in rescue and relief operations in the aftermath of total nuclear war became public. The plan reduced annual training days from sixty to forty-five and drastically cut back funding for summer camps, requiring those future camps to run at local training bases with Regular Force support. Militia signals and engineer units were deemed the only type with relevant civil defence military skills and equipment. Basic military training and discipline were still considered valuable in the civil defence context, but gunners, infanteers, and tankers were deemed to be of little use if they continued training in traditional combat skills. Map reading, first aid, small-arms training, and small-party task leadership were all thought useful building blocks for units employed in aiding civil authorities in a post-nuclear apocalypse.

By 1957 the stage had been set for a long, quiet battle between Ottawa and Militia units across Canada as represented largely through the Conference of Defence Associations. As if to endorse General Graham's scheme for the Militia, in October 1957 the Russians launched the Sputnik satellite, the first of its kind. The satellite was not much to celebrate, but the accomplishment was. It was now clear to military

Gunners of 3rd (NB) Regiment boarding a plane bound for summer training and firing practice at Camp Picton in the 1950s. (Loyal Company Association Collection)

planners that the Russians had missiles capable of delivering nuclear warheads to North America: the age of the intercontinental ballistic missile (ICBM) was born. The combination of the ICBM and thermonuclear warheads soon rendered any notions of fighting large-scale conventional war totally obsolete.

In 1958, New Brunswick's medium anti-aircraft regiments trained with their new radar-directed guns, while 12th Field Regiment spent its first, reduced training year refocused on civil defence training in earnest. Advocates for maintaining effective reserve forces won one small victory: a name change from civil defence to "national survival" training to highlight the military nature of the service, lest the change result in the complete civilianization of the Militia. Few could deny that an armed and disciplined force was necessary to assist in both rescue efforts and the restoration of civil order in a post-nuclear world. Lt.-Col. E.A. Grant's 12th Field Regiment ran local exercises on derelict or otherwise empty buildings in Moncton, Fredericton, and Woodstock, rescuing civilians trapped in "smashed" buildings. The cost was the complete elimination of artillery collective training beyond basic gun drills; even training hours allotted for basic gun drill dropped sharply. Captain Donald Cox saw morale in 89th Battery plummet during what he called the national survival "lost cause."

The introduction of national survival training accompanied another round of Militia funding cuts. The postwar economic boom ended in 1957, the year John Diefenbaker became prime minister. Deficits and unemployment rose sharply. While the Regular Army toyed with medium-range nuclear-tipped Honest John missiles in Europe as the new form of "heavy" artillery, the government began to slash much of the excess capability that had been built up over the previous decade, now that conventional war seemed less likely. "The re-equipping of the NATO brigade was a relatively low priority for the Tory government," Jack Granatstein wrote in his history of the Canadian army, "and the forces in Canada were even further down the list. For a soldier to get a pencil or a few sheets of paper by 1962 was a major feat, and exercises at Camp Borden found officers and soldiers training in broken-down jeeps without tops in pouring rain."

In these straitened circumstances – collapsing fiscal support and a combat role entirely undermined by the prospect of global nuclear annihilation – fighting to preserve Militia units at all became the challenge of the day. In New Brunswick, changes began as early as 1959, by which time it was clear that larger centres like Fredericton and Saint John maintained more units on paper than could be manned, equipped, or paid for. Some measure of consolidation was certainly necessary. The first to go, in August 1959, was 64th Light Anti-Aircraft Regiment from Moncton and Fredericton. The Regular Army had abandoned LAA years earlier, so perhaps the end of the 64th was no great surprise. Its personnel were absorbed into 1st Battalion of the Royal New Brunswick Regiment. Some devoted gunners no doubt found places in 12th Field Regiment. The other logical decision was a merger of 3rd (New Brunswick) and 23rd Medium AA Regiments. Maj.-Gen. M.P. "Paddy" Bogert, then head of Eastern Command, proposed the merger on the grounds that it was simply not economical to maintain two regiments in the same city, competing in the same recruit pool. During the war, in the Italian Campaign, Bogert had led the West Nova Scotia Regiment and later 2nd and 3rd Infantry Brigades, so he was familiar with New Brunswick's overseas batteries. There was no question that the old 3rd Regiment must survive. After all, 23rd Regiment was not only quite new, but it had formed in 1936 around 3rd Regiment's old 6th Battery when it converted to field artillery as 106th Battery. So that part of the amalgamation was easy; deciding which battery numbers survived was much harder. In the end, Bogert accepted the proposal that the 1920s battery numbers be restored to perpetuate the regiment's Great War heritage. On 1 September 1959, 23rd MAA Regiment ceased to exist, and 3rd (NB) MAA Regiment paraded 4th, 6th, and 15th Batteries.

Yet more name changes were on the way. As part of the 1959–60 wave of Militia cuts, the Royal Canadian Artillery Association lobbied successfully to have the word "artillery" inserted in unit titles to distinguish them clearly from engineer "field regiments." This was part of the resistance to the civil defence role taking precedence over corps training on guns and gunnery. Thus in 1960 the province's remaining two units were renamed 3rd (NB) Medium Anti-Aircraft Artillery Regiment (Militia) and 12th Field Artillery Regiment (Militia). The Saint John gunners now found themselves facing the same pressure as their field counterparts to shift to National Survival training.

In 1961, Brigadier Oland retired from the Militia, relinquishing command of New Brunswick Militia District 6. At the same time, Lt.-Col. R.F. "Reg" Sansom took command of 3rd (NB) MAA Artillery Regiment and Major Turnbull became his second-in-command. Sansom was a fine choice for the job, having served during the war in 2nd Heavy Anti-Aircraft Regiment and as second-in-command of 23rd HAA Regiment before the 1959 amalgamation. He was thus a combat-experienced heavy "bird gunner," ironically taking command at a time when the regiment's anti-aircraft role was approaching its end.

In those darkest days of the battle to demonstrate reserve artillery relevance, and at a time when Second World War vets no longer filled the ranks, Jim Turnbull recognized the need to get better at public affairs. In his civilian life he was part owner of the Fundy Broadcasting Corporation, which had just replaced its news director with an experienced young field reporter named Robert Lockhart. Turnbull gave Lockhart little choice but to come down to the Barrack Green Armoury and join the regiment as an officer in hopes of making him the unit's very own public affairs officer. According to regimental lore, when Lt.-Col. Sansom spotted Lockhart sporting lieutenant's pips on his shoulders and a gunner badge on his forage cap, he "exploded"! Sansom was not at all opposed to getting into the public affairs game, but he had no intention of carrying an officer who was not trained to command guns. Lockhart was immediately ordered to pack his gear and head to Gagetown to join in a basic gun numbers course with "W" Battery. His boss, Turnbull, let him go. Within a very short time, Lockhart had learned not just to crew a field gun, but to command first a troop and then a battery in the field, all while running an aggressive public affairs effort to let New Brunswickers know what their militia regiments were doing and why they mattered. The value of this effort would be proven in time.

The 3rd Regiment would need Sansom's passion and his powers of persuasion and Lockhart's media savvy, because the following summer (1962) marked the last year of anti-aircraft training for Militia gunners. The age of ICBMs made medium or heavy anti-aircraft guns designed to shoot down high-altitude bombers obsolete. Plans were thus put in train to convert the regiment to field artillery as part of a nationwide trend towards streamlining all militia artillery into a single common type. This new scheme was acceptable to Saint John's gunners, but conversion to field artillery threatened the regiment's 1959 battery numbering scheme. Their existing anti-aircraft battery numbers – 4th, 6th, and 15th – clashed with similarly numbered militia field batteries in Nova Scotia and Ontario. Again, General Bogert helped Lt.-Col. Sansom through the naming muddle and approved their second choice from the 1959 merger: numbers 104, 105, and 115. These all had NB connections, especially with southern New Brunswick.

General Bogert also helped with the regimental title. Earlier efforts to maintain "The Loyal Company" in 3rd Regiment's title had failed on the grounds that including "New Brunswick" as well was too cumbersome. But the regimental family understood that heritage, history, and community support were vital if the unit was to continue to exist in the face of further defence cuts. So they used the 1962 re-roling of the regiment to lobby for a return the Loyal Company name. General Bogert and the Army Directorate of History and Heritage in Ottawa were inclined to agree after a careful reading of Colonel Baxter's history of the regiment's first century instructed them that there had only been one "Loyal Company" of gunners in what is now Canada, and that it had become the "New Brunswick Regiment of Artillery" and then 3rd Regiment upon Confederation in 1867. Other artillery regiments certainly incorporated place names in their titles, including 7th Toronto and 5th British Columbia Regiments, although none had any claim to being the oldest continuously serving artillery regiment in Canada. If some part of the name had to drop, Bogert and the army historians argued, it should be "New Brunswick," for "The Loyal Company" was synonymous with gunners in the Loyalist province. Ottawa accepted the recommendations. In December 1962 the official title of the artillery unit in Saint John became 3rd Field Artillery Regiment (The Loyal Company), Royal Canadian Artillery. With that issue settled, New Brunswick now had two regiments of field artillery, the 3rd based in Saint John and the 12th – the venerable remnant of the old pre-1914 12th Field Brigade – based in Fredericton and composed of the 8th Battery in Moncton, 89th Battery in Woodstock, and 90th Battery in Fredericton.

In the early 1960s, Militia units in the province, still led by Second World War veterans, continued playing visible roles in the province even as their numbers shrank. Newspapers carried stories about annual inspections, church parades, and change-of-command parades. The 12th Field and 3rd Field Artillery Regiments – indeed, all Militia units in New Brunswick – sought new ways to demonstrate their relevance to the community and to fulfill their National Survival task by initiating special summer militia basic training programs for high school students. The voluntary program offered opportunities and employment for restless young men, and when it ended, many interested students enrolled in the sponsoring batteries. The program stimulated recruiting at a time when National Survival training had led many gunners to leave the service. The Royal Canadian Artillery Association complained to Ottawa that national survival training was too dull to attract and retain young gunners, and that after only two years many batteries across Canada carried members with no training on the guns. Some batteries, including those in New Brunswick, kept up some degree of gunnery skill with voluntary unpaid training over and above the approved. Both 3rd and 12th Field Regiments sought ways to make more time for "specific to corps" training on the guns on weeknights at drill halls and at the truncated summer training camps.

In those years, Fredericton served as the headquarters and central hub for 12th Field Artillery Regiment and home of 90th Battery at the Wagoneer's Lane Drill Hall. There, on 21 January 1963, detachments from 8th Battery in Moncton and 89th Battery in Woodstock travelled to join 90th Battery and Regimental Headquarters for a Change of Command parade and ceremony. Each battery brought its own band. The event attracted some attention in what was then still very much an artillery town. Great War 8th Battery veteran Albert Dodge, who had raised and commanded 105th Anti-Tank Battery out of St. George during the Second World War and then acted for a short time as second-in-command of 3rd Anti-Tank Regiment, RCA, in England, attended the ceremony as Honorary Lieutenant-Colonel. Command passed from Lt.-Col. E.A. Grant to Lt.-Col. L.G. Thompson, who had served with 4th Field Regiment in France and Germany during the Second World War and more recently as Grant's second-in-command. Since 1958, Grant had ably led 12th Field Regiment through the wave of cuts. Thompson took the regiment to Camp Gagetown that summer, where they managed a few days on the guns. To the displeasure of many, though, most of the training camp focused on "national survival" and basic recruit training. The week-long camp ended with a two-day nuclear re-entry exercise. Each battery trained and maintained emergency stores to assist the closest likely target city. For most gunners, that was the port of Saint John. However, 89th and 90th Batteries prepared to assist in the aftermath of a strike against Loring Air Base in northern Maine (just across the border from Grand Falls), a major US Air Force Strategic Air Command base, considered a key target for Soviet missiles.

Robert MacFarlane and Paul Hanson joined 89th Battery in their last high school years in the early 1960s and attended that 1963 camp. MacFarlane's father, Sergeant Marshall "Paddy" MacFarlane, had been overseas with the 89th during the war, and young Robert was eager to follow in his path. However, both young men had precious few opportunities to get near the battery's 105 mm howitzers, and spent most of their time with the "ropes and ladders" of National Survival training. MacFarlane recalled being "on top of every building in Woodstock including the fairgrounds grandstand on Island Park." To prepare for the 1963 summer re-entry exercise in Gagetown, they practised rescuing civilians trapped in smashed buildings. Back then, within the Gagetown training area, expropriated houses and ghost towns remained largely intact; they became National Survival practice grounds.

Lt.-Cols. Sansom and Thompson recognized that they needed to make more time for training on the guns if they were to keep members interested and maintain a strong enough skill base to offer any artillery value to Canada. Bob MacFarlane, Paul Hanson, and Bob Lockhart all recalled that in the mid-1960s, after the first years of experimentation with National Survival, both 3rd and 12th Field

Regiments quietly went about restoring the primacy of gunnery training and what they called "real soldiering" on their armoury floors, even though Ottawa still demanded that qualifications for promotion in artillery units remain weighted in favour of National Survival skills and knowledge.

By the 1960s, Gagetown was the major Canadian army base in eastern Canada, and increasingly the home to Militia summer training. It was therefore a difficult place to "bend" the training rules. So in the summer of 1964 the local Militia summer camps were held on the old exercise ground at Sussex, away from prying oversight by the Regular Force. The camp had fallen into disuse after 1958 when its lodger unit, the Black Watch (Royal Highland Regiment of Canada), moved to Gagetown. Nonetheless, there was ample space and enough infrastructure to support consecutive camps for units in New Brunswick's Militia Districts 5 and 6. Local newspaper reports indicate that 3rd and 12th Field Artillery Regiments both focused more on "specific to corps" artillery skills that summer than they had at the previous few summer camps in Gagetown. Instead of the familiar post-nuclear attack–re-entry into Saint John training exercise, the camp culminated in a major combined arms brigade field exercise.

Whatever New Brunswick gunners got away with at Sussex in 1964, in Ottawa plans to further shrink and reshape the Militia were already in train. Prime Minister Lester B. Pearson's new defence minister, Paul Hellyer, released his infamous White Paper in 1964. The document started the dissolution of the Canadian Army, Royal Canadian Navy, and Royal Canadian Air Force, along with their separate headquarters and administrative structures, with the goal of eventually combining them into the unified Canadian Armed Forces by 1968. Even though the resulting cost savings freed funds for much needed equipment modernization in all three services, the policy was politically explosive and eventually cost Hellyer his job. In the meantime, his 1964 White Paper also confirmed as policy that the Militia would be unsuitable for modern, come-as-you-are war in Europe. Military planners had decided there would never be time, as there had been in 1914 and 1939, for militia units to mobilize, train, and embark for overseas expeditions. By the time they did so, any conventional war would be over, or the world destroyed. Militia units would continue their internal security and National Survival tasks. The good news was that Hellyer wanted them to rethink training and organization for a new role of providing Regular Force units with trained individual reinforcements. The task left scope for ongoing "specific to corps" training on the guns, but it ended the idea that any New Brunswick battery – or regiment – would ever again deploy operationally overseas.

The 1964 White Paper and Militia reorganization also acted on the recommendations of the Commission on the Reorganization of the Canadian Army Militia, which was led by Brigadier E.R. Suttie, himself a veteran gunnery officer. Much like the Militia reform commissions before it, the Suttie Commission travelled across

Canada inspecting units and facilities in order to make hard choices about which ones should go and which should stay. In November 1964 the *Saint John Evening Times-Globe* reported that many units were to disband across Canada, but that the impact on New Brunswick would not be clear for some time yet. In fact, Ottawa planned to chop the number of Militia units from 323 to 241 nationwide. The artillery saw the largest cuts, with plans to reduce Militia gunners from thirty-six regiments and seven independent batteries to twenty-three and three respectively. Some disbanding units were earmarked for a new Supplementary Order of Battle, which in theory meant they could be reactivated should the need present itself: for most it spelled the end.

It did not take long for word to filter down from Ottawa. Within days of the *Evening Times-Globe* story, New Brunswick papers were reporting that National Defence Headquarters would be disbanding 12th Field Artillery Regiment based in Fredericton. This represented a contraction of NB gunner units from their postwar peak of four and a half regiments composed of fifteen batteries down to a single regiment of five (later three) three batteries in Saint John, where The Loyal Company had started it all in 1793. It was a balm that the storied and still popular 89th and 90th Batteries would be transferred to 3rd Field Regiment (The Loyal Company), joining Saint John's 104th, 105th, and 115th Batteries. The redoubtable old 8th Moncton Battery and 12th Field Regiment itself would be retired to the Supplementary Order of Battle. After nearly three-quarters of a century the province was in many ways back to where it began in the nineteenth century, when all artillery units served as one New Brunswick Regiment of Artillery.

But it is doubtful that simple seniority would have been enough to preserve even 3rd Field Regiment at this stage had it not been for effective lobbying by its well-connected patrons. The Royal Regiment of Canadian Artillery official historian, Lt.-Col. G.W.L. Nicholson, wrote that across the country successful militia artillery units had made it through the 1960s changes with "confidence inspired by past traditions, together with skilled leadership, determined effort, and the maintenance of the high standards that had characterized long years of efficient service." Moreover, the friendly competitive spirit that existed between New Brunswick's field and coast gunners, and between Saint John and "upriver" units, needed to be overcome. In 3rd Field Regiment, skilled leadership came from James Turnbull and the Honorary Colonel, Philip Oland. At forty-one years of age, Lt.-Col. Turnbull assumed command of the regiment from Lt.-Col. Sansom on 23 February 1965, in an elaborate change-of-command parade at the Barrack Green Armoury in Saint John. Throughout his term in command, Turnbull worked tirelessly to connect his dispersed batteries and make them feel part of the broader regimental family. He travelled to Woodstock and Fredericton to visit 89th and 90th Battery as often as possible, despite heavy commitments to his civilian career in the insurance

Battery Sergeant Major Herb Little and Lieutenant Paul Morrison pose in front of Sergeant Bob MacFarlane's gun detachment and their C-1 Howitzer at Woodstock's Island Park, 1 July 1967, before 89th Battery fired a Canadian centennial salute. (89th Battery Museum)

and broadcasting businesses. Turnbull also struggled to overcome animosity from upriver about the disbanding of 12th Field Regiment.

During that first year the several bands inherited by 3rd Field were amalgamated under the direction of newly promoted Captain Bruce Holder (Junior), who had taken over from his father the year before. And Turner made excellent use of the 1965 summer camp in Sussex. All five batteries attended, and they won the Royal Canadian Artillery Association's Mcdonald Trophy in competition with other units from Eastern Canadian Command. Just as in the previous summer, the camp concluded with a combined arms brigade exercise.

Barely a year after taking command, Turnbull faced another challenge when Ottawa reduced the regiment from five batteries to three. This time Saint John bore the brunt: 104th and 105th batteries were disbanded and folded into the 115th. This left the balance of the regiment outside the city, along the upper reaches of the Saint John River. Nonetheless, Peter Alward, son of Lt.-Col. Wallace Alward and himself a former member of the regiment and its historian in the 1960s, was content with what remained of the province's artillery after the dust settled. "Considering the many vicissitudes over the years," he wrote to Turnbull in 1967, "I do not think the Regiment could be better constituted than it is now." Alward felt that the 89th carried on the traditions of both the old days of the New Brunswick Brigade before

1874 (and earlier still, since the 89th pre-dated Confederation) and the now dormant 12th Field Regiment. The 90th also perpetuated 12th Field and had its own proud record of service from the Second World War. Alward wrote that "of course the 115th, having always remained with the 3rd provides the one remaining link with the past and the traditions of the Loyal Company." In the same letter he admitted he was sad about the loss of the old 4th and 6th Battery numbers, which were so tightly linked to the regiment's Great War achievements. He was not alone.

With plenty of support and guidance from many retired New Brunswick gunners still active within the regimental family, Lt.-Col. Turnbull organized a three-year run-up to The Loyal Company's 175th Anniversary celebrations, planned for May 1968. The party started in May 1966 in Woodstock. The 90th and 115th Batteries travelled upriver from Fredericton and Saint John to join Major R.B. Doucet's 89th Battery for a parade and dance to celebrate the entire regiment's 173rd birthday. The revered and talented Captain Bruce Holder led 3rd Field Regiment's new combined band through the occasion. The year, 1966, also coincided with the centennial of the Woodstock Battery, the only pre-Confederation field battery in the province – a great distinction in its own right. This major provincial event was the big news for that week in May.

A few months later, by a curious twist of fate, Ottawa increased funding for national-level artillery training. Summer camps were again held locally and were followed in October by a major national weekend practice and competition, held at the Royal Regiment of Canadian Artillery home station at Camp Shilo, Manitoba, and sponsored in part by the RCA Association. The 3rd Field Regiment (The Loyal Company) formed a composite battery made up of 107 officers and men, including 40 from RHQ and 115th Battery, 32 from 90th Battery, and 35 from 89th Battery. They all flew from Fredericton on the evening of 21 October, landed in Winnipeg on Saturday morning, and bused out to Shilo. They worked through gun drills and then fired on the ranges on Saturday and Sunday before loading up for the Winnipeg airport on Sunday night. Their plane brought them home to New Brunswick on Monday morning, with enough time for more than a few to report to work at their civilian jobs that day, however much exhausted. Anything was possible in the Jet Age. Clearly, much had changed for the regiment over the past 174 years. The long journey and work had paid off: the regiment placed third nationally in gun practice competition, which won them the Sir James Aitkens Challenge Cup from the RRCA. Captain Bob Lockhart of the composite battery reported extensively to the folks back home through local media.

The following May a grand 174th Birthday fête for the whole regiment was mounted in Fredericton. The festivities were clouded somewhat by the recent demise of 12th Field Regiment, but two hundred members attended the weekend event, from all three batteries including Fredericton's own 90th. The numbers suggest that despite the steady national decline in militia enrolments, Militia artillery

Lieutenant-Colonel Martin O'Leary was the last Second World War veteran commanding officer of 3rd Field Regiment in 1969. He later served as Honorary Lieutenant-Colonel. (Loyal Company Association Collection)

service was still popular in New Brunswick. The old guard of New Brunswick's artillery came out to help celebrate, including the aging but still strong George Gamblin, Ned Slader, and Albert Dodge, as well as the Honorary Colonel, Brigadier Oland. The celebration as always featured a parade, church services, and a dance at 90th Battery's Drill Hall. But the biggest show of all came off in May 1968 in Saint John to mark the 175th Birthday of The Loyal Company of Artillery. Ned Slader and Albert Dodge were on hand to represent their great generation. Three hundred members of the regiment turned out on parade, one detachment in Loyalist period uniforms, and were granted Freedom of the City by the Saint John City Council. It was a truly provincial celebration pulled off in fine style. James Turnbull, acknowledged by friends and colleagues as a master event organizer, would accept nothing less. Warm congratulatory messages flowed in from near and far, including from UNB President Colin B. Mackay, son of the Great War battery commander Colin Mackay, and from Maj.-Gen. Bruce Matthews, Commandant of the Royal Regiment of Canadian Artillery and one of Canada's most famous Second World War gunners. No message was more warmly received, however, than the one from the Captain General of the Royal Canadian Artillery, Her Majesty Queen Elizabeth, who thanked the "officers and men on their expression of continuing loyalty."

As it turned out, 1968 was an important transition year, for Militia gunners and for the entire armed forces. That February the Canadian Armed Forces Reorganization act was implemented and the three services – army, navy, and air force – were officially disbanded. New common uniforms and more militia cuts were looming. The good news was that transformation of the Militia role to a source of trained soldiers for the Regular Force facilitated the regiment's return to artillery proficiency after a decade of National Survival training. Between 30 June and 7 July, all batteries in the Maritimes not stood down by the Suttie Commission sent their officers and gunners in composite batteries to form 3rd Field Training Regiment for training in Gagetown. The summer camp training unit grouped 3rd Field Regiment's three batteries with Halifax's 1st Field and Yarmouth's 84th Independent Field Battery and sent them to the field under command of Lt.-Col. Jack de Hart from the Regular Force. The 2nd Royal Canadian Horse Artillery loaned the signals and observation post equipment to the training regiment, allowing a standard of training in gunnery not possible since the early 1950s. Bob Lockhart remembered de Hart as "a real driver He expected regular force gunnery standards and had us fire steady, all day, no pauses." Turnbull could not have been happier, and he formed an immediate professional and personal friendship with de Hart. The formal existence of 3rd Artillery Training Regiment lasted only a few years, but the practice of forming full batteries from Maritime Militia gunners equipped and trained to Regular Force standards for the busy summer training periods at CFB Gagetown continued for the rest of the century.

In 1969, Jim Turnbull was promoted full Colonel and given command of a southwestern New Brunswick Militia District, which, although in a state of flux, still loosely approximated the old District 6. As was standard practice then, his former second-in-command Major Martin T. O'Leary was promoted to Lieutenant-Colonel and took over 3rd Field in a cold January 1969 parade. O'Leary was the last Second World War veteran to command New Brunswick's Militia artillery. He had joined the infantry as a youth towards the end of the war, ended up as a replacement with the Algonquin Regiment in 1944, and was wounded in action in 1945. After coming home to Saint John he joined the postwar Militia with the short-lived New Brunswick Scottish, which maintained a company at the Saint John Garrison. Later he remustered as an anti-aircraft gunner with 23rd HAA Regiment and was commissioned as an officer in 1953. O'Leary stayed with 23rd Regiment through the 1959 amalgamation and in 1961 took command of 115th Radar Battery. He took the 115th through its conversion to 105 mm howitzers and through National Survival training in the early 1960s before becoming Turnbull's second-in-command in 1965. Like his many predecessors, O'Leary had an important civilian career as an auditor for the New Brunswick Workers Compensation Board. His Regimental Sergeant Major, Chief Warrant Officer "Stick" Holtom from Woodstock, was likewise the last Second World War veteran RSM.

In addition to taking command of what eventually became the Western New Brunswick Militia District, Colonel Turnbull also became the first RCA Association president from the Maritimes and therefore a key member of the Conference of Defence Associations. Turnbull had long been an active member, travelling each year with Brigadier Oland to Ottawa. Now it was his turn to carry on Oland's work, reminding Regular Force gunners and civilian policy-makers that the Militia artillery was still uniquely valuable to Canada. It was a crucial year for Turnbull, for in 1969, National Defence Headquarters tried again, as they had a decade earlier, to eliminate all "specific to corps" training in Militia artillery and armoured units, and focus them again entirely on National Survival (or "snakes and ladders") training. The RCA Association, the Royal Canadian Armoured Corps Association, and the CDA won that fight again, ensuring that gunners could train to be gunners first.

Unfortunately, neither Turnbull nor the CDA could stop Ottawa from cutting the Militia from 24,000 to 20,000, nor could he shield his own regiment from the impact. In 1969, Fredericton lost its long-standing gunner presence when 90th Battery was transferred to the Supplementary Order of Battle. Lt.-Col. O'Leary, 3rd Field Regiment, and the province of New Brunswick were now left with only 89th Battery in Woodstock and 115th Battery and the RHQ in Saint John. The regiment counted itself lucky, for a number of artillery units in other provinces were eliminated completely. That gunnery establishment of 1969 has remained in place ever since, making it the longest-standing unchanged order of battle for New Brunswick's artillery since the founding of the province in 1783.

The battle to keep the militia active, relevant, and funded carried on through the 1970s, with Turnbull leading the charge. In 1972 he was named an Officer of the Order of Military Merit in recognition of his lifetime of military service. In 1973 he took over as national Chairman of the Conference of Defence Associations, and a year later he retired his command of the Western New Brunswick Militia District. Of course, much like Brigadier Oland, after Turnbull took off the uniform officially he could be even more vociferous in the defence of Canada's Militia through the CDA. In those days he campaigned heavily for a Reserve Force employer support program, similar to the one in the United States, that would offer businesses incentives to allow employees time off for Militia training. Turnbull also continued to serve 3rd Field Artillery Regiment (The Loyal Company) after being named Honorary Lieutenant-Colonel in 1974. Brigadier Oland continued the fight at his side as Honorary Colonel. In those years they had especially strong support from the Saint John City Council. Bob Lockhart served as mayor of that city from 1971 until 1974 and then returned later for a second term. They proved a powerful trio.

The struggle to keep the Militia, and its training in combat roles, relevant was affected by developments in international affairs, NATO–Warsaw Pact relations, and changes in military technology. This time, however, the changes worked in the Militia's favour. By the 1970s the West and the Russians were deeply engaged in

Lieutenant-Colonel Ron Fitzpatrick and Major Ron Johnston observing a 3rd Field Regiment shoot in the 1970s. (89th Battery Museum)

strategic arms limitation talks (the "SALT talks"), and there was increasing anxiety that the credibility of the nuclear threat was eroding. In the 1960s, in response to the huge Soviet tank armies along the inner German border, NATO had reserved the right of first use of nuclear weapons to stop a massive Soviet conventional assault. Efforts had been made to scale nuclear weapons down, creating tactical nuclear weapons of small yield that might be used on Soviet mechanized forces. The gradual reintegration of West Germany into the community of democratic nations, and that country's increasingly important political and economic role in NATO, made the prospect of even a limited thermonuclear war in their country unthinkable. Yet NATO had disarmed so thoroughly that its conventional deterrence left it little except the tactical nuclear option should the Soviet army invade. It was widely understood, moreover, that "nuclear release" could not be confined to the battlefield and that even a limited use of tactical nuclear weapons could escalate quickly into a general thermonuclear war. As the use of nuclear weapons became more and more an "incredible" option, fears mounted that the Soviets might call NATO's bluff and force their way into the West by conventional means. That scenario would put NATO on the horns of a dreadful dilemma: capitulation or global Armageddon. To prevent this, NATO needed to raise the threshold of nuclear war by building up its conventional deterrence. So by the 1970s, conventional combat capability was needed again. For Canada this meant that its brigade in Europe needed to be modernized, and that the ACE mobile force slated for Norway needed new kit as well, and that both forces needed trained gunners. During the 1970s the augmentation role articulated in the 1964 White Paper – to provide trained gunners for Regular Force units on deployment – emerged as the dominant role for Militia gunners.

So in spite of a general apathy among Canadians with regard to defence matters and their own armed forces, 3rd Field Regiment stabilized and strengthened in the 1970s, first under Lt.-Col. Ed Bauer, then after 1973 under Lt.-Col. Ron Fitzpatrick. The 89th Battery's Bob MacFarlane was promoted to Chief Warrant Officer and appointed as Fitzpatrick's Regimental Sergeant Major. The pattern of selecting the commanding officer from Saint John and the RSM from Woodstock became somewhat routine and part of the solution for maintaining harmony between the 89th Battery "farm boys" and the 115th Battery "city boys."

Militia gunners in this troubled era benefited greatly from the call-outs to support the Regular Forces. In 1971, the RCA School moved from Shilo, Manitoba, to Base Gagetown to form part of the new all-arms Combat Training Centre in 1971. The school offered summer duty opportunities with "M" (Militia) Battery and/or with the Regular Force "W" Battery. Both fired all summer, supporting Regular Force courses, and in the process gave Militia gunners valuable time honing their skills on the guns in addition to meaningful summer employment.

More exciting still was the chance to travel to Europe. In the fall of 1974, 3rd Field Regiment sent thirteen (seven from Saint John and six from Woodstock) of the twenty-six Militia augmentees required in Germany for the annual NATO Fall Exercise "Reforger" (Return of Forces to Germany) rapid reinforcement drill. The regiment's Regular Force Support Staff Warrant Officer "Chappy" Wilson was already posted to Germany and Terry Sleep and Ron Wilson, from 115th Battery, were chosen to join him. By 1974 they were both well-qualified sergeants with extensive experience on "M" and "W" Batteries at Gagetown. For the Militia gunners accustomed to equipment and clothing shortages of every type, their new combat dress, boots, rucksacks, sleeping bags, and forage caps seemed like Christmas. After being briefed and properly attired, the Militia contingent flew to Ottawa and from there directly to Lahr, Germany, to reinforce 1st Regiment, Royal Canadian Horse Artillery (1RCHA).

Ron Wilson and Terry Sleep found that 1RCHA was a Regular Army unit full of sergeants and bombardiers but short on gunners. The Regular Force therefore employed all Militia augmentees in general labour duties in camp and in the field. When WO Chappy Wilson found out that Sleep and Wilson were assigned to kitchen duties, he immediately intervened, making clear to the command chain that this was an ineffective and inappropriate use of two well-qualified artillery sergeants. The episode was one in a wider campaign to demonstrate the Militia's value to the Regular Army in the decades after National Survival training had eroded

Reserve Force readiness. Soon after Wilson's intervention, Sleep and Wilson were assigned to crews of M-109 self-propelled 155 mm howitzers. Both were impressed at how the exercise took place across the German countryside, and in the same towns and villages they would be fighting to defend if the Cold War turned hot. In the end, the planeload of militia gunner augmentees proved a welcome addition to the undermanned 1RCHA, adding their enthusiasm and youthful energy to the regiment in exchange for training and experience. In important ways, the post–National Survival rebirth of the Militia artillery started with these call-outs. By the 1970s, NATO – including Canada – was striving to rebuild its conventional deterrence; war fighting, with all its attendant skills, was back in vogue. Wilson, Sleep, and others returned to Canada full of new knowledge and experiences to share in the armouries of Saint John and Woodstock. Their leadership and gunnery knowledge at the troop level helped energize the whole regiment.

Meanwhile, the RCA Association continued making individual gunnery skills and battery tactics a priority by supporting an annual competition during summer training camps. In 1973, 3rd Field Regiment tied for first place, earning the Commandant's Challenge Cup. It won first place again in the annual competitive exercise "Valley Road" in 1975, 1976, and 1977, all under the leadership of Lt.-Col. Fitzpatrick and CWO MacFarlane. Success in the Gagetown training area was all the more remarkable given the shortages the unit faced in every kind of equipment from radios to 2½-ton gun towers, combat uniforms, and even rain gear. "We did not do it for the money," Sleep recalled, "we got paid twice a year and the daily rate was poor compared to today." Ammunition was scarce, and there were no camouflage nets, no formal command posts, no helmets, and only Second World War webbing. The only modern equipment in the regiment were the FN C1 automatic rifle and C2 light machine-gun. Such was the legacy of more than a decade of militia National Survival training. Bob MacFarlane remembered that there were no ear protectors for Militia gunners: only Regular Force gunners got such luxuries. Sleep remembered how members struggled despite the shortages to maintain and improve their gunnery standards in the early 1970s. "We focused on the basics, studied the manuals and worked hard to gain experience and skill." New young gunners responded to the leadership provided by the junior NCOs who had gained experience in Germany. Sergeant Irving Wheeler from 89th Battery remembers how school let out early on Friday afternoons before planned training weekends in Woodstock so that 89th Battery members in their last year of high school could load trucks and hitch guns to make it to Gagetown in decent time.

The regiment was dealt a strange blow in the middle of this 1970s gunnery training revival when orders arrived in 1975 to strike "The Loyal Company" from its formal title. The reasons behind the decision remain vague but were possibly tied to the wave of similar moves to cut obvious ties to Britain. The Canadian government's efforts to distinguish its service personnel from their British counterparts in response to growing demands for UN peacekeeping missions may also have played a role. But undeterred as always by Ottawa's interference, the unit continued to identify itself, however unofficially, as 3rd Field Artillery Regiment (The Loyal Company), Royal Canadian Artillery.

Just as "The Loyal Company" was being sheered from the regiment's title, the first augmentees deployed on UN observer and peacekeeping missions. Sergeants Irving Wheeler and Dale Lawson of 89th Battery deployed to Egypt with the second UN Emergency Force (UNEF II) in 1974, set up to supervise the truce after the 1973 Yom Kippur War between Egypt and Israel. They formed part of the Canadian Transport Company. Not long after, following his first term as mayor of Saint John, Major Bob Lockhart deployed with the Canadian Airborne Regiment as part of the UN Force in Cyprus. The three set a new pattern for individual Militia augmentation on Regular Force operational deployments overseas. Sergeant Ron Wilson followed Wheeler and Lawson to Egypt on the next rotation in 1975. Pre-deployment training back then consisted of two weeks of refresher military training and four weeks of "on the job training" for roles in theatre, which for Lawson, Wheeler, and Wilson meant transport and logistics. All also had to hone their basic infantry skills, including requalifying on the FN C1 rifle. Attacks against Canadian headquarters and support troops during UN missions in the Congo and Cyprus served as a reminder that all soldiers deployed in the midst of war zones must be ready to protect themselves. Wilson later preached the value of basic marksmanship to all the soldiers he trained. Land mine awareness was also critically important in Egypt. Israeli and Egyptian units had laid some 23 million mines between the Suez Canal and the Sinai Desert in their recent war. Nearly all casualties suffered by UNEF II members between 1973 and 1979 were as a result of mines.

Wilson was one of eleven reservists from Atlantic Canada who leavened UNEF II in 1975. Their plane landed at Cairo's airport surrounded by multiple surface-to-air missile (SAM) batteries, which quickly put the situation in perspective. They moved from the airport by bus to the UN support base at Ismailiya (about seventy-two miles from Cairo) through rolling dunes and sweeping plains covered in rocks and scrub. Wilson's new boss was a navy Petty Officer in the Canadian Headquarters Unit, which commanded, supplied, and maintained the whole UN force, including contingents from many nations. The combination of sailors, aircrew, and Militia augmentees became a key Canadian Forces method for sustaining multiple rotations on long-term UN missions, especially among "purple" trades common to the three services. The tour passed quickly, but not without danger. Six UN soldiers died during Wilson's six-month stay, all killed by mines left on the battlefield they now observed. Although none of the dead were Canadian, it kept all hands alert to the dangers hidden in the Sinai sand. Mine awareness training had a deep impact on Wilson, who passed on the skill to others on his return from the desert.

New training and deployment opportunities overseas arrived at a time when a new generation of highly capable members were joining the regiment and proving themselves dedicated and willing to take up the torch from the now scarce Second World War veterans. Some, like Lou Cuppens, stayed long enough in the 1960s to learn the basics of soldiering before moving on. Cuppens served first in the regular artillery before transferring to the air force; he would cap his career as Deputy Commander of the North American Aerospace Defense Command (NORAD). The renewed emphasis on artillery training in the 1970s had attracted a strong new group of officers and NCOs, who drew on the experiences and energy of members returning from overseas service. The new batch of junior leaders included Kirk McGeachy, Ron Johnston, Fearon Currie, Joe Foote, David Boudreau, and Joe Linder.

They proved a dedicated lot. In early 1978, training and deployment demands in support of the Artillery School at Gagetown had drained the unit's budget by January. Lt.-Col. Fitzpatrick asked his officers and men if they would continue serving voluntarily through February and March to the end of the fiscal year. A similar situation arose in the 1980s, when once gain the officers and senior NCOs did not draw pay for a month. Times harkened back to the 1930s Depression years, when members of the regiment trained without pay out of their sense of duty to Canada. In the late 1970s and early 1980s most of the members continued to attend training nights on the armoury floor and to go on live-fire training weekends at CFB Gagetown, all in the name of maintaining and improving the regiment's skill at arms. That they did so spoke volumes about the regiment's spirit and trust in their leaders. This revival, too, resembled the 1920s, except this time it was not combat veterans driving the standard of excellence. Instead, a new generation of peacetime gunners were devoting themselves to the unit and delivering results. Their dedication to service continued through another wave of change begun in 1978, as Lt.-Col. Ron Johnston took over from Lt.-Col. Fitzpatrick. Both men helped get 3rd

A 3rd Field Artillery Regiment mess dinner, ca. 1979, after reductions and amalgamations reduced New Brunswick's four and a half artillery regiments to one. Left to right are Lieutenant-Colonel Ron Johnston, Honorary Colonel Philip Oland, Chief Warrant Officer Bob MacFarlane, and Honorary Lieutenant-Colonel James Turnbull.

(Loyal Company Association Collection)

Field Regiment ready for a new era of near constant global warfare in the aftermath of the Cold War.

In those last years of the Cold War, American planners in NATO began developing the Air–Land Battle Doctrine to revitalize conventional options for halting a Warsaw Pact invasion of Western Europe. The renewed emphasis on conventional forces encompassed reserve forces. Although increasingly the Canadian army welcomed the Militia as a pool to draw upon to fill out units, there was even talk again of full Reserve Force mobilization. Behind all of these ideas was the evident need for trained gunners. In the last years of the 1970s the Artillery School in Gagetown provided ample opportunities for 3rd Field members to serve in "M" and "W" Batteries. By then each was deploying with 125 officers and men serving six guns. While the RCHA batteries relied on the powerful M-109 155 mm self-propelled gun, which met the NATO standard, Militia gunners and those of the Artillery School batteries used the venerable C1 105 mm towed howitzers. They were directed by observers and Command Post staff using tabular firing tables, graphical firing tables, and plotter boards – all little changed since 1945. Nova Scotia batteries provided a good portion of those Gagetown crews, but 3rd Field provided large numbers as well, and the training opportunity was unsurpassed in Canada. Joe Linder, who enrolled in 89th Battery in Woodstock in 1976, spent the last years of the 1970s through to 1982 serving the Gagetown guns nearly full-time. For much of the year he and many others from 89th and 115th Batteries crewed with "M" and "W" Whiskey Batteries all week long during three seasons, and then joined their own batteries for weekend exercises and summer gun camps. Linder remembered that Militia gunner training standards were so high that Regular Force officers and NCOs could scarcely tell the difference. He ought to know, for in 1982 he transferred to the Regular Force. Linder never forgot his 89th Battery roots. Service with the Artillery School training batteries was essential for maintaining training standards in 3rd Field Regiment in the late 1970s, as defence spending on the Reserve Force had yet to catch up with the discussion about NATO conventional readiness. In 1979, 3rd Field had only enough funding and ammunition for two live-fire exercises. That year they placed second in the annual competition, finally breaking their long run of first place wins.

In 1980 an aging Brigadier Oland left his post as Honorary Colonel, turning it over to James Turnbull. Martin O'Leary stepped in as Honorary Lieutenant-Colonel. The influence of all three remained central to the well-being of the regiment. By the following summer, DND resources to support Militia training and make the new NATO Air–Land Battle conventional deterrence concept a reality slowly began to be felt. In the summer of 1981, composite 105 mm howitzer batteries from New Brunswick and Nova Scotia formed the Atlantic Artillery Regiment of three full batteries and deployed to the field with three more from Quebec. They joined with 1-52nd Artillery Regiment of the Maine National Guard, which was equipped with

The 3rd Field Artillery Regiment firing a Canadian-built C-1 105 mm from a well-dug-in pit at CFB Gagetown in the early 1980s. Plotting boards had given way to fire control computers to more quickly and accurately direct fire. (Loyal Company Association Collection)

155 mm howitzers, to form a full divisional artillery train. At the end of the summer concentration exercise at Gagetown, dubbed Atlantic Barbera, battery commanders coordinated divisional fire missions that included all nine batteries. The exercise succeeded only because it relied heavily on tractors, command posts, and other equipment borrowed from the Artillery School to replace rotting and rusty old 2½-ton prime movers and other aging machines held in the Militia vehicle parks. In the end it was all good: that year, 3rd Field placed first once again in the gunnery competition, winning the Commandant's Challenge Cup.

The 3rd Field Regiment's consistently high performance earned them a place in the Canadian army's new mobilization plan, which was rolled out in 1981. Late in the year, Lt.-Col. Johnston was informed that the regiment had been assigned the role of providing a complete light direct support battery of 105 mm howitzers to the Regular Force 5th Régiment d'artillerie légère du Canada (RALC) based in Valcartier, Quebec. Essentially, the force assembled within 3rd Field would form 5RALC's fourth battery should the nation go to Stage 3 of the new national mobilization plan. Major Gordon Moffitt, commander of 115th Battery, was slated to command the Operational Tasked (OPTASK) composite sub-unit to meet this assignment, made up of willing members from Saint John and Woodstock. Captains Kirk McGeachy, Pat Ervin, and Don Hawkes rounded out his command staff. The new task came with cutting-edge technology in the form of the HP41C Hewlett Packard Calculator. The new fire control computer replaced the old plotting boards pioneered by New Brunswick heavy and siege gunners during the Great War. The new machine electronically computed gun position and target data with remarkable speed and accuracy.

The 3rd Field Regiment's high-readiness mobilization task came with other welcome additions that benefited the whole regiment. The OP Tasked Battery was to be fully equipped to Regular Force battery standards. Everything from new towers, guns, and command post trucks to clothing began flowing into the unit in the 1980s. Unit FOOs and Command Post staff also benefited from training with the Invertron fire control video simulation trainer. In this way they could perfect and maintain their skills without expensive ammunition allotments, so that when they did head to the field to fire live, the regiment would make the rounds count. All of this had a positive impact on morale. The unit continued to perform to a routine high standard of skill-at-arms in the field, winning the Challenge Cup again in 1983.

That summer's Exercise Atlantic Barbera grew larger yet again. Most importantly, 5RALC joined the Eastern Canadian and Maine batteries, providing the Divisional Artillery Headquarters to coordinate the fire of forty-seven guns. Major Moffit's OP Tasked Battery airlifted into gun positions at the Blue Mountain gun camp at the southern end of the Gagetown training area with their C1 howitzers slung underneath Chinook helicopters. Captain Fearon Currie, serving as one of the regiment's FOOs, had the honour of directing all forty-seven guns on the first concentrated divisional "Mike" shoot that New Brunswick batteries had formed part of since the Second World War. Little more than a decade earlier, 3rd Field had had to sneak off to Sussex to do gunnery training; now they were managing the fire of a division's worth of artillery as part of a major readiness exercise to support NATO's crucial conventional deterrence. Fitzpatrick, Johnson, Moffit, and Currie – and Oland, Turnbull, and O'Leary – could take pride in that accomplishment. But as things turned out, the battle for survival was not yet won.

The revival of meaningful training in 3rd Field Regiment accompanied the usual slate of activities in support of communities. Gun detachments routinely spread across southern New Brunswick to support Remembrance Day commemorations on 11 November each year, and the regiment fired the annual twenty-one-gun Loyalist Days salute every May. Being the "senior" artillery unit in New Brunswick, 3rd Field Regiment retains the honour of firing the salute at the opening of the provincial legislature. It also fires the Royal Salute, as it did when the Prince and Princess of Wales visited Saint John in 1983 during the run-up to New Brunswick's bicentennial celebration. The following year, the regiment formed a central part of many bicentenary events, including a grand international tattoo put on in front of the Barrack Green Armoury for a week in the summer of 1984.

All the while, Lt.-Col. Johnston maintained the regiment's high standard on the gun line. Once again the unit placed first in the national competition exercise "Shellburst Valley," renamed from its former, less glamorous title "Valley Road." Training grew more sophisticated. In the mid-1980s the regiment worked far more closely coordinating fires with their infantry and armoured regiment combined arms partners; this included providing trained officers to form fire support coordination cells in all combined arms "combat teams" and directing fires for infantry mortar groups from 2nd Royal New Brunswick Regiment and Nova Scotia's Princess Louise's Fusiliers.

By 1985 the tempo of training throughout New Brunswick's militia had altered considerably to meet the new NATO requirement for high-readiness forces in Europe backed by strong reserves. Nowhere was this more apparent than in 3rd Field Regiment, now led by Lt.-Col. Gordon Moffitt. Major Fearon Currie took command of the OP Task Battery. Ammunition was plentiful, and this, along with all the new technological enhancements, enabled crews to reach ever higher levels of proficiency. The HP41C first-generation fire control computer was replaced by the MILIPAC battery fire control computer, which was powered by a cutting-edge military-pattern 386 computer chip. The machine computed meteorological data, gun position geography, battery centre grid data, observation post locations, and target data with incredible speed so that Command Post staff could issue fast and accurate fire orders to the gun line. The MILIPAC computer arrived along with new laser range finders, which further enhanced speed and accuracy to make rounds count. Confidence within the regiment grew during those years of Militia training revival. Often during training weekends in Gagetown, 3rd Field Regiment gunners and officers faced jibes from their Regular Force counterparts about being "weekend warriors" or "after-supper" soldiers. During those years they served The Loyal Company in the tradition of Cyrus Inches, King Hazen, and Neil McElvey. Patrick Ervin ran a successful law practice besides being an efficient artillery officer, and was able to bark back at Regular Force jibes: "I have a civilian career with special expertise, and I can do 80% of your job on top of that – what exactly can you do outside of the Artillery?"

In the late 1980s the regiment received a steady flow of new equipment, including gun tractors, C-7 rifles, and C-9 light machine-guns. All of this was part of the 1987 Canadian Defence White Paper plan to grow the Canadian regular and reserve ground forces to meet expanded NATO commitments. Plans included increasing the Reserve Force back to numbers not seen since the 1950s. As a start, the regiment recruited to more than 200 all ranks after hovering around 160 for some decades. They also began thinking about whether to recall batteries from the Supplementary Order of Battle or stand up new batteries in communities with recruiting potential. Some favoured restoring 90th Battery in Fredericton, but others saw merit in establishing a battery in St. Stephen in Charlotte County, where no other Militia unit then existed and recruiting competition was nil. Of course, that area had long been associated with 3rd Field Regiment, dating back to the old nineteenth-century New Brunswick Regiment of Artillery and through both world wars.

At the height of the 1980s expansion, Major Fearon Currie was promoted to Lieutenant-Colonel and took command, while Colonel Johnston took command of the Western New Brunswick Militia District. Both now played significant roles in resisting Regular Force proposals to convert 3rd Field back to an air defence role and equip it with Blowpipe shoulder-fired missile launchers. NATO's new Air–Land Battle Doctrine called for powerful air defence artillery forces to protect manoeuvring field armies in Europe. The Royal Canadian Artillery Air Defence School was re-established along with 119th Air Defence Battery, this time in Chatham, New Brunswick, alongside the fighter base. Currie and Johnston were not entirely dismissive of the idea of converting to the air defence role, but they rejected the Blowpipe option. If the move came, they wanted armoured self-propelled Air Defence Anti-Tank System (ADATS) missile launcher, which would keep the regiment on the cutting edge of artillery development – and in close association with the new school in Chatham. The ADATS system, mounted on M-113 armoured personnel carriers, had already been adopted by 127th Battery in the newly formed 4th Air Defence Regiment, RCA, deployed with the Canadian brigade in Germany; this provided it with powerful anti-air and anti-tank capability from the same missile. But the request for the expensive vehicles and missile system died, and 3rd

The 3rd Field Regiment bicentennial celebrations in 1993. Saint John Mayor Elsie Wayne inspects 115 Battery escorted by Major David Boudreau. During the ceremony, Wayne was made an honorary gunner. (Loyal Company Association Collection)

Field maintained its 105 mm guns. That enabled Currie to get back to the task of maintaining and improving the regiment's operational readiness – a task made both difficult and possible due to constant demands to provide gunners to support Gagetown's artillery school.

Not long after the Berlin Wall fell in 1989, followed closely by the collapse of the Soviet Union and the Warsaw Pact, it became apparent to governments in all NATO countries that large, standing, forward-deployed military forces in central Europe were no longer necessary. Most if not all of the expansion and re-equipping programs laid out in the 1987 Defence White Paper had been cancelled by 1991. Defence reductions began despite indications that the post–Cold War world promised to be uncertain and violent. By 1992 the Canadian government had introduced a large-scale force reduction plan. Canada's NATO brigade in Germany was disbanded, and the Regular Force Royal Regiment of Canadian Artillery was cut by half. Regular Force members retired by the hundreds. As they returned to civilian life, some found "homes" in reserve units, including 3rd Field.

The 3rd Field Regiment, along with sister units in Nova Scotia, did their best to weather this newest wave of defence cutbacks and carry on their tradition of maintaining a pool of trained gunners. In 1993 that tradition in New Brunswick reached the ripe old age of 200. With cutbacks causing concern all around, Lt.-Col.

The 3rd Field Regiment parades its colours during the Saint John 1993 Bicentennial rededication ceremonies, which culminated at the city's Stone Church. (Loyal Company Association Collection)

Currie struck a committee that included Brigadier Oland, Colonels Turnbull and O'Leary, and Hon. Lt.-Col. Neil McKelvey to plan for Loyal Company bicentennial celebrations. Those plans included inviting none other than the Captain General herself, Queen Elizabeth. While that request was rejected, they did manage to secure participation from the Master Gunner of St. James Park, General Sir Martin Farndale, as the reviewing officer for the 1993 Loyalist Days Parade, who would receive a twenty-one-gun salute. Bicentennial activities included Freedom of the City parades in Woodstock and Saint John, as well as a church parade to rededicate the colours at Saint John's Stone Church. During the latter ceremony, on behalf of the city, Mayor Elsie Wayne presented new replica colours to the regiment and in return was made an honorary gunner. Lieutenant Shawn McPherson received the Queen's Colours, guarded by Sergeant Ron Wilson. Captain Warren Smith took hold of the Regiment's Colours, guarded by Sergeant Norm Mason. Lt.-Col. Currie's slate of activities carried right through the summer, culminating on 20 August in a sunset ceremony and mini-tattoo with the special guest being Commander Land Forces Atlantic Area Brig.-Gen. A.R. MacDonald. The following day, the regiment once again exercised its Freedom of the City of Saint John. This time the reviewing officer was the Commander-in-Chief of the Canadian Armed Forces and the Governor General of Canada, His Excellency the Right Honourable Ramon J. Hnatyshyn, P.C., C.C. C.M.M. After the parade, the Governor General unveiled a plaque at the Barrack Green Armoury commemorating the regiment's achievement of "200 Years Loyal." The day ended with a ball at the Trade and Convention Centre with the Lieutenant Governor of New Brunswick as the special guest.

The celebrations offered a pleasant distraction for Currie and his colleagues from the trouble that lay ahead. The end of the Cold War seemed to have brought with it, in American theorist Francis Fukuyama's words, "the end of history." Nearly a century of strife and tension was over, Germany was unified, the countries of Eastern Europe were independent, and Russia – modernizing, democratizing, and Westernizing – was a welcome partner in the creation of a new, peaceful world. Everyone expected to garner a "peace dividend" by slashing now unnecessary defence spending. Canadians, who had spent their peace dividend years before, were no different. Ironically, the cuts came just as the latest new artillery technology reached 3rd Field, including the L2 Magellan GPS receivers. The introduction of digital GPS technology revolutionized the artillery world in the same way gridded maps had at the outbreak of the Great War. The technology enabled instant and precise gun and target location data to feed into firing solutions. This took artillery accuracy to new heights and virtually eliminated the need to bracket targets with fire and adjust until precision was reached.

Sergeant Ron Wilson's gun detachment posing in front of their C-3 105 mm howitzer at CFB Gagetown in the 1990s. (Loyal Company Association Collection)

The geodesy and geomatics revolution – propelled by New Brunswick gunners turned scientists – occurred at the same time that myriad small wars, most of them civil wars, exploded around the post–Cold War world. Even as the Canadian Army endured the force reduction plan, it went to war in a half-dozen places, from the former Yugoslavia to Somalia, Rwanda, and Cambodia, in addition to fulfilling its ongoing UN commitments in Cyprus and the Middle East. The shrinking Regular Force units could meet the demand only by relying heavily on the Reserve Force to fill out their ranks to full strength.

Thanks to the work of Oland, Turnbull, Mckelvey, and scores of others, the Militia was there when needed. Among the most noteworthy of those post–Cold War UN peace missions were the ones in the former Yugoslavia in the 1990s. They marked a shift away from Cold War classical UN peacekeeping *between* sovereign nations towards peace support or peace enforcement *within* dissolving states. These new missions required more heavily armed troops who were prepared to use deadly force not just for self-protection, but to enforce peace agreements and protect innocent civilians. Between 1992 and 2004, 3rd Field Regiment dispatched dozens of its members to fill out Regular Force units rotating into the former Yugoslav republics. The first contingent, assembled in 1993, was among the largest and joined one of the most famous Canadian army rotations in the Balkans – the one based on 2nd Battalion, Princess Patricia's Canadian Light Infantry. Together they made history around a little Croatian village named Medak.

Five trained and experienced bombardiers were selected, including Kent Campbell, Tri Pham, Jeff Godin, Ray Birt, and Brad Wilson. Campbell had been with the regiment since 1989 and by 1992 had qualified as a gun detachment second-in-command. Pham, the son of Vietnamese immigrants, had joined in 1990 straight out of Kenebecasis Valley High School. His father had served as an artillery sergeant in the South Vietnamese army. In the winter of January 1993, the five gunners travelled to Winnipeg for pre-deployment training as infanteers to help fill out rifle companies in 2nd Battalion, PPCLI. The five were parcelled out to various elements of the battlegroup to serve as riflemen, along with nearly 400 reserve soldiers from across Canada. Campbell was assigned to 4 Platoon in "Bravo" Company while Pham went to 10 Platoon in Delta Company. They trained to operate in a mechanized infantry role, riding in M-113 armoured personnel carriers armed with .50-calibre heavy machine-guns. Their PPCLI battlegroup formed part of Canada's second rotation into Croatia, relieving 3rd Battalion of the Patricias in late March 1993.

In the spring and summer of 1993 the five gunners participated in the often tense disarmament of former warring parties in northern Croatia. This required a great deal of diplomacy, as well as iron nerves as they searched vehicles for hidden weapons at checkpoints, but in the end their efforts were rewarded with acts of kindness from a grateful population. Campbell recalled many unauthorized but "culturally mandatory" sips of slivovitz, homemade plum brandy. Their task changed tremendously in September, during the last month of their tour, when the UN Force Commander ordered the Canadian battlegroup to southern Croatia to implement the Medak Agreement. This involved inserting a UN force onto a battlefield between the Croatian army and the Serb Krajina militia to impose a ceasefire and restore security for the UN protected area around the Serbian enclave. The 2PPCLI Battlegroup was chosen for the mission, reinforced by two French mechanized infantry companies.

The result of this deployment in September 1993 was the so-called Battle for the Medak Pocket, Canada's most intense engagement since Korea, followed by a grisly investigation of Croatian ethnic cleansing in the Serbian enclave. Bombardier Pham remembers rolling into the Medak sector, which resembled "a war zone from a movie, with houses blown up and burned out." Bombardier Kent Campbell understood that this new kind of peacekeeping meant they were "to protect people who were being ethnically cleansed, to get in the middle and get shot at." But unlike most traditional UN peacekeeping missions, the Canadians shot back in the Medak Pocket. Medak typified the new type of overseas deployment and was the harbinger of an uncertain future. The violent reality of the new peacekeeping remained unknown in Canada in the 1990s, although a decade afterwards, all serving and retired members of the 2PPCLI battlegroup received the Commander-in-Chief's Commendation for their service, some at an official ceremony in Winnipeg presided over by Governor General Adrienne Clarkson. Tri Pham received his in a small, poignant ceremony in Saint John with his proud father.

Back in Canada, Lt.-Col. Currie reached the end of his tenure in command in 1994 and turned the regiment over to Lt.-Col. Allison Gallop. Currie was promoted full Colonel and, as was often the case, took command of what was now the New Brunswick–Prince Edward Island Militia District. Lt.-Col. Gallop had begun his army service as a gunner in 89th Battery before undertaking a long Regular Force career with both 1RCHA and 2RCHA. He carried on the tradition of high gunnery standards set by the regiment's previous commanding officers and brought 3rd Field Regiment back to its first-place standings in Exercise Shellburst Valley competitions. That same year, Warrant Officer Tom Watters joined the regiment as part of the regular support staff.

Together Currie and Gallop, backed in the shadows by Jim Turnbull, took on the newest challenge to 3rd Field Regiment's existence – the Special Commission on Reserve Restructuring. Currie testified before the committee in 1995. The commission did away with the militia district system and replaced it with more balanced all-arms brigade groups. The 3rd Field Regiment thus became the artillery element in 37 Canadian Brigade Group, supporting units from New Brunswick and Newfoundland. The commission tied the future survival and viability of every Militia unit to its ability to recruit and retain members. Dropping below 75 percent

In the late 1990s the regiment's venerable C-1 105 mm howitzers were replaced with refurbished and modernized C-3s, seen here firing on exercise at the US Army National Guard training centre at Fort Pickett, Virginia. (Loyal Company Association Collection)

establishment would mean extinction. Thankfully, service in both 89th and 115th Batteries remained popular in the 1990s despite defence cutbacks. In fact, service became more attractive to the latest generation of recruits as new clothing and equipment flowed into the units and more soldiers deployed overseas on peace and stability missions. Realistic weekend training and annual summer concentrations as part of the Atlantic Artillery Regiment continued to draw new members and maintain standards among the large number of long-service NCOs and officers.

The mid-1990s militia reorganization included a brief return of guns to Moncton. In 1996, 4th Air Defence Artillery Regiment reactivated as a "Total Force" unit made up of regular and reserve force members. The Air Defence Artillery School moved from Chatham to Gagetown, bringing 119th Air Defence Battery (an independent unit now combining guns, ADATS, and personnel returned from Germany) with it. Regimental Headquarters and 128th Air Defence Battery stood up in Moncton by re-roling 32 Service Battalion and mixing them with air defence gunners back from Germany. The 89th Battery's Major Dave Henley became Battery Captain of 128th Battery in Moncton, having served in Germany and the Persian Gulf attached to 4th Air Defence Regiment in 1990–91. In the post–Cold War world some questioned the future of air defence artillery in Canada. Others saw 4th Air Defence Regiment as a testing ground for new technologies and capabilities, including target acquisition, surveillance, and air support coordination. Indeed, reactivating the unit in New Brunswick laid important groundwork so that gunners from the province could meet the first great conflict of their third century.

Turnbull, Currie, and the rest of the 3rd Field family won this latest battle for survival, and then almost immediately lost one of the regiment's greatest champions: in 1996, Brigadier General Philip Oland died. The entire regiment attended his funeral at Saint John's Stone Church. Captain Joe Foote commanded the detail of regimental pallbearers, and Lieutenant Shawn McPherson guarded the Brigadier's cap and medals in the procession. Oland's service had made an impact and propelled the regiment into its third century. He could rest easy, duty done.

But as Oland would have understood, the struggle to survive in a rapidly changing world was never over. As the promised of post–Cold War peace began to unravel in the 1990s, opportunities for deployments overseas as Regular Force augmentees – especially in tasks suited to the professional skills of the men and women of 3rd Field Regiment – actually increased. One of the first came in 1996, when NATO took responsibility for peace enforcement in the former Yugoslavia with combat-ready forces. Canada's mechanized battlegroup in Germany, in the process of coming home, deployed to Bosnia complete with an artillery battery of new LG1 light 105 mm howitzers. The accuracy now possible in the digital age, coupled with the high threat levels posed by former warring parties, meant that artillery still had a role to play in the new era of peace enforcement. Events over the next two decades would reinforce that trend. Indeed, if anything, increasing global instability simply highlighted the need for combat-capable, readily deployable reserves. More opportunities arose for reserve gunners and officers to take Regular Force training, including artillery survey and forward air controller (FAC) courses. The job was well suited to artillery officers trained in the art of forward observation for directing supporting fire. Captain Warren Smith and Major Joe Foote were the first two officers to qualify in the role. Foote got the chance to practise his new craft at the summer training concentration in 1997, during which he directed eight bomb- and rocket-laden CF-18 fighters on a close support strike, adding weight to the Atlantic Artillery Regiment's fire plan.

The increasingly high standard of Reserve Force training and readiness in the 1990s, made possible because of close cooperation with the Artillery School in Gagetown and greater seamlessness with the Regular Force, became a challenge in the late 1990s. As the demand for Canadian troops overseas increased, the Regular Force began routinely inviting qualified and experienced reserve members into their ranks through the new Direct Component Transfer program. In an era when the regiment's survival depended on maintaining fixed numbers of trained gunners, NCOs, and officers, the Regular Force often absorbed as many 3rd Field members as the regiment could recruit to fill the vacancies on the armoury floors. The problem was exacarbated by a clumsy new Canadian Forces recruiting system

Master Corporal Michelle Casey, on operations in Bosnia-Herzegovina, 2001. Casey was the first female member of the Regiment to deploy overseas. (Loyal Company Association Collection)

imposed on the reserve army that held up its new application files for months on end. Meanwhile, well-trained members moved into the Regular Force by the dozen. Among them was Warren Smith, who transferred into 5RALC in the mid-1990s, taking his substantial skill set and leadership experience with him. In 1999, Smith deployed to Bosnia as one of 5RALC's FOOs and FOCs supporting the Canadian all-arms battlegroup within NATO's Stabilization Force.

By then, Lt.-Col. Kirk McGeachy had assumed command from Lt.-Col. Gallop and was carrying on the effort to recruit enough new members to maintain the regiment's establishment, which had fallen by 2000 to 102 all ranks. Colonels Turnbull and McKelvey made the case loudly in Ottawa that numbers were low precisely *because* the regiment was so effective at producing trained gunners for war. And war was exactly what the Canadian army was up to, given the explosion in the number of peace and stability missions asked of it by the government since 1992. The 3rd Field Regiment did its share both by "lending" augmentees to those missions and by growing the regular Royal Regiment of Canadian Artillery to meet the demand. One of its members was Master Corporal Michelle Casey, who in 2001 became the first female member to deploy overseas on active operations. Casey served as a finance clerk, in an era when women were now being welcomed in the combat arms. Casey was as known for her dedication to efficient unit administration as she was to soldiering. Since joining the regiment in 1993, she had taken every opportunity to learn to serve the guns, including qualifying as a gun tower driver. She insisted on taking the more demanding Combat Leadership Course instead of the leadership course designed for service support trades members. Her skill-at-arms training prepared her well for Bosnia, where she did double-duty as a headquarters clerk and as part of the battle-ready camp quick reaction force.

The officers and members of 3rd Field Regiment survived the perils of the Cold War by never giving up on their mission to serve New Brunswick and Canada. The Great War veterans had kept New Brunswick's artillery spirit burning through the desperate days of the Depression; Philip Oland, James Turnbull, Reg Sansom, and a score of others were the great mentors and advocates through the dark days of the Cold War. In the end, the Cold Warriors won their fight, too. As a new era of Canadian peace and stability missions around the world began at the dawn of a new century, the Militia was ready once again to help.

Conclusion

Afghanistan: The Regiment's Latest Test, 2001–12

The outraged shock stirred around the globe by the 11 September 2001 attacks on New York and Washington was followed quickly by operations to root out the perpetrators' support. The trail led to Afghanistan. Two decades of war against the Soviets followed by bitter civil war had left Afghanistan largely under the control of fundamentalist Islamic forces known as the Taliban. Their deep religious conservatism put the Taliban at odds with modernity and with the West, whose ideas they considered heretical. The UN had already sounded the alarm about the dangers that Taliban rule posed to Afghanistan's people. When the even more extreme terrorist group known as al-Qaeda began using Afghanistan as a base from which to launch attacks on the United States, the international community led by the UN set out to destroy al-Qaeda and to restore Afghanistan to the community of nations. Little did anyone know that this would set the stage for Canada's longest overseas conflict and a new test for 3rd Field Artillery Regiment (The Loyal Company). Eventually – nearly halfway through that gruelling campaign – a steady flow of gunners began leaving the armouries of Woodstock and Saint John with rucksacks and duffels packed for war.

On 11 September 2001, 3rd Field Regiment responded as it had in previous times of crisis. Lt.-Col. McGeachy and his RSM, Chief Warrant Officer Watters,

The Salute Troop on parade in Fredericton during the Queen's visit in 2002. Honorary Colonel James Turnbull and Honorary Lieutenant-Colonel James McKelvey are flanked on the left by Battery Sergeant Major Joe Linder and on the right by Captain Shawn McPherson. (Loyal Company Association Collection)

activated the Regimental Operations Centre, and members stood-to in readiness for a call to assist. That call did not arrive for five years. At the end of that fateful September in 2001, Lt.-Col. Joe Foote took command of the regiment with new orders to secure the armouries, ensuring they were manned around the clock to protect weapons and equipment and in readiness to mobilize soldiers to respond to any crisis. Beyond that, the regiment continued supporting the Regular Force as it had since 1992 by training gunners and helping fill Canadian commitments in Bosnia and Kosovo that carried on through 2004.

At first, therefore, the war in Afghanistan had little direct impact on 3rd Field Regiment. The focus within the regiment in the early twenty-first century was, as it had been before, on battery-level operations. The ultimate aim of training was to mass 3rd Field's guns with those of 1st Field Regiment and 84th Battery from Nova Scotia at CFB Gagetown during the summer in order to fire regimental missions against a conventional enemy in a war between nation-states. The operationally tasked high-readiness battery of the last decade remained the centrepiece, even as their name changed to "Mission Battery." They also did their best to prove to the world that Canada and the Commonwealth would continue to exist, undeterred by well-publicized al-Qaeda threats against Western nations. In October 2002 the regiment proudly stood to their guns to fire the twenty-one-gun salute during the visit of Her Majesty Queen Elizabeth.

Overseas, pressure built slowly in Afghanistan. Canada sent an infantry battalion in early 2002 as part of American-led efforts to root out al-Qaeda and remove the Taliban from government. Overthrowing the Taliban, with much help from its indigenous enemies, was the easy part. Bringing peace and stability to a nation habituated to war and generally hostile to foreigners proved a long and ultimately intractable task. After the initial deployment in 2001–2, Canada deployed in and around the Kabul area from 2003–5 to help stabilize the new Afghan government and allow the difficult task of rebuilding the war-shattered nation to begin.

Members of the regiment watched the first smouldering years of nation-building and war in Afghanistan from the sidelines. By 2004 the new operational reality had begun to creep into summer training exercises, which featured threats from improvised explosive devises and suicide bombers. Close cooperation with New England National Guard units continued to feature in regimental activity, injecting multinational authenticity that mirrored NATO Alliance activity abroad. That summer, Lt.-Col. Foote and CWO Watters hatched a scheme with the New York Air National Guard to airlift the guns into firing positions hitched under American UH-60 Black Hawk helicopters. Sergeant Ron Wilson's detachment won the honour of first to fly. This would prove a common method of moving guns in Afghanistan. Realistic training and experimentation with applying modern, long-range, accurate artillery support to a dispersed counter-insurgency campaign also proved

New York Air National Guard UA 60 Black Hawk helicopter ferrying a 3rd Field Regiment C-3 105 mm howitzer on exercise in 2004. (Loyal Company Association Collection)

The first 81 mm mortar course run by the regiment in 2006 in preparation for deploying 3rd Field gunners to Afghanistan. The course officer, Captain Tom Watters, is in the front row, fourth from the left. (Loyal Company Association Collection)

worthwhile as much as it foreshadowed the future. In the near future, several exercise participants would put their air mobile artillery skills to the combat test.

In 2005 the Canadian government announced plans to expand the nation's commitment to Afghanistan. For Afghanistan to have any hope for the future, the international community would have to expand NATO's International Security and Assistance Force (ISAF) and the UN Assistance Mission. In particular, it was clear that aid and reconstruction must flow into southern Afghanistan rather than just the more populous north. It was also clear by then that the Taliban and other forces resistant to both Western presence in the country and the new government in Kabul were strongest in the south. So Canada joined the United Kingdom, the Netherlands, Romania, and the United States in what was expected to be a more dangerous mission to protect and support the government of Afghanistan as it tried to rebuild the southern provinces. Canada took on one of the toughest challenges of all – the Taliban spiritual homeland in Kandahar province.

While all this was happening in 2005, Lt.-Col. Foote passed command of 3rd Field Regiment back to Lt.-Col. McGeachy for a second term. CWO Watters commissioned from the ranks to Captain and became Regimental Operations Officer. His place was taken by Joe Linder, who had returned to the regiment in 2002 after retiring from twenty years with the Regular Force. Linder first returned to serve as Battery Sergeant Major in his hometown of Woodstock, until promoted to Chief and appointed as RSM. This leadership team readied the regiment for war.

The deployment of a Canadian battlegroup to Kandahar in 2006 to join the Canadian Provincial Reconstruction Team established there in 2005 changed everything for the Canadian army. The word "war" was no longer whispered – it was embraced – and for both the Regular Force and the Reserve Force it fundamentally changed how they trained for the next six years. The officers and senior NCOs of The Loyal Company were to be trained in full spectrum operations (FSOs) in the new contemporary operating environment (COE); they would require proficiency with new and ever evolving tactics, techniques, and procedures (TTPs), from house clearing and fighting in built-up areas to convoy and counter-IED drills.

For the first time since Korea, the Canadian army was in a shooting war, and it would require all of its resources, including the reserves, to win it. Every rotation of a new Canadian task force into Kandahar included hundreds of Reserve Force augmentees. The largest single deployment of reserve gunners from New Brunswick to go to Afghanistan – indeed the largest single deployment of gunners from NB to combat overseas since 1945 – went early, joining a battlegroup built around 2nd Battalion, Royal Canadian Regiment, from CFB Gagetown in 2007. The 2RCR battlegroup formed the core of Canada's third rotation in Kandahar, known by the less than glamorous administrative title of Task Force 1-07. Ten members of 3rd Regiment were selected, representing 10 percent of its strength at the time, including many of the most experienced soldiers. One of these, Captain Amanda Clutesi, was assigned to ISAF HQ in Kabul. Bombardier John Greer and Master Warrant Officer Kendall McLean were assigned to the Provincial Reconstruction Team (PRT), Greer as part of the headquarters staff and McLean as a Civil–Military Affairs detachment commander. Master Corporal Sean O'Dell joined the National Support Element (NSE) as a logistics technician. The remaining six members prepared, for the first time since 1945, to deploy into action as gunners. Bombardiers Bradley Blinn, David Eggert, Mark Golder, Melvin Clark, Joseph Robinson, and Gunner Joseph Hosford were all chosen to join Major Dan Bobbit's D ("Dragon") Battery of 2nd Royal Canadian Horse Artillery.

Bobbit was a professional gunner and an excellent leader who quickly earned the respect and loyalty of his militiamen. He too had begun his service as a Maritime militia officer with the West Nova Scotia Regiment. Melvin Clark remembered how Bobbit regularly walked the gun line, getting to know his gunners individually. "D" Battery was equipped with six brand-new American-built M777 155 mm howitzers capable of firing an array of ammunition types out to nearly 40,000 metres with tremendous precision. Of "medium" size at 155 mm, the howitzer was light and compact. It reversed on its wheels, which made it shorter to tow and light enough to hitch under a helicopter. The battery also deployed with 81 mm medium mortars.

Pre-deployment training for reserve force augmentees and all members of the task force had come a long way since the days of Egypt and the former Yugoslavia. The 3rd Field Regiment's contingent headed first to Aldershot, Nova Scotia, in mid-2006 for refresher training on basic soldiering and small-arms training. Some Regular Force gunners treated the augmentees with customary distance until they

Gunner Joseph Hosford in front of M777 155 mm howitzer positions at Forward Operating Base Sper'wan Ghar, Kandahar province, 2007. (Loyal Company Association Collection)

realized how well qualified most were for their jobs. "Everyone wears the same cap badge," Eggert recalled, and wore the same kit and rank badges, "because they are all artillerymen." By 2006, Eggert had been in uniform for a decade; Bombardiers Clark and Golder had been with the regiment closer to two, and MWO McLean was into his third. Indeed, the whole 3rd Field Regiment contingent possessed a great deal of artillery and general soldiering experience among them.

From Aldershot the force moved to Petawawa for mission-specific training. The six members heading over as gunners took a conversion course on the M777 and 81 mm mortars. As in 1914 and 1939, they quickly proved that basic gunnery knowledge, skills, and talent are transferrable to new weapon systems. After the conversions, the six were spread among the three two-gun troops in Dragon Battery. Clark, Robinson, and Hosford were assigned to A Troop, Blinn to C Troop, while Golder and Eggert served in B Troop, Golder with the Troop Command Post and Eggert with Sergeant Sydney Barnes's gun 15D. The crew included a number of reservists, all of whom Eggert felt proved themselves capable of serving alongside their Regular Force mates. Eggert earned a spot as a loader after demonstrating that he could muscle the heavy 155 mm rounds quickly and carefully into the breach. After mastering the gun, they had a live-fire exercise in Gagetown with mortars and howitzers in direct support of the troops they were to fight alongside: 2RCR and

Afghanistan: The Regiment's Latest Test, 2001–12 | 435

Afghanistan

Bombardier Mark Golder walking B Troop's gun line in Helmand province. Golder was one of six 3rd Field Regiment gunners who served with Major Dan Bobbit's Dragon Battery, 2nd Royal Canadian Horse Artillery, on Task Force 1-07 in Afghanistan. (Loyal Company Association Collection)

its attached squadrons of tanks, reconnaissance troops, and armoured engineers. The last stop for the whole task force – including 2RCR Battlegroup, its attached artillery, the Provincial Reconstruction Team, and the National Support and Command Elements – was the Canadian Manoeuvre Training Centre in Wainwright, Alberta, in November 2006 for collective training based on exercise scenarios designed from the latest lessons learned in Kandahar. McLean, Greer, and O'Dell joined the task force there to practise civil affairs and service support functions in an operational environment. As fate would have it, this training took place at the beginning of an early and particularly cold prairie winter. However, it did put the battlegroup through its final certifications for deployment. The gunners of Dragon Battery returned to barracks "physically fit and ready to go."

In February 2007 the Task Force began flying to Afghanistan in stages, first to Camp Mirage in Dubai and then by CC-130 Hercules into Kandahar Airfield (KAF), to relieve the 1RCR Battlegroup. The last leg into Kandahar was uneventful, until the Hercules plunged evasively down to the airfield, launching flares as part of its anti-missile protection procedure. Clark recalled the blast of intense heat off the tarmac and wondered whether Afghanistan was always going to be that hot. In fact, the Kandahar late-winter winds they were about to feel blew quite cool, especially at night. After landing in the dark of night, shuffling down the ramp and into a bullet-riddled Russian hangar, Eggert recalled thinking, "Now we're in the shit."

Dragon Battery members were briefed on the latest Taliban improvised explosive device (IED) tactics, drew night vision goggles and small-arms ammunition, and set out for their new homes out in the Arghandab River "green belt" west of Kandahar city. There they took over gun positions, observation posts, vehicles, and other equipment from "E" Battery, 2RCHA. A Troop relieved its counterpart at a small forward operating base at Sperwan Ghar in the heart of Panjwayi district. Eggert and B Troop deployed to the larger FOB Ma'Sum Ghar on the northern edge of Panjwayi, overlooking the Arghandab River; from there, they could reach deep into Zharey district.

For the next six months, Dragon Battery delivered supporting artillery fire in a very different kind of war. The enemy operated hidden among the Afghan population that Canada's Task Force Kandahar had come to protect and help. Harming innocent Afghans or damaging their property was out of the question, especially since the populations of Zharey and Panjwayi districts along the fertile Arghandab River had just returned after heavy fighting there forced them to flee in the fall of 2006. "Our job," according to Eggert, "was to provide fire support for the combat

Bombardier Melvin Clark (left) ready to board a Danish Chinook in southern Afghanistan, 2007.
(Loyal Company Association Collection)

operations taking place in our vicinity." But those actions were being fought against small enemy detachments practising classic guerilla warfare tactics, with ambushes and IEDs. To fight this kind of enemy, Dragon Battery often lit the night sky with illumination rounds to reveal Taliban cells planting IEDs. The guns also ranged in on Taliban fighters running in the open after being driven from villages by Canadian troops. Major Bobbit insisted that his gunners always apply their fire with the utmost care and precision when operating in the densely populated agricultural heartland of Kandahar. Circumstances were very different in more sparsely populated and Taliban-dominated regions farther north and west of the Arghandab green belt.

In April 2007, NATO Regional Command South ordered the Canadian Task Force to detach Dragon Battery's B Troop to the British FOB Robinson near Lashkar Ghar in Helmand province. From there they were to reinforce British and American troops taking the offensive in the heart of the Taliban and drug gang dominated opium fields in Helmand. Getting there meant hitching guns underneath Royal Air Force Chinook helicopters. The gun crew did their own rigging and harnessing, a task Eggert was no stranger to. The war in Helmand was different: after landing, B Troop's two "Triple 7s" fired steadily for two weeks. At times, in response to desperate calls for support from British and American FOOs, they unleashed barrages that Eggert thought might "rip your ears out." Rounds left both of B Troop's barrels at a rate not seen by Canadian gunners since Korea. Taliban mortar crews tried unsuccessfully to hit back.

For the most part, the new M777s performed well, but a century of technological advances in gunnery could not eliminate all inherent risks posed by handling high-explosive shells and propellant. On 13 April 2007 a primer casing blew up on Bombardier Eggert's gun, setting off others and rupturing the primer magazine. Sergeant Sydney Barnes and two other members of the crew were wounded or burned by the flash. The whole detachment was stunned by the blast. A medic went to work on Barnes's injuries until the radio crackled with another call for fire from a British unit locked in a firefight. Undaunted by their injuries, the whole crew followed Barnes to the second gun and prepared it to fire. Major Bobbitt described Barnes's "singular focus on his mission [as] in the finest traditions of the Artillery Corp and of the Canadian Forces."

Not long after deploying to Helmand Province, B Troop learned that call sign 22 Bravo, a LAV III armoured vehicle carrying a Hotel Company section, struck a massive IED. Six infantrymen were killed and two severely wounded on the terrible Easter Sunday of 2007. The entire task force felt the blow. However, news from Helmand that same week that B Troop shells inflicted heavy casualties on the Taliban near FOB Robinson steeled Canadian resolve to carry on the mission. Bombardier Golder recalls how "we were all hurting from the loss of 22B. When word came back to us that our effective fire on the enemy had raised the spirit of the entire

An M777 or "Triple 7" 155 mm howitzer from Golder and Eggert's B Troop firing from Forward Operating Base Robinson in support of hard pressed British and US troops, April 2007.
(Loyal Company Association Collection)

battlegroup, it gave us a sense of worth. We were in the fight and we were making a difference."

While B Troop supported British and American troops in Helmand, A Troop, including Bombardiers Clark, Robinson, and Gunner Hosford, drove to western Kandahar province and built a fire base in the open desert in Maywand district. From there, their guns supported 2RCR's mechanized combat team, comprised of H Company in LAV-3 armoured fighting vehicles and the tanks of A Squadron, Lord Strathcona's Horse. A Troop spent almost forty-two days in their remote location, where supplies were scarce. They lacked water in particular, and many times there was no water for washing or shaving. The day heat was nearly 60 degrees Celsius, and it was possible to cook rations in ammo boxes left in the sun. Nonetheless, they helped protect H Company combat team from nighttime Taliban rocket attacks and answered all their calls for fire.

Eggert recalled that after fighting season opened in May 2007, "everyone wanted the Canadian guns." A Troop eventually relieved B Troop supporting the British and Americans in Helmand, which rejoined C Troop in Kandahar province. In fact, all three troops were ferried around southern Afghanistan rigged underneath

British or Dutch Chinooks, and even American Black Hawks. The 3rd Field Regiment's personnel travelled to each new firing position "loaded for bear" with personal weapons and ammunition. They almost always operated at a distance from the infantry and armoured troops they supported, so they needed to stand ready to defend their own gun positions with infantry weapons. They delivered every kind of artillery fire mission in every kind of terrain, from craggy mountains and desert flats to the lush green farm country of the Arghandab Valley. They helped prove to all that modern artillery had an important role to play in counter-insurgency operations.

The 3rd Field Regiment's other contribution to TF1-07 was Bombardier J. Greer and WO Kendall McLean, who deployed with the provincial reconstruction team (PRT) based at Camp Nathan Smith in Kandahar city. Greer worked on the headquarters staff supporting the PRT commander, Lt.-Col. Rob Chamberlain, himself a gunner and former commanding officer of 1RCHA. WO McLean led one of the PRT's civil–military affairs (CIMIC) detachments, which had been assigned to reach out to Kandahar's communities to help restore basic infrastructure, including roads, wells, and the traditional but highly effective local irrigation network. The aim in 2007 was to help rebuild Kandahar's economy: local community leaders would be mobilized to help with project planning, and thousands of unemployed Kandaharis would do the work; all of this would help restore governance and civil society. McLean, an experienced soldier from a farming background along the Saint John River, was an ideal choice to work with the locals. He roamed around the province in an RG-31 mine-proofed wheeled armoured vehicle, along with a force protection detachment of Royal 22e Regiment infanteers. McLean's detachment, seldom more than eight soldiers, lived mostly out in the FOBs, sharing the dangers there from Taliban rocket and mortar attacks, and sharing routine camp security duties.

By the summer of 2007, Task Force 1-07 members had much to be proud of. They had taken the fight to Taliban strongholds and made great strides in helping Kandaharis rebuild their war-torn province. But that effort was really just getting started. It would take many more years to make Kandahar a functioning part of a viable Afghan nation, all while criminal gangs, the Taliban, and corrupt officials challenged Afghan government authority. Nonetheless, Canadian soldiers carried out orders from Ottawa to do their best to protect and rebuild Kandahar. When Task Force 1-07's tour in Kandahar ended, they turned responsibility over to Task Force 3-07 based on a battlegroup formed from units of 5e Groupe-brigade mécanisé du Canada from CFB Valcartier. X Battery from 5e Régiment d'artillerie légère du Canada (5RALC) provided the artillery component commanded by former New Brunswick gunner Major Warren Smith.

Like their predecessors in 1919 and 1945, the new group of 3rd Field Regiment wartime veterans brought experience and knowledge back to their armouries in

A 3rd Field Regiment funeral party loads Honorary Colonel James Turnbull's casket aboard a 25-pounder for his last ride with his beloved unit, 2010. (Loyal Company Association Collection)

the fall of 2007, helping to inspire a new generation of gunners. The following year, newly promoted Lt.-Col. Shawn McPherson took over command from the long-serving Kirk McGeachy. Only two months later, McGeachy was killed in a tragic accident and laid to rest with full military honours. It was a tough way for McPherson to commence his tenure in command; nonetheless, he set out with his RSM, CWO Joe Jordan, to maintain the unit's high gunnery standard, which in itself would help ready the next 3rd Field augmentees to head off to Afghanistan. For the next four years, from 2008 through 2011, 3rd Field Regiment formed a close working relationship with the Gagetown-based 4th Air Defence Regiment (now a fully Regular Force unit), which undertook responsibility for providing much of the unmanned aerial vehicle (UAV) capability to Canada's task forces in Kandahar. The 3rd Field Regiment's proximity to 4th Air Defence Regiment's home made the partnership practical. The Canadian UAV Squadron in Kandahar was mix of air force and army artillery personnel similar to the army cooperation and artillery observation squadrons of past wars. They operated camera-equipped flying machines of varying shapes, sizes, and types, all used for observation, reconnaissance, evidence gathering, surveillance, and target acquisition – tasks quite familiar in the gunner world. The Loyal Company deployed at least one soldier on every rotation of 4th AD Regiment's UAV Squadron until the cessation of combat operations in 2011.

The first batch of 3rd Field Regiment members to join the UAV Squadron included Master Bombardier Greg Jones and Bombardiers Jeff Andrews and Mike

Burns. They began pre-deployment training with 4th Air Defence Regiment in 2008, readying for service with Task Force 1-09. Their training included mastering the newer gunner arts of launching, flying, retrieving, and maintaining unmanned aerial vehicles. Their Kandahar deployment in March 2009 followed the 2008 Independent Panel on Canada's Future Role in Afghanistan, chaired by John Manley. The Manley Report recommended significant military reinforcements and aid resources for Task Force Kandahar from both Canada and other NATO countries. Task Force 1-09 benefited from those reinforcements; for example, it was provided with a much larger UAV Squadron equipped with more Boeing ScanEagles and ground control stations, subdivided into troops and four-gunner sections that could deploy into the field at FOBs in the far corners of Kandahar province. Bombardiers Andrews and Jones witnessed the signs of NATO reinforcement when their UAV Section deployed to the new US Army FOB Ramrod in Maywand district, thus establishing a substantial standing NATO presence along the vital Highway 1 between Kandahar and Helmand. Other members of 3rd Field Regiment followed them on subsequent UAV Squadron rotations, including Bombardier Melvin Clark, who went back for his second tour in Kandahar with Task Force 1-10.

By the end of the first decade of the new millennium, 3rd Field Regiment had settled into a steady pace of providing skilled volunteers for Canada's long war in Afghanistan. The wartime flow of resources back in Canada helped make regimental life back in New Brunswick vibrant even as Canadians seemed to lose interest and patience with the campaign in Afghanistan. In 2009 the Loyal Company made history by appointing Major Chantal Bérubé to command 115th Battery, making her the regiment's first female battery commander. In 2010 the regiment joined the city of Saint John in its 225th Anniversary celebrations. That year, John Irving became the new Honorary Colonel, carrying on the tradition of his predecessors as the regiment's champion and voice in the community and in the halls of power in Ottawa. Irving quickly became a force for acknowledging the regiment's historical contribution to New Brunswick and the nation. He had joined the regimental family at a critical time. Almost as if he knew his regiment was in good hands, Colonel James Turnbull took his last breaths in October 2010. He was buried with military honours, his flag-drapped coffin delivered to his church on a 25-pounder gun carriage, his band playing and his gunners marching behind, a fitting and emotional goodbye to a great "Loyal Gunner." McPherson and Irving, backed by a vibrant Loyal Company Association, including dedicated former gunners and officers like Al Gallop, Fearon Currie, and Joe Foote, carried on Philip Oland and James Turnbull's work.

The decision to make 2012 the final year to be included in this book was based upon the extremely significant events that took place within the regiment that year. Just prior to these, the regiment held a change of command between Lt.-Col. Shawn McPherson and the incoming CO Lt.-Col. Stephen Strachan, who came to the regiment having served thirty years in the regular force and nine with the reserves. During 2012, the regiment exchanged its colours by retiring the C3 105 mm howitzer and taking delivery of the LG1 105 mm Howitzer. It also introduced the 81 mm mortar as a secondary indirect fire system. The year saw the retirement of the MLVW gun tractor after twenty-six years of service; it was replaced by the MSVS gun tractor.

The regiment also received a War of 1812 Banner acknowledging the participation of 1st and 2nd Battalions of the Charlotte County Regiment, which deployed troops in Saint Andrews, New Brunswick, to counter potential American coastal raids. The most significant event of the year, however, came in October, when, thanks to the efforts of Honorary Colonel Irving and the regiment's many supporters in the community, including all levels of government, the Minister of National Defence restored "(Loyal Company)" to the regiment's official name. By restoring its name, the federal government officially acknowledged the clear link between 3rd Field Regiment and the original Loyal Company formed in 1793, laying to rest any arguments about the pedigree of the oldest continuously serving artillery regiment in Canada.

From the first rumble of guns in South Africa in 1899 through two world wars and the threat from a third, through to the most recent test in South Asia, 3rd Field Regiment always answered the nation's call to defend Canadians and their allies. Through over 200 years of service at home and overseas, the value of maintaining effective reserve units to reinforce and grow the Canadian army regular artillery in times of emergency has been proven time and again. The most recent overseas contribution from 3rd Field Artillery Regiment (The Loyal Company) proves that. In 2013, five seasoned gunners deployed for the last phase of Canada's involvement in Afghanistan, dubbed Operation Attention. The five included MWO McLean and Master Bombardier Burns returning for their second tours. It was their gunnery skill, gifts for teaching, and experience serving with the Royal Canadian Artillery School that mattered most this time, for they were deploying as part of Canada's mission supporting the Afghan National Army (ANA) training system. Their job was not to teach Afghan gunners themselves, but to coach Afghanistan's Artillery School instructors so that the new fledgling army could take control of and grow its own future.

Appendix 1

Commanding Officers of The Loyal Company, 1793–2016

Captain John Colville, 1793–1808
Captain Andrew Cruikshank, 1808–15
Captain James Potter, 1815–21
Captain David Waterbury, 1821–22
Captain John Waterbury, 1822–26
Captain Thomas Barlow, 1826–38
Lt.-Col. Richard Hayne, 1838–65
Lt.-Col. Stephen Kent Foster, 1865–83
BrLt.-Col. Martin Hunter Peters, 1883–85
Lt.-Col. John Russell Armstrong, VD, 1885–97
Lt.-Col. George West Jones, VD, 1897–1902
Lt.-Col. Walter Woodworm White, VD, 1902–7
Lt.-Col. John Babington McCaulay Baxter, VD, 1907–12
Lt.-Col. Beverley Robinson Armstrong, VD, 1912–20
Lt.-Col. William Henry Harrison, DSO, 1920–22
Lt.-Col. Norman P. McLeod, MC, VD, ADC, 1922–26
Lt.-Col. George Alexander Gamblin, MC, VD, 1926–30
Lt.-Col. Edward Merritt Slader, VD, 1930–34

Lt.-Col. Henry F. Morrisey, ED, ADC, 1934–38
Lt.-Col. James Gilbert Hart, OBE, ED, 1938–40
Lt.-Col. William Wallace Alward, 1940–41
Lt.-Col. Ken J. Partington, ED, 1941–42
Lt.-Col. William Wallace Alward, 1942–48
Lt.-Col. Phillip Warburton Oland, 1948–52
Lt.-Col. David B. Armstrong, ED, 1952–56
Lt.-Col. William N. Anderson, CD, 1956–59
Lt.-Col. Bernard L. McCarthy, CD, 1959–61
Lt.-Col. Reginald F. Sanson, CD, 1961–65
Lt.-Col. James H. Turnbull, OMM, CSU, CD, 1965–68
Lt.-Col. Martin T. O'Leary, CD, 1969
Lt.-Col. Martin N. Parker, CD, 1970–71
Lt.-Col. Ed A. Bauer, CD, 1971–73
Lt.-Col. Ronald M. Fitzpatrick, CD, 1973–78
Lt.-Col. Ronald W. Johnston, CD, 1978–83
Lt.-Col. Gordon L. Moffitt, CD, 1984–88
Lt.-Col. Fearon Currie, CD, 1988–94
Lt.-Col. Al Gallop, CD, 1994–98
Lt.-Col. D. Kirk McGeachy, CD, 1998–2001
Lt.-Col. Joe Foote, CD, 2001–5
Lt.-Col. D. Kirk McGeachy, CD, 2005–8
Lt.-Col. Shawn I. McPherson, CD, 2008–11
Lt.-Col. Stephen B. Strachan, CD, 2011–15
Major Louigi Andreola, CD, 2015–

Appendix 2

Regimental Sergeants Major, 1866–2016

Sgt. Major Samuel Hughes, 1866–1900
Sgt. Major John C. Edwards, 1900–08
WO1 Horace Brown, 1908–10
WO1 George Day, 1910–12
WO1 Edward M. Slader, 1912–14
WO1 Robert McMillan, 1919–23
WO1 Phillip Griffin, 1923–33
WO1 James Stackhouse, 1933–38
WO1 Frederick B. Pike, 1938–41
WO1 Robert Milligan, 1941–45
WO1 Thomas Keleher, 1946–49
WO1 Garfield Noftell, 1949–53
WO1 Thomas Keleher, 1953–57
WO1 Raymond Campbell, 1957–58
WO1 Douglas Glasier, 1958–61
WO1 Fred McCarthy, 1961–63
WO1 Leo Donovan, 1963–67
WO1 Fergus Price, 1967–71
Regt. Sgt. Major, J.A.R.P. McDonald, CD, 1972–73
CWO Robert McFarland, CD, 1974–84

CWO Paul P. Claessen, CD, 1984–89
CWO Glen L. McLean, CD, 1989–91
CWO Larry B. Samms, CD, 1991–93
CWO Paul P. Claessen, CD, 1993–94
CWO D. Rod Croucher, CD, 1994–96
CWO Kenneth J. Norman, CD, 1996–99
CWO Frank Gimple, CD, 1999–2000
CWO Tom N. Watters, CD, 2000–5
CWO Joe Linder, CD, 2005–7
CWO Joe Jordan, MMM, CD, 2007–11
CWO Rene Parker, CD, 2011–13
CWO Mike Louvelle, CD, 2013–16
CWO Kendall McLean, CD, 2016–

Note on Sources

The book has been compiled from myriad sources, and it is not possible to list them all here. They include the obvious war diaries and official reports, published histories – official, regimental, and otherwise – and memoirs and monographs pertinent to the subject. All of the principal authors drew from their extensive holdings of documents collected for other projects, and Windsor, Sarty, and Milner have many times walked the landscapes described in the book (except for South Africa). New collections of materials not yet archived in any public institution were also found and used extensively, especially the Turnbull Papers. Amidst the mountain of material the latter contain are draft notes for two chapters (pre-1914 and the interwar years) of an unpublished history prepared by Peter Alward in the 1960s.

The 3rd Field Regiment (The Loyal Company) was fully engaged in this project from the outset. Lt.-Col Shawn McPherson conducted an extensive interview project for the final two chapters, and the Loyal Company Association, with its many retired officers and NCOs, contributed to the writing at every stage.

The standard official histories were consulted extensively for this book, including:

G.W.L. Nicholson, *The Gunners of Canada: The History of the Royal Regiment of Canadian Artillery*, 2 vols. (Toronto: McClelland and Stewart, 1967, 1972).

G.W.L. Nicholson, *Official History of the Canadian Army in the Second World War*, vol. 2: *The Canadians in Italy* (Ottawa: Queen's Printer, 1956).

G.W.L. Nicholson, *Official History of the Canadian Army in the First World War: Canadian Expeditionary Force 1914–1919* (Ottawa: Queen's Printer, 1962).

C.P. Stacey, *Official History of the Canadian Army in the Second World War*, vol. 3: *The Victory Campaign* (Ottawa: Queen's Printer, 1960).

C.P. Stacey, *Official History of the Canadian Army in the Second World War*, vol. 1: *The Army in Canada, Britain and the Pacific* (Ottawa: Queen's Printer, 1955).

Chapter 1

Library and Archives Canada (LAC), Annual Reports of the Department of Militia and Defence 1895–1914.

Public Archives of New Brunswick (PANB), James Turnbull Papers, 3rd Field Regiment Collection: Draft notes on the history of 3rd NB Regiment of Artillery, 1893–1914.

E.M. Slader, *From the Victorian Era to the Space Age* (Saint John: NB Historical Society, 1973).

Chapters 2–5 (Defence of Saint John during the war)

Home defence Militia units did not keep war diaries during the Great War until late 1917. Fortunately, 3rd Regiment's collection at the New Brunswick Museum includes many personnel and other administrative files for the Composite Battery that garrisoned Partridge Island in 1914–18. The monthly pay lists, along with the daily orders for the Composite Battery for the entire war period, are available at Library and Archives Canada (LAC), RG 9 IIF9, boxes 928–30 and 1103–4, and these have fleshed out gaps in the NBM collection. For the latter part of the war, the war diaries for Military District 7, November 1917–19 (RG 9 IIID3, boxes 5062–63), and for 9th Siege Depot Battery, 1916–18 (RG 9 IIID3, box 5064), provided much essential information. A fundamental source is the main National Defence Headquarters file for the defence scheme for Saint John, which survives for the period 1918–40 and includes excellent notes for the period before 1918 (file HQS 12, pts. 4–7, RG 24, boxes 1234, 2269–70).

Chapters 2–5 (the Western Front)

LAC RG 9 war diaries including: 1st Canadian Heavy Battery; 2nd Canadian Field Brigade; 3rd Canadian Field Brigade; 1st Canadian Divisional Ammunition Column; 2nd Canadian Divisional Ammunition Column; 1st Canadian Divisional Artillery; Headquarters, Canadian Corps Heavy Artillery; 2nd Brigade, Canadian Garrison Artillery; 3rd Brigade, Canadian Garrison Artillery; 4th Canadian Siege Battery; 6th Canadian Siege Battery; 8th Canadian Siege Battery; 9th Canadian Siege Battery.

8th Hussars Museum, Sussex, NB: 8th Canadian Hussars Museum files; Great War Diary of Lt.-Col. Keltie Kennedy

PANB James Turnbull Papers, 3rd Field Regiment Collection: 4th Overseas Siege Battery in the Great War.

Newspapers

Moncton Times; *Saint John Standard*; *Saint John Globe*; *Fredericton Daily Gleaner*

Published Works

E.M. Slader, *From the Victorian Era to the Space Age* (Fredericton: New Brunswick Historical Society, 1973).

F.G. Green, *A History of the 6th Canadian Siege Battery, France Belgium, and Germany: 1916–1919* (Sackville: 6th Siege Battery Association, 1968).

Chapter 6

PANB James Turnbull Papers, 3rd Field Regiment Collection: Draft notes on the history of 3rd NB Regiment of Artillery, 1919–39; 3rd Field Regiment Collection, Orders books, Correspondence; Royal Canadian Artillery Association Annual Reports.

Published Works

E.M. Slader, *From the Victorian Era to the Space Age* (Saint John, NB: New Brunswick Historical Society, 1973).

F.G. Green, *A History of the 6th Canadian Siege Battery, France Belgium, and Germany: 1916–1919* (Sackville, NB: 6th Siege Battery Association, 1968).

G.W.L. Nicholson, *The Gunners of Canada: The History of the Royal Regiment of Canadian Artillery*, vol. 1: *1534–1919* (Toronto: McClelland & Stewart, 1967).

Chapter 7

LAC RG 24 includes war diaries for all of the units that garrisoned Saint John, and the Headquarters, Defended Port of Saint John for 1940–45, with material from army administrative files and reports in RG 24 at LAC and in the Army Kardex collection at the Directorate of History and Heritage. RG 24 also contains the Reports of Proceedings of HMCS *Captor II*, the RCN base in Saint John during the war.

This chapter also drew on research carried out for Marc Milner and Glenn Leonard, *New Brunswick and the Navy: Four Hundred Years,* New Brunswick Military Heritage Project, vol. 16 (Fredericton: Goose Lane, 2010); Roger Sarty and Doug Knight, *Saint John Fortifications, 1630–1956*, New Brunswick Military Heritage Project, vol. 1 (Fredericton: Goose Lane, 2003); and Roger Sarty, *The Maritime Defence of Canada* (Toronto: Canadian Institute of Strategic Studies, 1996).

Chapters 8–10

LAC War Diaries: 8th Field Battery; 28th Field Battery; 89th Light Anti-Aircraft Battery; 90th Anti-Tank Battery; 103rd Anti-Tank Battery; 104th Anti-Tank Battery; 105th Anti-Tank Battery; 1st Anti-Tank Regiment; 1st Light Anti-Aircraft Regiment; 2nd Canadian Field Regiment; 3rd Anti-Tank Regiment; 5th Field Regiment; 6th Anti-Tank Regiment; 7th Anti-Tank Regiment; 1st Canadian Division Headquarters; 2nd Canadian Infantry Brigade; 3rd Canadian Division Headquarters.

Canadian Forces Directorate of History and Heritage

1st Anti-Tank Regiment, Royal Canadian Artillery; 3rd Anti-Tank Regiment, RCA [Major R.H. Barker], 3rd Anti-Tank Regiment Association, n/d.

"History of the 3rd Anti-Tank Regiment, RCA, October 1st 1940 – May 5th 1945" [Major R.H. Barker]. "History of 5 Cdn Fd Regt, R.C.A. From 1 Sep 39 to 31 Jul 45 World War II," n.d.

Public Archives of New Brunswick, 3rd Field Regiment Collection

"History of 105th ATK Bty, RCA," by Major Walter Love, Walter Love Papers.

A.A. Dodge diary, Walter Love Papers.

Newspapers

St. Croix Courier; *Campbellton Graphic*; *Moncton Times*; *Saint John Standard*; *Saint John Globe*; *Fredericton Daily Gleaner*

Interviews

Ken Newell, 3rd Anti-Tank Regiment

Published Work

6th CDN Anti-Tank Regiment, Royal Canadian Artillery, Regimental History (n.p., n.d.; copy at University of Toronto Library).

Gordon Brown, DSO, MID, NBL, and Terry Copp, *Look to Your Front … Regina Rifles, a Regiment at War: 1944–45* (Waterloo, ON: Laurier Centre for Military, Strategic and Disarmament Studies, 2001).

Terry Copp, *The Brigade* (Mechanicsburg: Stackpole Books, 2007).

———. *Cinderella Army: The Canadians in Northwest Europe, 1944–45* (Toronto: University of Toronto Press, 2006).

———. *Fields of Fire: The Canadians in Normandy*, 2nd ed. (Toronto: University of Toronto Press, 2014).

D.W. Falconer, *Battery Flashes of W.W.II* ([Victoria, BC]: privately published, 1985).

Donald Graves, *South Albertas: A Canadian Regiment at War* (Montreal: Robin Brass Studio, 1998).

Marc Milner, *Stopping the Panzers: The Untold Story of D-Day* (Lawrence: University Press of Kansas, 2014).

G.W.L. Nicholson, *The Gunners of Canada*, vol. 2: *1919–1967* (Toronto: McClelland & Stewart, 1972).

Brian Reid, *Named by the Enemy: A History of the Royal Winnipeg Rifles* (Montreal: Robin Brass Studio, 2010).

Chapters 11 and Conclusion

PANB, 3rd Field Regiment Collection, James Turnbull Papers, correspondence files.

Royal Canadian Artillery Association Annual Reports, 1946–2008.

Interviews with former members of the regiment

Tim Bishop, David Boudreau, Michelle Casey, Melvin Clark, Donald Cox, Lou Cuppens, Fearon Currie, David Eggert, Joseph Foote, Allison Gallop, Mark Golder, Paul Hansen, Greg Jones, Joseph Linder, Norman Mason, Carrie McCollum, Robert McFarlane, Kendall McLean, Wayne McLean, Shawn McPherson, Elaine Osborne, Tri Pham, Terry Sleep, Tom Watters, and Ronald Wilson.

Newspapers

Moncton Times; *Saint John Telegraph-Journal*; *Fredericton Daily Gleaner*

Published Works

Lee Windsor, David Charters, and J. Brent Wilson, *Kandahar Tour: Turning Point of Canada's Afghan Mission* (Toronto: John Wiley, 2008).

Acknowledgements

Books are usually the work of many hands, and this one is no exception. It has been years in the making. HCol. James Turnbull and HLCol. Neil McKelvey of 3rd Field Regiment (The Loyal Company) worked tirelessly on the concept of a book marking the second hundred years of the Regiment and its soldiers. The vision is now complete. Although they are no longer with us, the Loyal Company Association along with 3rd Field Artillery Regiment RCA (The Loyal Company) would like to say: "Your work is done," "End of Mission," "Stand-easy."

Credit needs to be given to the late Peter Alward, a son of Lt.-Col. W.W. Alward, who compiled some excellent early draft chapters, which we found in Colonel Jim Turnbull's papers. Peter, and his brother John Alward of Halifax (former commanding officer of the 1st [Halifax] Field Regiment, RCA) guided Roger Sarty when he began his studies of coast artillery in the late 1960s and early 1970s. Roger is also indebted to the important research undertaken by former Parks Canada historian Ron MacDonald on all aspects of Saint John's coastal fortifications, which was for development of the Carleton Tower National Historic Site.

Thanks to Tom McLaughlin and Borden McClellan at the 8th Hussars Museum in Sussex for helping to access Keltie Kennedy's invaluable diary. To Lt.-Col. Robert Lockhart for gathering photographs and providing insight on the Cold War years. Special thanks to James Turnbull and Derek Oland, who helped assemble documents and photographs related to both their fathers; to Sharon Macdonald of New Glasgow, NS, for sharing Major Walter Love's wonderful document collection on 105th Battery; to Ken Newell of Springfield, NB, for sharing his memories of 3rd Anti-Tank Regiment, his maps of the unit's movements, and his copy of the regimental history; to Elspeth Leger of Moncton, who shared her information on

104th Battery; and to Catherine Reid of the Newcastle Public Library, who kindly went home and brought to us her father's wonderful photo albums of 28th Battery prior to 1939.

Many of our UNB undergraduate and graduate students helped research this project at archives across New Brunswick and in Ottawa. In particular we must thank Nancy Carvell, Matthew Douglass, Thomas Gordon, Thomas Littlewood, Alex Fitzgerald-Black, Patrick Proctor, and Joseph Zeller. The Gregg Centre's Dr. Cindy Brown both coordinated student research efforts and joined in the process herself. Bobbi Milner trolled NB newspapers to help fill in gaps in our knowledge. During overseas study tours over the past three summers, dozens of our students, too many to name, have helped investigate New Brunswick gunner battlefields and test hypotheses on the ground in Sicily, Italy, France, Belgium, Germany, and the Netherlands. We thank them, and many other NB students, including those of Mark Perry at Hampton and recently KV high schools, for their work on the biographies of soldiers killed on active service. We have relied extensively on their work.

Having excellent research support virtually on call in Ottawa was invaluable. Sarah Cozzi located and copied more than 1,000 pages of material at Library and Archives Canada and the Directorate of History and Heritage on the organization and operations of 3rd Regiment at home during both world wars. She also supplied most of the war diaries for the Northwest Europe campaign of the Second World War. Doug Knight of Ottawa has long shared his expertise in artillery with the Gregg Centre and undertaken research in response to especially challenging questions, including helping enormously with photos. Roger Nason and Vern Faulkner (editor of *The St Croix Courier*) helped locate information on 105th Battery.

Catherine Reid of the Newcastle Public Library, Clive Law of Service Publications, Clive Prospero-Brooks of the RCA Museum in Shilo, Manitoba, Josh Smith of the Provincial Archives of New Brunswick, Steve Harris and Warren Sinclair of DHH in Ottawa, Cor de Graaf of the Leiden Regional Archives, Leiden, Netherlands; Bruce Jackson of St. Stephen; Bob Lockhart; and Jennifer Longon and Gary Hughes of the NBM all helped track down and supply photos. Mike Bechthold at Wilfrid Laurier University Press helped with everything from maps and photographs to layout and ultimately produced a fine product.

We are certain that, given the length and complexity of this project, we have neglected to mention more than a few people who – like all of those named above – were unstinting with their time and enthusiastic in their support. If you are one of these, we apologize.

The book committee of the Loyal Company Regimental Association was fully engaged throughout the entire process. The authors would like to thank them for their support and patience. Our working relationship was entirely professional, and the committee gave the authors full rein to tell the story as we found it. The committee included Al Gallop, Fearon Currie, Joe Foot, Shawn McPherson, Steve Strachan, John Irving, Michael Louvelle, and Tom Watters. Joseph Linder, Bob MacFarlane, and Paul Hanson all helped tremendously with pulling 89th Battery's unique story from Woodstock. The authors especially wish to acknowledge the dedication of Captain Thomas Watters, a long-serving member of the regiment. Tom helped gather sources and photographs and interview candidates and kept the project on track. We are grateful to Shawn McPherson and Kendell French for compiling the interviews that formed the basis for the final chapters of the book, and to Brent Wilson for his work and expertise on the pre-1914 period. Special thanks to HCol. John K. Irving, whose determination to get this book done was the driving force behind the project.

Although this is the work of many hands, and the book belongs – rightly enough – to The Loyal Company and all the gunners of New Brunswick over the last 223 years, the authors are responsible for whatever errors or omissions remain. We would like to leave one final thought. It was expressed by Captain Lawrence Wilmot, Chaplain of the West Nova Scotia Regiment, to Mr. Luke Amos, father of Gunner Ralph Amos, the last New Brunswick gunner killed in Italy during the Second World War: "We who remain owe a heavy debt to those who have fallen, to see to it that a better world is built upon more enduring foundations" (courtesy of Terry Amos).

Index

Page references in *italic* indicate illustrations and maps.

Aberdeen, Earl of (John Campbell Hamilton-Gordon), 6
Adamson, Ray, 311
Afghanistan, 429–43; 3rd Field Artillery Regiment, 429, 432–34, 440–41; 4th Air Defence Regiment, 441, 442; Afghan National Army (ANA) training system, 443; Canada's deployment in, 431, 432–33, *436*, 436–38, 443; Dragon Battery, 437, 438; Forward Operating Base Sper'wan Ghar, *434*; infrastructure rebuilding, 433, 440; Islamic forces, 429; Kandahar Airfield (KAF), 436; Manley Report, 442; map, *435*; National Support Element (NSE), 433; nation-building in, 431; NATO reinforcement, 442; personal accounts about, 438–39; Taliban tactics, 437, 438; war in Helmand province, 438; war in Kandahar province, 439–40; weather conditions, 439
Aiken, R.J., 277
Air Defence Anti-Tank System (ADATS), 418
Aitkens, James, 405
Alderson, Lt.-Gen. E.A.H., 39, 49, 61
Alexander (Gunner), 289
Alexander, W.J., 133
Allaby, Percy, 119
Allen, Lawrence, 33, 65, 92, 95, 104, 120, 174

Allen, Maj. L.T., 52
Alward, H.C., 174, 179
Alward, Lt.-Col. Wallace, 174, 216–17, 221, 233, 391
Alward, Peter, 404–5
Amirault, Joseph, 293
Amos, Nelson, 289
Amos, Ralph, 333
Anderson, Maj.-Gen. T.V., 217
Anderson, Maj./Lt.-Col./Col. S. Boyd: *46*; commander of 19th Battery, 15, 28, 31; commander of New Brunswick field batteries, 176; District Officer Commanding of New Brunswick Militia District, 179; letters of, 48–49; military career, 46; promotion, 70; on Western front, 36
Anderson, W.N., 396
Andrews, Jeff, 441
Anglin, W.A.I., 174
Anti-Aircraft Artillery Training Centre, 221, 228
anti-aircraft gunners training, *248, 249*
Archibald, I.F., 174
Armstrong, Capt./Lt.-Col. Beverley Robinson: *50*; advocacy for Canadian overseas representation, 51–52; commanding officer 3rd Regiment, 21, 24; laying up of the colours ceremony in Saint John's church, 181; mili-

458 | Index

tary career, 50; retirement, 174; *Saint John Globe* report about, 25–26; in Transvaal contingent, 8, 11–12
Armstrong, D.B., 393
Armstrong, Lt.-Col. John Russell, 5, 8, 52, 98, 106, 129–30
Armstrong, T.E.G., 181
Ashton, Maj.-Gen. E.C., 207
Ashwood, C.S., 95
Askin, Cyril, 344
Atlantic Artillery Regiment, 414, 416
Attis, Joseph, 293

Bailey, James, 332
Ballantyne, Charles, *142*
Barker, Lt., 121
Barker, Maj. Louis: 4th Siege Battery funeral, *117*; accomplishments, 174; battle of Arras, 149; battle of Somme, 74–75, 84, 86, 87; battle of Ypres Salient, 131; commanding officer of 3rd New Brunswick Regiment, 52, 64, 65, 66, 153, 166; replacement, 242; Vimy Ridge, 121, 139
Barnes, Charles, 315
Barnes, Sydney, 438
Barracks Green Armories, *20*
Barry, C.J., 319
Barton, Capt. A.E., 15
Barton, Maj. Arthur, 176
battles, pre-1914: Paardeberg, 8–9, 10
BATTLES, 1914–1918: Amiens, 143–46, map, *145*; Arras, Second Battle of; 147–53, map, *150*; Artois, Second Battle of, 57–58; Aubers Ridge, 54–57; Cambrai, 161–65, map, *162*; Canal du Nord 155–60, map, *157*; Givenchy, 57–59; Hill 70, 121–30; Jutland, 65–66; Loos, 61–63; Mount Sorrel, 72–74; Neuve Chapelle, 36–38; Passchendaele, 130-33; Somme, 77–96, map, *78*; St-Eloi craters, 67–69; Vimy Ridge, 106–21, map, *103, 112*; Wytschaete–Messines Ridge, 67–68; Ypres, First Battle of, 39; Ypres, Second Battle of, 40–51, map, *42*
BATTLES, 1939–1945: Agira, 291–92; Battle-group Chill, 366; Bulge, 373; Caen, 345, 348, 349, 350; Carpiquet, 346–48, 350; Coriano Ridge, 327–29, *328*; Falaise, 356–61; Groningen, 379; Gustav and Hitler Lines, *316*; Hochwald, 376; Lamone River, 332–33; Leonforte-Assoro, 287–90; Liri Valley, 317–19; map, *282, 300, 304*; maps, *364, 369*; Monte Cassino, 312, 315, 317; Moro River, 299–305, *303, 304*; Operation Olive, *326*; Ortona, 307–12; Regalbuto, 292–93; Sangro River, 298–99; Scheldt, *364, 366–71, 369*; Valguarnera, 286
battles, post–Cold War: Medak Pocket, 423
Bauer, Ed, 410
Baxter, Capt./Lt.-Col. John "J.B.M.," 5, 181
Beach, P., 119
Beeman, William, 143
Belyea, Abner, *19*
Bemrose, David, 289, 312
Bennett (Bombardier), 290
Bennett, Lt. C.S., 175
Bennett, Lt. H.F., 175
Benson, Thomas, 98
Bérubé, Chantal, 442
Bidlake, Cyrus, 161
Bidlake, Geoff, 161
Bidlake, Walter Geoffrey, 161
Birt, Ray, 422
Black, R.S., 125
Blackey, Maj./Lt.-Col. J.A., 256, 261, 262, 271, 272
Blinn, Bradley, 433
Bobbit, Dan, 433, 438
Boer republics, 7
Boer War. *See* Second Boer War
Bogert, M.P., 398, 399–400
Borden, Frederick, 6
Boudreau, Art, 306
Boudreau, David, 413, *419*
Bovard, John, 30
Boyd, C.W., 121
Boyer, J.M., 246
Brewer, Frank, *9*, 154
Bridges, H.A., 175
British Empire: German's naval blockade of, 34; military reform, 2; relations with US, 6, 172; Royal Navy, 5
Brown, A.E., 175
Brown, K.A., 175
Brown, K.J., 396
Brown, Orville, *284,* 293

Brownfield, H.O.N., 255
Bruce, Lt. H.A., 33
Bruce, Lt. John Adams, 64, 116, 153, 174
Bruce, R.H., 175
Bryce, T.B., 120
Buck, Frank, *9*
Burnett, Capt./Maj. Hugh, *257,* 300, 302, 310, 311, 319, 324
Burns, Mike (Bombardier), 441–42, 443
Burns, Sgt. M.L., 347
Burstall, Henry, 35, 39, 41, 57, 61, 100, 177
Byng, Julian, 69, 100, 155

Caldow, W.L., 174
Call, Lt.-Col. R., 3
Callum, E.A., 146
Calnek, S.H., 253
Cameron, Norman, *9*
Campbell, Douglas, 306
Campbell, Kent, 422, 423
Campbell, Maj. J., *193*
Campbell, Maj. N.D., 349
Campbell, Maj. S.J., 246
Canada: contribution to NATO deterrent force, 382; corvette-building program, 225; defence programs, 196–97, 198–99; First World War mobilization, 25; League of Nations and, 192–93; Militia Act of 1868, 2; National Resources Mobilization Act (NRMA), 228–29; overseas missions, 422; relations with US, 5; Reserve Force, 383, 392–93; Second Boer War, 7, 9–10; survey of garrison towns, 197–98
Canadian Armed Forces Reorganization act, 407
Canadian Artillery: mechanization and reorganization of, 180, 183–85; modern technology, 421, 422
Canadian Artillery Association, 179, 183, 187–88, 189–90
Canadian Militia Act centennial celebration, 395–96
Canadian Occupation Force in Germany, 165, *165,* 165–66, *166*
Carter, T. Le M., 299
Casey, Michelle, 426, *426,* 426–27
Chamberlain, Rob, 440
Chantilly Conference, 67

Chase, J. Stanley, 250
Chill, Kurt, 366
Church, W.G., *32*
Churchill, Winston, 294
Clark, C., 286
Clark, Capt., 108
Clark, Maj. Gerald, 391
Clark, Melvin, 433, 434, *437,* 442
Clark, Vernon, 158
Clarke, Bertram, 250
Clarke, James Gordon, 291
Clarkson, Adrienne, 423
Claxton, Brooke, 384
Clutesi, Amanda, 433
Clynick, A.B., 269, 296, 300, 312
Cobham, Arthur, 83
Coffey, Lt. Gordon W., *194,* 253
Cold War, 381–419; aircraft recognition training, *388*; air defence artillery regiments, 387–88; artillery's public affairs, 399; blockade of West Berlin, 386; Canadian Armed Forces Reorganization act, 407; Canadian defence plans, 384, 390, 418; coastal fortifications, 386; defence against Soviet submarines, 386–87; end of, 421; Exercise Atlantic Barbara, 416–17; fall of Berlin Wall, 419; first thermonuclear test, 391–92; Hellyer's White Paper, 402; Kennedy Commission's recommendations, 392–95; Korean War, 390–91; mobilization plan of Canadian army, 416; mutually assured destruction (MAD), 383; national survival training, 398; overseas deployment opportunities, 413; peacekeeping missions, 412; political and economic role of NATO, 409–10; practice-firing in Halifax, 386; regiment bands, 385–86; reorganization of Militia, 396, 408; Reserve Forces, 383, 392–93; role of conventional military forces, 383; Royal Canadian Artillery School (Anti-Aircraft), 388; Russia's launch of Sputnik satellite, 396–97; status of Canadian Militia, 384–85, 393–94, 396–97, 398–99, 400, 402–3; strategic arms limitation talks (SALT), 409; threat of Soviet bombers, 387–88; training of New Brunswick artillery regiments, 382, 388, 389, 392, 396, 397, 401–2, 404, 405, 413

Cole, C.L., *277*
Cole, Minden, 65
Comeau, Joseph Arthur, 49
Connell, W.A., 105
Constantine, C.F., 179
Cooper, W.T., 389
Copp, Terry, 349
Costigan, R., 10
Cox, Donald, 391, 393, 397
Craig, Harold, 139
Craig, J., 395
Crawford, Stanley, 5
Creelman, Lt.-Col., 43, 46, 49
Crerar, Harry, 45, 265
Critchlow, D., 250
Crocker, R., 183
Crocker, Randolph, 60, 67
Cronjé, Pieter Arnoldus, 8
Crooker, Randolph, *24*
Crosby, J.M., 389
Cummings, Donald, 75
Cunard, Charlie, 28
Cuppens, Lou, 413
Curley, William, 45
Currie, Lt.-Col. Fearon, 413, 416, 417, 418
Currie, Lt.-Gen. Arthur, 121, 129, 151, 155, *163*
Currie, Maj. David, 358, 359

Daley, D.H., 146
Daughney, Ralph, 346, 347
Davison, William, 163
Delaney, S.C., *277*
Devenne, F.E., 396
Devine, L.A., 256
Dibblee, F.H.J., 15
Dick, W.C., 322
Dickie, J.R., 242
Dineen, Sgt., 360
Doane, J.E., 179
Dodge, Alfred, 28
Dodge, Lt./Capt./Maj. Albert: accomplishments, 174; celebration of the 174th anniversary of the 3rd Field Regiment, 406; commander of the 105th Anti-Tank Battery, 256, 261, 401; commanding officer of the 3rd NB Heavy Brigade, 175, 179; illness, 255; military career, 253; militia service, 170; photograph among NB Dragoons, *194*; preparations for Nazi attack, 253–54; salute of thirteen guns from Reeds Point, 177; training in Petawawa camp, 181
Doetzell (Gunner), 107
Donahue, William, 8
Doucette, William Joseph, 310, 311
Douglas, Charles, 65
Downing, Frank, 293
Drew, G.A., 192
Drury, Charles William, 7, 10
Duff, Graham, 139
Dumas, Herman, 344
Dunbar, M.D., *277*
Dunn, W.L., 292
Dunphy, A.E., 369
Dysart, Harry, *9*

Earle, E., 179
Eayrs, James, 188
Edgar, W.H., *32*
Edgar, W.S., 347
Edwards, Jack, 28
Eggert, David, 433, 434, 439
Elizabeth II, Queen of England, 391, 430
Elkins, W.H.P., 221
Ellis, H.G.E., 230
Ervin, Patrick, 416, 418
Evans, Lt./Capt. Gerald Charles, 283, *289*, 290, 301, 309, 312
Everett, Allen, 177
Everett, Fred, *9*
Ewing, W.C, 174

Fairweather, Lt./Capt. Jack (J.H.A.), 52, 64, 86, 116–17, 175, 178
Fallon, M.A., 311
Farndale, Martin, 55, 420
Fawcett, Earle, 327
Ferguson, J.H., *309*
Ferguson, R.B., 309
Firlotte, D.G., 358
First World War: Allied Expeditionary Force in Russia, 167, 168, *168*, 170; ammunition supply, *152*; armistice, 164–65; Britain's "precautionary" telegram, 24–25; Canada's defence preparations, 26–27; Canadian

artillery, organization of, 23–24; Canadian occupation forces, 165; contemporary accounts, 164–65; *Dornfontein* incident, 226; German control of the sky, 101; German offensive of 1918, 139, 140; German strategy, 74; Halifax garrison, 32–33; Hindenburg Line, *147*; King George's visit of Canadian front, 122; Marshal Fosh's plan, 146–47; Mount Kemmel, assault on, 68; Neuville-St-Vaast, German attack on, 70; New Brunswick's gunners in, 23, 33–34, *34*, 35, 54, 59, 97, 137–38; Nivelle Offensive, 101; Operation Michael, 139; postwar settlement in south Pacific, 172; refugees, 47–48; siege warfare, 59, 143; submarine warfare, 98–99, 141–43; transportation, *152*; Western Front map, *22*; winter on Salisbury Plain, 33. *See also* battles, 1914-1918

Fitzpatrick, Lt.-Col. Ron, *409*, 410, 413
Flagle (Gunner), 300
Flowers, Lt. J.R., 358, 359
Foch, Ferdinand, 147
Foote, Joe, 413, 425, 430, 432
Forbes, A.A., 250
Fort Dufferin, 217–18, 223, 233
Forward Observation Officers (FOOs), 19, 34, 46, *82*, *114*, *127*, 240, *351*
Foster, G.C.L., 174
Fournier, E.J., 179
Fraser, Kenneth Alexander, 319
French Navy, 226
Fullerton, Frank, 267, *284*, 286, 293, 299, 303

Gagetown Artillery School, 414, 425
Gallop, Allison, 423
Gamble, George, 139
Gamblin, Capt./Maj./Lt.-Col. George: 158th anniversary of the 3rd (NB) Regiment, 391; 174th anniversary of the 3rd (NB) Regiment, 406; battle of Amiens, 144, 146; commanding officer of the 2nd Divisional Ammunition Column, 60, 71; commanding officer of the 3rd (New Brunswick) Heavy Brigade, 175; photograph, *32*; promotion to Lt.-Col., 181; vice-presidents of the Canadian Artillery Association, 187; Vimy Ridge, 119
Garland, Charles, 77, 79
garrison artillery: definition of, 4
Gaskin, Cyrus, 121, 161
Geary, Fred, 69
George VI, King of England, 391
Gilbert, A.B., 189
Gillies, Lt.-Col. John, 266
Gillin, F.J., *277*
Gillis, A.A., 262
Glanville (Gunner), 154
Glew, George, 9
Godin, Jeff, 422
Golder, Mark, 433, 434, *436*
Goldsworth, William, 132
Gomez, D., 378
Good, Capt./Maj./Lt.-Col. William C., 9, 10, 12, 15
Gough, Gen. Hubert, 84, 92, 94
Graham, Dominick, 61
Graham, Howard, 394
Granatstein, Jack, 398
Grant, H.A. (Gunner), 124
Grant, Lt.-Col. E.A., 397, 401
Grassick, G.A., 352
Gray, Andrew, 171
Great Depression, 187, 188–89
Great War. *See* First World War
Green, Clarence, 250
Green, Steve (Gunner), 92, 96, 124, 131, 154, 164
Greer, John, 433, 436, 440
Grey, Harold, 9
Gunn, Fred, 48, 49
Gutelius, F.P., 174
Gwatkin, W.G., 27, 171

Hague, Lt.-Col. Harry, 269, 283, *284*, 302
Haig, Gen./FM Douglas, 54, 56, 71
Halifax, NS, 25, 27, 32–33
Hall, Frank, 30
Hall, Harry, 9
Hamm, Frank, 119
Hanson, Paul, 401
Harkness, D.S., 250

Harpell, Michael, 119
Harper, William, 118
Harris, J.L.W., 242
Harrison, Charles, 5
Harrison, Lt.-Col. Harry, *33*, 60, 87, 175, 177
Harrison, Maj./Lt.-Col. W.H. "Harry," 21, 27, 31, 32, 173, 174
Harrison, Maj. William A., 175
Harrison, R.A., 367, 372
Harrison, Walter A., *32*
Hart, Cpl. James, 120
Hart, Jack de, 407
Hart, Lt./Maj./Lt.-Col./Col. J.G. "Gil," 178, 179, 187, 216, *216*, 221, 391
Hatt, John *325*
Hawkes, Don, 416
Hayes, C., 175
Hayes, Ralph, 28
Hayne, Richard, 180
Hazen, Allie, *9*
Hazen, D. King, 174
Hazen, Douglas, 69
Hazen, James, 69
Hellyer, Paul, 402
Henley, Dave, 424
Hennessy, Thomas, 59
Henry, L.J., 266
Henty, G.A., 17
Hicks, Ainsley, 43
Hipwell, Jack, 70
Hnatyshyn, Ramon J., 420
Hoffmeister, Bert, 323
Holden, J.W., 161
Holder, Bruce, Jr., 404, 405
Holder, Bruce, Sr., 386
Hooper, Rufus, 305
Hope, E., 295
Hopper, E.A., 125
Hornby, R.S. Phipps, 32
Horne, Henry, 76, 151
horse transport, *61*
Horwell, Sgt., 199
Hosford, Joseph, 433, *434*
Howard, Spencer, 120
Howe, Adrien, 306
Hughes, Robert, *9*, 17
Hughes, Sir Samuel, 13, 27, 28, 129

Hunter, William, 83
Hutchison, G.O., 283
Hutton, E.T.H., 15
Huxford, C.P.H.E., 220

Iarocci, Andrew, 59
Inches, Cyrus: Aubers Ridge, 54; Canal du Nord, 158; civilian career, 170; commander of the 15th Heavy Battery, 175; Hill 70, 123; letter on battle of Loos, 63; personal accounts, 54, 57, 100; promotion to Major, 107; recognition, 174; Somme, 75, 86; training in Valcartier, QC, 28; transfer to 1st Heavy Battery, 30, 69; transfer to Corps Reserve, 178
Irving, John, 442
Italian Campaign, 294–336; Allied artillery in Liri Valley, *311*; Allied strategy, 295–96; ammunition and supplies delivery, 313–14, *314*; attack on Pontecorvo fortress, 319–20; British units, 328, 329; Canadian artillery bunker, *313*; Canadian position behind Mount Trocchio, *318*; casualties, 306, 311, 315, 319, 323, 327, 333, 334; contemporary accounts, 306–7, 310–11, 317, 320, 323, 333; fight for Bagnacavallo, 333; fire support to 1st Canadian Division infantry, *295*; Florence, attack on, 323; German resistance, 295–96, 301–3, 305, 318–19, 321, 325, 330; Gothic Line, 321, 323, 325, 327, 328; Green Line I defence belt, 324; Gustav Line, *316*, 317; Hitler Line, 317, 319, 322; last months of, 330–35; Loyal Edmonton Regiment, 296; map, *300*; mobile warfare on road to Rome, 320; Motta Montecorvino, 296; newspapers on, 308–9; New Zealand units, 317, 323, 328; observation posts, *306*; Operation Baytown, 294–95; Operation Chesterfield, 319–20; Operation Chuckle, 332; Operation Diadem, 315, 317; Operation Olive, 324, *326*; planning, 294; retreat from Ortona sector, 315; role of New Brunswick's artillery, 334; Royal Canadian Army Service Corps trucks, *314*; San Fortunato Ridge, capture of, 330; San Leonardo, attack on, 302, 305; San Martino Ridge, 329–30; Second Mediterranean

Contingent, 312–13; shortages of infantry, 321–23; trench warfare, 312; vehicle losses, 301–2; weather conditions, 305

Jaillet, Joseph, 329
Jarvis, E.P., *245*
Johnson, V.C., *32*
Johnston, Ron, *409*, 413, *413*
Joncas, Laurier, 293
Jones, Capt. F.C., 8, 12, 14
Jones, George, 5
Jones, Greg, 441
Jones, R.K., 175
Jones, R.V., 176
Jordan, Joe, 441
Judd, F.C., 393

Kelly, Lawrence, 28, 59
Kennedy, A.A., 288
Kennedy, Howard, 392
Kennedy, Keltie: Ancre river heights, 94, 95; on French hospitality, 100; Lieutenant-Colonel, 242; personal accounts, 92, 100; Vimy Ridge, 104, 109, 112, 115
Kenney, William, *9*
Kent, G.L., 231
Kerr, Lt. Bill, 86
Kerr, Lt. Gordon, 52, 64, 95
Kesselring, FM Albert, 322
Kimball, Keith, 323
King, Lt.-Col. William, 68
Kirkpatrick, Fred, 8
Kitchener, 1st Earl (Horatio Herbert), 64
Knowlan (Gunner), 323

Landry, E.H., 133
Laurier, Wilfrid, 18
Lawlor, J.W., 176
Lawlor, T.W., 12
Lawson, J.H. (Gunner), 133
Lawson, Lt. Hugh, 126, 161
Lawson, Sgt. Dale, 412
Leach, Dick, 72, 80
Leighton, Wheeler, *9*
Linder, Joe, 413, *430*, 432
Lipsett, Lt.-Col. Louis James, 44
Little, Charles, 327
Little, Herb, *404*
Locket, A.E., 28
Lockhart, Robert, 399, 401, 405, 407, 408, 412
Lofstrom, Frank, 283, 302
Love, Capt./Maj. Walter: 105th Battery's training, 253–54, 255; commanding officer, 261–62; D-Day, 338–39; military career, 195, 253; Nijmegen Salient, 372; Operation Charnwood, 348–49; photograph, *194*; Regimental Quartermaster, 256
Ludendorff, Erich, 144
Lutes, Edwin, 59
Lynn, W.P., *9*

MacAdam, Walter, 133
MacBrien, J.H., 179
MacCafferty, Wallace, 329
MacDonald, A.R., 420
MacDonald, E. Ross, 306
MacDonald, Herb, 92, 93, 115, 118–19
MacDonald, S.K.L., *32*
MacDougall, F.V., *309*
MacFarlane, James, 329
MacFarlane, Kenneth Foster, 319
MacFarlane, Marshall, 401
MacFarlane, Robert, 401, 410, 411, *413*
Mackay, Colin B., Jr., 406
MacKay, Lt./Maj. Colin, 33, 143, 154, 174, 391
Mackenzie King, William Lyon, 196, 267
MacLaren, David, 120
MacLaren, I.N.M., 175
MacLean, M.Y., 389
MacLeod, Maj./Lt.-Col. Norman, *32*, 137, 175, 178, 179, 181
MacMillan, Cyrus, 138
MacMillan, F.S.C., 367
MacMullen, W.F., 373
MacRae, Chester, 347
MacRae, J.F., 120
Magee, Frank: Aubers Ridge, 54; in Canadian Expeditionary Force, 30, 34, 35; commanding officer, 21, 25, 97, 136; departure to the Great War, 28; Foreign Service Battery, 27; Neuve Chapelle, 35; photographs, *165*; promotion to Lieutenant-Colonel, 107; recognition, 174; Somme offensive, 75; wounds, 71, 75

Magee, R.D., 174
Malley, Leo, 334
Manderville, Malcolm, 333
Manley, John, 442
Marley, Henry, 8
Mason, Norm, 420
Matthews, Bruce, 286, 291
McAdam, Murray, 69
McCallum (Gunner), 154
McCarthy, D., 199
McClaskey, Vernon, 121
McCordick, Edward, 242
McCurdy, F.B., 129
McCutcheon, C.L., 140
McDougall, George, 41
McGeachy, Kirk, 413, 416, 426, 432, 441
McGowan, Maj. J.T., 21, 174, 177
McInerney, Harold, 58
McKelvey, James, *430*
McKelvey, Neil, 233, 395, 420
McKinnon, Lt., 358, 359
McKinnon, Sgt. Neil, 41
McLaren, Donald, 391
McLean, Harry, *9*
McLean, Kendall, 433, 434, 440
Mclean, Lt.-Col. A.T., *193*, 195
McLeod, George Frederick, 12
McLeod, Norman P., 11
McMullen, George, 31
McNair, J.B., 174
McNaughton, Brig.-Gen. A.G.L., 125, 151, 171, 189, 192–94, 219, 265
McNaughton, Robert Duncan, 171
McPherson, Shawn, 420, 425, *430,* 441, 442
Megill, W.J., 354, 363
Melanson, A.G., 323
Merritt, Lt., 181
Militia: centennial celebration of Militia Act, 395–96; ceremonial role, 177; during Cold War, 384–85, 393–94, 396–97, 398–99, 400, 402–3; funding, 6, 188–89, 398–99; during Great Depression, 188–89; during the Great War, 170–71; Interwar period (1919–1939), 170–71; local communities and, 391; reforms, 5, 14–15; reorganizations, 172, 181–82, 191–93, 396–97, 408, 424–25

Militia Act of 1868, 2
Miller, Leslie, 48
Mills, Ira, 47
Milner, William C., 381
Minto, 4th Earl of (Gilbert John Elliot-Murray-Kynynmound), 14
Mispec Point: 4th Battery training, *215*; 7.5-inch gun, *212*; battery guns, 215; coast artillery cuts, 232, 233; communication line, 214; counter-bombardment battery, *211*; Huxford's inspection of, 220–21; observation post, 214–15; Port War Signal Station, 214
Moffitt, Gordon, 416, 417
Moller, E.C., 125
Mollins, Clyde, 41
Moncton, NB, 50–51, 176
Moncton Times war reports, 60
Montgomery, Bernard Law, 276, *289,* 294
Morlock, Maj. John Forbes, 263–4, 349, 367
Morrisey, Lt./Maj./Lt.-Col. Henry, 178, 188, 196
Morrison, E.W.B., 98, 171
Morrison, Paul, 404
motor transport, 183–85
Mowat, Farley, 303, 320, 333
Mowat, Oliver, 167, 168
Munich agreement, 200
Munro, Chester, 327
Munro, Ross, 290, 291, 307
Murdoch, Lt., 289, 290, 312
Murray, W. (Gunner), *277*

Netherlands, Liberation of the: attacks on Aurich and Emden, 379; Canadian artillery, 335–36, *365*; contemporary accounts, 335; Operation Plunder, 378; preparation for parade in Leiden, *377*
New Brunswick: map of, *xx*; Royal visit to, 14; South African War Memorial, 9
New Brunswick's gunners: ceremonial activities, 6; in the First World War, 23, 33–34, *34,* 35, 54, 59, 97, 137–38; postwar careers, 381–82
Nicholson, G.W.L., 403
Nicks, Sgt. Maj., 207
Nighswander, Lt.-Col. E.D., 263, 363
Nivelle, Robert, 101
Nixon, Capt./Maj. A.B., 347, 372, 376
Norman, W.C., 372

North Atlantic Treaty Organization (NATO): Air–Land Battle Doctrine, 414; creation of, 382; International Security and Assistance Force (ISAF), 432

Northrup, Alexander, 117

Northrup, Leigh, 121

Northwest Europe Campaign, 337–80; Allied forces operations from Caen to Argentan, *355*; anti-tank actions, 351–52, 373, 375, 377–78; assault on Walcheren, 371; attack on Boulogne, 362, 363; attack on Calais, 365; attack on Sluis, 368–70; attack on Tilley-la-Campagne, 352; Breskens Pocket, 365, 368, 370–71; Campbellton gunners, 358–59, *368*; Canadian POWs, 359; Canadian troops on the move, *360, 361, 364, 368*; Cap Gris Nez, attack on, 365; capture of Woensdrecht, 367; capture of Xanten, 376; casualties, 349, 354; contemporary accounts, 337–38, 344, 352, 359, 361, 362–63, 375, 379; D-Day, 337, 338–40; field artillery battery command post, *348*; final months of, *374*, 379–80; German resistance, 340–41, 344, 345, 347, 357, 366, 378; gun positions along the Scheldt River, *362*; landing on Juno Beach, 338–40; liberation of Belgium, 365–67; liberation of Cherbourg, 345; liberation of Normandy, *342, 343*–44; liberation of Rouen, 361; North Nova Scotia Highlanders, 343; observation posts, *351*; Operation Atlantic, 350–52; Operation Blockbuster, 375, 376; Operation Charnwood, 348–49; Operation Market Garden, 372; Operation Plunder, 378; Operation Totalize, 352–54, 356; Operation Tractable, 354, 356; Operation Veritable, 375–76; Operation Windsor, 345–47; Polish forces, 352–53, 356, 357; winter patrol in Nijmegen Salient, *372*, 372–73

North-West Rebellion of 1885, 2, 3

observation balloon, *152*

O'Dell, Sean, 433, 436

Ogilvie, G. Hunter, 10, 11

Oland, Capt./Maj./Lt.-Col./Col./Brig. Philip: anniversaries of the 3rd Field Regiment, 406, 420; civilian career, 383; commanding officer in anti-aircraft battery, 230; D-Day landing, 345, 346–47; death and funeral, 425; leadership, 403; overseas service, 233, 368; photographs, *389, 413*; promotions, 389–90, 393; recognition, 427; Regiment's band and, 385–86; retirement, 399

Oland, J.E.W., 224

O'Leary, Launce, 58

O'Leary, Martin, 383, *406,* 407, 414, 420

Olive, Harry, 250

O'Neill, W.J., 133

Otter Commission, 171–73, 181–82

Ottey, L.C.D., 262

Owens, F., 69

Page, L.F., 196

Parker, George, 9

Parker, J.J., 266

Parsons, Brig.-Gen., 190

Partington, K.J.B., 222

Partridge Island: aerial views, *236, 237*; batteries, 52, 97–98, 205; communication line, 214; concrete gun positions, 142–43; defence role of, 99, 206–7; fortifications, 219–20, 236–38; gun-firing practices, 218–19; Huxford's inspection, 220–21; navy signals detachment, 211; observation post, 220, 238; Port War Signal Station, 211; preparation for U-boat attacks, 143

Patchell, Holly, 31

Patchell, Sgt. Maj., 31, 53

Patterson, George, 47

Pearkes, Maj.-Gen., 250

Pemberton, J.B., 179

Penhale, John, 28

Peters, W.J., 181

Pham, Tri, 422, 423

Phin, Lt.-Col. J.P., 270, 271, 273, 274, 343, 372

Pidgeon, D.F., *32*

Piers, Lynd, 295

Pike, H., 181

Pitman, J.S., 146

Plummer, Alfred, 133

Polleys, Fletcher, 50

Polleys, Ned, 50

Pond, L.C., *245*

Popow, Fred, 47

Portal, Air Chief Marshal Sir Charles, 81–82
Porter, H.J., *277*
post–Cold War era: air defence artillery, 424–25; defence reductions, 419; peace enforcement in former Yugoslavia, 425; September 11 attacks, 429; UN peace missions, 422
Pottle, Arthur, 233
Prince, J.W., 64
Pritchard, Lt.-Col., 81
Puddington, E.R., 175
Puddy, Ed, 28
Purkis, Lt. W.T., 343, 347

Quebec Conference, 272, 294

Rankin, G.A., 293
Rawlings, John, 8
Ray, Lt. L.N., 344, 356
Reid, Robert, *193*
Richard, Edgar, 250
Ricketts, G.A., 179
Ricketts, J.A., 179
Riddell, Bill, 344
Ring, Capt./Maj. Roy, 52, 64, 133, 153, 174
Ritchie, H.H., 187
Roberts, W.F., 393
Robertson, Herbert, 119
Robertson, Jim, 113
Robinson, Jack, 60
Robinson, Joseph, 433
Robinson, Roy, 60
Roome, R.E.G., 246
Royal Canadian Air Force (RCAF), 208–9, *209*, 210, 217, 231
Royal Canadian Artillery (RCA) Air Defence School in Gagetown, 410, 418, 419, 424
Royal Canadian Artillery Association, 398–99, 411
Royal Canadian Navy (RCN), 208, 210, *224*
Royal Flying Corps, 62, 80
Rudic, Christopher, 28
Russian Bolshevik Revolution, 136, 167
Rutherford, R.W., 25
Ryan, H., 146
Rycroft, J.G., 98
Ryder, T.E., *32*

Saint John: 175th Birthday of The Loyal Company of Artillery, 406; Barracks Green Armories, *20*; closure of forts, 386; coast gunnery training, 199; commercial importance, 4, 25; Committee of Public Safety, 141; defence of, 25, 27, 207; departure of troops to the Great War, 33, *51*, 65; fortress, *198*; Otter Commission in, 172–73; survey of, 197–98; threat of U-boat attacks, 133–34, 140–42
Saint John Fusiliers, 205, 208
Saint John Globe, 25
Saint John in the Second World War, 203–38; aerial photo, *209*; anti-aircraft defence, 231–32; army garrison, 232–34; artillery courses, 222; coastal defence mountings, 217–18; Courtenay Bay breakwater position, *234*; defensively equipped merchant ships (DEMSs), 224–25; Drydock and Shipbuilding facilities, *210,* 225; Fire Command Post, 223; foreign vessels in, 225; Fort Dufferin, 223, 235; fortifications, 218, 221, 223–24, 235–36; German patrols, 227; government's defence plan, 204–6; gun-firing practices, 218–19; harbour and cargo docks, *206*; Huxford's visit to, 210–21; inner harbour defences, 222–23, 235; Inspector Anderson's visit, 217; Lt.-Col. Hart as defence commander, 216; Mispec Point batteries, *211,* 213–14; navy signals detachment on Partridge Island, 211; observation posts, *234,* 235; role of Navy, 208, 210–12; Royal Canadian Air Force (RCAF), 208–10, 217; searchlight operations, 207, 218; U-boat operations near, 226–27, 228, 234–35
Sansom, Ernest W., 254
Sansom, Lt.-Col. R.F., 399, 400, 427
Sayre, J.E., 31
Scott, A.H., 323
Scott, F.G., 160
Screeton, G.E., 317
Scullin, C.B., 344
Seaforth Highlanders of Canada, 284, 288, 299, 302, 309, 319
Searle, George, 9
Second Boer War, 7–8, 9, 11

Second World War, 203–380; artillery mobilization, 241–42; beginning of, 201; British Army in North Africa, 258; Burgess, capture of, 359; Canada's declaration of war, 205; Canadian coast defence program, 205, 215–16; Canadian forces overseas, 245, 249, 252–53; capitulation of France, 244–45; characteristic of, 239; D-Day, 275–76; Exercise Spartan, 264–66; German air forces, 203–4, 205; German Navy, 203–4, 205, 215, 225–26; German patrols in Canadian waters, 227–28; Germany's assault on Britain, 217; Germany's "Blitzkrieg" of 1940, 244; gun production, 229; Japan's attack on US, 226; Japan's surrender, 238; landings at Dieppe, 263; Luftwaffe attack on London, 250; Mediterranean Theatre, 283; mobilization during, 203, 240–41; Operation Fortitude, 276, 277; Operation Husky, 269, 281; Operation Overlord, 278; Salo Republic, 330; success of Allied forces in Normandy, 324; training during, 221–22, 260, 263; Unites States enters, 226; victory in Europe, 238. *See also* battles, 1939–1945; Italian Campaign; Netherlands, Liberation of the; Northwest Europe Campaign; Sicily, invasion of

Secord, R.W., 120

Sewell, Jack, 69

Shackleton, Clayton, 327

Shaw, J.F., 233, 234

Shephard, M., 161

ships: SS *Alfreda*, 218; *Bismarck*, 225, 226; HMCS *Brunswicker*, 210; HMS *Calcutta*, 177; HMCS *Captor II*, 210; CGS *Cartier*, 212; SS *Cornwallis*, 235; HMS *Hampshire*, 66; HMS *Isis*, 99; HMS *Jervis Bay*, 204, 225; *Dornfontein*, 141, 142; SS *Fort Binger* (French Navy), *226*; HMT *Laconia*, 204; HMCS *Moncton*, 224; HMCS *Niobe*, 99, 205, 238 RMS *Olympic*, 65; HMT *Queen Mary*, 272; HMS *Ramilles*, 225; HMCS *Venosta*, 212; HMCS *Vernoe*, 212; *Tirpitz*, 226; SS *Skottland*, 226; SS *Urla*, *206*.

Siberian Field Force, 167, 168

Sicily, invasion of: American forces, 285–86, 293; attack on Monte della Forma, 286, *287*; Canadian forces, 267–68, 283–84, 289–90, 293–94; contemporary accounts, 293; German retaliation, 290–91, 293; Italian Blackshirt Legion counterattack, 285; map, *282*; Nissoria Ridge, 291; Operation Husky, 281, 283, 284–85

Simonds, Gen. G.G., 286

Simonds, Lt., 179

Simpson, Alfred, 8

Sinclair, Capt. V.G., 323

Sinclair, Lt. Reed, 161

Sinclair, Maj. J.M., 324, 327

Slade, Jim, 28

Slader, Edward "Ned": *190*; 174th Birthday fête of 3rd Regiment, 406; Albert, 80; Canal du Nord, 156; civilian career, 170; exercise at Petawawa, 190; Hill 70, 126; military career, 17, 175, 187, 190; Mount Sorrel, 72; promotions, 70, 139; recognition, 174, 391; recruiting mission, 28; Somme offensive, 76, 79; Vimy Ridge, 107, 113, 115; Western front, 35, 44, 47; wounded, 161

Slater, Maj. H.R., 350, 358, 359

Sleep, Elwood, 305

Sleep, Terry, 410–11

Smith, Maj. S.B., 260, 314, 315, 335

Smith, Robert, *9*

Smith, Warren, 425, 426

Special Commission on Reserve Restructuring, 423

Spinney, J.O., *194*

Spottiswood, W., 295

Sprague, Frank, 8

Stackhouse, Jim, 28, 81

Starkey, J.S., 146

Steeves, Clifford, 293

Steeves, E.O., *277*

Steeves, Henry, 69

Steeves, James, 5

Steeves, Noah, 30, 48, 68–69

Stewart, J.R., 146

Stone, George, 69

Story, Fred, *224*

Strachan, Stephen, 442

Strang, L.J., 179

Suttie, E.R., 402

Sypher, Roy, 373

468 | Index

Talbot, George, 47
Tambling, G.T., 132
Thompson, Jim, 315
Thompson, L.G., 401
Tibbits, A.S., 9
Tingley, Harvey, 43, 49
Todd, P.S.A., *246*, 247
Towe, Sgt. John, 286, 290, 312
training camps: Debert, 255; Deseronto, 7, 14; Gagetown, 382, 392, 396, 407, 410, *421*; Petawawa, 16, 25, 178–79, *195*, 247; Picton, 388; Shilo, 405; Sussex, 3; Utopia, 392; Valcartier, QC, 28, *29*; Whitley (England), 34
Treatt, B.D.C., 197
Tremblay, T.L., 233
Trites, Leonard, 293
Troy, J.A., 277
Turnbull, B.W., 175
Turnbull, Eber H., 137, 175
Turnbull, James: commanding officer, 399, 403–4, 407; death, 442; funeral, *441*; Loyal Company bicentennial celebrations, 420; Loyal Company's 175th Anniversary celebrations, 405–6; military and civilian career, 395; overseas service, 233, 315; parade in Fredericton, *430*; photographs, *389, 413*; president of RCA Association, 408; promotion to Colonel, 407; recognition, 383, 408, 427; training camps, 396
Turner, Gordon, 48, 154

U-boats, 227–28, 234–35, 269
UN Assistance Mission, 432
UN Emergency Force (UNEF II), 412
United States: Japan's attack on, 226; Loring Air Base, 401; relations with Britain, 6, 172; relations with Canada, 5
units and formations
– 1st Canadian Army, 264–66, 277, 352–53, 356–57, *364*, 378
– 1st Divisional Ammunition Column, 70, *73*, 75
– 1st Regiment, Royal Canadian Horse Artillery (1RCHA), 410–11
– 1st Searchlight Battery, 207, 218
– 2nd Divisional Ammunition Column: arrival on Western front, 61; Cambrai, 164; departure to First World War, 33; formation of, 31; officers of, *32*; return to Canada from the Great War, *169*; Somme offensive, 87; Vimy Rigde, 100, 101, 106, 107, 119
– 4th Royal Canadian Horse Artillery, 392
– 6th Canadian Infantry Division, 16
– I Canadian Corps, 298, 320, 321, 323, 327–29, 333–34
– II Canadian Corps, 337, 371
– 26th (New Brunswick) Battalion, *33*, 60, *169*
ANTI-AIRCRAFT AND AIR DEFENCE ARTILLERY:
1st Light Anti-Aircraft Regiment, 248–49, 260, 265, 298–99, 317, 322, 334; 3rd (NB) Heavy Anti-Aircraft Regiment, 387, *387*, 389, 391; 3rd (NB) Medium Anti-Aircraft Artillery Regiment (Militia), 399; 4th Air Defence Artillery Regiment, 424; 4th Air Defence Regiment, 441, 442; 8th Anti-Aircraft Battery, 208, 229–30; 22nd Anti-Aircraft Regiment, 231; 23rd Heavy Anti-Aircraft Regiment, 385, 387–88, 389; 25th Light Anti-Aircraft Battery, 230–31, 232; 64th Light Anti-Aircraft (New Brunswick) Regiment, 384, *385*, 398; 89th Anti-Aircraft Battery, 266–67, 317, 333
ANTI-TANK REGIMENTS
– 1st Anti-Tank Regiment, RCA (former 1st Canadian Field Brigade): designation, 242; Field Artillery tractor, *301*; Italian Campaign, 268–69, *297*, 312, 314; training in England, 243–44, *244*, 257
– 3rd Anti-Tank Regiment; battery composition, 255, 275; exercise Beaver, 260; Gorman attacks on, 260–61; gun drills, 256, 257–58, 273–74; Northwest Europe Campaign, 337, *338*, 340, 343, 344, 345, 349–50, 354, 356, 361, 376–77; preparation for D-Day, 270–71, 274, 275, 276; relationship with Americans, 273; training, 255–56, 271; weapons, 257, 274, *346*
– 6th Anti-Tank Regiment; battery composition, 272; equipment and ammunition, 272–73; Northwest Europe Campaign, 350, 354, 360, 361, 362, 370, 376; training, 262, 271, 272
– 7th Anti-Tank Regiment: guns, 258–59; Italian Campaign, 296–98, 315, 322;

in Netherlands, 335; Petworth village incident, 259, *259*; provisional infantry battalion, 335; training, *265*
- 62nd Anti-Tank Regiment, RA, 340, 343, 348, 349, 350
- 90th Anti-Tank Battery, 242, 243–44, 250, 251, 259, 267
- 104th Anti-Tank Battery: commanding officer, 256; Italian Campaign, 312, 314, 315, 317, 320, 327, 328, 334–35; reorganization, 257
- 105th Anti-Tank Battery: casualties, 261; early days, 253; gun drills, 257–58; New Brunswickers in, 262; Northwest Europe Campaign, 337, 338–39, 344–45, 348, 354, 356, 363
- Army Group, Royal Artillery (AGRA), 384

ARTILLERY, CORPS: anti-tank regiment, 256; attack on Lens, 121–22; batteries, 97; commanding officer, 61, 69, 121; creation of heavy artillery, 130, 143; formation of, 61; Headquarters, 61; Hill 70, 127–28; Mount Sorrel, 72–73; reinforcement, 71; Somme offensive, 87; training, 70; Ypres, 67, 74

ARTILLERY, FIELD
- 2nd Canadian Field Brigade: Aubers Ridge, 57; Givenchy, 58–59; mobilization in Second World War, 241; Neuve Chapelle, 36, 38; reorganization of, 31; Second Battle of Ypres, 39, 41, 43, 44, 46–47, 49; Vimy Ridge, 106
- 2nd Field Regiment: departure to England, 242; invasion of Sicily, 291; Italian Campaign, 269, *298, 299, 307,* 318, *321, 331,* 333–34
- 3rd Field Brigade, 39, 41, 43, 44, 45
- 3rd (NB) Field Regiment (The Loyal Company): 174th Birthday fête, 405–6; 175th anniversary celebrations, 405, 406; Afghanistan war, 429, 430, *432,* 432–34, 440–41; ammunition, 191; anti-aircraft organization, 395; Barracks Green Armories, *20;* batteries, *19,* 52, 97–98, 182; becomes 3rd (NB) Coast Brigade, 199; becomes 3rd (NB) Coast Regiment (Reserve), 384, 389; becomes 3rd Field Artillery Regiment (The Loyal Company), 400; becomes 3rd Field Artillery Regiment (The Loyal Company), Royal Canadian Artillery, 400; becomes 3rd (NB) Medium Brigade, CRA (The Loyal Company of Artillery), 180, 191–92; becomes 3rd "New Brunswick" Heavy Brigade, Canadian Garrison Artillery, 19; becomes 3rd "New Brunswick" Regiment (Heavy Brigade), 19; becomes 3rd "New Brunswick" Regiment, Canadian Garrison Artillery, 20; becomes 3rd (New Brunswick) Regiment, Canadian Garrison Artillery, 6; bicentennial celebrations, *419,* 419–21, *420;* Canadian army's mobilization plan and, 416; ceremonial duties, 6, 14, 417; coast defence role, 25; colours of, 180, 181; commanding officers, 217, 222, 423, 430, 442; Composite Battery, 55, 98, 133–34; defence of Saint John, 205, 207, 208, 212–13, 221, 223; deployment in former Yugoslavia, 422–23, 425–26; fire control technology, 416, 417–18; flags, 180–81; gathering in Admiral Beatty Hotel, *200,* 201; glorious history of, 1–2; implementation of cutting-edge technology, 416; media attention to, 25–26, 34; militia duties, 13; at Mispec Point, 213–14; modernization of, 6–7, 17; as New Brunswick Battalion of Garrison Artillery, 5, *9;* officers of, *389;* organization of, 21; overseas operations, 413, 426–27; parades, *13,* 181, 185–86; participation in NATO Fall Exercise "Reforger," 410; peacekeeping missions, 412, 422; personal accounts about, 411; in post–Cold War era, 419–27; primary sources about, 449–52; Radar Battery, 395; ranks, 216; recruitment, 17, 27–28, 31, 98, 200; reduction of batteries, 403–4; reduction of personnel in 1943, 233; Remembrance Day commemorations, 417; removal "The Loyal Company" from title, 411–12; reorganizations, 17–18, 19–20, 173–74, 195–96, 423–24; restoration of "The Loyal Company" title, 443; Second Boer War, 7–8; "Shellburst Valley" national competition, 417; training, 14, *14,* 19, 28–30, 187, 190, 196, 199–201, *397,* 413, *415,* 416–17; "Valley Road" exercise, 411;

veteran members, *390*; War of 1812 Banner, 443; weapons and equipment, 18, 20, 21, 417, 443
- 3rd Field Training Regiment, 407
- 4th Field Brigade, 176
- 4th Medium Battery, Canadian Artillery (Howitzer), 183
- 5e Régiment d'artillerie légère du Canada (5RALC), 440
- 5th Field Brigade, 69–70, 106
- 5th Field Regiment; batteries, 248; commanding officers, 263; departure to England, 247; formation of, 246–47; Northwest Europe Campaign, 349–51, 354, 356, 361–62, 367, *372, 373*, 375–76, 378; Operation Overlord, 278–79; qualification of gunners, 264; training, 247–48, *252*, 263, 277–78, *278*
- 5th Régiment d'artillerie légère du Canada (RALC), 416
- 5th Westmount Battery, 106
- 6th Canadian Field Brigade, 53, 69, 106
- 6th Howitzer Brigade, 67, 68, 69
- 7th Battery, 241, *292*
- 7th Brigade, 343, 348
- 8th Field Battery; commanding officer, 267; defence of Saint John, 231; departure to England, 242; gunners' lunch, *264*; guns and equipment, 243, 260; invasion of Sicily, 285, 291, 293; Italian Campaign, 296, 300, *307*, 311, 312, 317, 324, 328, 334; liberation of the Netherlands, 335–36; training, *243*, 250–51, *251, 258*
- 8th Field Regiment (Self-Propelled), 315
- 8th Moncton Battery, 106, 401
- 9th Brigade, 340, 343, 348
- 10th (Woodstock) Field Battery, 2–3, 163, 177
- 11th Battery, 163
- 12th Field Artillery Regiment, 345, 385, 396, 397, 399, 401
- 12th (Newcastle) Field Battery, 2–3, *24*, 154, 183
- 12th Field Brigade (former 4th Field Brigade); during Cold War, 384; interwar period, 177, 186; organization and battery composition, 71, 176, 195; Somme offensive, 86, 87; Thiepval Ridge, 90; training, *184, 185*, 186; Vimy Ridge, 106
- 15th (Saint John) Battery, 183, 218–19
- 16th Brigade, 167
- 19th (Moncton) Field Battery, 15, *15*, 24, 31
- 22nd Howitzer Battery, 106, 119
- 23rd Field Brigade, 194–95
- 23rd Field Regiment, 384, 389
- 23rd Howitzer Battery, 53, 60, 67, 69–70, 87, 90, 101, 106
- 28th/89th Field Battery, 247, 248
- 28th (Newcastle) Battery; commanding officer, 183; Loos offensive, 101; Mount Kemmel, 68; in Netherlands, *370*; Northwest Europe Campaign, 349, *363*, 367, 379; reorganizations, 67, 183, 393; Second World War mobilization, 240, 241; Somme offensive, 87, 90; teatime, *250*; training, *182, 186*, 186–87, *191*, 251–52; Vimy Ridge, 106; at Westenhangar Race Course, *277*
- 65th Depot Battery, 167
- 68th Battery, *168*
- 89th Field Battery, 177, 241, 247, 401
- 90th (Newcastle) Battery; becomes 28th (Newcastle) Battery, 177; commanding officer, 176
- 90th Field Battery (Howitzer): Change of Command parade and ceremony, 401; commanding officer, 242; in England, 243; formation, 186; invasion of Sicily, 291, 293; Italian Campaign, 296, 300–301, 305, 311, 312, 324, 328, 331–32, 334; Second World War mobilization, 241; training, 186–87
- 103rd Battery, 377, 393
- 104th Field Battery, 245–46
- 105th (St. George) Battery: mobilization, 253–54; in the Netherlands, *371, 377*, 378–79; Petawawa camp, *194*
- 115th Radar Battery, *394*
- 128th Air Defence Battery, 424
- 245th Battery, 349

ARTILLERY, GARRISON, 23–24, *155*
- 2nd Garrison Brigade: Arras, 148, 149, 151–52, 153; Cambrai, 161, 164; Canal du Nord, 156, 159, 160; Vimy RIdge, 138
- 3rd Garrison Brigade, 156, 159, 163, *163*
- 3rd (NB) Regiment of, 5, 6–8, 24

ARTILLERY, HEAVY
- 1st Heavy Battery: Arras, 149, 151, 153; Cambrai, 164; Canal du Nord, 156, 159; detachment from 1st Canadian Division, 38; guns, 138; Hill 70, 122, 126; Loos, 61, 62, 63; Neuve Chapelle, 36, 37; Passchendaele, 131; Somme offensive, 71, 75–76, 77, 79, 80–83, 87, 88, 89, 94; Vimy Ridge, 106, 112, 113, 115
- 2nd Canadian Heavy Artillery Group, 121, 122
- 2nd Canadian Heavy Battery, 31, *37*, 60, 71, 97
- 3rd (NB) Heavy Brigade, 19, 174, 175–80, 182, 183
- 4th Heavy Battery, 207, 213
- 15th Heavy Battery, 174, 175, 179, 216–17
- 23rd Heavy Artillery Group, 77
- 48th Heavy Battery, 62
- Canadian Heavy Artillery Groups, 100, 107, 130, 143

ARTILLERY, SIEGE BATTERIES
- 1st Siege Battery, 65
- 2nd Siege Battery, 137
- 4th Siege Battery; Arras, 151, 153; becomes 131st Siege Battery, 100; Cambrai, 163–64; Canal du Nord, 155–56, 158–59; competition of Canadian Artillery Association, 179; Corps Reserve, 175; departure to Western front, 65; in England, 66; formation of, 52; guns, *66, 83*; Hill 70, 122, 123, 125; parade in Saint John, *51*; reorganization, 137–38; return to Canada from Western front, *169*; Somme offensive, 84, 86, 88, 90, 91–92, 94, 96; summer camp, 179; Vimy Ridge, 101, 102, 104–5, 106, *107*, 109, 113, 118, *119*, 121
- 5th Siege Battery, 137–38
- 6th Siege Battery: Arras, 149, 151, 153; arrival to England, 66; becomes 2nd Brigade, 136; becomes 167th Siege Battery, 100; Cambrai, 164; Canal du Nord, 155, 158–59, *160*; departure to Western front, 65; gunners at rest, *136*; guns, *66, 83*, 137, *138*; Hill 70, 124, 125, 126; as part of Canadian Occupation Force, 166; Passchendaele, 131, 132; perpetuation of the 4th Medium Battery to, 183; personnel, 175; reunion dinner, *200*; Somme offensive, 92, 96; training, 74; Vimy Ridge, 100, 101, 102, 104–5, 106, *107,* 109, 111, 113, 118–19, 120
- 7th Siege Battery from Montreal, 106, 109, 138
- 9th Siege Battery, 109, *125*
- 10th Siege Battery, *173,* 182
- 12th Siege, 182

CANADIAN DIVISIONS, 1914–1918
- 1st Canadian Division: ammunition delivery, 44–45, *45*; casualties, 40–41; challenges of bad weather, 30; commanding officer, 39; departure to Great War, 30; Neuve Chapelle, 35–36; reliefs-in-place practice, 39; reputation, 48; Western front, 33–34, 35; Ypres, 38–39, 49
- 2nd Canadian Division, 60, 67–68, 87, 164
- 3rd Canadian Division, 69, 71, 87
- 4th Canadian Division, 96

CANADIAN DIVISIONS, 1939–1945
- 1st Canadian Infantry Division: 1st Canadian Infantry Brigade, 283, 307, 318; 2nd Canadian Infantry Brigade, 288, 290, 292, 296, 301, 307; casualties, 250; invasion of Sicily, 267, 271; Italian Campaign, 269, 270, 291, 298–99, 305–6, 312, 319, 323, 334; Mediterranean Theatre, 283; Operation Husky, 285; training in England, 242–43, 250–51
- 2nd Canadian Infantry Division: Exercise Crescendo, 270; landings at Dieppe, 263; in Normandy, 337, 349–50; Northwest Europe Campaign, 349, 350, 354, 356, 361, 362, *365*; Operation Fortitude, 277; preparation for D-Day, 276
- 3rd Canadian Infantry Division; arrival in England, 256; in Normandy, 349–50; Operation Overlord, 278; preparation for D-Day, 275, 276; training, 271, 273
- Loyal Edmonton Regiment, 285–86, 288, 289, 309, 319
- New Brunswick Field Artillery: 2nd (Special Service) Battalion, 7–8; 4th (NB) Brigade, 3, 15, 16–17, 24; deployment for action, *4*; E Battery, 7, *9,* 10–11; modernization, 17
- North Nova Scotia Highlanders, 343

– North Shore (New Brunswick) Regiment, 241, 368–70
– Royal Regiment of Canadian Artillery (RCA), 239–40, 246–47, 395–96
– Seaforth Highlanders infantry, 284, 288, 299, 302, 309
– Siberian Field Force, 167, 168

OTHER UNITS AND FORMATIONS
  – Australian-New Zealand Corps (ANZACs), 82, 83, 131, 144; 13th Australian Brigade, 86; Australian 6-inch battery, 84
  – British Army: 51st Highland Division, 96, 149; XIII Corps, 79; XV Corps, 76, 79, 80, 82; British Heavy Artillery Groups, 71; British Reserve (Fifth) Army, 84, 94, 95; Royal Flying Corps, 62, 80
  – German Army: 1st Parachute Division, 305, 307–8, 327; 2nd SS Panzer Corps, 345; 12th SS Panzer Division, 341, 343; 21st Panzer Division, 340; 29th Panzer-Grenadier Division, 327; 90th Panzer-Grenadier Division, 302–3, 305, 307; air forces, 203–4, 205; Navy, 197, 203–4, 205, 225–26
  – South African and New Zealand units, 323; 2nd New Zealand Division, 328
  – United States Army: 3rd US Army, 357; 104th "Timberwolf" Division, *368*

UN peacekeeping missions, 422
Upton, William, 285, 286

Van Buskirk, Robert, 306
Varendorf, Amelung von, 227
Vassie, William, 28, *32*, 75, 174
Verdun, 67, 74
Victoria, Queen of England, 11
Vidal, Col. Beaufort Henry, *3*

Waddingham, Sgt. R., 347, 376
Wainwright, Stanley, 132
Walker, Don, 344
Wallace, Sgt., 112
Walsh, E.D., 179, 230
Walton, C.W., 181
Warman, Roy, 250
Warneford, H.M., 125

Warr, A.H., 312
Warrell, Sgt., 301
Wasson, William Barker, *74*
Watters, Tom, 423, 432, *432*
Wayne, Elsie, *419*
WEAPONS: 2-pounder gun, 258, 332; 3.7-inch gun, *387*; 4.5-inch field howitzer, 53–54, 68; 4.7-inch gun, *26*; 6-inch 26-cwt medium howitzer, 65, *124, 128, 132*, 137, *140, 148, 160, 173*; 6-pounder gun, 258–59, *261, 265, 295*, 338, *339, 346, 360*; 7.5-inch gun at Mispec Point, *212*; 8-inch BL (breech-loading) Mark VI howitzer, 65, *66, 119*; 8-inch heavy howitzer, 66, 74, 76, *83*, 92, 105, *107*, 137, *142*, 151, *156*; 9.2-inch heavy howitzer, 65, 66, *80*; 17-pounder gun, *271, 297, 301*, 310, 343, 349, *353, 368*, 373, 375; 18-pounder cartridges, *75*; 25-pounder gun, *266, 270, 328, 373*; 40 mm Bofors, 260, *268, 308*; 60-pounder gun, *29, 37, 76*, 144, 146; 81 mm mortar, *432*, 433; 105 mm gun, 396, 419; American M-10 tank destroyer, 315, 319, 322; American self-propelled 3-inch guns, 273; British 18-pounder gun, *21, 182*; British BL (breech-loading) 4.7-inch gun, *18, 35, 41, 55, 63, 75*; C-1 howitzer, *404*; C-3 105 mm howitzer, *421, 424, 431*; German 5.9-inch howitzer, 37, 38, 65, *113*; German 10.5 cm field howitzer, *115*; German 21 cm Mörser, 65, *120*, 124, 125, *158*; German trench mortars and artillery, *159*; M-10 self-propelled 3-inch anti-tank gun, 322, *325*, 340, *341*, 344, *366*; M777 155 mm howitzer, 433, *439*; UA 60 Black Hawk helicopter, *431*
Welch, Robert, *9*
Welsh, Maj. Arthur George, 251, *257*, 289, 290, 302, 309, 311–12, 324, 330
West, Herb A., 33, 52, 95, 174
Wetmore, Allen, 133
Wetmore, Barton, 64
Wetmore, Bruce, 105
Wetmore, H.D., 95
Wetmore, Lt. G.B., 52, 105
Wetmore, Percy W., 98, 128, 174

Wheaton, J.A., 121
Wheeler, Harold, 250
Wheeler, Irving, 411, 412
White, A.T., 119
White, Doug, 137, 143, 175
White, W.W., 181
Whitebone, Ernie, 28
Wiley, Yank, 161
Williams, Charlie, 28
Wills, Kenneth, *125,* 130, 143, 154, 170
Wilson, Brad, 422
Wilson, Ron, 410–11, 412, 420, *421*
Winslow, H.O., 120
Winslow, John D., 168, 170
Winsor, William, 146
Withers, Fred W., 8–9
Wood, T.V., 344
World War I. *See* First World War
World War II. *See* Second World War
Wright, Maj. G., 265, 313

Zamer (Gunner), 289
Zavitz, Ross, 333, 334